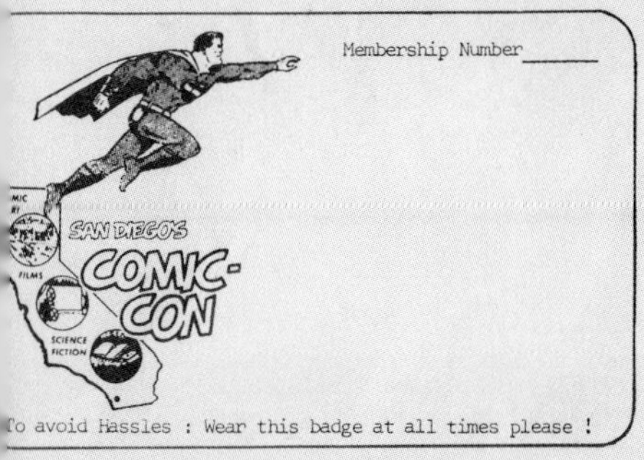
Membership Number______
SAN DIEGO'S
COMIC-CON
FILMS
SCIENCE FICTION
To avoid Hassles : Wear this badge at all times please !
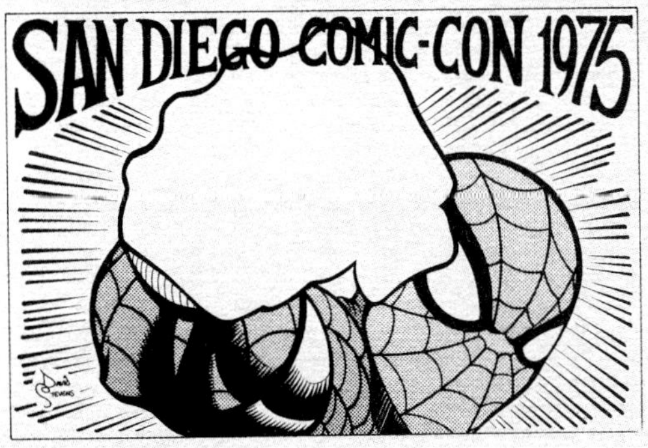
SAN DIEGO COMIC-CON 1975
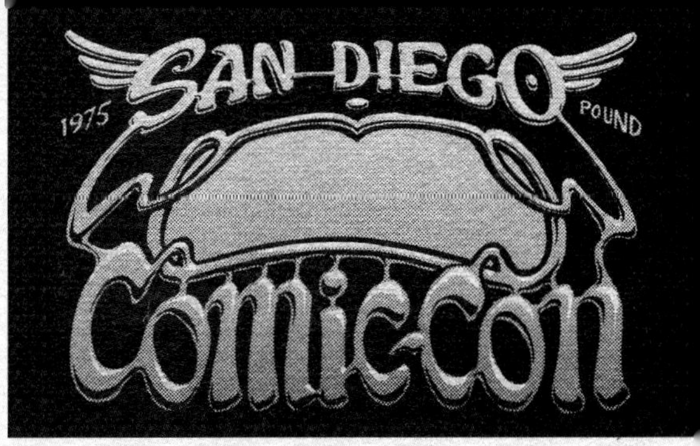
1975
SAN DIEGO
POUND
Comic-con
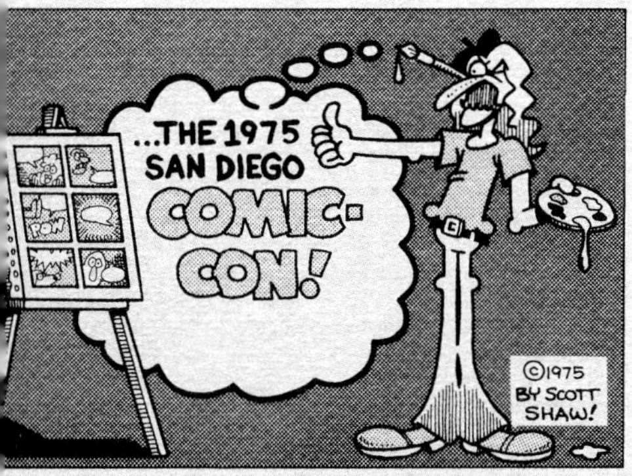
...THE 1975 SAN DIEGO COMIC-CON!
©1975 BY SCOTT SHAW!
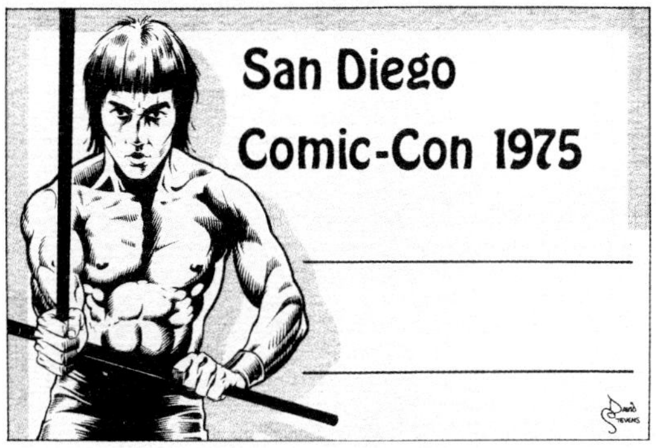
San Diego
Comic-Con 1975
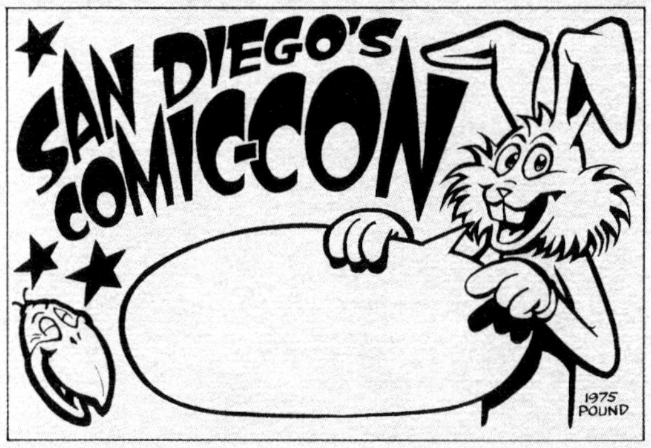
SAN DIEGO'S COMIC-CON
1975 POUND
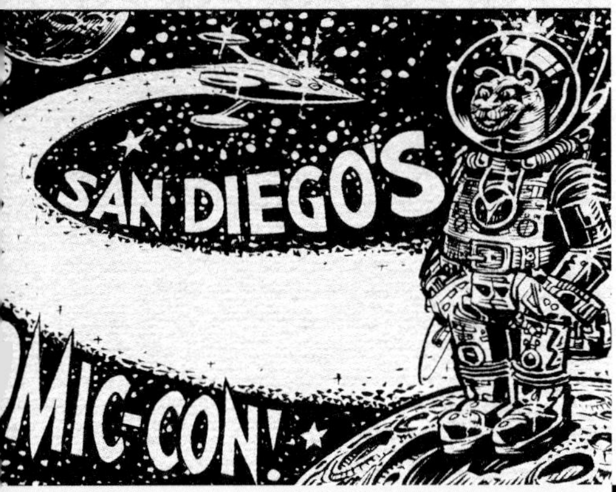
SAN DIEGO'S
MIC-CON!
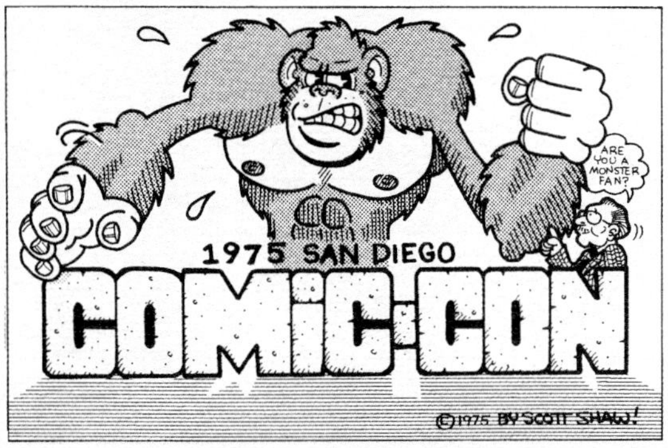
ARE YOU A MONSTER FAN?
1975 SAN DIEGO
COMIC-CON
©1975 BY SCOTT SHAW!
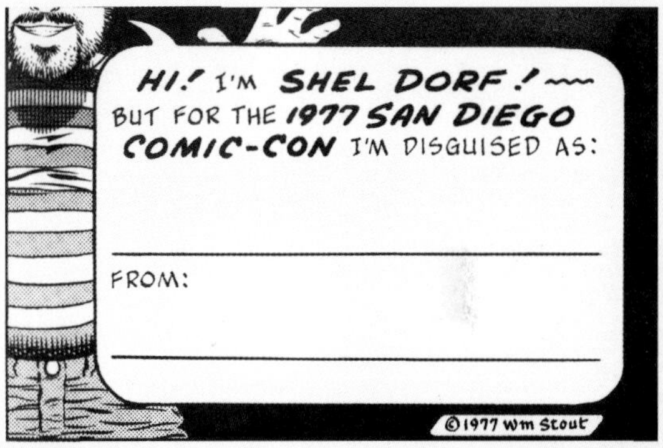
HI! I'M SHEL DORF! ~~
BUT FOR THE 1977 SAN DIEGO COMIC-CON I'M DISGUISED AS:
FROM:
©1977 Wm Stout
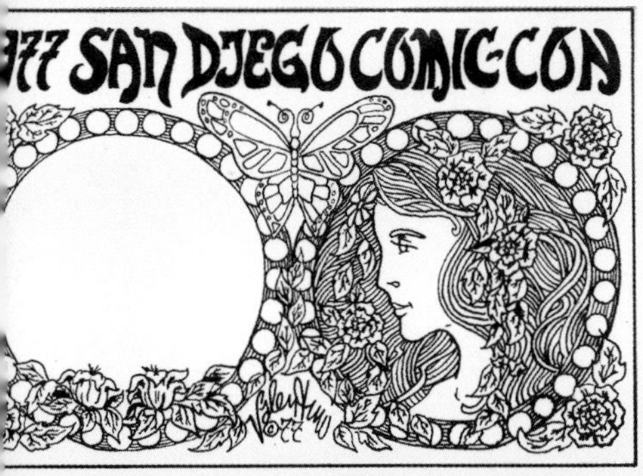
77 SAN DIEGO COMIC-CON
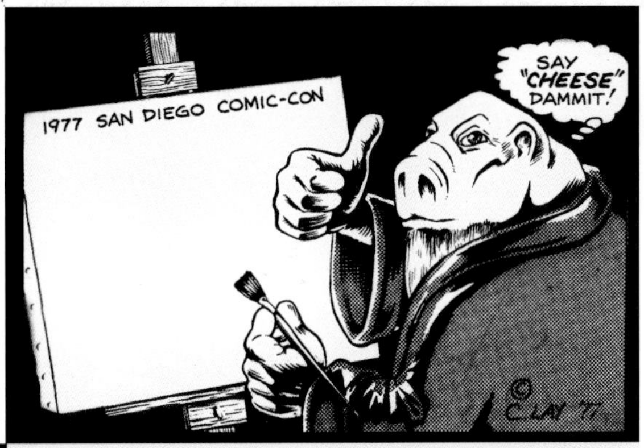
1977 SAN DIEGO COMIC-CON
SAY "CHEESE" DAMMIT!
© C. LAY '77
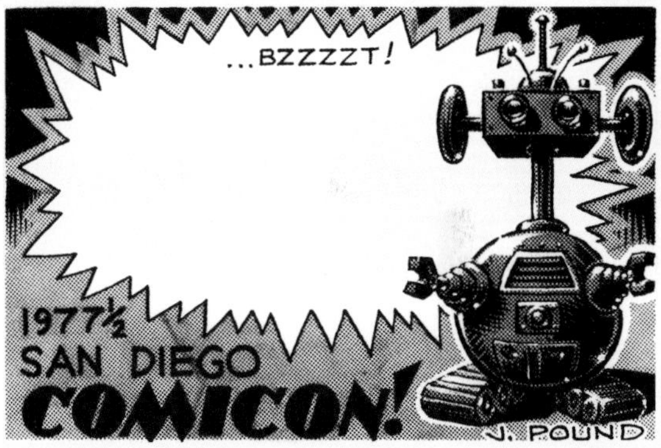
...BZZZZT!
1977½ SAN DIEGO COMICON!
J. POUND
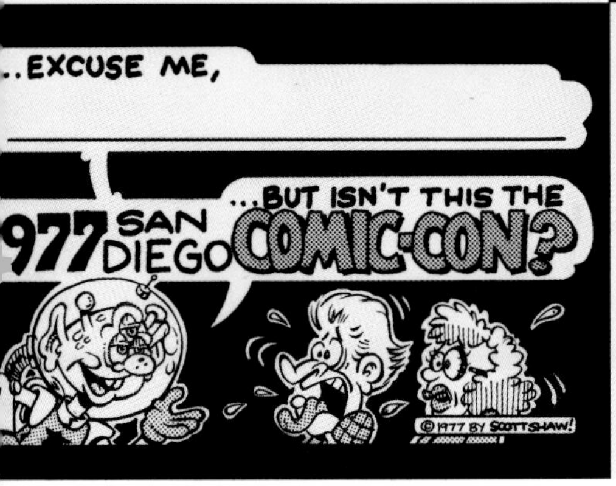
..EXCUSE ME,
...BUT ISN'T THIS THE
977 SAN DIEGO COMIC-CON?
©1977 BY SCOTT SHAW!
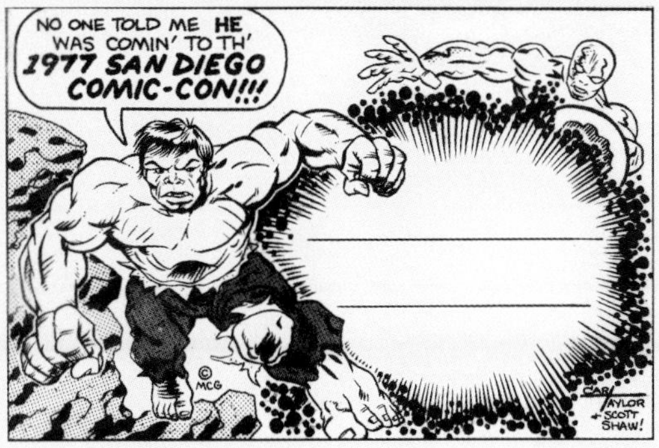
NO ONE TOLD ME HE WAS COMIN' TO TH' 1977 SAN DIEGO COMIC-CON!!!
© MCG
CARL TAYLOR + SCOTT SHAW!
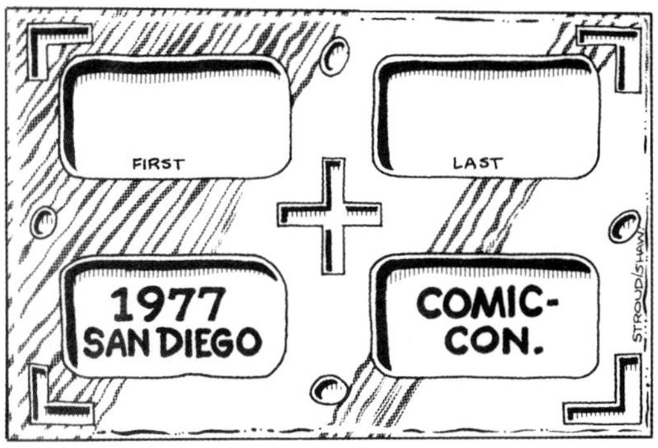
FIRST
LAST
1977 SAN DIEGO
COMIC-CON.
STROUD/SHAW
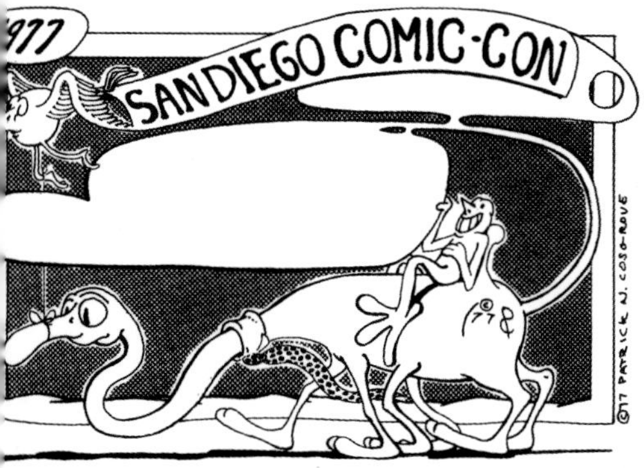
1977
SAN DIEGO COMIC-CON
©77 PATRICK N. COSO-ROVE
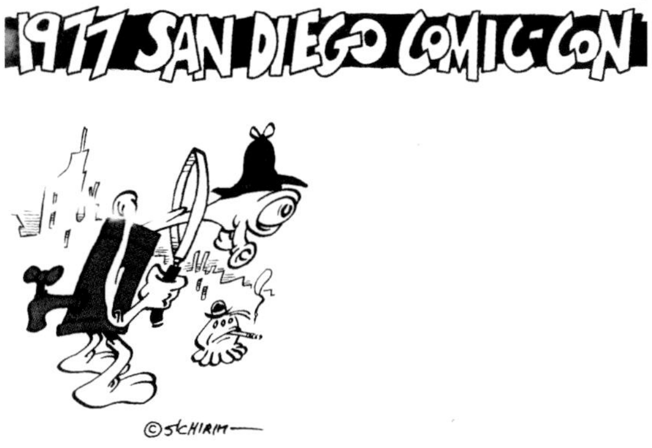
1977 SAN DIEGO COMIC-CON
©SCHIRM
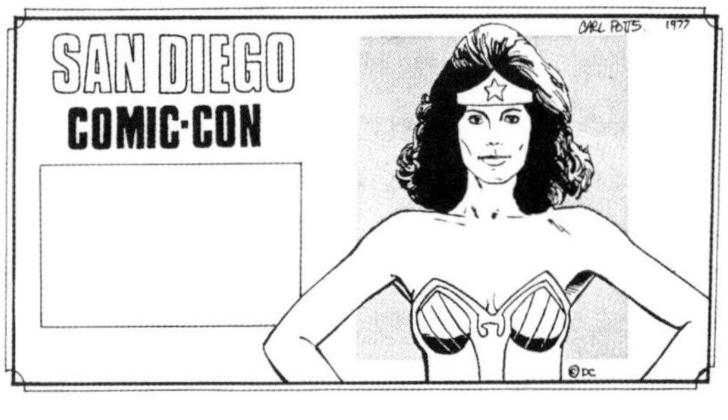
CARL POTTS 1977
SAN DIEGO
COMIC-CON
©DC

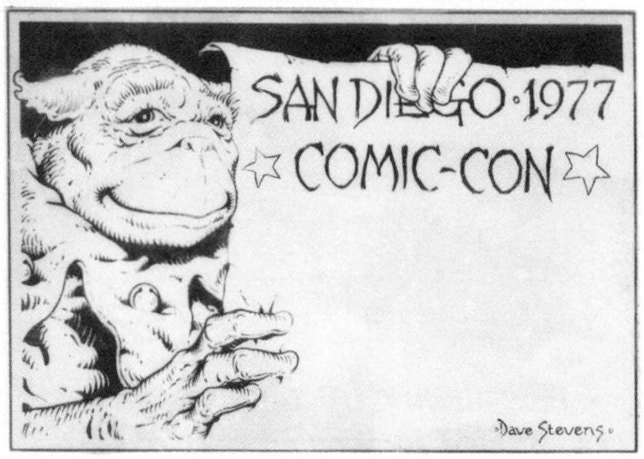
SAN DIEGO·1977
☆COMIC-CON☆
Dave Stevens

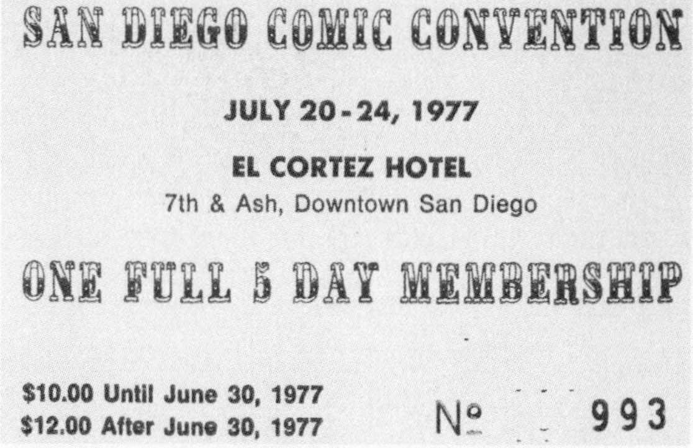
SAN DIEGO COMIC CONVENTION
JULY 20-24, 1977
EL CORTEZ HOTEL
7th & Ash, Downtown San Diego
ONE FULL 5 DAY MEMBERSHIP
$10.00 Until June 30, 1977
$12.00 After June 30, 1977
№ 993

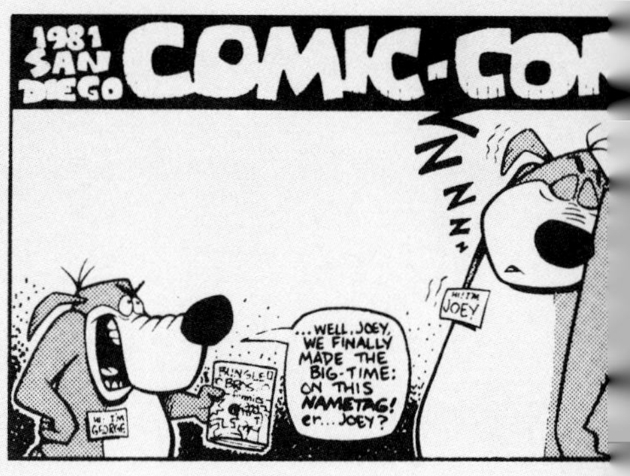
1981 SAN DIEGO COMIC-CON
...WELL, JOEY, WE FINALLY MADE THE BIG-TIME: ON THIS NAMETAG! er...JOEY?

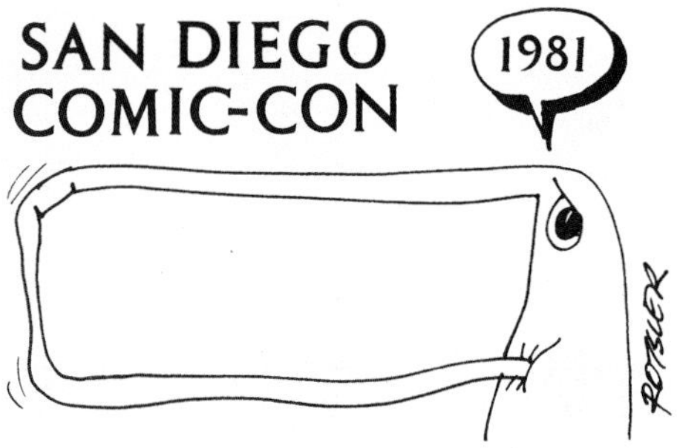
SAN DIEGO COMIC-CON
1981

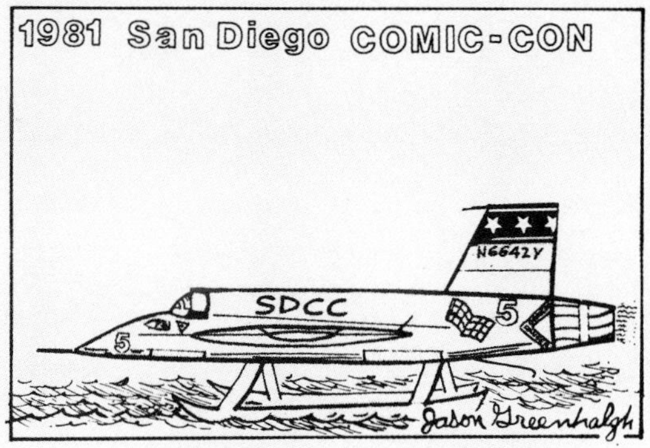
1981 San Diego COMIC-CON
N6642Y
SDCC
Jason Greenhalgh

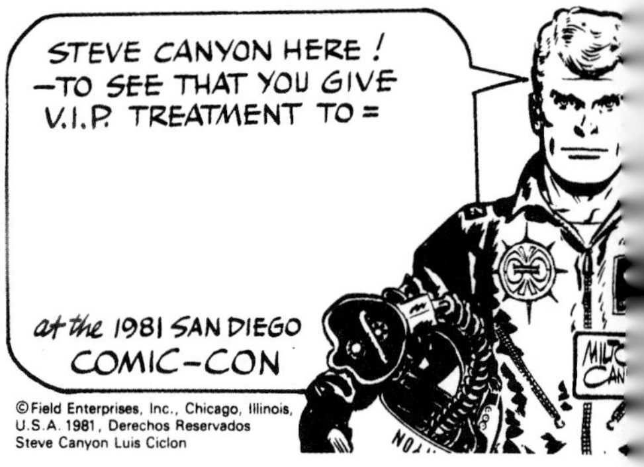
STEVE CANYON HERE ! —TO SEE THAT YOU GIVE V.I.P. TREATMENT TO =
at the 1981 SAN DIEGO COMIC-CON
©Field Enterprises, Inc., Chicago, Illinois, U.S.A. 1981, Derechos Reservados
Steve Canyon Luis Ciclon

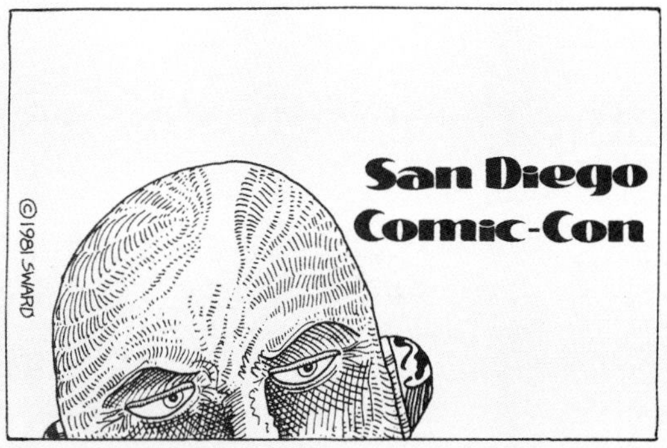
San Diego Comic-Con
© 1981 SWARD

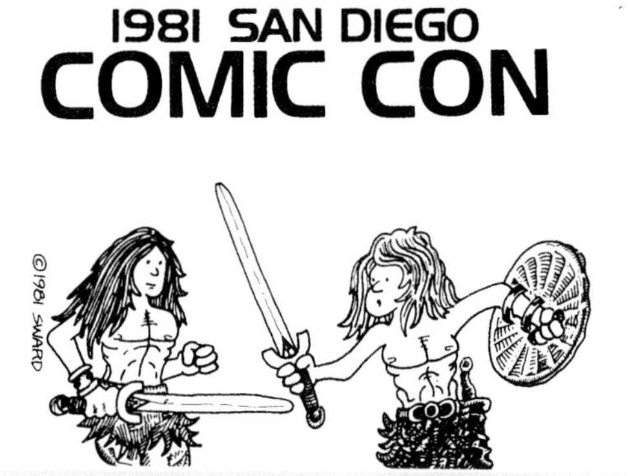
1981 SAN DIEGO
COMIC CON
© 1981 SWARD

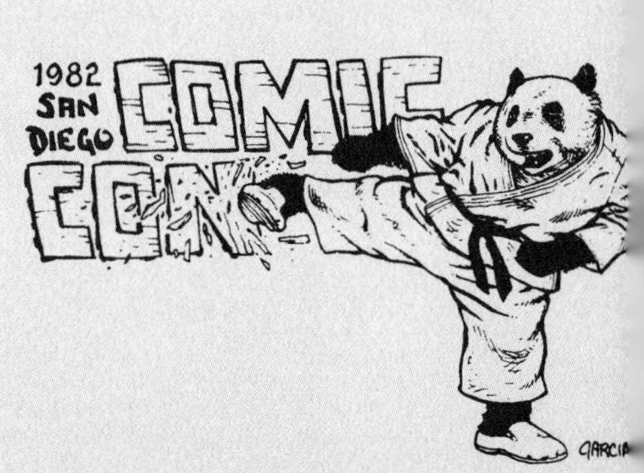
1982 SAN DIEGO COMIC CON

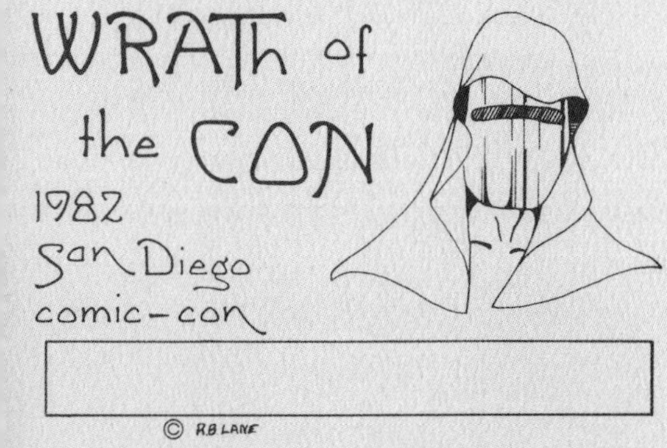
WRATh of the CON
1982 San Diego comic-con
© RB LANE

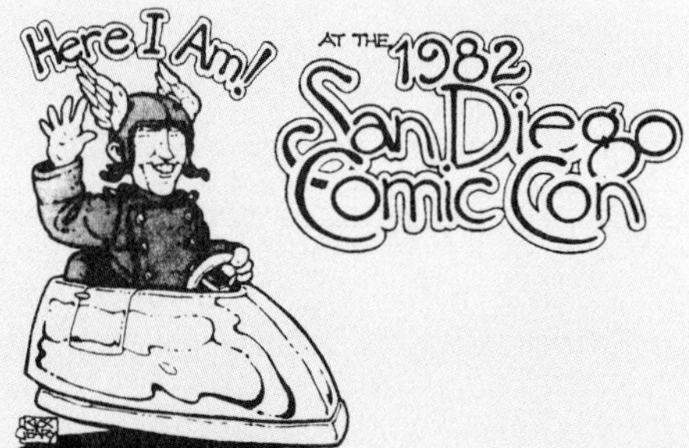
Here I Am!
AT THE 1982 San Diego Comic Con

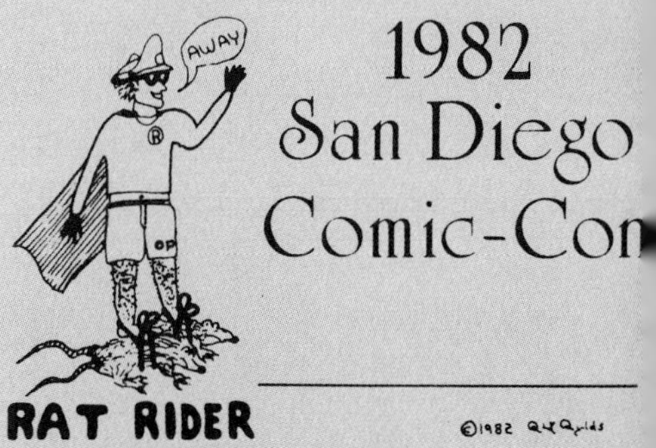
AWAY
1982 San Diego Comic-Con
RAT RIDER

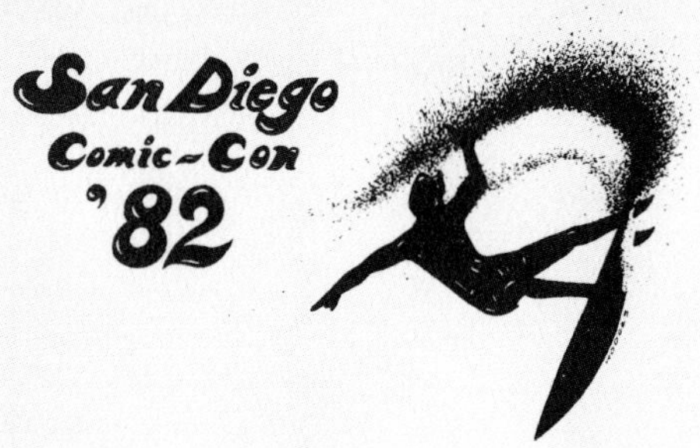
San Diego Comic-Con '82

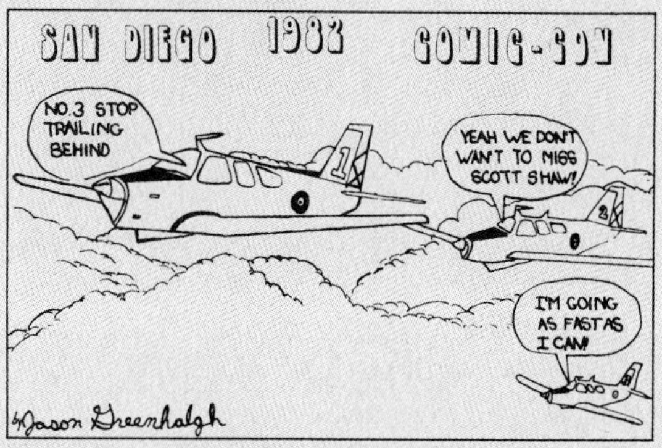
SAN DIEGO 1982 COMIC-CON
NO.3 STOP TRAILING BEHIND
YEAH WE DON'T WANT TO MISS SCOTT SHAW!
I'M GOING AS FAST AS I CAN!
by Jason Greenhalgh

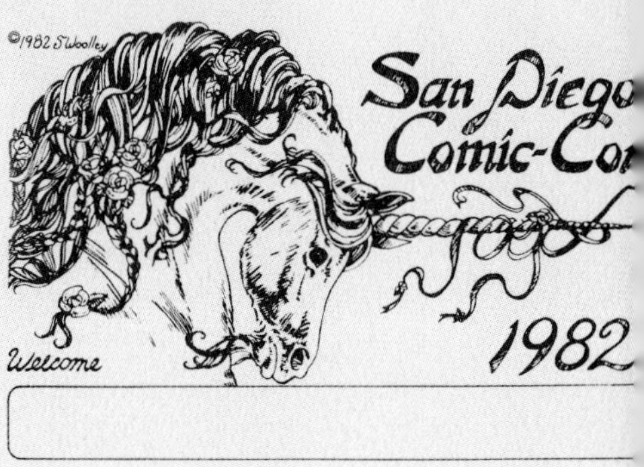
©1982 S.Woolley
San Diego Comic-Con
Welcome
1982

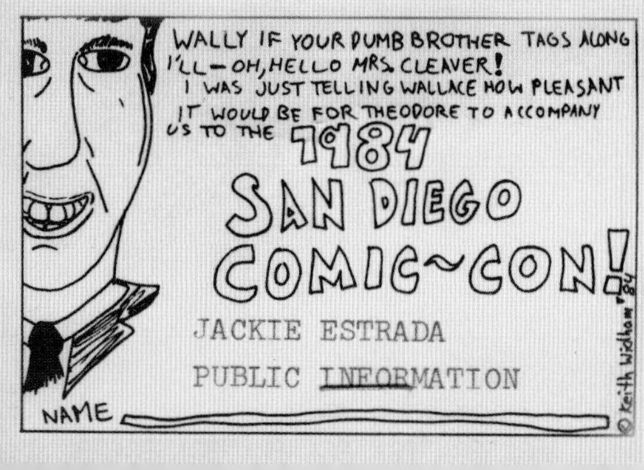
WALLY IF YOUR DUMB BROTHER TAGS ALONG
I'LL—OH, HELLO MRS. CLEAVER!
I WAS JUST TELLING WALLACE HOW PLEASANT IT WOULD BE FOR THEODORE TO ACCOMPANY US TO THE 1984
SAN DIEGO COMIC~CON!
JACKIE ESTRADA
PUBLIC INFORMATION
NAME
© Keith Wilson '84

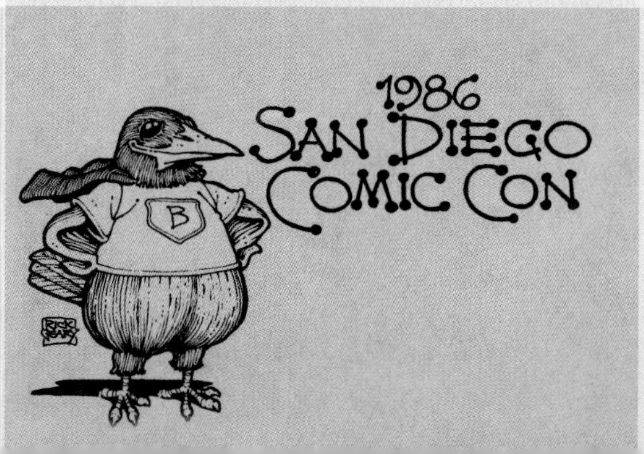
1986 SAN DIEGO COMIC CON
B

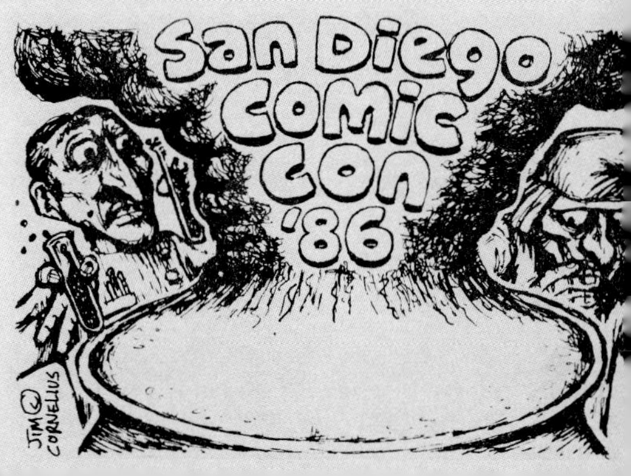
San Diego Comic Con '86
JIM Q CORNELIUS

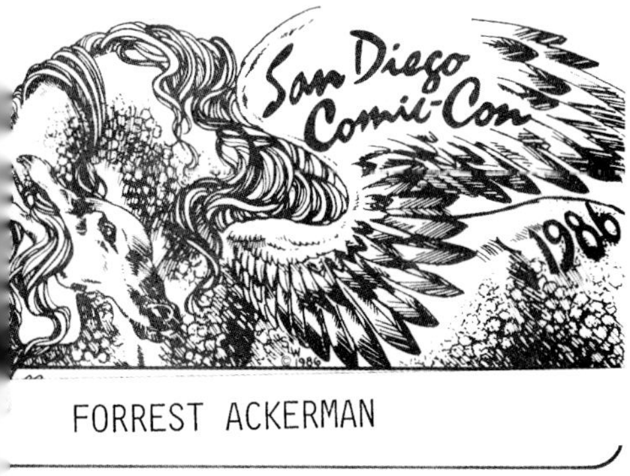
San Diego Comic-Con
1986
FORREST ACKERMAN

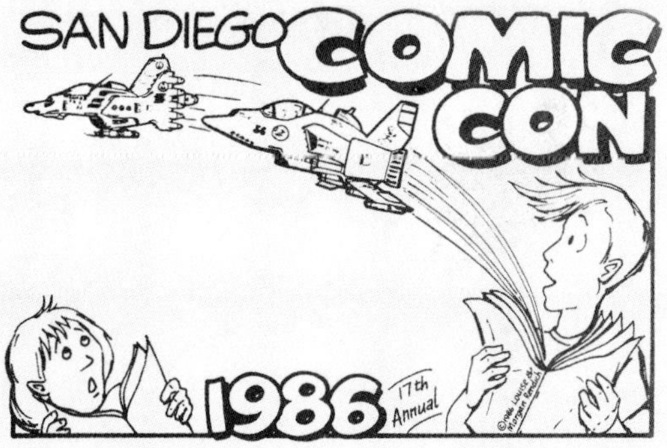
SAN DIEGO COMIC CON
1986
17th Annual

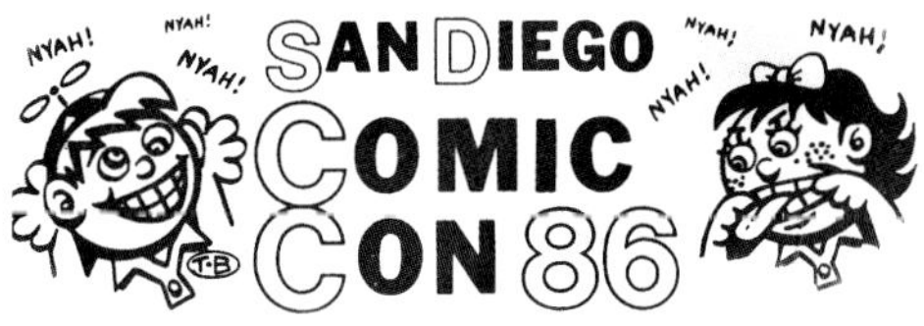
NYAH!
NYAH!
SAN DIEGO COMIC CON 86
NYAH!
NYAH!
NYAH!

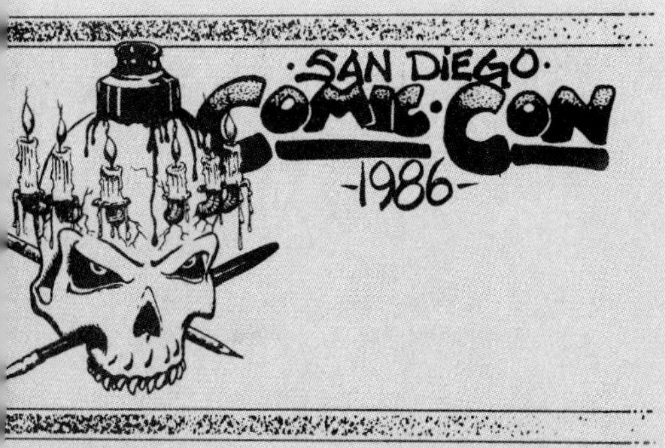
SAN DIEGO COMIC·CON
-1986-

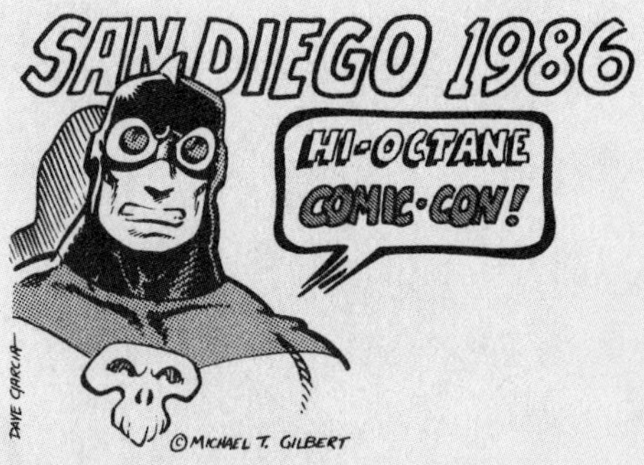
SAN DIEGO 1986
HI-OCTANE COMIC-CON!
DAVE GARCIA
©MICHAEL T. GILBERT

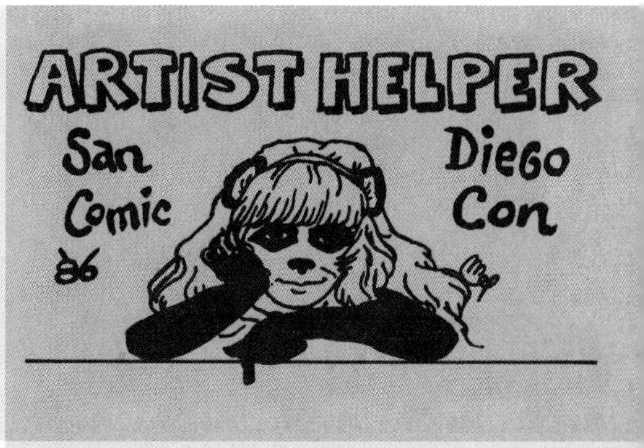
ARTIST HELPER
San Comic 86
Diego Con

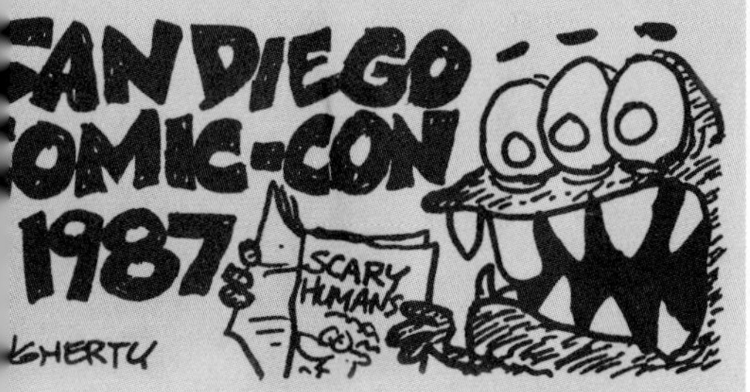
SAN DIEGO COMIC-CON 1987
SCARY HUMANS

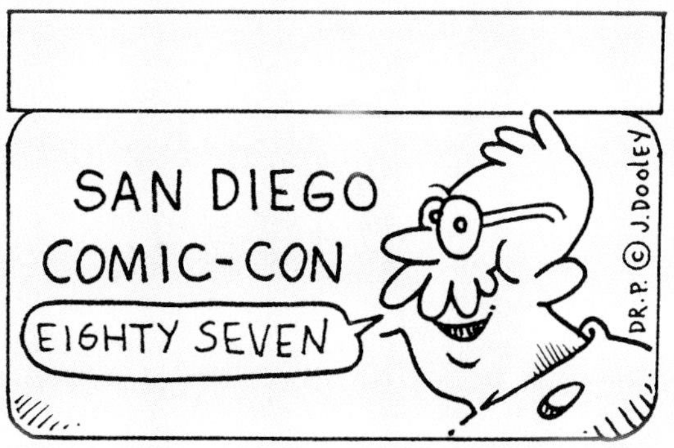
SAN DIEGO
COMIC-CON
EIGHTY SEVEN
DR. P. © J. DOOLEY

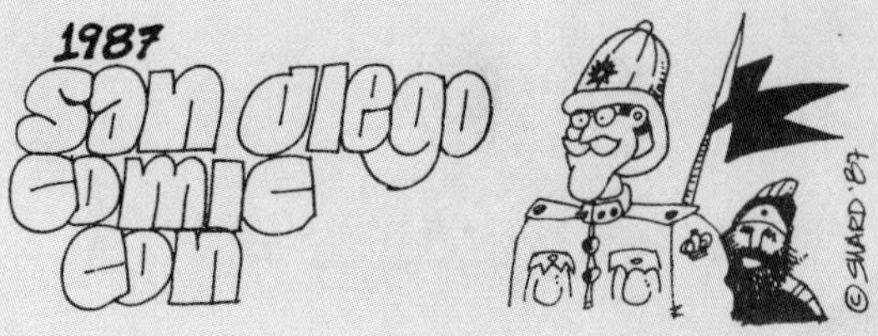
1987
san diego comic con
© SHARD '87

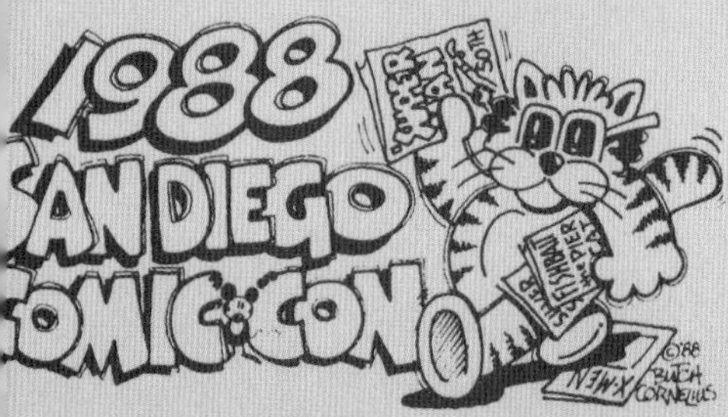
1988
SAN DIEGO
COMIC·CON
©88 BUTCH CORNELIUS

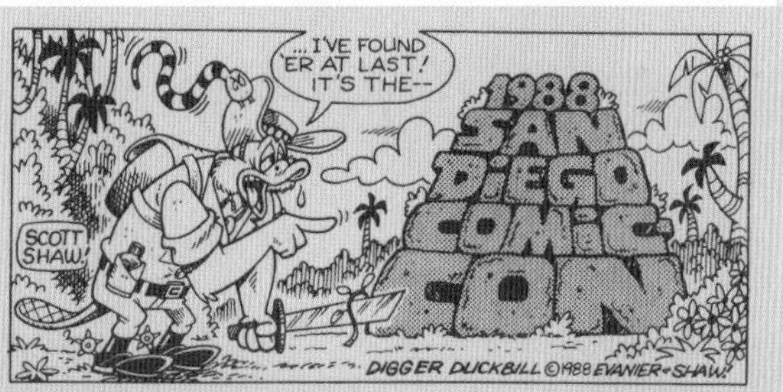
...I'VE FOUND 'ER AT LAST! IT'S THE--
1988 SAN DIEGO COMIC CON
SCOTT SHAW!
DIGGER DUCKBILL ©1988 EVANIER+SHAW!

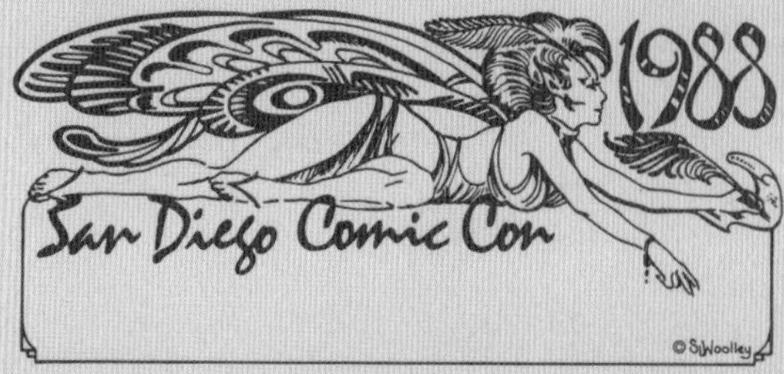
1988
San Diego Comic Con
© S.Woolley

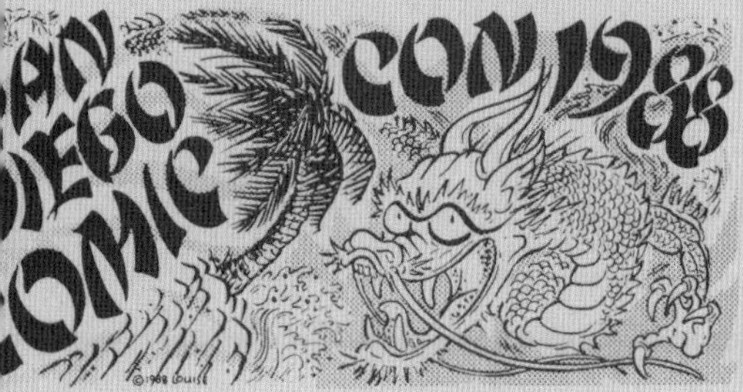
SAN DIEGO COMIC CON 1988

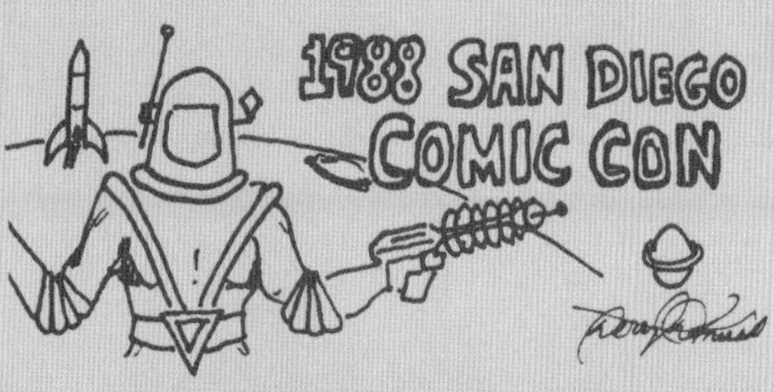
1988 SAN DIEGO
COMIC CON

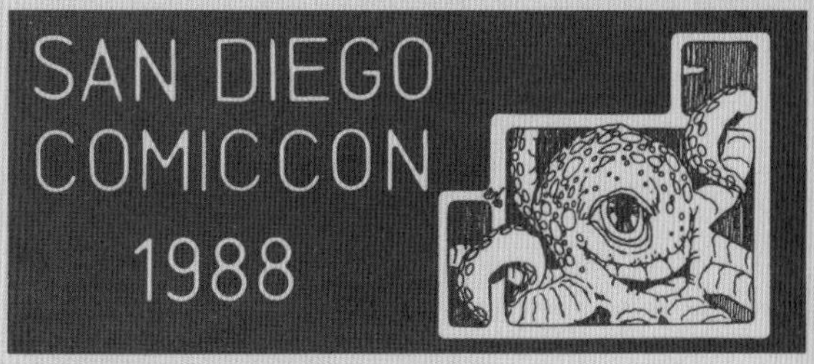
SAN DIEGO
COMICCON
1988

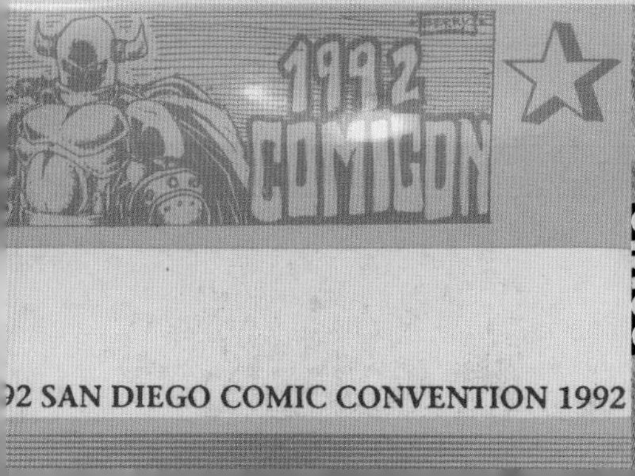
1992
COMICON
92 SAN DIEGO COMIC CONVENTION 1992

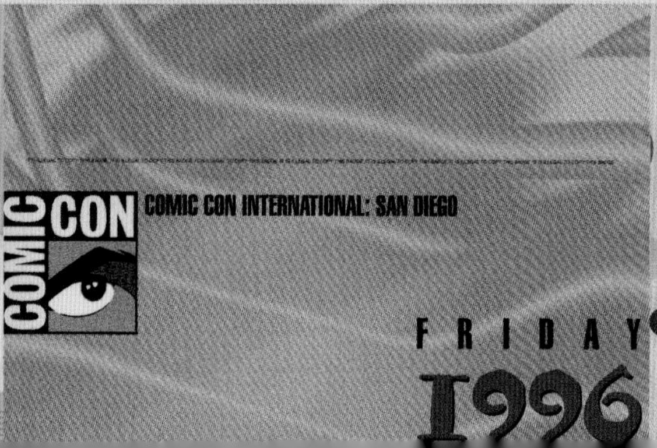
COMIC CON
COMIC CON INTERNATIONAL: SAN DIEGO
FRIDAY
1996

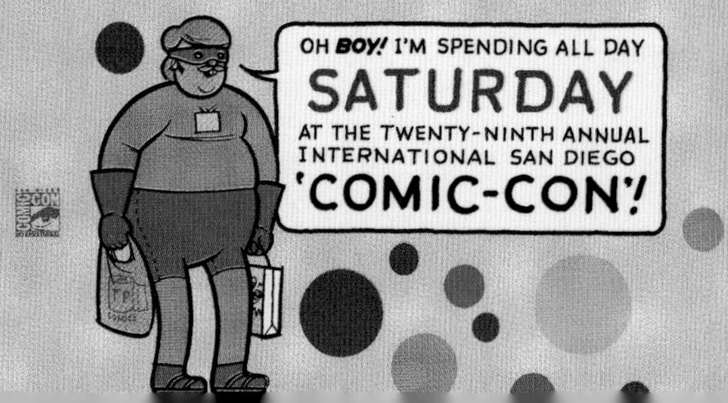
OH BOY! I'M SPENDING ALL DAY
SATURDAY
AT THE TWENTY-NINTH ANNUAL
INTERNATIONAL SAN DIEGO
'COMIC-CON'!

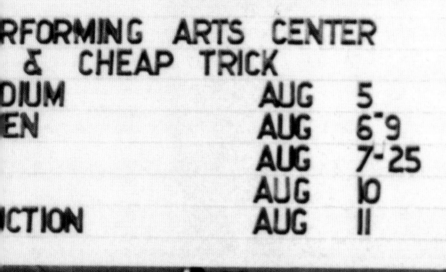

RFORMING ARTS CENTER
& CHEAP TRICK
DIUM   AUG 5
EN   AUG 6-9
                    AUG 7-25
                    AUG 10
CTION   AUG 11

BOX OFFICE

S.

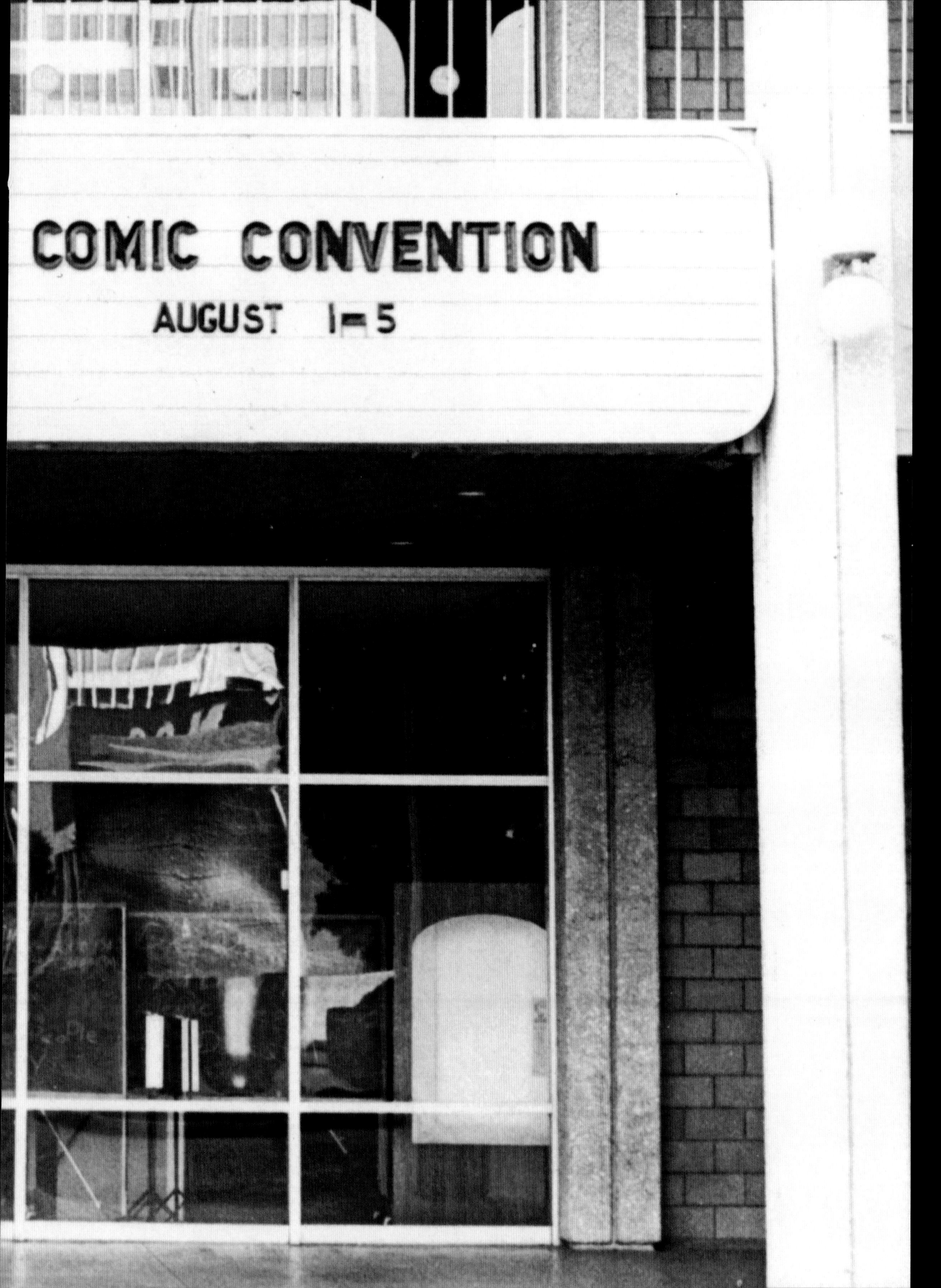
COMIC CONVENTION
AUGUST 1-5

SAN DIEGO COMIC CON INTERNATIONAL

COMIC-CON®

40 YEARS OF ARTISTS, WRITERS, FANS & FRIENDS

FOREWORD BY RAY BRADBURY

CHRONICLE BOOKS
SAN FRANCISCO

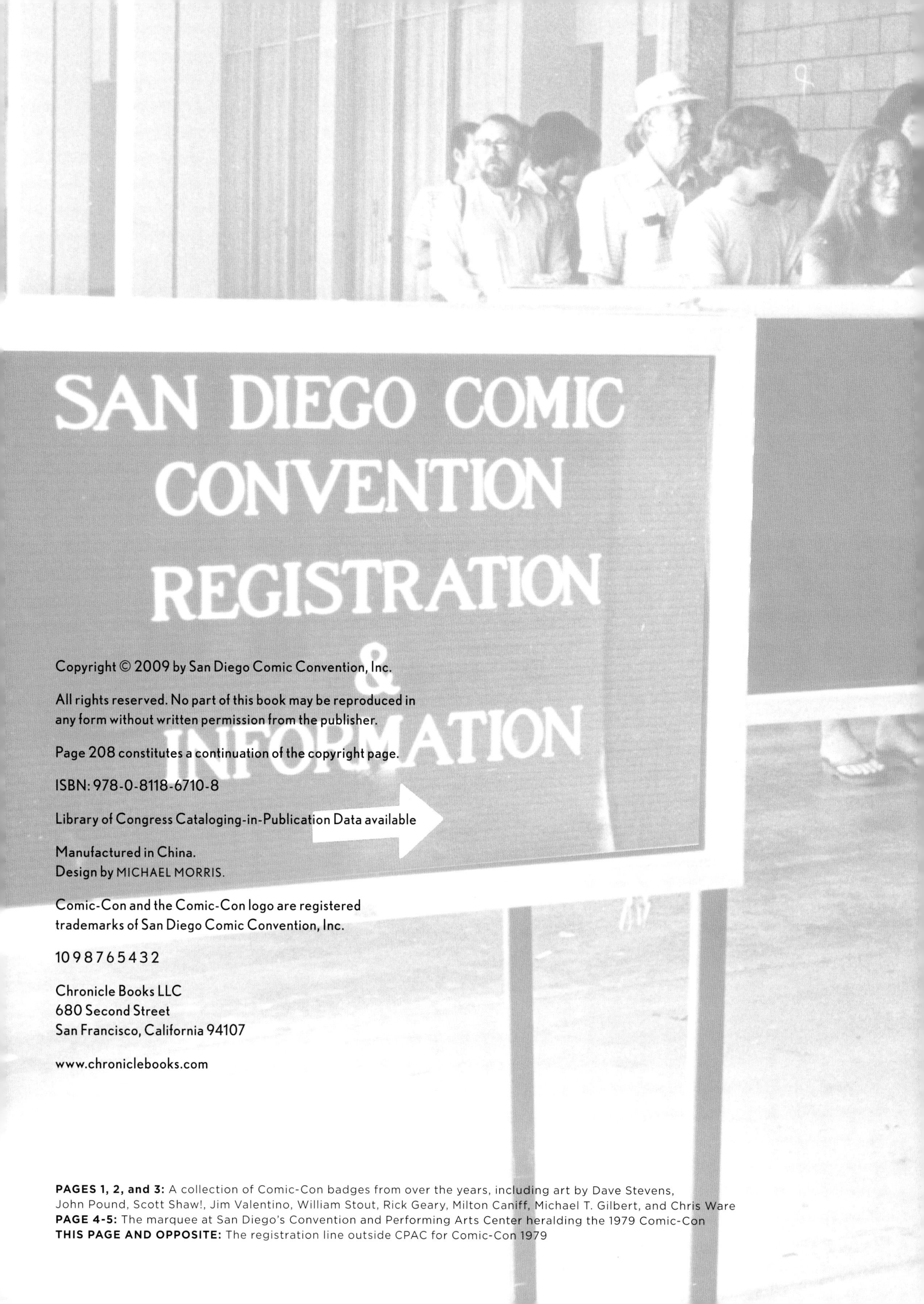
SAN DIEGO COMIC
CONVENTION
REGISTRATION
&
INFORMATION

Page 208 constitutes a continuation of the copyright page.

ISBN: 978-0-8118-6710-8

Library of Congress Cataloging-in-Publication Data available

Manufactured in China.
Design by MICHAEL MORRIS.

10 9 8 7 6 5 4 3 2

Chronicle Books LLC
680 Second Street
San Francisco, California 94107

www.chroniclebooks.com

PAGES 1, 2, and 3: A collection of Comic-Con badges from over the years, including art by Dave Stevens, John Pound, Scott Shaw!, Jim Valentino, William Stout, Rick Geary, Milton Caniff, Michael T. Gilbert, and Chris Ware
PAGE 4-5: The marquee at San Diego's Convention and Performing Arts Center heralding the 1979 Comic-Con
THIS PAGE AND OPPOSITE: The registration line outside CPAC for Comic-Con 1979

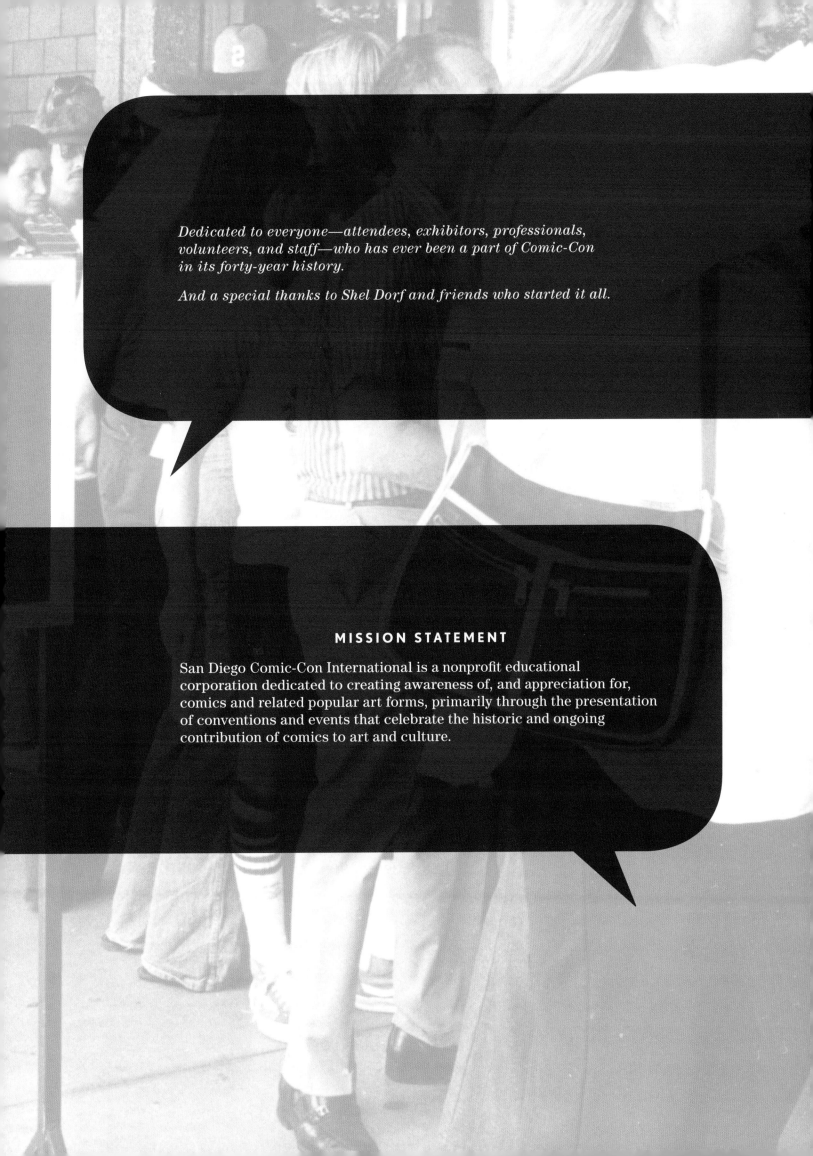

Dedicated to everyone—attendees, exhibitors, professionals, volunteers, and staff—who has ever been a part of Comic-Con in its forty-year history.

And a special thanks to Shel Dorf and friends who started it all.

MISSION STATEMENT

San Diego Comic-Con International is a nonprofit educational corporation dedicated to creating awareness of, and appreciation for, comics and related popular art forms, primarily through the presentation of conventions and events that celebrate the historic and ongoing contribution of comics to art and culture.

SAN DIEGO'S GOLDEN STATE COMIC-CON

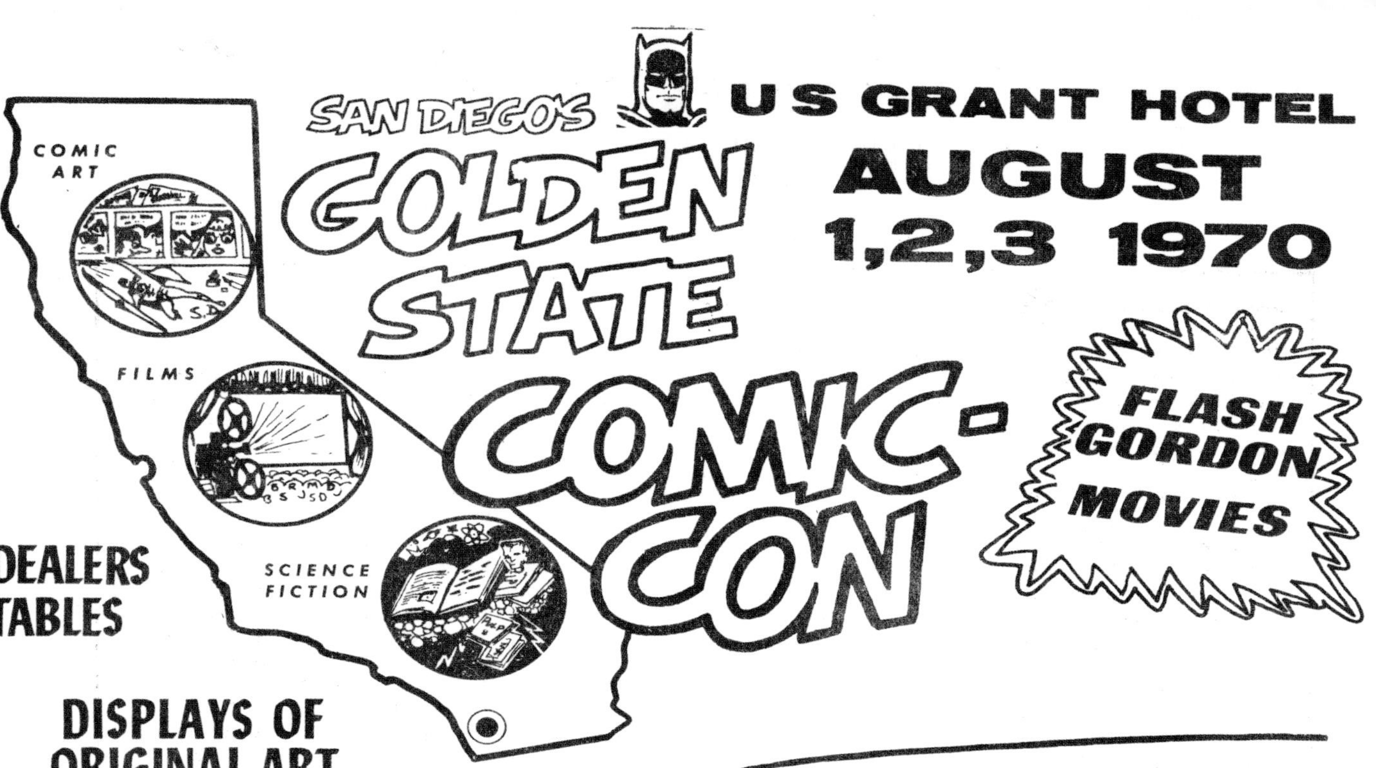
COMIC ART
FILMS
SCIENCE FICTION

U S GRANT HOTEL

AUGUST 1,2,3 1970

FLASH GORDON MOVIES

DEALERS TABLES

DISPLAYS OF ORIGINAL ART AND FAN ART

-JACK KIRBY-
...Yes, JACK KIRBY will be appearing in person

appearing in person
A.E. VanVOGT
Renown SCI-FI Writer
EARL KEMP
Editor GREENLEAF and ADVENT Publishers

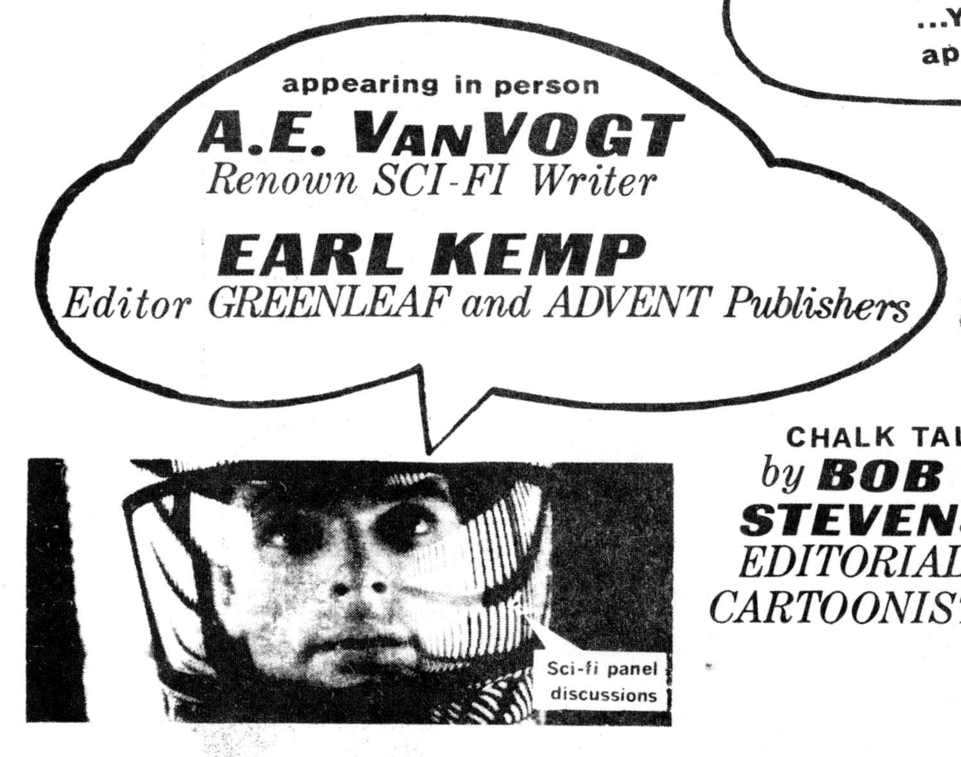
Sci-fi panel discussions

CHALK TALK
by **BOB STEVENS**
EDITORIAL CARTOONIST

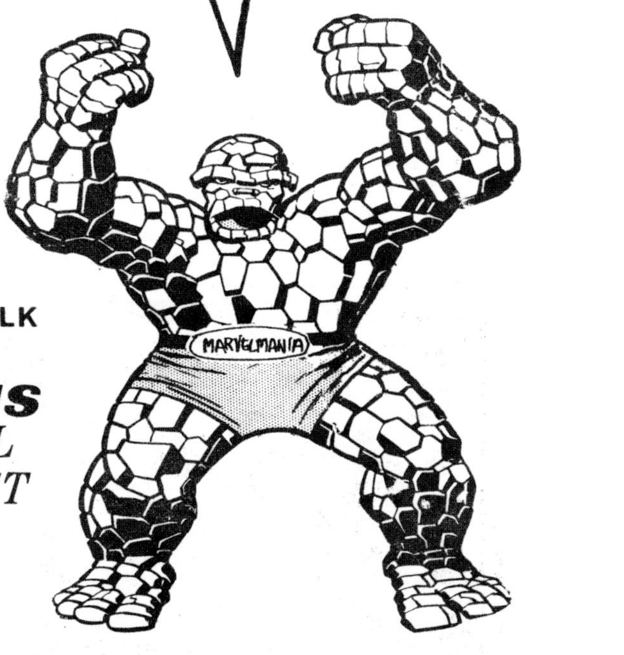
MARVELMANIA

----CLIP OUT AND MAIL---------------------------------- **Admission** ------------------------------

To: SDGS COMIC-CON
P.O. BOX 23182
SAN DIEGO, CALIF.
92123

ENCLOSED IS $_____ FOR ____DEALERS TABLES
($10.00 each)

_______ ☐ ***$3.50 for 3 days***

_______ ☐ **SUPPORTING MEMBERSHIP** (NON-ATTENDING)-$2.00

Make out checks and Money Orders to:
SAN DIEGO'S GOLDEN STATE COMIC-CON

TICKETS AT THE DOOR – $5.00

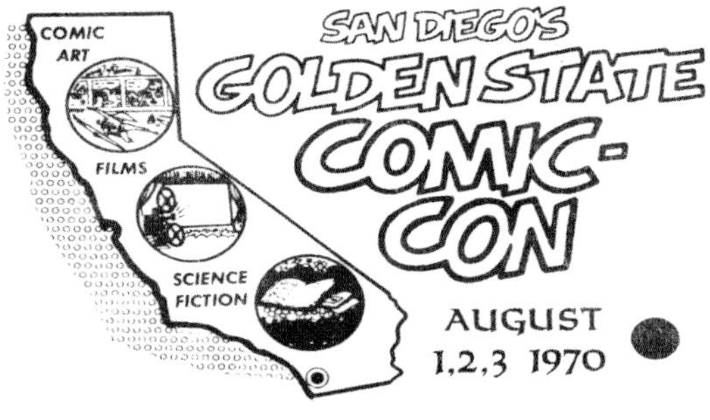
SAN DIEGO'S
GOLDEN STATE
COMIC-CON
COMIC ART
FILMS
SCIENCE FICTION
AUGUST
1,2,3 1970

Name:_______________ Age:_____

Address:_______________

City:__________ State:__________ Zip:______

(FILL OUT THE HOTEL RESERVATION CARD AND RETURN)

CONTENTS

FOREWORD BY RAY BRADBURY 13

PRESIDENT'S MESSAGE 15

INTRODUCTION 18

THE 1970s   20

Jack Kirby 32
Forrest J Ackerman 37
A Short History of Comic Conventions 40
The Many Facets of Comic-Con International......44
Ray Bradbury..49
Underground Comix Creators at Comic-Con........52
Robert A. Heinlein Blood Drive...........................56
Notable Guests 58

THE 1980s   60

Will Eisner 67
Dave Stevens..75
Sergio Aragonés 78
Rick Geary 80
The Will Eisner Comic Industry Awards 84
Comic Book Expo 86
Masquerade...92
Notable Guests 94

THE 1990s   96

Neil Gaiman.. 103
Con/Fusion 105
Comic-Con Is Truly International...................... 106
APE: The Alternative Press Expo 112
Frank Miller... 114
Comic-Con Publications................................ 120
The Official Comic-Con T-shirt 136
Comics Arts Conference 148
Notable Guests 150

THE 2000s   152

Will Eisner Spirit of Comics Retailer Award....... 157
Mark Evanier 161
WonderCon 162
Volunteers 172
Jim Lee 178
Notable Guests 180

APPENDICES   183

Will Eisner Comic Industry Awards.................... 184
Will Eisner Hall of Fame 195
Will Eisner Spirit of Comics
    Retailer Award.................................. 196
Inkpot Awards.. 197
Bob Clampett Humanitarian Award 200
Bill Finger Award for Excellence
    in Comic Book Writing...................... 201
Russ Manning Most Promising
    Newcomer Award 202
Comic-Con Icon Award........................203

AFTER WORDS 204

ACKNOWLEDGMENTS 206

PHOTO CREDITS 207

OPPOSITE: A poster for the first Comic-Con in 1970

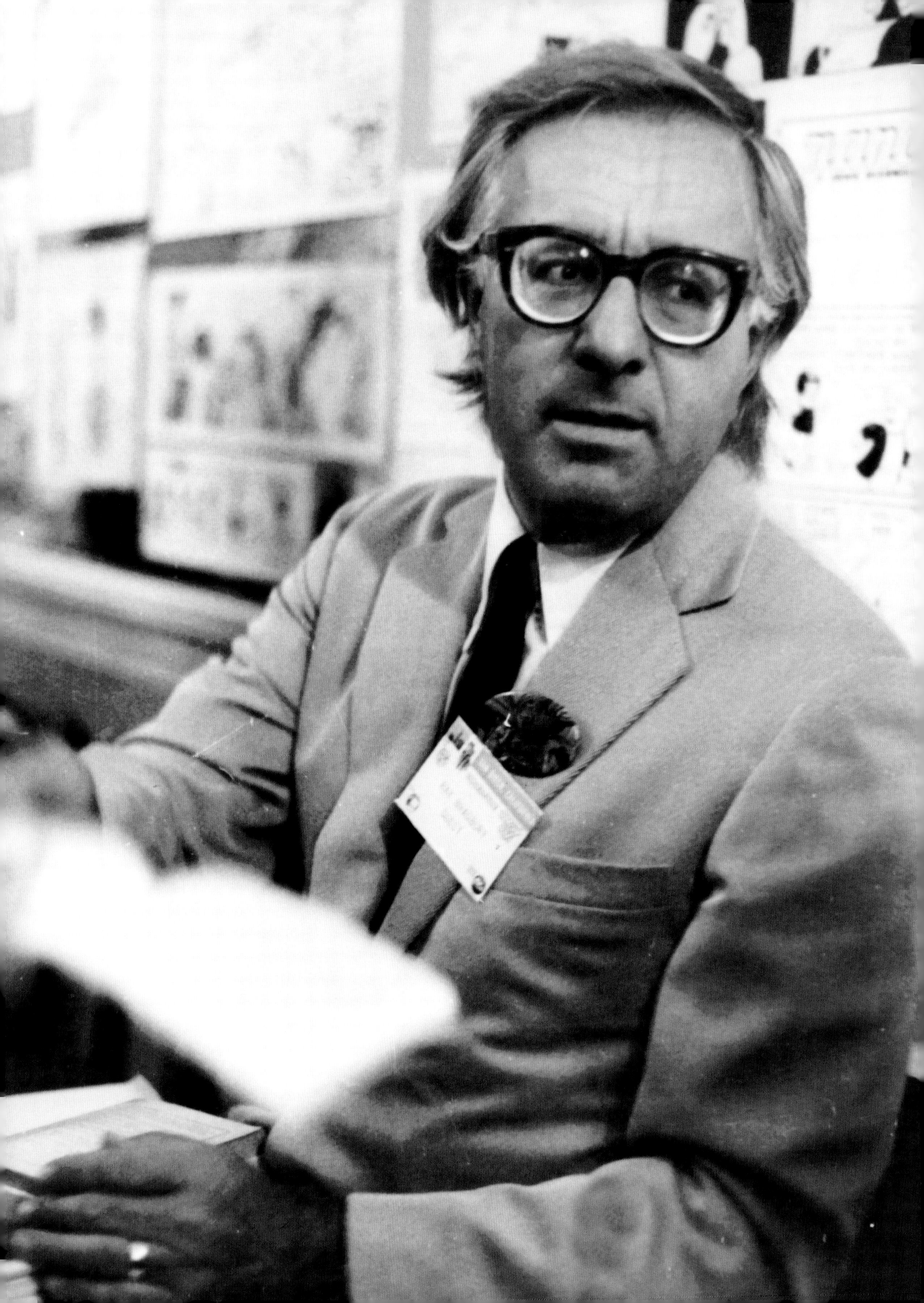

FOREWORD

I first started collecting comics when I was twelve years old and fell in love with the work of Hal Foster. I collected the *Tarzan* strips from the Sunday paper, as well as *Prince Valiant*, every week for many years.

When I was twenty-six and had published my first book, I wrote to Hal Foster and told him how much I loved him.

He responded by giving me one of his original large Sunday illustrations, which I still have here at the house.

When I was in my late forties, I was asked to come down to San Diego to attend the first Comic-Con at the El Cortez Hotel. I was part of a group of about three hundred people, if you can believe that. The fascinating thing about this was that these people all loved illustration. We were all very happy being there and enjoying one another's company.

It's still a wonderful experience for me to attend Comic-Con, now with tens of thousands of people, and to be able to look around at all these people who share my love for the history of illustration.

During the next year I will have three graphic novels printed—*The Martian Chronicles*, *Fahrenheit 451*, and *Something Wicked This Way Comes*—and I hope to be able to celebrate these graphic novels with all the wonderful people at the 2009 Comic-Con.

BEST FROM
Ray Bradbury
1976!

RAY BRADBURY
OCTOBER 9, 2008

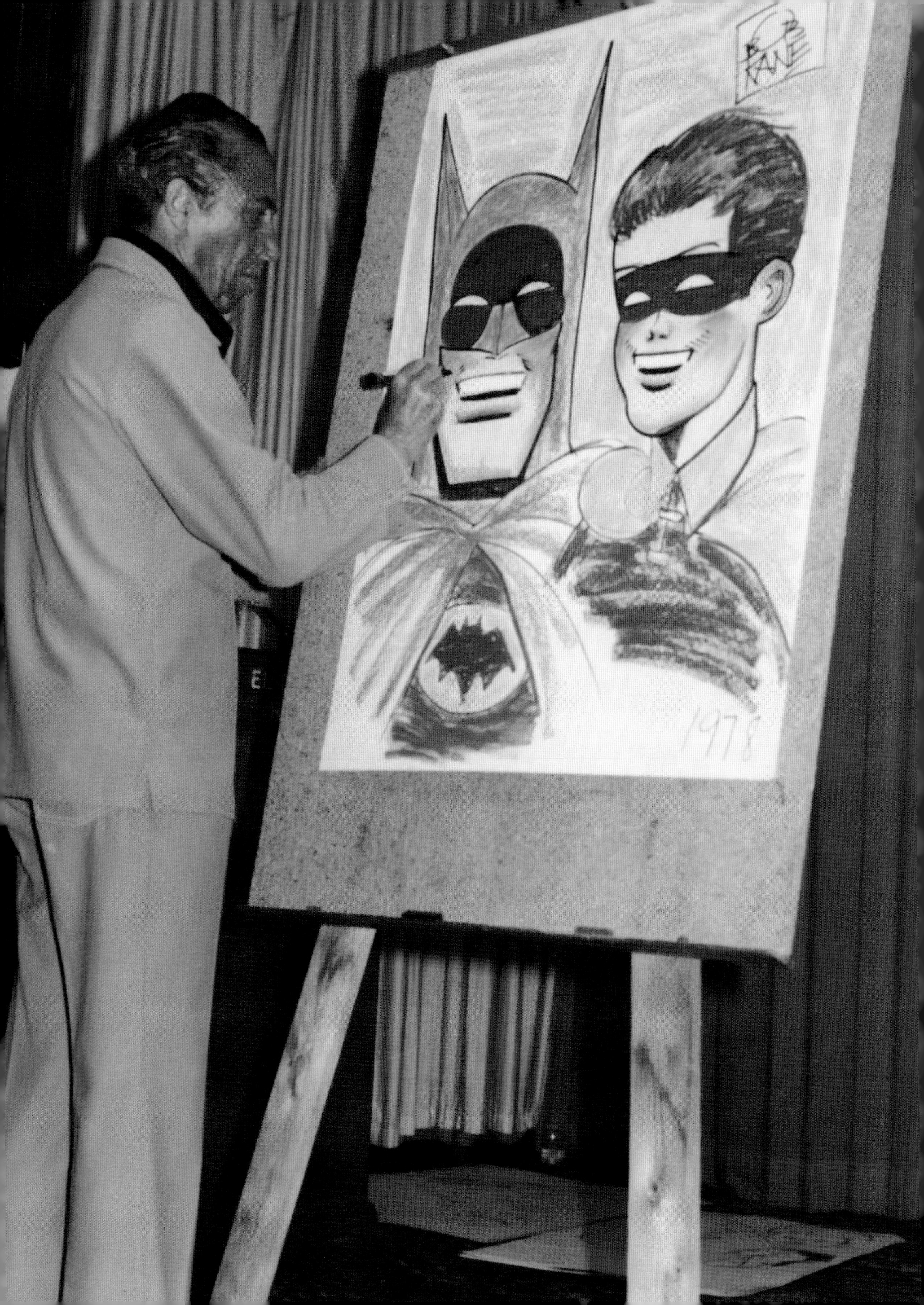
1978

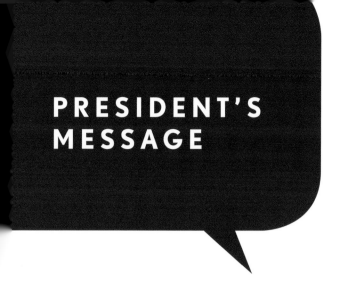

PRESIDENT'S MESSAGE

CONVENTION FACILITIES
DRESS ROOM
STAR TREK HEADQUARTERS
MULTIPLE ART SHOWS
CARTOONISTS DISPLAYS
WRITERS SEMINARS
GAMES ROOMS
MOVIES, SPEAKERS
ONE LARGE DEALERS ROOM
FREE PARKING FOR HOTEL GUESTS WITH IN & OUT PRIVILAGES
BEACH LEVEL MEETING ROOMS
HI-RISE
BARCELONA ROOM
MADRID ROOM
TOLEDO ROOM
LOBBY
ENTRANCE
WEST PARKING
EAST PARKING

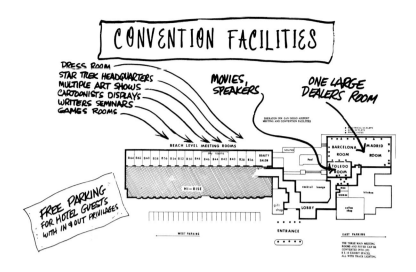

Comic-Con International. There was a time when few knew the name.

Today the scenario is a little different. With mainstream magazine covers, newspaper headlines the world over, and television news shows covering Comic-Con, there doesn't seem to be many who haven't heard the name.

Like so many people involved in organizing this amazing event, I started volunteering for Comic-Con when I was a teenager and the gathering was small. It still surprises me how many people have heard about Comic-Con now. Some know the story of our humble beginnings, how that first convention attracted three hundred people and was held in the basement of a downtown hotel almost forty years ago.

While the show now welcomes more than one hundred twenty-five thousand people annually and attracts worldwide attention, few are aware—or remember—that there was a time when we struggled to make ourselves known. Encouraging people to attend Comic-Con over the course of these four decades wasn't always an easy task. We tried a variety of ways to get our message across to the general public.

The constraints of a limited budget had us try classified advertising in newspapers, very limited radio ads, and even a local television commercial featuring a man dressed as the Mighty Thor, complete with hammer.

I don't think we'll ever know for sure if Thor was the reason for our continued increase in attendance so many years ago. But one thing is for certain: The event catered to a whole new area of popular arts that, until then, had only barely been tapped.

Forty years ago we embarked on a journey to bring wider recognition to comic books and comic art, fantasy literature, and film. Our intentions were modest and stemmed from a profound appreciation for those media. And that continues to this day. But what a different day it is.

Film received its due recognition as a historic and artistic treasure when the United States Congress created the National Film Registry. Fantasy literature has perhaps never been more popular as fantasy novels reach number one on many best-seller lists for weeks at a time, and movies turn those books into multimillion-dollar epics. Comic books have not only reached a wider audience as publications are being translated into different languages and a host of different mediums, but they are now widely accepted in the mainstream for their value as art and entertainment as well. This uniquely American art form now boasts a diverse group of publications and genres that range from superhero comics to independent

OPPOSITE: Batman co-creator Bob Kane drawing the Caped Crusader and Robin at the 1978 Comic-Con
ABOVE: The layout of the 1973 Comic-Con at the Sheraton Hotel, Harbor Island

and self-published books. The medium is restricted only by the imagination of its creators, which is seemingly limitless.

But this book is not a history of the comics industry. This book is not even an all-encompassing chronicle of Comic-Con. Instead, it's a photo- and art-filled stroll through time, an opportunity to look back at some of the people, places, and events that helped make Comic-Con International what it is today.

In reviewing the photographs and art included in these pages, a part of me realizes that so much of this happened before many of our current attendees were even born. But a bigger part of me gets lost in these wonderful memories: the times we had, the friends we made, and the fun we continue to have in organizing what is, for me, the best event in the world.

Enjoy.

JOHN ROGERS
PRESIDENT
COMIC-CON INTERNATIONAL

OPPOSITE: The El Cortez Hotel in downtown San Diego, home of Comic-Con for most of the 1970s

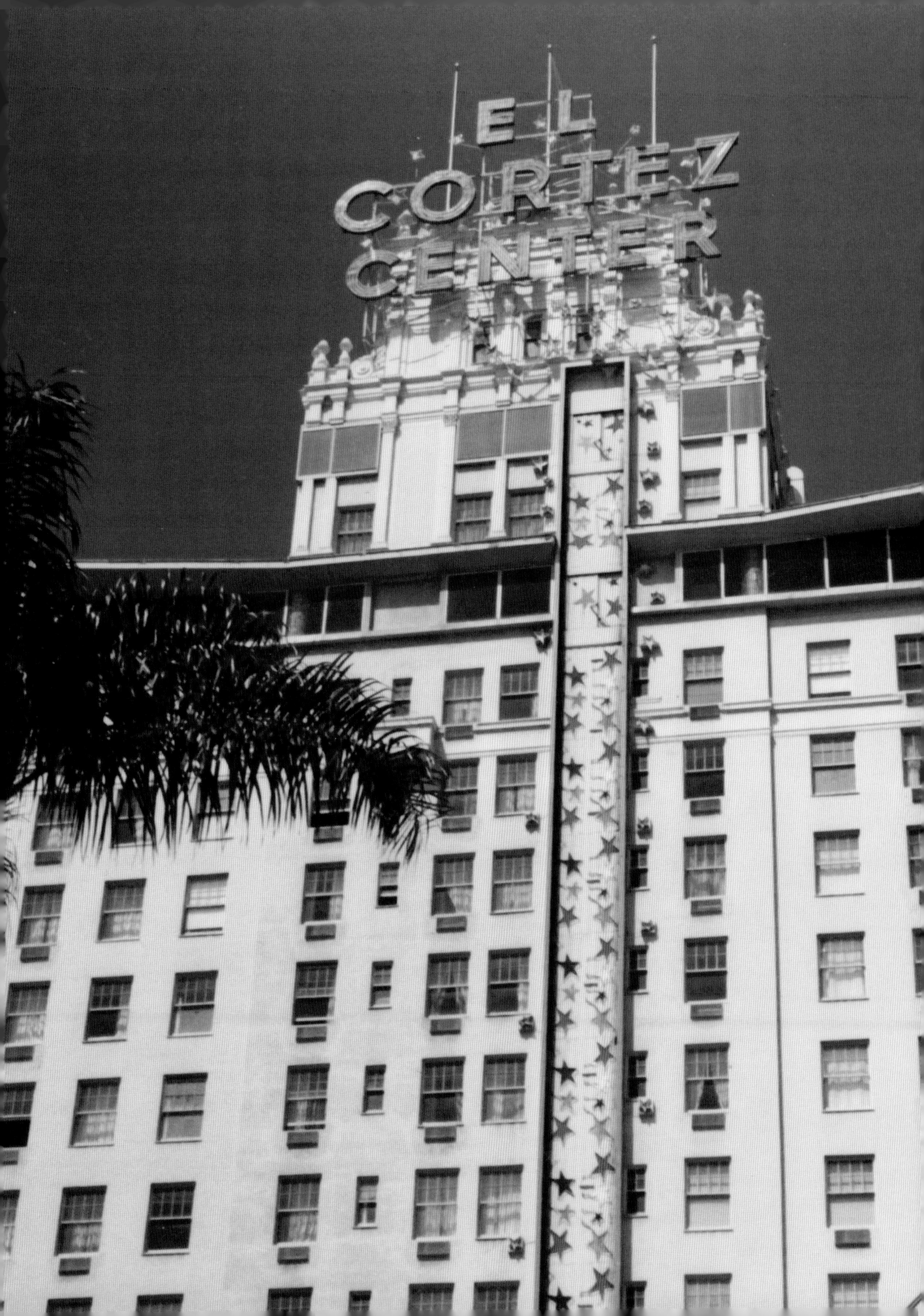
EL
CORTEZ
CENTER

INTRODUCTION

Some people liken it to Brigadoon, the mythical Scottish village that appears for one day every one hundred years and then vanishes again into the mist. Others bring up the tale of the blind men and the elephant: Each man touches a different part of the giant animal and walks away with his own impression of what an elephant is.

Both analogies are true for the San Diego Comic-Con. The timeframe is a bit more manageable: It appears once a year for four days and then vanishes. Each attendee would probably tell you something different about his or her own personal experiences at the event. To some, it's all about comics: hunting down that missing back issue, meeting their favorite writer or artist, finding that incredible piece of original art that they can't live without. For others, it's about movies, television, animation, gaming, anime, toys, action figures, fine art, or any number of things from a list that's almost endless. The truth is, Comic-Con is a convention that combines numerous elements of the popular arts under one roof. Much like the tale of the blind men and the elephant, Comic-Con is all of these different things at the same time. But the common thread is simple: It's a gathering of men, women, and children drawn together by the magic of creativity and the age-old tradition of storytelling, especially in comics, but including other areas of the popular arts—movies, television, animation, and science fiction and fantasy, to name just a few. And that's the way it was planned to be from the very beginning, back in 1970, almost forty shows ago.

The founders of Comic-Con laid it all out at the start, with a trio of graphics in the very first logo for San Diego's Golden State Comic-Con: "Comic Art, Films, Science Fiction." The show started with three hundred attendees. In 2008 more than one hundred twenty-six thousand people—attendees, professionals, exhibitors, volunteers, and staff—were present at an event that sold out weeks in advance. That incredible leap of attendance occurred over almost forty years and throughout a few location changes in the general vicinity of San Diego (most of them downtown). Those years include an amazing amount of comics and pop-culture history. Thousands of comic book writers and artists; science fiction and fantasy authors and illustrators; and movie, television, and animation stars—in front of and behind the camera—have made the trip to Comic-Con in that time span.

Some of those people, especially those who worked in the comics industry over the seventy-five years since the debut of the American comic book, would never have had a chance to meet their fans. Comic-Con has actively sought out the writers and artists from the rich heritage of comic books and strips and presented them to the public. Many of these creators labored anonymously and were discovered by individual fans and collectors and brought to Comic-Con to meet, for the very first time, the people who adore their work.

This book is about those people and everyone who came to see them. It's a pictorial history of a convention that has gone from a small local gathering of fans to an international event with a name recognized around the world. Say *Comic-Con* in this day and age, and most people know you're talking about that show that takes place in San Diego each summer. Comics, once the object of affection for a small group of discerning collectors and aficionados, has become a mainstream phenomenon, finally recognized as the art form it's been from its inception as well as an

THIS PAGE AND OPPOSITE, TOP: The Comic-Con logo from its earliest days (from left) as both the Golden State and West Coast Comic-Con, Rick Geary's toucan logos, and the current version
OPPOSITE, BOTTOM: Charles Schulz Snoopy cartoon from the 1974 program book

exciting form of entertainment. Comics have a history of being a vibrant and diverse medium of storytelling. Comics writers and artists create entire universes with a blend of words and artwork on paper that is unparalleled in any other medium. The folks running Comic-Con have long recognized the rich history and incredible potential of the art form, and have presented the medium to a wider audience as part of the nonprofit organization's mission statement, to create awareness of and appreciation for comics and related popular art forms. Along with its sister shows, WonderCon and APE (the Alternative Press Expo), Comic-Con has continued *the* grassroots effort to tell the world about comics, an effort that was started some forty years ago by a dedicated group of volunteers.

Over the four decades of the event, one thing has remained the same at Comic-Con: The convention is an event run by fans. In 2008 more than two thousand volunteers helped run the show alongside full-time staff members, the board of directors, and members of the Comic-Con committee. It's the incredible dedication of these people—all of them fans who give their time and effort to the Herculean task of putting

on this event—that remains one of the most tangible constants of the convention over the years.

This book will take you back through the past thirty-nine Comic-Cons through photographs and art from the Comic-Con archives. If you've been to the convention, you're in for an enjoyable trip down memory lane. And if you've never been to Comic-Con in San Diego, it's a bit hard to describe, but you don't need a mythical Scottish village or an elephant to get the idea. Just turn the page and enjoy the journey.

I LOVE COMIC CONVENTIONS, BUT I ALWAYS END UP DRINKING TOO MUCH ROOT BEER...

THE 1970s

When the first "San Diego's Golden State Comic-Con" was held in the basement of San Diego's U. S. Grant Hotel in 1970, the three hundred people gathered there could never have imagined what was in store for the show's future. Comics and science fiction fans' dreams had finally come true when the first-ever comic convention happened on the West Coast. The three-day event consisted of a dealers' room (the precursor to what is currently known as the Exhibit Hall where a "deal"—or a trade—could be made) with old comic books and memorabilia for sale, a meeting room with programs featuring the special guests (Jack Kirby, Ray Bradbury, A. E. van Vogt), an Art Show highlighting editorial cartoons by Bob Stevens, a charity Art Auction, a Marvelmania booth, and film screenings. There was even a program book with a wraparound Jack Kirby cover. The cost for all three days? A mere $3.50 in advance. Admission jumped to a whopping $5.00 at the door.

COMIC-CON'S ORIGINS

For that first Comic-Con to happen, a lot of things had to fall into place. Yes, there had been comic conventions in other cities (SEE A Short History of Comic Conventions, page 40), but never before in San Diego. An amazing confluence of fan groups occurred in the area in the mid-1960s that made the

ABOVE: Superman by Curt Swan and Murphy Anderson from an early 1970s program book
LEFT: An illustration by artist John Pound from the first Comic-Con program book in 1970
OPPOSITE: Detail from the first program book cover, by Jack Kirby

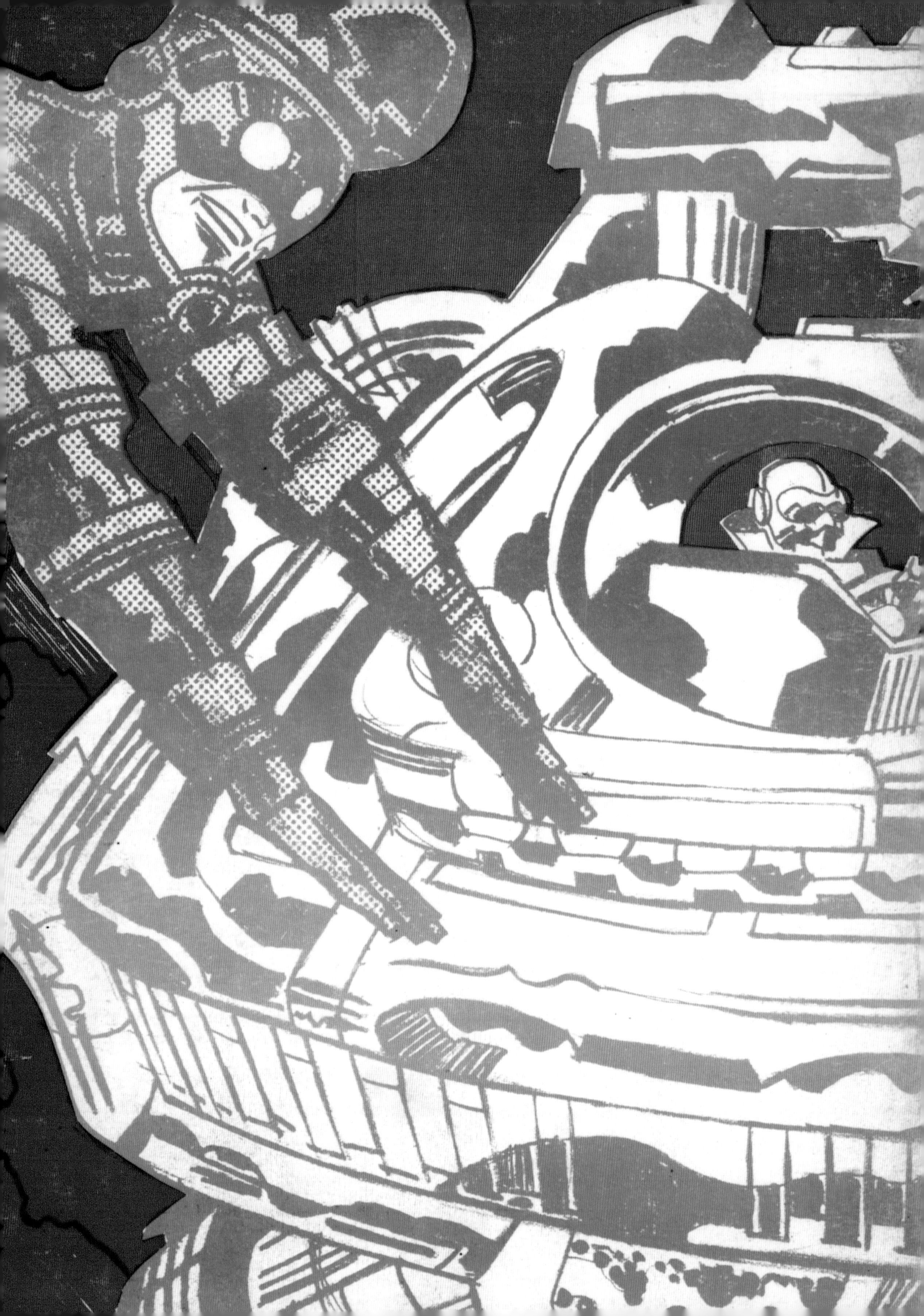

convention—in hindsight—seem almost inevitable. The first group consisted of teenaged fans Scott Shaw! (yes, the exclamation point is part of his name), Greg Bear, John Pound, Roger Freedman, Bill Richardson, and others calling themselves the Underground Film Society, a confederation of comics, movie, and science fiction enthusiasts. In addition to publishing mimeographed fanzines, their activities included a field trip to Los Angeles to meet Forrest J Ackerman, the writer/editor behind fan-favorite magazine *Famous Monsters of Filmland* and the possessor of one of the largest collections of movie and science fiction memorabilia in the world. These teens eventually joined with a group of science fiction fans, the San Diego Science Fantasy Society, which included Ken Krueger (a member of science fiction's First Fandom, an organization of science fiction fans active in fandom for more than twenty years as of the late 1950s), collector and dealer John Hull, and fans Dave Clark and John Paul. The combined group called themselves the ProFanests (more informally, the Woodchucks, after Carl Barks's "Junior Woodchucks," a Boy Scouts–like group featured in his Donald Duck stories). They met at Krueger's Ocean Beach bookstore to discuss their interests.

Meanwhile, another group of fans were meeting occasionally to talk about their love of old comic books. That group included Bob Sourk, Richard Alf, Bill Lund, Barry Alfonso, and Mike Towry. A chance meeting between Bob Sourk and Scott Shaw! (an aspiring cartoonist and self-described "funnybook freak") led to Scott's attending one of those comics get-togethers. The special guest at that meeting was Shel Dorf, a recent transplant from Detroit who had helped organize that city's Triple Fan Fair, one of the first comic conventions in the country. Shel was a freelance graphic designer who had developed contacts with a number of cartoonists and other celebrities. Before long Shel was arranging trips for the fan group (which now included many of the Woodchucks) to visit Jack and Roz Kirby in their home in the Los Angeles area. Kirby found the kids interesting enough to immortalize five of them—Shaw!, Pound, Alfonso, Towry, and Lund—as the rock band "The San Diego Five-String Mob" in *Superman's Pal Jimmy Olsen*, one of the comics he was doing at the time.

Inspired by the Kirby visits and Shel's other contacts and past experience with putting on conventions, the fan group decided to put on its own local show. But first they needed some money, so they held a trial one-day event at the U. S. Grant Hotel in downtown San Diego as a fund-raiser. That show, on March 21, 1970, featured talks by the two special guests—Forrest J Ackerman and comic book artist Mike Royer (most famous for his inking of Jack Kirby's work)—and a showing of the 1925 silent film *The Lost World*. The small four-page program for the show listed Bob Sourk and Richard Alf as the co-chairmen and Shel Dorf as founder and adviser. The booklet was prophetic in its introduction: "The years to come will see us grow, and San Diego will take its rightful place in the world of fandom."

The minicon not only raised needed funds but generated interest in what is considered the first-ever San Diego Comic-Con, the three-day event held

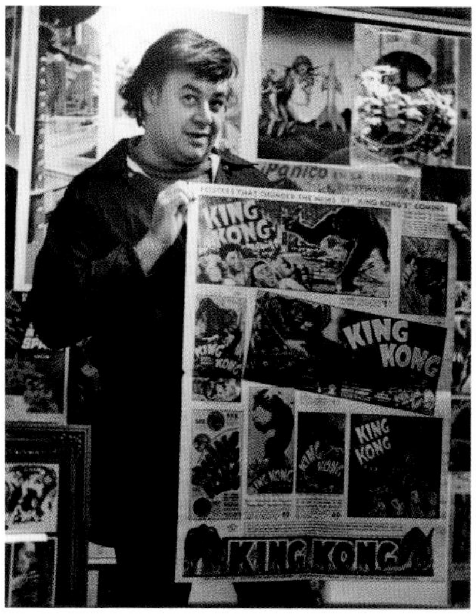
KING KONG

LEFT: One of Comic-Con's founders, Shel Dorf, shown with the type of movie memorabilia present even at the early conventions

August 1–3, 1970. The summer show—with Jack Kirby as the big draw and science fiction writers Ray Bradbury and A. E. van Vogt as additional guests— was considered a success by the convention committee. They scheduled a second year for Comic-Con at an unusual venue: the campus of the University of California, San Diego. About eight hundred people showed up for the three days, including many who took advantage of the low cost of staying in the dorm rooms. The guests and programs over this weekend illustrate that, from the start, Comic-Con embraced science fiction/fantasy, film, animation, and comic strips, along with comic books. The special guests from both the minicon and the first Comic-Con—Kirby, Bradbury, Ackerman, and Royer—were back and joined by comics artists, science fiction authors and illustrators, animators, and even actor Kirk Alyn, who played Superman in the 1940s serials.

A NEW HOME AT THE EL CORTEZ

In 1972 Comic-Con moved to the location most fondly remembered by longtime attendees: the El Cortez Hotel. The venerable downtown landmark had every- thing: a separate convention facility for the dealers' room and programs (con- nected by a walkway over the street), inexpensive sleeping rooms, a funky glass elevator to the roof, a courtyard pool, and a nearby Denny's. The El Cortez was home to Comic-Con throughout the rest of the 1970s (with one brief sidetrack in 1973 to the Sheraton Harbor Island, due to a late start in planning that left the convention committee scrambling to find a venue). The show underwent a name change to San Diego's West Coast Comic Convention in 1972, before settling on the official name of San Diego Comic-Con in 1973. In 1975 the committee added a "Part II" in November—an additional three-day event, which made it the longest Comic-Con ever—with guests including George Pal and actor Jock Mahoney, for the low admission price of $1.00.

Even at this early stage of the convention, Comic-Con became the place to be for both fans and pros. Comic book legends Stan Lee, Will Eisner, Carl Barks, and Superman creators Jerry Siegel and Joe Shuster; science fiction giants Robert A. Heinlein and Theodore Sturgeon; animation greats Bob Clampett, Chuck Jones, Mel Blanc, and June Foray; and comic strip superstars Milton Caniff and Charles Schulz all made their first appearances at the event in the early 1970s. Movies were also part of the mix, not only in the form of sixteen-millimeter classics being shown in the films room at all hours, but also with appearances by directors Frank Capra and George Pal and actors Chuck Norris, Walter Koenig, and Adam West. In 1974 *The Golden Voyage of Sinbad* had its world premiere at Comic-Con, and *Doc Savage* had an advance screening in 1975. In 1976 Lucasfilm's Charlie Lippincott gave the first-ever presentation about *Star Wars*—a year before the film's debut. A huge audience turned out three years later when Lucasfilm sent Craig Miller with a preview of *The Empire Strikes Back*.

THE BEGINNING OF FAN-FAVORITE TRADITIONS

Many other Comic-Con traditions began in the 1970s. The annual Masquerade costume contest got under way in 1974, as did Comic-Con's own Inkpot Awards, presented at a banquet to the event's special guests in recognition of achievement in their individual fields. The Robert A. Heinlein Blood Drive got its start in 1977, with donors getting to meet the famed science fiction author (SEE Robert A. Heinlein Blood Drive, page 56), and the first Japanese animation (anime) screening room debuted in 1978, showing videotapes supplied by Toei Animation.

Carried over from many science fiction conventions, the Art Show became a part of Comic-Con, too. Featuring the art of many talented professionals and amateurs, it became a showcase for comics, science fiction, and fantasy paintings, drawings, and even sculpture. At various times, the Art Show in the 1970s included paintings by Carl Barks, original drawings by Basil Wolverton and Milton Caniff, Steranko's covers for *The Shadow* paperbacks, Robert Williams's lowbrow art canvases, *Little Annie Fanny* originals by Harvey Kurtzman and Will Elder, and early works of Dave Stevens (*The Rocketeer*), who was the Art Show coordinator in 1975.

To help raise funds for the show, artist Jack Katz (*The First Kingdom*) came up with the idea of holding an Art Auction, with all the works being created on the spot. Easels were set up next to the El Cortez pool, and fans could watch as their favorite artists produced original pieces that were immediately auctioned off. One lucky bidder paid $250 for an original Joe Shuster Superman. The Art Auction continued over the next three decades as a part of Comic-Con.

EXPANSION AND GROWTH

As the 1970s progressed, more and more comics professionals from around the country were making their way to San Diego and the guest list expanded every year, including everyone from Golden Age comic book creators like Bob Kane, C. C. Beck, and Gardner Fox to top writers and artists for the major companies, such as Neal Adams, John Buscema, Joe Kubert, and John Romita. In addition, a large contingent of underground comics ("comix") creators descended on Comic-Con in 1978, partly to hang out with their mentor, Harvey Kurtzman. Those cartoonists included *The Fabulous Furry Freak Brothers* creators Gilbert Shelton and Dave Sheridan, *The Checkered Demon* creator S. Clay Wilson, and *Trashman* creator Spain Rodriguez (SEE Underground Comix Creators at Comic-Con, page 52). And marking Comic-Con as the place to be even in the 1970s, visionary author and psychologist Timothy Leary appeared in 1977 and blew attendees' minds on a panel with science fiction authors Theodore Sturgeon and George Clayton Johnson (co-author of *Logan's Run*).

Comic-Con's dealers' room also grew. Fans could find not only a wider number of old comics, but also original artwork, collectible toys and games, movie memorabilia, pulps, science fiction/fantasy books and art, and other pop culture treasures. By 1974 the room had grown to more than one hundred tables, and by 1978 the demand for space was so high that a second dealers' room was opened on the ground floor of the El Cortez. In addition to such longtime dealers as Bud Plant, Russ Cochran, Bruce Hamilton, Mile High Comics, the American Comic Book Company (Terry Stroud and David T. Alexander), Greg Pharis, Bob Beerbohm, the Carter brothers, the Schanes brothers, Tony Raiola, and dealers' room coordinator Tom French, several artists presented and sold their art at their own tables, most notably Jim Steranko and Filipino artists Alfredo Alcala, Ernie Chan, and Nestor Redondo.

During the 1970s the convention committee expanded greatly as people were needed to run all the different areas of the show. In 1975 the event became a nonprofit, with Shel Dorf as president of the board of directors and Richard Butner as executive vice president. Besides Dave Stevens, some of the committee members who went on to notable careers included best-selling science fiction author Greg Bear, comics writer/artist Jim Valentino (co-founder of Image Comics), Dark Horse Comics licensing director David Scroggy, cartoonist/animator Scott Shaw!, cartoonist John Pound (Garbage Pail Kids), and scream queen Brinke Stevens (a.k.a. Charlene Brinkman, who later appeared in B movies such as *Teenage Exorcist* and *Mommy*).

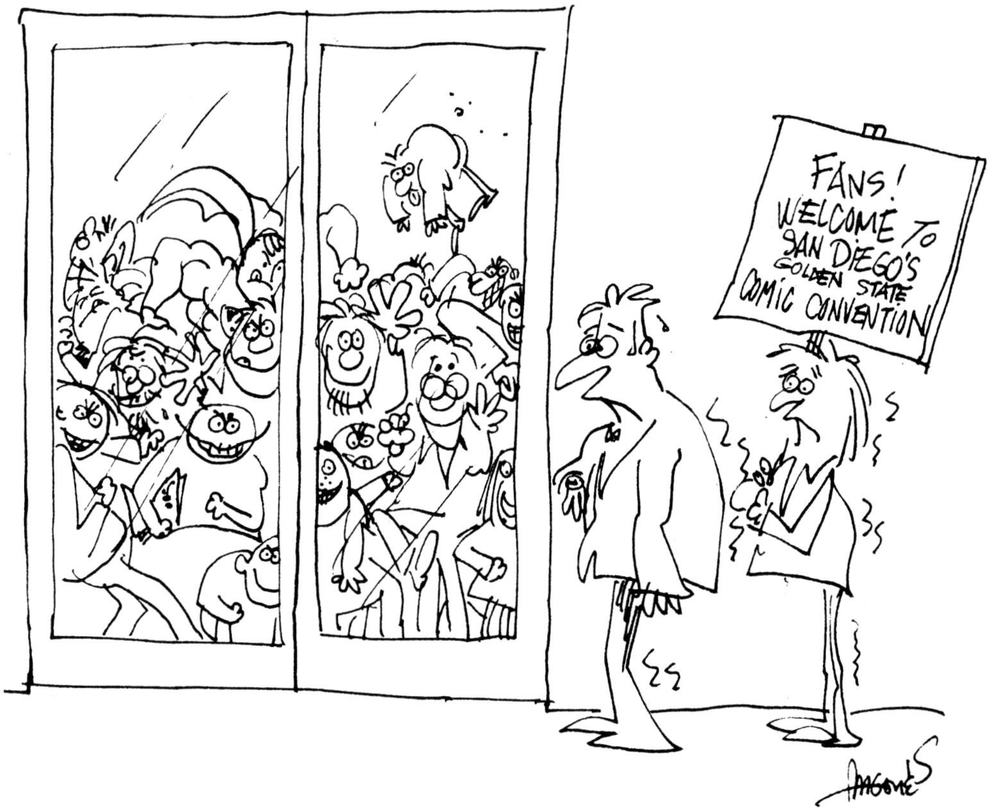
FANS!
WELCOME TO
SAN DIEGO'S
GOLDEN STATE
COMIC CONVENTION
ARAGONÉS

ABOVE: The first piece of art Sergio Aragonés made for Comic-Con, from the 1971 program book. Thirty-eight years later, Sergio is still making drawings for the convention, including the cover for this book.

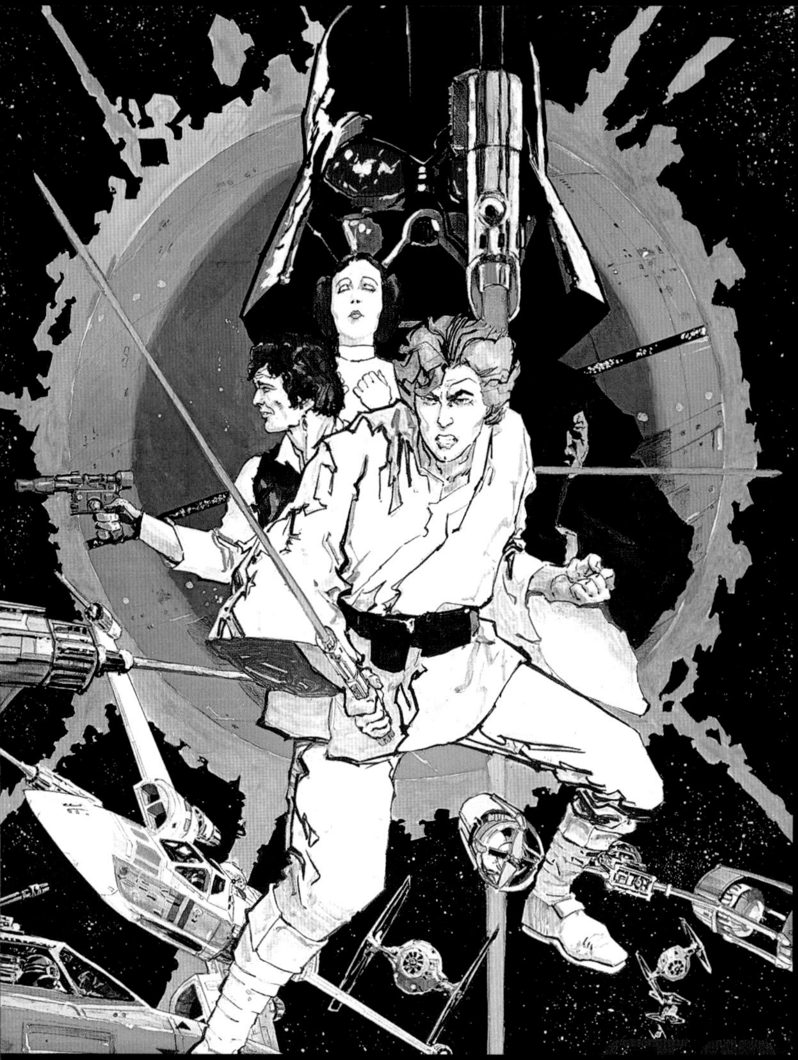

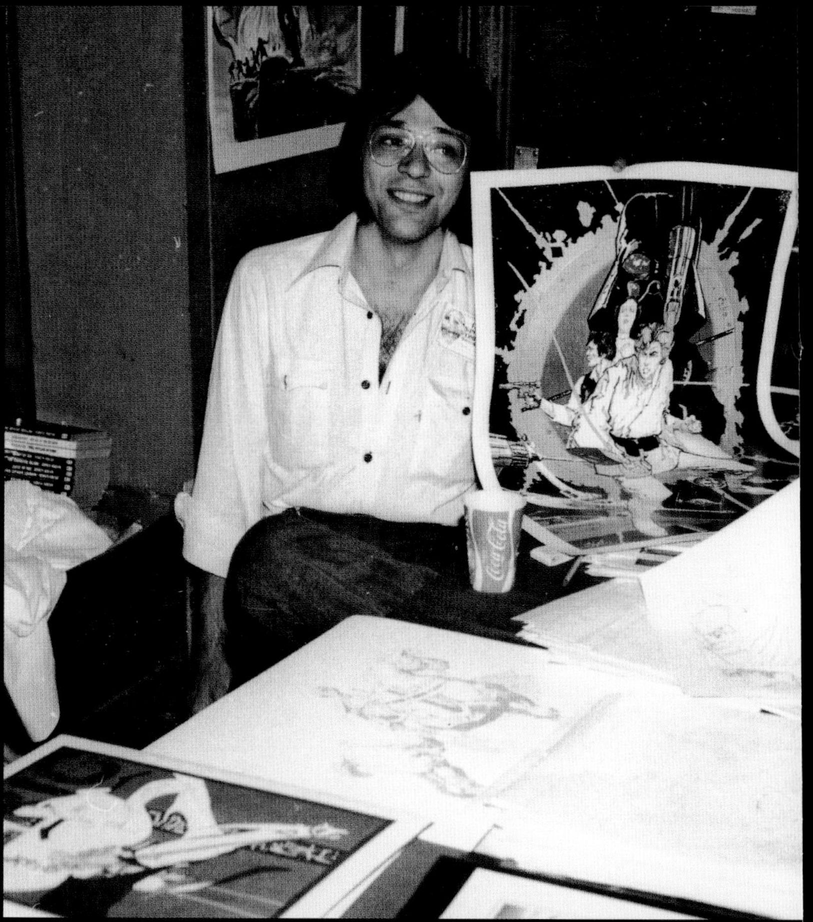
Coca-Cola

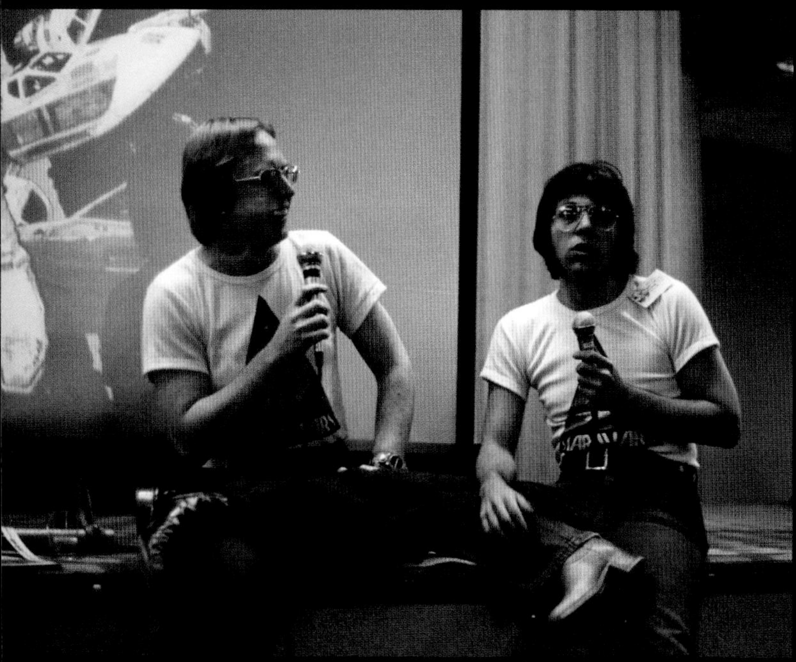
STAR WARS

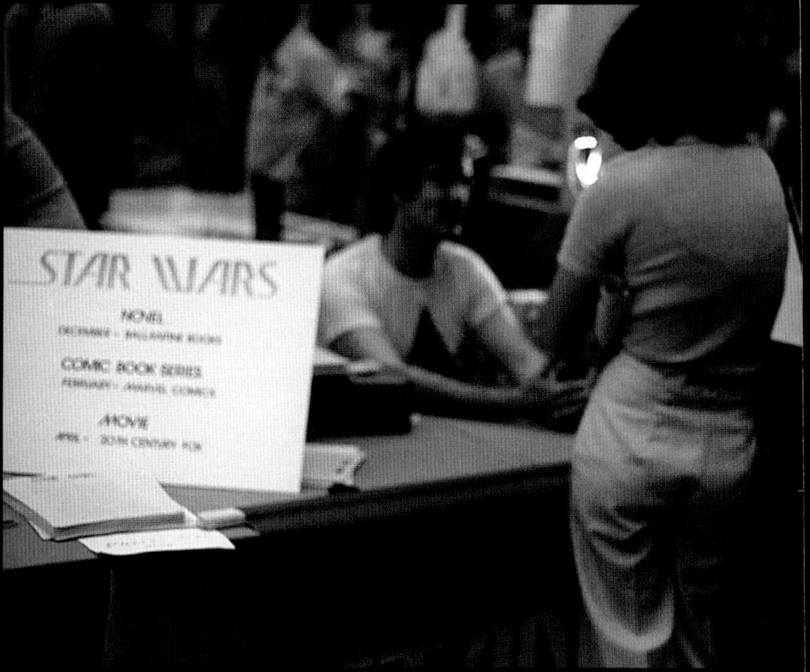
STAR WARS
NOVEL
COMIC BOOK SERIES
MOVIE

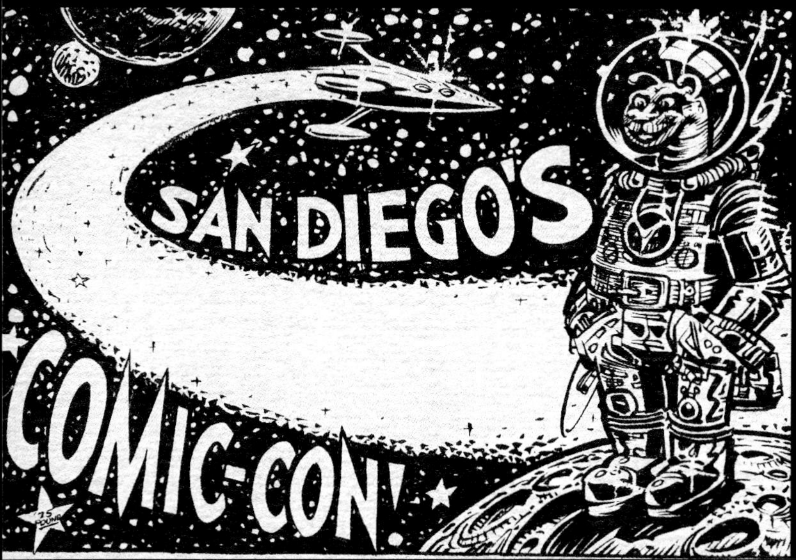
SAN DIEGO'S
COMIC-CON!

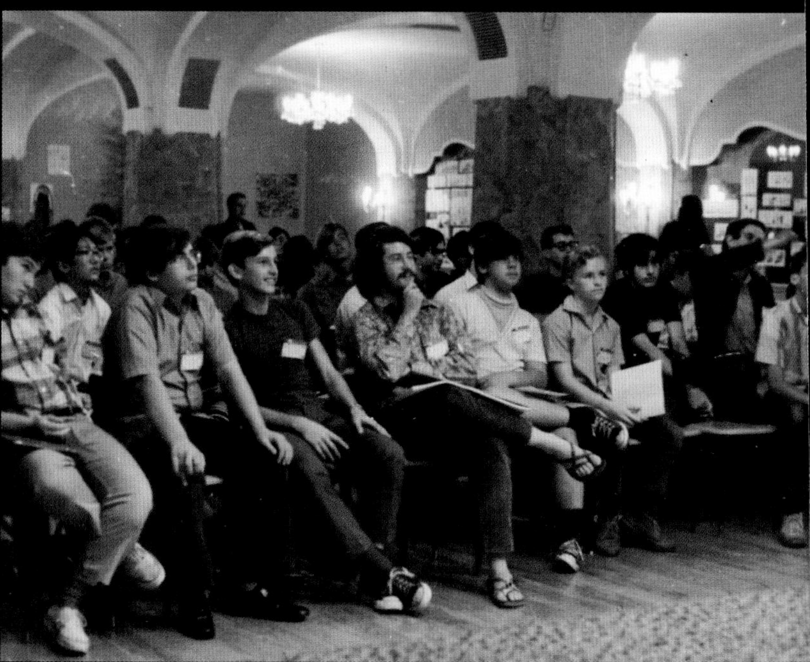

Star Wars made an early impact at Comic-Con, first having a presence at the convention in 1976, a year before the movie opened.
OPPOSITE, TOP ROW, FROM LEFT: The first art for the movie was a limited-edition poster with art by Howard Chaykin; Howard with the poster **MIDDLE ROW, FROM LEFT:** Roy Thomas and Howard Chaykin, writer and artist for Marvel's *Star Wars* comic book, talking about the project; Lucasfilm's Charlie Lippincott at the *Star Wars* table in the 1976 Dealers' Room **BOTTOM ROW, FROM LEFT:** John Pound art for a 1975 badge; an enraptured crowd at an early 1970s program

CLOCKWISE FROM TOP LEFT: A pinup by Dennis the Menace creator Hank Ketcham, one of the many syndicated cartoonists who submitted art for the 1970s program books; this 1979 map shows the Comic-Con layout at the San Diego Convention and Performing Arts Center; ads from the program book, both from 1979 and both proclaiming "still number 1" status for the "Big Two"

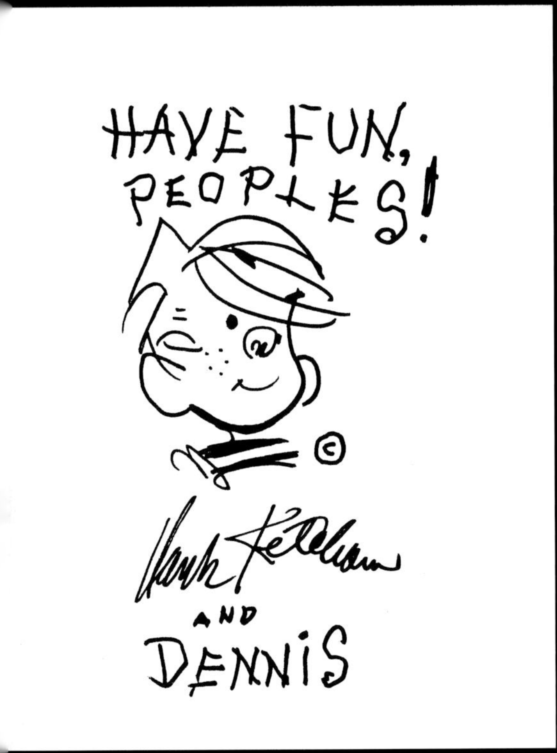
HAVE FUN, PEOPLES!
©
Hank Ketcham
AND
DENNIS

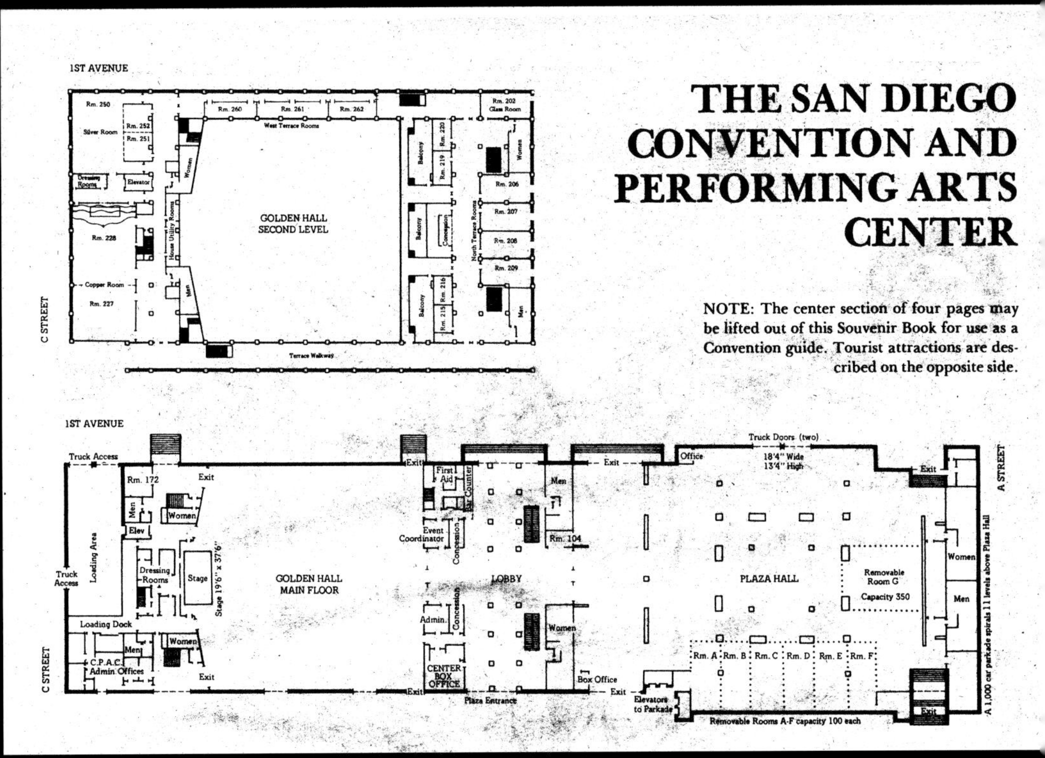
THE SAN DIEGO CONVENTION AND PERFORMING ARTS CENTER
NOTE: The center section of four pages may be lifted out of this Souvenir Book for use as a Convention guide. Tourist attractions are described on the opposite side.
1ST AVENUE
C STREET
GOLDEN HALL SECOND LEVEL
GOLDEN HALL MAIN FLOOR
LOBBY
PLAZA HALL
A STREET
Truck Access
Loading Dock
Stage
Plaza Entrance
Removable Rooms A-F capacity 100 each

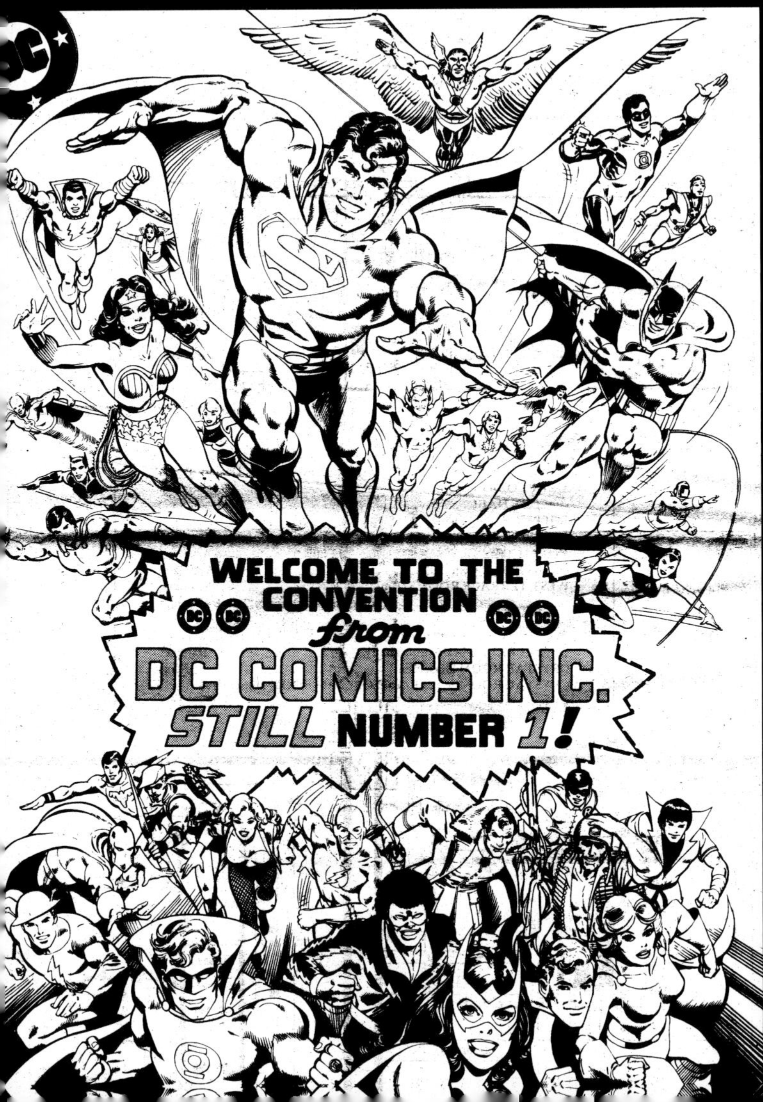
WELCOME TO THE CONVENTION
from
DC COMICS INC.
STILL NUMBER 1!

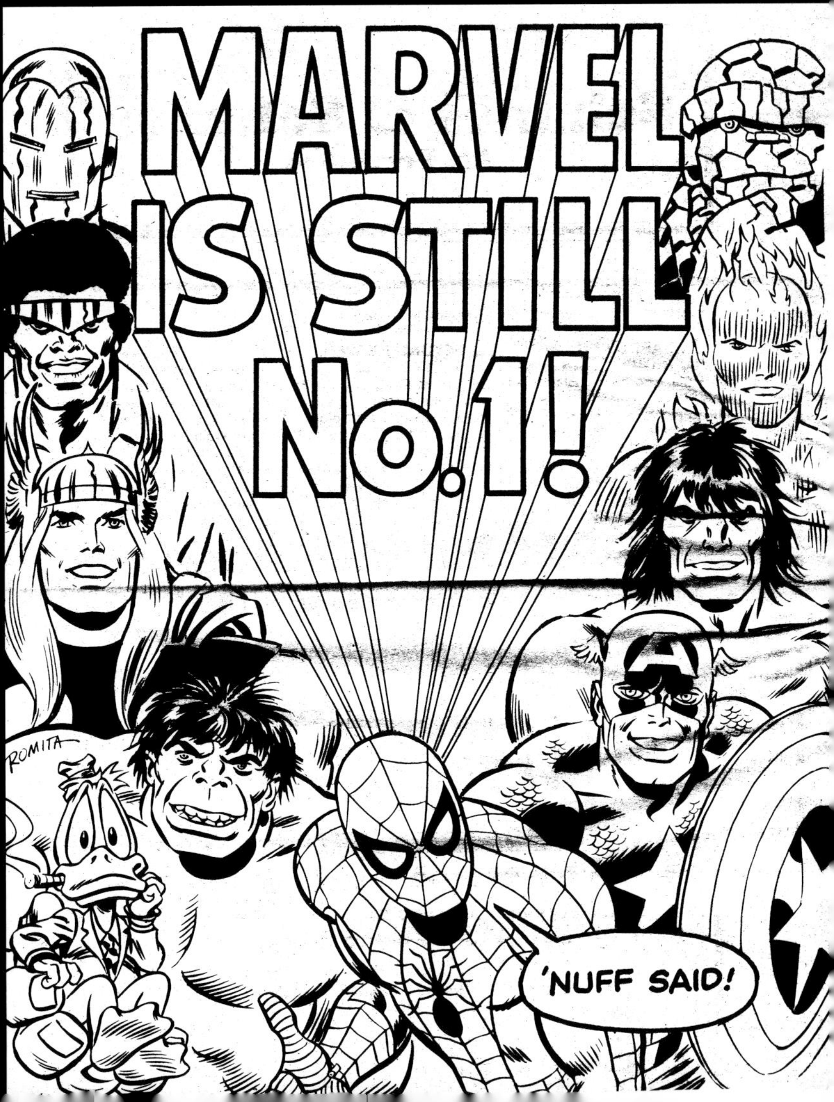
MARVEL IS STILL No.1!
ROMITA
'NUFF SAID!

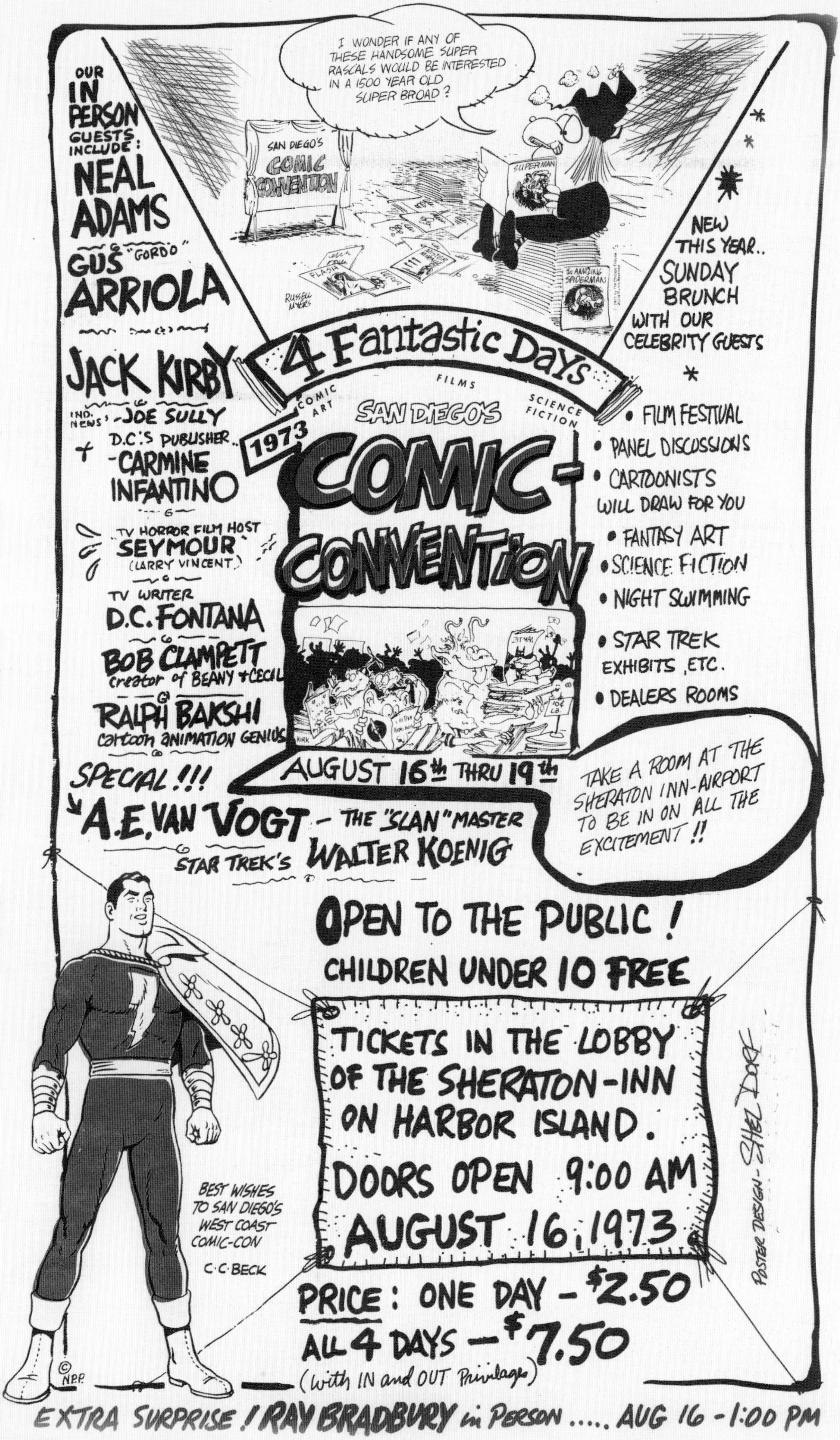
I WONDER IF ANY OF THESE HANDSOME SUPER RASCALS WOULD BE INTERESTED IN A 1500 YEAR OLD SUPER BROAD?
SAN DIEGO'S COMIC CONVENTION
SUPERMAN
FLASH
THE AMAZING SPIDERMAN
RUSSELL MYERS
OUR IN PERSON GUESTS INCLUDE:
NEAL ADAMS
GUS "GORDO" ARRIOLA
JACK KIRBY
IND. NEWS - JOE SULLY
+ D.C.'S PUBLISHER - CARMINE INFANTINO
TV HORROR FILM HOST "SEYMOUR" (LARRY VINCENT)
TV WRITER D.C. FONTANA
BOB CLAMPETT creator of BEANY + CECIL
RALPH BAKSHI cartoon animation GENIUS
NEW THIS YEAR.. SUNDAY BRUNCH WITH OUR CELEBRITY GUESTS
4 Fantastic Days
COMIC ART
FILMS
SCIENCE FICTION
SAN DIEGO'S
1973
COMIC-CONVENTION
AUGUST 16th THRU 19th
• FILM FESTIVAL
• PANEL DISCUSSIONS
• CARTOONISTS WILL DRAW FOR YOU
• FANTASY ART
• SCIENCE FICTION
• NIGHT SWIMMING
• STAR TREK EXHIBITS, ETC.
• DEALERS ROOMS
SPECIAL!!!
A.E. VAN VOGT - THE "SLAN" MASTER
STAR TREK'S WALTER KOENIG
TAKE A ROOM AT THE SHERATON INN-AIRPORT TO BE IN ON ALL THE EXCITEMENT!!
OPEN TO THE PUBLIC!
CHILDREN UNDER 10 FREE
TICKETS IN THE LOBBY OF THE SHERATON-INN ON HARBOR ISLAND.
DOORS OPEN 9:00 AM
AUGUST 16, 1973
BEST WISHES TO SAN DIEGO'S WEST COAST COMIC-CON
C.C. BECK
© N.P.P.
POSTER DESIGN - SHEL DORF
PRICE: ONE DAY - $2.50
ALL 4 DAYS - $7.50
(with IN and OUT Privilages)
EXTRA SURPRISE! RAY BRADBURY in PERSON ..... AUG 16 - 1:00 PM

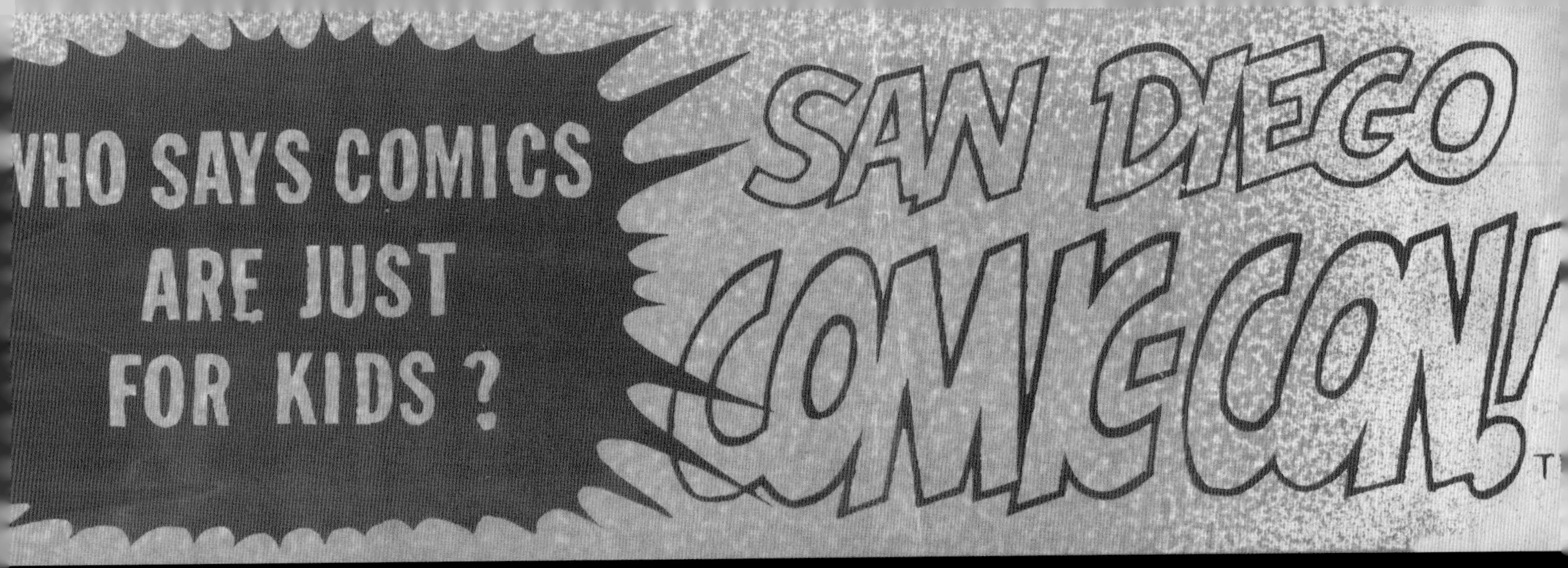
WHO SAYS COMICS ARE JUST FOR KIDS?
SAN DIEGO COMIC-CON!

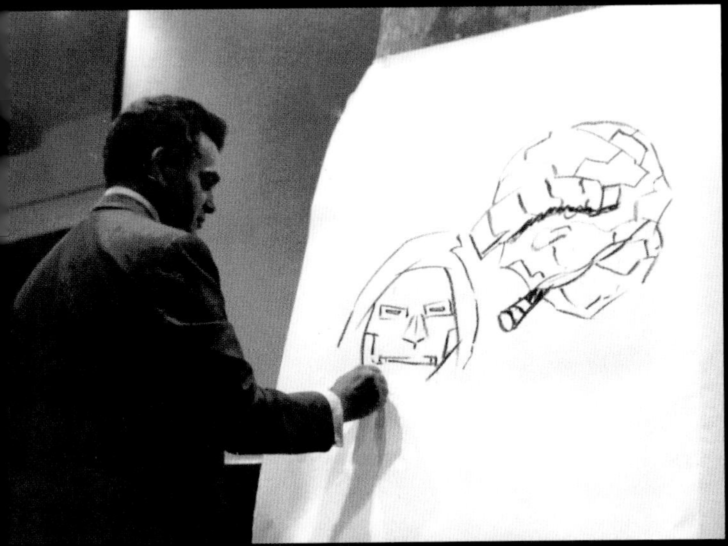

OPPOSITE: A hand-lettered poster for the 1973 Comic-Con, designed by Shel Dorf **ABOVE:** An early bumper sticker advertising Comic-Con—it took some persuading in the early 1970s to convince the general public that comics aren't just for kids **LEFT:** Jack Kirby sketches Dr. Doom and the Thing at the very first Comic-Con in 1970 **BELOW:** A 1979 underground comix panel with (left to right) David Scroggy, Ron Turner, Denis Kitchen, and Spain Rodriguez

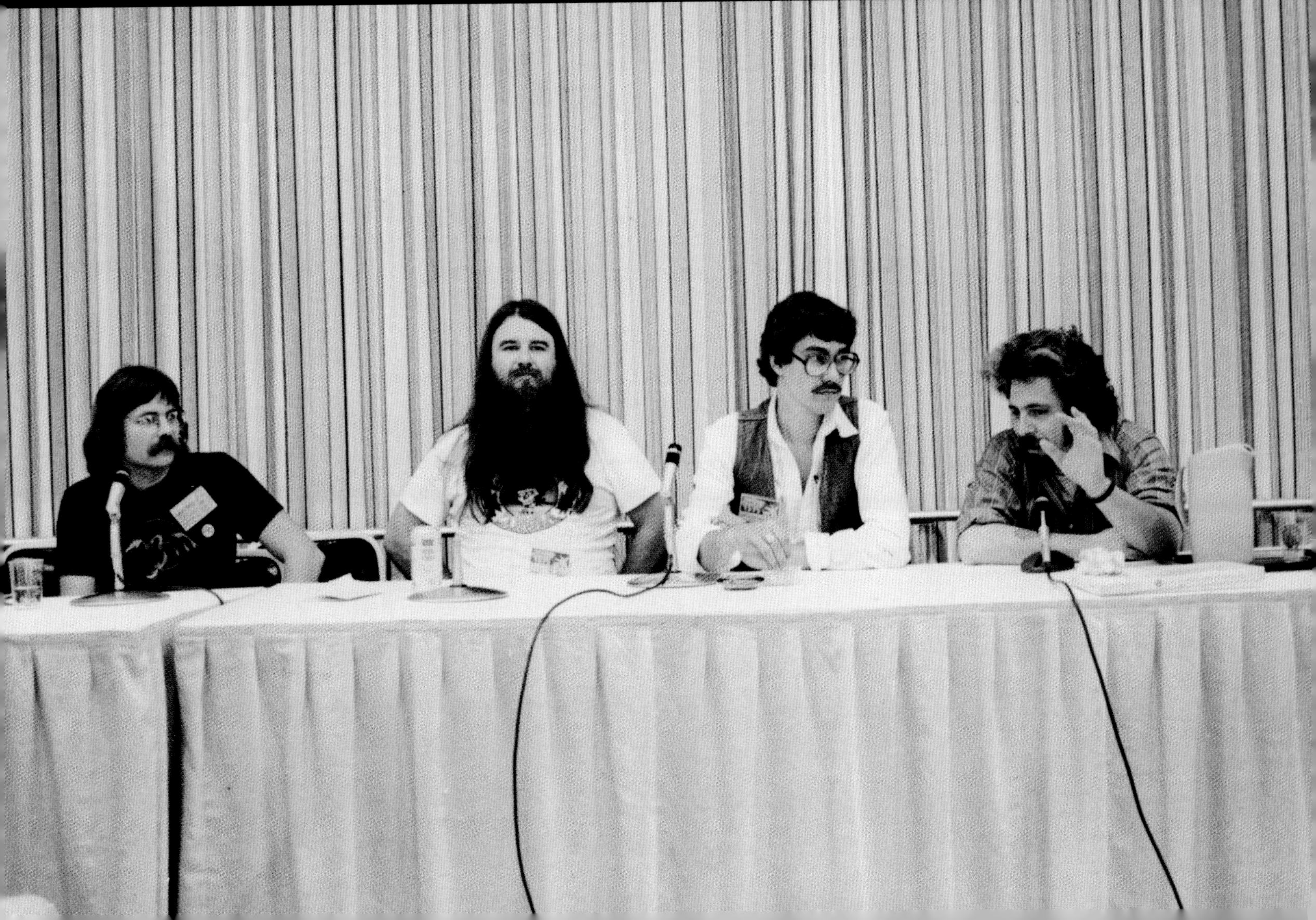

BELOW: A hand-drawn badge by comics writer/artist Jim Valentino **RIGHT:** One of the first pieces of art Dave Stevens produced for Comic-Con, featuring Marvel's Captain Marvel, from 1974 **BOTTOM:** A rare jam piece featuring (left to right) Broom-Hilda, by Russell Myers; Snoopy and Linus, from *Peanuts*, by Charles M. Schulz; and the Demon, by Jack Kirby **OPPOSITE, TOP LEFT:** Two badge designs from the 1970s. The green one is from one of the earliest Comic-Cons, and the 1977 one is by Scott Shaw! **TOP RIGHT:** Jackie Estrada's handwritten list from the 1974 program book recording the numerous pros (besides the special guests) who attended the show **BOTTOM RIGHT:** Broom-Hilda creator Russell Myers sketching onstage **BOTTOM LEFT:** The art on the doors outside the Convention and Performing Arts Center in 1979 certainly grabbed this young fan's attention

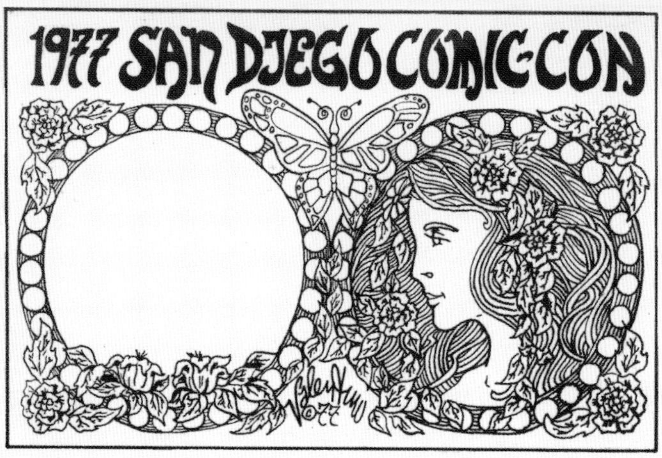
1977 SAN DIEGO COMIC-CON

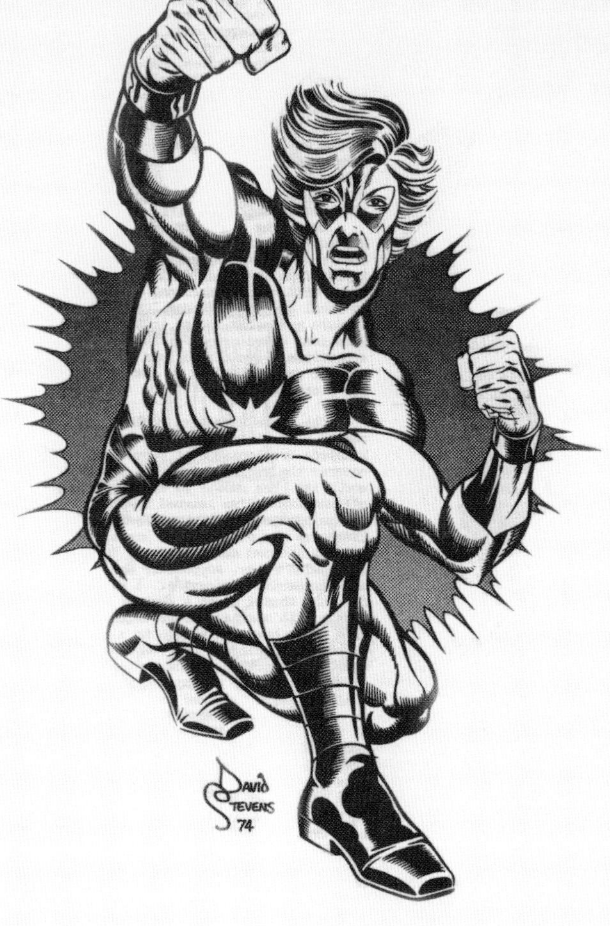
DAVID STEVENS '74

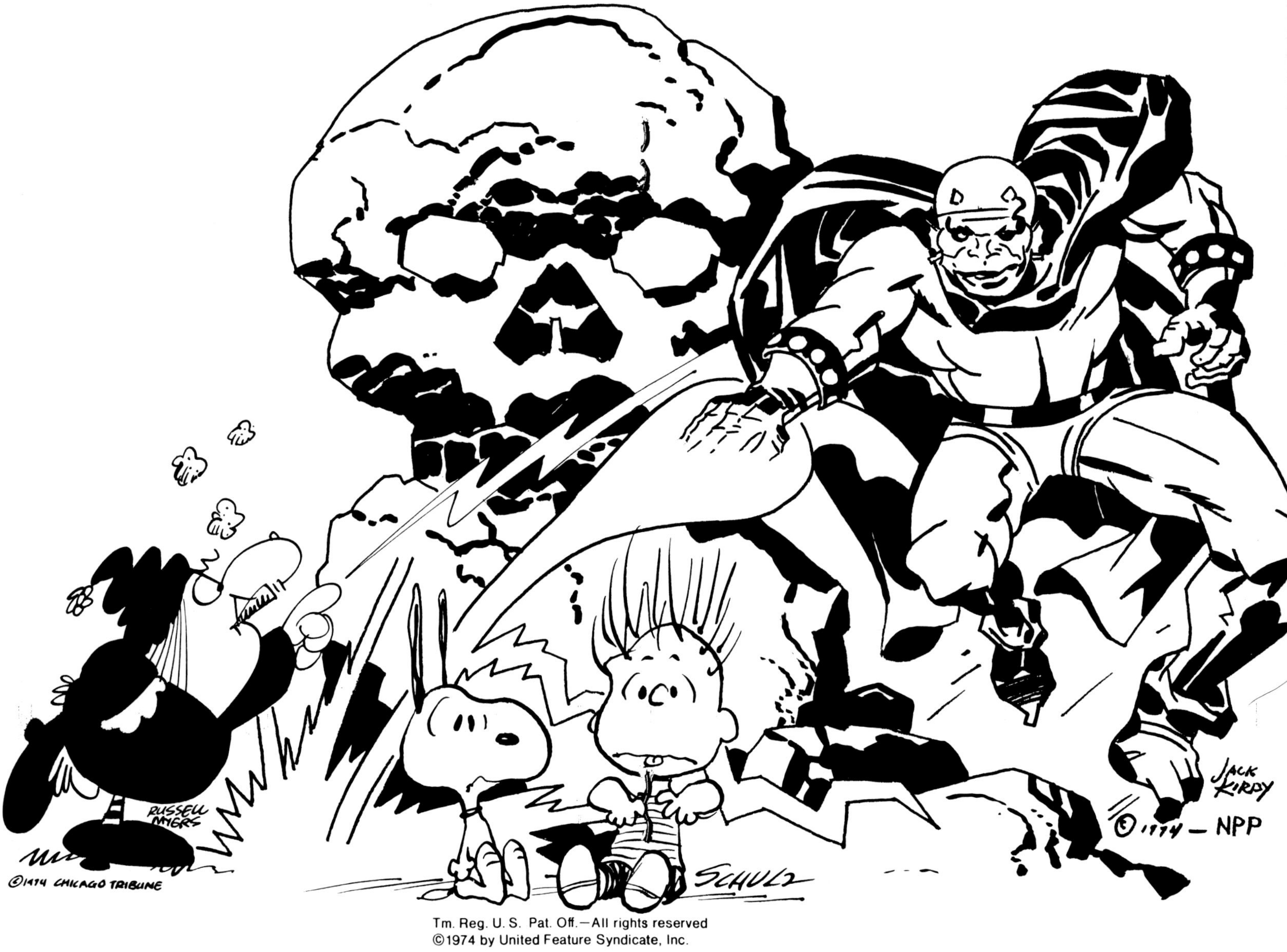
RUSSELL MYERS
©1974 CHICAGO TRIBUNE
SCHULZ
JACK KIRBY
©1974 — NPP
Tm. Reg. U. S. Pat. Off.—All rights reserved
©1974 by United Feature Syndicate, Inc.

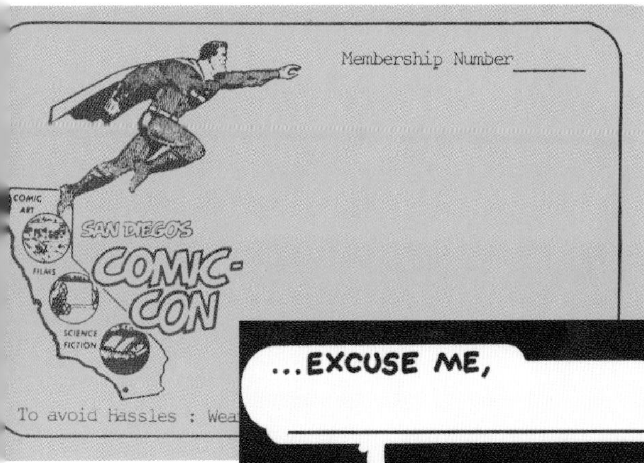
Membership Number______
COMIC ART
SAN DIEGO'S
COMIC-CON
FILMS
SCIENCE FICTION
To avoid Hassles : Wea

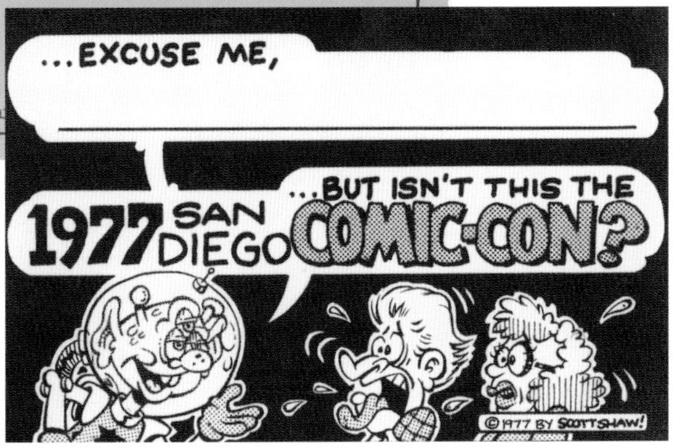
...EXCUSE ME,
...BUT ISN'T THIS THE
1977 SAN DIEGO COMIC-CON?
©1977 BY SCOTT SHAW!

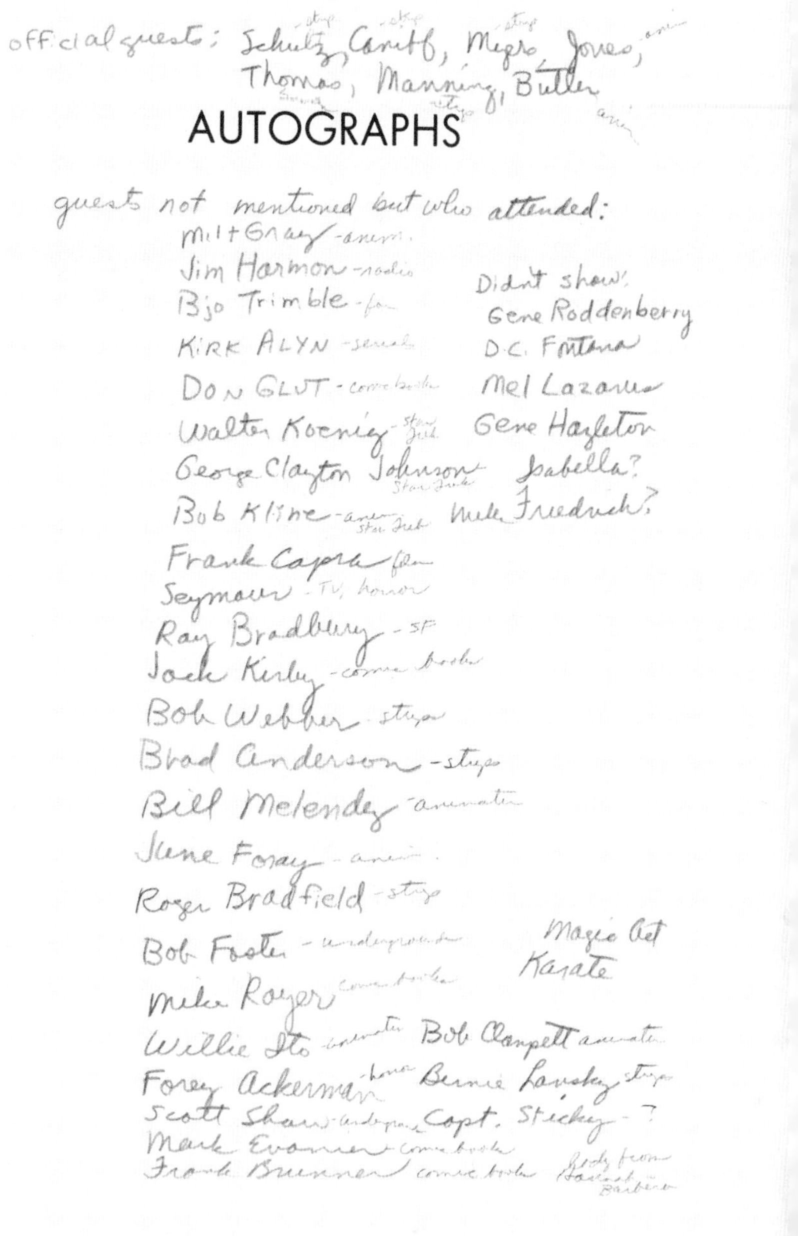
official guests: Schulz, Caniff, Megro, Jones, Thomas, Manning, Butler

AUTOGRAPHS

guests not mentioned but who attended:

Milt Gray - anim.
Jim Harmon - radio
Bjo Trimble - fan
Kirk Alyn - serials
Don Glut - comic books
Walter Koenig - Star Trek
George Clayton Johnson - Star Trek
Bob Kline - anim. Star Trek
Frank Capra - film
Seymour - TV, horror
Ray Bradbury - SF
Jack Kirby - comic books
Bob Webber - strips
Brad Anderson - strips
Bill Melendez - animation
June Foray - anim.
Roger Bradfield - strips
Bob Foster - underground
Mike Royer - comic books
Willie Ito - animation
Forry Ackerman - horror
Scott Shaw - underground
Mark Evanier - comic book
Frank Brunner - comic books

Didn't show:
Gene Roddenberry
D.C. Fontana
Mel Lazarus
Gene Hazelton
Isabella?
Mike Friedrich?

Magic Act
Karate

Bob Clampett animation
Bernie Lansky strips
Capt. Sticky - ?
Body from Hanna Barbera

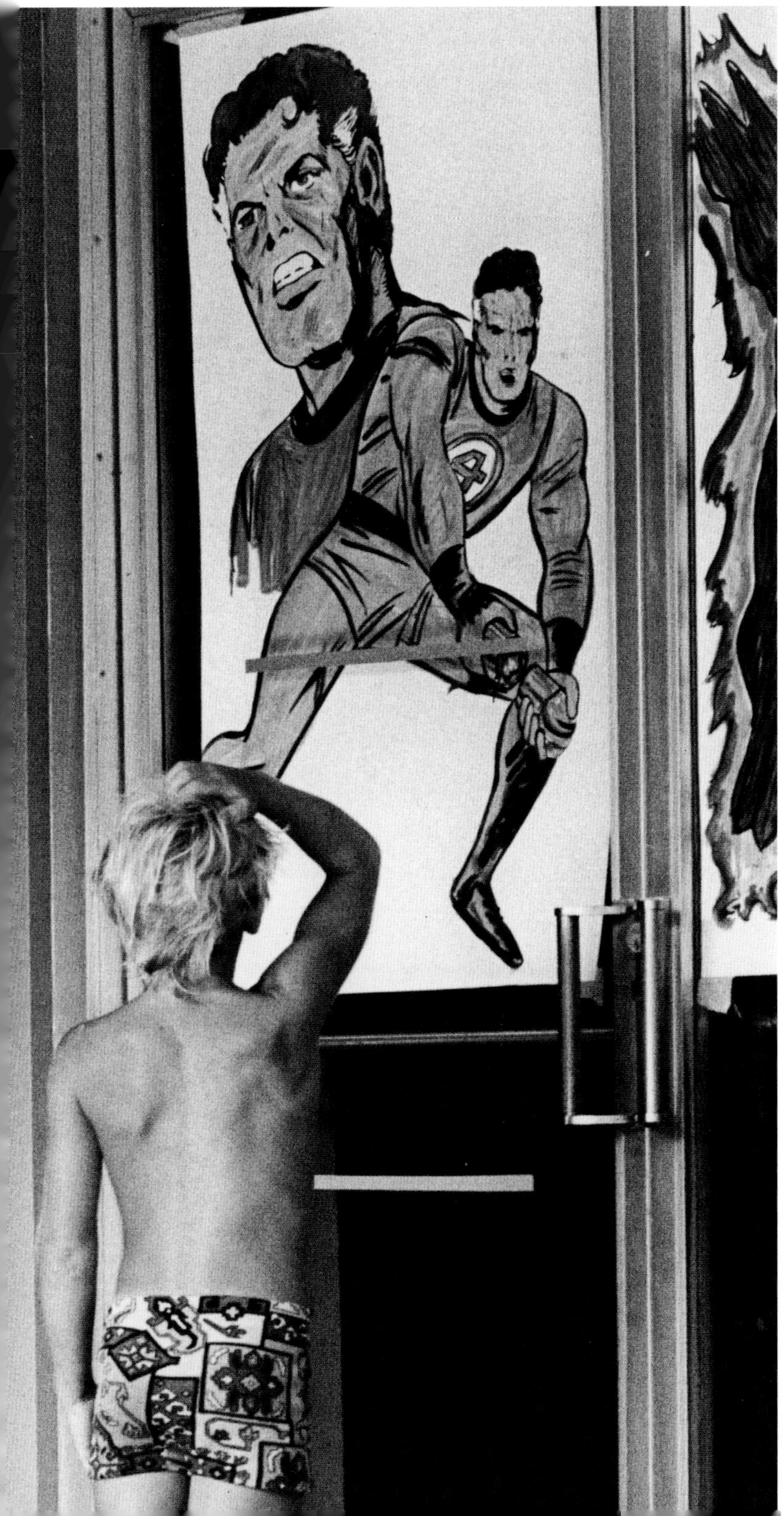

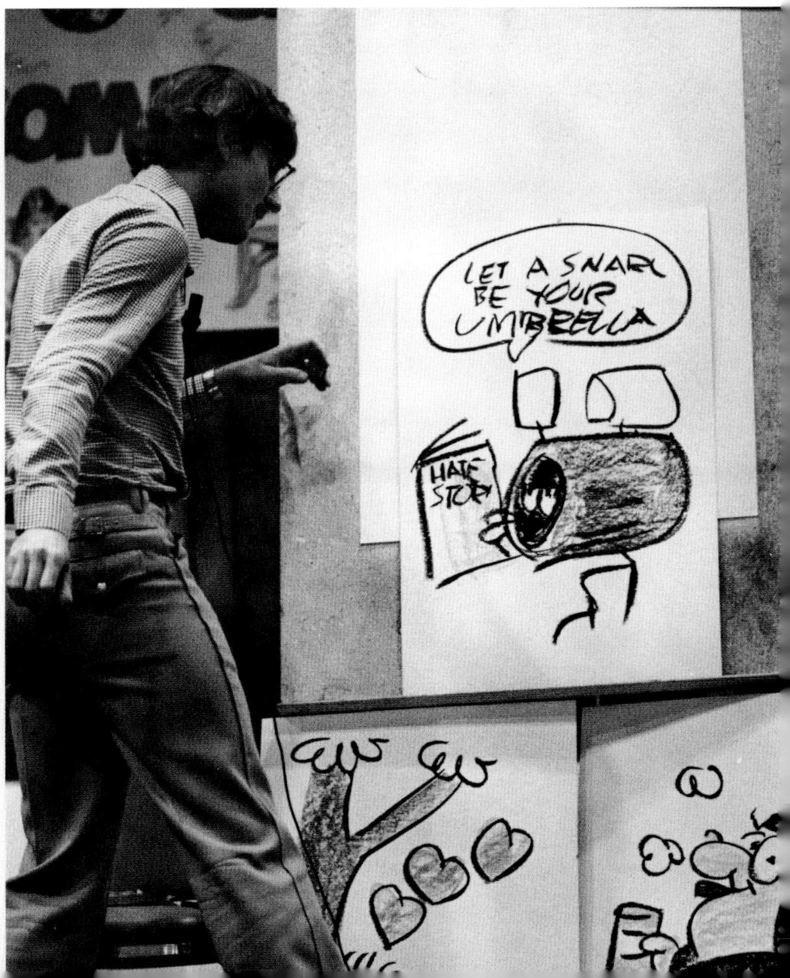
LET A SNARL BE YOUR UMBRELLA

JACK KIRBY (1917-1994)

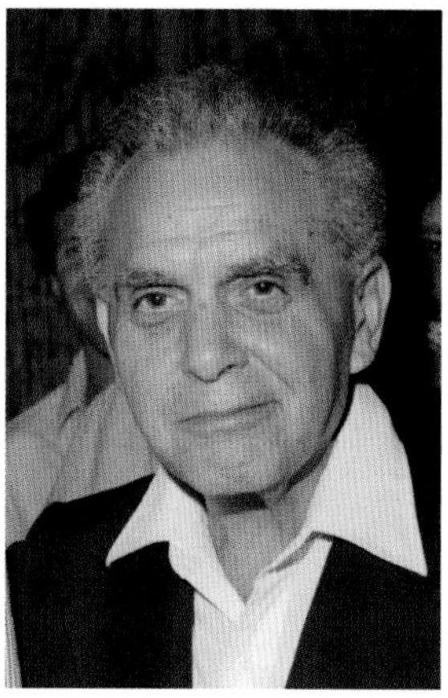

IN 1971 comic book artist Jack Kirby said, "This is the future, not just of comics but of all media. Movie studios are going to come to this convention every year to see what's new."* He was talking about the San Diego Comic-Con.

Kirby was a visionary in many ways, a man whose work at times seemed to channel the future. Among the pantheon of comics characters to which he gave life were the Fantastic Four, the Incredible Hulk, and the Mighty Thor—and the superlative adjectives before each name fit. They were all fantastic, incredible, and mighty. Kirby made them that way.

Jack Kirby was born Jacob Kurtzberg in 1917 in New York City. With partner Joe Simon, he pioneered a new kind of comics storytelling, with figures often breaking out of panels and across pages. Simon and Kirby co-created numerous characters—including Captain America—and even started the romance comics genre with titles such as *Young Romance* and *Young Love* in the 1940s. In the 1960s, Kirby co-created, along with Stan Lee, many of the superhero characters that formed the Marvel Universe, revitalizing and revolutionizing the comics industry. Besides the Fantastic Four, Hulk, and Thor, Kirby knocked readers' socks off with the Silver Surfer, the Avengers, Black Panther, and the original X-Men, to name just a few. In the early 1970s, Kirby created his *Fourth World* series for DC, a groundbreaking epic saga spanning three interconnected but separate titles (*New Gods*, *Forever People*, and *Mister Miracle*); many of the characters from that series are still part of the DC Universe today.

When Jack and his family moved to the Los Angeles area in the late 1960s, he opened his home to fans. Both he and his beloved wife, Roz, were endlessly patient and kind to fans who stopped by—sometimes unannounced—to look at his work and talk to their favorite comics artist. When a group of those visiting fans from San Diego started San Diego's Golden State Comic-Con in 1970, Kirby was their first choice to invite as a guest. Fans at that first show were treated to a Kirby chalk-talk in which he introduced some of his new *Fourth World* characters, including Scott Free and Big Barda (from *Mister Miracle*).

San Diego soon became his home away from home each year, and Jack and Roz attended every Comic-Con from 1970 through 1993, save one (1981). He provided the covers for two of the first three program books (1970 and 1972), and contributed art to many more. He became such a part of the Comic-Con family that special birthday parties were thrown for him on the occasions of his seventieth and seventy-fifth birthdays (in 1987 and 1992). The "King of Comics" was always available to participate in panels, to speak to his fans, to encourage new talent, or to take a spin across the dance floor with Roz at after-hours parties. Kirby's willingness to take time to talk to his fans is legendary, and he was awarded the Bob Clampett Humanitarian Award in 1993 for his many efforts in mentoring writers and artists.

Jack was right about Comic-Con's future. Sadly, he didn't live long enough to see the big-budget movies made from some of his most famous creations. Films such as *Fantastic Four, The Incredible Hulk, X-Men*, and *Iron Man* all had their "coming-out parties" at Comic-Con, showcasing special footage and cast members for the first time.

Jack Kirby holds a special place in Comic-Con history. Each year Comic-Con presents a "Jack Kirby Tribute Panel," moderated by Kirby's friend and biographer Mark Evanier and featuring writers and artists speaking about Kirby's influence on comics and on their own work. Even today, fifteen years after his death, Kirby's spirit and creativity remain a constant presence at the convention.

* Quoted in Mark Evanier, "The Timeless Jack Kirby," 2004 Comic-Con International Souvenir Book

EXCLUSIVE!

Jack Kirby's New Characters for DC

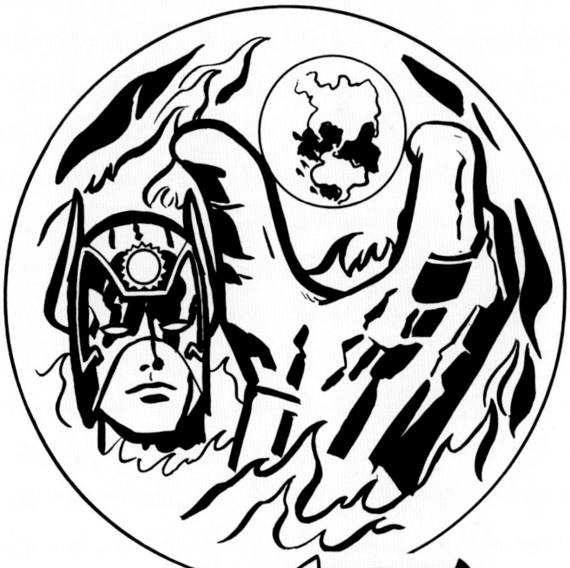

THE NEW GODS

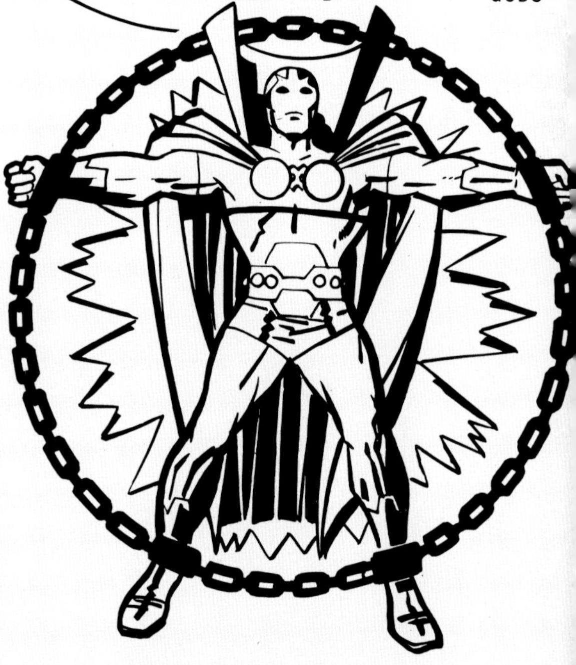

MR. MIRACLE

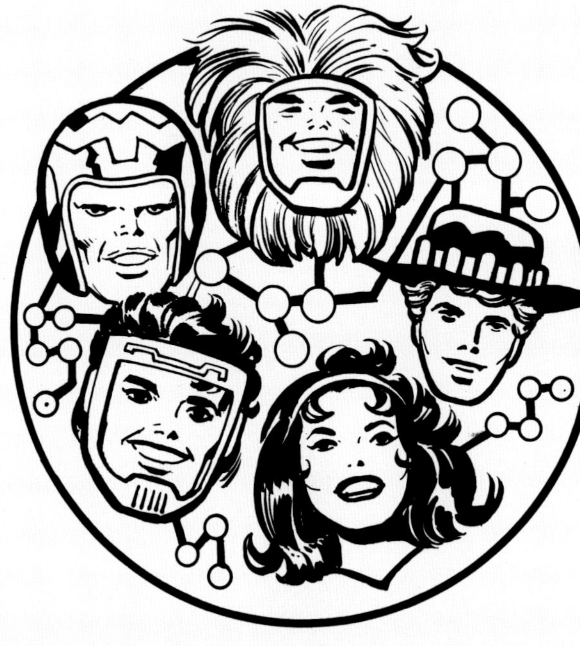

THE FOREVER PEOPLE

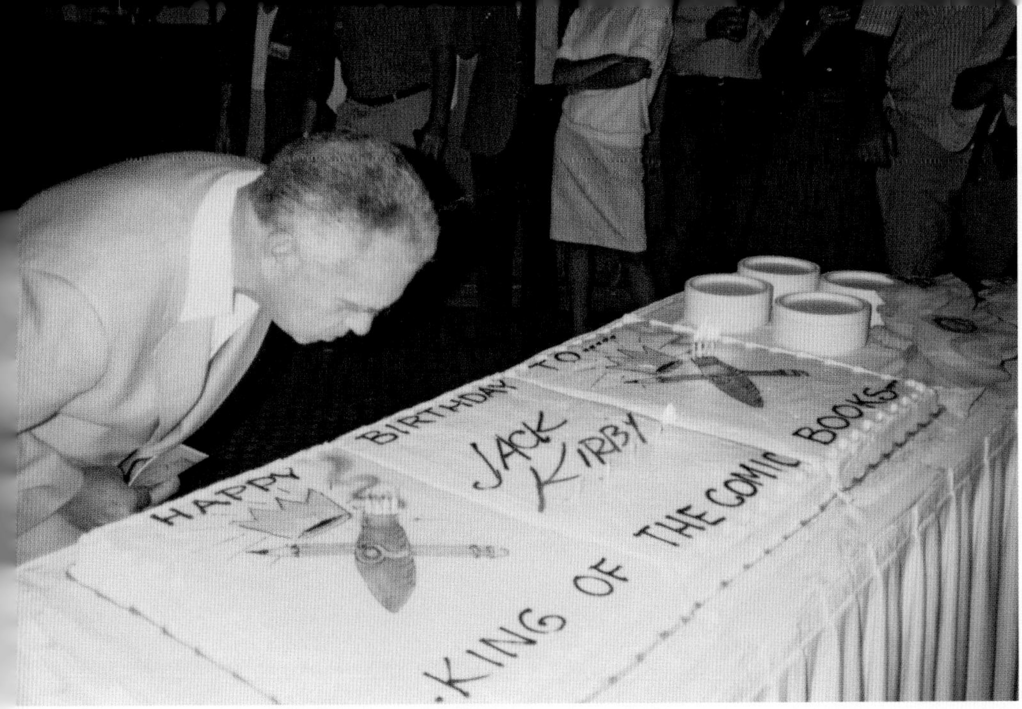
HAPPY BIRTHDAY TO.....
JACK KIRBY
KING OF THE COMIC BOOKS

“I went to Jack Kirby’s seventy-fifth birthday party and met him. It was like meeting a relative you had always heard stories about and finally got to meet at a family reunion.”

–JILL THOMPSON

WRITER/ARTIST, *SCARY GODMOTHER, THE SANDMAN*

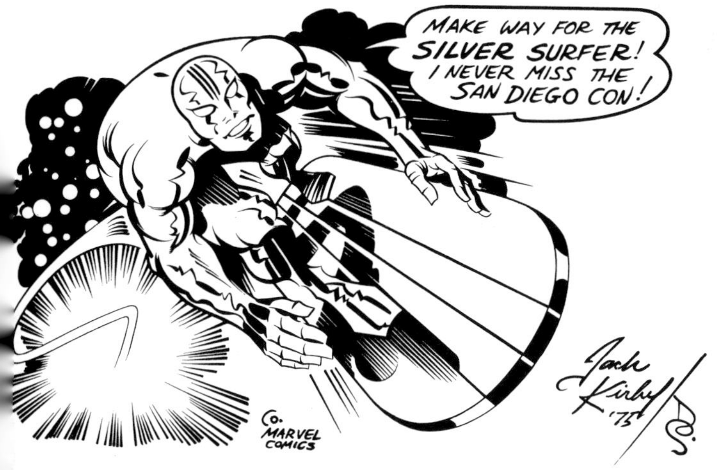
MAKE WAY FOR THE SILVER SURFER! I NEVER MISS THE SAN DIEGO CON!
Jack Kirby '75
©. MARVEL COMICS

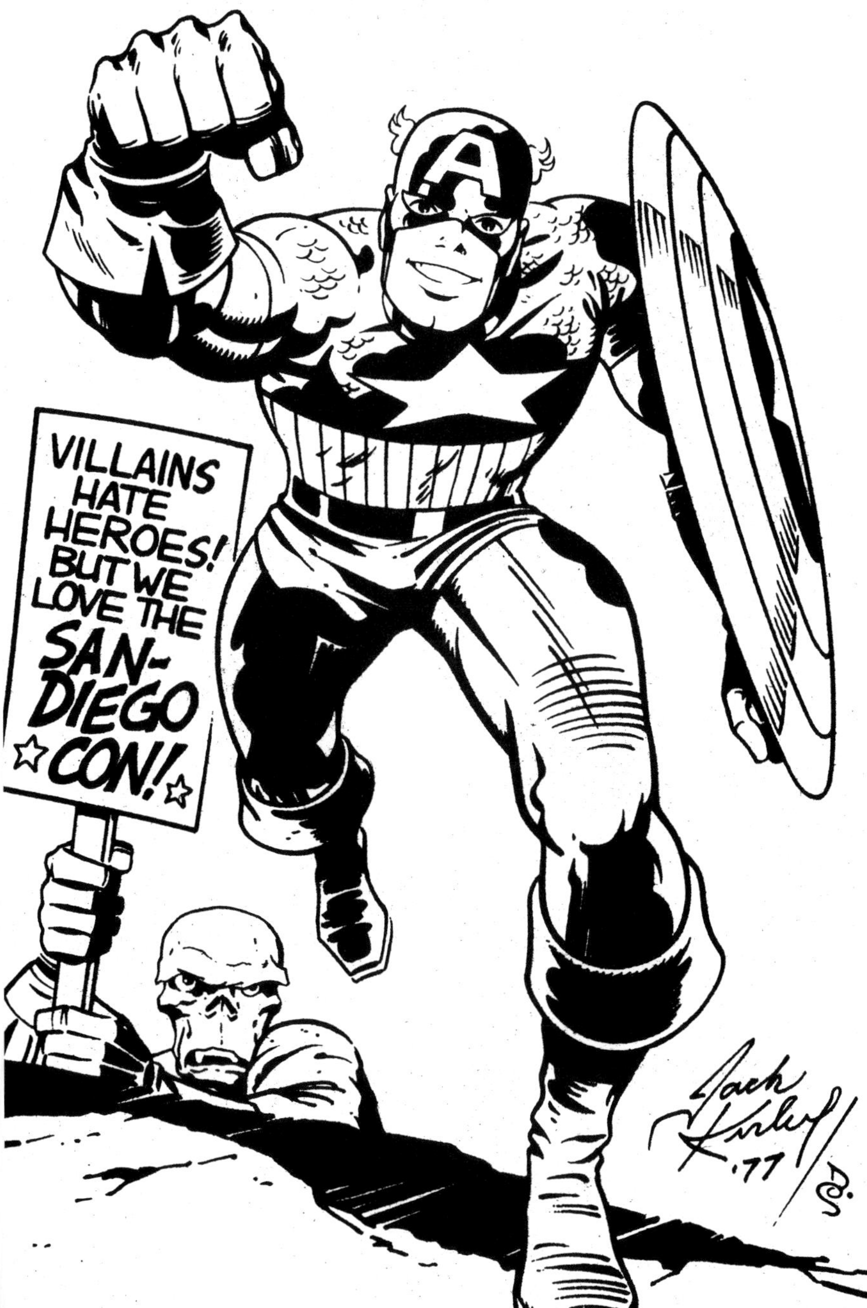
VILLAINS HATE HEROES! BUT WE LOVE THE SAN-DIEGO CON!
Jack Kirby '77
© MARVEL COMICS

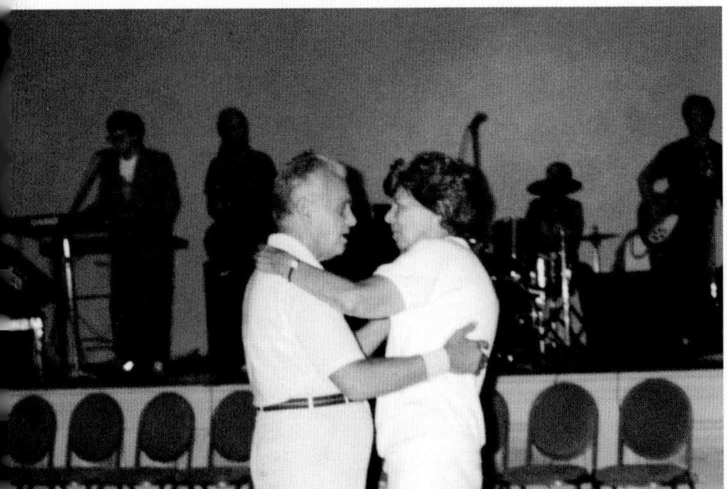

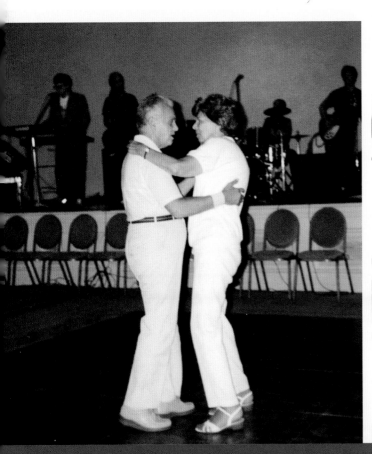

OPPOSITE: An exclusive sneak peek at Jack Kirby’s new *Fourth World* characters, from the 1970 program book
CLOCKWISE FROM TOP LEFT: Kirby at his seventieth birthday party at the 1987 Comic-Con; Captain America sketch from 1977 by Kirby, inked by Dave Stevens; Kirby and his wife, Roz (who had as many fans as the King of Comics did), dancing at Comic-Con’s twenty-fifth anniversary party in 1989; Silver Surfer sketch from 1975, also inked by Dave Stevens

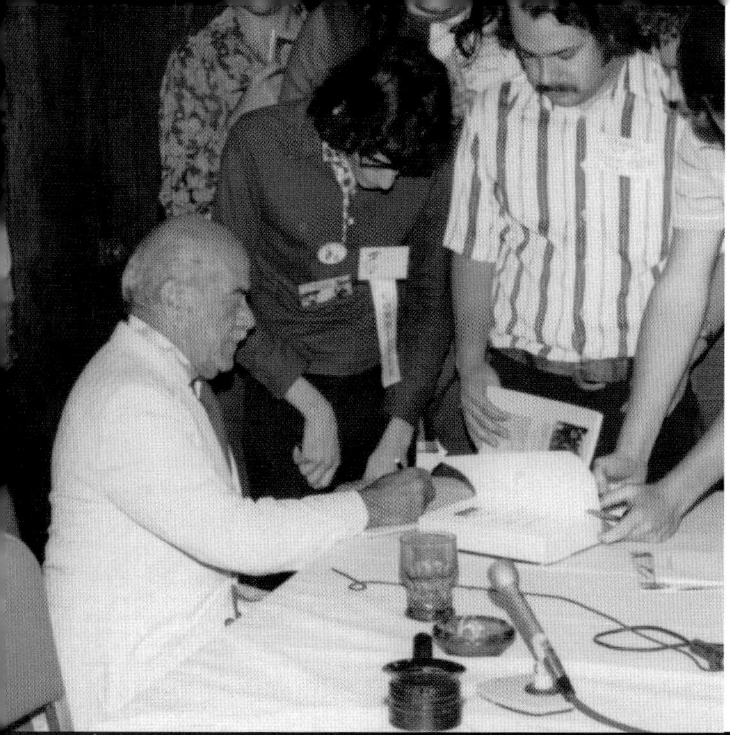

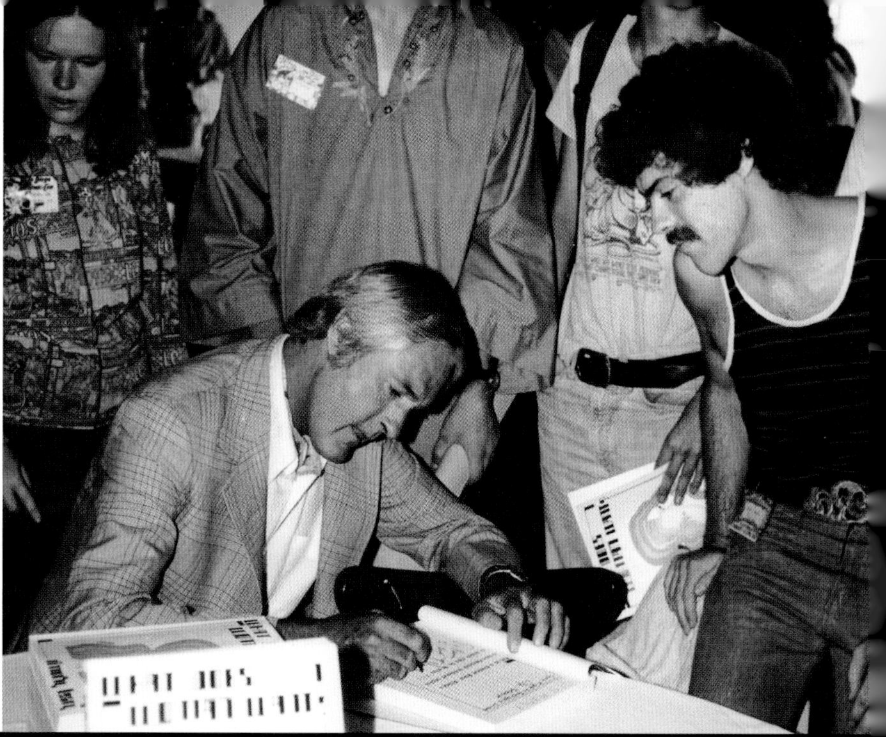

ABOVE LEFT: Famed Hollywood director and Comic-Con guest Frank Capra (*It's a Wonderful Life*) signing for fans, including Barry Alfonso and Scott Shaw! in 1974 **ABOVE RIGHT:** 1960s counterculture legend Timothy Leary, a guest at the 1975 convention **BELOW:** A veritable comics Who's Who from the first Inkpot Awards banquet (left to right): Russell Myers (*Broom-Hilda*), Charles M. Schulz (*Peanuts*), Russ Manning (*Tarzan*), Roy Thomas (*Conan*), and Milton Caniff (*Steve Canyon*)

OPPOSITE, CLOCKWISE FROM TOP LEFT: A Batman sketch by Bob Kane for the 1977 program book; San Diego mayor Pete Wilson (left) presenting Comic-Con's Richard Butner (center) and Shel Dorf (right) with a proclamation marking Comic Arts Week in San Diego in 1976; Charles M. Schulz (center) with fans at the 1974 convention; a Nancy and Sluggo sketch by creator Ernie Bushmiller; a shot of the dealers' room in the early 1970s; Art Show coordinator Clayton Moore with Ron Graham's incredible Basil Wolverton original art exhibit, part of the Art Show in 1974; voice actor Daws Butler greeting fans

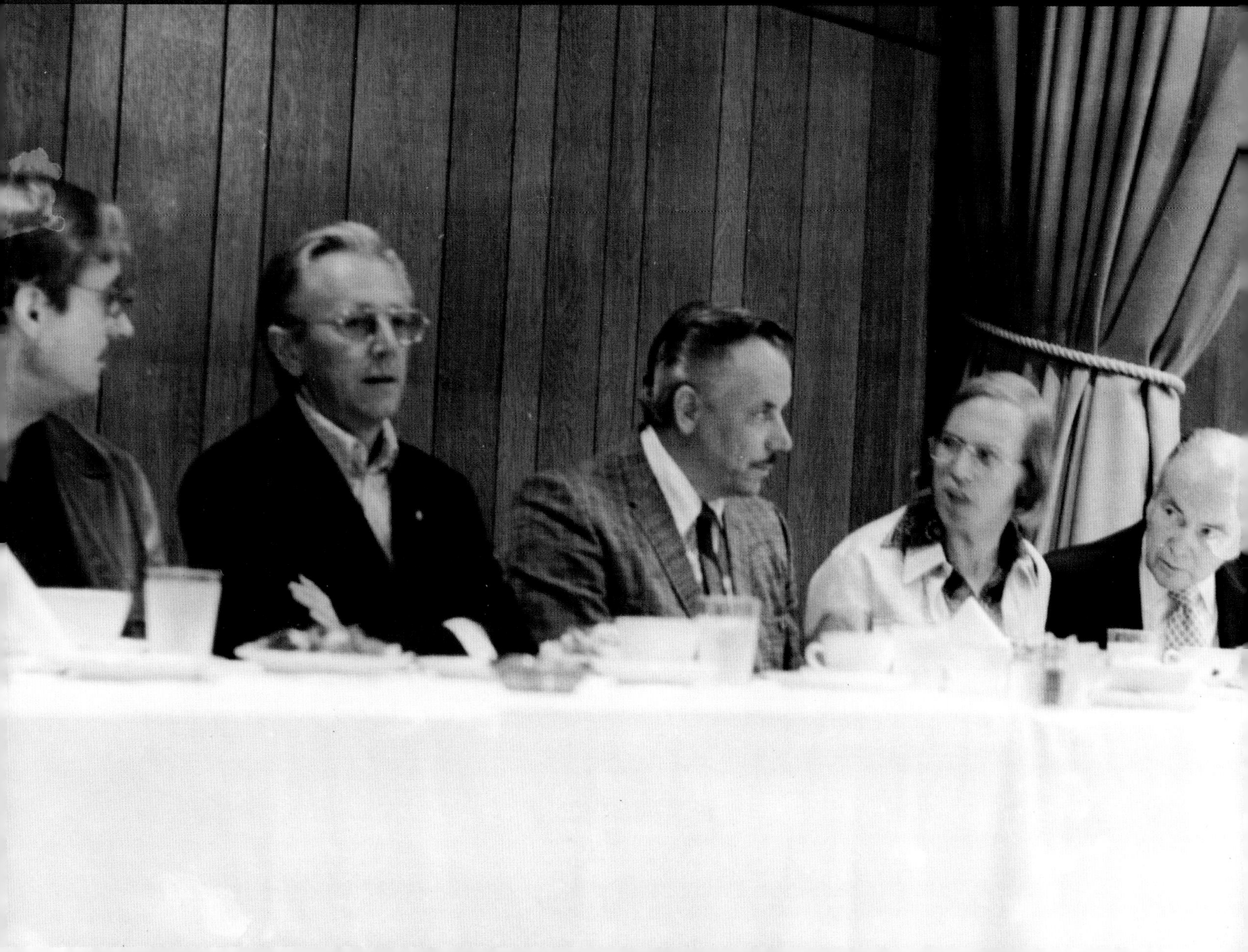

"BATS" WISHES TO 1977 SAN DIEGO COMIC-CON!

BOB KANE 1940

RON GRAHAM'S WALKERTON COMIC JULI 1974 to 1974

THOMAS NAST (1840-1902)

WORLD'S UGLIEST MAN CONTEST

BASIL WOLVERTON

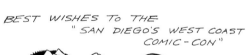

BEST WISHES TO THE "SAN DIEGO'S WEST COAST COMIC-CON"

"NANCY"   "SLUGGO"

AND ERNIE BUSHMILLER

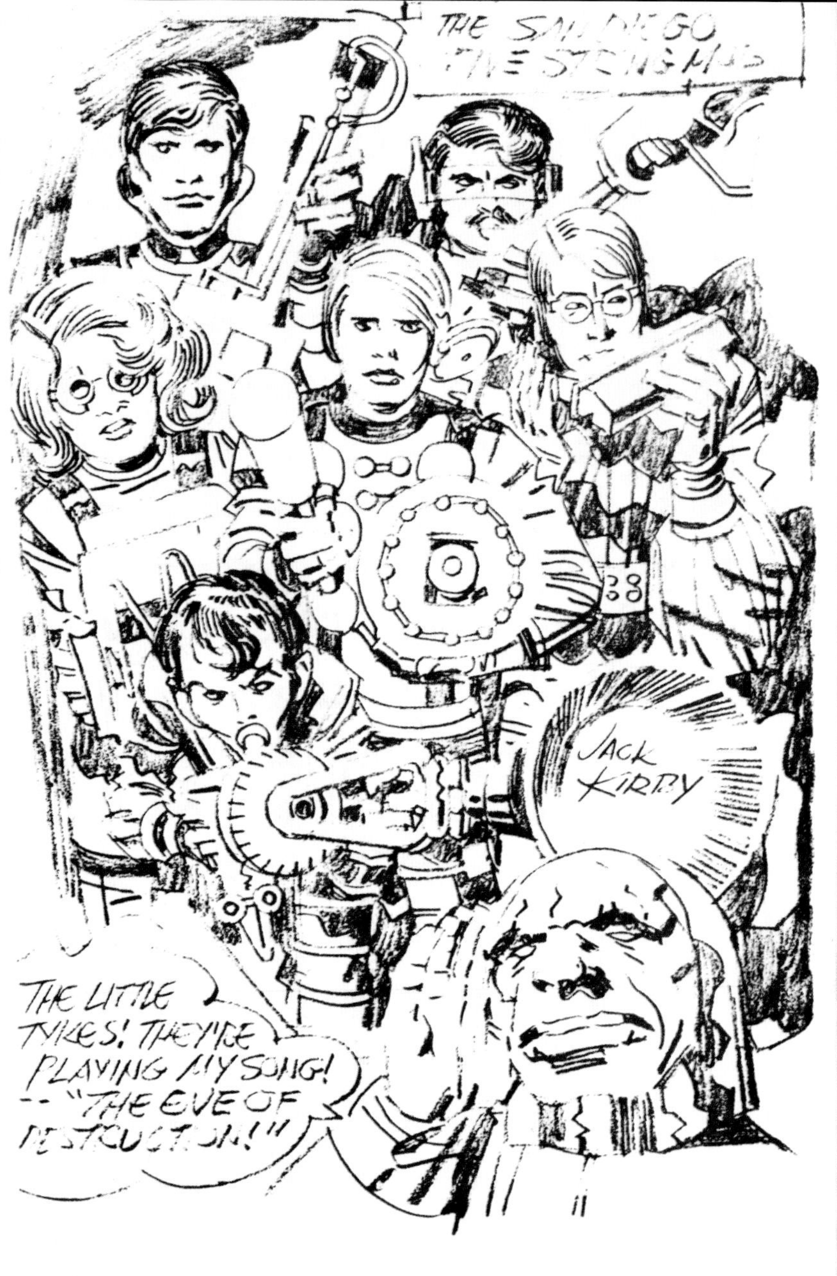
JACK KIRBY
THE LITTLE TYKES! THEY'RE PLAYING MY SONG! -- "THE EVE OF

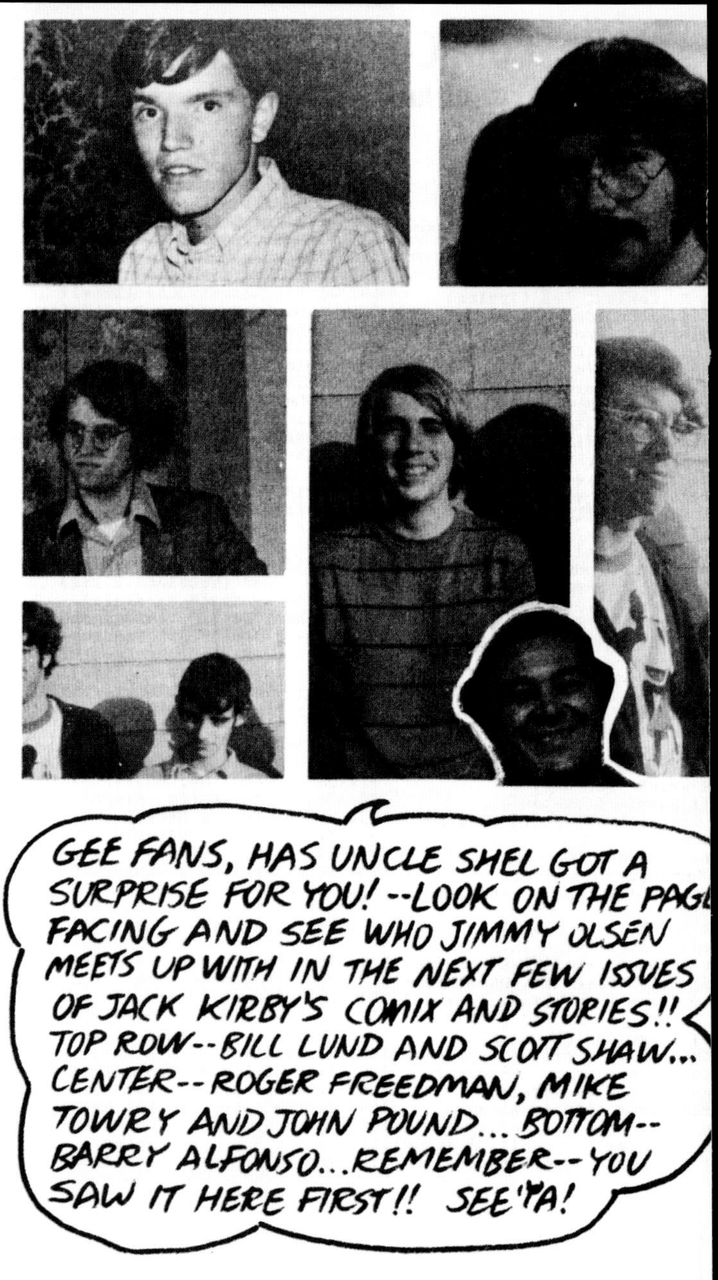
GEE FANS, HAS UNCLE SHEL GOT A SURPRISE FOR YOU! --LOOK ON THE PAG FACING AND SEE WHO JIMMY OLSEN MEETS UP WITH IN THE NEXT FEW ISSUES OF JACK KIRBY'S COMIX AND STORIES!! TOP ROW--BILL LUND AND SCOTT SHAW... CENTER--ROGER FREEDMAN, MIKE TOWRY AND JOHN POUND... BOTTOM--BARRY ALFONSO...REMEMBER--YOU SAW IT HERE FIRST!! SEE'YA!

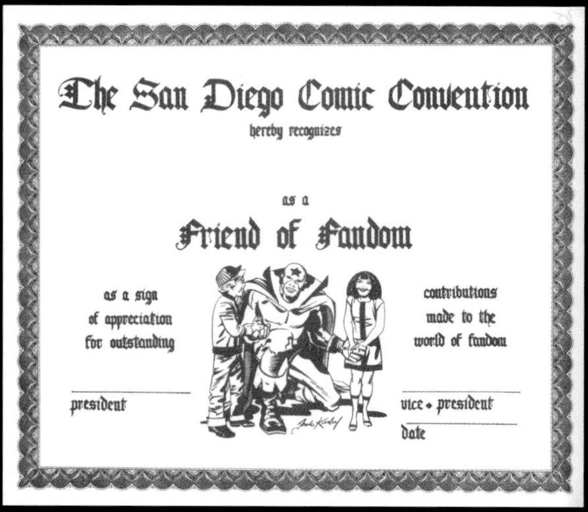
The San Diego Comic Convention

hereby recognizes

as a

Friend of Fandom

as a sign of appreciation for outstanding contributions made to the world of fandom

president vice • president

date

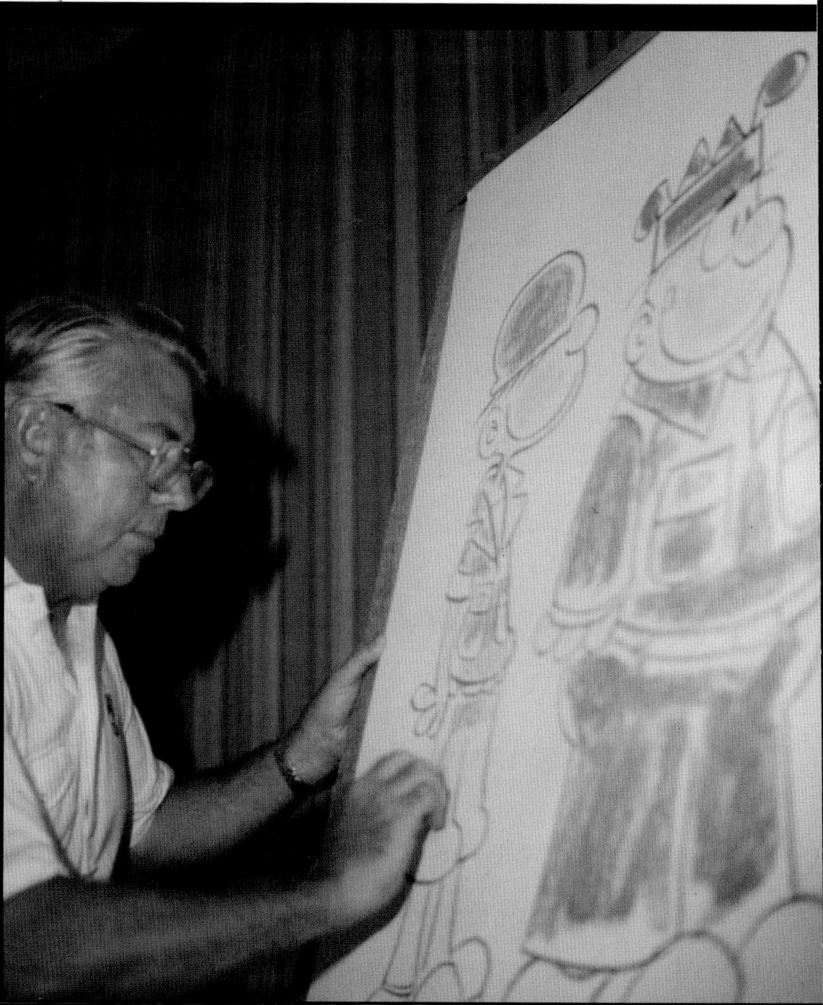

TOP: A two-page spread from the 1970 program book showing the five Comic-Con committee members whom Jack Kirby immortalized in comics form in *Superman's Pal Jimmy Olsen* **ABOVE:** Jack Kirby art for Comic-Con's Friend of Fandom certificates, originally given out along with the Inkpot Awards **RIGHT:** Cartoonist Mort Walker sketching his signature creations Beetle Bailey and Sarge at the 1979 show **OPPOSITE, TOP TO BOTTOM:** A page from the 1970 program book showing scenes from the fund-raising minicon held earlier that year—Forry Ackerman was one of the guests, along with Mike Royer (shown with drawings in top right photo); Forry with Ken Krueger (center) and science fiction author A. E. van Vogt (right) at the first Comic-Con in 1970; Forry speaking to his fans at another 1970s Comic-Con—he was a perennial guest since the first one

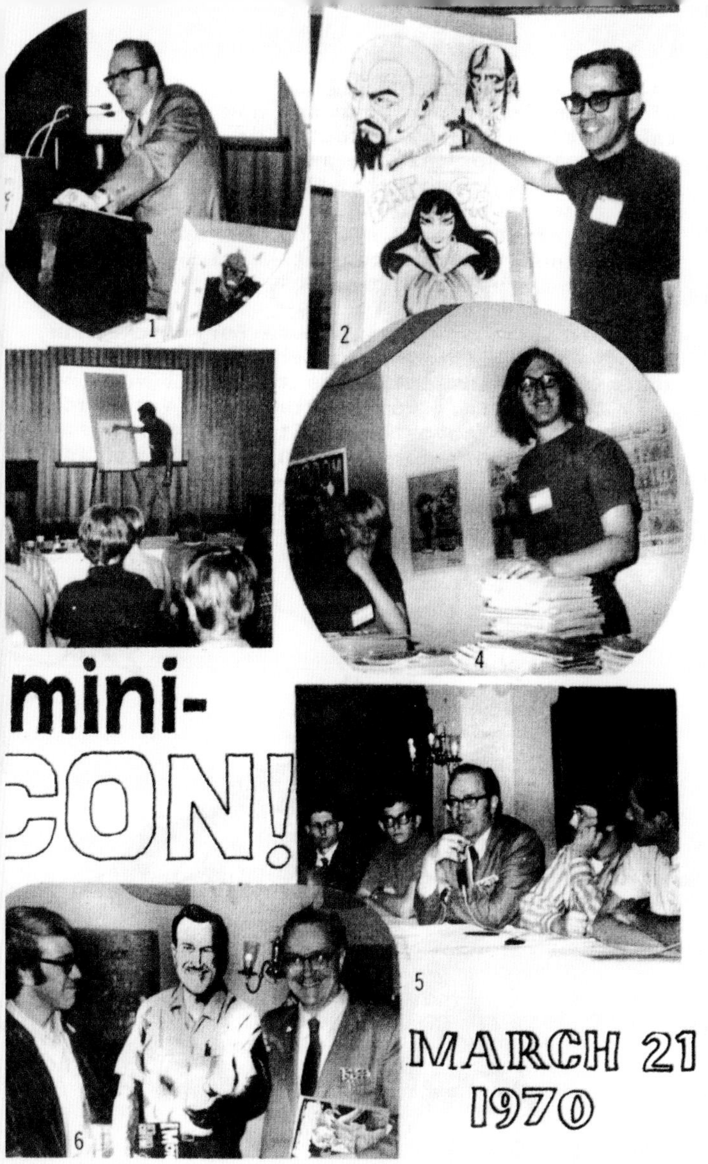
mini-
CON!
MARCH 21
1970

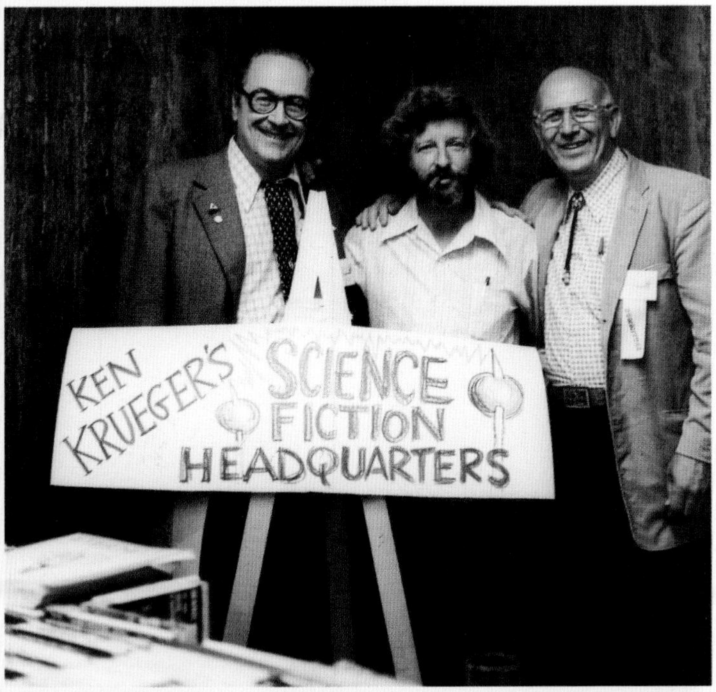
KEN KRUEGER'S SCIENCE FICTION HEADQUARTERS

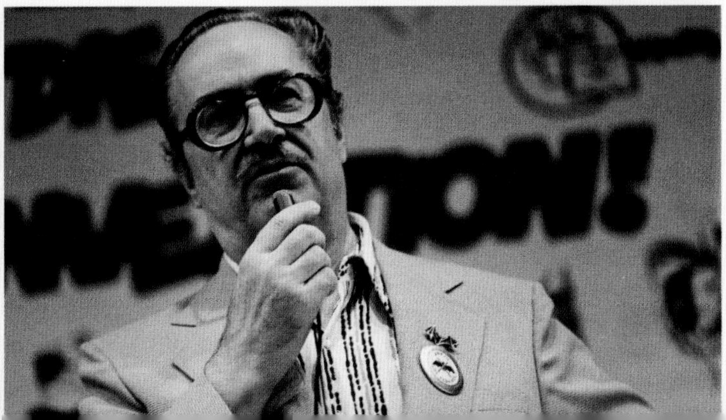

FORREST J ACKERMAN (1916-2008)

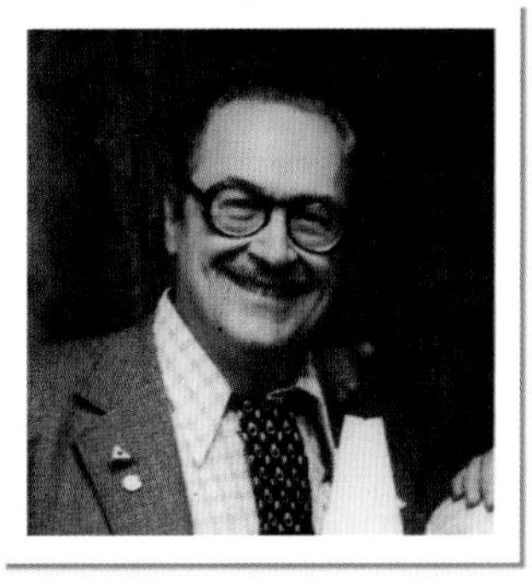

IF HIS IDOL, Lon Chaney, was known as "The Man of a Thousand Faces," then Forrest J Ackerman must surely be "The Man of a Thousand Names." Known to his legion of fans as 4SJ, 4E, Dr. Acula, FJA, and Forry, this major fan took his fannish ways and turned them into his career.

Starting as a literary agent in 1948—his clients would include A. E. van Vogt and Hugo Gernsback—Forry is best known for being the editor of the hugely popular monster magazine *Famous Monsters of Filmland*. Beginning in 1958, and published by James Warren, *Famous Monsters* tapped into the growing monster craze sweeping the country. When televisions started to show up in just about every household in the 1950s, the glowing box needed programs, and Universal Pictures released its classic monster films—*Dracula*, *Frankenstein*, *The Wolf Man*, et al.—to an eager television-viewing public. Many kids gladly jumped on the monster bandwagon, seeing the classic (and sometimes not-so-classic) films for the first time.

Forry's magazine surfed that wave of monster enthusiasm. His gentle, pun-inflected style of humor, along with his amazing collection of photographs and incredible knowledge of the films and their stars, made *Famous Monsters* an instant hit. Forry became the king of the monsters, or at least their most avid public relations person. Many a modern-day filmmaker and author—Steven Spielberg, George Lucas, and Stephen King, to name just a few—credit *Famous Monsters* as a seminal influence in their young lives.

But Forry's love of all things science fiction, horror, and fantasy didn't stop with *Famous Monsters*. His Hollywood home was stuffed to the rafters with memorabilia from the films and books he loved, and he opened that home to anyone who wanted to visit the "Ackermansion, in Horrorwood, Karlifornia." His amazing collection at one time included items such as life masks molded from the faces of Boris Karloff, Bela Lugosi, and Vincent Price, among others, and the legendary Lon Chaney's personal makeup kit, which the actor used to craft his startling on-screen personas.

Forry was at the very first Comic-Con in 1970, the minicon in March of that year that was held to raise money to put on a bigger show. Ackerman was an old hand when it came to science fiction fandom, having attended the first Worldcon in 1939. He was an almost constant presence at Comic-Con since that first minicon, participating in panels, signing autographs, and meeting with his many fans up through the 2008 show. In 1984 Bob Clampett's widow, Sody, presented him with Comic-Con's first Bob Clampett Humanitarian Award for his mentoring of talent.

In recent years, Comic-Con attendees have had the major treat of seeing Forry together with two of his dearest friends: Ray Bradbury and Ray Harryhausen. The three legends appeared on panels together in 2005 and 2006, regaling the audience with amazing stories (pun intended—*Amazing Stories* was the first science fiction magazine Forry purchased more than eighty years ago, which set him on his incredible path). At the 2008 Comic-Con, Forry was on hand, along with publisher James Warren, to celebrate the fiftieth anniversary of *Famous Monsters*. Sadly, it turned out to be Forry's last appearance at a convention. He passed away on December 4, 2008, at the age of ninety-two.

Comic-Con and all of comics and science fiction fandom are richer for having had Forry Ackerman as a friend.

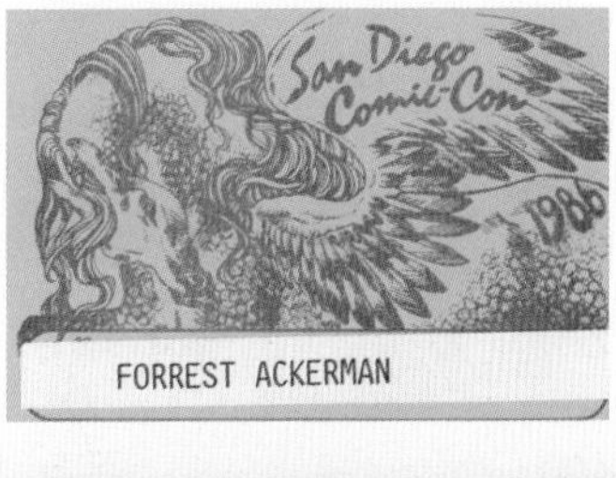
San Diego Comic-Con
1986
FORREST ACKERMAN

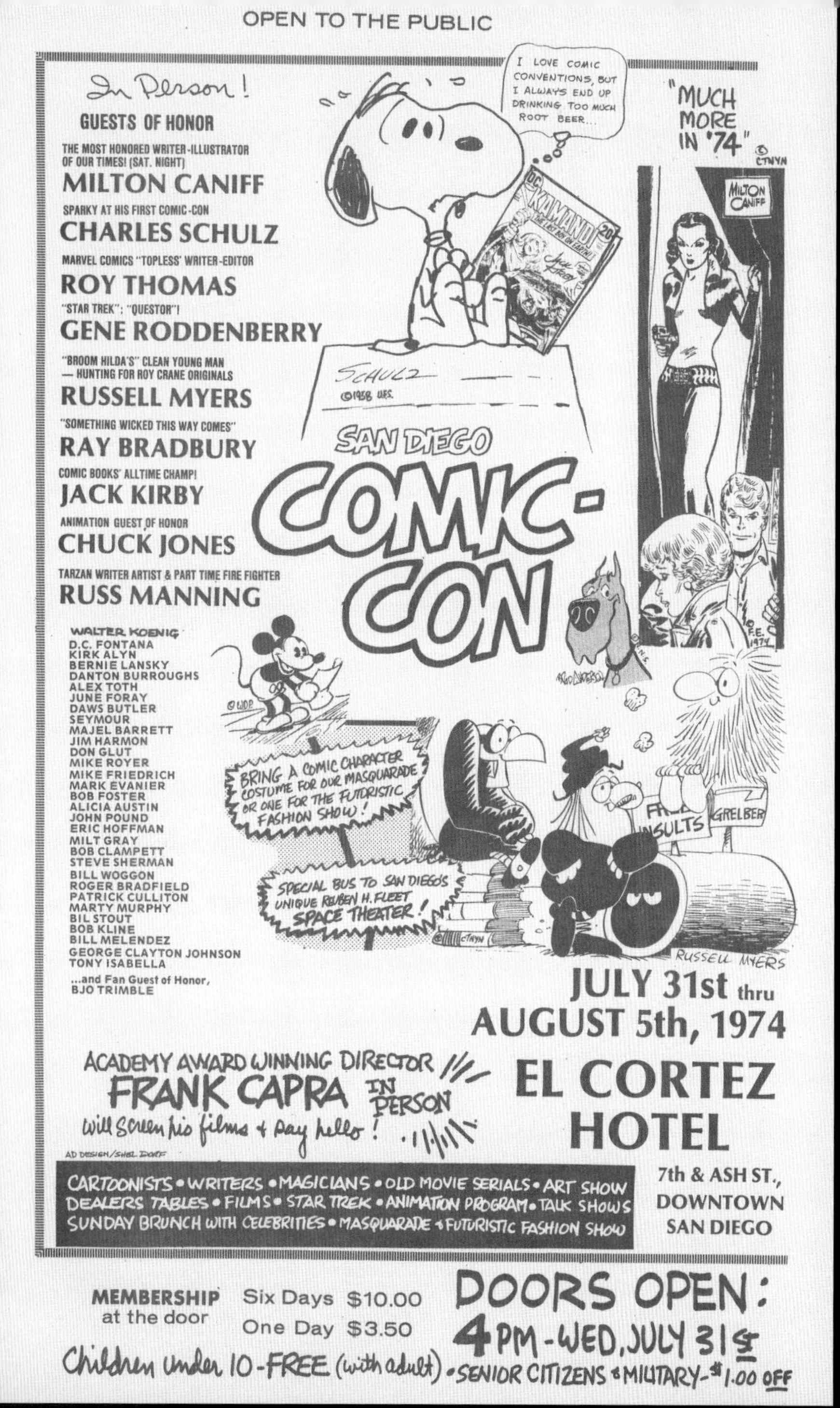
OPEN TO THE PUBLIC
In Person!
GUESTS OF HONOR
THE MOST HONORED WRITER-ILLUSTRATOR OF OUR TIMES! (SAT. NIGHT)
MILTON CANIFF
SPARKY AT HIS FIRST COMIC-CON
CHARLES SCHULZ
MARVEL COMICS "TOPLESS" WRITER-EDITOR
ROY THOMAS
"STAR TREK"; "QUESTOR"!
GENE RODDENBERRY
"BROOM HILDA'S" CLEAN YOUNG MAN — HUNTING FOR ROY CRANE ORIGINALS
RUSSELL MYERS
"SOMETHING WICKED THIS WAY COMES"
RAY BRADBURY
COMIC BOOKS' ALLTIME CHAMP!
JACK KIRBY
ANIMATION GUEST OF HONOR
CHUCK JONES
TARZAN WRITER ARTIST & PART TIME FIRE FIGHTER
RUSS MANNING
WALTER KOENIG
D.C. FONTANA
KIRK ALYN
BERNIE LANSKY
DANTON BURROUGHS
ALEX TOTH
JUNE FORAY
DAWS BUTLER
SEYMOUR
MAJEL BARRETT
JIM HARMON
DON GLUT
MIKE ROYER
MIKE FRIEDRICH
MARK EVANIER
BOB FOSTER
ALICIA AUSTIN
JOHN POUND
ERIC HOFFMAN
MILT GRAY
BOB CLAMPETT
STEVE SHERMAN
BILL WOGGON
ROGER BRADFIELD
PATRICK CULLITON
MARTY MURPHY
BIL STOUT
BOB KLINE
BILL MELENDEZ
GEORGE CLAYTON JOHNSON
TONY ISABELLA
...and Fan Guest of Honor, BJO TRIMBLE
I LOVE COMIC CONVENTIONS, BUT I ALWAYS END UP DRINKING TOO MUCH ROOT BEER...
"MUCH MORE IN '74"
MILTON CANIFF
SCHULZ
SAN DIEGO
COMIC-CON
BRING A COMIC CHARACTER COSTUME FOR OUR MASQUARADE OR ONE FOR THE FUTURISTIC FASHION SHOW!
SPECIAL BUS TO SAN DIEGO'S UNIQUE REUBEN H. FLEET SPACE THEATER!
RUSSELL MYERS
JULY 31st thru AUGUST 5th, 1974
ACADEMY AWARD WINNING DIRECTOR FRANK CAPRA IN PERSON will screen his films & say hello!
EL CORTEZ HOTEL
AD DESIGN/SHEL DORF
CARTOONISTS • WRITERS • MAGICIANS • OLD MOVIE SERIALS • ART SHOW
DEALERS TABLES • FILMS • STAR TREK • ANIMATION PROGRAM • TALK SHOWS
SUNDAY BRUNCH WITH CELEBRITIES • MASQUARADE & FUTURISTIC FASHION SHOW
7th & ASH ST., DOWNTOWN SAN DIEGO
MEMBERSHIP at the door
Six Days $10.00
One Day $3.50
DOORS OPEN: 4PM-WED, JULY 31st
Children under 10-FREE (with adult) • SENIOR CITIZENS & MILITARY-$1.00 OFF

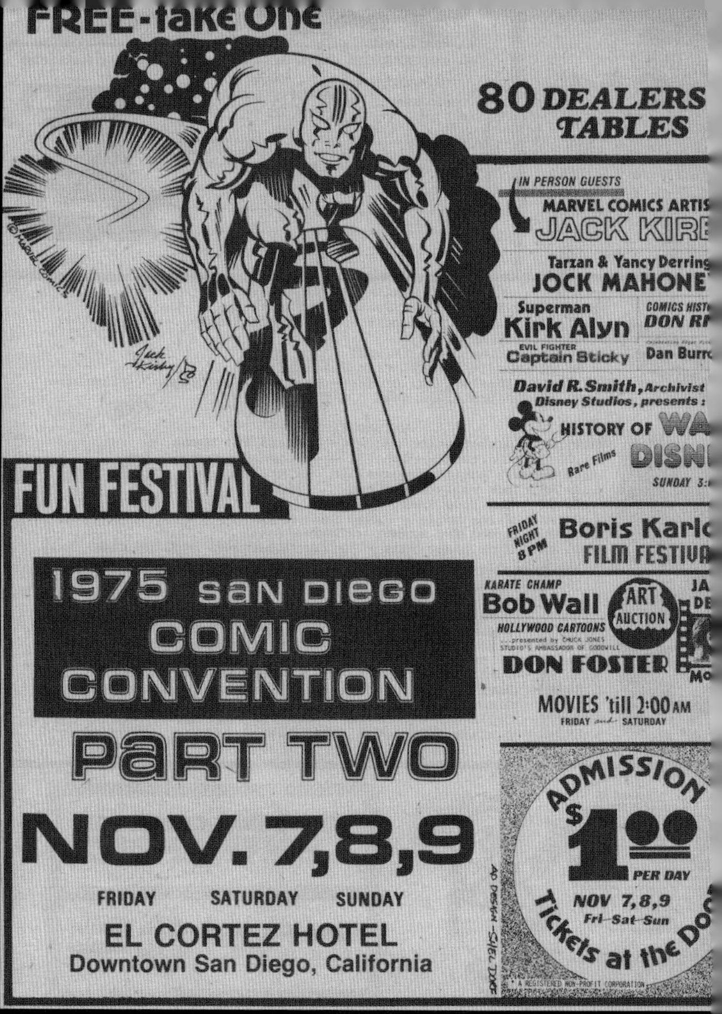
FREE-take One
80 DEALERS TABLES
IN PERSON GUESTS
Tarzan & Yancy Derring
JOCK MAHONE
Superman
Kirk Alyn
EVIL FIGHTER
Captain Sticky
David R. Smith, Archivist
Disney Studios, presents :
FUN FESTIVAL
FRIDAY NIGHT 8PM
Boris Karlo
KARATE CHAMP
Bob Wall
ART AUCTION
HOLLYWOOD CARTOONS
DON FOSTER
MOVIES 'till 2:00 AM
FRIDAY and SATURDAY
1975 san DIEGO COMIC CONVENTION
PaRT TWO
NOV. 7,8,9
FRIDAY SATURDAY SUNDAY
EL CORTEZ HOTEL
Downtown San Diego, California
ADMISSION $1.00 PER DAY
NOV 7,8,9
Fri-Sat-Sun
AD DESIGN-SHEL DORF

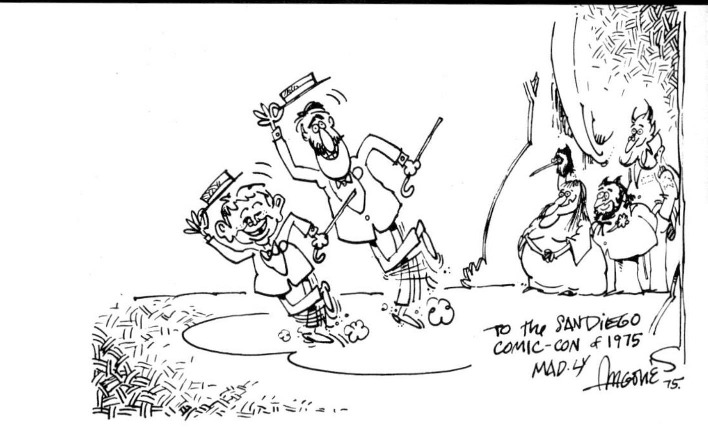
TO the SAN DIEGO COMIC-CON of 1975
MAD. 4
ARAGONES 75.

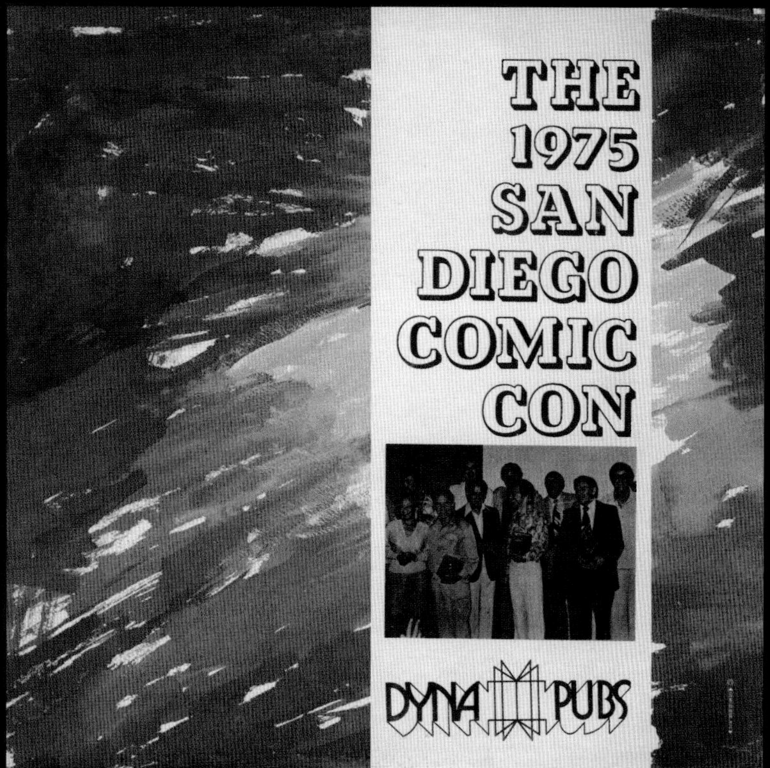
THE 1975 SAN DIEGO COMIC CON
DYNA PUBS

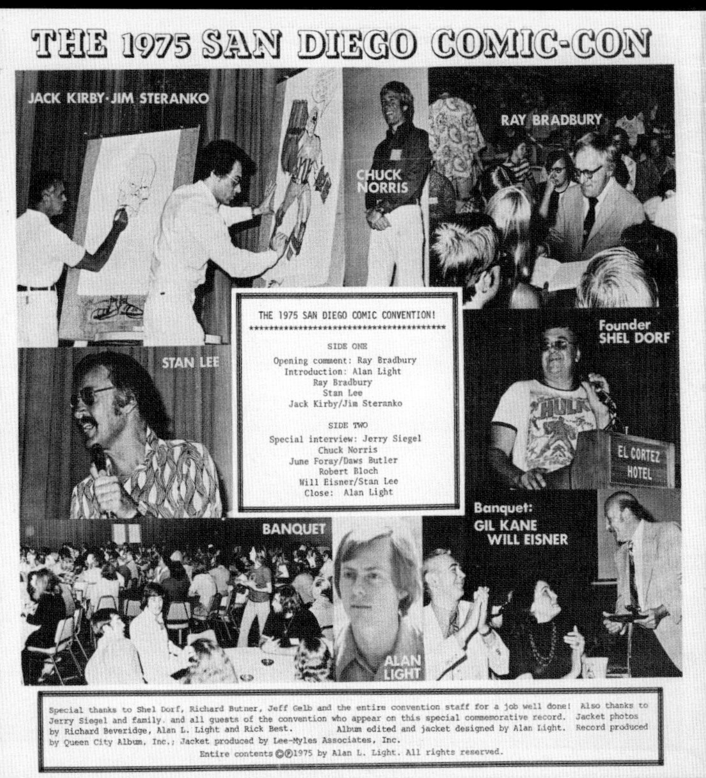
THE 1975 SAN DIEGO COMIC-CON
JACK KIRBY • JIM STERANKO
CHUCK NORRIS
RAY BRADBURY
STAN LEE
Founder SHEL DORF
EL CORTEZ HOTEL
BANQUET
Banquet: GIL KANE WILL EISNER
ALAN LIGHT
THE 1975 SAN DIEGO COMIC CONVENTION!
SIDE ONE
Opening comment: Ray Bradbury
Introduction: Alan Light
Ray Bradbury
Stan Lee
Jack Kirby/Jim Steranko
SIDE TWO
Special interview: Jerry Siegel
Chuck Norris
June Foray/Daws Butler
Robert Bloch
Will Eisner/Stan Lee
Close: Alan Light
Special thanks to Shel Dorf, Richard Butner, Jeff Gelb and the entire convention staff for a job well done! Also thanks to Jerry Siegel and family, and all guests of the convention who appear on this special commemorative record. Jacket photos by Richard Beveridge, Alan L. Light and Rick Best. Album edited and jacket designed by Alan Light. Record produced by Queen City Album, Inc.; Jacket produced by Lee-Myles Associates, Inc.
Entire contents ©℗1975 by Alan L. Light. All rights reserved.

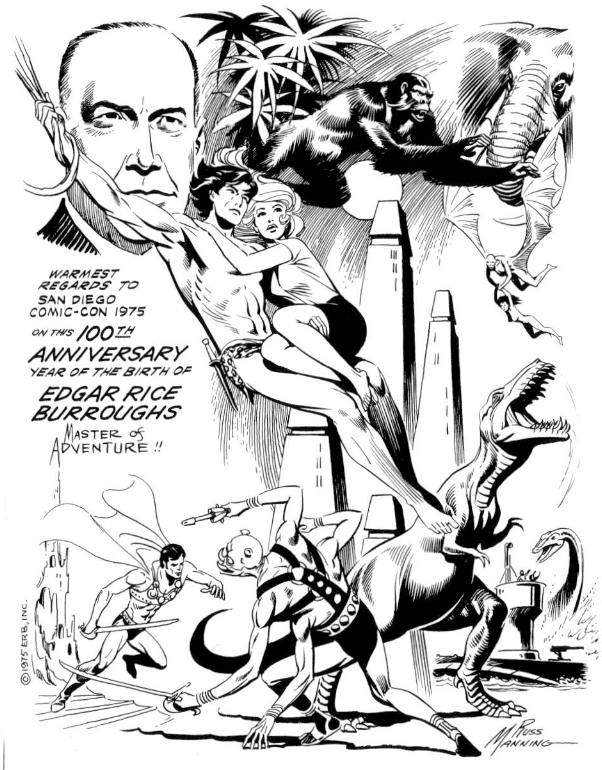
WARMEST REGARDS TO SAN DIEGO COMIC-CON 1975
ON THIS 100TH ANNIVERSARY YEAR OF THE BIRTH OF
EDGAR RICE BURROUGHS
MASTER OF ADVENTURE!!
©1975 ERB, INC.
Russ Manning

OPPOSITE, CLOCKWISE FROM TOP LEFT: A poster for the 1974 Comic-Con ("Much More in '74"); a 1975 flyer for the Part II event held in November; Sergio Aragonés bringing some friends to the 1975 show in an original sketch; back and front of one of Comic-Con's rarest items: *The 1975 San Diego Comic Con*, a record album produced by Alan Light's Dyna Pubs, featuring recordings of some of 1975's programs **CLOCKWISE FROM ABOVE LEFT**: Russ Manning's tribute to the hundredth birthday of Edgar Rice Burroughs, produced for the 1975 program book; a 1977 drawing by Rick Geary, one of his first contributions to Comic-Con; this photo from 1975 proves the allure of boxes and boxes of comics is a Comic-Con constant; a 1979 comic strip by fan-favorite Fred Hembeck; Marie Severin's 1975 caricature of Stan Lee; an actual ticket for a full five-day (yes, five!) membership in 1977, for the princely sum of $10

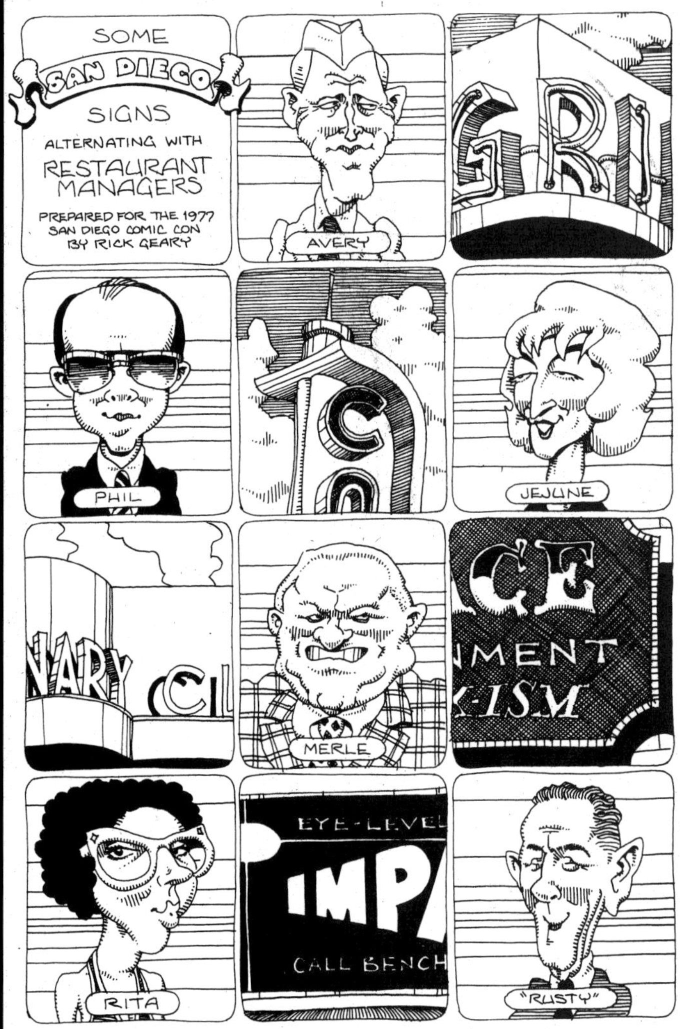
SOME
SAN DIEGO
SIGNS
ALTERNATING WITH
RESTAURANT MANAGERS
PREPARED FOR THE 1977 SAN DIEGO COMIC CON BY RICK GEARY
AVERY
PHIL
JEJUNE
MERLE
RITA
EYE-LEVEL
IMP
CALL BENCH
"RUSTY"

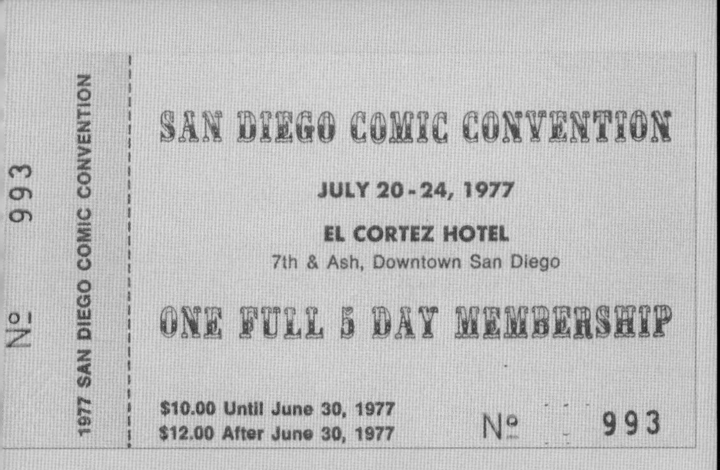
1977 SAN DIEGO COMIC CONVENTION
No 993
SAN DIEGO COMIC CONVENTION
JULY 20-24, 1977
EL CORTEZ HOTEL
7th & Ash, Downtown San Diego
ONE FULL 5 DAY MEMBERSHIP
$10.00 Until June 30, 1977
$12.00 After June 30, 1977
No 993

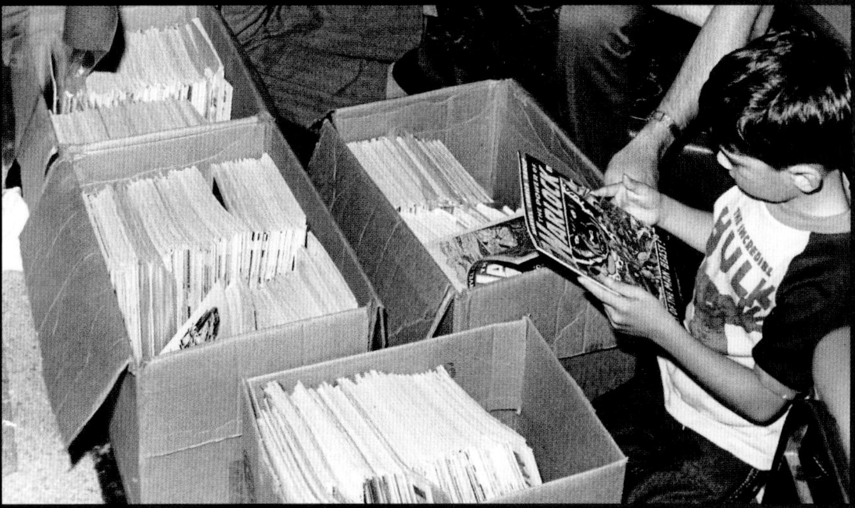

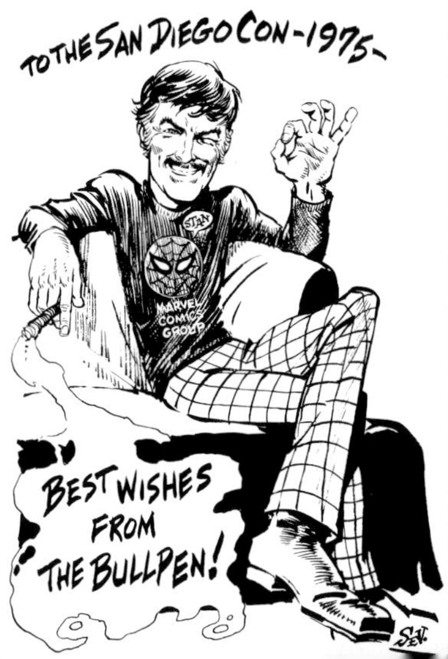
TO THE SAN DIEGO CON - 1975 -
MARVEL COMICS GROUP
BEST WISHES FROM THE BULLPEN!

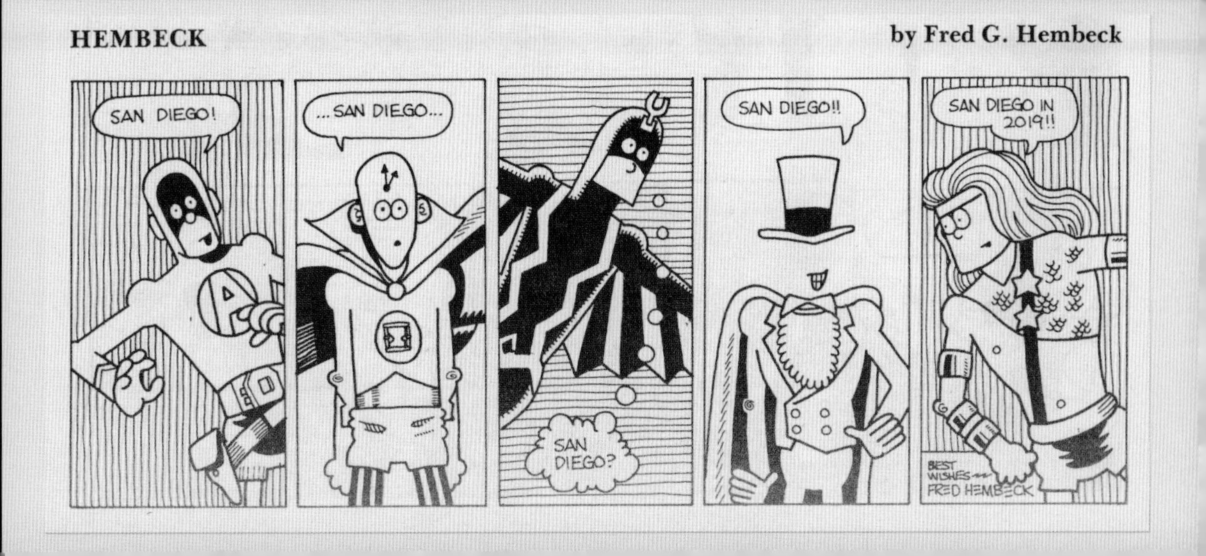
HEMBECK
by Fred G. Hembeck
SAN DIEGO!
...SAN DIEGO...
SAN DIEGO?
SAN DIEGO!!
SAN DIEGO IN 2019!!
BEST WISHES FRED HEMBECK

A SHORT HISTORY OF COMIC CONVENTIONS

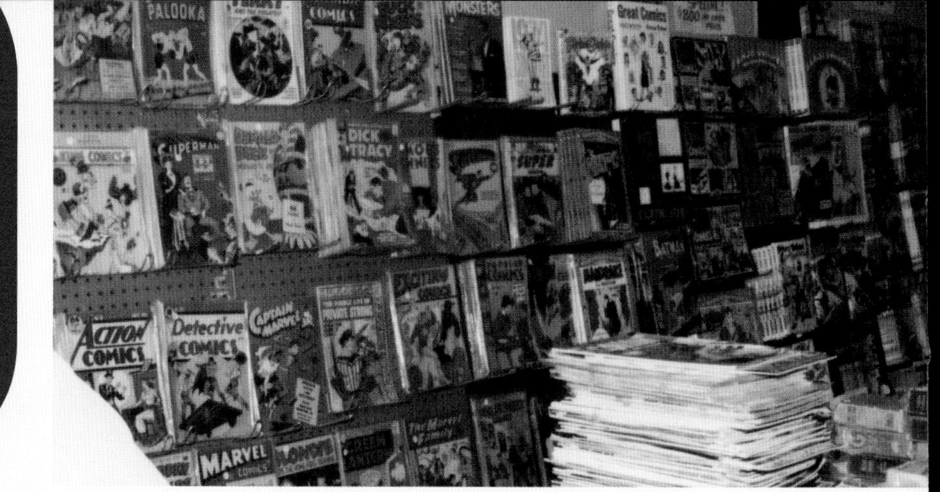

Although San Diego Comic-Con has become the largest gathering of comics fans in the country, it wasn't the first. In the early 1960s, comics fandom started to bubble to the surface. With the return of the DC heroes at the start of the Silver Age of Comics and the advent of the "Marvel Age of Comics," fans started to publish fanzines about the resurgence of costumed heroes. They discovered like-minded people in the letters columns of comics. DC editor Julius Schwartz plugged fanzines such as *Alter-Ego* (edited by Jerry Bails and soon-to-be comics pro Roy Thomas) and *The Comics Reader* (also started by Bails, but taken over by other people, including another future pro, Paul Levitz). Suddenly, fans became aware that they were not alone.

The idea of fans getting together to share their interests wasn't new; science fiction fan conventions started in the late 1930s. Worldcon, the best known of the science fiction conventions, dates back to 1939. The first real comics presence at a convention was at the 1960 Worldcon in Los Angeles, when Dick and Pat Lupoff appeared as Captain Marvel and Mary Marvel. The Lupoffs produced *Xero*, one of the early comic fanzines. In 1962, at Worldcon in Chicago, more comic fans dressed up as superheroes, including a group costumed as the Justice Society of America, and Don and Maggie Thompson—publishers of the fanzine *Comic Art*—as Ibis the Invincible and his assistant, Taia.

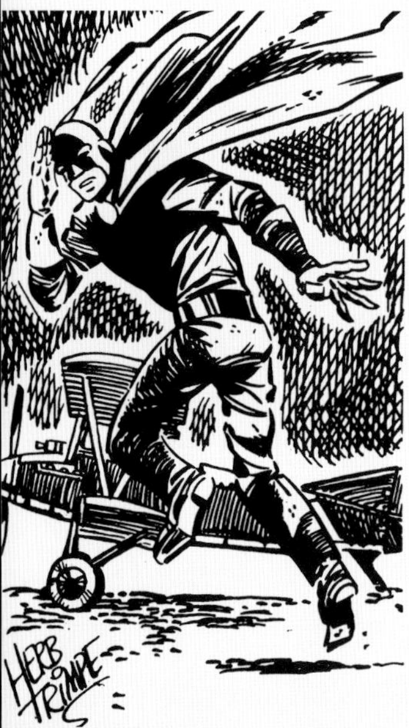
HERB TRIMPE

In 1963 Jerry Bails (whom many regard as the father of comics fandom) invited everyone who sent in a ballot for the Alley Awards (an early award for excellence in comics given out in his *Alter-Ego* fanzine) to come to his home in Warren, Michigan, to help count the votes. Though not a "convention" per se, the "Alley Tally Party," as it was known, was probably the earliest gathering of comics fans in one place. In May 1964, in nearby Detroit at a downtown hotel, two enterprising teenagers, Dave Szurek and Bob Brosch, held what some consider the first actual comic convention. More than seventy people attended, and the makings of the

TOP: Comic-Con's dealers' room, a treasure trove of old comics **ABOVE:** Phantom Eagle art by Herb Trimpe for the 1970 program book
OPPOSITE, LEFT: A Sunday brunch event in 1975, with artist Gil Kane, in light coat, in the far right of the photo, just below center
RIGHT: A dealer specializing in original art at the 1979 Comic-Con

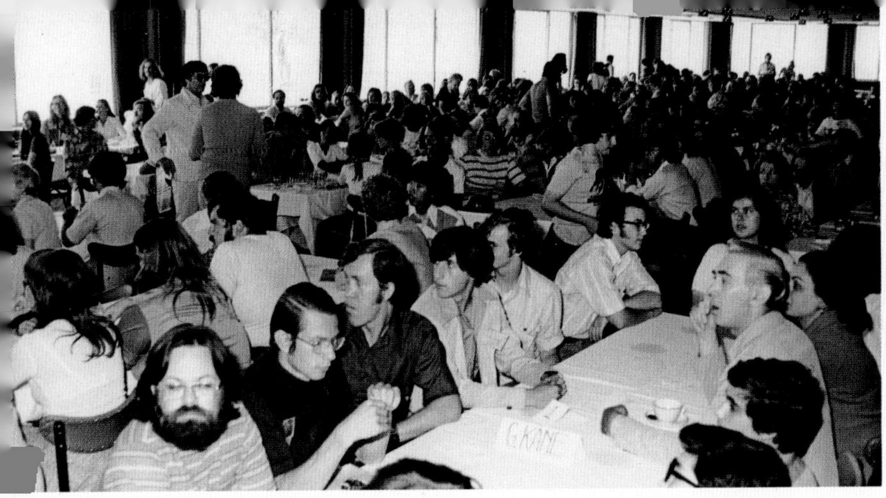

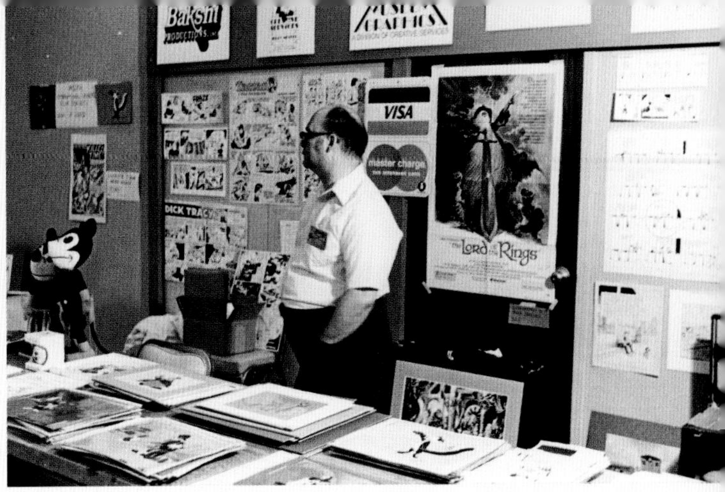
Bakshi
VISA
master charge
DICK TRACY

classic comic convention model were already in place: about a dozen dealers selling comics, featured guest speakers (including Jerry Bails and Shel Dorf), and the screening of a movie, the 1936 science fiction classic *Things to Come*, based on H. G. Wells's novel. The comic convention had been born.

In July of 1964, in New York City, Bernie Bubnis organized the New York Comicon. A one-day affair, the event attracted unofficial representatives from Marvel Comics (an intern named Dave Twedt, famed secretary Flo Steinberg, and Spider-Man artist Steve Ditko, making his first and only comic convention appearance). As comics historian Bill Schelly wrote in his book *The Golden Age of Comic Fandom*, "the 1964 New York Comicon has traditionally been considered the first real comicon, perhaps because of the presence of three representatives from Marvel and the number of well-known fans and dealers in attendance."

The year 1965 saw the creation of the Detroit Triple Fan Fair, which was co-chaired by Shel Dorf and featured a logo boasting "fantasy literature, films, comic art"—a precursor to the same concept in San Diego five years later. In New York City, the Comicon continued under the Academy of Comic Arts and Sciences and, in another few years (as the New York Comic Art Conventions) under the legendary Phil Seuling, who took his annual Fourth of July events to new heights. Regional conventions popped up all over the country, and many cities, including New York, Chicago, Los Angeles, Seattle, Orlando, Detroit, Pittsburgh, Columbus, and Charlotte, still have shows to this day. San Diego's Comic-Con remains the longest-running, continuously held comic convention.

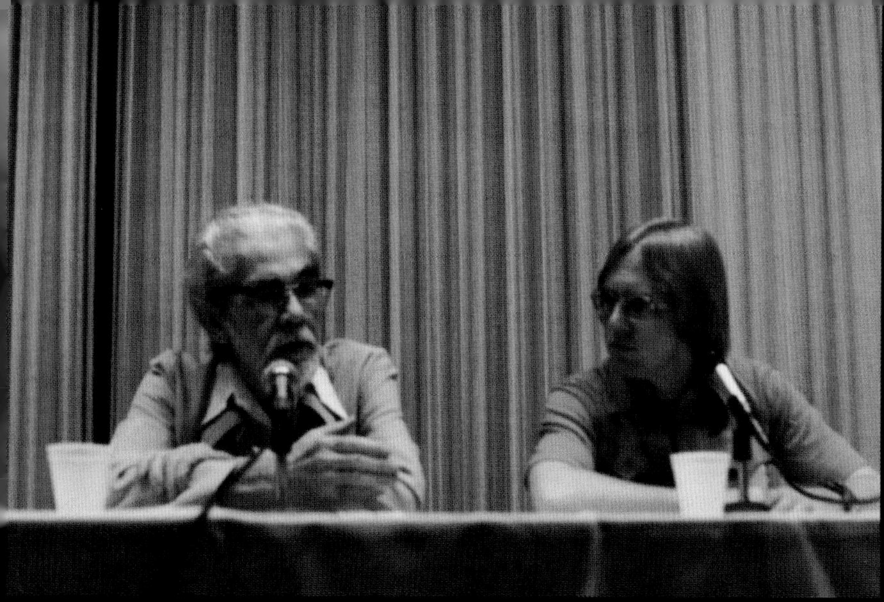

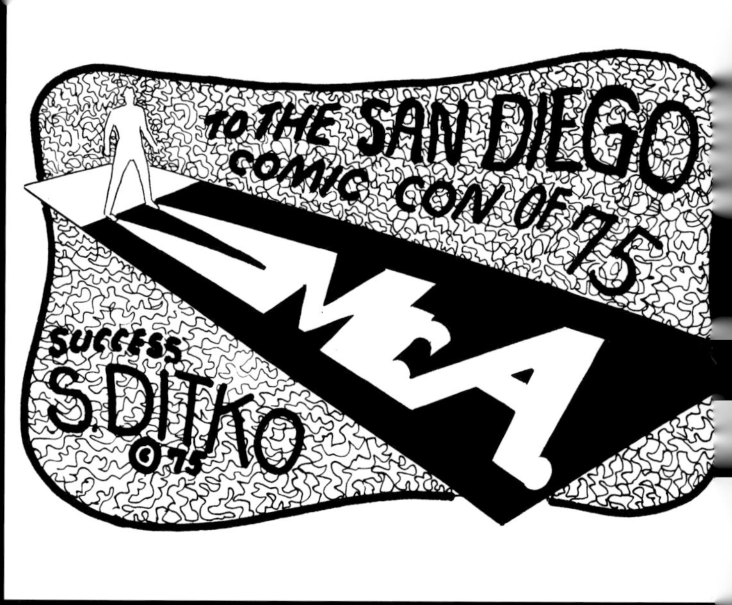
TO THE SAN DIEGO
COMIC CON OF '75
Mr. A
SUCCESS
S.DITKO
©75

CLOCKWISE FROM TOP LEFT: Captain Marvel artist C. C. Beck (left) being interviewed by Roy Thomas (right) at the 1976 show; an original Steve Ditko Mr. A piece for the 1975 program book; committee member Jackie Estrada (left) and Comic-Con vice president Richard Butner (right) in 1979; programming coordinator David Scroggy (left) with author George Clayton Johnson (*Ocean's 11*, *Logan's Run*); Jim Steranko sketching Captain America in 1975 **OPPOSITE, CLOCKWISE FROM TOP LEFT:** Actress Brinke Stevens (nee Charlene Brinkman) was a constant presence and Masquerade contributor in the 1970s; Tarzan, by Russ Manning (1970); "A Brief History of San Diego Fandom," also from 1970; Peter Parker and Aunt May, by John Romita (1975)

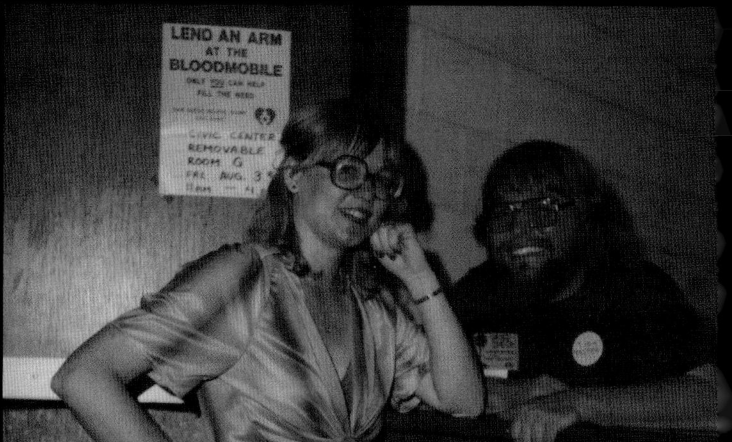
LEND AN ARM
AT THE
BLOODMOBILE
ONLY YOU CAN HELP
FILL THE NEED
CIVIC CENTER
REMOVABLE
ROOM G

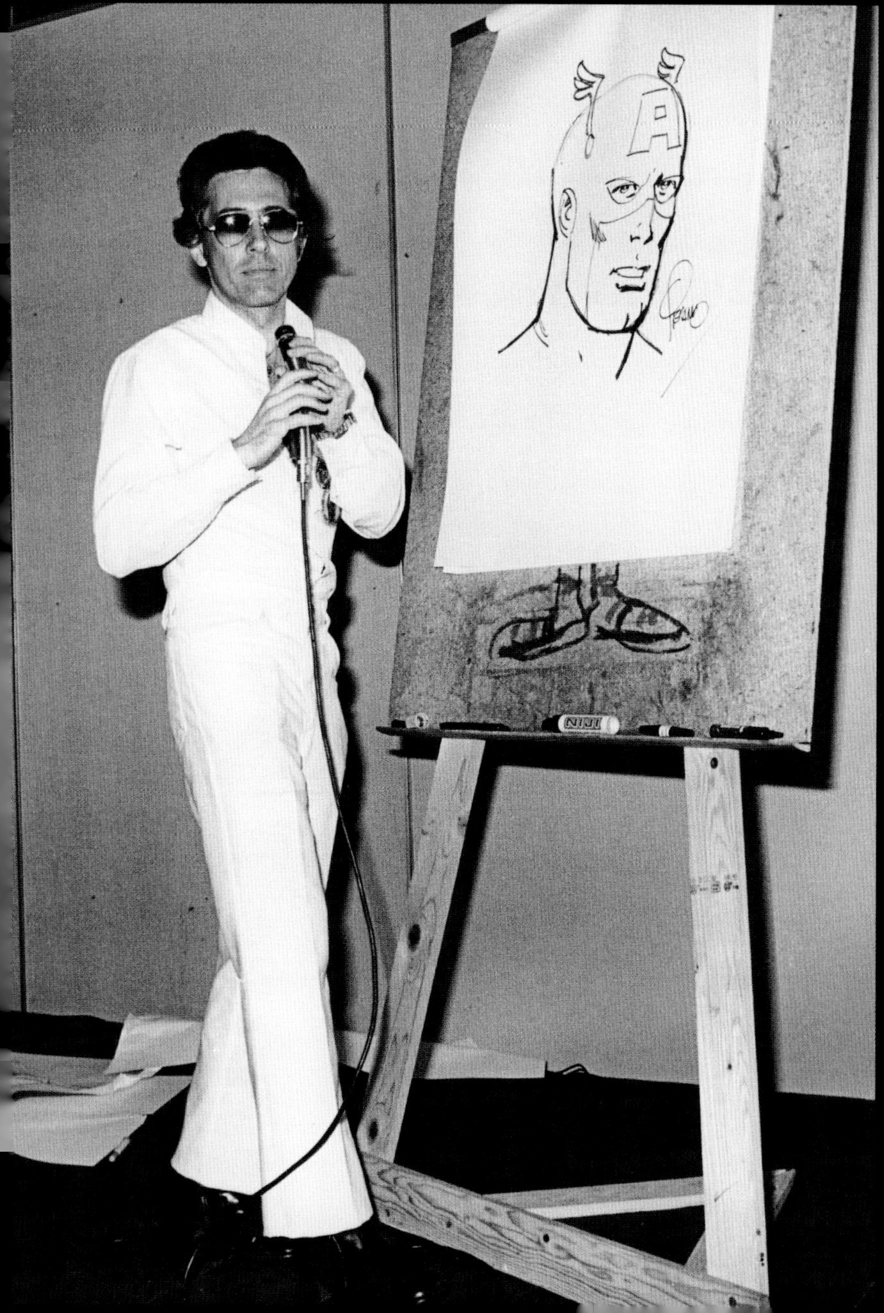
NIJI

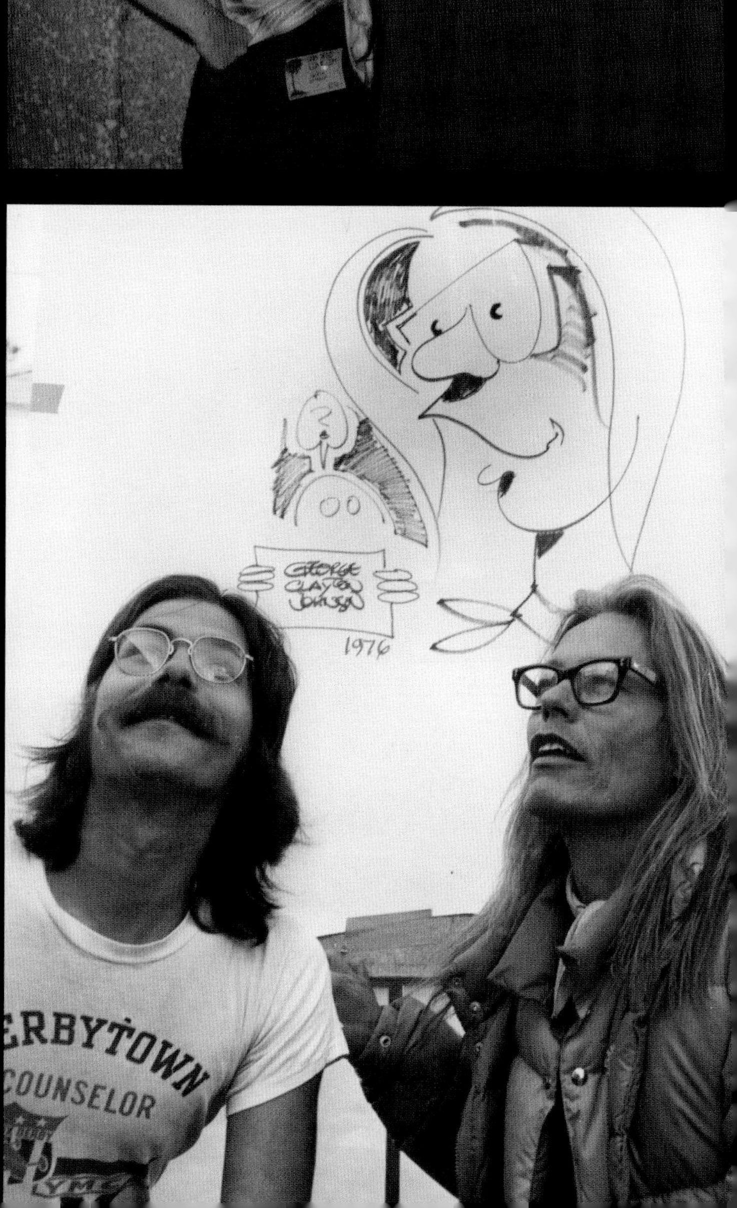
GEORGE CLAYTON JOHNSON
1976
ERBYTOWN
COUNSELOR

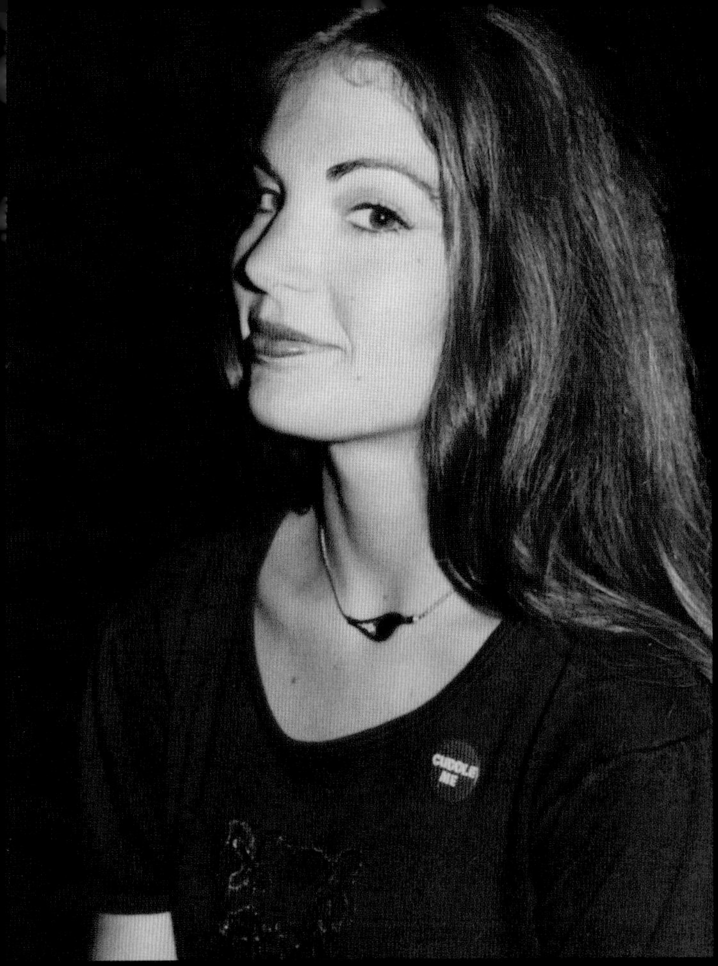

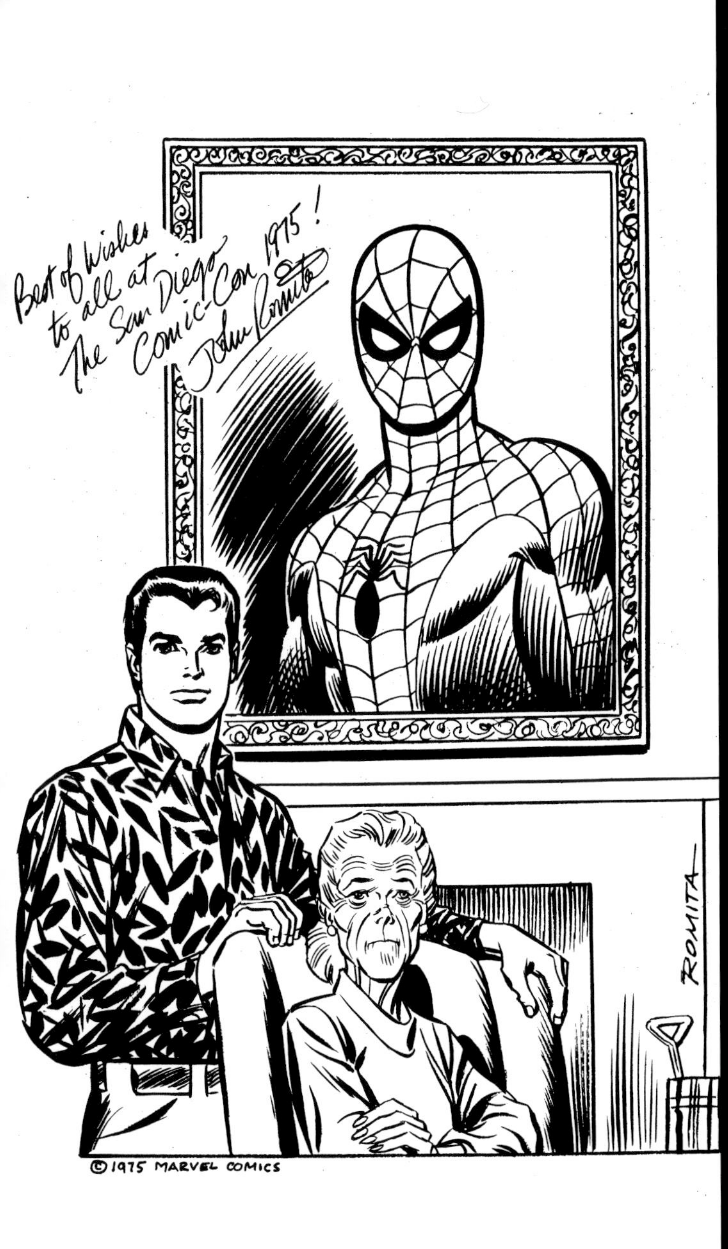
Best of wishes to all at The San Diego Comic-Con 1975!
John Romita
ROMITA
©1975 MARVEL COMICS

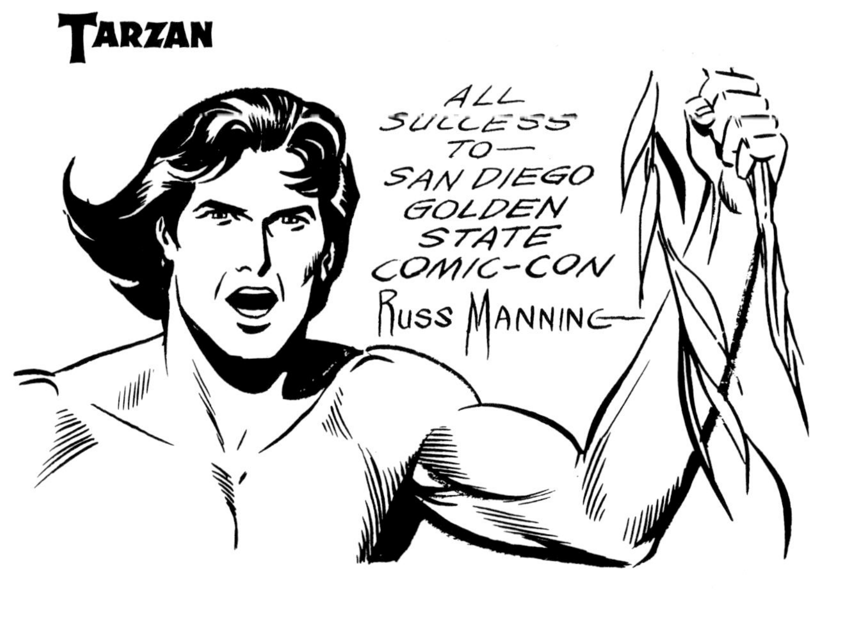
TARZAN
ALL SUCCESS TO— SAN DIEGO GOLDEN STATE COMIC-CON
RUSS MANNING

A BRIEF HISTORY OF SAN DIEGO FANDOM

San Diego fandom reaches back to at least 1952, for we know that the San Diego Science Fantasy Society, under the chairmanship of Roger C. Nelson, hosted Sou-Westercon -Westercon V- at the U.S. Grant Hotel. This was the first American SF con to have attendence reach one thousand. Later, in 1963, John Hull formed the San Diego Science Fiction Society. Although Westercon XIX is officially listed as having no sponsor, the S.D.S.F.S., under the leadership of Dennis Smith and John Hull, hosted the con here in San Diego in 1966. At the 1969 Westercon, in Santa Monica, San Diego fandom was re-organized with the refounding of the San Diego Science Fantasy Society, through the joint efforts of John Paul, Ken Krueger, and Dave Clark. This group, which later became known officially as the San Diego ProFanEsts and unofficially as the Wood-chucks, included many from the ranks of the previous S.D.S.F.S. and authors Harry Harrison and G. C. Edmondson.

The second main branch of San Diego fandom began in 1966 when a group of high school students led by Ron Cearns founded the Society of the Friends of Hobbits, a Tolkien organization. At its peak, the Society was represented on fourteen high school and four college campuses. In the spring of 1969, they hosted their own mini-mini-con, with 47 members. That summer, the Hobbits met the Woodchucks through Ed Meskys, the Man from Niekas, Thain of the Tolkien Society of America.

In the fall of 1969, San Diego comic fandom emerged as several persons led by Shel Dorf and Richard Alf met through Barry Alfonso, founded a club, and thought about possibly holding a convention. After running into the Woodchucks, their plans grew to last March's Mini-Con and has now resulted in San Diego's Golden State Comic-Con. The Hobbits, as the San Diego branch of the Mythopoeic Society, have joined with the rest of San Diego fandom in supporting this convention. Now that the SDGSCC is a reality, we are all working hard on next year's con and are making plans for Westercon 27. Remember - SAN DIEGO IN '74.

THE MANY FACETS OF COMIC-CON INTERNATIONAL

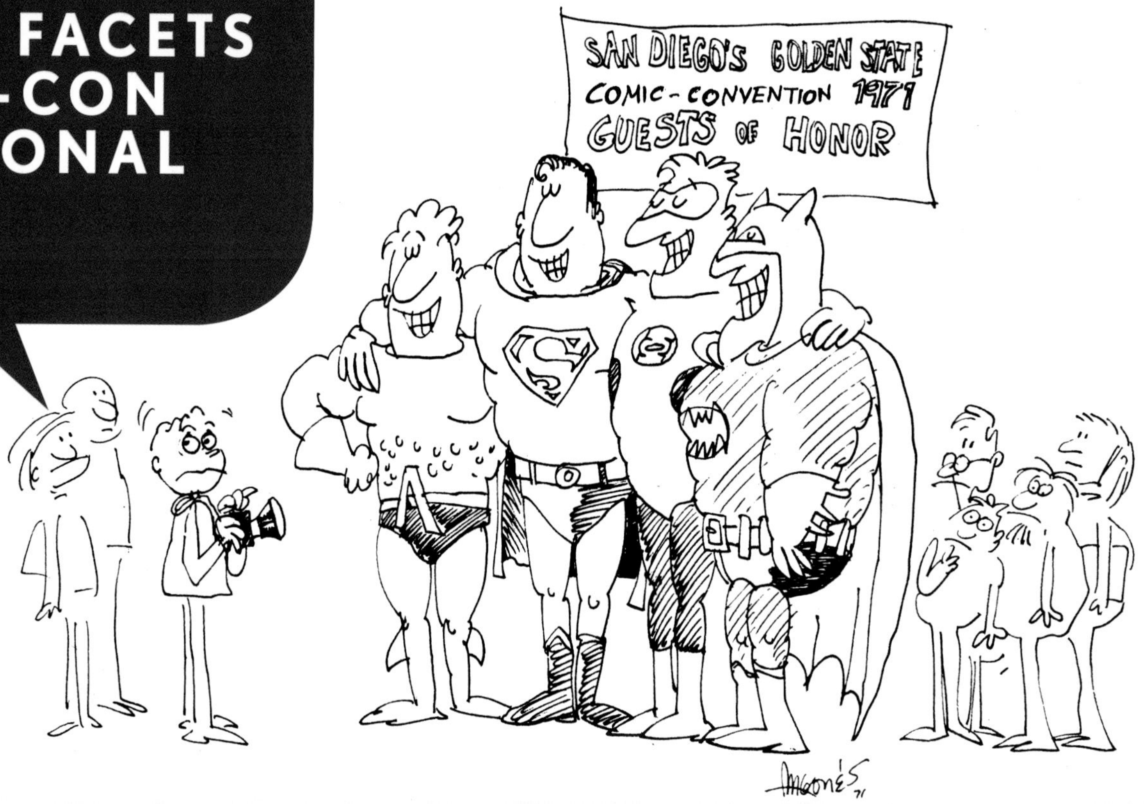
SAN DIEGO'S GOLDEN STATE
COMIC-CONVENTION 1971
GUESTS OF HONOR

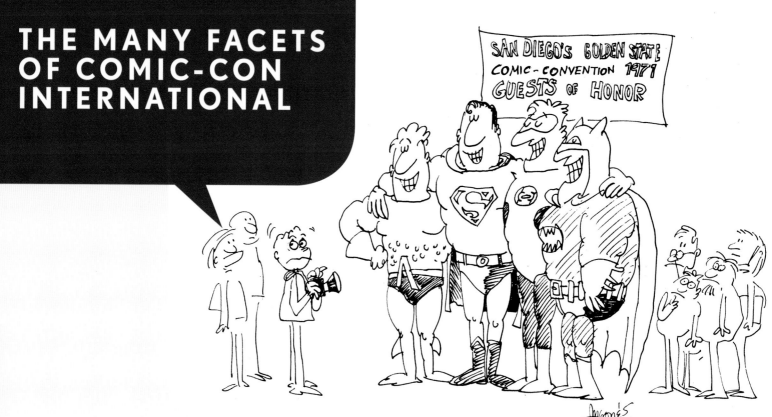

Comic-Con is a convention made up of many facets, any one of which could be considered a separate event in itself. Here's a look at some of those incredible elements that make up the country's largest comics and popular arts show.

ANIME

Japanese animation, or anime, screenings have been a part of Comic-Con since almost the beginning of the event. Early imports of anime programs from Japan such as *Astro Boy*, *Gigantor*, *8 Man*, and *Kimba the White Lion* made their way into television syndication in the mid-1960s, creating a fervent fan base in the United States. In 1978 the first screenings debuted at Comic-Con. Videotapes were provided by Japan-based Toei Animation, the producer of programs such as *Devilman*, *Mazinger*, *Captain Harlock*, and many more. Those early screenings resulted in many anime and manga creators visiting Comic-Con over the next few decades, including Osamu Tezuka (*Astro Boy*), Monkey Punch (*Lupin III*), Rumiko Takahashi (*Urusei Yatsura*), and Tite Kubo (*Bleach*).

Anime became a separate department at Comic-Con in 1998, devoted to obtaining and screening the very best the industry has to offer. As the amount and quality of anime imports has grown over the years, so has the number of followers, helping to create the related phenomenon of cosplay (short for "costume play"), in which people dress as their favorite anime, manga, and comics characters. In recent years, anime screenings have grown to encompass three separate rooms at Comic-Con, which run from when the doors first open each morning until late into the night. Premieres, sneak peeks, and old favorites dominate the schedule and, as usual at Comic-Con, you never know what might pop up and surprise you.

ABOVE: A cartoon by Sergio Aragonés for the 1971 program book, combining a few facets of the show into one image: comics, photo opportunities, and—literally—superstars

ARTISTS' ALLEY

Imagine an Exhibit Hall filled with table after table of some of your favorite comics artists selling original art, sketchbooks, prints, and books and doing sketches for you while you watch—that's what Comic-Con's Artists' Alley is like. Created in 1986, this area is given over each year to an incredible assortment of top talents from comics and science fiction/fantasy. It's one of the places at Comic-Con where fans can meet and greet some of their idols, and even get a sketch or that rare piece of original art.

ART SHOW

The idea of an art show at Comic-Con most likely came from science fiction conventions, where the displays of artwork by both fans and professionals have been mainstays. Comic-Con's Art Show was there from the first event in 1970—which featured the editorial cartoons of the *San Diego Evening Tribune*'s Bob Stevens, along with comics pieces. Over the years, the Art Show has featured works by many talented amateurs and professionals, and quite a few of the amateurs have gone on to become pros. Additional space has been devoted to displays of art by such comics legends as Carl Barks and Basil Wolverton as well as Jim Steranko's paintings for the paperback reprints of the old pulp magazine series *The Shadow*. In more recent years, the Art Show has showcased a wide variety of mediums, from drawings and paintings to sculpture, jewelry, and 3-D work. Many of these pieces are available for purchase, giving Comic-Con attendees the opportunity to take home a beautiful, one-of-a-kind piece of art.

AUTOGRAPHS

Getting your favorite writers and artists to sign a particularly treasured comic or book has always been a part of the fan experience. The Autograph Area is filled with fan favorites from all areas of the popular arts, including comics, science fiction and fantasy, movies, animation, and television. You never quite know whom you might see in the giant Autograph Area at Comic-Con. It could be a favorite television star (such as Richard Hatch from *Battlestar Galactica*) or a scream queen (such as the one and only Elvira), or a national treasure such as Noel Neill (Lois Lane on television's *Adventures of Superman*), or a noted science fiction author such as Ray Bradbury. Comic-Con's Autograph Area also serves as "signing central" for authors, artists, and celebrities after their panel appearances.

EXHIBIT HALL

It's one of the yardsticks that any convention is measured by: the size and scope of its exhibit hall. The Exhibit Hall was originally known as the "dealers' room" when it was a part of the first Comic-Con in 1970, but the number of exhibitors has grown exponentially over the years. Of course, comics have always been the centerpiece of the Exhibit Hall, with dealers selling old and new comic books and related items, and publishers promoting new comics and books. But from the beginning, exhibitors have specialized in other materials as well, including movie memorabilia, collectible toys, and original artwork. Over the years, the Exhibit Hall has grown to encompass every aspect of the popular arts world, including publishers of all sizes (in the Publishers' Area, the Independent Press Pavilion, the Small Press Area, and Artists' Alley), manga and anime producers, action figure and toy companies, video-game and role-playing game producers, movie and television studios, art book publishers and retailers, movie memorabilia and DVD sellers, and jewelry and apparel retailers, all with an almost endless mix of products (and more often than not, much-coveted free stuff!). From its humble beginning with just a few dealers in 1970 to its four-hundred-sixty-thousand-plus-square-foot shoppers' paradise today, Comic-Con's Exhibit Hall is a must-see part of the show for every attendee.

GAMES

With the rise of popular games such as Dungeons & Dragons, it was only natural that gaming would become an important part of Comic-Con. From the mid-1970s on, gamers have been coming to Comic-Con, and to accommodate them the convention created the first dedicated gaming area in 1983. That space grew over the years and now encompasses most of the mezzanine area at the San Diego Convention Center and a large space at the convention's host hotel for late-night games. In the 2000s, Comic-Con saw an increasing influx of video-game companies wanting to reach out to the event's fabled fan base. These days, games at the show include everything from role-playing card games to miniatures, from video games to LARP (live-action role-playing). Some Comic-Con attendees now come solely for the gaming aspect of the show, and many major tournaments and gaming companies figure prominently in both the game schedule and in the Exhibit Hall.

PORTFOLIO REVIEW

It's the dream of a lot of Comic-Con attendees: to be "discovered" by a comics publisher and draw their favorite comics characters. From the 1990s onward, the convention has provided a dedicated space for Portfolio Review, featuring not only some of the top comics publishers, but also other related companies in the popular arts, including movie and animation studios and video-game and role-playing game companies. The Portfolio Review process gives attendees a chance at some real openings in their chosen careers and an opportunity for an honest evaluation of their work, helping them refine and hone their skills for that next big break.

PROGRAMMING

Another very public "face" of Comic-Con is its rich and extensive program schedule. From the beginning, the event has showcased panel discussions, chalk-talks, and presentations geared toward the comics, science fiction/ fantasy, movie, animation, and television fan. Comic-Con regularly invites special guests from comics and all aspects of the popular arts to be featured in programs. Each year, special programming themes are selected in advance, and guests are invited who have taken part in the events and whose works have inspired this special recognition. Those themes have included everything from the fiftieth anniversaries of such comics touchstones as EC Comics, Superman, Batman, and Captain America to celebrations of the vast world of editorial cartoons in a presidential election year. They have encompassed looks back at the 1960s; at the seminal comics year of 1986,

when comics "grew up" (*Maus, Batman: The Dark Knight Returns*, and *Watchmen*); and even Comic-Con's own anniversaries. Another important part of programming at the event is the hands-on workshops and seminars. From attorney Michael Lovitz's "Comic Book Law School," to San Diego artist and teacher Jeff Watts's life-drawing classes—and everything in between, including panels on all aspects of comics creation and publishing—these special discussions and demonstrations underscore Comic-Con's ongoing commitment to showcasing educational programs.

Programming has continued to grow over the years from a handful of events at that very first Comic-Con (which included discussions on the history of comics, underground comics, and censorship; talks by special guests Ray Bradbury, Jack Kirby, and A. E. van Vogt; and movie screenings featuring *Flash Gordon* serial chapters and Laurel and Hardy shorts), to more than 450 events in 2008. In recent years, Comic-Con has run fifteen separate tracks of programs each day of the four-day convention, in rooms ranging in size from two hundred to sixty-five hundred seats. At any given time, there are more than eighteen thousand seats available in the programming rooms (most of them full), and something is sure to be on the schedule that would make even the most discerning fan want to attend a must-see presentation.

RIGHT: The program schedule for the first Comic-Con in 1970, showing that all the familiar programming elements were there from the beginning **OPPOSITE:** By 1977 the program schedule had grown much larger but still included the Comic-Con staples: comics, science fiction, movies, special guests, and even old-time radio (*The Jim Harmon Radio Show*, on the middle panel, bottom row). Rick Geary provided the art, one of his earliest pieces for the convention.

- PROGRAM -

SATURDAY

9:00	Registration / Hucksters rooms open
11:00	Opening Address
11:30	Movies: "Angor Love", "Two Tars" (Laurel and Hardy)
1:00	History of Comics
2:00	Jack Kirby
3:00	Flash Gordon Movie, "Purple Death"
4:00	Auction
5:00	Ray Bradbury
6:00	Dinner Break
7:00	"Comics and Censorship" Open discussion
8:00	"Angora Love", "Two Tars"

SUNDAY

9:00	Registration / Hucksters rooms open
11:00	Movie: "The Gladiator", Joe E. Brown
12:00	Lunch
1:00	Auction
2:00	Bob Stevens
3:00	Earl Kemp
4:00	"Amateur Publishing for Fun and Profit"
5:00	A. E. Van Vogt
6:00	Dinner Break
7:00	"Underground Comics and Pornographic Science Fiction" Open discussion
8:00	More movies – til you tire (Incl. "Bomba The Jungle Boy")

MONDAY

9:00	Registration / Hucksters rooms open
11:00	Cartoonist Chalk Talk
12:00	Lunch
1:00	Movie: "The Man From Beyond" (1922) written, produced and starring Harry Houdini with Nita Naldi
2:30	Fantasy Fandom Panel
3:30	Auction
4:30	Flash Gordon Movie: "Purple Death"
6:00	Closing Remarks

1977
SAN DIEGO
COMIC CON

PROGRAM

WEDNESDAY, JULY 20

9:00 Dealers' registration (Cent.)
10:00 Dealers' setup (Cent.)
2:00 Registration opens (Cent. foyer)
   Dealers' Room opens (Cent.)
3:00 Films begin (Car.)
9:00 Eric Hoffman Presents Serial Classics (Car.)
   Registration closes
   Dealers' Room closes

FILM SCHEDULE

Some of the films being shown at the convention have been included in this schedule, but a more complete listing can be found posted outside the Caribbean Room. The special Film Noir program will be held throughout the convention and will be kicked off Thursday night at 8:30 in the Caribbean Room.

BLOOD DRIVE

Thursday the Cotillion Room will be *the* place to be. Artists will be doing drawings, belly dancers will be doing their thing, Patrick Culliton will be performing magic tricks, and convention guests will be wandering in and out. The price of admission to all this entertainment is one pint of blood for the San Diego Blood Bank. In addition to being entertained, blood donors will receive packets of goodies and will have a chance to chat with Robert A. Heinlein.

Note: Times and programs are subject to change, so please check the program listing in the registration area (Century Room foyer) each day for changes in the schedule.

KEY TO ABBREVIATIONS:

Car. = Caribbean Room
Cent. = Century Room
Cot. = Cotillion Room
Int. = International Room

THURSDAY, JULY 21

9:00 Registration opens (Cent. foyer)
   Dealers' Room opens (Cent.)
9:30 Films begin: *Behind the Mask* (Car.)
10:00 Keynote Address--Forry Ackerman (Int.)
10:30 Robert A. Heinlein (Int.)
11:00 Jack Katz and the First Kingdom (Int.)
   Blood Drive opens (Cot.)
   Film Room closes till 2:30
12:00 Art Show opens (Don Room)
   Byron Preiss: Weird Heroes and Fiction Illustrated--with Chaykin, Steranko, others (Int.)
1:00 Producing and Selling a Comic Strip-- Richard Lynn, Mell Lazarus, Shel Dorf (Int.)
2:30 Musical Tribute to Fleischer Studios-- Leslie Cabarga (Int.)
   Film: *Ocean's 11* (Car.)
3:00 Betty Boop Meets Smegma the Barbarian (Int.)
   Blood Drive closes
3:30 The Sergio Aragones Hour (Int.)
4:30 George Clayton Johnson reads from his works (Int.)
5:30 Super 8 Symposium--featuring classic films, including the original *King Kong* (Car.)
6:00 Women in the Comics--Trina Robbins (Int.)
7:00 Esoteric Comics slide show--Scott Shaw (Int.)
8:00 The Art of Rick Griffin--slide show by Joel Milke (Int.)
   Art Show closes
8:30 Film Noir--Carl Macek (Car.)
9:00 Film Noir movies begin (Car.)

   Registration and Dealers' Room close at 9:00 p.m.

   Special Midnight Show: History of Sex in the Comics (Cot.)-- no one under 18 admitted

FRIDAY, JULY 22

9:00 Registration opens (Cent. foyer)
   Dealers' Room opens (Cent.)
   Art Show opens (Don Room)
   Film: *Lost World of Sinbad* (Car.)
10:00 Bill Blackbeard (Int.)
10:30 Film: *The Black Book* (Car.)
11:00 Alternative Publishing Panel--Walter Bachner, Ron Turner, Mike Friedrich, others (David Scroggy, moderator) (Int.)
12:00 Artists' Panel--Don Rico (moderator), Frank Brunner, Jack Katz, Alfredo Alcala, others (Int.)
   Middle Earth Publications Q&A (Cot.)
12:30 Film: *Masque of the Red Death* (Car.)
1:00 Tarzan Panel--Russ Manning, Joe Kubert, Roy Thomas (Int.)
   Bob Kane Slide Show--Bob Kane & Shel Dorf (Cot.)
2:00 WSA meeting (Cot.)
2:30 Humor Panel--B. Kliban, Harvey Kurtzman, Bill Scott, others (Mark Evanier, moderator) (Int.)
3:00 Shadow Secret Society Meeting--Walter Gibson, Jim Steranko, Ed Noonchester (Cot.)
   Film: *Scarlet Street* (Car.)
4:30 Theodore Sturgeon reads from his works accompanied by artists William Stout, Larry Todd, Jack Katz, others (Int.)
   Film: *Invasion of the Body Snatchers* (Car.)
6:00 International Room closes down for Masquerade setup
   Film premiere: *Amanaman* (Car.)
8:00 Art Show & Registration close
8:30 MASQUERADE (Int.) featuring Gabriel Wisdom as Thor; music by Corky Carroll; and "Funeral for a Friend," dance presentation by Charlene Brinkman & Company

FRIDAY, JULY 22 (cont.)

9:00 Dealers' Room closes
Midnight: *Rocky Horror Picture Show* (Car.)

SATURDAY, JULY 23

9:00 Registration opens (Cent. foyer)
   Dealers' Room opens (Cent.)
   Art Show opens (Don Room)
   Film: *Scarlet Pimpernel* (Car.)
10:00 Marvel Panel--Jack Kirby, Roy Thomas, others (Int.)
10:30 Incas & Iguanas: An Expedition to the Galapagos and Peru--Wm Stout (Cot.)
   Film: *Judex* (Car.)
11:30 Creators' Panel--Joe Shuster, Bob Kane, Jack Kirby (Roy Thomas, moderator) (Int.)
   Illustration as Fine Art--Phil Garris, Michael Kaluta, John Pound, Wm Stout (Cot.)
12:00 Auction by the pool
1:00 The Shadow--Walter Gibson, Steranko (Int.)
   Foreign Artists in American Comics-- Alfredo Alcala, Ernie Chan, Pablo Marcos, Rudy Nebres (Ed Noonchester, moderator); plus Victor Silver on the Mexican comics industry (Cot.)
1:30 Secrets and Scandals of the TV Industry --Mark Evanier & Stanley Ralph Ross (Cot.)
2:00 The Making of Star Wars--Charles Lippincott (Int.)
3:00 The Jim Harmon Radio Show (Cot.)
   Film: *T-Men* (Car.)
4:00 Dialogue: Theodore Sturgeon & Robert A. Heinlein (Int.)
   Jack Katz Chalk Talk (Cot.)
   5:00 The Harvey Kurtzman Show, with Wm Stout & Clay Geerdes (Int.)
   King Tut's Tomb slide show--Walt Daugherty (Cot.)

SATURDAY, JULY 23 (cont.)

5:00 Films end in Caribbean Room for banquet setup
6:00 Stan Lynde (Cot.)
7:00 Registration closes
   Dealers' Room closes
8:00 BANQUET, featuring the Inkpot Awards & an appearance by Carl Barks; Sergio Aragones, Master of Ceremonies.
   UFO Research Group: Meeting and Films Presentation (Int.)
   Art Show closes
10:00 Superman program--John Field (Int.)
Midnight: "2001: A Splice Odyssey"--3 hours of film trailers (Int.)
Midnight: Special showing of *Allegro Non Troppo* at Ken Theater, San Diego

SUNDAY, JULY 24

9:00 Registration opens (Cent. foyer)
   Dealers' Room opens (Cent.)
   Art Show opens (Don Room)
   Films begin (Int.)
10:00 CELEBRITY BRUNCH, featuring chalk talks by guests (Car.)
1:00 Bob Clampett Animation Special (Int.)
1:30 The Magic of Houdini--Patrick Culliton and Walter Gibson (Cot.)
2:00 Films resume in Caribbean Room
2:30 Jay Ward Program--Bill Scott & June Foray (Int.)
4:00 Film: *Destination Moon*, with commentary by George Pal & Robert Heinlein (Car.)
6:00 Dealers' Room closes
   Art Show closes
   Films continue until projector and/or projectionist breaks down

MONDAY, JULY 25

Planning begins for the 1978 San Diego Comic Convention

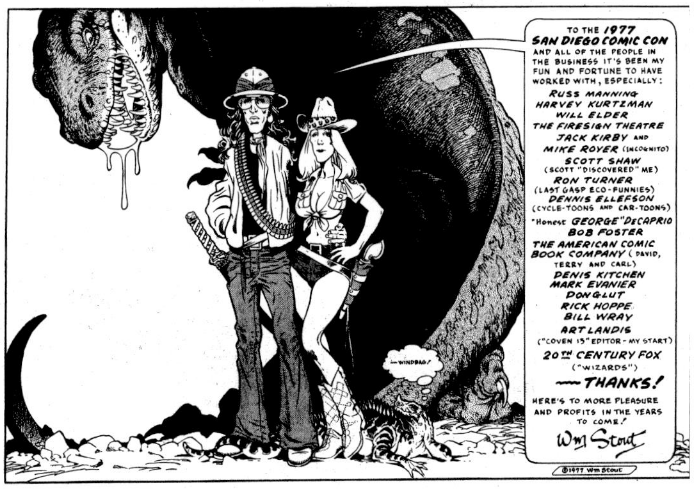
TO THE 1977 SAN DIEGO COMIC CON AND ALL OF THE PEOPLE IN THE BUSINESS IT'S BEEN MY FUN AND FORTUNE TO HAVE WORKED WITH, ESPECIALLY:
RUSS MANNING
HARVEY KURTZMAN
WILL ELDER
THE FIRESIGN THEATRE
JACK KIRBY AND
MIKE ROYER (INCOGNITO)
SCOTT SHAW
(SCOTT "DISCOVERED" ME)
RON TURNER
(LAST GASP ECO-FUNNIES)
DENNIS ELLEFSON
(CYCLE-TOONS AND CAR-TOONS)
"Honest GEORGE" DeCAPRIO
BOB FOSTER
THE AMERICAN COMIC BOOK COMPANY (DAVID, TERRY AND CARL)
DENIS KITCHEN
MARK EVANIER
DON GLUT
RICK HOPPE
BILL WRAY
ART LANDIS
("COVEN 13" EDITOR - MY START)
20TH CENTURY FOX
("WIZARDS")
—THANKS!
HERE'S TO MORE PLEASURE AND PROFITS IN THE YEARS TO COME!
Wm Stout
©1977 Wm Stout
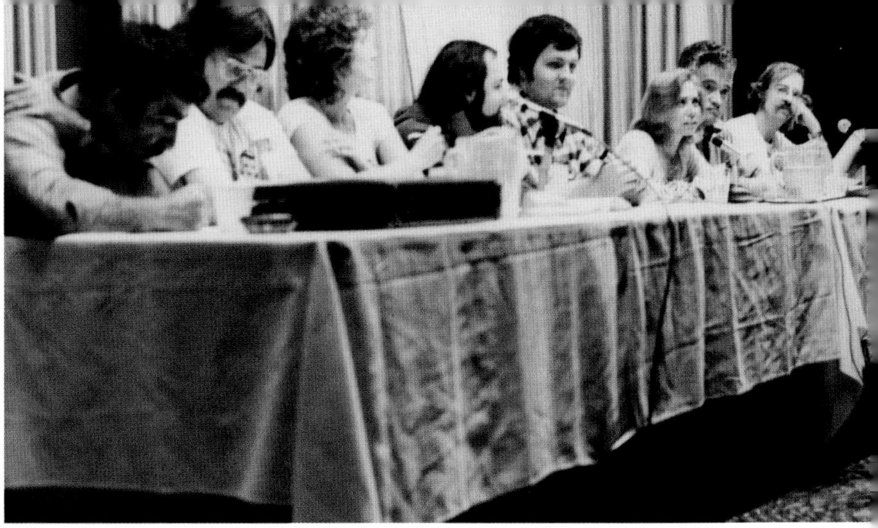
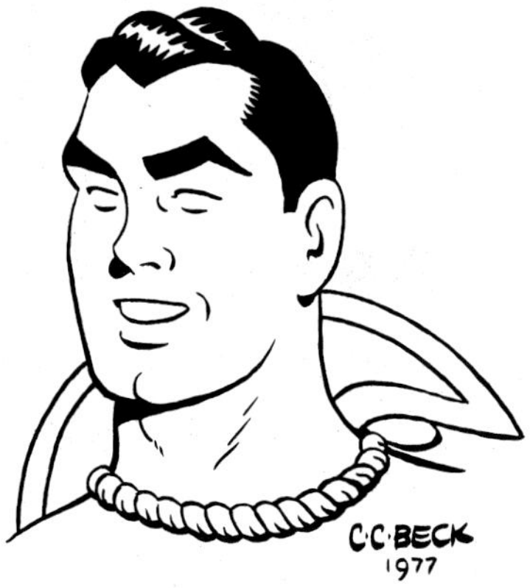
C.C. BECK
1977
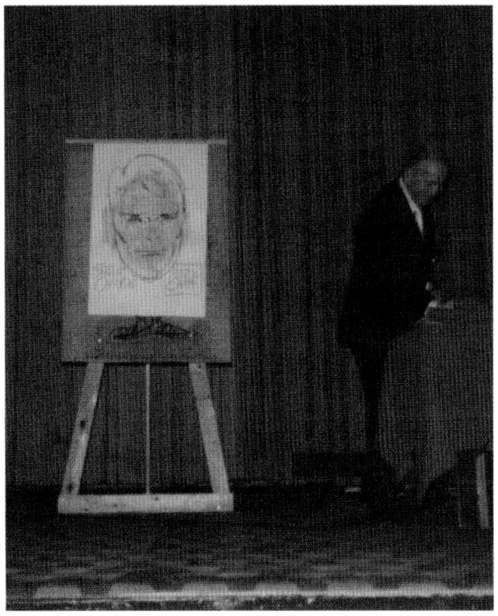
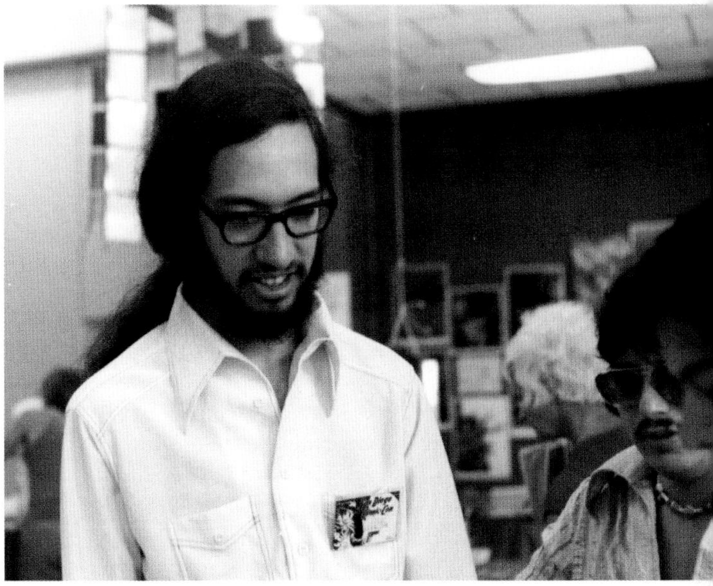
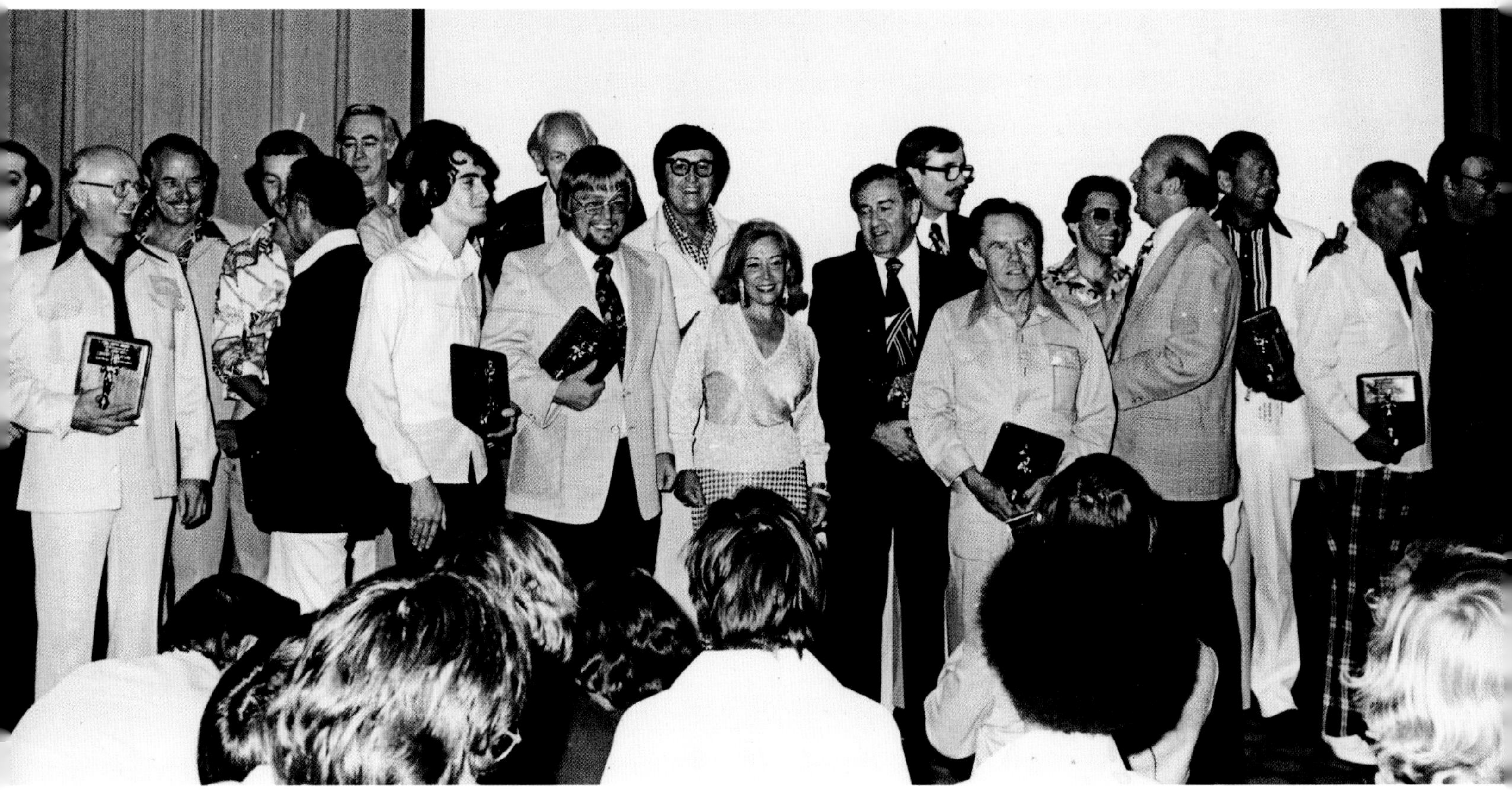

TOP ROW, FROM LEFT: William Stout art from 1977; a panel at the 1978 Comic-Con that included (left to right) Sergio Aragonés, Scott Shaw!, Lee Marrs, (unidentified), Mark Evanier (who was no doubt the moderator), June Foray, Russ Heath, Dan O'Neill, and Shary Flenniken **MIDDLE ROW, FROM LEFT:** A Captain Marvel sketch from 1977 by C. C. Beck; Milton Caniff sketching Steve Canyon in 1973; comics artist Steve Leialoha at the 1976 show **BOTTOM**: Recipients and presenters at the 1975 Inkpot Awards: (left to right) Brad Anderson, Russ Manning, Jim Starlin, Jack Kirby, Gil Kane, Barry Alfonso, Dick Moores, Richard Butner, Bob Clampett, June Foray, Jerry Siegel, Russell Myers, Daws Butler, Jim Steranko, Will Eisner, Robert Bloch, George Pal, and Shel Dorf **OPPOSITE, LEFT, TOP TO BOTTOM:** Ray Bradbury at Comic-Con in the mid-1970s; Bradbury with fans in the early 1970s; Bradbury in 2007 at his "Spotlight" panel **OPPOSITE, TOP RIGHT:** Ray Bradbury portrait by Milton Caniff

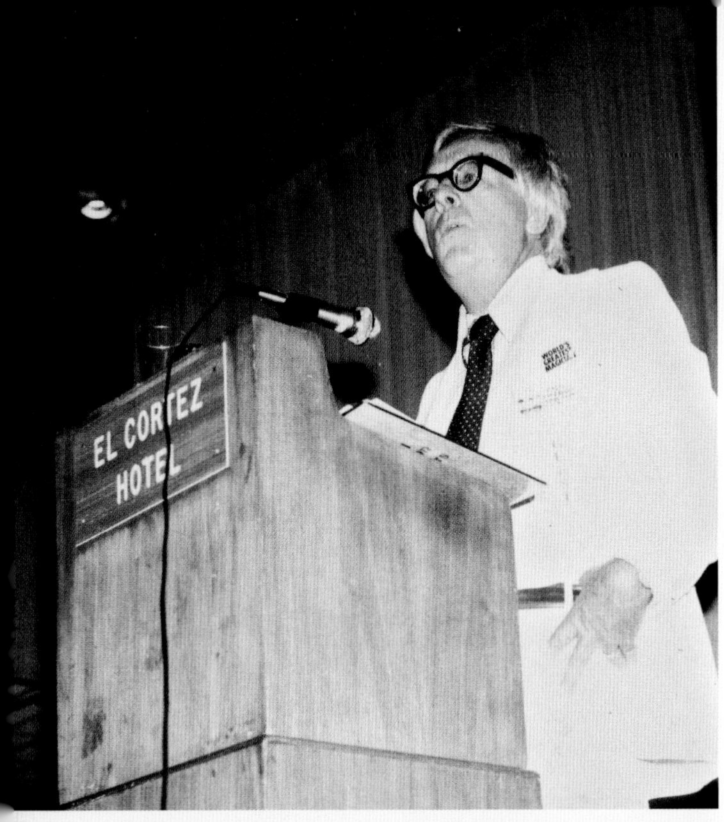
EL CORTEZ
HOTEL

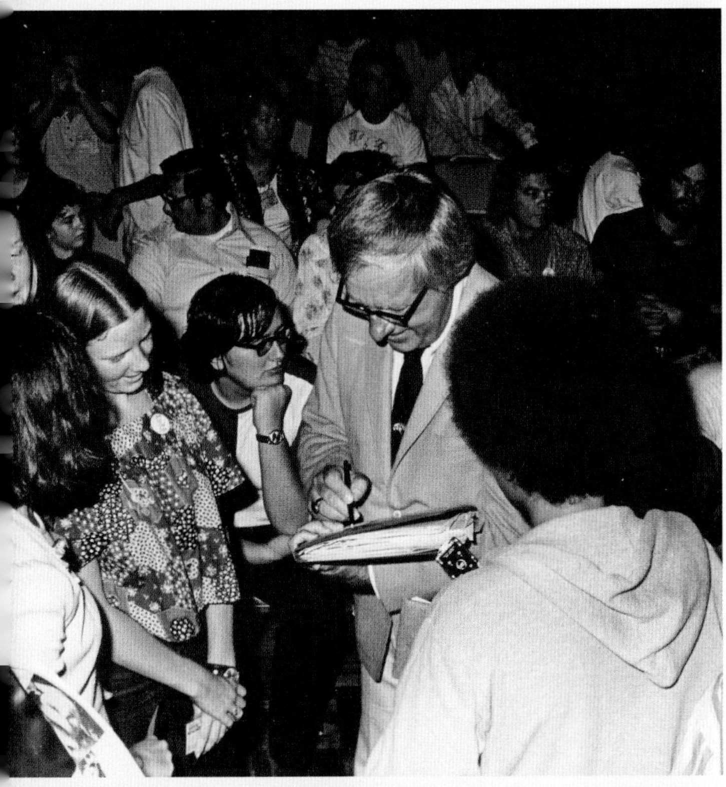

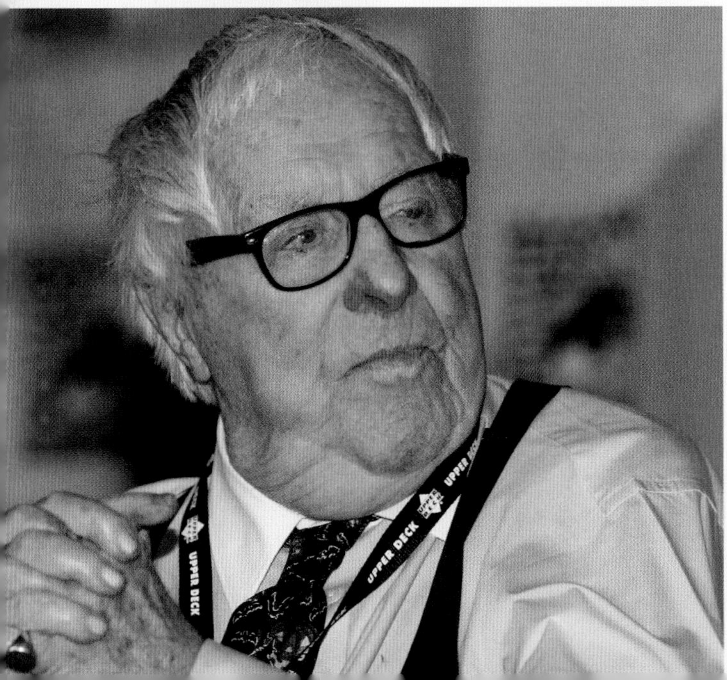
UPPER DECK

RAY BRADBURY

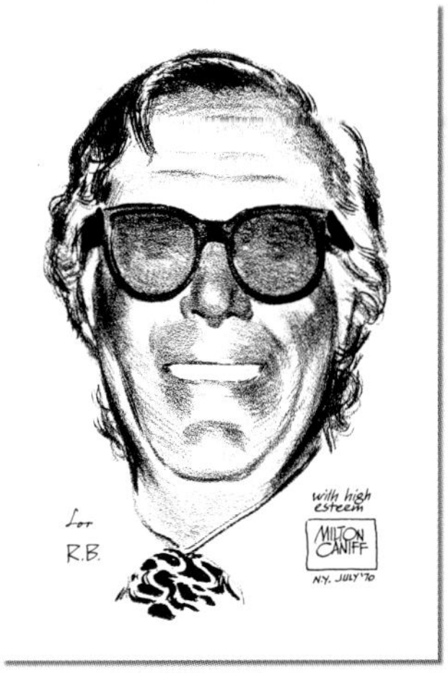
For
R.B.
with high
esteem
MILTON
CANIFF
N.Y. JULY '70

WIDELY REGARDED as one of the greatest American fiction writers of the twentieth century, Ray Bradbury was a special guest at the very first Comic-Con in 1970.

But before he became the dean of science fiction authors, Bradbury was first and foremost a fan. Born in 1920, the young author-to-be fell madly in love with comic strips at the wise old age of nine. In the 1980 Comic-Con program book, Bradbury revealed his love of comics in an essay titled "What Comic Strips Mean to Me." He wrote, "I have never got over the initial impact of Buck Rogers on my life, and I am grateful for his explosion in my midst sometime in the year 1929 when the newspaper thudded against the screen door of my home in Waukegan, Illinois, and I walked out to pick up my destiny—the first Buck Rogers strip . . . From that day forward I did not walk to pick up the newspaper, I dashed, I ran, I streaked! I held my breath all day, waiting for the incredible moment when I opened the paper and was in love all over again."

Bradbury moved to Los Angeles with his family when he was thirteen. He began to publish stories in science fiction fanzines in 1938 and became involved with L.A. science fiction fandom with the Clifton's Cafeteria Science Fiction Club. Here he met lifelong friend Forrest J Ackerman, who went on to become a writer's agent and the editor of *Famous Monsters of Filmland*. Bradbury sold his first professional story in 1941, and his first collection of short stories, *Dark Carnival*, appeared in 1947. He was off and running with a career that included books, comic book adaptations (most notably in the EC Comics line), movies (including those based on his work and screenplays he adapted, such as John Huston's *Moby Dick*), and television. His most notable fiction work includes *The Martian Chronicles*, *Fahrenheit 451*, *Dandelion Wine*, and *The Illustrated Man*. He was the host of *Ray Bradbury Theater* on television, for which he adapted sixty-five of his short stories. Bradbury was the recipient of the 2004 National Medal of Arts award and a special citation from the Pulitzer Board in 2007 "for his distinguished, prolific, and deeply influential career as an unmatched author of science fiction and fantasy."

At Comic-Con Bradbury has been a perennial special guest since that first show. He received the Bob Clampett Humanitarian Award in 1987 for his efforts in mentoring and encouraging talent. Over the past decade, Bradbury has visited Comic-Con each Saturday, taking part in a "Spotlight" panel and signing autographs. In recent years he's teamed up with his dear friends Forry Ackerman and movie special-effects legend Ray Harryhausen on panels to talk about all the things they love. For many fans at Comic-Con, there's no more eagerly awaited moment than when Ray Bradbury takes the stage.

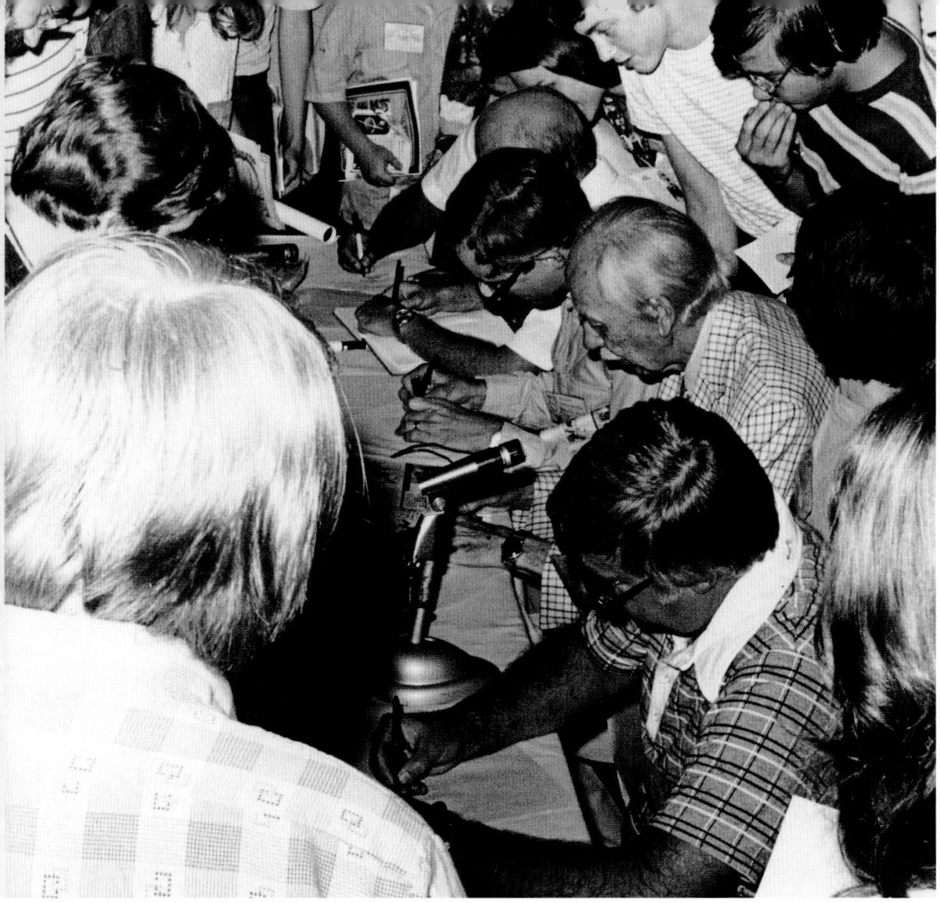

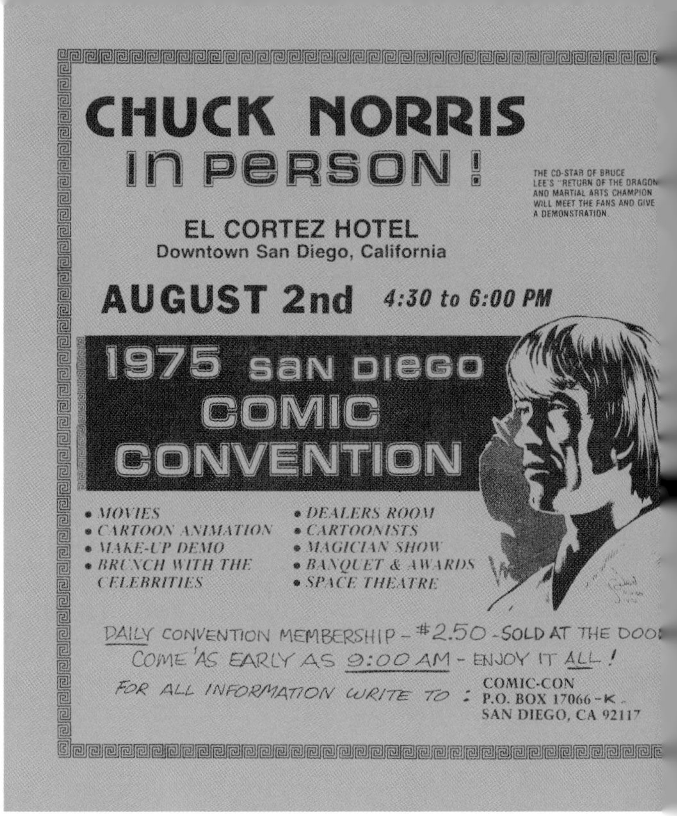
CHUCK NORRIS
IN PERSON!
THE CO-STAR OF BRUCE LEE'S "RETURN OF THE DRAGON" AND MARTIAL ARTS CHAMPION WILL MEET THE FANS AND GIVE A DEMONSTRATION.
EL CORTEZ HOTEL
Downtown San Diego, California
AUGUST 2nd
4:30 to 6:00 PM
1975 SAN DIEGO
COMIC
CONVENTION
• MOVIES
• CARTOON ANIMATION
• MAKE-UP DEMO
• BRUNCH WITH THE CELEBRITIES
• DEALERS ROOM
• CARTOONISTS
• MAGICIAN SHOW
• BANQUET & AWARDS
• SPACE THEATRE
DAILY CONVENTION MEMBERSHIP - $2.50 - SOLD AT THE DOOR
COME AS EARLY AS 9:00 AM - ENJOY IT ALL!
FOR ALL INFORMATION WRITE TO:
COMIC-CON
P.O. BOX 17066-K
SAN DIEGO, CA 92117

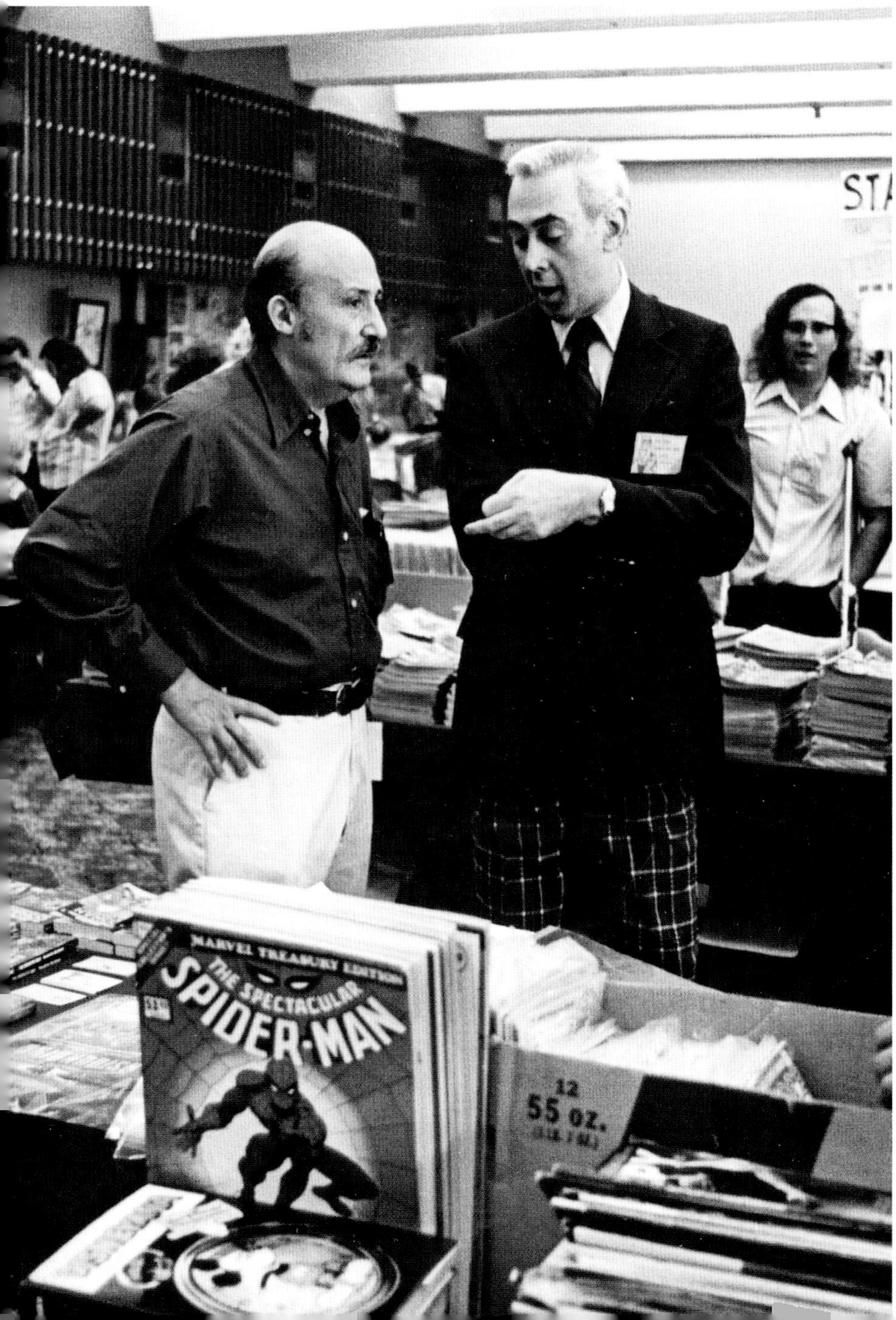
MARVEL TREASURY EDITION
THE SPECTACULAR
SPIDER-MAN
12
55 oz.

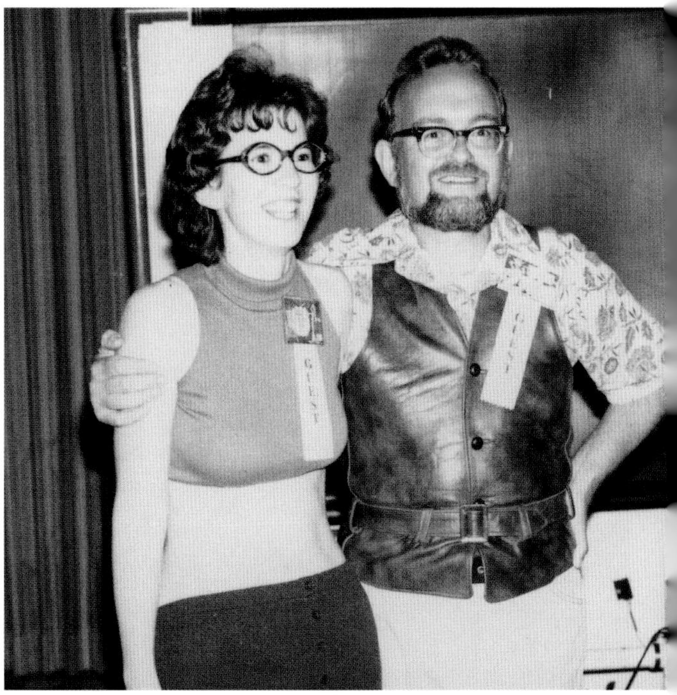

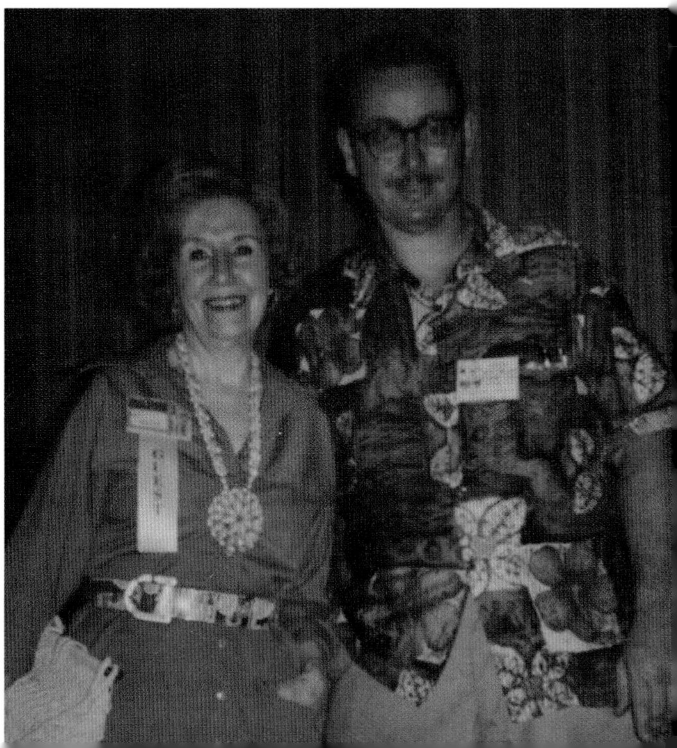

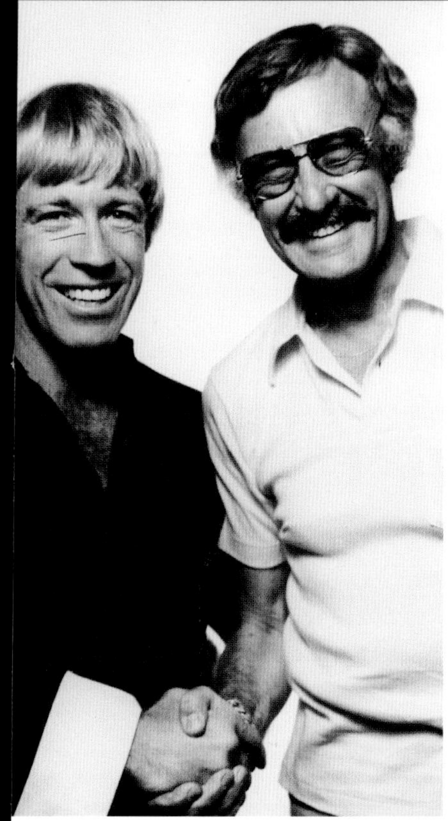

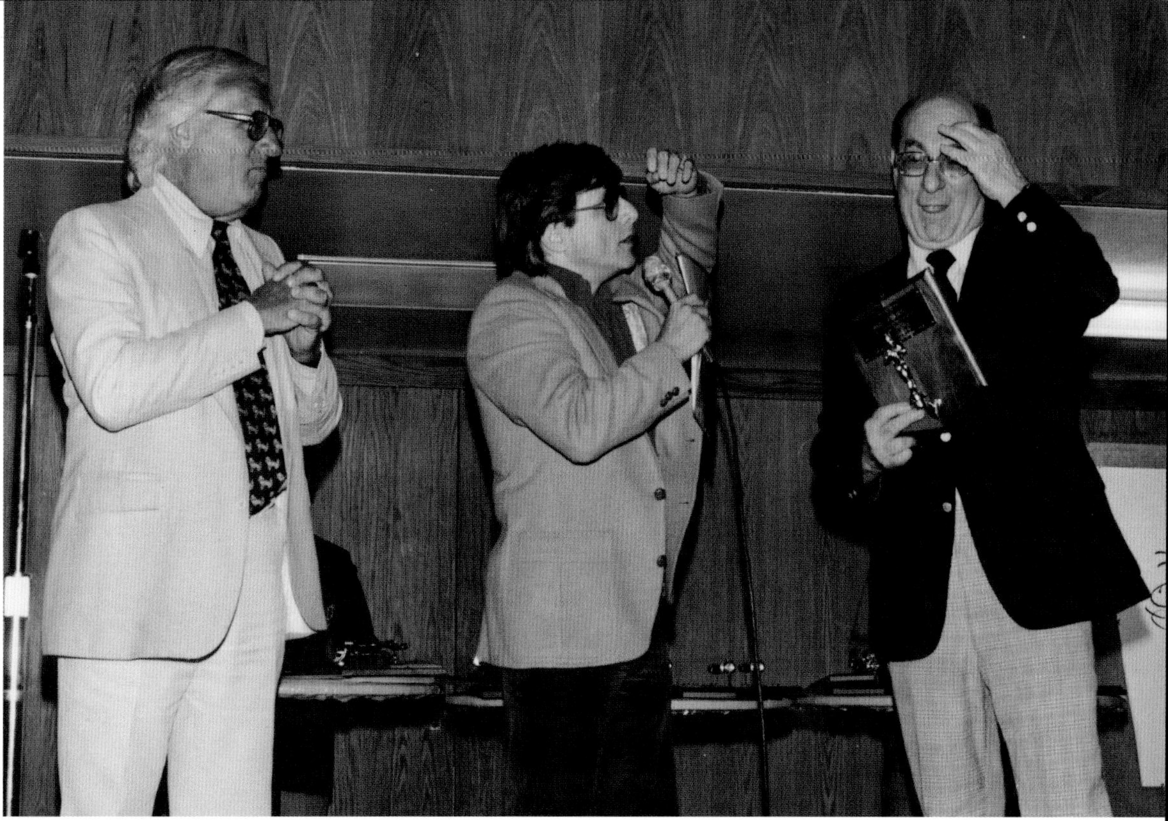

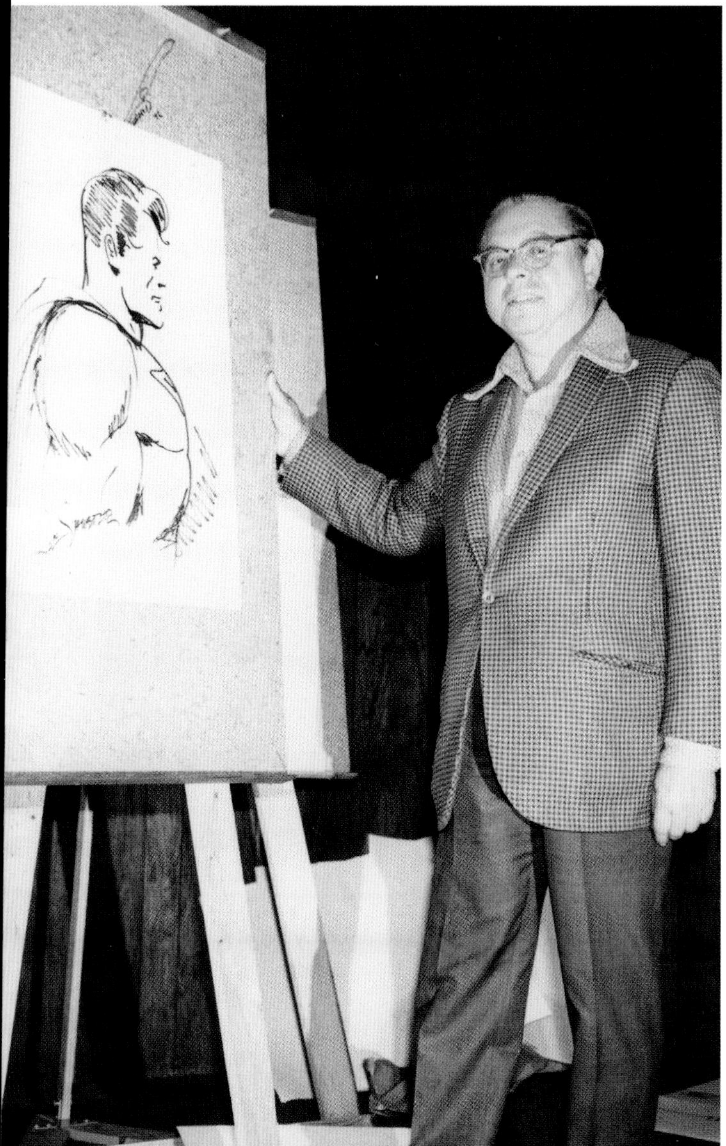

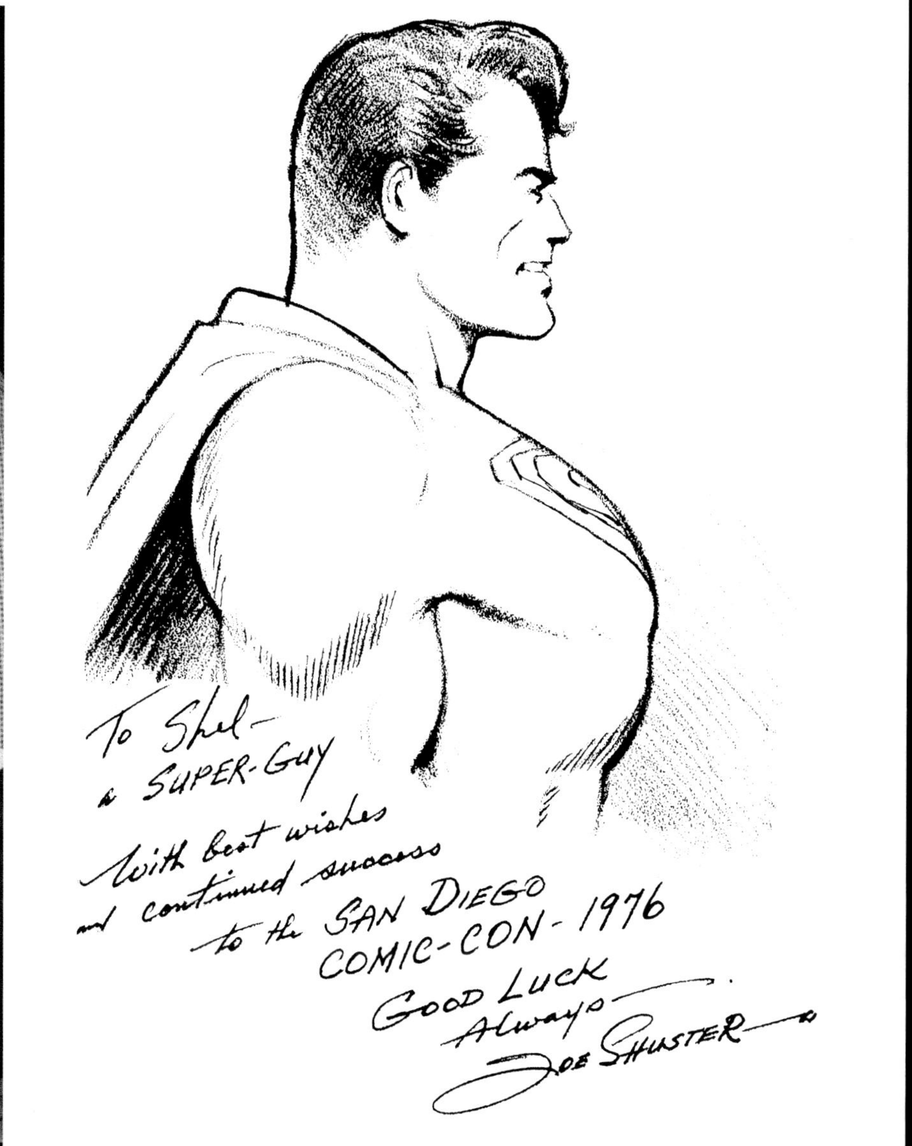
To Shel—
a SUPER-GUY
With best wishes
and continued success
to the SAN DIEGO
COMIC-CON - 1976
GOOD LUCK
Always—
JOE SHUSTER

OPPOSITE, CLOCKWISE FROM TOP LEFT: *Gasoline Alley* artist Dick Moores (center) signing for fans in 1975; a flyer heralding the appearance of soon-to-be superstar Chuck Norris; comics fandom pioneers Maggie and Don Thompson at Comic-Con in 1975; Brenda Starr creator Dale Messick (left) with an unidentified fan in 1975; comics legends Will Eisner (left) and Gil Kane (right) talk in the dealers' room, also in 1975, the first time both attended the event

CLOCKWISE FROM TOP LEFT: Chuck Norris (left) meeting Stan "The Man" Lee (right) in 1975; Ray Bradbury (left) and Harlan Ellison (center) awarding DC Comics' legendary editor Julius Schwartz (right) his Inkpot Award in 1976; a Superman sketch similar to the one co-creator Joe Shuster is drawing on stage in 1976, at left

UNDERGROUND COMIX CREATORS AT COMIC-CON

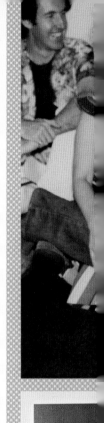

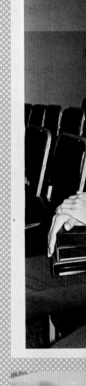

AT THE TIME that Comic-Con began, underground comix were experiencing their golden age. Sold through head shops and via mail order, these comics resembled regular comic books in format only, as their themes and artwork challenged the typical reader's concept of the medium. Drugs and sex ran rampant in these publications, which grew out of the 1960s counterculture. A majority of the titles came from small publishers in San Francisco, such as Don Donahue's Apex Novelties (which published several R. Crumb titles), Ron Turner's Last Gasp Eco-Funnies (*Slow Death Funnies*, *Wimmen's Comix*), Fred and Kathe Todd's Rip Off Press (*The Fabulous Furry Freak Brothers*), Gary Arlington's San Francisco Comic Book Company (*Bogeyman Comics*, *Man from Utopia*), and the Berkeley-based Print Mint (*Yellow Dog*, *Zap*). Undergrounds came from other parts of the country as well, including Chicago (Jay Lynch's *Bijou Funnies*), Milwaukee (Denis Kitchen's Krupp Comic Works), and Los Angeles (Bill Spicer's Los Angeles Comic Book Company).

In the early 1970s, many Comic-Con committee members were big underground comix fans, and a few were even involved in undergrounds (the first chairman, Ken Krueger, published *Gory Stories Quarterly*, and both Scott Shaw! and John Pound contributed to that and to other comix). Committee member David Scroggy had lots of contacts in the comix world as well, while dealers such as Bud Plant, Bob Beerbohm, George DiCaprio, and Ron Turner could be counted on to have a variety of comix for sale at the show. All those folks made a compelling case for underground cartoonists to make the trek from San Francisco down to San Diego to be a part of Comic-Con.

The first major underground guest at Comic-Con was Rick Griffin in 1976. One of the original *Zap* artists, Griffin was known not only for his psychedelic posters and album cover art but also for creating Murph the Surf in *Surfer Magazine*. In 1977 one of the best-known female comix creators, Trina Robbins (*Wet Satin*, *Wimmen's Comix*), was a guest, and several other underground artists could be spotted at the show, including Lee Marrs (*The Adventures of Pudge, Girl Blimp*), Greg Irons (Fillmore posters, *Slow Death Funnies*), Shary Flenniken (*Trots and Bonnie*, *Air Pirates Funnies*), and Larry Todd (*Dr. Atomic*, *Dr. Time*).

But the banner year for comix creators at Comic-Con was 1978. The big incentive for many of them to attend was the opportunity to meet one of their idols: special guest Harvey Kurtzman. Many considered Harvey to be the godfather of the underground movement, as his *MAD* comics and work for EC Comics in general had been a seminal influence on these cartoonists. Short of R. Crumb (who was invited but declined), just about every major name in undergrounds was at the show: Dave Sheridan and Gilbert Shelton (*The Fabulous Furry Freak Brothers*); S. Clay Wilson (*Zap*, *The Checkered Demon*); Spain Rodriguez (*Zap*, *Trashman*); Paul Mavrides (*The Fabulous Furry Freak Brothers*, founding member of Church of the SubGenius); Melinda Gebbie (*Wimmen's Comix*, *Tits & Clits*); George Metzger (*Moondog*); Ted Richards (*Dopin' Dan*, *Air Pirates Funnies*); Terry Richards (*Wimmen's Comix*); minicomic pioneer Roger May; Dan O'Neill (*Air Pirates Funnies*); Larry Rippee (*Mondo Snarfo*, *Commies from Mars*); Bob Foster (*Myron Moose*); poster artist Stanley Mouse; Shary Flenniken and Lee Marrs, in return appearances; photographer and chronicler of the underground movement Clay Geerdes; publishers Ron Turner, Don Donahoe, and Denis Kitchen; and distributor George DiCaprio, who brought his young son Leo with him to Comic-Con. (Leo would go on to his own fame as actor Leonardo DiCaprio.)

In subsequent years, more underground cartoonists made appearances at Comic-Con, including Robert Williams (*Zap*, *Coochie Cootie*), Howard Cruse (*Barefootz*, *Gay Comix*), Dori Seda (*Lonely Nights Comics*), Larry Welz (*Cherry Poptart*), R. L. Crabb (*Weirdo*, *Snarf*), Guy Colwell (*Inner City Romance*, *Doll*), Art Spiegelman (*Young Lust*, *Arcade*), Jack Jackson (Rip Off Press co-founder, *God Nose*, *Comanche Moon*), Bill Griffith (*Zippy the Pinhead*), and Diane Noomin (*Wimmen's Comix*, *Twisted Sisters*, *DiDi Glitz*).

A number of female underground cartoonists became frequenters of Comic-Con in the 1980s and early 1990s. They included Angela Bocage, Joyce Farmer, Krystine Kryttre, Caryn Leschen, Lee Binswanger, Carol Tyler, Phoebe Gloeckner, Leslie Sternbergh, Carol Lay, Roberta Gregory, and Mary Fleener. Most of these women had their work published in the *Weirdo* or *Twisted Sisters* anthologies. These high-profile anthologies brought attention to the wide variety of work being done by women cartoonists, who found a welcome environment at Comic-Con.

Underground comix laid the foundation for a number of today's comics' best features. They fostered the do-it-yourself mentality that is prevalent in comics publishing today, from minicomics to high-end art books, and also presented an "anything goes" philosophy when it came to storytelling. The roots of today's self-publishing and small press movements—not to mention the ability to tell stories across a wide spectrum of subject matter—were established by the groundbreaking underground cartoonists who forged the way in the late 1960s and into the decades that followed.

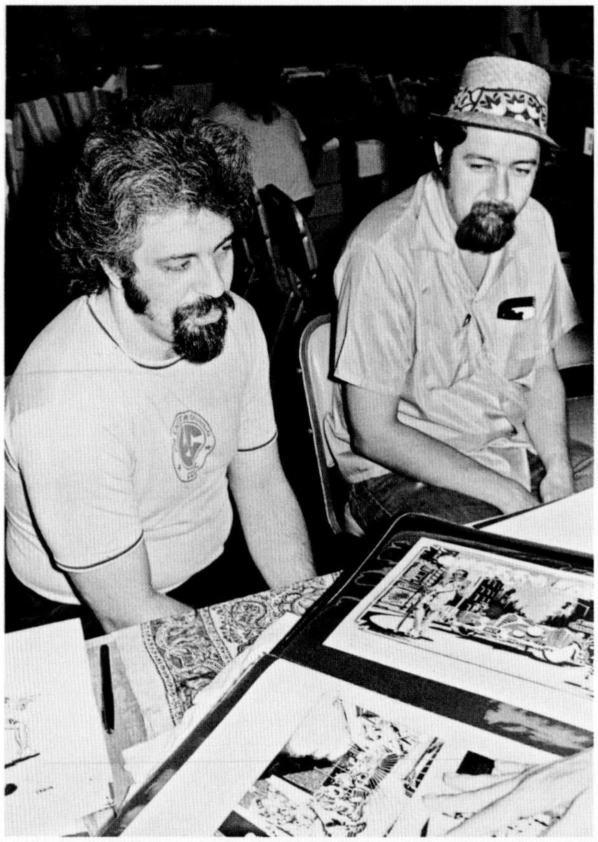

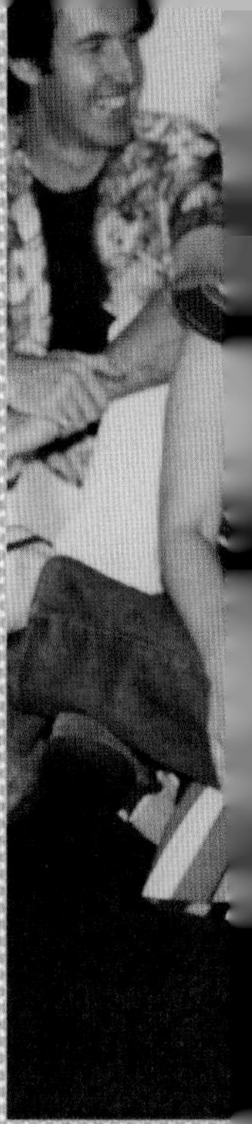

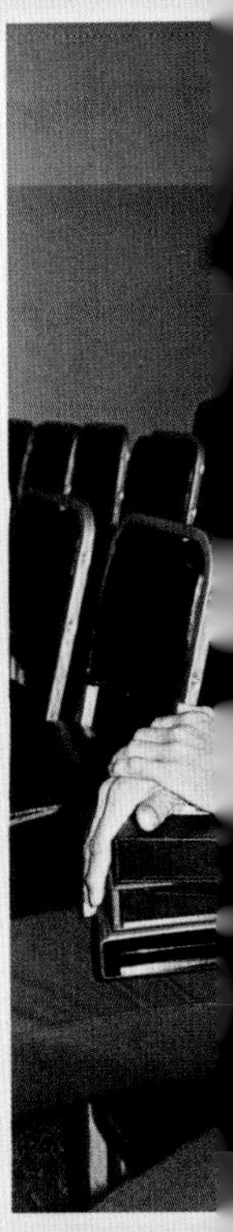

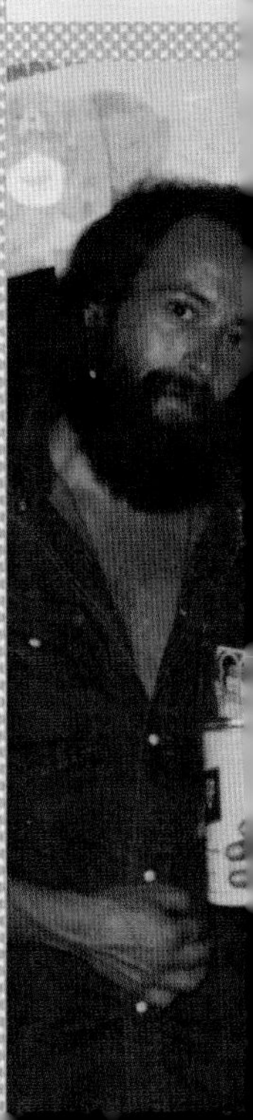

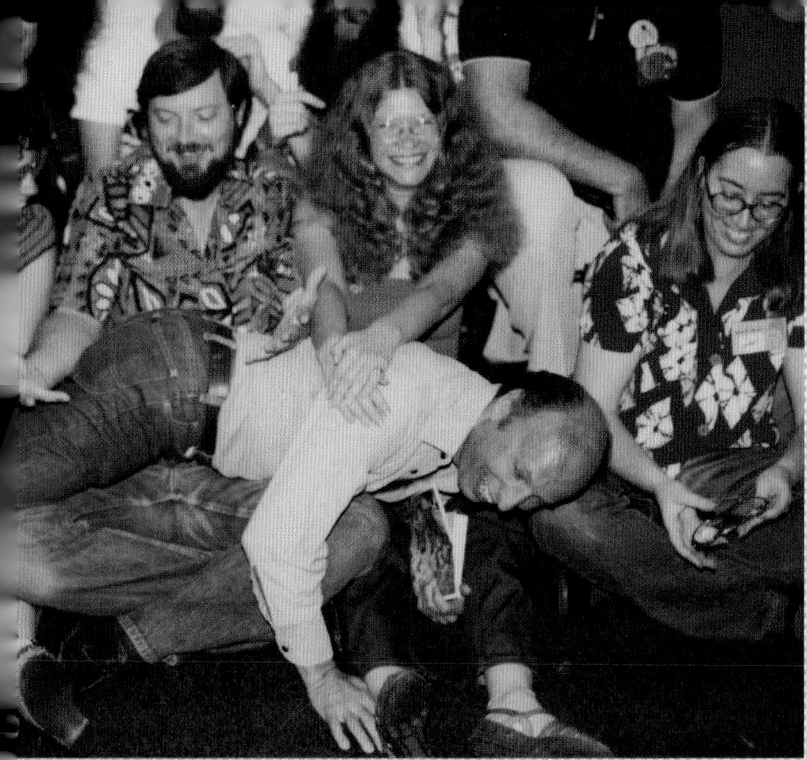

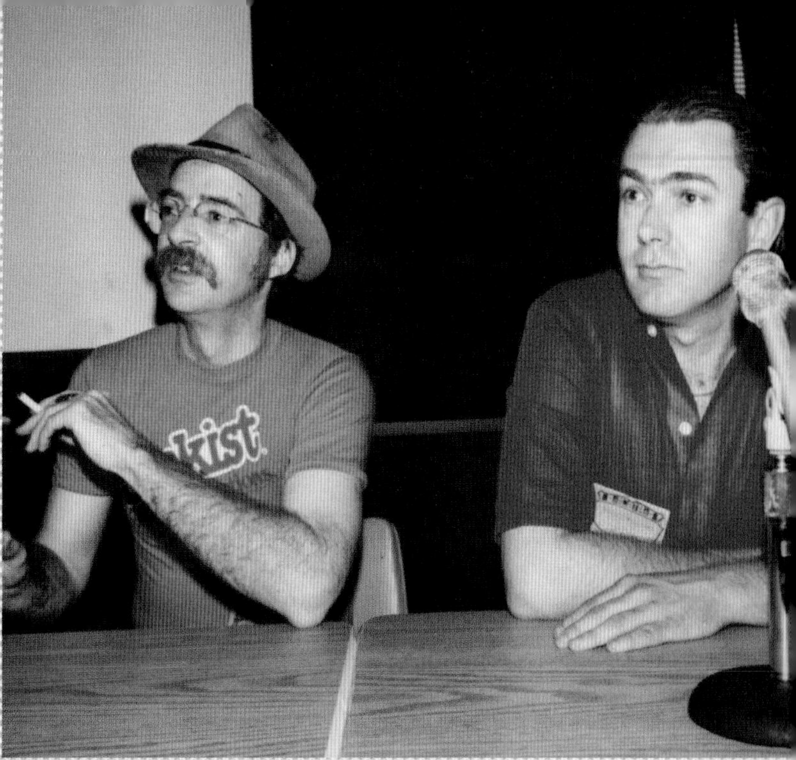
kist

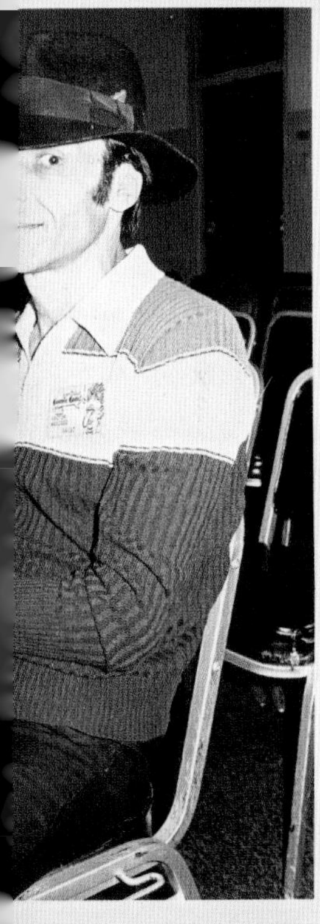

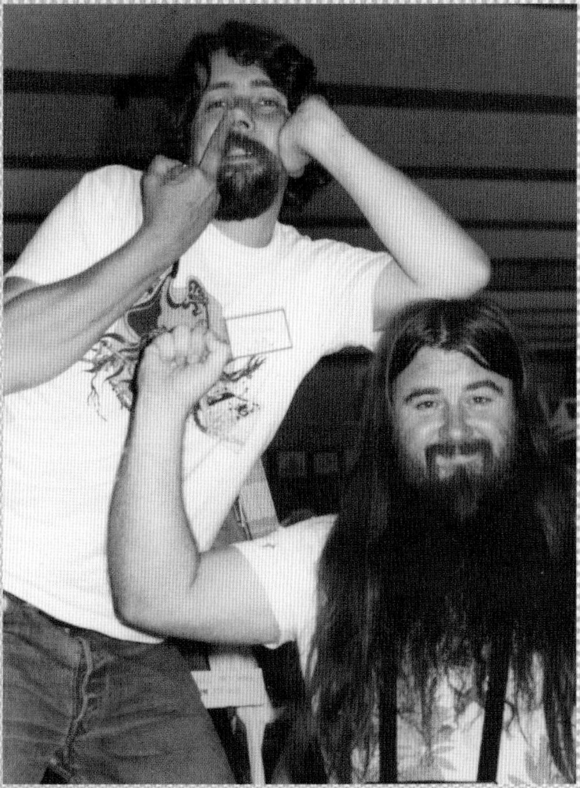

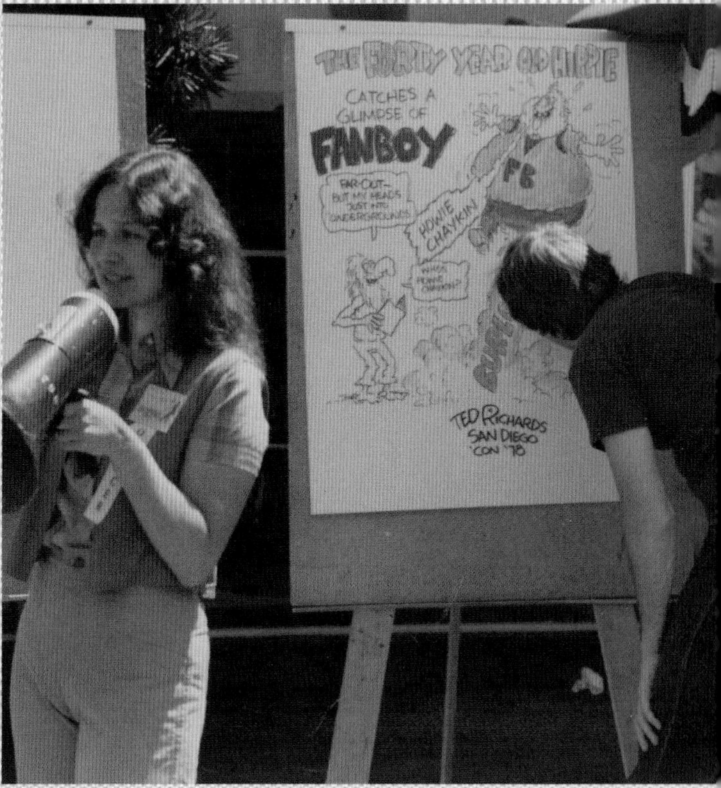
THE FORTY YEAR OLD HIPPIE
CATCHES A GLIMPSE OF
FANBOY
HOWIE CHAYKIN
TED RICHARDS
SAN DIEGO
'CON '78

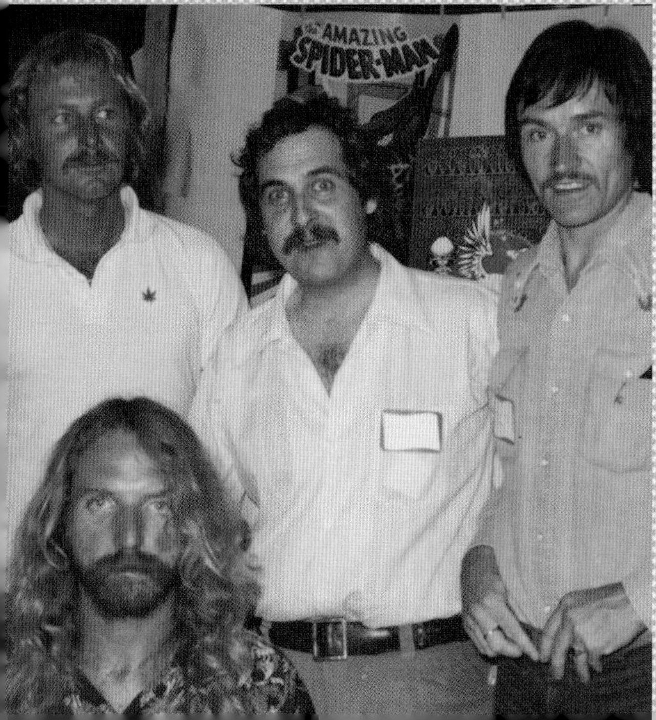
THE AMAZING SPIDER-MAN

OPPOSITE: Spain Rodriguez (left) and S. Clay Wilson (right) **TOP ROW, FROM LEFT:** Harvey Kurtzman cavorting with (left to right) Melinda Gebbie, Bob Foster, Trina Robbins, and Carol Lay and other underground comix creators at the 1978 Comic-Con; Dan O'Neill (left) and Robert Williams (right) on a panel about the underground scene **MIDDLE ROW, FROM LEFT:** Victor Moscoso; S. Clay Wilson (left) and comix publisher "Baba" Ron Turner (right); Ted Richards drawing for the Art Auction while Comic-Con committee member Wendy All takes bids **LEFT:** Rick Griffin (front) at the 1976 Comic-Con, flanked by his art agent, Gordon McClelland (far left) and album cover artist Neon Park (second from right). (The other two men are unidentified.) **OVERLEAF:** "Women of the Underground" article from the 1977 Comic-Con program book

Women of the Underground

by Clay Geerdes

Women have been drawing comic strips and books since the early days of the medium, but they have never had the promotion and public attention given to male artists. Whether this neglect has had to do with the male-oriented nature of the industry or with the introversion of the women is subject to debate; but there is no disputing the fact that the situation began to change in the 1960s with the advent of women's liberation and a more aggressive feminism.

In 1969 a Berkeley women's collective known as "It Ain't Me Babe!" published a regular periodical of women's news and events in tabloid form. The paper lasted fifteen issues and was the forerunner of the current *Plexus*. Most of the covers and a lot of the advertising art in *It Ain't Me Babe!* came from the talented hand of a young woman named Trina Robbins.

Trina came to the Bay Area in the late 1960s from New York City, where she had been the owner of a successful East Village boutique called Broccoli. Her first published cartoon was an ad for her store. In subsequent ads, she expanded her cartoons, eventually leading into a strip for *The East Village Other*. When the *Other* decided to produce a color comic section titled "Gothic Blimpworks," editor Vaughn Bode talked to Trina about doing a regular story. The result was *Pantha*.

The underground comix were ubiquitous in the Bay Area when Trina arrived, and when someone suggested doing a comic book to raise money for the collective, Trina got into it right away. The result was the first underground comic by and about women. It was published in May of 1970 by Ron Turner at Last Gasp Eco-Funnies. Trina drew characters such as Sheena, Little Lulu, Mary Marvel, and Wonder Woman on the cover to symbolize that the women super-heroines were fighting back; that was the theme of the issue. A couple of years later, Patricia Moodian arrived in San Francisco and edited the first issue of *Wimmen's Comix*. Lee Marrs came on the scene with her adventures of Pudge, Girl Blimp, and Joyce Sutton Farmer and Lyn Chevli started Nannygoat Productions, publishing their own comix. Throughout the early 1970s the women's comix movement continued to grow and expand.

In April 1973, the first underground comix convention was held in Berkeley; it was there that the first women's comix panel was inaugurated. Moodian, Marrs, Shelby, Trina, Chevli, Sharon Rudahl, and Joyce Farmer were on the panel. The meeting of these women from various parts of the country started an association that has continued to produce a new genre of comix in America.

Lee Marrs, Sharon Rudahl, and Trina Robbins.

Of the women cartoonists, Trina has produced the most solo books to date, with titles such as *Girl Fight* (two issues), *All Girl Thrills*, and *Trina's Girls Women*. Her work has appeared in nearly all of the women's titles, from *Manhunt* to the recent quality paperback anthology of women's humor, *Titters*. Her art has been shown at all three Berkeley Comic Conventions, and recently she joined in a show with Sharon Rudahl and Lee Marrs at Art For Art's Sake in San Francisco.

The women's comics are as varied as those drawn by men, but they tend to be less symbolic and more concerned with women's personal experiences and fantasies. *Wimmen's Comix* has a rotating editorship and each issue has a theme. The sixth issue, for example, was a women's history issue, and the stories were reminiscent of the "Wonder Women in History" tales that appeared in the *Wonder Woman* quarterly in the 1940s. The seventh issue, edited by Dot Bucher and Melinda Gebbie, was about women outlaws. Gebbie wanted the women artists to confront their inability to cope with violence—to deal with their latent aggression. Tarpe Mills, who drew *Miss Fury* in the 1940s, would have had no problem with the subject.

The movement has lead to a breakthrough in publishing for many of the women. Their work has begun to appear more often in slick magazines that were previously the exclusive territory of male artists. Those who adhere closely to popular feminine stereotypes get more commercial work than those who violate those advertising images. Lee Marrs' character Pudge was rejected by *Ms. Magazine*, whereas Trina's more "acceptable" character Lulu appeared on the cover of *High Times*.

Women underground cartoonists have learned that printers (all male) have different standards for them than they have for men. When Denis Kitchen of Krupp Comic Works in Milwaukee took *Wet Satin* in to be printed, his Wisconsin printer said no. *Wet Satin* was a collection of women's sex fantasies drawn by Trina, Melinda Gebbie, and others. The printer figured it was all right for men to draw sex-oriented subjects but that "women shouldn't be doing things like that." Kitchen had the comic printed in California.

It has taken seven years, but Trina, Lee, Sharon, Melinda, Shelby, Dot, Shary Flenniken, Aline Kominsky, and the gang have begun to make a big dent in the public psyche. Read their books. Let them know what you think. They get mail at P.O. Box 212, Berkeley, CA 94702.

Clay Geerdes publishes Comix World, *an information newsletter that functions as an ongoing history of and commentary on alternative comics in America and abroad. It is available monthly from him at 915 Indian Rock Road, Berkeley, California 94707.*

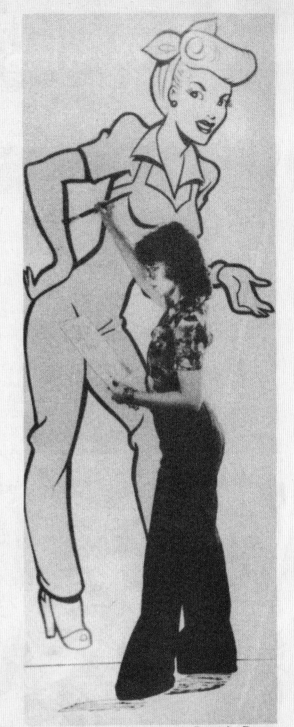

Trina Robbins and her character Rosie the Riveter.

THE FURTHER FATTENING ADVENTURES OF PUDGE GIRL BLIMP
©'76 BY LEE MARRS-
BURP
WANTED: EARN UP TO $45 @ HR.! ♀ TO BE TRAINED AS PROFESSIONAL MASSEUSE. CALL 32 POLK ST.
OH BOY!
TOPLESS! BOTTOMLESS! NO COVER!
ALL-NITE ★ WIERDO SPECIAL
MASSAGE
32
EDNA'S SCHOOL OF SWEDISH MASSAGE?
O.K. KID. YA SUPPLIES IS DEDUCTED FROM YA FOIST WEEK'S PAY. REMEMBER: DA CUSTOMER IS ALLUS RIGHT.
YES, MR. EDNA, SIR.
MACHO OIL

Lee Marrs' Pudge has appeared in a number of publications, including three issues of her own comic.

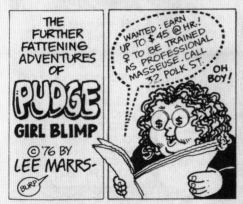

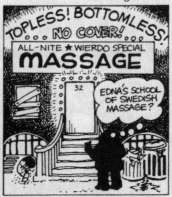

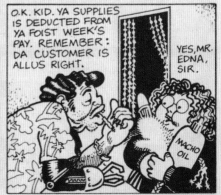

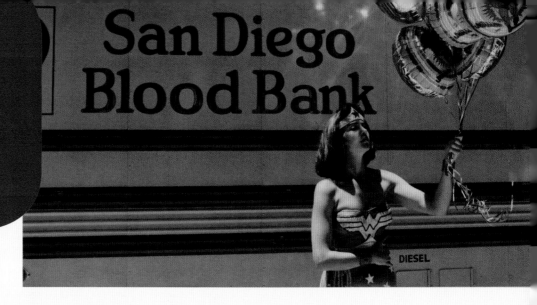

ROBERT A. HEINLEIN BLOOD DRIVE

San Diego
Blood Bank
DIESEL

For science fiction fans, few names are as stellar as Robert A. Heinlein's. From *Starship Troopers* to *Stranger in a Strange Land*, Heinlein was the dean of science fiction writers. Unfortunately, he rarely attended conventions, so his readers had few opportunities to meet the master in person.

Then in the early 1970s, Heinlein had a life-threatening illness and needed many pints of a rare blood type. He felt he owed his life to the donors, so when asked to be a guest at the 1976 Worldcon in his hometown of Kansas City, Missouri, he agreed—but with one specific stipulation: He would only sign autographs for people who donated blood.

The San Diego Comic-Con committee, which had been trying to get Heinlein as a guest for years, approached the author with an offer to hold a blood drive in San Diego in the hopes that he would consent to being a guest and help promote the first Comic-Con Blood Drive. In 1977 Heinlein agreed to be a guest, and Comic-Con's version of the Robert A. Heinlein Blood Drive was launched. That first Blood Drive saw donors giving blood while being entertained by a belly-dance troupe and later by cartoonist Leslie Cabarga playing old-time piano and Golden Age comic artist C. C. Beck strumming his guitar. Blood donors were personally greeted by Heinlein, who signed their books. As a bonus, science fiction author Theodore Sturgeon was at Robert's side, signing copies of his own novel *Some of Your Blood*. One lucky attendee even won a rare original drawing by Heinlein during the Art Auction later that weekend.

make a difference in life.
The Power of ONE
At Comic-Con July 26-July 29
San Diego Blood Bank
make a difference in life.

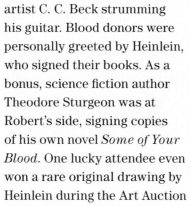

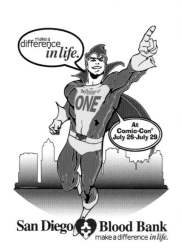

Although Heinlein was never able to visit Comic-Con again, he gave his blessings to making the Blood Drive an annual event. When the convention moved to the Convention and Performing Arts Center, the San Diego Blood Bank's bloodmobile was a familiar site on the curb outside the lobby. Many of the special guests would make a point of visiting and chatting with donors to thank them for their contributions.

In subsequent years, blood donors have received increasing benefits for participating in the Heinlein Blood Drive. They receive a special T-shirt and goodie bags filled with comics and other items provided by exhibitors and are entered in a raffle for some big-ticket items. In 2008 one lucky donor won an exclusive Honda Element with graphics featuring Captain America designed by Marvel Comics. Other bonus gifts added in recent years are limited-edition action figures from Diamond Select Toys and other Comic-Con exhibitors.

After Comic-Con moved to the San Diego Convention Center, the Blood Drive expanded to encompass more days of the show, and it now operates the full four days. It has become the San Diego Blood Bank's longest-running blood drive, and over its thirty-two-year history, Comic-Con donors have given 7,538 pints of blood. In 2008 the pints collected numbered 1,070, making that year's Heinlein Blood Drive the second-biggest donation event in San Diego's history. Over the years, the compassion and generosity of Comic-Con's attendees, professionals, and exhibitors and their donations to the Robert A. Heinlein Blood Drive have had a lasting impact on the San Diego area.

Robert A. Heinlein Santa Cruz, California 95060

31 August 1978

Dear David Scroggy,

Thanks for the report on the blood drive; you certainly did a job on it!

I have written to Shel about next year. If my health permits me to travel at all, I intend to help out at the inaugural SF blood drive in England at Seacon, 37th WSFC, 21-25 Aug '79 . . and need to be in Paris & London & Milan before that. But those plans might change. Be sure of this: We will be at the SD Comic-Con every year we can; it was the <u>best</u> fun of any con we've ever attended.

Good wishes! [signature]

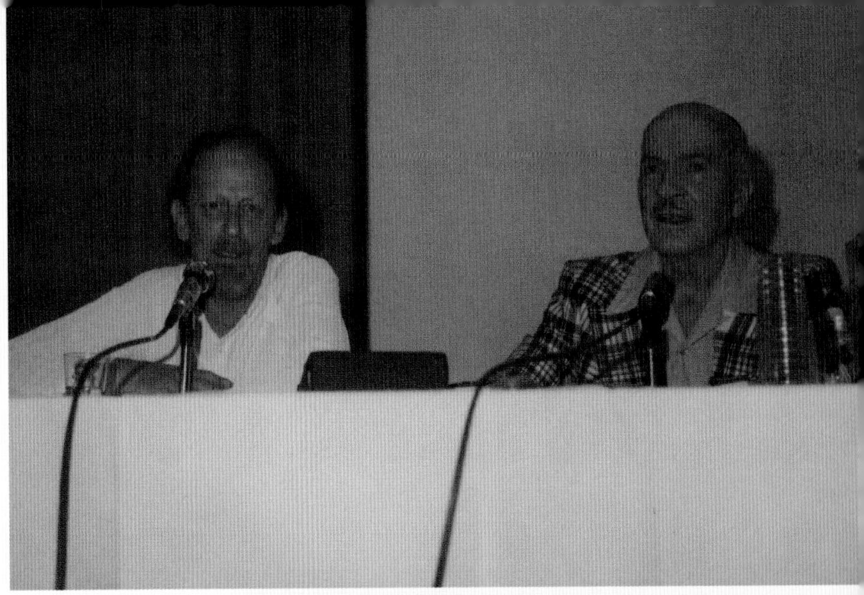

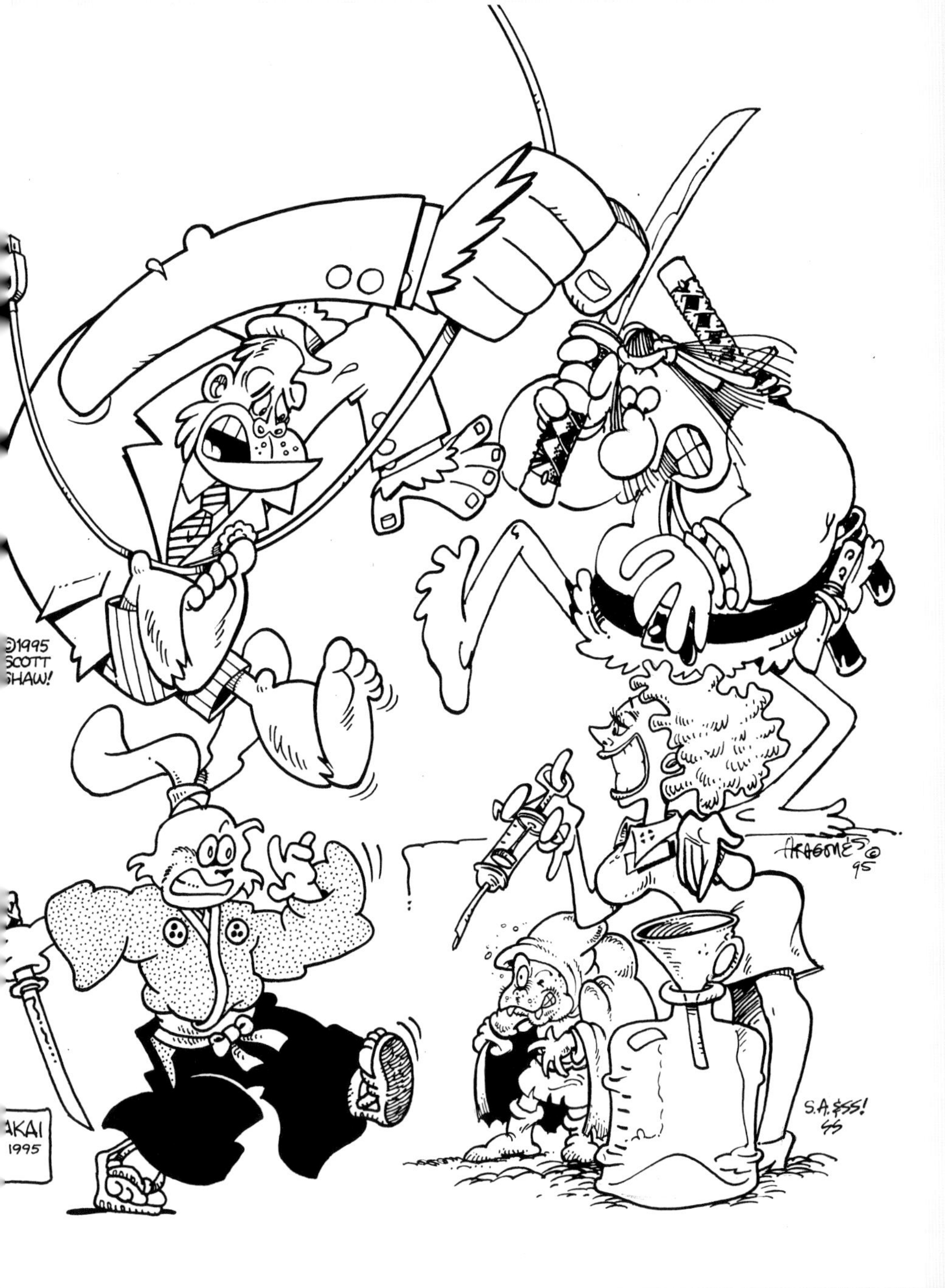
ARAGONÉS © 95
S.A.$$S!

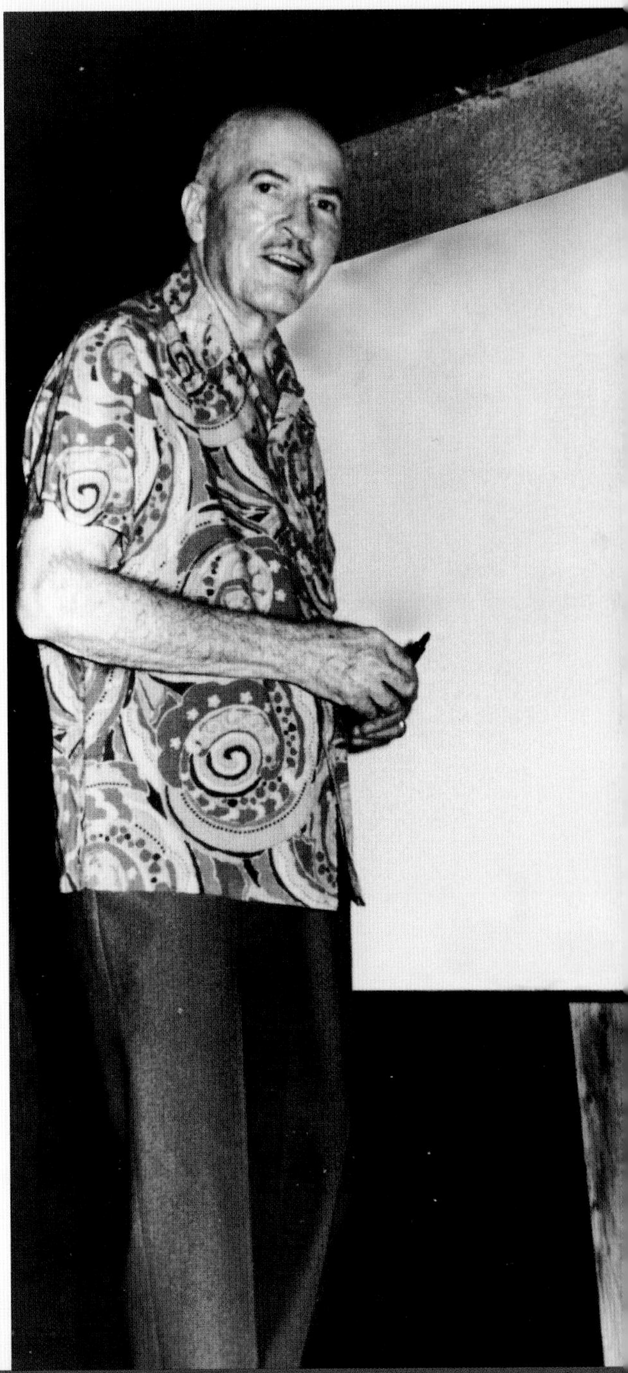

OPPOSITE, TOP: Wonder Woman drawing attention to the Blood Drive in 1985 **OPPOSITE, BOTTOM:** 2007 Blood Drive T-shirt art by John Smallwood-Garcia **CLOCKWISE FROM TOP LEFT:** A personal note from legendary science fiction author Robert A. Heinlein; science fiction author Ted Sturgeon (left) with Heinlein (right) on a panel in 1977; Heinlein sketching at the Sunday brunch; a jam piece done for the Blood Drive in 1995 by Scott Shaw!, Sergio Aragonés, and Stan Sakai

NOTABLE GUESTS

PEOPLE MAKING THEIR FIRST APPEARANCES AS SPECIAL GUESTS AT COMIC-CON IN THE 1970s . . .

1970
MINICON

FORREST J ACKERMAN (a.k.a. "Mr. Science Fiction"): editor, *Famous Monsters of Filmland*; creator, *Vampirella*; member of science fiction's First Fandom

MIKE ROYER: inker for Jack Kirby's *Fourth World* books, penciller and inker for Gold Key Comics, assistant to Russ Manning

COMIC-CON 1

RAY BRADBURY: science fiction author, *The Martian Chronicles*, *Something Wicked This Way Comes*, *Fahrenheit 451*

JACK KIRBY (a.k.a. "The King of Comics"): comics artist; co-creator, Captain America, Fantastic Four, the X-Men, Incredible Hulk, the Avengers, Thor; creator, *New Gods* series

A. E. VAN VOGT: science fiction author, *Slan*, *The Voyage of the Space Beagle*

1971
COMIC-CON 2

KIRK ALYN: actor, *Superman* and *Blackhawk* serials

LEIGH BRACKETT: science fiction author, *The Sword of Rhiannon*, *The Long Tomorrow*; screenwriter, *The Big Sleep*, *Rio Bravo*

EDMOND HAMILTON: comics and science fiction author, Superman and Captain Future novels, *City at World's End* (married to Leigh Brackett)

1972
COMIC-CON 3

BOB CLAMPETT: animation director, *Looney Tunes*; creator, *Beany and Cecil*

HARRY HARRISON: science fiction author, *Stainless Steel Rat* series; *Bill, the Galactic Hero* series; and novel *Make Room! Make Room!*

KATHERINE KURTZ: fantasy author, the Deryni novels, *The Adept*

MELL LAZARUS: syndicated cartoonist, *Miss Peach*, *Momma*

1973
COMIC-CON 4

NEAL ADAMS: comic book artist, *Batman*, *Deadman*, *Green Lantern/Green Arrow*

D. C. FONTANA: television writer and story editor, *Star Trek*

JUNE FORAY: voice actress, *The Rocky and Bullwinkle Show*

MIKE FRIEDRICH: comic book writer, *Justice League of America*, *Iron Man*, *Captain Marvel*

CARMINE INFANTINO: comics artist, *Flash*, *Adam Strange*; DC Comics editorial director (1967–1971) and publisher (1971–1976)

1974
COMIC-CON 5

MAJEL BARRETT: actress, played Christine Chapel on *Star Trek*

MILTON CANIFF: cartoonist and creator, *Terry and the Pirates*, *Steve Canyon*

FRANK CAPRA: movie writer and director, *Mr. Smith Goes to Washington*, *It's a Wonderful Life*

CHUCK JONES: animation director, Bugs Bunny and Road Runner cartoons

WALTER KOENIG: actor, played Pavel Chekov on *Star Trek*

RUSS MANNING: comic book and syndicated comic strip writer and artist, *Magnus, Robot Fighter*; *Tarzan*

RUSSELL MYERS: syndicated cartoonist and creator, *Broom-Hilda*

CHARLES M. SCHULZ: syndicated cartoonist and creator, *Peanuts*

1975
COMIC-CON 6

ROBERT BLOCH: fiction author, *Psycho*

WILL EISNER: cartoonist and creator, *The Spirit*

MARK EVANIER: writer, Disney and Gold Key comics

GIL KANE: comic book and cover artist, *Green Lantern*, *The Amazing Spider-Man*

STAN LEE: Marvel Comics editor and writer, co-creator of *The Fantastic Four*, *The Amazing Spider-Man*, *The X-Men*

CHUCK NORRIS: action movie actor

JERRY SIEGEL: comic book writer and co-creator of *Superman*

JIM STARLIN: comic book writer and artist, *Captain Marvel*, *Warlock*

JIM STERANKO: comic book writer and artist, *Nick Fury, Agent of S.H.I.E.L.D.*; *Captain America*

THEODORE STURGEON: science fiction author, *More Than Human*

COMIC-CON 6, PART II (HELD NOVEMBER 7–9)

JOCK MAHONEY: actor, Tarzan films, *Yancy Derringer* television series

GEORGE PAL: producer and director, *When Worlds Collide*, *War of the Worlds*, *Doc Savage*

1976

COMIC-CON 7

SERGIO ARAGONÉS: *MAD* magazine cartoonist

MEL BLANC: voice actor, *Looney Tunes*, Bugs Bunny, Daffy Duck

RICK GRIFFIN: artist of underground comix, psychedelic posters, and album covers

DALE MESSICK: syndicated comic strip artist and creator, *Brenda Starr*

JOE SHUSTER: comic book artist and co-creator, *Superman*

NOEL SICKLES: syndicated comic strip artist, *Scorchy Smith*

1977

COMIC-CON 8

CARL BARKS: comic book writer and artist, *Donald Duck*; creator of Uncle Scrooge

C. C. BECK: comic book artist, *Captain Marvel*

WALTER GIBSON: pulp magazine writer, *The Shadow*

ROBERT A. HEINLEIN: science fiction author, *Starship Troopers*, *Stranger in a Strange Land*, *The Moon Is a Harsh Mistress*

MICHAEL W. KALUTA: comic book artist, *The Shadow*, *Starstruck*

BOB KANE: co-creator, *Batman*

B. KLIBAN: cartoonist, *Kliban Cats*

JOE KUBERT: comic book writer, artist, and editor, *Sgt. Rock*, *Hawkman*, *Tor*

HARVEY KURTZMAN: cartoonist; *MAD* magazine creator; EC Comics writer, artist, and editor; *Frontline Combat*, *Two-Fisted Tales*

STAN LYNDE: syndicated comic strip artist and creator, *Rick O'Shay*

ALEX NIÑO: Filipino comic book artist, *House of Mystery*, *House of Secrets*, *Heavy Metal* characters

TRINA ROBBINS: underground comix writer/artist and comics historian

BILL SCOTT: writer, *The Rocky and Bullwinkle Show*; voice of Bullwinkle J. Moose

ROY THOMAS: writer/editor, *The Avengers*, *Conan*, *All-Star Squadron*; early member of comics fandom; editor of fanzine *Alter-Ego*

1978

COMIC-CON 9

JOHN BUSCEMA: comic book artist, *Conan*, *The Avengers*

HOWARD CHAYKIN: comic book and graphic novel writer/artist, *Cody Starbuck*, *Star Wars* comics, *The Stars My Destination*

SHARY FLENNIKEN: underground comix writer/artist and creator, *Trots and Bonnie*

ALAN DEAN FOSTER: science fiction author, *Icerigger*; *Star Wars* and *Star Trek: The Animated Series* novelizations

GARDNER FOX: Golden and Silver Age comic book writer, *Justice League of America*

STEVE GERBER: comic book writer, *The Defenders*, *Man-Thing*, *Howard the Duck*

RUSS HEATH: comics artist, *Sgt. Rock*, *Haunted Tank*

BURNE HOGARTH: syndicated comic strip writer/artist, *Tarzan*

GRAY MORROW: book illustrator and cover artist, syndicated adventure comic strip artist, comic book artist, *Creepy*, *Eerie*

CLARENCE NASH: voice actor, Donald Duck

GRIM NATWICK: artist/animator, *Snow White and the Seven Dwarfs*, *Betty Boop*

WENDY PINI: comic book writer/artist/creator, *Elfquest*

BORIS VALLEJO: fantasy painter/illustrator

1979

COMIC-CON 10

KELLY FREAS: science fiction and *MAD* magazine painter/illustrator

VICTOR MOSCOSO: poster and underground comix artist, *Zap*

NESTOR REDONDO: Filipino comic book artist, *Swamp Thing*, *Rima*

MARSHALL ROGERS: comic book artist, *Batman*, *Doctor Strange*

JOHN ROMITA: comic book artist, *The Amazing Spider-Man*, *Captain America*

MORT WALKER: syndicated cartoonist, *Beetle Bailey*, *Hi and Lois*

LEN WEIN: comic book writer/editor; co-creator, Wolverine, Swamp Thing

MARV WOLFMAN: comic book writer/editor, *Tomb of Dracula*, *The Amazing Spider-Man*, *Nova*

> "What I still love about Comic-Con is that I can't walk twenty feet without running into someone I know. Where else can I see all of the artists we work with in one place surrounded by all of their amazing work? But what I've grown to love most is the feeling from the fans. For five glorious days they are with their people."
>
> **—RUTH CLAMPETT**
> DAUGHTER OF FAMED ANIMATION ARTIST AND DIRECTOR BOB CLAMPETT (*LOONEY TUNES*, *MERRY MELODIES*)

THE

STAY PUFT

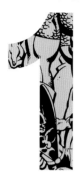

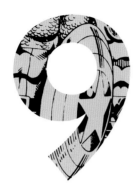

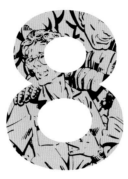

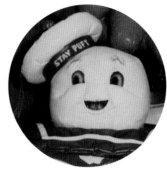

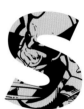

In 1979 Comic-Con moved to more spacious quarters, the Convention and Performing Arts Center (CPAC), in the heart of downtown San Diego. With the exception of a one-year return to the El Cortez in 1981, the convention stayed there until 1990. The show at first occupied half of CPAC, what was known as the facility's Exhibit Hall, but by the end of the decade it had expanded across the lobby to also include the giant Golden Hall. The sprawling CPAC facility had a massive outdoor plaza complete with fountain, a wide lobby for the registration area, and plenty of programming rooms upstairs.

SEE YA THERE!
SAN DIEGO
1980
COMIC CON
VIVA MAD!
MAD ABOUT MAD!
IN MAD WE TRUST
INCURABLY MAD
SHOOTIN' MAD
MAD MARGINALS
MAD AS A HATTER

ESTABLISHING NEW TRADITIONS

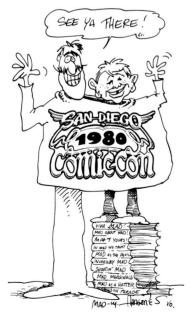

One of the major developments during the 1980s was the establishment of the Comic Book Expo (SEE page 86), a separate trade show held prior to the opening day of Comic-Con, to recognize the fact that more and more publishers and comic book retailers were using the show to do business in the burgeoning direct market. With the coming of the Expo, fans encountered "professional-style" booths that would become the anchors at Comic-Con, as exhibitors at the trade show kept their set-ups for the rest of the weekend's event.

A number of Comic-Con traditions began in the 1980s, including the major awards programs: the Russ Manning Most Promising Newcomer Award in 1982, the Bob Clampett Humanitarian Award in 1984, and the Will Eisner Comic Industry Awards in 1987 (SEE page 84). The first dedicated gaming area debuted in 1983, as did a children's activities room. Artists' Alley was created

TOP: The Stay Puft Marshmallow Man appeared in 1988 to promote the *Ghostbusters* comic book **ABOVE:** Sergio Aragonés and his old pal Alfred E. Neuman in this sketch from 1980, featuring the logo designed by artist John Pound **OPPOSITE:** Archie Comics saluted Comic-Con in 1989 with a special issue of *Pep*

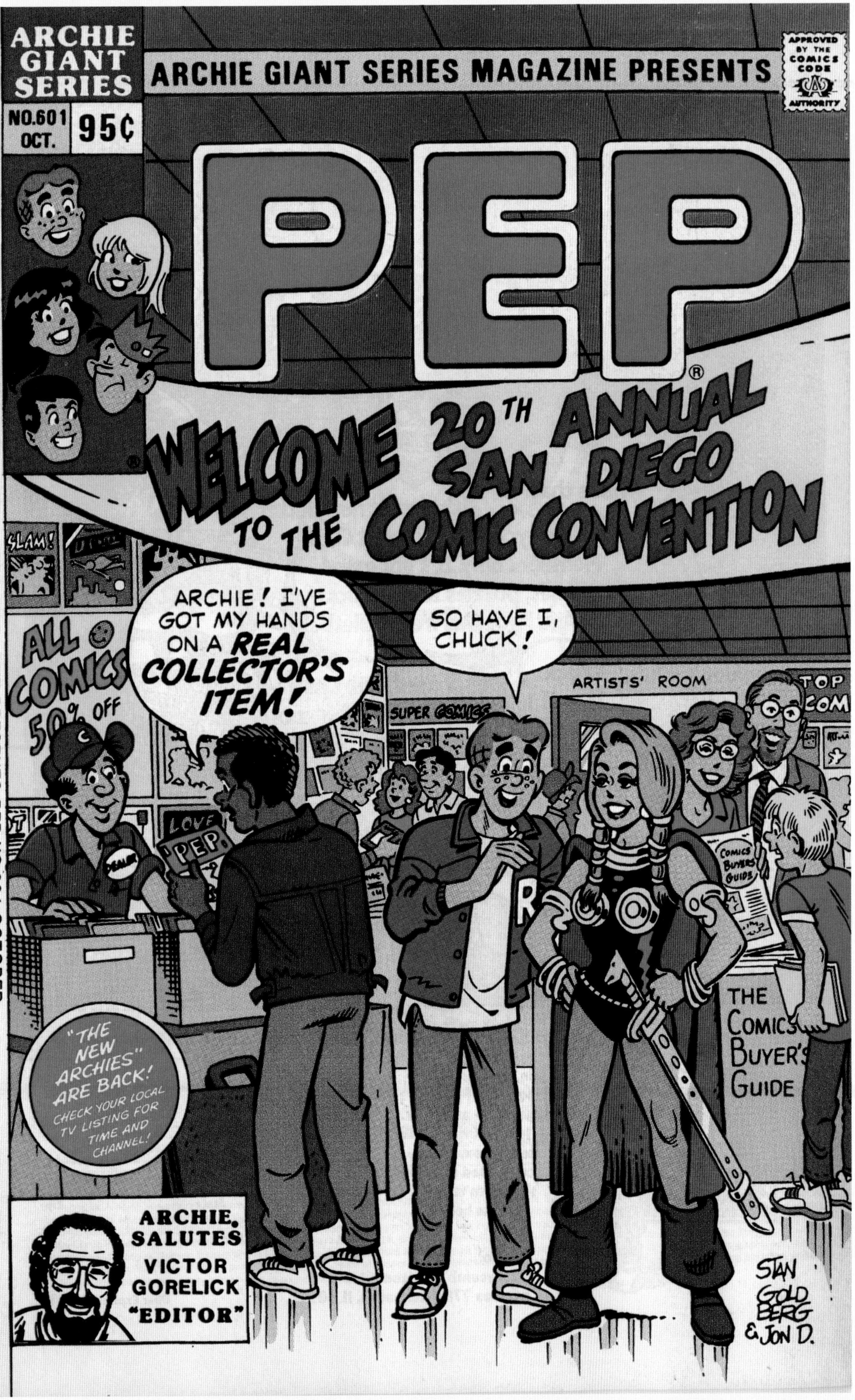
ARCHIE GIANT SERIES
ARCHIE GIANT SERIES MAGAZINE PRESENTS
APPROVED BY THE COMICS CODE AUTHORITY
NO.601 OCT.
95¢
PEP®
WELCOME TO THE 20TH ANNUAL SAN DIEGO COMIC CONVENTION
SLAM!
ALL COMICS 50% OFF
ARCHIE! I'VE GOT MY HANDS ON A REAL COLLECTOR'S ITEM!
SO HAVE I, CHUCK!
ARTISTS' ROOM
SUPER COMICS
TOP COM
LOVE PEP
DEALER
COMICS BUYER'S GUIDE
THE COMICS BUYER'S GUIDE
"THE NEW ARCHIES" ARE BACK! CHECK YOUR LOCAL TV LISTING FOR TIME AND CHANNEL!
ARCHIE, SALUTES VICTOR GORELICK "EDITOR"
STAN GOLDBERG & JON D.

ARCHIE GIANT SERIES MAGAZINE PRESENTS PEP NO.601 OCTOBER

in 1986 and included an autograph signing area. In 1987 the first at-show Events Guide was published, while 1988 saw the introduction of the Disabled Services Department and the official Japanese animation (anime) programming track.

INTO THE DECADE . . .

The hallmark of 1980 was the appearances of two very diverse contingencies: manga artists from Japan and alternative artists from *National Lampoon*. The Japanese delegation, headed by superstar Osamu Tezuka (*Astro Boy*, *Phoenix*) and including Go Nagai and Monkey Punch, held a reception at the U. S. Grant Hotel "in order that the American and Japanese comic-art and cartoon artists may become better acquainted." The *Lampoon* cartoonists—Shary Flenniken, Mary Wilshire, Sam Gross, B. K. Taylor, M. K. Brown, and Rick Geary—had a prominent spot in the Exhibit Hall where they created a giant poster. The juxtaposition of such widely varying comics groups coming together in the same place showcased what a "big tent" Comic-Con was becoming and would continue to be in the future. All aspects of the comics world were drawn to the event.

In 1981 Comic-Con made a brief return to the El Cortez, where the event permanently shrank from five days to four. Voice actor and announcer Gary Owens was MC for the Masquerade, and everyone was wearing masks provided by Disney to promote its upcoming *Condorman* film. Comic-Con's first film festival, showcasing original films from student and independent filmmakers and featuring cash prizes, drew thirty entries. Officially called the "Fantasy, Horror and Science Fiction Film Festival," the event accepted sixteen-millimeter and Super 8 film entries, with the winners selected by a panel of judges who awarded cash prizes totaling $600. The festival featured some incredible films, many of them animated.

The convention was scaled back in 1982 because of budget concerns; the film screenings and programs were held in breakout rooms on the Exhibit Hall floor and the Souvenir Book was on newsprint. The five thousand fans didn't seem to notice, as they came to see guests like Frank Miller, Will Eisner, Carl Barks, and Chuck Jones, and they packed into the basement at the Hotel San Diego to see a special preview of the upcoming *Star Wars* movie, *Revenge of the Jedi* (which became *Return of the Jedi* before its release the following year).

In 1983 programming themes were introduced, with the first theme being a look back at the 1960s. For the first time no banquet was held; the Inkpots were given out in an evening ceremony at the Hotel San Diego. And those staying at that hotel could tune in to CCTV (Comic-Con's closed-circuit TV programming) to see an early-morning talk show and late-night movies.

The 1984 Comic-Con was the earliest ever (June 28–July 1) because of the summer Olympics in Los Angeles. Dr. Raoul Duke and His All-Human Orchestra were a popular part of the entertainment at the Masquerade, which was MC'd by Sergio Aragonés. This was Shel Dorf's last Comic-Con as president, as he left to devote more time to his own professional career.

Alan Moore made his only U.S. convention appearance at the 1985 event and was on hand for the first-ever Jack Kirby Awards (which later evolved into the

Eisner Awards). This was also the year Comic-Con set up an office with a full-time general manager, and Rick Geary's toucan character was adopted as the official Comic-Con logo.

In 1986 the Masquerade, which had been on Friday nights, was moved to Saturdays, where it's been ever since, while the Inkpot banquet moved to the Friday slot. The newly instituted Artists' Alley had seventy-five creators taking turns at the eighteen tables available.

Harlan Ellison was the star at the 1987 show, enthralling a packed hall with his two-hour presentation titled "A Brimstone and Hellfire Afternoon with Harlan Ellison." Joyce Brabner promoted her *Real War Stories* with a performance by Country Joe in a roped-off area of Golden Hall. A special highlight for many pros that year was the surprise seventieth birthday party for Jack Kirby at the Hotel San Diego.

In 1988 Comic-Con reached new heights as it expanded its exhibit space into Golden Hall, which became the publishers' booths area. The after-banquet entertainment was provided by Seduction of the Innocent, a created-for-Comic-Con band consisting of actors Bill Mumy and Miguel Ferrer, writer Max Allan Collins, artist Steve Leialoha, and musician Chris Christensen. The Masquerade was held at the Civic Theatre, and a special party was held to celebrate Superman's fiftieth anniversary.

The decade ended with a major jump in attendance—from eight thousand in 1988 to eleven thousand in 1989. The twentieth Comic-Con was celebrated with a luau-themed Inkpot Awards banquet (with Hawaiian shirt contest) and a party at the U. S. Grant, complete with a giant toucan-shaped cake and music by Seduction of the Innocent. Attendees were left with the memorable sight of Jack and Roz Kirby gracing the dance floor.

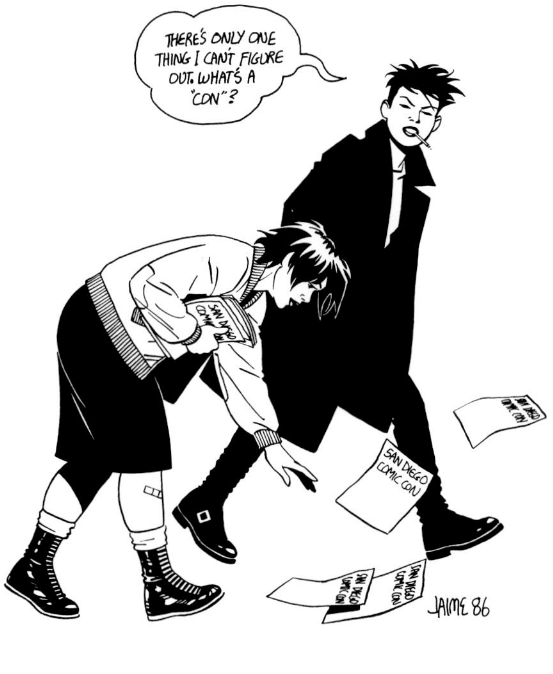
THERE'S ONLY ONE THING I CAN'T FIGURE OUT. WHAT'S A "CON"?
SAN DIEGO COMIC CON
JAIME 86

ABOVE: Drawing of *Love and Rockets'* Maggie and Hopey by Jaime Hernandez, from the 1986 Souvenir Book. One of the first indie comics hits, the Hernandez Brothers' *Love and Rockets* is still going strong today.

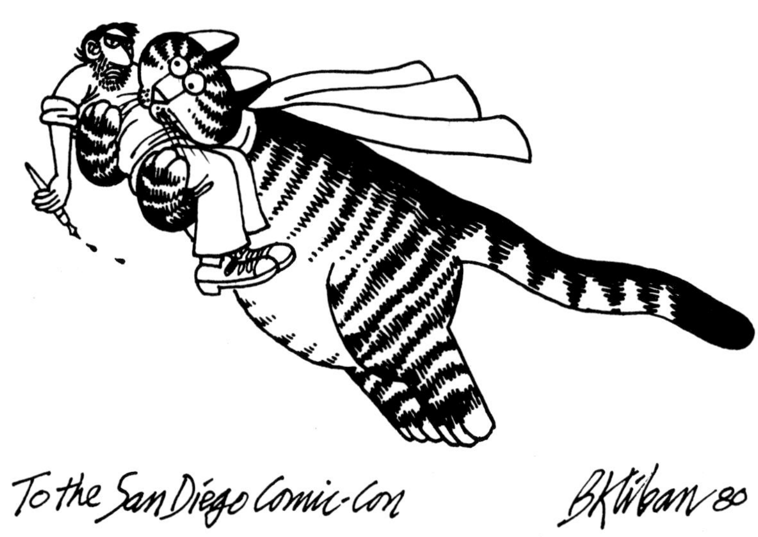
To the San Diego Comic-Con
BKliban 80

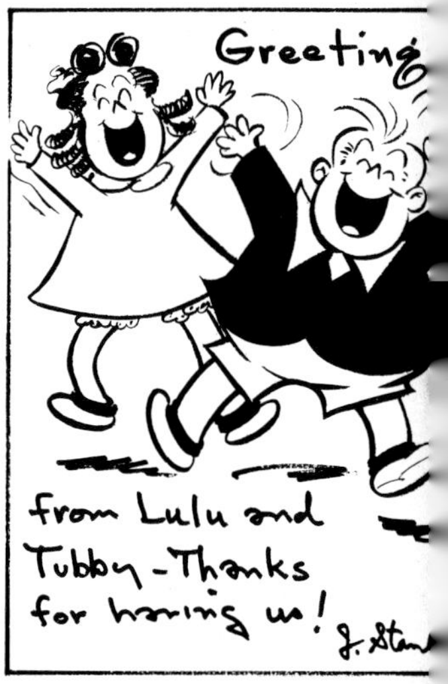
Greeting
from Lulu and Tubby - Thanks for having us!

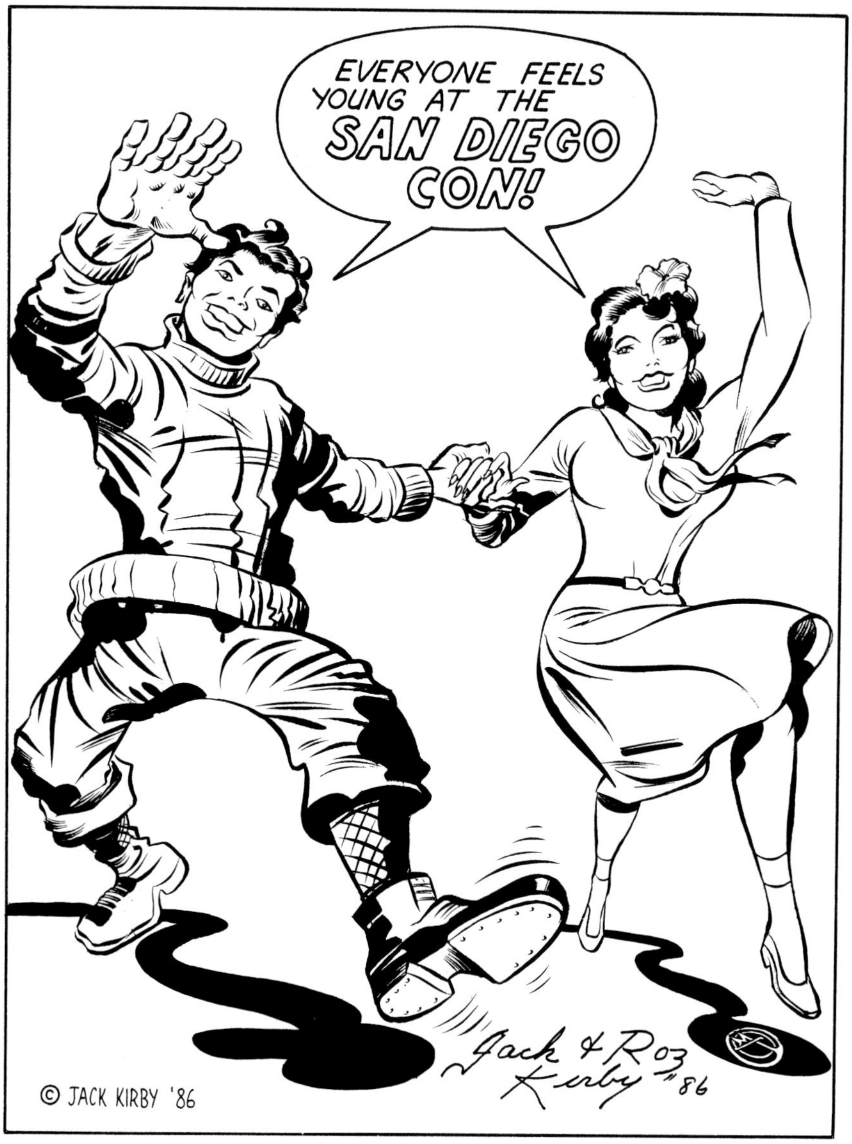
EVERYONE FEELS YOUNG AT THE SAN DIEGO CON!
Jack & Roz Kirby '86
© JACK KIRBY '86

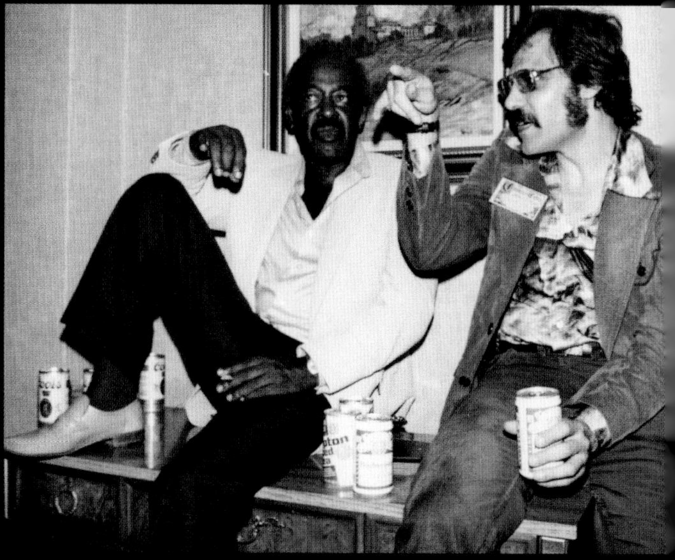

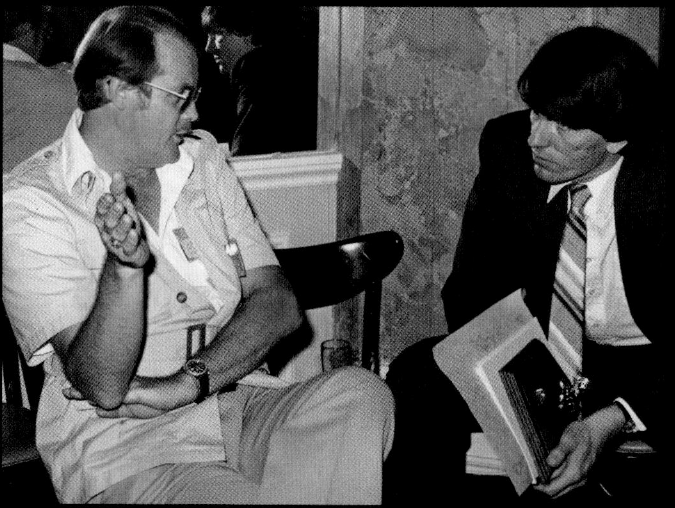

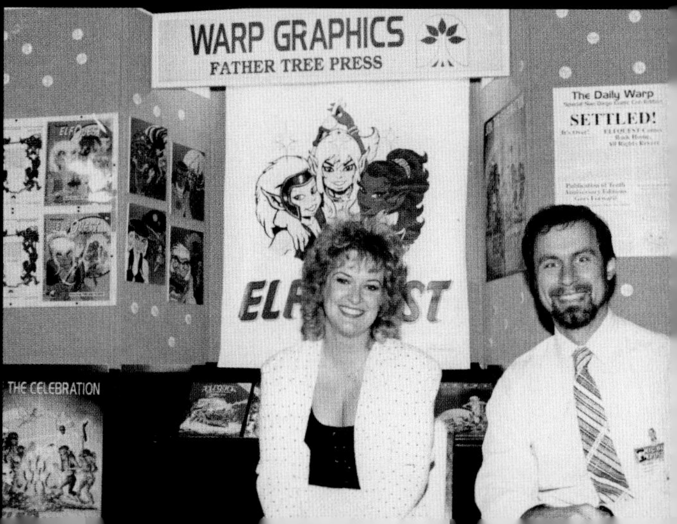
WARP GRAPHICS
FATHER TREE PRESS
The Daily Warp
SETTLED!
THE CELEBRATION

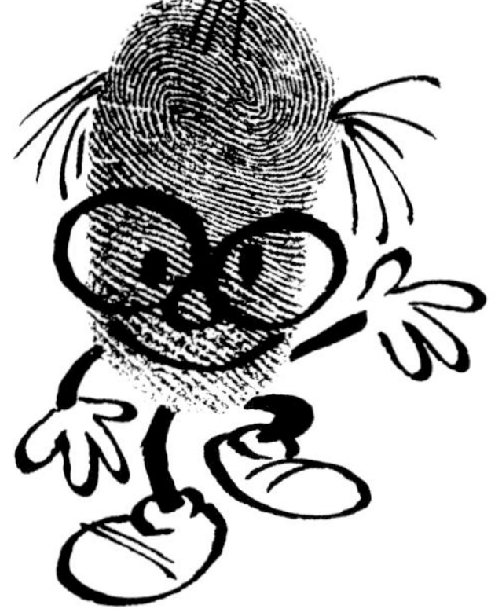

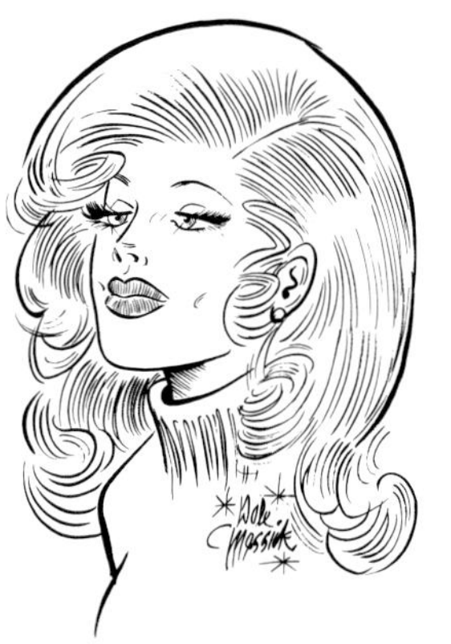

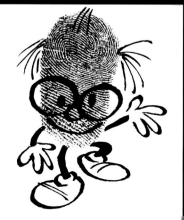

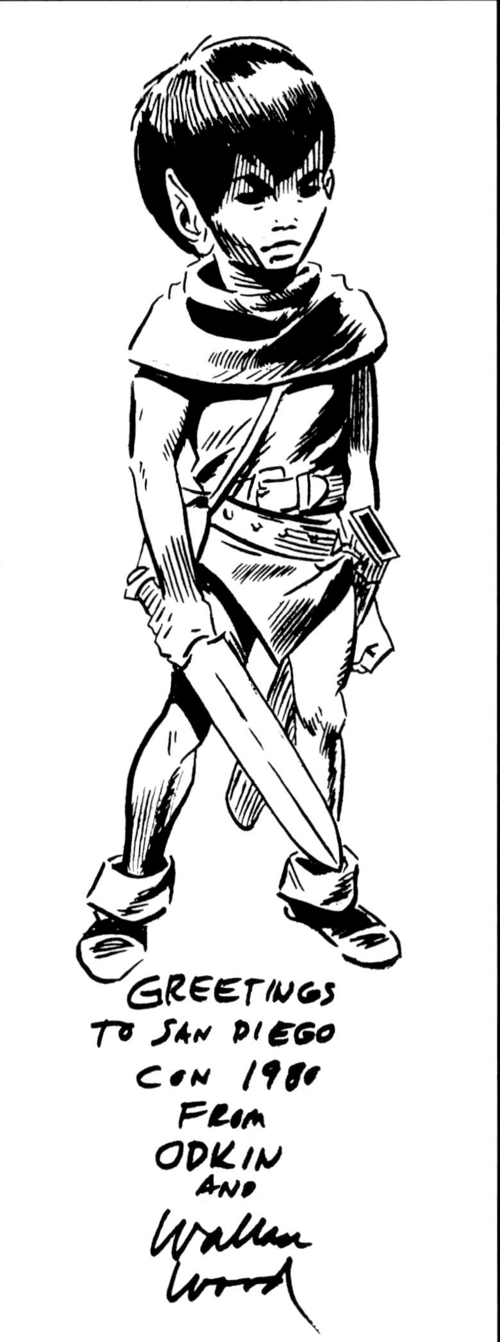
GREETINGS TO SAN DIEGO CON 1980 FROM ODKIN AND
Wallace Wood

What comic strips mean to me

By Ray Bradbury

There simply is no way to estimate the importance of comic-strip collecting in my life. The combination of comics, films, and magicians, plus carnivals, probably shaped me forever. The things I drank in from films and cartoon strips, especially, were to help me with my work when I finally made it to the movie studios when I was 32.

Reading the comics and collecting them gave me the shorthand that screenwriters need to make points, prove metaphors, and do it with swift economy. The lessons I learned from Buck Rogers and Flash Gordon—setting scenes, cutting dialogue to the bone—were put to use when I worked on It Came From Outer Space (as author of the 99-page treatment) and my first screenplay, Moby Dick, for John Huston.

I have never got over the initial impact of Buck Rogers on my life, and I am grateful for his explosion in my midst sometime in the year 1929 when the newspaper thudded against the screen door of my home in Waukegan, Illinois and I walked out to pick up my destiny—the first Buck Rogers strip published that year—with Buck trapped in a mine, coming out to find himself in the Future, and with Wilma leaping through the air on her jumping-belt. Was ever a love joined so quickly? Did ever anyone stay in love so long?

From that day forward I did not walk to pick up the paper, I dashed, I ran, I streaked! I held my breath all day, waiting for the incredible moment when I opened the paper and was in love all over again.

Kids made fun, I took on embarrassment, and tore up the strips. A month later, empty, I burst into tears, asked myself what was wrong. The answer: Buck Rogers gone, and a life not worth living.

Damn! I must have cried. Or darn, anyway.

And started collecting Buck Rogers all over again.

Since that day I have never listened to anyone about my tastes. I have said to hell with others and their pontifical airs and gone on collecting and saving and loving.

The next year it was Tarzan, full of Egyptians and dinosaurs and fabulous cats, drawn by Harold Foster. I still have all of those bright Sunday panels put away in my basement, where I can look at, touch, and, by God, smell them! They smell very fine, thank you, because in them I know are hidden away the incenses of Tutankhamen and the great lion-house odors of Africa. My sense of their beauty and rightness remains the same today, fifty years later. Harold Foster was and is one of the giants who lived amongst us working in this fresh new field.

The year 1934 brought Flash Gordon and a new and exciting love. Now there were three things to look for every Sunday! Buck, Tarzan, and Flash! What a rich life!

And, in 1937—the incredible first panels of Prince Valiant, all of which I stashed away. I have some 40 years of Valiant saved up now, and during those years I wrote my admiration to Harold Foster, and was rewarded by having him send me two immense Sunday panel originals. We still correspond on occasion—especially at Christmas. And I have not changed my opinion of him, right on down the line. For me, he will remain the absolute top.

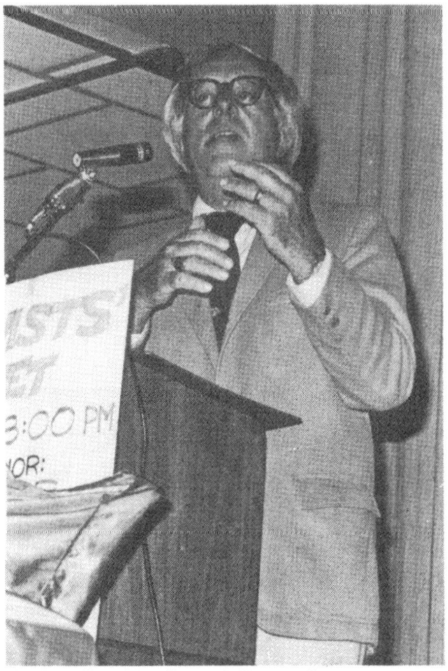

Author Ray Bradbury talks to Con gathering.

There's not much more to add, except to point out that along with those others, I saved a good supply of 1932-33 Popeyes and Mickey Mouses, a shelf full of big little books, all of the original Little Orphan Annie books, some Mutt and Jeff, Alley Oop, you name it. And, when I was 26, Charles Beaumont, the fantasy writer, arrived in my life, aged 16, and we traded panels of Terry and the Pirates.

So there you have the raw and unashamed facts. I was hooked, I am hooked, I will always be hooked on my first great love. Daily strips, Sunday panels—to the artform and its creators, my undying gratitude! ■

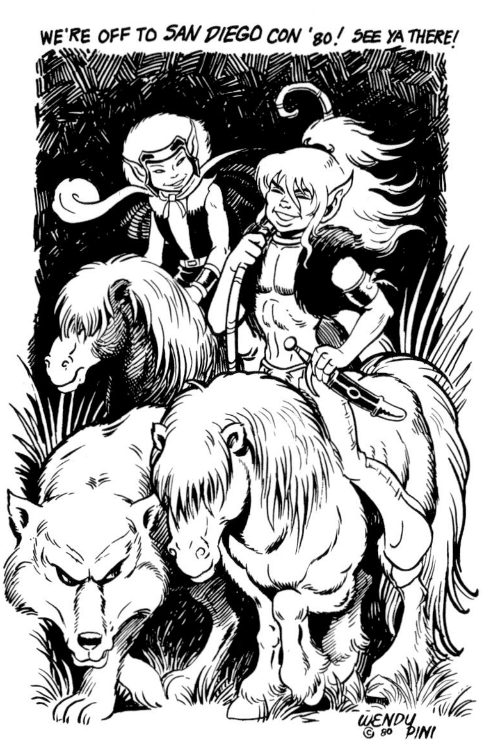
WE'RE OFF TO SAN DIEGO CON '80! SEE YA THERE!
WENDY PINI © 80

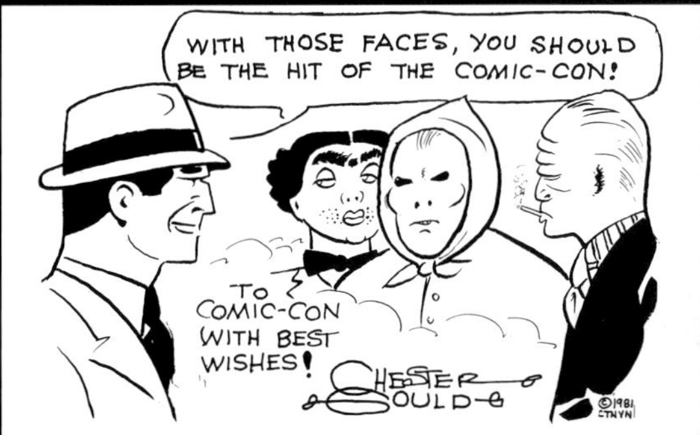
WITH THOSE FACES, YOU SHOULD BE THE HIT OF THE COMIC-CON!
TO COMIC-CON WITH BEST WISHES!
CHESTER GOULD
©1981 CTNYNI

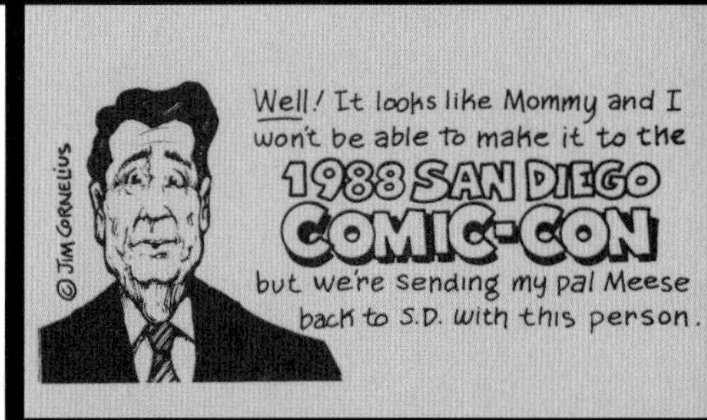
© JIM CORNELIUS
Well! It looks like Mommy and I won't be able to make it to the
1988 SAN DIEGO COMIC-CON
but we're sending my pal Meese back to S.D. with this person.

OPPOSITE, CLOCKWISE FROM TOP LEFT: One of B. Kliban's trademark cats, drawn for the 1980 program book; Little Lulu and Tubby, by their comic book writer/artist, John Stanley; *Wee Pals* creator Morrie Turner (left) with journalist Malcolm Schwartz (right); science fiction author Jerry Pournelle (left) talking with Marvel Comics editor-in-chief Jim Shooter (right) at a party in 1980; Wendy and Richard Pini (*Elfquest*) at their WARP Graphics booth in 1988; a sketch of Brenda Starr by Dale Messick; animator Ward Kimball's self-caricature from his guest appearance in 1987; Jack and Roz Kirby cutting a rug in a drawing by the King from 1986 **CLOCKWISE FROM TOP LEFT:** Art by comics great Wallace Wood, whose only appearance at Comic-Con was in 1980; Ray Bradbury's "true confession" from the 1980 program book; the only way for President Reagan to appear at Comic-Con: on a 1988 badge illustrated by Jim Cornelius; Dick Tracy confronting a rogues gallery in a sketch by creator Chester Gould; a 1980s self-publishing success story, *Elfquest*, drawn by co-creator Wendy Pini

PROGRAMS

THURSDAY

10:00 Registration opens.
Dealers' room opens.

1:00 IT'S LONELY AT THE TOP: What is it like to be responsible for a major comic book company? Dick Giordano and Jim Shooter discuss the joys and pains. (Hammett)

2:00 MARVEL PLOT-A-THON: Mark Gruenwald and Marvel editors tell how they develop a plot. Then it's your turn to suggest a plot for your favorite Marvel character and to get the response of the panel. (Hammett)

3:00 ARCHIE/RED CIRCLE: They've published the adventures of the red-headed teen for decades, and now they've reentered the superhero field. Find out what's ahead from Richard Goldwater, Michael Silberkleit, and Rich Buckler. (Hammett)

3:00 SYMPOSIUM ON SUPERHERO ROLE-PLAYING: Game designers Steve Perrin and Steve Peterson share their insights into successful gamesmanship. (Chandler)

4:00 DC PREVIEW 1: Among the exciting new DC projects you'll hear about are *Infinity, Inc.*, *Atari Force*, *The Redeemer*, and *Star Raiders*. Hosted by Mike Flynn, with appearances by Joe Kubert, Roy Thomas, Gerry Conway, and Jose Luis Garcia-Lopez. (Hammett)

6:00 THE IMAGERY OF ROBERT WILLIAMS: The celebrated artist will again share his view of the world with us. In keeping with the 60s theme, he will focus on his work with Ed "Big Daddy" Roth, George Barris, and underground comix. (Hammett)

7:30 JUNGLE JUDD'S SENSATIONAL SOMETHING FOR EVERYONE ESOTERIC SLIDE SHOW: How many publishers can you name that have done strange, weird, or simply bad comics? Jungle Judd knows them all, and he'll prove it as he explores the "injury to the intellect" motif and much, much more! (Continental Room, Hotel San Diego)

9:00 Registration closes.
Dealers' room closes.

10:00 BOUND TO PLEASE II: You loved it when we presented version I two years ago, so we tied down Carl Macek and forced him to do a new, improved version! Just make sure you're not too tied up to attend! (Continental Room, Hotel San Diego)

FRIDAY

10:00 Registration opens.
Dealers' room opens.

10:00 ROBERT A. HEINLEIN BLOOD DRIVE: The Bloodmobile will be parked in front of the convention center (on Third Avenue) to take your donations. Donors will receive a bounty of goodies--comic books, magazines, and tons more--for their contribution. Closes at 3 p.m.

11:00 THE DIRECT SALES MARKET: New methods of distributing comics are having far-reaching effects on the industry. Find out what's happening from Rick Felber (First Comics), Mike Flynn (DC), Carol Kalish (Marvel), and Michael Silberkleit (Archie/Red Circle). (Hammett)

11:30 THE WORLD OF VICTOR MOSCOSO: A look at the 60s work of this pioneering underground comix and poster artist. (Tin)

Noon JOURNALISM AND THE FAN PRESS: What is the role of the fan press? Where does reporting end and muckraking begin? What is valid criticism? These and other questions will be discussed by Mike Catron, Mike Flynn, Bob Greenberger, Carol Kalish, Maggie Thompson, and Cat Yronwode. (Hammett)

12:30 THE 60s: DECADE OF CHANGE: Clay Geerdes recalls the 60s as they were, illuminating the developments in society that helped shape our current situation. (Tin)

1:00 THE INDEPENDENT PRESS: Sometimes you have so much faith in your own comics that you just have to publish them yourself. This look at such projects will include representatives from Comico, Just Imagine, Texas Comics, Americomics, and more. (Hammett)

1:30 WEIRD HORRORS, TOR, AND THE THREE STOOGES: THE ST. JOHN STORY: A fond look back at St. John Comics, one of the most interesting publishers of the early 1950s. Hosted by Ray Zone and bringing back together St. John principals Norman Maurer and Joe Kubert. (Tin)

2:00 ADULT THEMES IN COMICS: Panel discussing how restrictions on taboo themes are changing and how best to handle them. With Jo Duffy, Archie Goodwin, Bruce Jones, Denis Kitchen, Denny O'Neil, and moderator Dr. Bill Wilson. (Hammett)

2:30 HOW I BROKE INTO SF: Learn the mystical secret of selling your novels and stories from Greg Bear, John Brizzolara, Ray Feist, Robert Wilfred Franson, and Vernor Vinge. (Tin)

3:30 RAY BRADBURY: An hour with the great fantasist. What more need be said? (Hammett)

4:00 THE GREAT CON FEUD: We swipe the format from Family Feud to present our own version, featuring teams for Marvel and DC fighting it out for the championship of the known universe! (To be taped for showing over Hotel San Diego closed-circuit TV.) (Tin)

4:30 DUNE: Frank Herbert's SF classic is about to become the most expensive movie ever made. Paul Sammon takes us behind the scenes. (Hammett)

5:00 BIG FEET AND FLOPPY EARS: Funny animals are a major part of the history of comics. Arn Saba moderates this look at the continuing tradition, joined by Floyd Gottfredson, Bob Clampett, Chase Craig, Mark Evanier, and Scott Shaw!. (Tin)

7:00 MASQUERADE: Comic-Con's famous costume contest, this year MC'd by the multitalented Arn Saba. Opening act: Raoul Duke and his All-Human Orchestra. Admission for the masquerade and dance following is $2 for con members, $5 for others. Tickets available at Box Office. (Golden Hall)

9:00 Registration closes.
Dealers' room closes.

9:30 60s DANCE: Following the masquerade, the floor will be cleared for a 60s dance featuring the mod sounds of MANUAL SCAN, with light show by George DiCaprio. Wear your best paisley. YOU MUST BE 17 OR OLDER TO STAY FOR THE DANCE (city ordinance). (Golden Hall)

COMIC ART SEMINARS

The Comic-Con's famous workshops will be held in the Balboa Room, on the 4th floor of the Hotel San Diego. Registration is $5 per seminar, payable at the door.

Friday: HARVEY KURTZMAN on comic art storytelling. 10 AM to noon.

TOM ORZECHOWSKI on lettering. 2:00 to 4:00.

Saturday: LEE MARRS on computer graphics in animation. 10 AM to noon.

CHET MOORE on commercial art applications. 2:00 to 4:00.

SATURDAY

10:00 Registration opens.
Dealers' room opens.

10:00 BRINKE STEVENS: The up-and-coming star (who hosts "Late Night Thrills" on the convention's closed-circuit TV) will be signing autographs in the lobby.

10:30 WHO'S ON FIRST? Last year we brought you a sneak preview of a new comics line. Now we find out how things are going and what is to come. With Mike Gold, Bruce Patterson, Joe Staton and friends. (Tin)

11:00 GRIM NATWICK: The creator of Betty Boop and master animator with both Disney and Fleischer talks about his amazing career. (Hammett)

11:30 AT HOME WITH THE THREE STOOGES: Joan Howard Maurer, daughter of the late Moe Howard, talks about her father, her uncles Curly and Shemp, and her adopted uncle Larry. She is joined by her husband, Norman Maurer, who produced several Stooges films in the 60s. Special showing of rare home movies. (Tin)

11:30 CARTOON FANTASY ORGANIZATION: All members of CFO and anyone interested in the club are encouraged to attend this meeting. (Chandler)

Noon ART AUCTION I: Our friendly and oh-so-persistent auctioneer Dave "The Beast" Davis is putting the arm on the pros for some really special art pieces to auction. Many artists will be on hand to draw while you watch. Bring money! (Lobby area, all afternoon)

Noon THE MAN BEHIND LITTLE ANNIE FANNY: Harvey Kurtzman, responsible for *Mad*, *Help!*, EC's acclaimed war comics, and Playboy's perennial blonde will hold a question-and-answer session. (Hammett)

12:30 WHAT'S NEW WITH THE UNDERGROUNDERS? Baba Ron Turner brings together UG comix creators to discuss their current projects and talk about the evolution of comix since the 60s. (Tin)

1:00 GEORGE PEREZ: The artistic star of *The New Teen Titans* presents a slide show covering his career, including never-before-seen material. (Hammett)

2:00 DOUGLAS ADAMS: Stick a fish in your ear and bring a towel, as the author of *The Hitchhiker's Guide to the Galaxy* talks about his best-selling trilogy and upcoming film version. Mike Gross of Ivan Reitman Productions will also be on hand to talk about the film. (Hammett)

2:00 KATY CON: Special "miniconvention" for Katy Keene fans, featuring Katy's creator, Bill Woggon. Also on hand to honor Katy will be Craig Leavitt, Barb Rausch, and the folks from Archie Comics. (Chandler)

3:00 BOB CLAMPETT: The celebrated animator presents a special program on *Beany and Cecil*, his popular 60s TV show. (Copper)

3:30 WARNER'S FILM PREVIEW: Our friend from Warner Bros., Jeff Walker, provides sneak previews of *Cujo*, *The Right Stuff*, *Never Say Never Again*, and *Greystoke*. (Hammett)

4:00 DEALING WITH CREATIVE RESTRICTIONS: Should a creator be forced to stay within certain limits and boundaries? Mark Stadler questions Harvey Kurtzman and B. Kliban. (Tin)

4:30 FLOYD GOTTFREDSON AND MICKEY MOUSE: The man who signed Walt Disney's name on Mickey's newspaper strip for over 40 years talks about his career. (Hammett)

5:30 PACIFIC SPECIFICS: Those fine folks from San Diego's own comics company will be active throughout the convention, but we'll pin them down here to discuss ongoing and upcoming projects. (Hammett)

7:00 Registration closes.
Dealers' room closes.

8:00 COCKTAIL PARTY: The bar is open for no-host cocktails, and a good time's to be had by all (all over age 21, anyway). The bar is in the Regency Room of the Hotel San Diego. Then wander downstairs to the . . .

9:00 INKPOT AWARDS CEREMONY. Once again the Comic-Con takes an opportunity to honor those who have been of special value to the popular arts. Everyone is encouraged to join in the salute. (Continental Room)

SUNDAY

10:00 Registration opens.
Dealers' room opens.

10:30 MARS: Joe Staton presents a sneak preview of this new book, coming in the fall from First Comics. (Hammett)

11:00 IF IT'S SO GOOD, HOW COME IT ONLY LASTED SIX ISSUES? Ever wonder why some characters make it big in TV, radio, and movies but fail in comics? We'll hear some theories from Louise Jones, Dick Giordano, Al Milgrom, and Marv Wolfman. (Hammett)

11:30 SO YOU KNOW THE 60s: John Javna, author of a new book on the 60s, will have a trivia quiz for all of you who can remember that far back. (Tin)

Noon ART AUCTION II: What's that? You've still got money in your wallet? Have we got deals for you! The art auction continues until we run out of art. (Lobby)

Noon PSYCHEDELIC COMICS: Ray Zone presents a slide show covering psychedelic art in comics, posters, and the popular arts. (Hammett)

12:30 DON BLUTH: Animator Don Bluth, with associates Gary Goldman and John Pomeroy, will discuss his studio, their first feature film, their animated video game (*Dragon's Lair*), and future projects. Followed by a screening of *The Secret of NIMH*. (Copper)

12:30 DC PREVIEW 2: Once again Mike Flynn takes us for a look at new DC comics, this time *Thriller* and *Vigilante*. On hand will be Trevor von Eeden, Robert Loren Fleming, and Marv Wolfman. (Tin)

1:00 HUMOR AND SF: Are these terms mutually exclusive? Panel with Greg Bear, Douglas Adams, Dave Brin, Bill Rotsler, and Vernor Vinge. (Hammett)

1:30 THE AMAZING KLIBAN: No, he's not going to pull a cat out of his hat, but the popular cartoonists will answer your questions about his work. (Tin)

2:00 THE NEW TEEN TITANS: Marv Wolfman, George Perez, and Len Wein discuss one of DC's hottest books. (Hammett)

2:30 TOTAL ECLIPSE: Jan and Dean Mullaney provide insights into the way that Eclipse does comics. Many artists and writers for the line will participate. (Tin)

3:00 GEORGE LUCAS: Got your attention, eh? Dale Pollock, author of *Skywalking*, the best-selling bio of Lucas, will be on hand to explain what it takes to write about a modern film genius. (Hammett)

3:00 Registration closes.

3:30 UNCANNED SAMMON: Paul Sammon, yet another San Diego boy made good, previews the new SF comedy film he has produced. (Tin)

4:00 TALK BACK: All right, people, here's your chance to voice your opinions, objections, praises, or whatever at those who put on the con. Volunteers to help next year also accepted! (Hammett)

5:00 Dealers' room closes.

The program directors wish to thank the SFWA for their assistance in arranging our science fiction programming.

CHILDREN'S ROOM

A variety of interesting and challenging activities will be available to kids young and old in the special Children's Room at the Hotel San Diego. Hours are from 10 AM to late in the evening. Leave your little ones or stay yourself--it's all free! (Rotary Room, 3rd floor)

FINDING THE ROOMS: All convention events are located in the convention center unless otherwise noted. The CHANDLER and HAMMETT rooms are in Plaza Hall (the dealers' room). TIN and COPPER are upstairs in the convention center.

NOTICE: Taping or other reproduction of convention events without written permission is prohibited. For information and release forms, see Mike Pasqua, convention events coordinator.

ABOVE: The 1983 Comic-Con program schedule **RIGHT:** A Kirby sketch from 1981 showing his first creator-owned character, Captain Victory, published by Pacific Comics **BELOW:** When legends meet: Harvey Kurtzman (left) and Jack Kirby (right) **OPPOSITE, TOP LEFT:** The Spirit at Comic-Con in 1987, via this Will Eisner sketch **TOP RIGHT:** Eisner with his wife, Ann **BELOW:** Jeff Smith (left) and Kurt Busiek (right) tried their best to get Eisner to sit down during the Eisner Awards ceremony, presenting him with a throne in 1998. Right after this photo was taken, Will was up again and stood through this and every other presentation, year after year **OVERLEAF:** This giant collage poster was produced in 1986, with photos by Jackie Estrada and design by Kate Kane

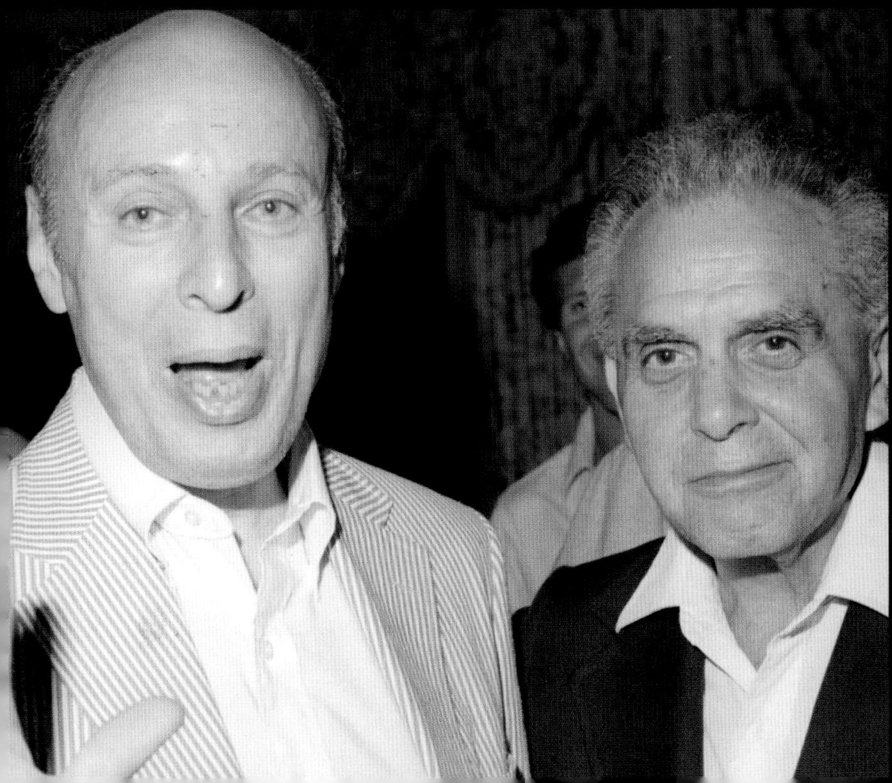

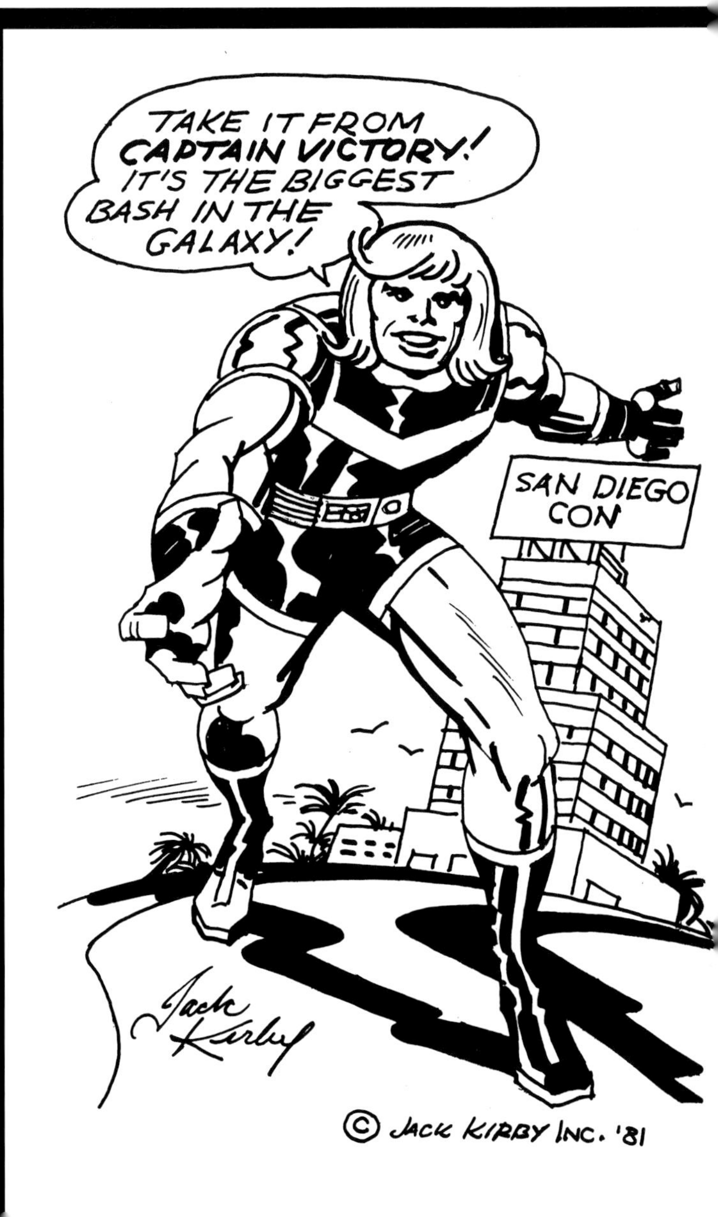
TAKE IT FROM CAPTAIN VICTORY! IT'S THE BIGGEST BASH IN THE GALAXY!
SAN DIEGO CON
Jack Kirby
© JACK KIRBY INC. '81

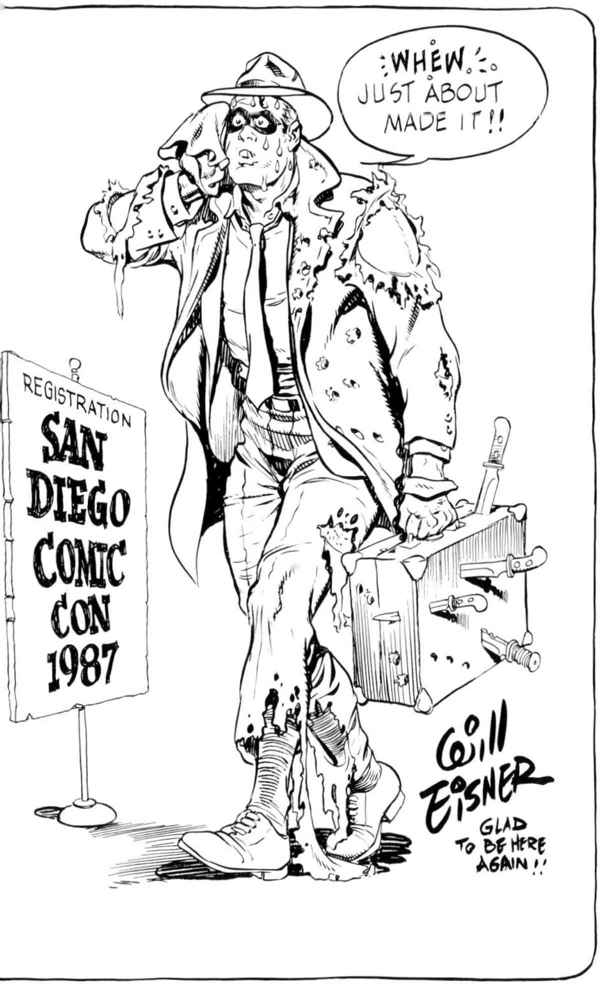
WHEW.
JUST ABOUT MADE IT!!
REGISTRATION
SAN DIEGO COMIC CON 1987
Will Eisner
GLAD TO BE HERE AGAIN!!

WILL EISNER (1917–2005)

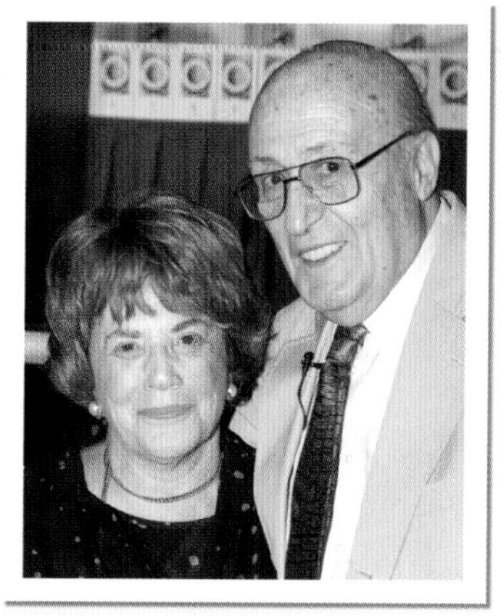

WILL EISNER will always epitomize the best of the comics medium, both as a creator and as a person. Eisner's career spanned eight decades, during which he was a pioneer not only in the beginning of the comic book industry but also later, in the creation of graphic novels.

Eisner was best known as the creator of *The Spirit*, a comic strip that appeared in a Sunday supplement in newspapers during the 1940s and early 1950s. In the seven-page stories that appeared each week, he experimented with a number of storytelling techniques that were hugely influential on later comics creators. Comics fans also knew him for having run one of the first comics "shops" that produced everything from superhero to western to jungle comics for a number of publishers during the Golden Age of comics. His shop is credited with creating Sheena, Queen of the Jungle; Dollman; and Blackhawk, among other characters.

In the 1950s and 1960s, Eisner had left the comic book world to produce publications for the U.S. Army and a number of other clients. But a revival of *The Spirit* through a series of reprints in the late 1960s and early 1970s brought him back to the comics industry. *The Spirit* was eventually published in a number of reprint series from Warren Publishing and Kitchen Sink Press (with new covers provided by Eisner) and in *The Spirit Archives* from DC Comics, a complete, chronological reprint in deluxe hardback format, bringing him a new audience. In the late 1970s, Eisner made a shift in his career. He became one of the first creators of the graphic novel, or book-length comics work. His first such book, *A Contract with God*, appeared in 1978. That was followed by several works in the 1980s, most notably *The Dreamer* (1986), a thinly veiled autobiographical depiction of his early days in the comics industry. Eisner was prolific with his graphic novel work throughout the 1990s and into the new century. His final graphic novel, *The Plot: The Secret Story of the Protocols of the Elders of Zion*, was published after his death.

Eisner first came to Comic-Con in 1975. He drew the wraparound cover for the Souvenir Book that year and received an Inkpot Award. By the mid-1980s Eisner (often accompanied by his wife, Ann) had become a regular guest at Comic-Con, and beginning in 1988 he had a regular role to play at the show: appearing onstage at the Will Eisner Comic Industry Awards to personally congratulate each recipient. He lent his name to the awards because he strongly believed that more attention should be drawn to the wide variety of high-quality works being produced in his beloved medium. He also strongly believed that the retailers who made a special effort to promote and sell those works and to advance the comics medium should have their own award, which is why he proposed the Will Eisner Spirit of Comics Retailer Award in 1993.

Will received a few awards himself at Comic-Con. In 1994 he was given the Bob Clampett Humanitarian Award, and over the years he was nominated for twelve Eisner Awards and won five of them (two for archival *Spirit* collections, two for original graphic novels, and one for his nonfiction book *Graphic Storytelling*).

At the show, Eisner was always easily accessible to fans and pros alike. On his panel appearances he could be counted on to offer historical information about comics, basic how-to's on creating comics, and insights on the direction of the industry. He was at home talking about everything from the international comics scene to alternative and indie comics. He was always on top of whatever was happening in business areas such as distribution and publishing, and he never hesitated to give advice to aspiring cartoonists. Whether he was signing autographs at a booth, strolling through the Exhibit Hall, or socializing at an industry party, he made time for anyone who wanted to speak with him, and he treated all with respect.

Will Eisner passed away in January of 2005, just two months shy of his eighty-eighth birthday. But his legacy lives on at Comic-Con, both in the awards given in his name and in the thousands of pros and fans who had the opportunity to learn from him.

"I was given the honor of giving the Eisner Award for Best Graphic Novel. Among the nominees was Will Eisner himself. I said to the audience, 'I don't know which is worse: being nominated for the Eisner and being up against Will Eisner, or being Will Eisner and losing the Eisner.' The delightful smile and laugh that got out of Eisner (and the collective breath of relief from the other nominees) was gratifying to say the least. And of course Eisner won."

—MAX ALLAN COLLINS

WRITER, *DICK TRACY, BATMAN, ROAD TO PERDITION*; SEDUCTION OF THE INNOCENT BAND MEMBER

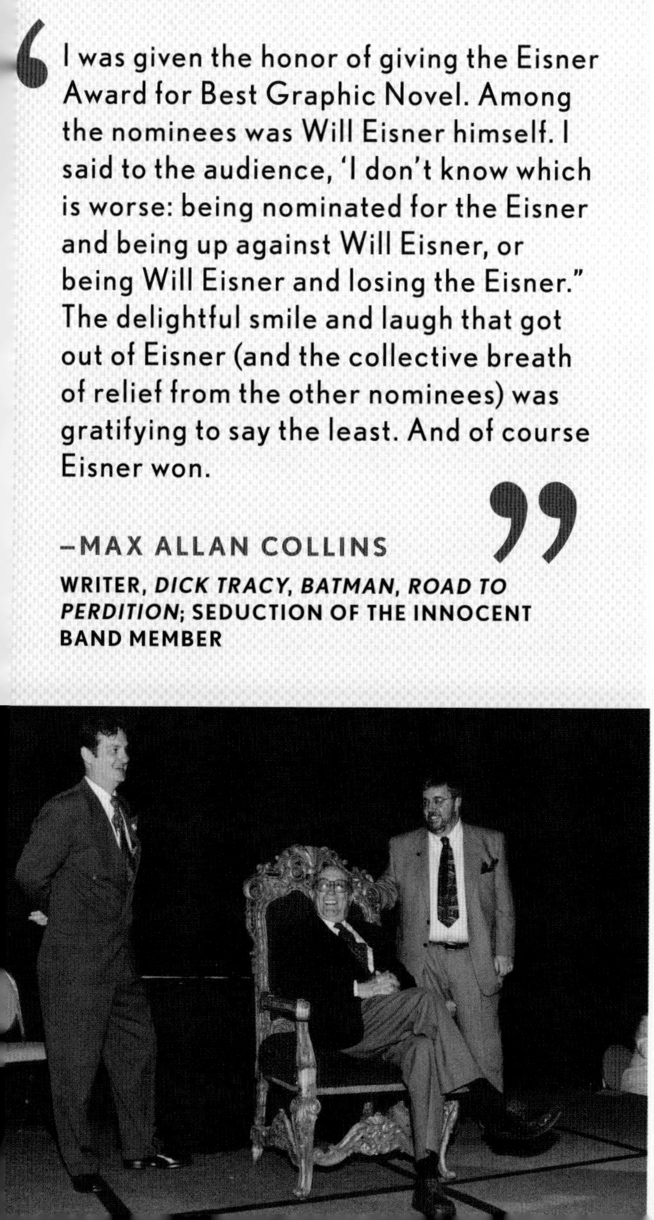

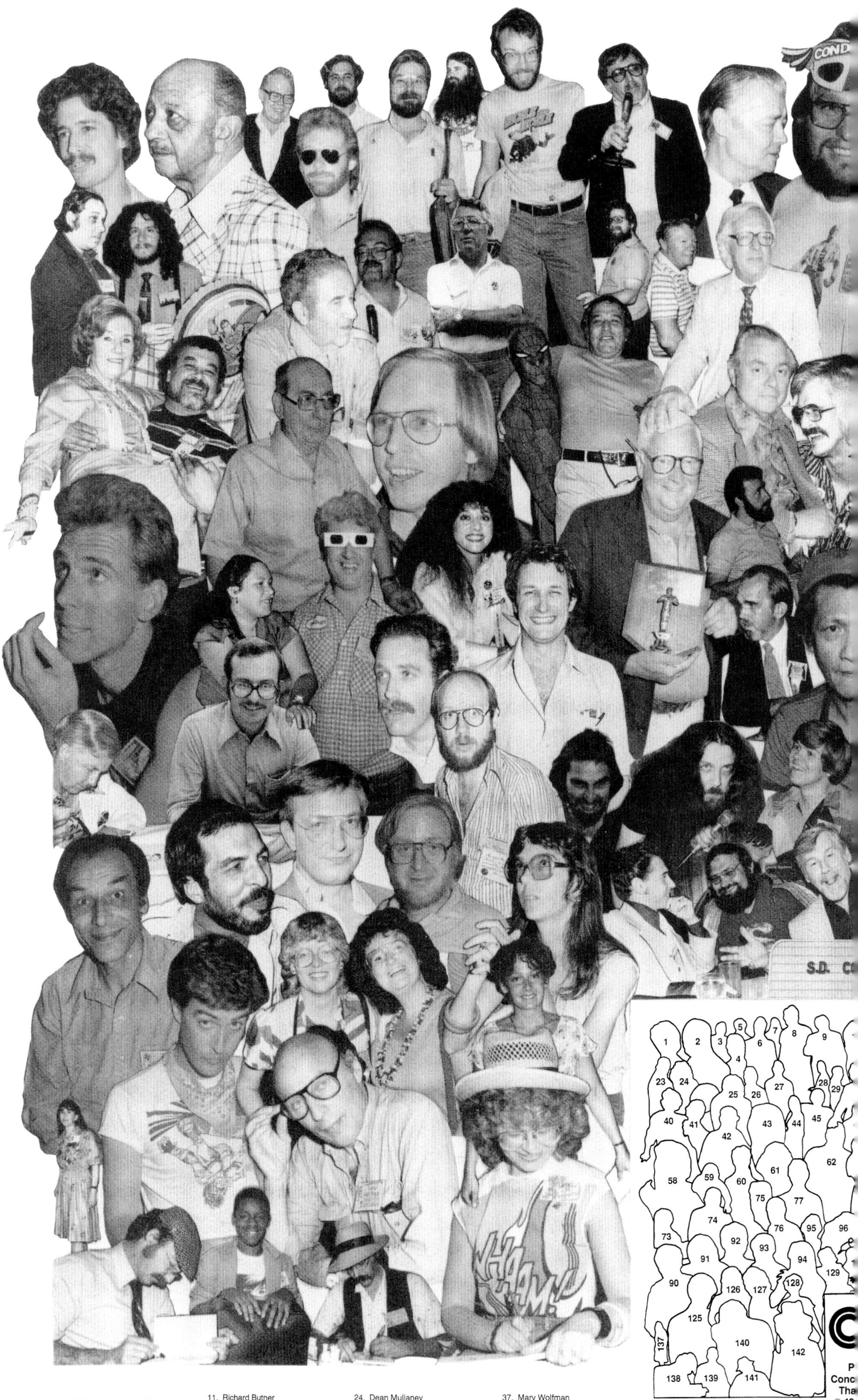
S.D. CO
1 2 3 4 5 6 7 8 9
23 24 25 26 27 28 29
40 41 42 43 44 45
58 59 60 61 62
75 77 74 76 95 96
73 92 93 91 94 129
90 126 127 128
125 137 140 142
138 139 141
P
Conc
Tha
© 19

List of Names Corresponding to Numbered Outline:

1. Tom Yeates
2. Mel Blanc
3. Kelly Freas
4. Bill Mumy
5. Michael Kaluta
6. David Scroggy
7. Ron Turner
8. John Pound
9. Dick Giordano
10. Murphy Anderson
11. Richard Butner
12. Chris Claremont
13. Gil Kane
14. Bob Layton
15. Robt. Williams
16. David Brin
17. Terry Beatty
18. Max Collins
19. Wendy Pini
20. Robert Shayne
21. Richard Pini
22. Phil Lasorda
23. Eric Hoffman
24. Dean Mullaney
25. Jerry Siegel
26. Don Thompson
27. Mort Walker
28. Bill Messner-Loebs
29. Clay Geerdes
30. Ray Bradbury
31. Paul Smith
32. Kate Crabb
33. Barb Rausch
34. Bill Woggon
35. Craig Leavitt
36. Joshua Quagmire
37. Marv Wolfman
38. Howard Chaykin
39. Dori Seda
40. Dale Messick
41. Shel Dorf
42. Julius Schwartz
43. Roy Thomas
44. Spider-Man
45. John Romita
46. Joe Shuster
47. Rick Geary
48. Sergio Aragones
49. Gary Groth
50. Clarence Nash
51. Jim Shooter
52. Shary Flenniken
53. Bruce Jones
54. Larry Niven
55. Kirk Alyn
56. Jerry Pournelle
57. Jenette Kahn
58. Steve Rude
59. Vicky Goulart
60. Ray Zone
61. Sharman Di V
62. Jack Davis
63. Steve Schane
64. Carol Lay
65. Paul Sammon
66. S. Clay Wilsor
67. Gary Arlingtor
68. Don Donohue
69. Jack Katz

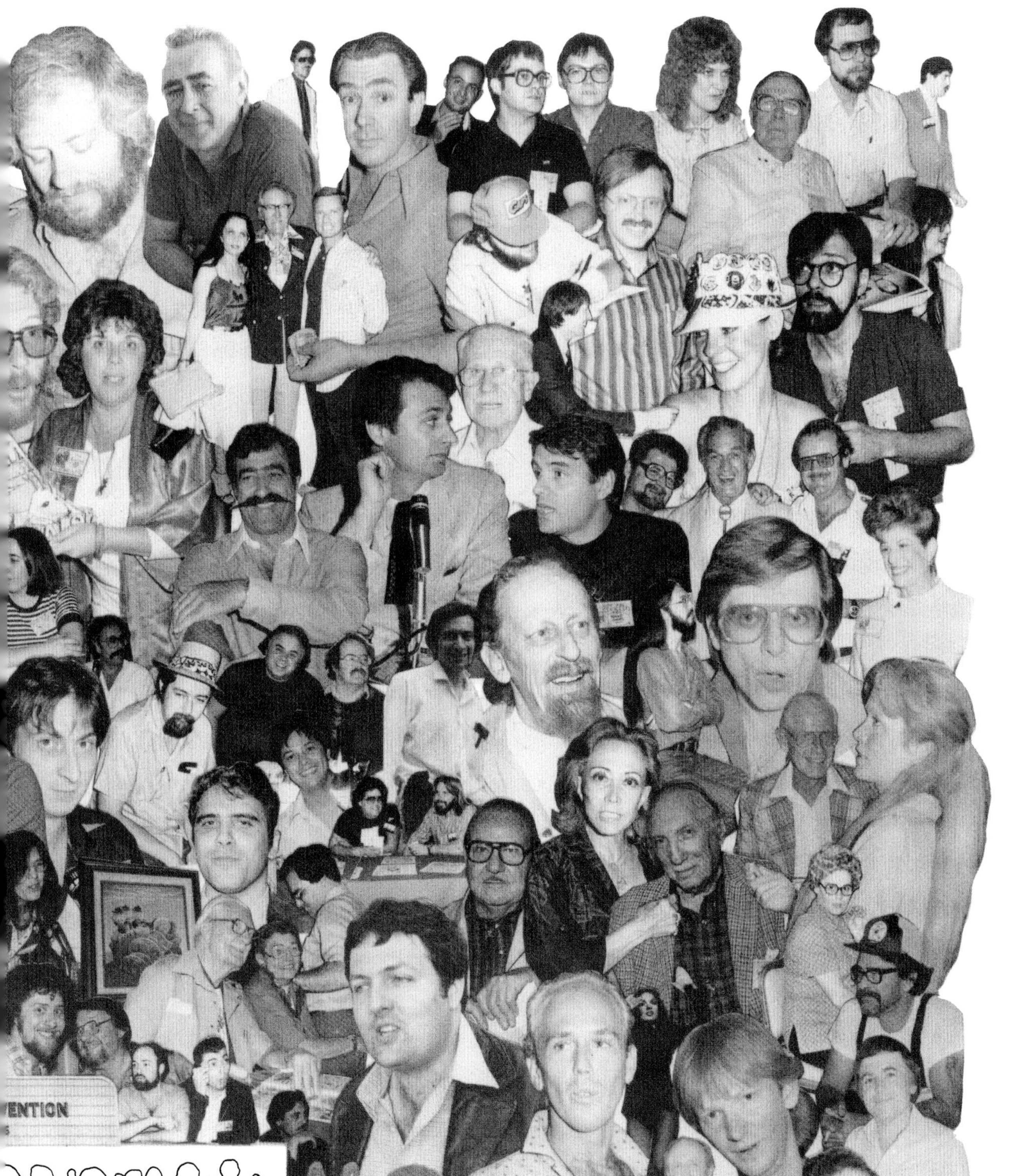
ENTION

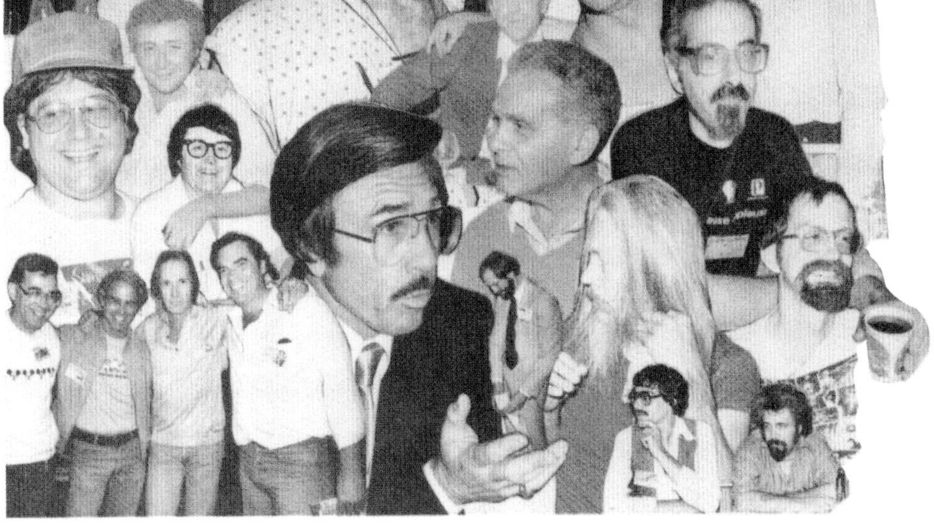

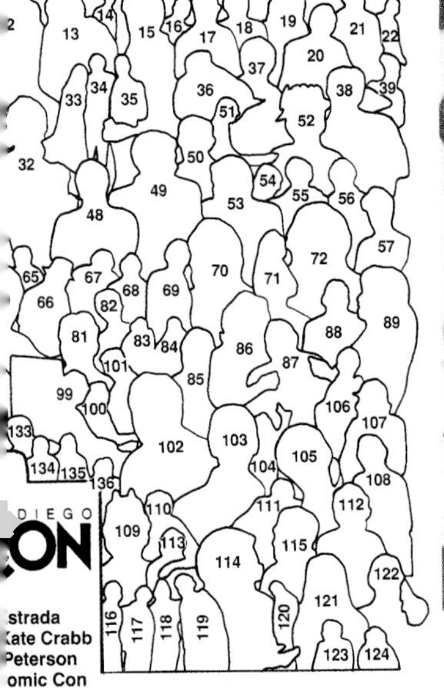

strada
Kate Crabb
Peterson
omic Con

70. Theodore Sturgeon
71. Steve Leialoha
72. Harlan Ellison
73. Don Christensen
74. Greg Bear
75. Al Gordon
76. Steve Englehart
77. Marshall Rogers
78. Ed Nizyborski
79. Alfredo Alcala
80. Frank Miller
81. Valentino
82. Phil Yeh
83. John Koukoutsakis
84. Bob Chapman
85. Burne Hogarth
86. June Foray
87. Jack Cummings
88. Bil Keane
89. Elaine Lee
90. Victor Moscoso
91. B. Kliban
92. Bob Burden
93. Dan O'Bannon
94. Deni Loubert
95. George Di Caprio
96. Alan Moore
97. Barry Short
98. cat yronwode
99. Carl Barks
100. Gare Barks
101. John Rogers
102. Mark Evanier
103. Bill Sienkiewicz
104. Brinke Stevens
105. Art Adams
106. Virginia French
107. Tom French
108. Walter Koenig
109. Scott Shaw!
110. Mike Smith
111. Bob Beirbaum
112. Larry Marder
113. Bob Clampett
114. Gary Owens
115. Jack Kirby
116. Mike Royer
117. Al Williamson
118. David Carradine
119. Patrick Culliton
120. Mike Catron
121. George Clayton Johnson
122. Roger May
123. Denis Kitchen
124. Spain
125. Dave Stevens
126. Jackie Estrada
127. Lee Marrs
128. Mary Wilshire
129. Steranko
130. Captain Sticky
131. Alex Toth
132. Len Wein
134. Gilbert Hernandez
135. Jaime Hernandez
136. Carl Macek
137. Maggie Thompson
138. Dan O'Neill
139. Reggie Byers
140. Harvey Kurtzman
141. R.L. Crabb
142. Trina Robbins

TOP ROW, FROM LEFT: Teenage Mutant Ninja Turtles co-creator Peter Laird at the 1986 show; a Kevin Eastman/Peter Laird sketch of the Turtles as Marvel characters from the same year's Souvenir Book **MIDDLE ROW, FROM LEFT**: A Harvey Kurtzman 1985 sketch with the artist picturing himself as the Hulk; Harvey Pekar manning the *American Splendor* table in Artists' Alley in 1986 **BOTTOM ROW, FROM LEFT:** Matt Groening signing at his table in Artist's Alley, along with an announcement for his signing (right) **OPPOSITE, CLOCKWISE FROM TOP LEFT:** Writer/artist Scott McCloud in 1987; a Jerry Robinson Batman sketch; Steve Rude's drawing of the "World's Finest" superteam in 1989; the 1983 Comic-Con tickets poster, predicting a sellout year; a 1988 badge by Rick Geary **PAGE 72:** A capsule of the Comic-Con experience by artist Brent Anderson (later known for *Astro City*) for the twentieth annual Comic-Con in 1989 **PAGE 73:** A 1985 jam piece by three artists who went on to much bigger things: Steve Purcell (*Sam & Max, Freelance Police*), Mike Mignola (*Hellboy*), and Arthur Adams (*Longshot*, pictured, and *Monkeyman and O'Brien*)

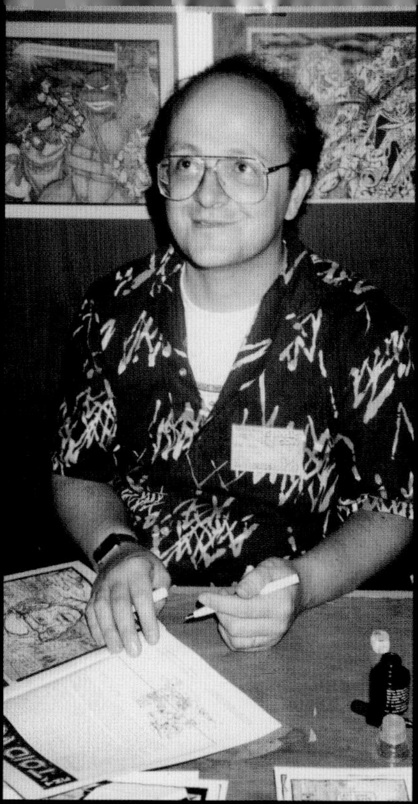

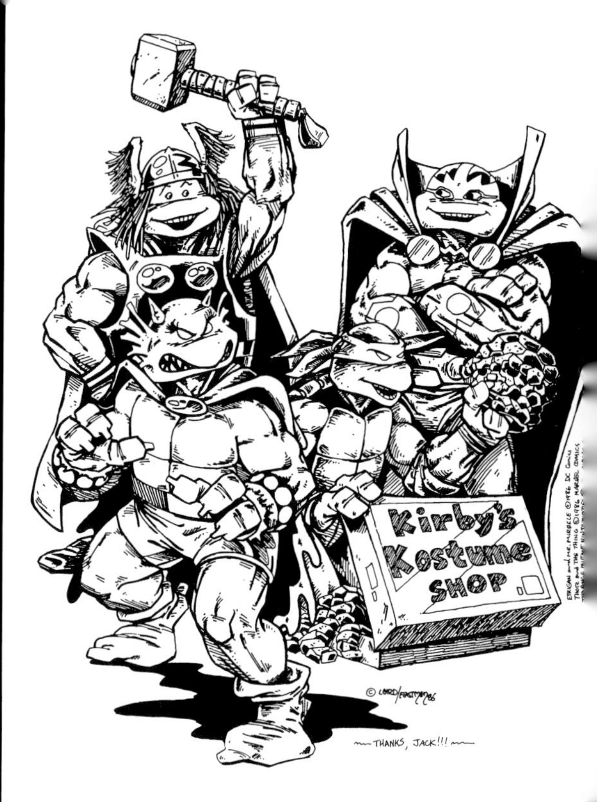
Kirby's Kostume SHOP
THANKS, JACK!!!

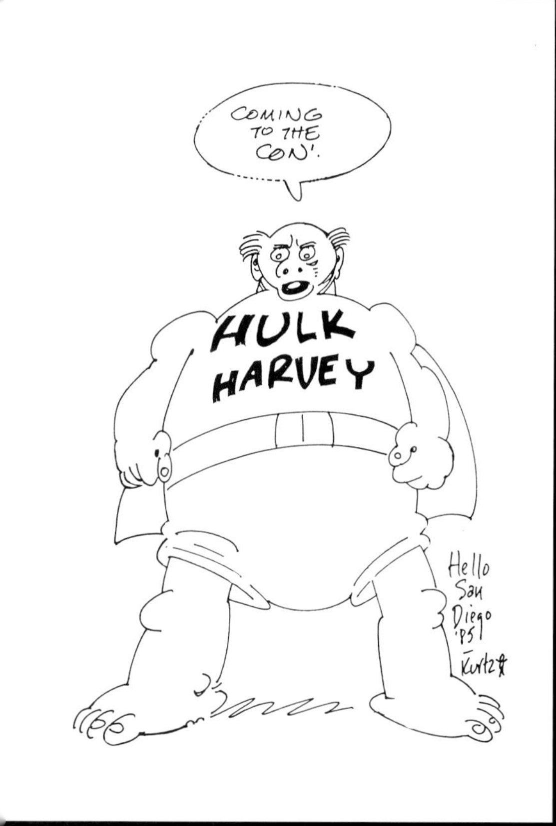
COMING TO THE CON'.
HULK HARVEY
Hello San Diego '85 Kurtz

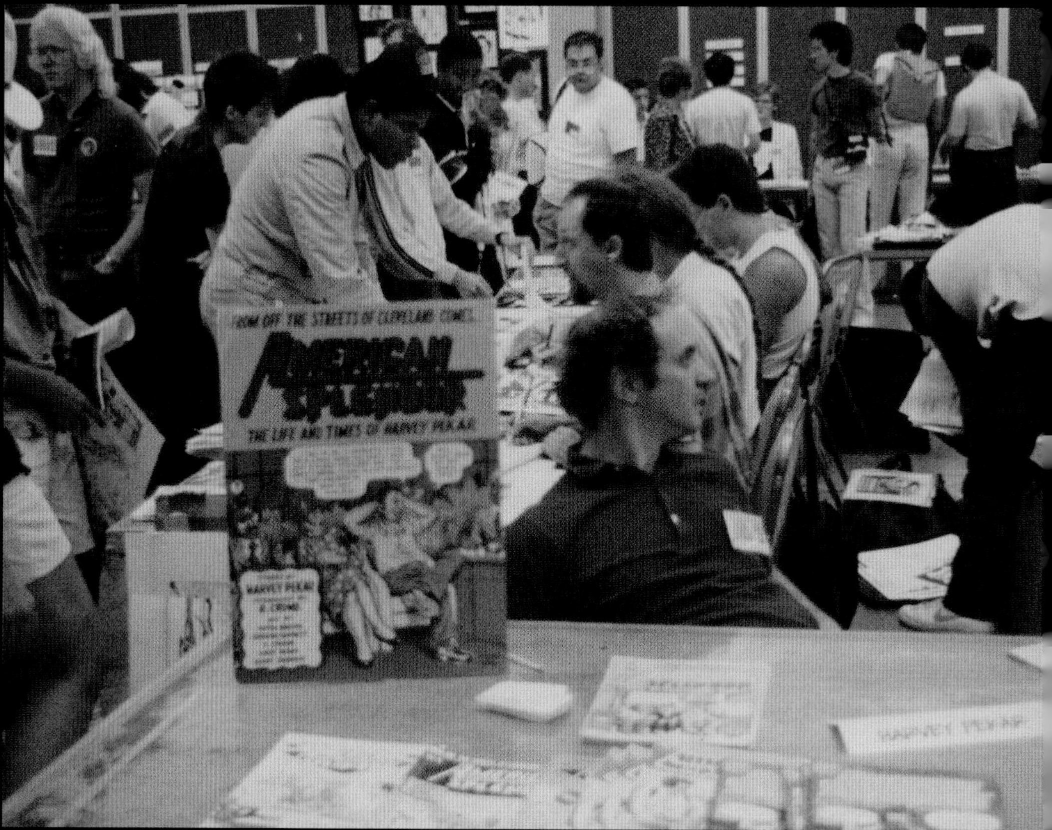
FROM OFF THE STREETS OF CLEVELAND COMES...
AMERICAN SPLENDOR
THE LIFE AND TIMES OF HARVEY PEKAR

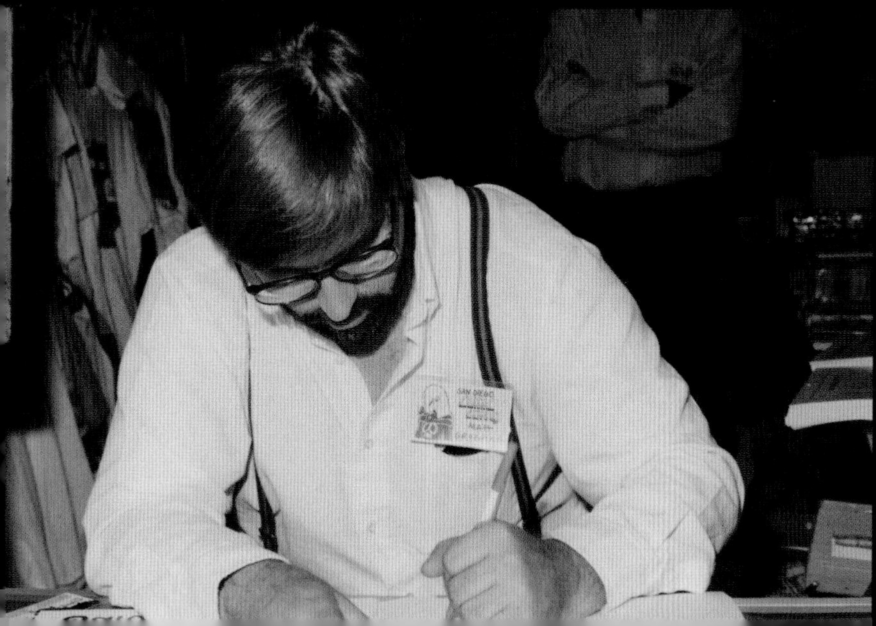

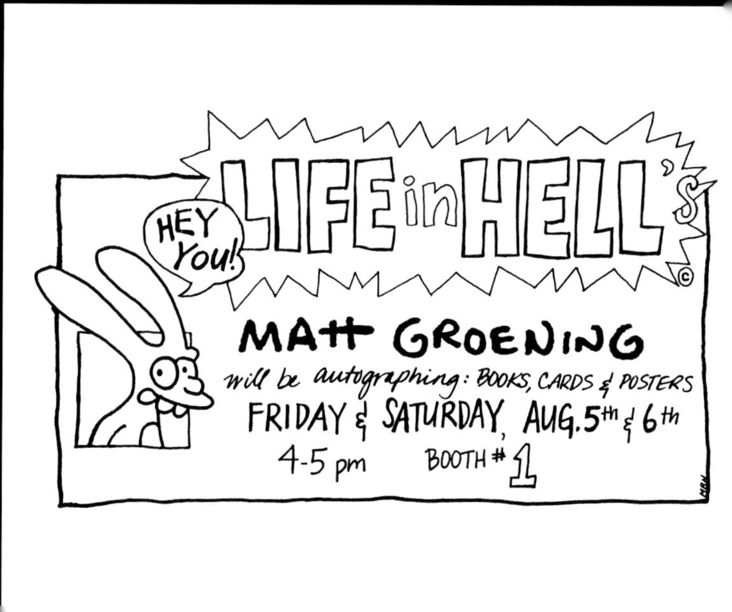
HEY YOU!
LIFE in HELL'S
MATT GROENING
will be autographing: BOOKS, CARDS & POSTERS
FRIDAY & SATURDAY, AUG. 5th & 6th
4-5 pm BOOTH # 1

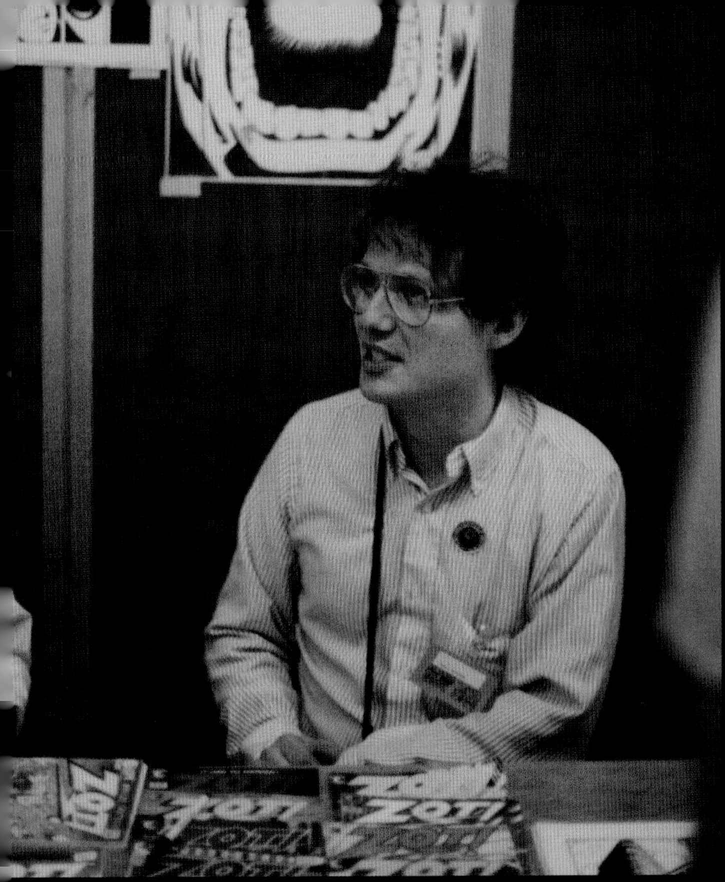
ZOT!

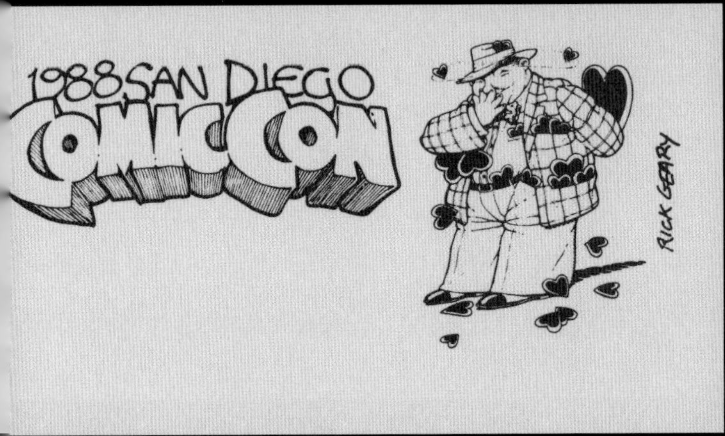
1988 SAN DIEGO
COMIC CON
RICK GEARY

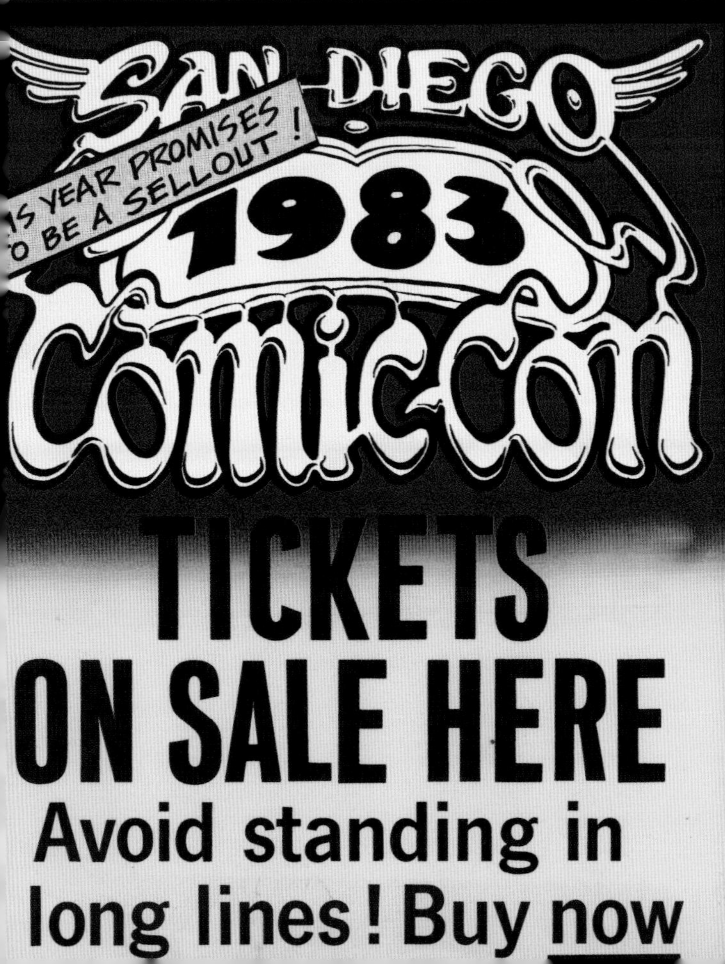
SAN DIEGO
IS YEAR PROMISES
O BE A SELLOUT !
1983
Comic Con
TICKETS
ON SALE HERE
Avoid standing in
long lines! Buy now

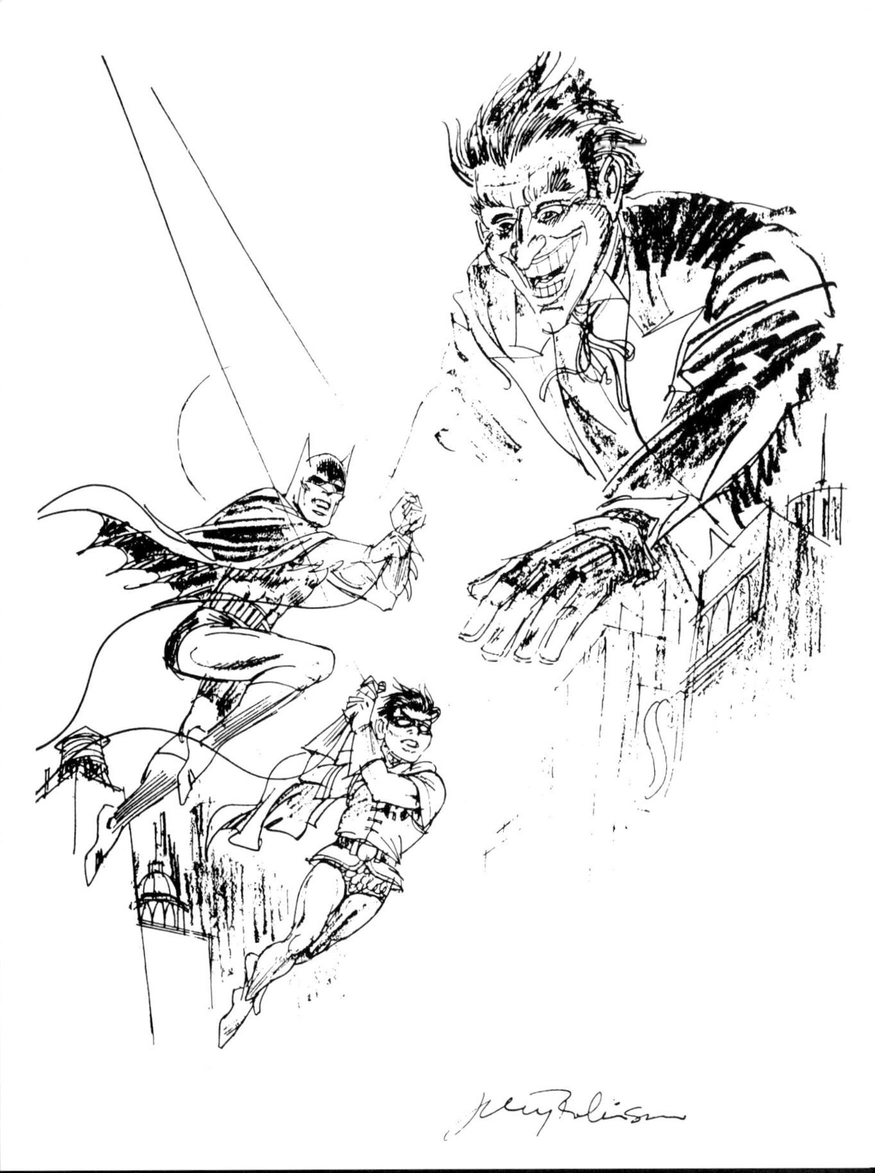

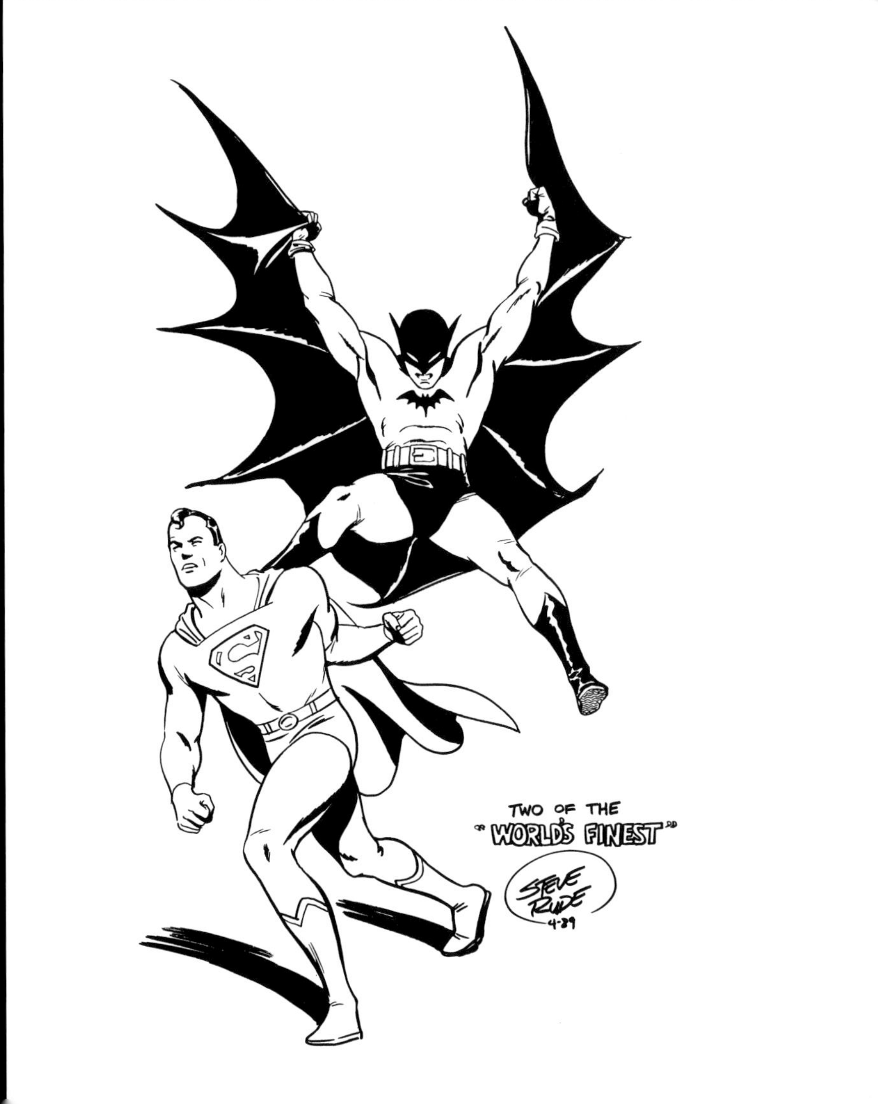
TWO OF THE
"WORLD'S FINEST"
STEVE RUDE
4-89

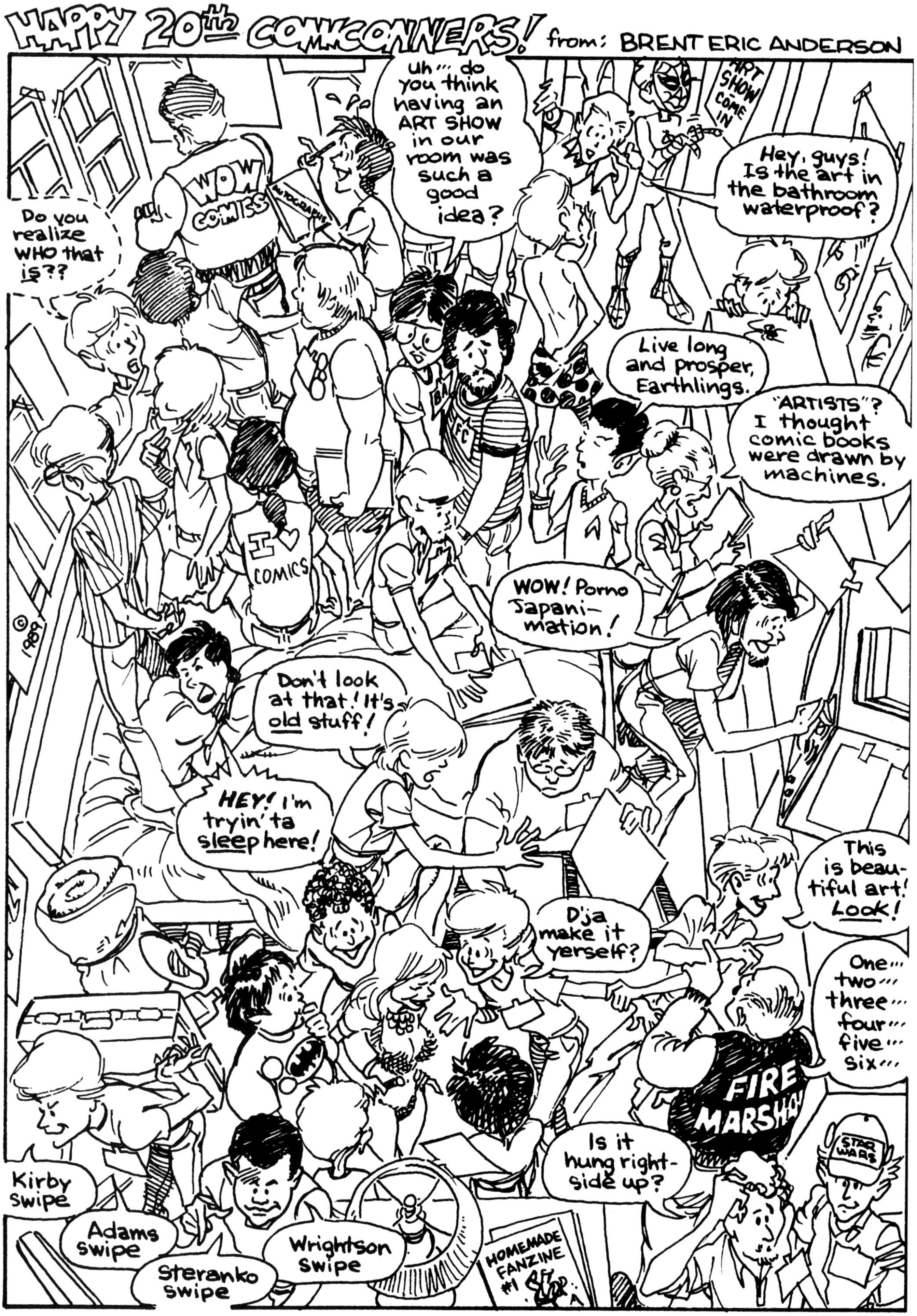
HAPPY 20th COMICONNERS! from: BRENT ERIC ANDERSON
WOW COMICS
AUTOGRAPHS
Uh… do you think having an ART SHOW in our room was such a good idea?
ART SHOW COME IN
Hey, guys! Is the art in the bathroom waterproof?
Do you realize WHO that is??
Live long and prosper, Earthlings.
"ARTISTS"? I thought comic books were drawn by machines.
I ♥ COMICS
WOW! Porno Japani-mation!
Don't look at that! It's old stuff!
HEY! I'm tryin' ta sleep here!
D'ja make it yerself?
This is beau-tiful art! Look!
One… two… three… four… five… six…
FIRE MARSHALL
Is it hung right-side up?
STAR WARS
Kirby swipe
Adams swipe
Steranko swipe
Wrightson swipe
HOMEMADE FANZINE #1

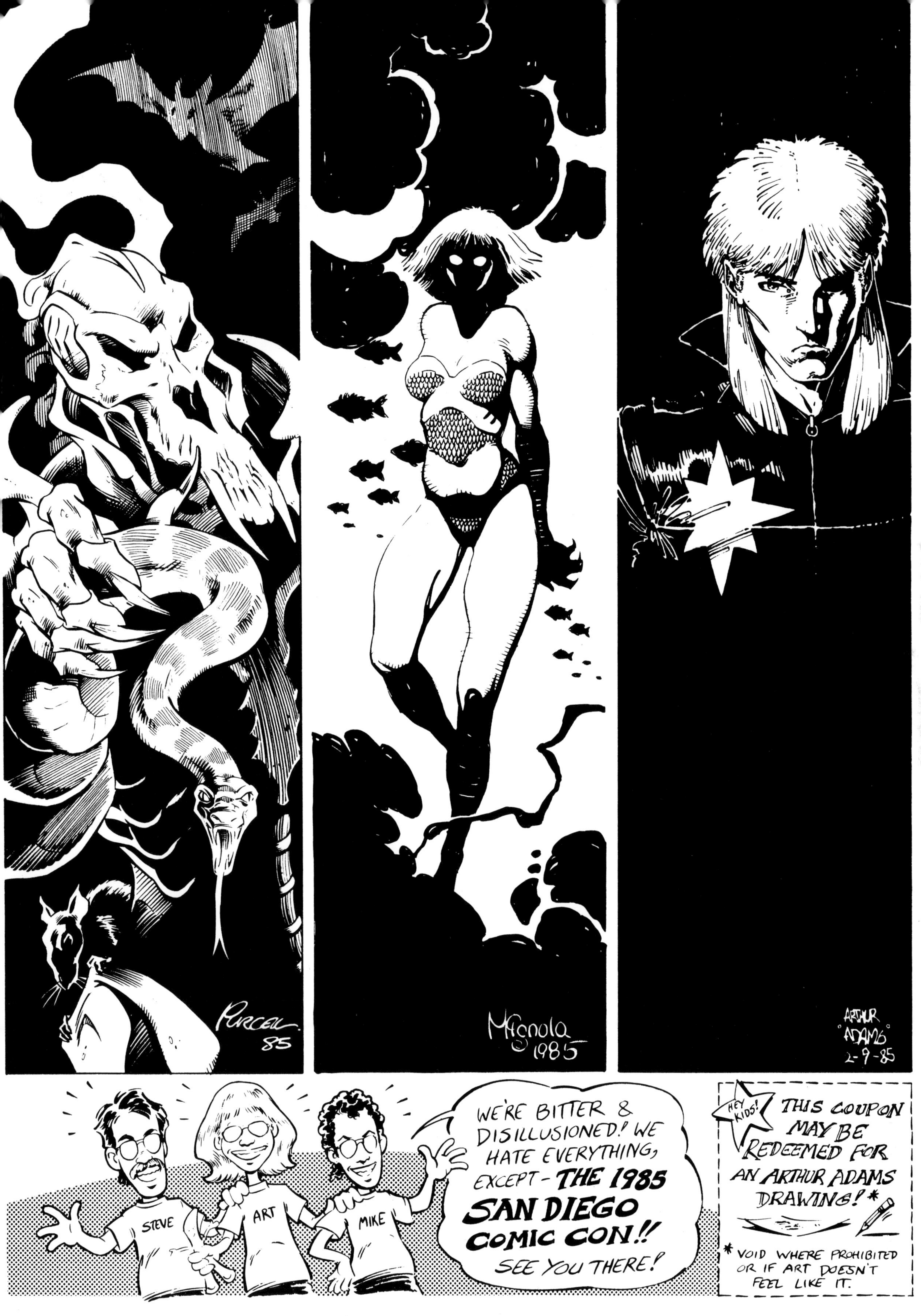
PURCELL 85
MIGNOLA © 1985
ARTHUR ADAMS 2-9-85
STEVE
ART
MIKE
WE'RE BITTER & DISILLUSIONED! WE HATE EVERYTHING, EXCEPT - THE 1985 SAN DIEGO COMIC CON!! SEE YOU THERE!
HEY KIDS!
THIS COUPON MAY BE REDEEMED FOR AN ARTHUR ADAMS DRAWING! *
* VOID WHERE PROHIBITED OR IF ART DOESN'T FEEL LIKE IT.

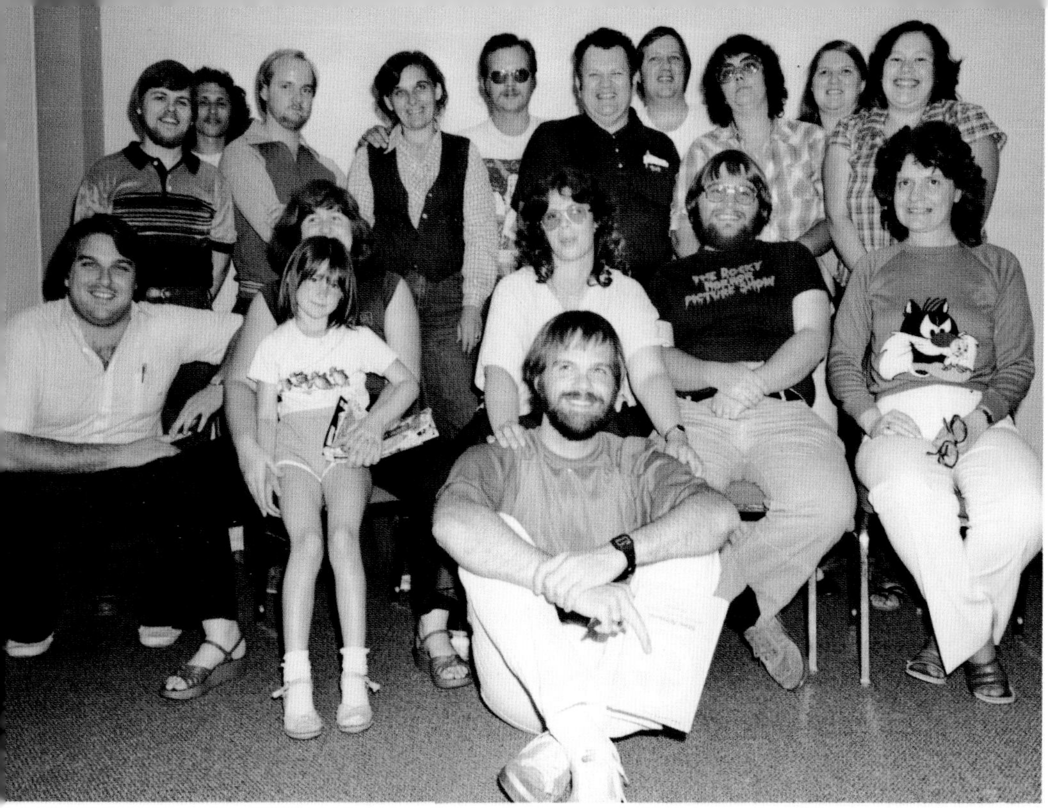

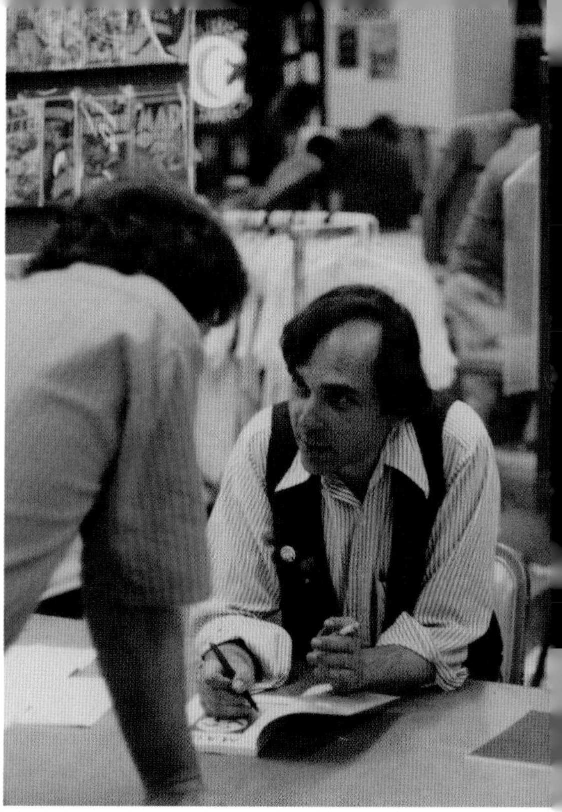

ABOVE LEFT: Members of the Comic-Con Committee in 1983: (back row, from left) Barry Short, Mike Amron, Jerry Williams, Kathy Davis, Dave Davis, Gene Henderson, (unidentified), Maeheah Alzmann, Mikee Reynante, and Vicky Kelso; (middle row, from left) Mark Stadler, Fae Desmond with daughter Maija, Janice Guy, Richard Butner, and Mary Henderson; (front) Larry Geeck **ABOVE RIGHT:** *Maus* creator Art Spiegelman in 1987 **RIGHT:** science fiction author Poul Anderson with his 1986 Inkpot Award **BELOW LEFT:** Alan Moore (with Jack Kirby, right) making his only U.S. convention appearance at Comic-Con in 1985 **BELOW RIGHT:** *The Hitchhiker's Guide to the Galaxy*'s Douglas Adams, a special guest at Comic-Con in 1983 **OPPOSITE, TOP TO BOTTOM:** Dave Stevens's stunning Sheena art for the 1981 program book was also used as the first official Comic-Con T-shirt; Bob Chapman (left) and Dave Stevens (right) at Comic-Con in 1982; Stevens's program book contribution for 1978 **OVERLEAF:** No one got into creating art for the Souvenir Books more than Scott Shaw!, one of the founding members of Comic-Con. Here's his 1989 contribution, celebrating twenty years of Comic-Cons.

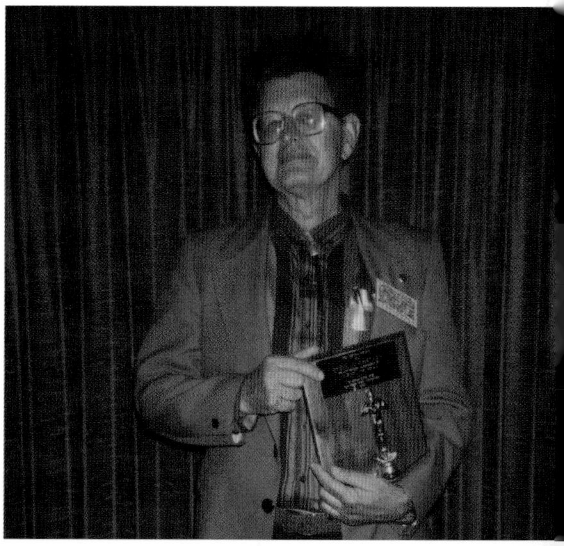

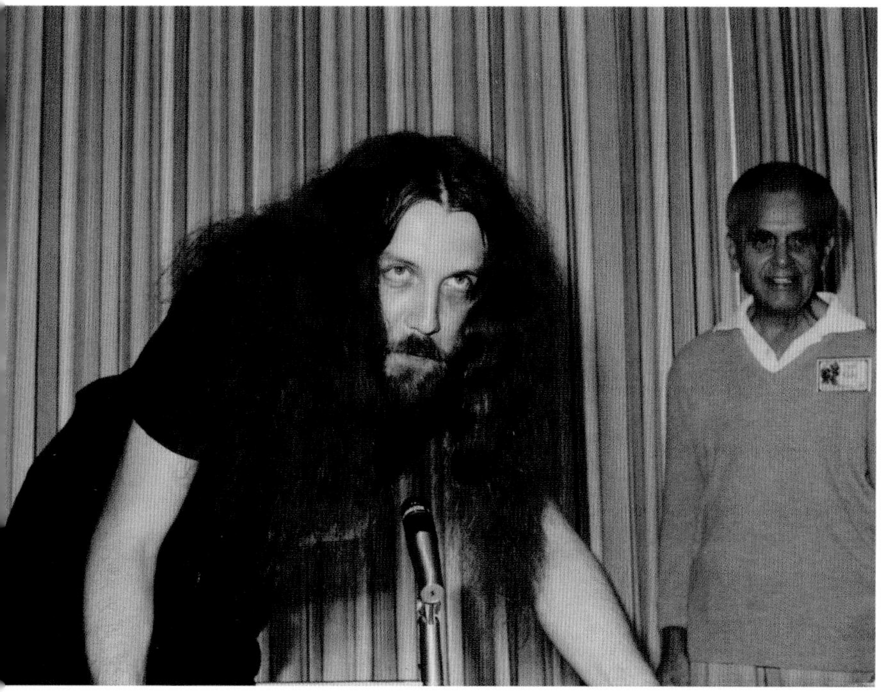

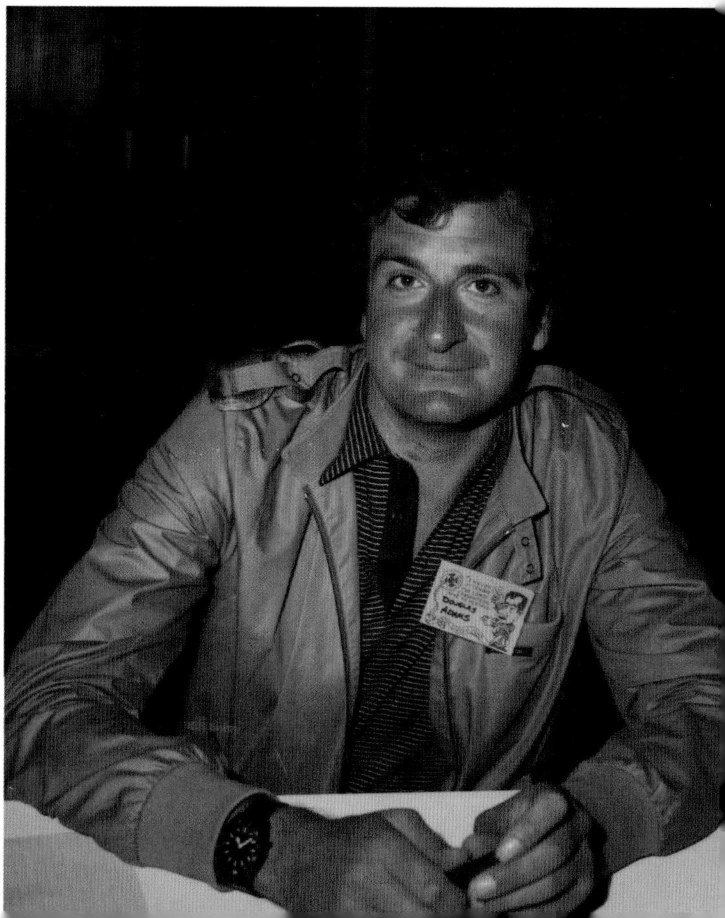

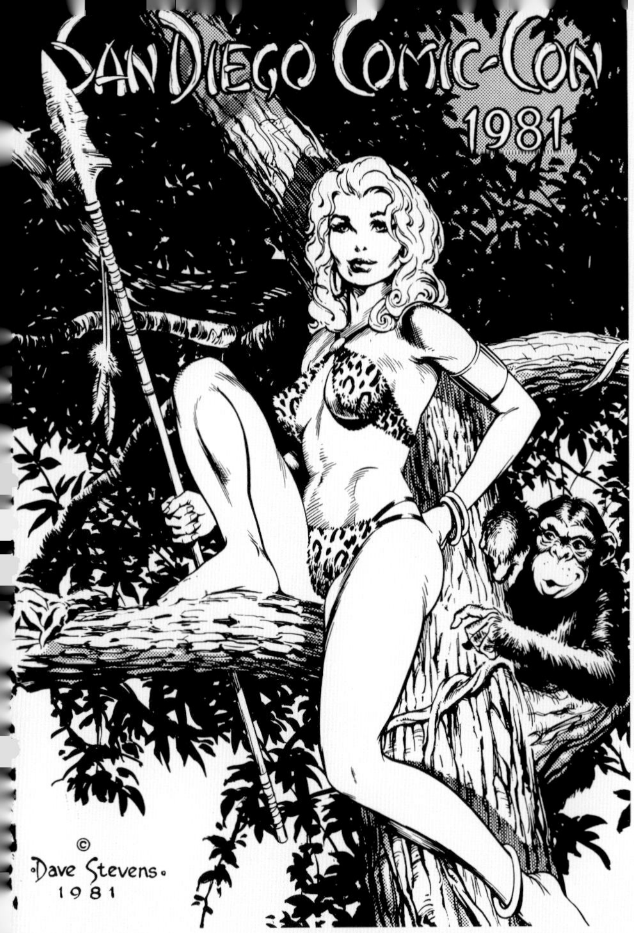
San Diego Comic-Con
1981
©
Dave Stevens
1981

DAVE STEVENS (1955–2008)

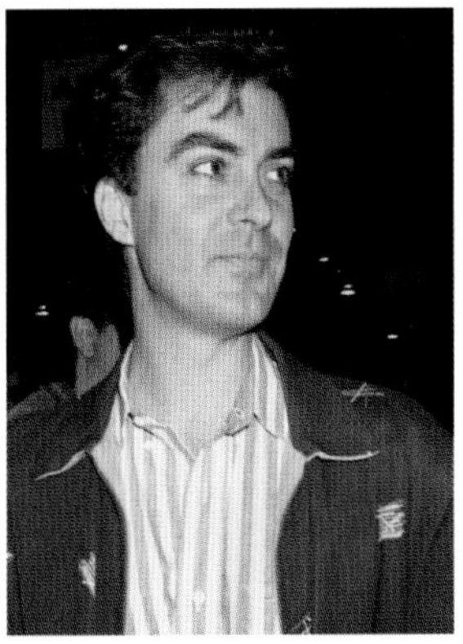

THERE ARE TWO THINGS everyone agrees on about Dave Stevens, the creator of *The Rocketeer*: (1) He was one of the most talented comic artists ever to pick up a pencil, and (2) he was one of the nicest guys they've ever met.

Dave was born in 1955 in Lynwood, California, and grew up in Portland, Oregon; as a teenager he moved with his family to the San Diego area. He was a student at San Diego City College when he went to his first Comic-Con back in the early 1970s. It wasn't long before he became more involved, running the Art Show and providing cover art (including depictions of Doc Savage and Nick Fury) and spot illustrations for the Progress Reports.

Dave made lots of permanent friends in his years with Comic-Con. Then vice president Richard Butner drove Stevens to his first comics job interview. Dave got the job, assisting Russ Manning on the *Tarzan* syndicated comic strip. When Comic-Con helped institute the Russ Manning Most Promising Newcomer Award in 1982 after Manning's death, Dave appropriately was the first recipient.

By the late 1970s Stevens had moved to Los Angeles, working in animation and later sharing a studio with artists Richard Hescox and William Stout (someone else he had originally met at Comic-Con). It was through Stout that the pulp-loving Stevens got a big assignment that was right up his alley: storyboarding sequences for Steven Spielberg's *Raiders of the Lost Ark*. Artistic opportunities continued when, shortly thereafter, Dave did the storyboards for Michael Jackson's classic "Thriller" video. But Dave was working on his own projects, too, and in 1982 one of them burst onto the comics scene like it was jet propelled.

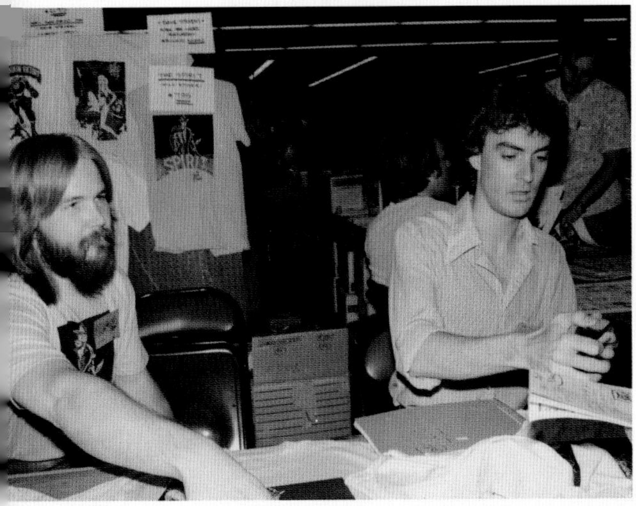

It was. *The Rocketeer* was a comic book series that forever placed Dave firmly in the ranks of comics superstars. It was another Comic-Con pal, David Scroggy (who handled programming at the event in the late 1970s), who asked Stevens to create a back-up feature for *Starslayer*, which Scroggy was editing for Pacific Comics. The retro hero combined all the things Stevens loved: old movie serials, airplanes, jalopies, diners, and, of course, beautiful women. Dave modeled his female lead after pinup legend Bettie Page, causing a whole new generation of fans to discover her. Dave's depiction of the 1950s pinup queen in *The Rocketeer* helped bring Bettie back into the public eye. He later became friends with her and helped her receive her rightful share of royalties from products that utilized her image.

Bob Chapman, who later started Graphitti Designs (producers of the official Comic-Con T-shirts since 1981), owes the existence of his company to Dave. While Bob was producing the 1981 Sheena, Queen of the Jungle Comic-Con T-shirt, which featured Dave's artwork, a friendship and collaboration developed. It led to the production of *The Rocketeer* limited-edition prints (ofttimes featuring Bettie Page), numerous screen-printed T-shirts, cloisonné pins, and statues, as well as a limited-edition, deluxe hardcover collection of the first five *Rocketeer* comics episodes in 1985. The items proved to be so popular that Graphitti Designs went on to become one of the industry's leading suppliers of T-shirts, prints, and collectible items.

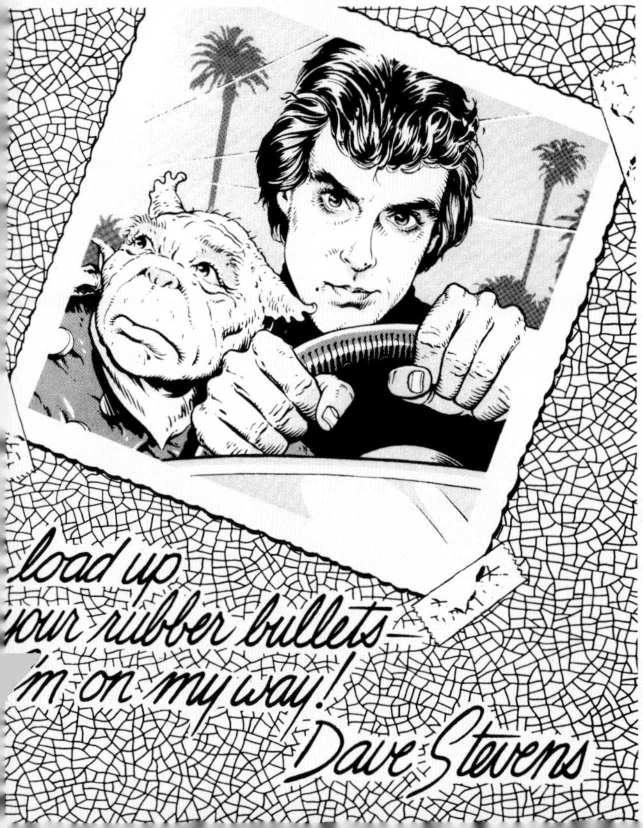
load up
our rubber bullets—
m on my way!
Dave Stevens

In the late 1980s, *The Rocketeer* was picked up by Disney as a feature film. Dave was heavily involved with the production of the movie, which starred Bill Campbell in the title role, and was given executive producer and creator credits when the film was released in 1991. In April of that same year, *Entertainment Weekly* ran a full-page feature on Dave, spotlighting him as a rising star.

Dave was a fixture at Comic-Con for more than thirty-five years. For many years he could be found at his Bulldog Studios booth, next to the booths of pals Bill Stout, Jim Silke, and John Koukoutsakis. Dave spent the last ten years of his life battling a rare form of leukemia. He died on March 10, 2008. Dave Stevens was the archetypal fan who went on to become a hugely successful professional. He was the poster child for the aspiring artist who made good, was able to do what he loved for a living, and refined his talents to become an artist's artist, all the while influencing the generation who followed.

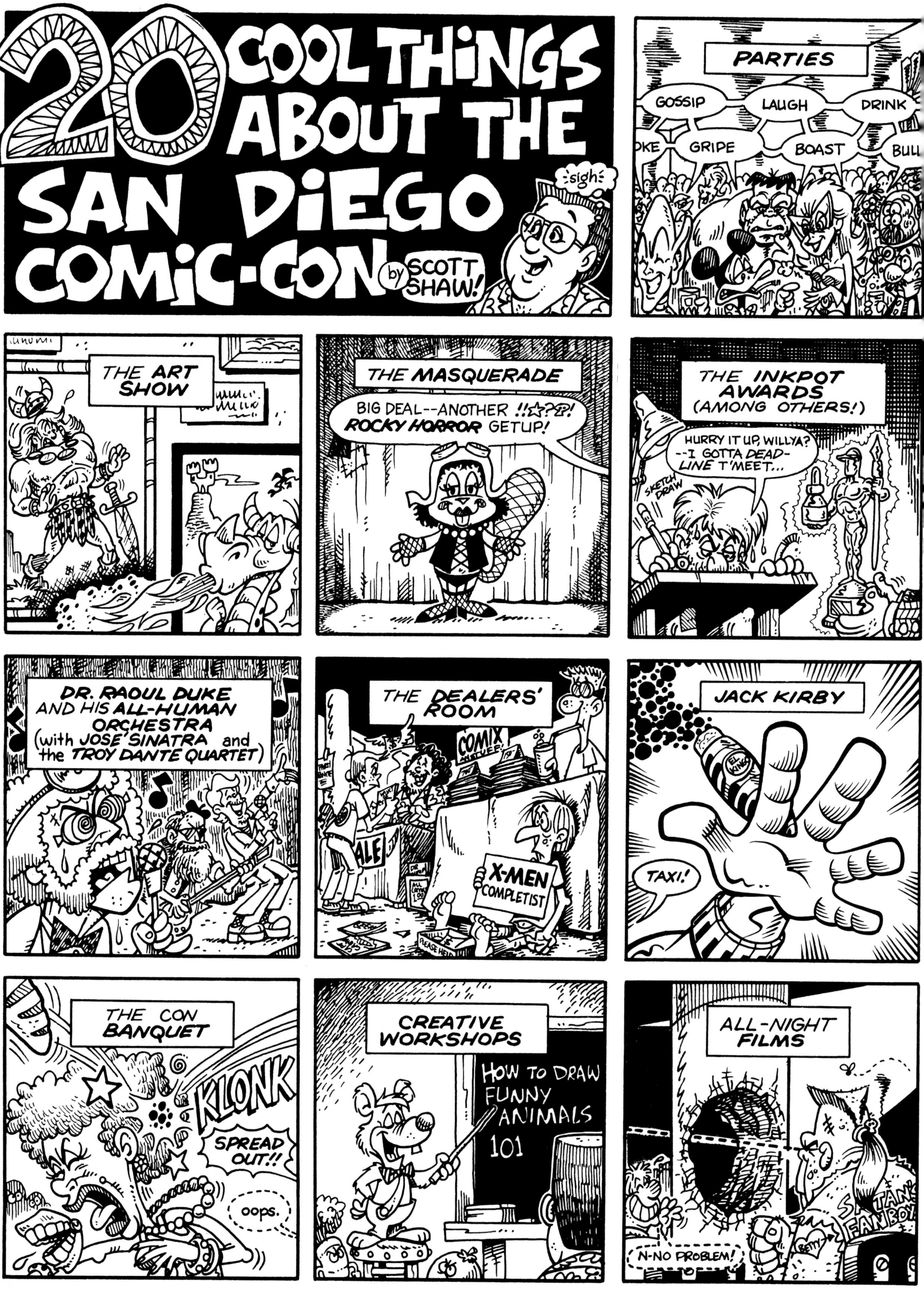
20 COOL THINGS ABOUT THE SAN DIEGO COMIC-CON
by SCOTT SHAW!
sigh
PARTIES
GOSSIP
LAUGH
DRINK
GRIPE
BOAST
THE ART SHOW
THE MASQUERADE
BIG DEAL--ANOTHER !!☆?!?! ROCKY HORROR GETUP!
THE INKPOT AWARDS (AMONG OTHERS!)
HURRY IT UP, WILLYA? --I GOTTA DEAD-LINE T'MEET...
SKETCH DRAW
DR. RAOUL DUKE AND HIS ALL-HUMAN ORCHESTRA (with JOSE SINATRA and the TROY DANTE QUARTET)
THE DEALERS' ROOM
COMIX
X-MEN COMPLETIST
JACK KIRBY
TAXI!
THE CON BANQUET
KLONK
SPREAD OUT!!
oops.
CREATIVE WORKSHOPS
HOW TO DRAW FUNNY ANIMALS 101
ALL-NIGHT FILMS
FANBOY
N-NO PROBLEM!

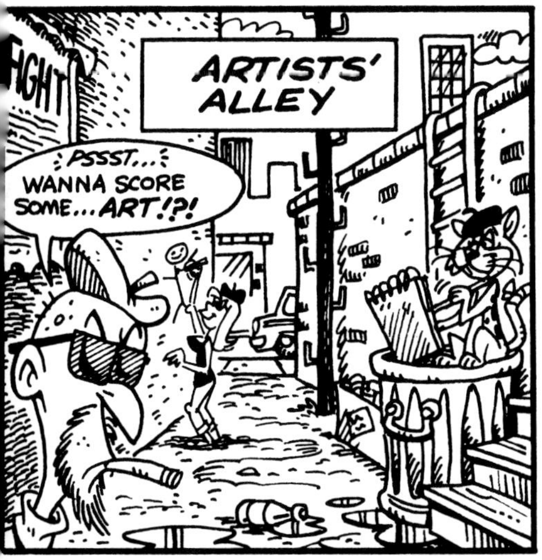
ARTISTS' ALLEY
PSSST... WANNA SCORE SOME... ART!?!

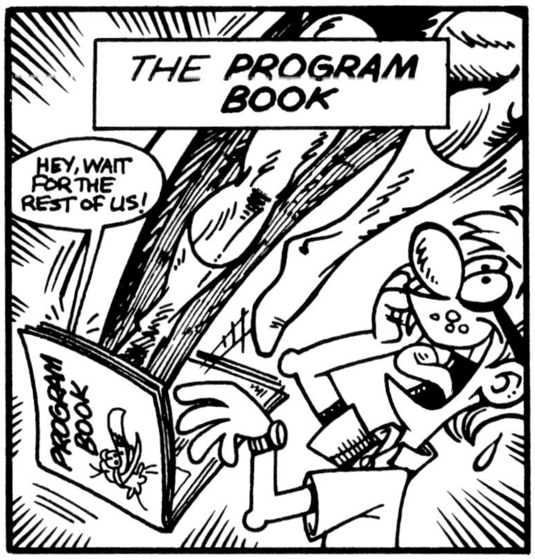
THE PROGRAM BOOK
HEY, WAIT FOR THE REST OF US!
PROGRAM BOOK

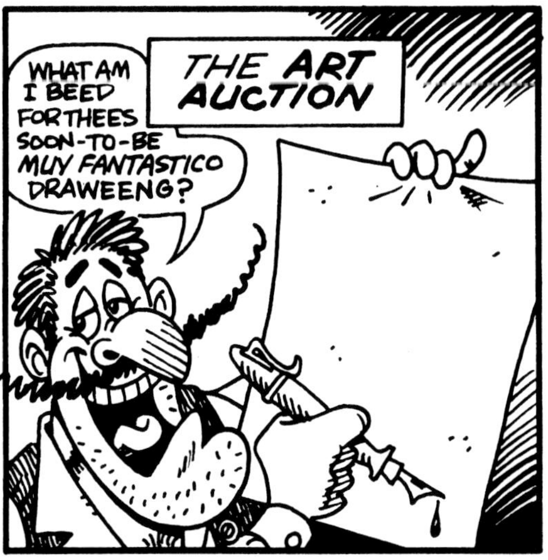
THE ART AUCTION
WHAT AM I BEED FOR THEES SOON-TO-BE MUY FANTASTICO DRAWEENG?

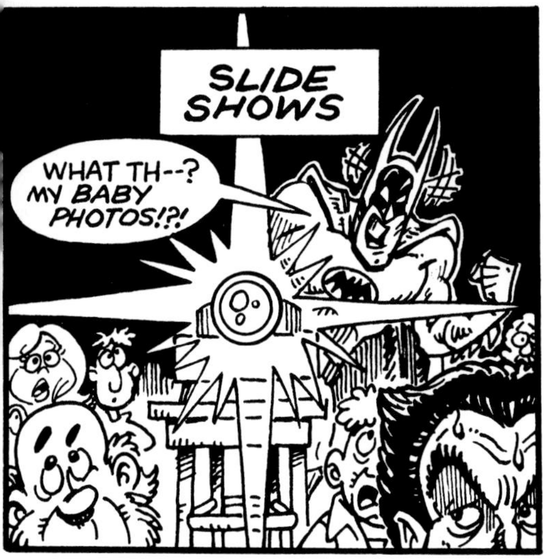
SLIDE SHOWS
WHAT TH--? MY BABY PHOTOS!?!

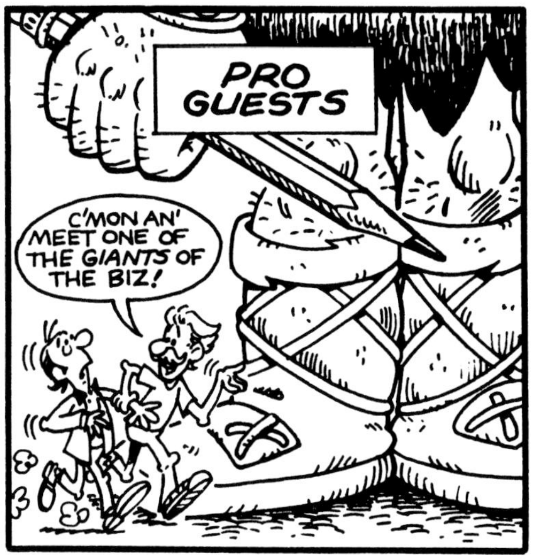
PRO GUESTS
C'MON AN' MEET ONE OF THE GIANTS OF THE BIZ!

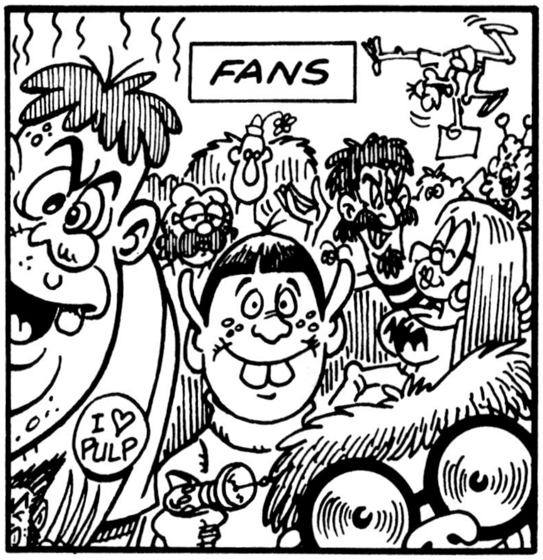
FANS
I ♥ PULP

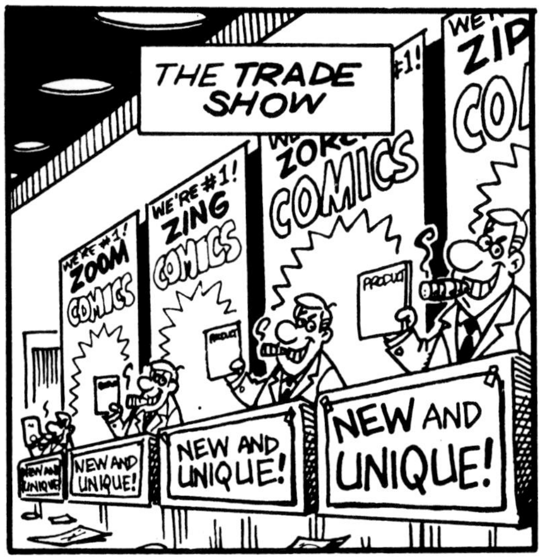
THE TRADE SHOW
WE'RE #1! ZOOM COMICS
WE'RE #1! ZING COMICS
ZORK COMICS
NEW AND UNIQUE!
NEW AND UNIQUE!
NEW AND UNIQUE!

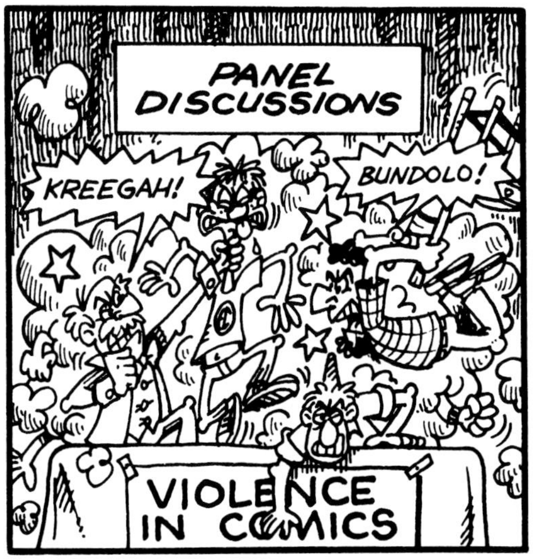
PANEL DISCUSSIONS
KREEGAH!
BUNDOLO!
VIOLENCE IN COMICS

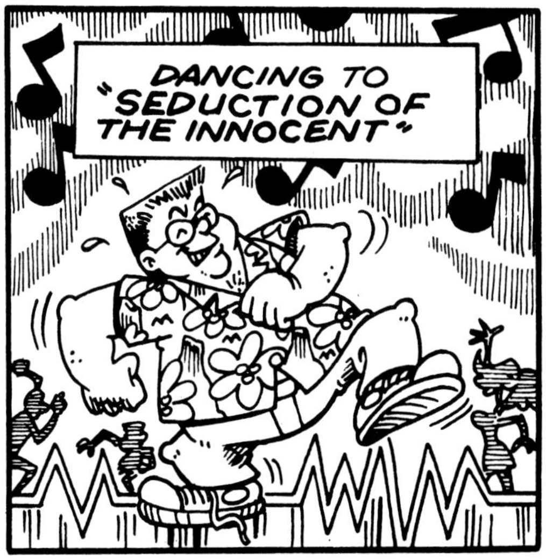
DANCING TO "SEDUCTION OF THE INNOCENT"

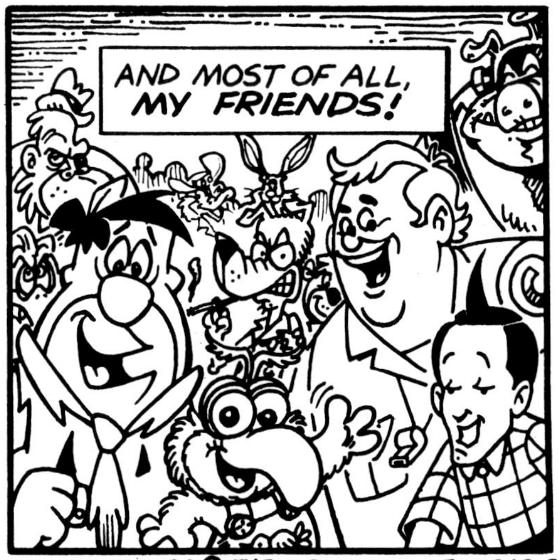
AND MOST OF ALL, MY FRIENDS!

...INCLUDING...

...JACKIE ESTRADA... BOB CLAMPETT... JOHN POUND... RON TURNER... KEN KRUEGER... DAVE STEVENS... BILZO RICHARDSON ... BUD PLANT ... AL WILLIAMSON... SERGIO ARAGONÉS... HARLAN ELLISON... RICHARD BUTNER... JIM CORNELIUS... RICK GEARY... STAN SAKAI... DAVE THORNE... DON DOUGHERTY... KRIS ADAMS... TED STURGEON... B. KLIBAN... PAT CULLITON... RAY BRADBURY... TERRY STROUD... JAN TONNESEN... TONY RAIOLA... ARN SABA... ROGER FREEDMAN... GREG BEAR... BOB FOSTER... DAVID T. ALEXANDER... MARK EVANIER... JON HARZ... ALISON BUCKLES... JACK DICKENS... DON CHRISTENSEN... DAVID SCROGGY... FAY DESMOND... JIM ENGEL... DAVE GIBSON... RAY ZONE... ROBT. WILLIAMS... *AN' LOTS MORE!!*

THANKS FOR 20 GREAT YEARS--!! SCOTT SHAW!

SERGIO ARAGONÉS

ASK ANYONE who's been attending Comic-Con for any length of time "Who's the most beloved professional at the show?" and nine times out of ten, the answer will be Sergio Aragonés.

Sergio has been a regular part of Comic-Con since 1976, when he was not only a special guest but also drew the cover of the Souvenir Book. At that time the cartoonist was working primarily for *MAD* magazine, drawing the marginal cartoons and occasional features as he had been doing since 1963. But he was also known to comics fans for co-creating the western series *Bat Lash* for DC Comics in the late 1960s and contributing to DC's humor title *Plop!* in the early 1970s.

In the El Cortez Hotel days of Comic-Con, the gregarious and debonair artist entertained attendees and his fellow pros with stories of being a professional clown in Mexico, acting in the Redd Foxx movie *Norman, Is That You?* (he played a hotel desk clerk), and his experiences on television's *Laugh-In*, as well as tales of world travel with *MAD* publisher Bill Gaines and the rest of the *MAD* crew.

With the rise of the direct market in the comic book industry in the 1980s, Sergio was at the forefront of creator-owned work with his original title *Groo the Wanderer*, published by local San Diego company Pacific Comics. When Pacific closed their doors, Sergio (along with co-plotter/writer Mark Evanier) took the book to Eclipse and then to Marvel's Epic imprint, where it ran for 120 issues. After a brief period with Image, *Groo* finally found a home in recent years at Dark Horse Comics, making it one of the longest-running creator-owned titles.

Over the years Sergio has always been happy to do whatever Comic-Con asks of him, whether MC'ing the Masquerade (in 1984), drawing caricatures of recipients at the Inkpot banquets (in the early 1980s), creating original pieces for the Art Auction, or providing artwork for things like the volunteer T-shirts and the 2007 Events Guide cover. For more than a decade he has presented the Hall of Fame category at the Will Eisner Comic Industry Awards. A Hall of Fame winner himself, he is also the proud owner of six other Eisner Awards, an Inkpot Award (1976), and a Bob Clampett Humanitarian Award (1990).

Sergio continues to contribute to every issue of *MAD*, and his work has been collected in dozens of books that are popular around the world. Most recently he co-wrote (with Evanier) the ongoing comic book series *Will Eisner's The Spirit* for DC Comics and created the cover for this book.

Sergio can always be found in the Exhibit Hall at Comic-Con, next to longtime pal Scott Shaw! He can also be found at the annual "Quick Draw" panel, where Evanier tries to stump Sergio, Shaw!, and a guest cartoonist with challenging topics. Not only a perennial guest at Comic-Con, Sergio Aragonés is also a yearly guest at WonderCon in San Francisco (Comic-Con's sister event).

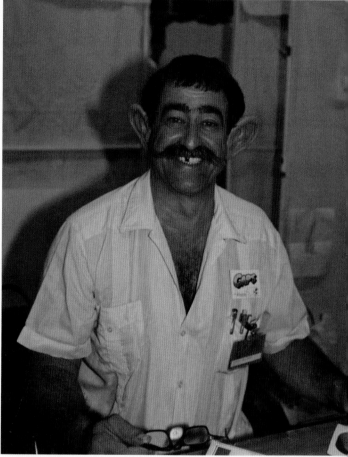

> " Osuma Tezuka, the most popular cartoonist in Japan and the most prolific in the world. "
>
> —SERGIO ARAGONÉS
> CARTOONIST, *MAD* MAGAZINE
> (On the most memorable person he's met at Comic-Con)

CLOCKWISE FROM TOP LEFT: Sergio Aragonés (right) with Roy Thomas (left) in 1980; Sergio meeting his famous creation *Groo the Wanderer* in the flesh—sort of—in 1989; Sergio doing his best to look like his "employer," Alfred E. Neuman of *MAD* magazine **OPPOSITE:** Sergio's twentieth-anniversary tribute to Comic-Con in 1989

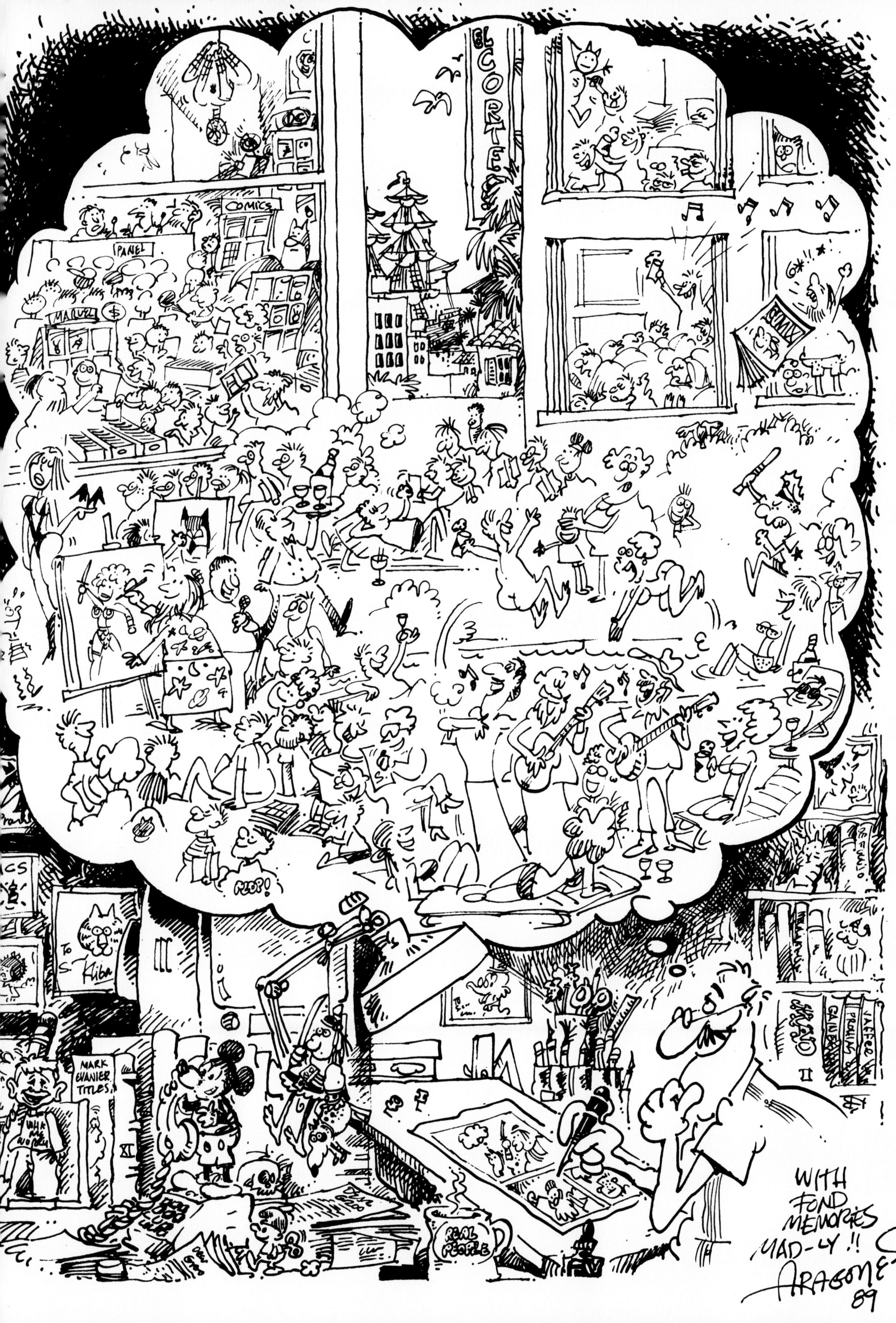
EL CORTES
COMICS
PANEL
PLOP!
MARK EVANIER TITLES
REAL PEOPLE
WITH FOND MEMORIES MAD-LY !!
ARAGONÉS 89

RICK GEARY

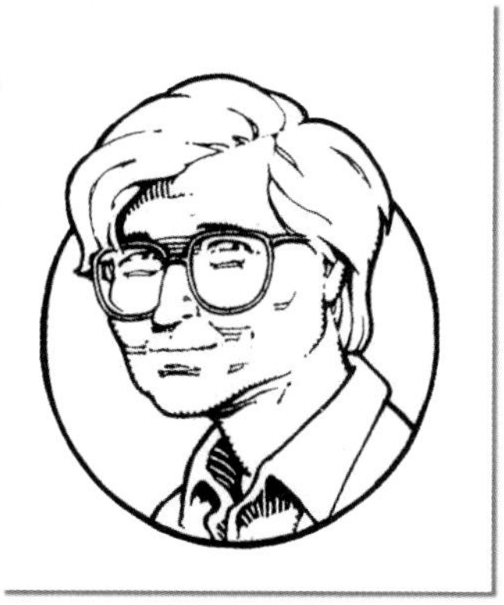

IF COMIC-CON has a resident artist, it would have to be cartoonist and graphic novelist Rick Geary, who has designed and illustrated many key art pieces for the show over the years.

Geary, a contributor to such magazines as *Heavy Metal* and *National Lampoon*, moved to San Diego from Kansas City in the late 1970s and quickly established himself as one of the area's top cartoonists.

Over the last three decades, Geary's signature quirky style has graced a variety of remarkable works, from children's books to *Classics Illustrated* adaptations to the revived *Gumby*. He is perhaps best known for his *Treasury of Victorian Murder* series of graphic novels for NBM, which examine the underpinnings of such historical incidents as the assassination of Abraham Lincoln, the Lizzie Borden case, and the murders of Jack the Ripper. His most recent book, *The Lindbergh Child*, is the first in a new series called *A Treasury of XXth Century Murder*. Geary has also garnered critical acclaim for his graphic biography *J. Edgar Hoover*.

For Comic-Con, Geary designed the lively toucan illustration that was the event's first real logo and illustrated mascot, and he adapted the bird into many variations over the years. He also created the "Expo Boy" as a graphic element for Comic-Con's industry trade show, the Comic Book Expo. In addition, Geary drew the cover for the 1983 Souvenir Book as well as regular yearly contributions for that publication, and has provided illustrations for postcards and other material for Comic-Con. Most recently, he redesigned the convention's signature Inkpot Award, making a new character out of a familiar artist's tool, a bottle of ink.

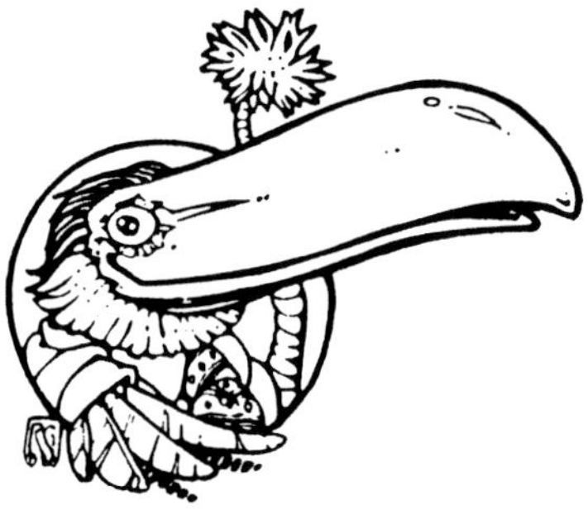

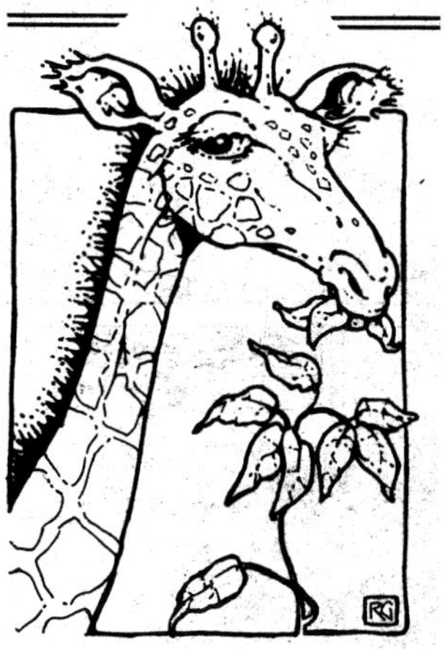

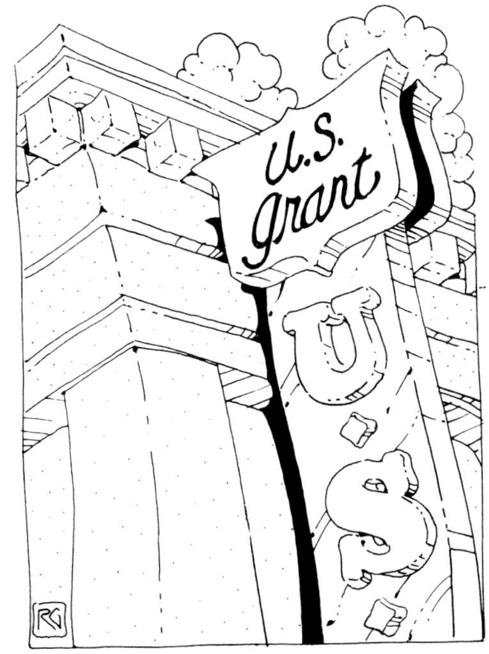
U.S. Grant

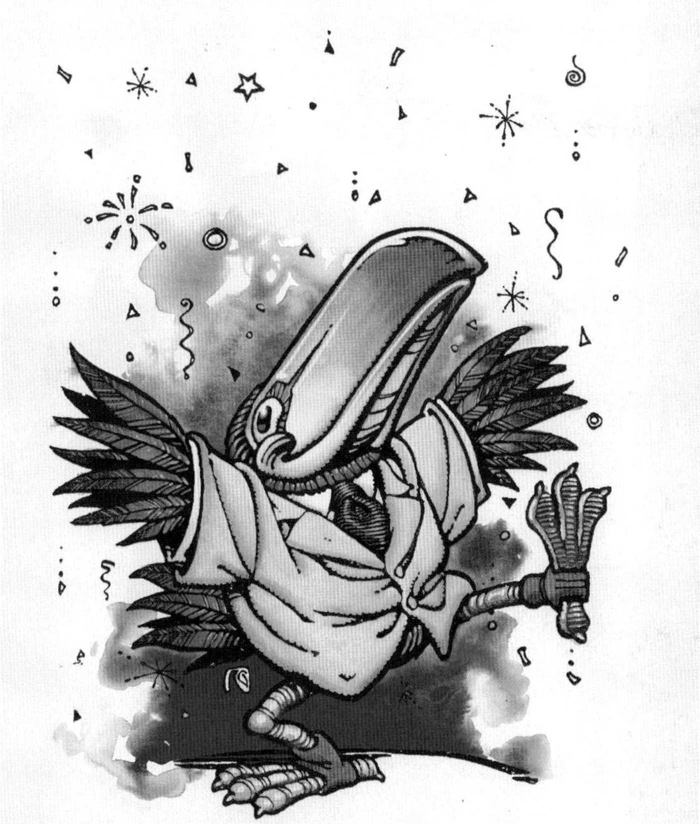

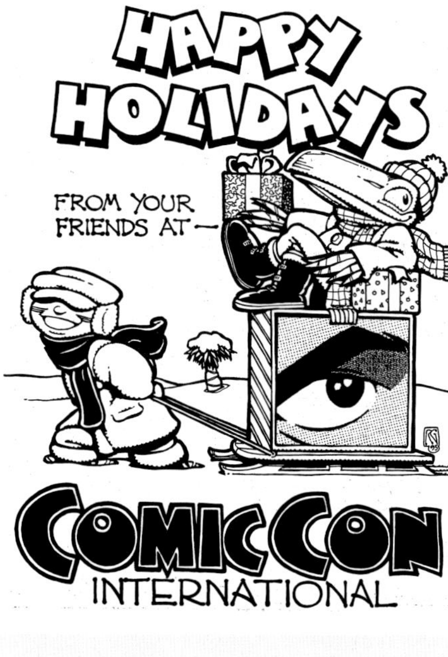
HAPPY HOLIDAYS
FROM YOUR FRIENDS AT—
COMIC CON
INTERNATIONAL

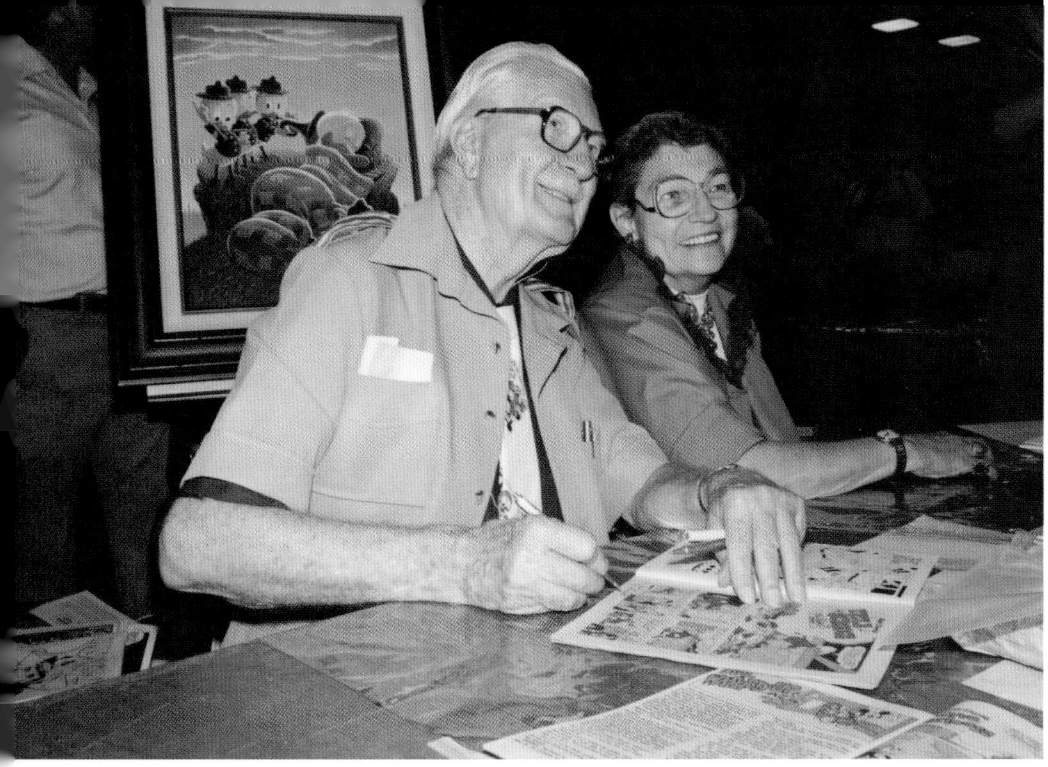

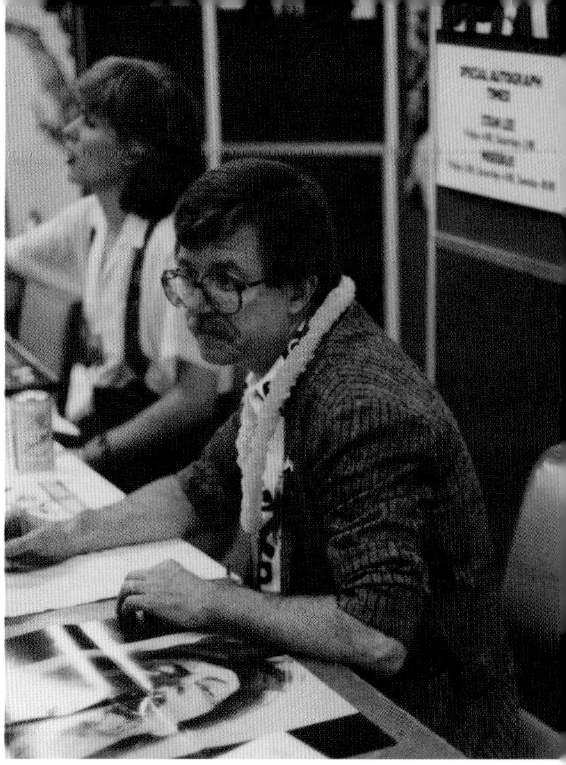

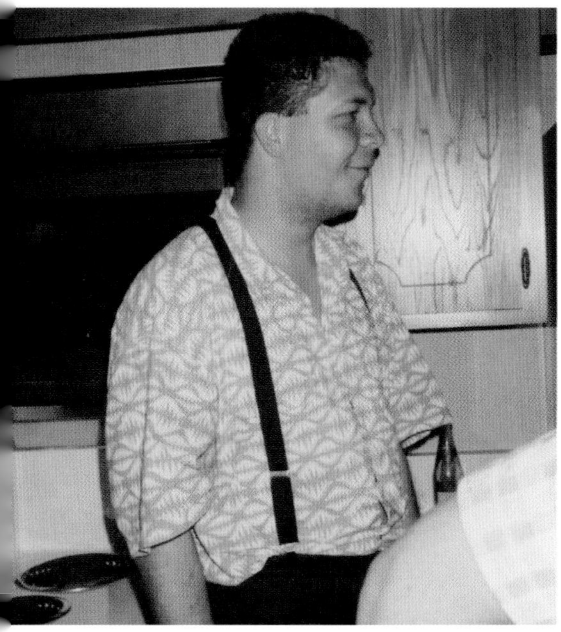

OPPOSITE, CLOCKWISE FROM TOP LEFT: Rick Geary's self-portrait; the Comic-Con toucan from 1992; two early pieces by Geary illustrating an article about what to do in San Diego in 1979; Geary's late-1990s Comic-Con Christmas card; a 1995 hand-painted drawing of the toucan that has graced many Comic-Con publications and announcements

CLOCKWISE FROM TOP LEFT: Legendary Disney comics writer/artist Carl Barks (*Donald Duck*, *Uncle Scrooge*) and his wife, Garé, at Comic-Con in 1980; Carol Kalish (left) and Archie Goodwin (right) at the Marvel booth in 1987; artist/animator Chuck Jones at the convention in 1980; Superman co-creators Jerry Siegel (left) and Joe Shuster (right) in 1983; Mike Mignola in 1988; a young Kyle Baker at an after-hours party in 1988

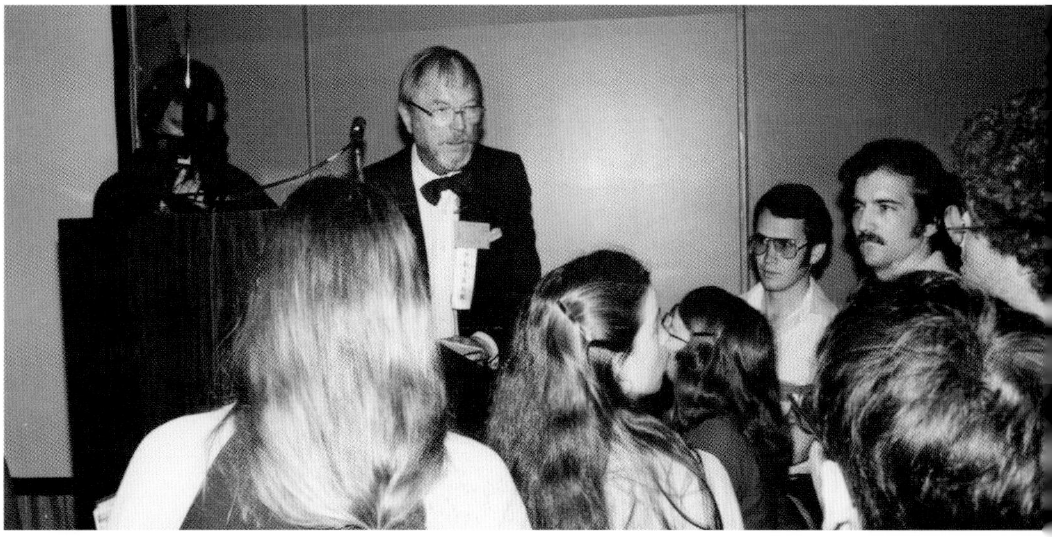

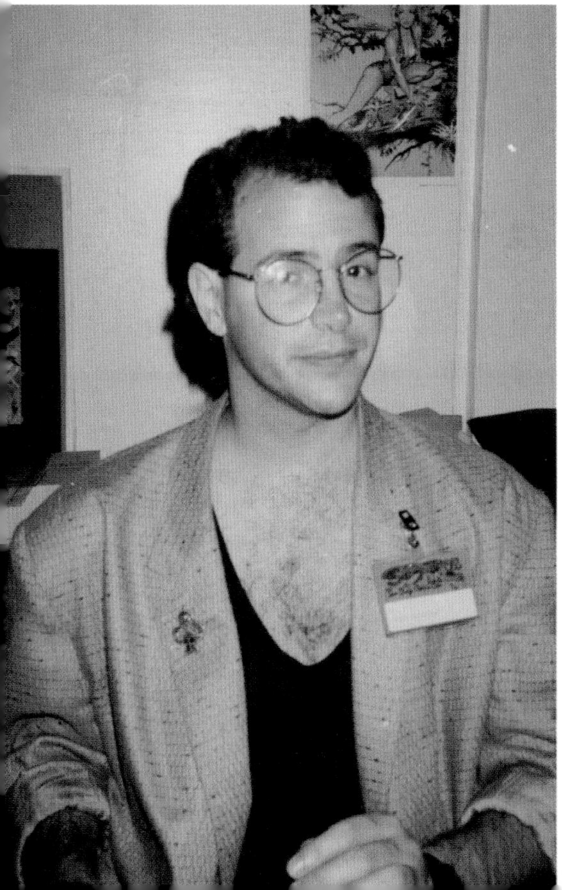

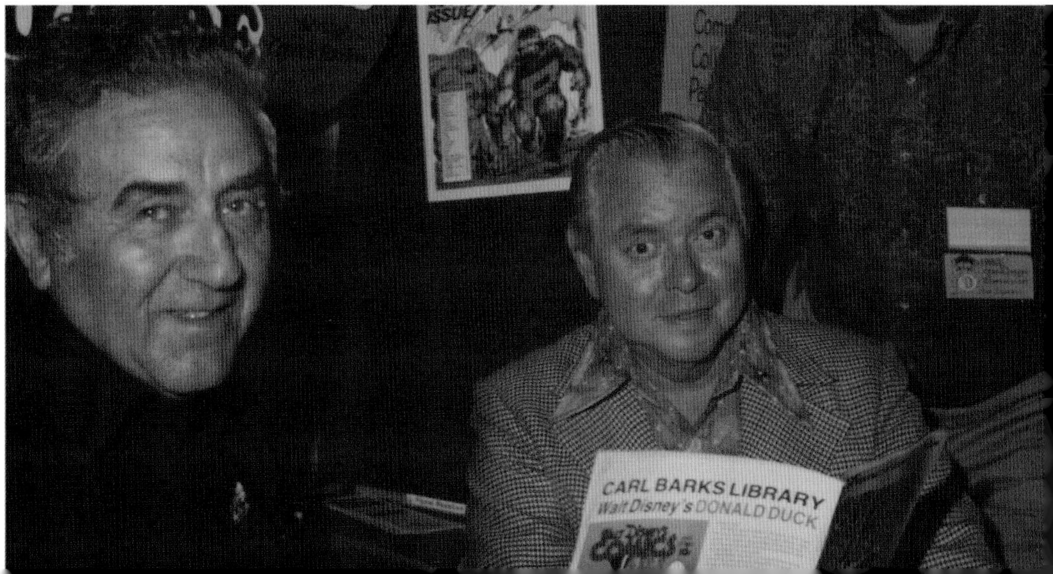
CARL BARKS LIBRARY
Walt Disney's DONALD DUCK

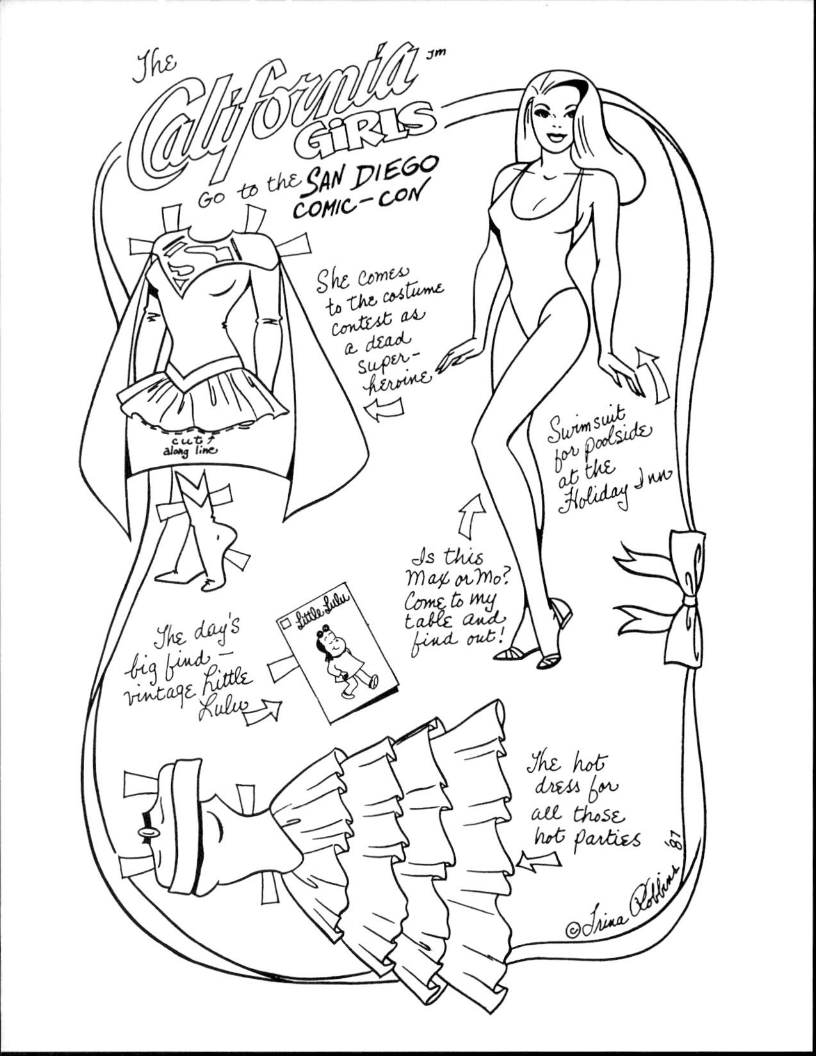
The California Girls TM
Go to the SAN DIEGO COMIC-CON
She comes to the costume contest as a dead super-heroine
cut along line
Swimsuit for poolside at the Holiday Inn
Is this Max or Mo? Come to my table and find out!
The day's big find — vintage Little Lulu
Little Lulu
The hot dress for all those hot parties
©Trina Robbins '87
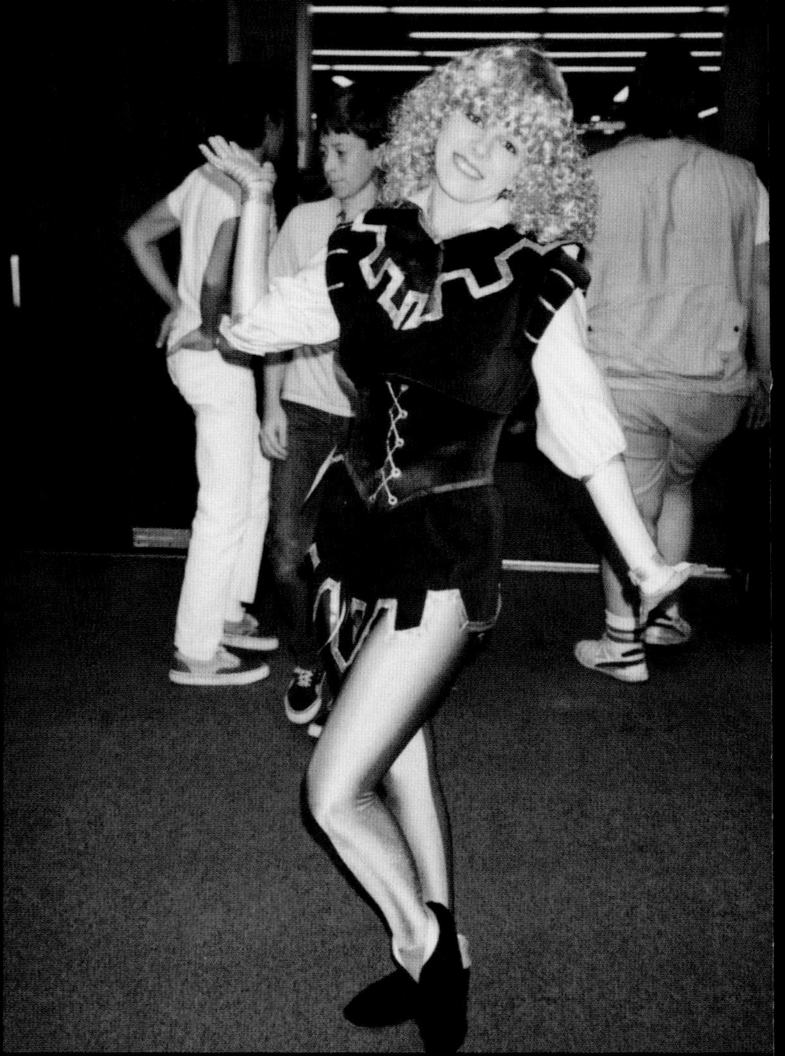

CLOCKWISE FROM TOP LEFT: Trina Robbins's *California Girls* paper dolls for the 1987 Souvenir Book; future VP of events Robin (Doig) Donlan in a 1987 Masquerade costume she made; legendary comics creators Murphy Anderson (left) and Jerry Siegel (right) at Comic-Con in 1983; writer/editors Marv Wolfman (left) and Len Wein (center) with actor/musician Bill Mumy (right) at the show in 1985; **OPPOSITE:** A DC Comics ad welcoming everyone to the 1989 Comic-Con, drawn by Denys Cowan

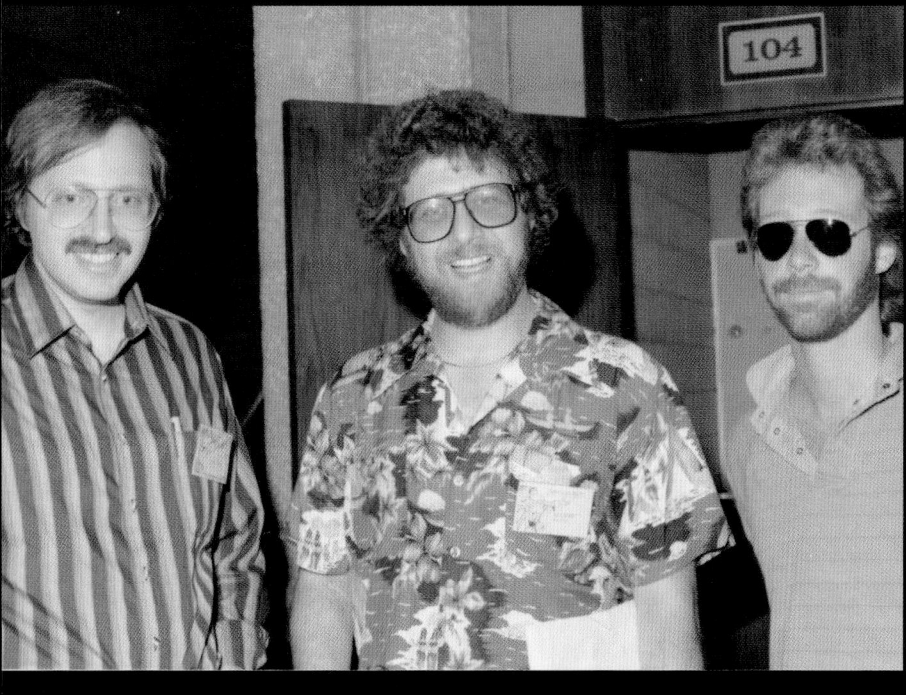
104
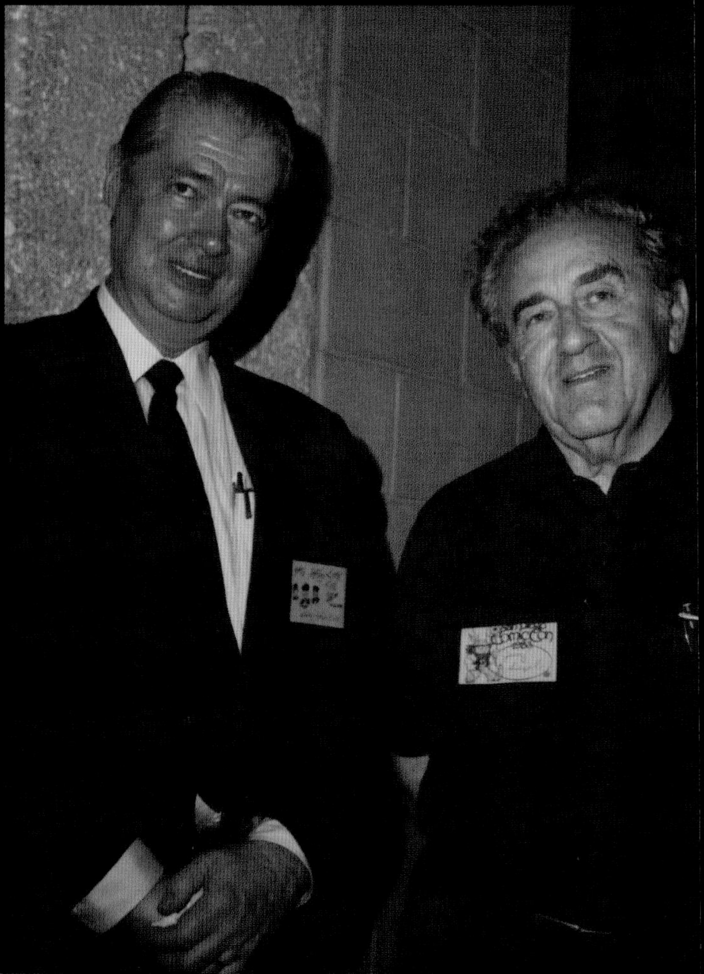

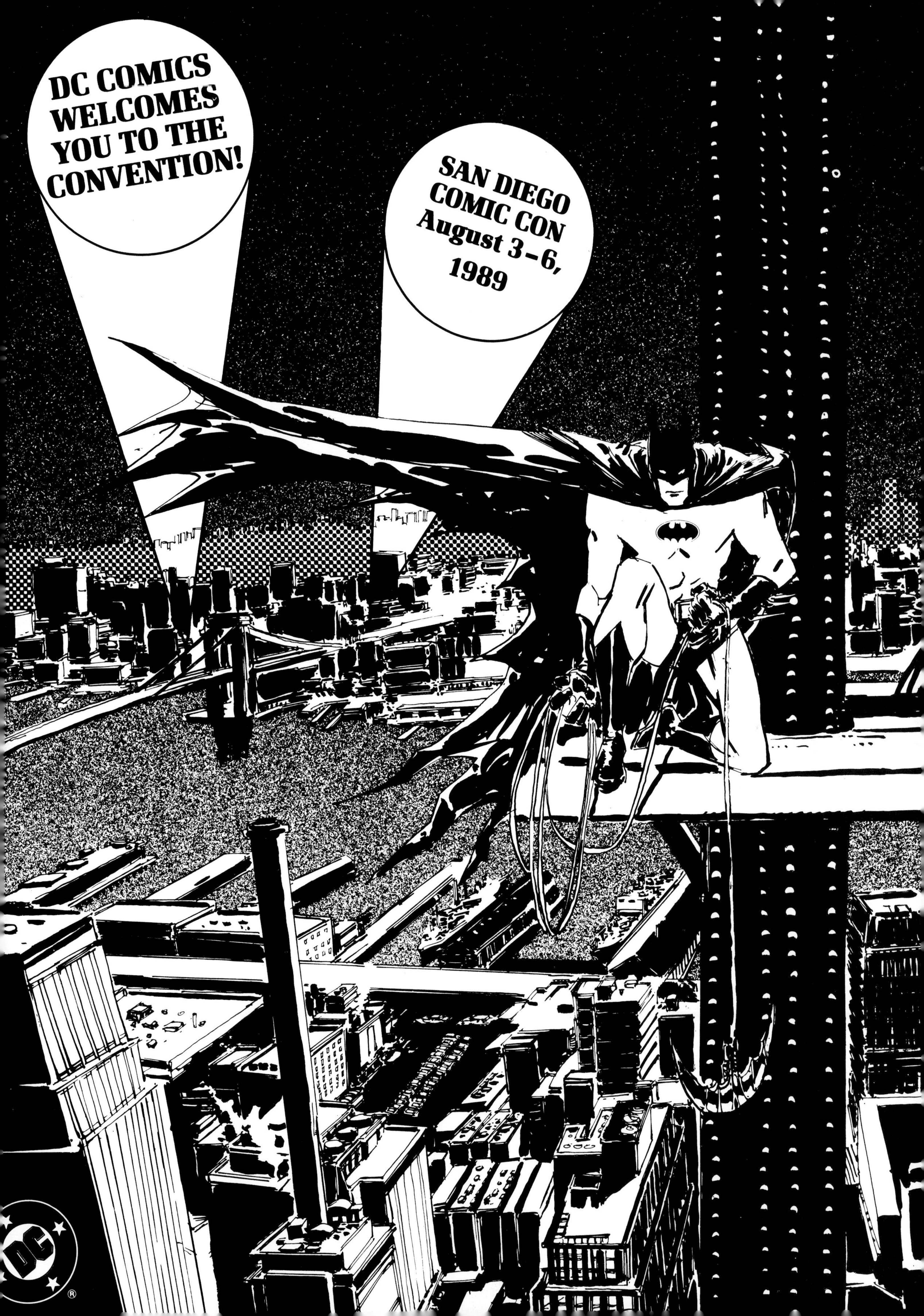
DC COMICS WELCOMES YOU TO THE CONVENTION!
SAN DIEGO COMIC CON August 3–6, 1989

THE WILL EISNER COMIC INDUSTRY AWARDS

THE OSCARS OF COMICS

WILL EISNER COMIC INDUSTRY AWARDS

The Will Eisner Comic Industry Awards, considered the Oscars of the comic book industry, are presented each year in a gala ceremony at Comic-Con. Named for renowned cartoonist Will Eisner (creator of *The Spirit* and several award-winning graphic novels; SEE page 67), the awards feature more than two dozen categories covering the best publications and creators of the previous year. A blue-ribbon five-person committee selects nominees from thousands of entries submitted by publishers and creators. The nominees are placed on a final ballot, which is then voted on by members of the comic book industry, including writers, artists, and other creators, publishers, editors, retailers, and distributors.

But the Eisner Awards were not always the Eisner Awards. At one point they were the Kirby Awards—sort of.

Back in 1984, Fantagraphics Books instituted the Jack Kirby Awards to honor the best works and creators in comics. The administrator of the awards was Dave Olbrich, a Fantagraphics employee. The awards were given out beginning in 1985 in an event at Comic-Con, with Kirby himself on hand to congratulate the winners.

When Olbrich left Fantagraphics for other pursuits in 1987, the Kirby Awards ended and two new awards programs were born: Fantagraphics started the Harvey Awards (named after cartoonist and *MAD* creator Harvey Kurtzman) and the Will Eisner Comic Industry Awards. Set up as a nonprofit organization, the Eisners continued at Comic-Con, with Will Eisner onstage to hand out the awards. The first Eisners were awarded in 1988 for works published in 1987. Olbrich administered the awards for two years and took a break in 1990. At that time it was proposed that Comic-Con take over and underwrite the awards, as the responsibilities involved in administering had grown. The first Will Eisner Awards given out under Comic-Con auspices occurred in 1991, with Jackie Estrada as the new administrator.

OPPOSITE, TOP LEFT: The 1985 Jack Kirby Award winners: (back row, left to right) Dave Stevens, Alan Moore, Don Thompson, and Jerry Bingham; (front row, left to right) Jack Kirby, cat yronwode, Dick Giordano, and awards administrator Dave Olbrich **TOP CENTER:** Brad Meltzer (left) accepting the 2008 Eisner Award for Best Single Issue (*Justice League of America* #11) from Samuel L. Jackson (right) **TOP RIGHT:** The Eisner Trophy **BOTTOM LEFT:** Frank Miller in 1995 with one of his Eisner Awards, for Best Limited Series for *Sin City* **BOTTOM CENTER:** Will Eisner in 2002 with his award for Best Archival Collection, for *The Spirit Archives* **BOTTOM RIGHT:** Todd Klein with one of his fifteen Best Lettering Eisner Awards; he's won more Eisners than any other comics creator

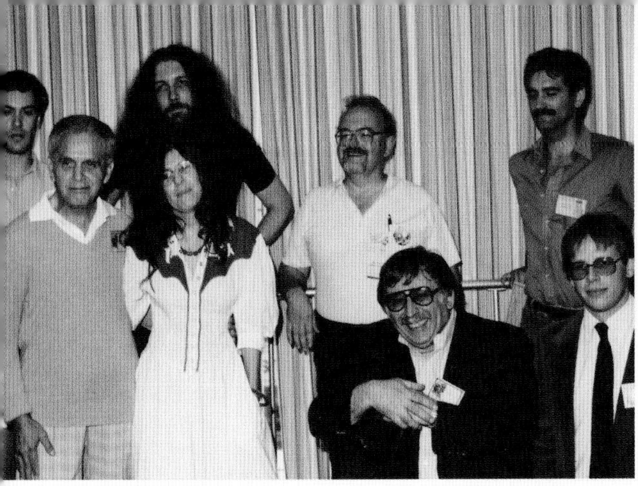

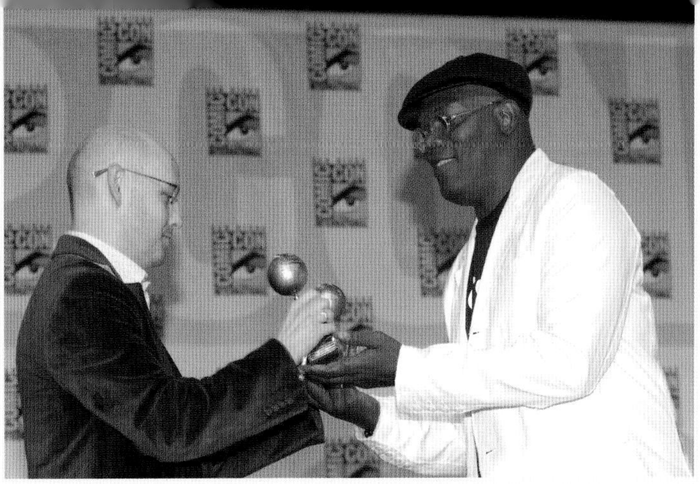

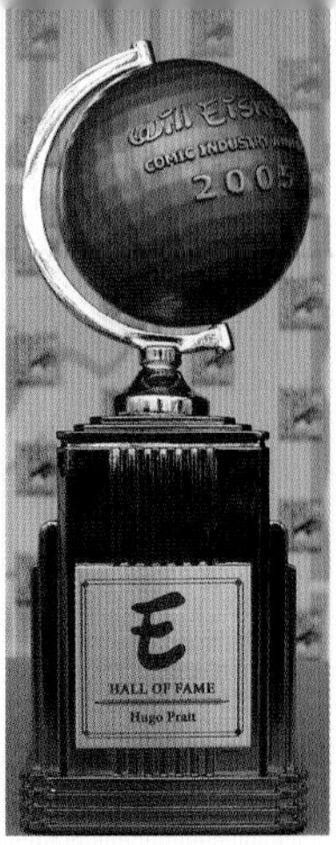
HALL OF FAME
Hugo Pratt

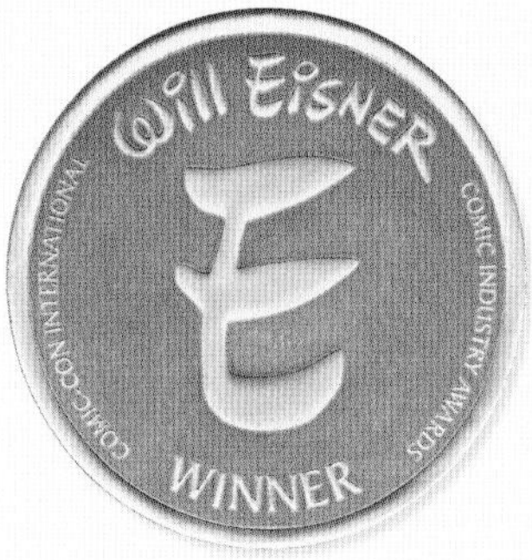
Will Eisner
Comic-Con International
Comic Industry Awards
Winner

The awards ceremony had its first keynote speaker in 1995, when Neil Gaiman set the tone for the evening by addressing the nature and meaning of awards. In subsequent years, memorable keynote speakers have included Dave Gibbons, Frank Miller, and novelist Michael Chabon, who made an eloquent plea for better comics for kids.

Over the last few years, the Eisner ceremony, now the big event at Comic-Con on Friday night, has been MC'd by Bill Morrison (creative director of Bongo Comics) and features celebrity presenters and multimedia graphics projected on multiple screens. But the focus remains on the works and creators being honored by the event. The list of nominees is treated as a shopping list by fans of comics and graphic novels who are looking for the best material being published, while publishers proudly display the Eisner Award logo on their nominated and winning books.

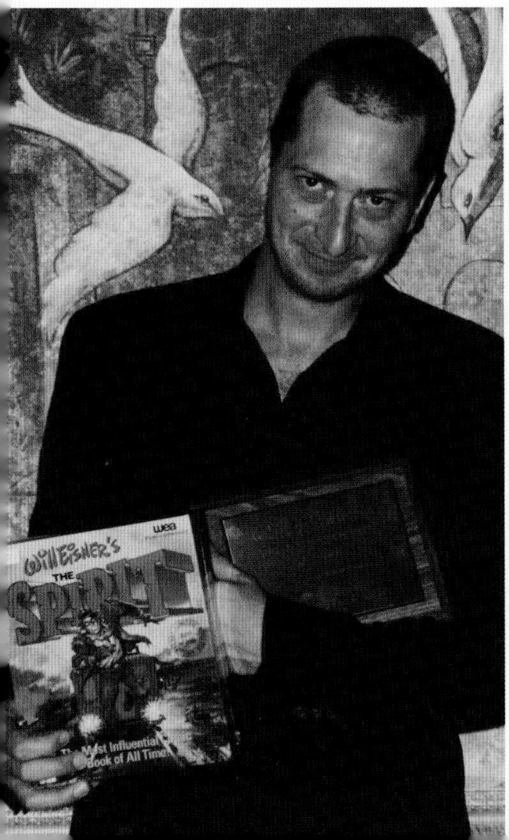
Will Eisner's
The Spirit

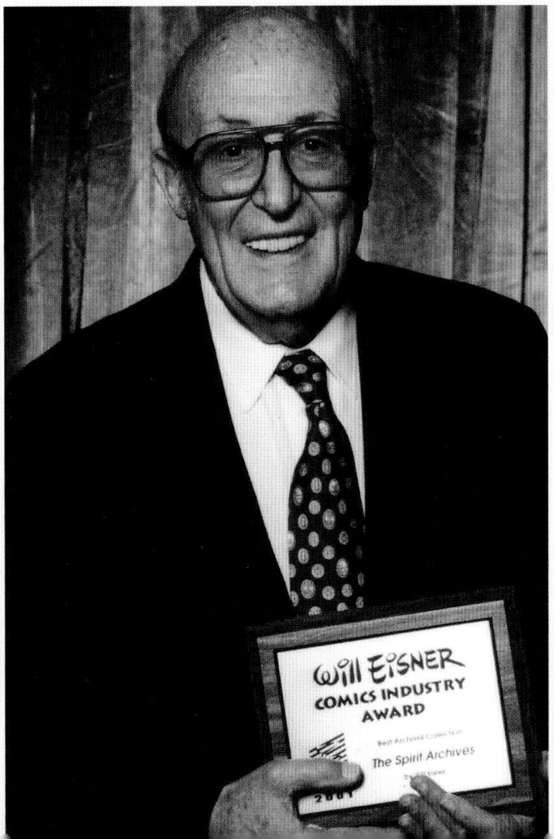
Will Eisner
Comics Industry
Award
The Spirit Archives

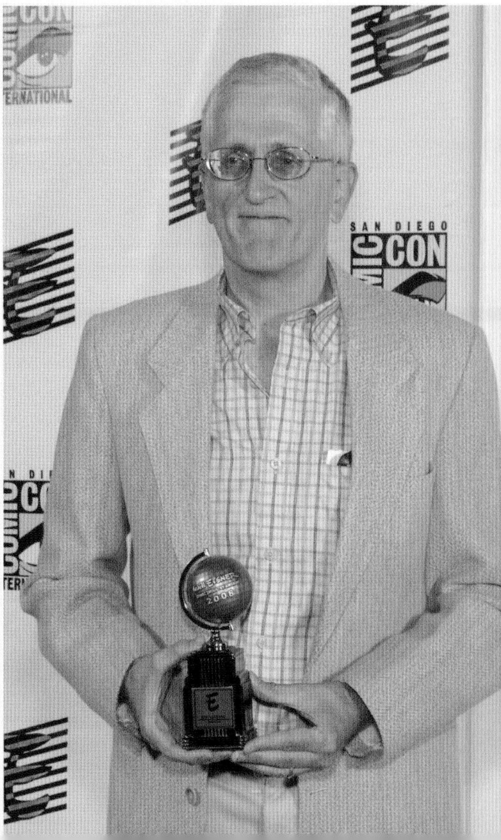
San Diego
Comic Con

COMIC BOOK EXPO

COMIC BOOK EXPO · JULY 24-26, 1995

REINVENTING BUSINESS
...*Again*

The comics industry changed drastically in the late 1970s and early 1980s. The traditional means of distribution for comics were fading as newsstands began to drop comic books to make room for more profitable magazines.

At the same time, comics shops started to sprout up around the country. A whole new network of distribution was set up, and a new portion of the comics industry was born—the direct market—due largely to the pioneering efforts of comic convention promoter Phil Seuling, whose New York Comic Art Convention set an early high standard for fan gatherings. Seuling approached Marvel and DC Comics with a daring plan: to distribute directly to the new network of comics shops gathering steam nationwide, with books offered on a nonreturnable basis.

By the mid-1980s, the direct comics market was ready for a national trade show. Various publishing representatives suggested an event that would bring both the publishers and the retailers together. One such person was Carol Kalish, who was Marvel Comics' direct sales manager. She contacted Comic-Con about setting up such an event, and in 1984 the Comic Book Expo was born.

The Expo quickly became "a trade show for the entire industry," and was shepherded for most of its first ten years by Expo director David Scroggy. Exhibitors included comics publishers and distributors, gaming and trading card companies, printers and service bureaus (including those that specialized in such comic book staples as coloring), and manufacturers of T-shirts, action figures, and other items such as store displays and fixtures. A retailer-based schedule of programs included everything from company presentations about new products to detailed information on how to help run a small business, including personal time management, employee and tax advice, technology, marketing, and much more. Most important, the Expo became a place where retailers could meet and network with each other and company representatives, exchange ideas, and discuss what their peers were doing, an important asset for the still relatively newborn comic retailing industry.

Running for the two days preceding Comic-Con each year, the Expo started in the basement of the U. S. Grant Hotel, a few blocks away from the Convention and Performing Arts Center. In the 1990s, when Comic-Con moved into the new San

TOP: Rick Geary's cover for the 1995 Comic Book Expo program book **ABOVE:** Expo Boy, by Rick Geary **OPPOSITE, TOP LEFT AND RIGHT:** Variations on Rick Geary's Expo Boy **TOP CENTER:** Carol Kalish, Marvel Comics' direct sales manager in the 1980s, who pushed for a national expo for the comics industry **BOTTOM:** Three more Expo program covers, (from left) 1999 (Rick Geary), 1998 (Sergio Aragonés), and 1997 (Will Eisner)

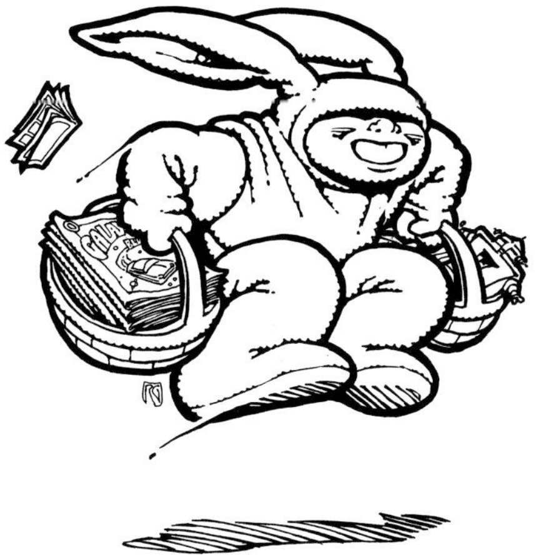

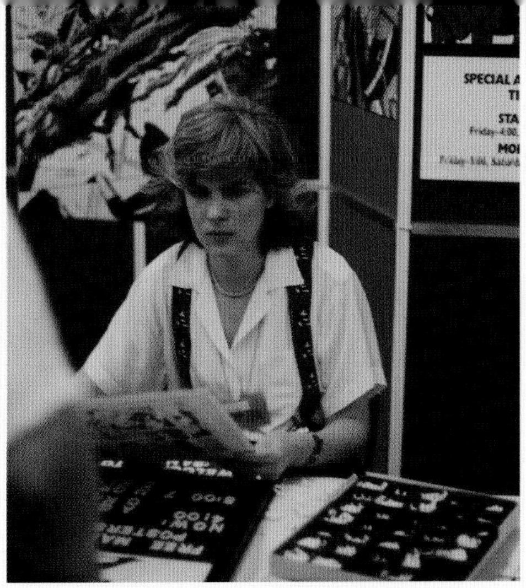

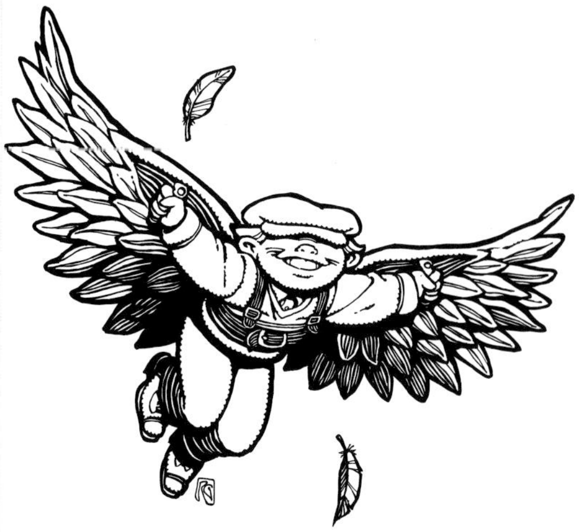

Diego Convention Center, the Expo became the anchor of the Exhibit Hall, with the rest of the event built around it.

For many years, the Expo offered incredible signed and numbered limited-edition art prints to all qualified attendees. Those prints included art by Dave Stevens (1991, *The Rocketeer*), Geof Darrow (1992, *Big Guy and Rusty the Boy Robot*), Arthur Suydam (1993, *Mudwogs*), Jeff Smith (1994, *Bone*), Charles Vess (1995, *Stardust*), Frank Miller (1996, *Sin City*), Alex Ross (1997, *U.S.*), John Romita and John Romita Jr. (1998, *Spider-Man and Thor*), Yoshitaka Amano (1999, *Sandman: The Dream Hunters*), Will Eisner (2000, *The Spirit of Collecting*), and Frank Cho (2001, *Kidnapped*). Graphitti Designs produced the prints.

The final year for the Comic Book Expo was 2001. With the size of Comic-Con growing exponentially, much of the business that had been taking place at the Expo began to shift to the larger event. The need for the Expo became less necessary to the retailers and exhibitors. To facilitate the transition to a combined show, retailer programs and events were added to Comic-Con programming.

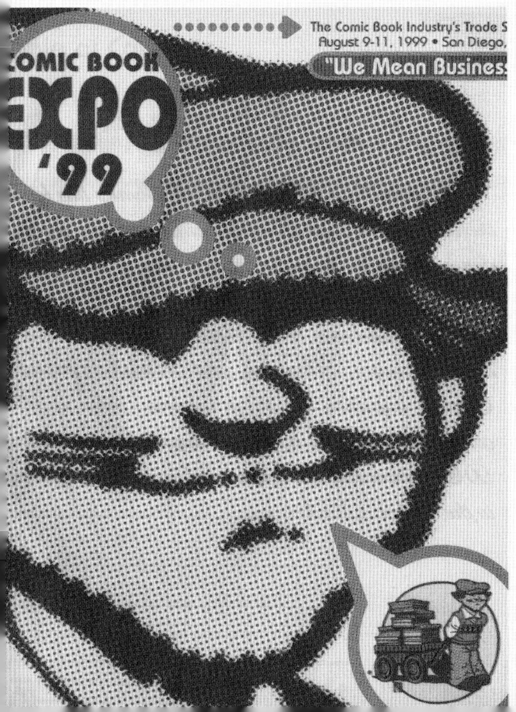
August 9-11, 1999 • San Diego,
'99

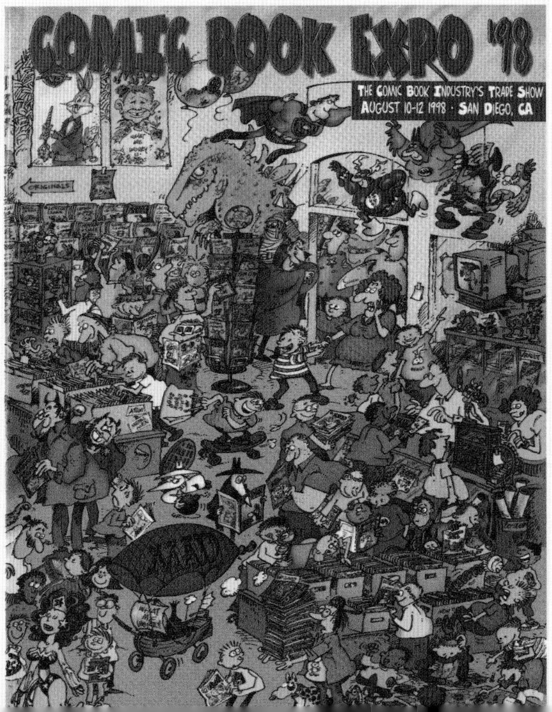
COMIC BOOK EXPO '98
THE COMIC BOOK INDUSTRY'S TRADE SHOW
AUGUST 10-12 1998 : SAN DIEGO, CA

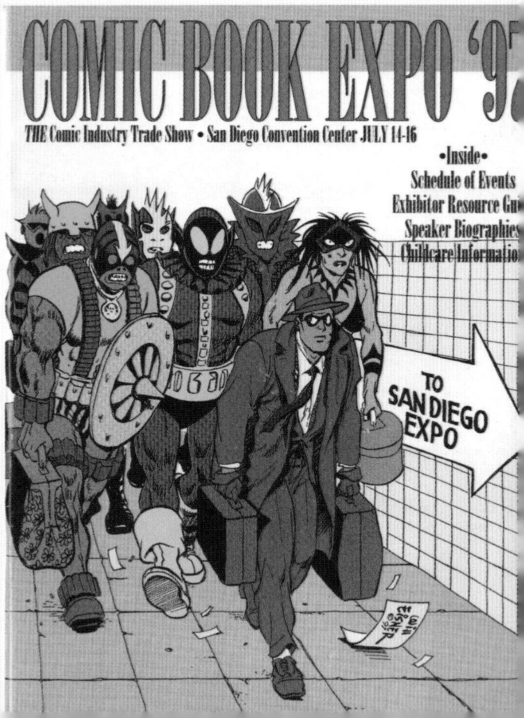
THE Comic Industry Trade Show • San Diego Convention Center JULY 14-16
•Inside•
Schedule of Events
Speaker Biographies
TO SAN DIEGO EXPO

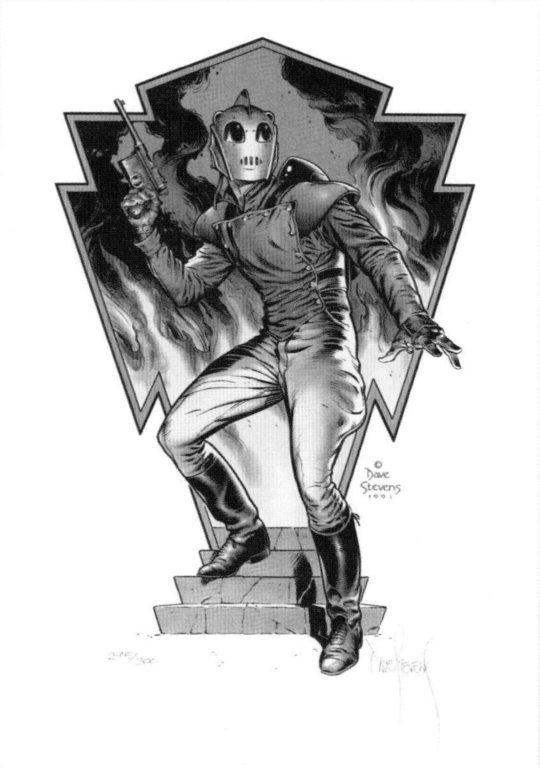
©
Dave
Stevens
1991

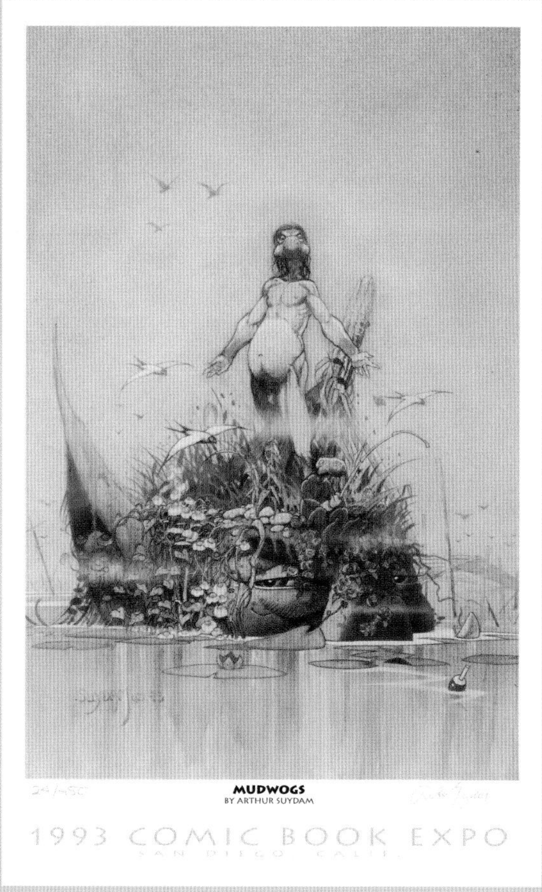
MUDWOGS
BY ARTHUR SUYDAM
1993 COMIC BOOK EXPO
SAN DIEGO CALIF.

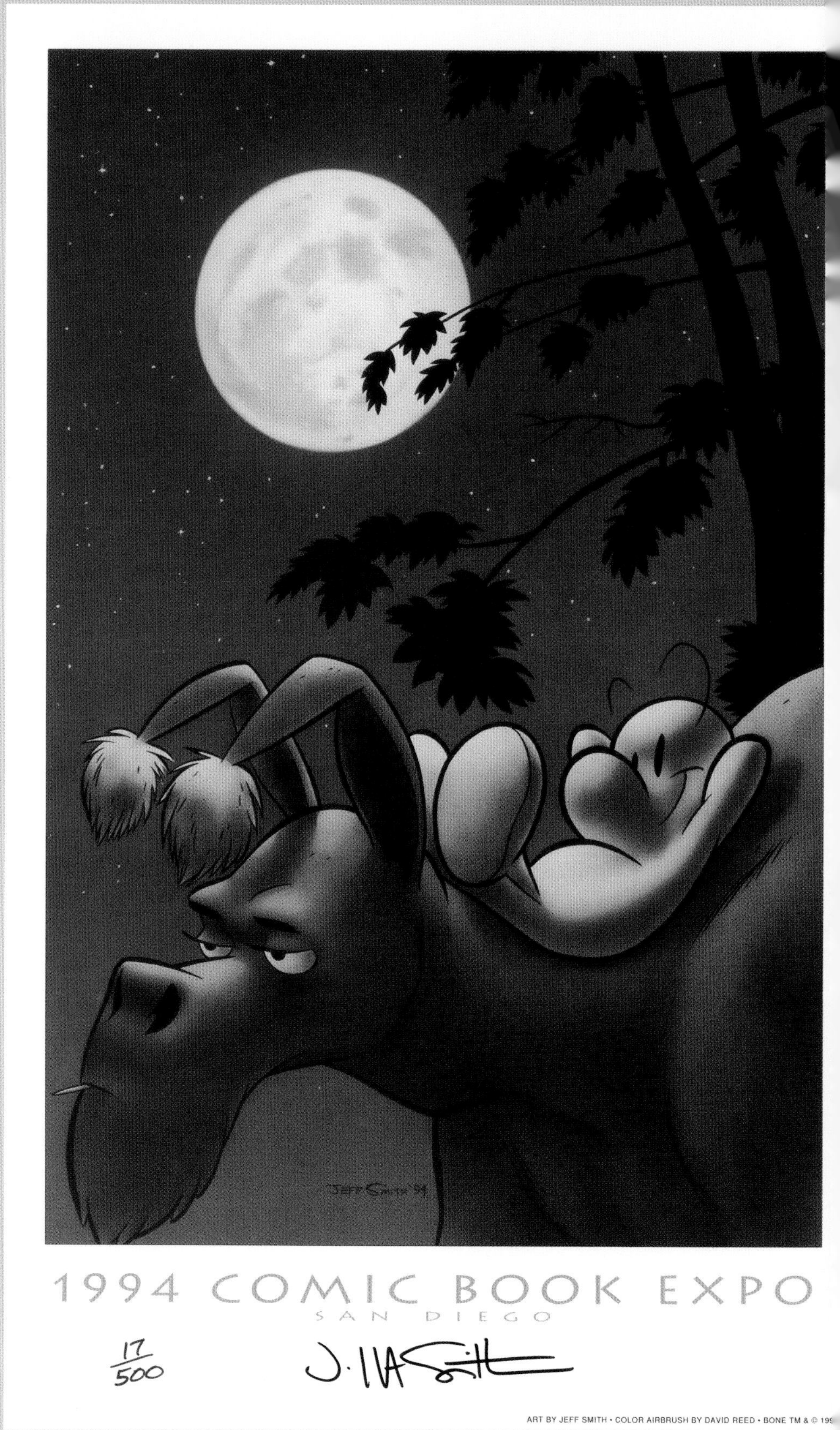
JEFF SMITH '94
1994 COMIC BOOK EXPO
SAN DIEGO
17/500
ART BY JEFF SMITH • COLOR AIRBRUSH BY DAVID REED • BONE TM & © 199

ABOVE, TOP LEFT: The first Expo print in 1991 featured the Rocketeer by Dave Stevens **BOTTOM LEFT:** 1993: Mudwogs, by Arthur Suydam **ABOVE RIGHT:** 1994: Bone, by Jeff Smith **OPPOSITE:** 1992: The Big Guy and Rusty the Boy Robot, by Geof Darrow

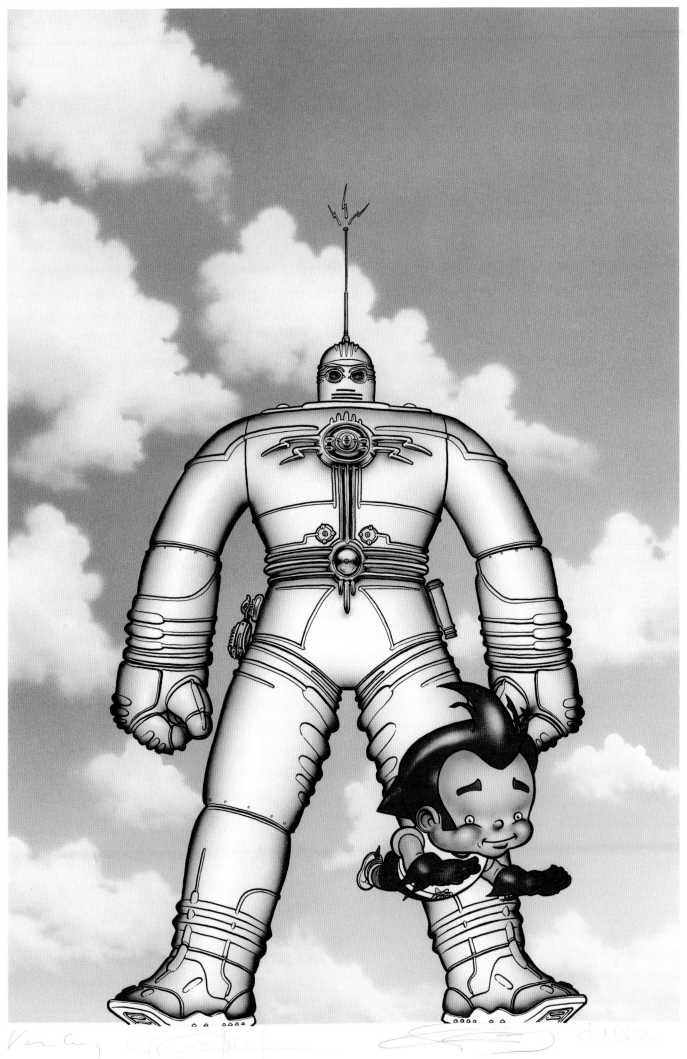

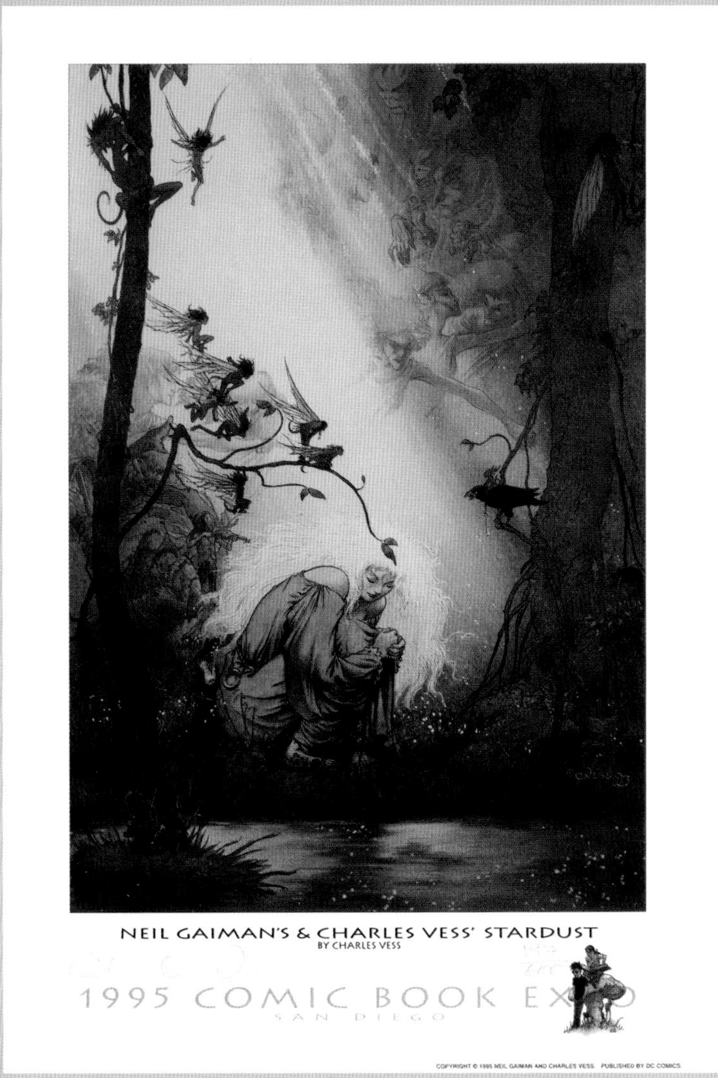
NEIL GAIMAN'S & CHARLES VESS' STARDUST
BY CHARLES VESS
1995 COMIC BOOK EXPO
SAN DIEGO
COPYRIGHT © 1995 NEIL GAIMAN AND CHARLES VESS. PUBLISHED BY DC COMICS.

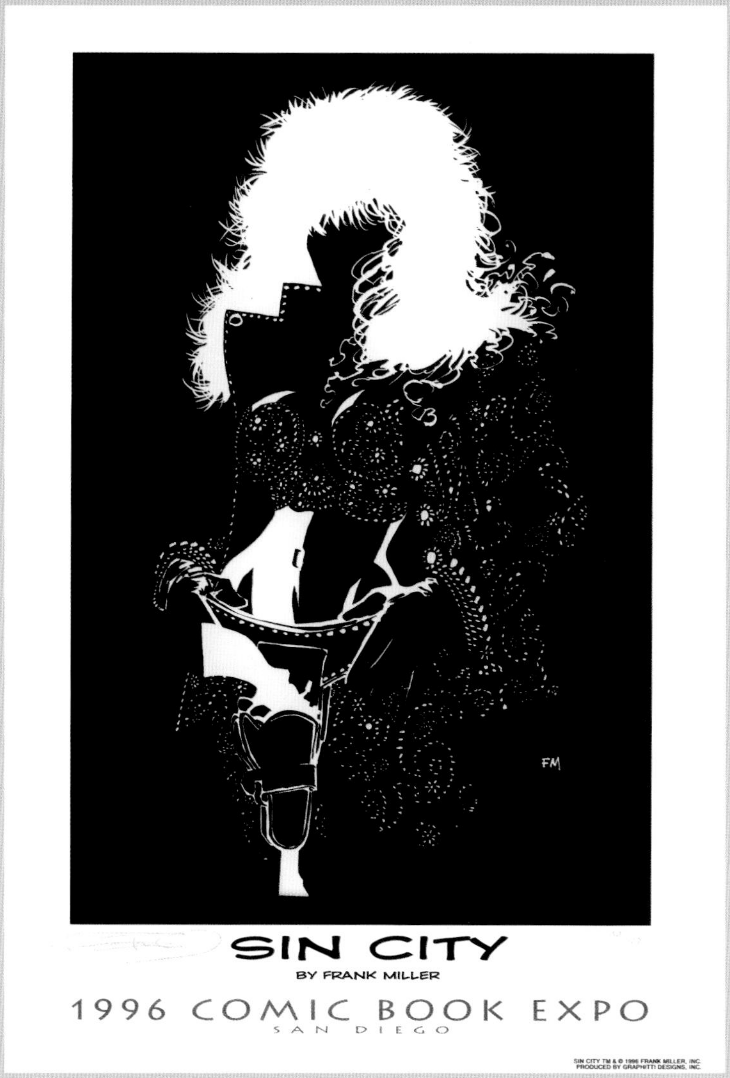
FM
SIN CITY
BY FRANK MILLER
1996 COMIC BOOK EXPO
SAN DIEGO
SIN CITY TM & © 1996 FRANK MILLER, INC.
PRODUCED BY GRAPHITTI DESIGNS, INC.

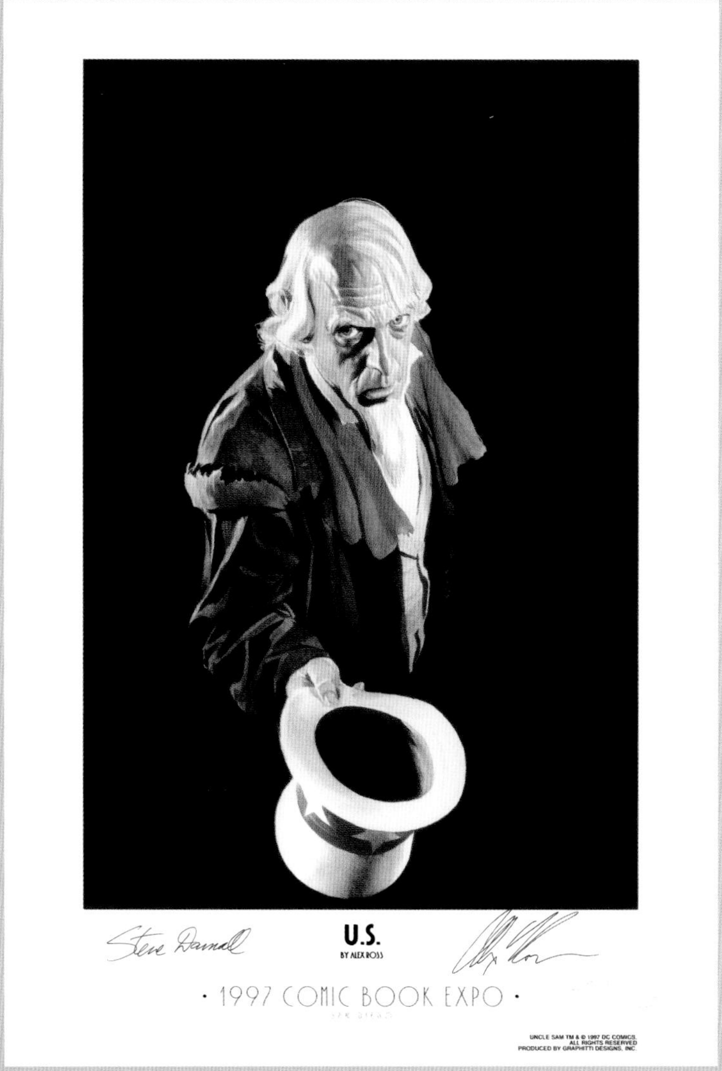
U.S.
BY ALEX ROSS
· 1997 COMIC BOOK EXPO ·
UNCLE SAM TM & © 1997 DC COMICS.
ALL RIGHTS RESERVED
PRODUCED BY GRAPHITTI DESIGNS, INC.

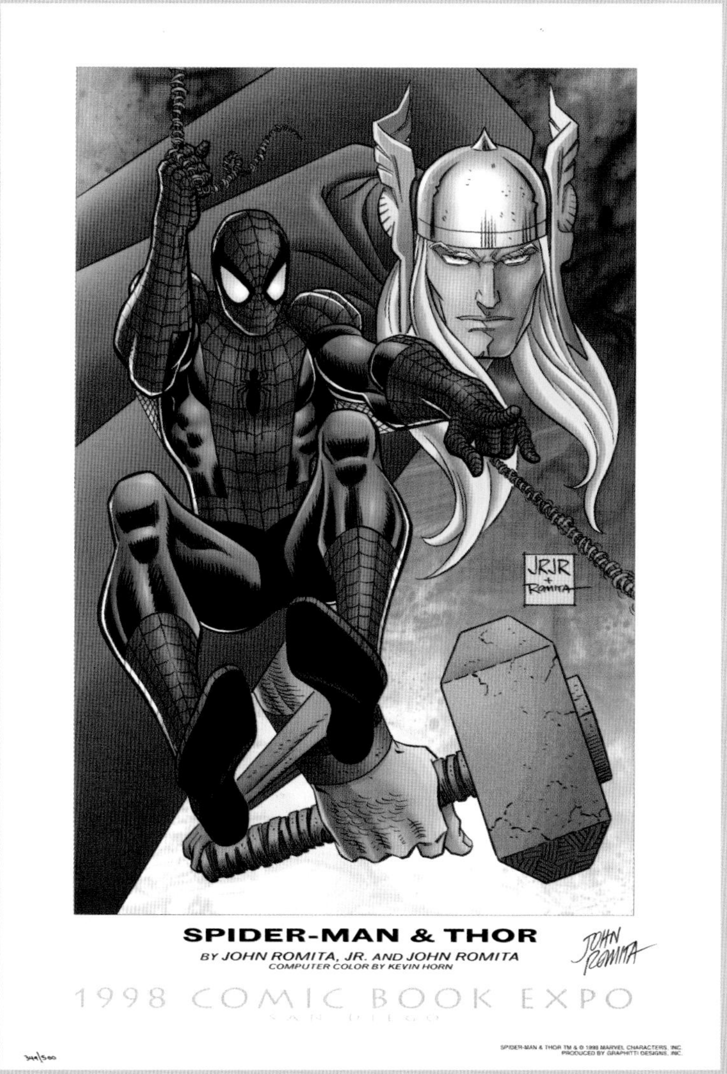
JRJR + ROMITA
SPIDER-MAN & THOR
BY JOHN ROMITA, JR. AND JOHN ROMITA
COMPUTER COLOR BY KEVIN HORN
1998 COMIC BOOK EXPO
SAN DIEGO
SPIDER-MAN & THOR TM & © 1998 MARVEL CHARACTERS, INC.
PRODUCED BY GRAPHITTI DESIGNS, INC.

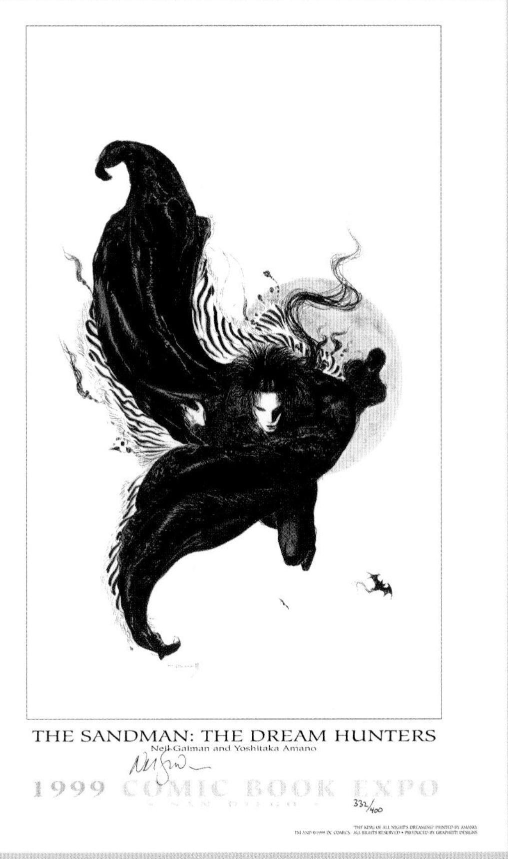
THE SANDMAN: THE DREAM HUNTERS
Neil Gaiman and Yoshitaka Amano
1999 COMIC BOOK EXPO
• SAN DIEGO •
332/400
"THE KING OF ALL NIGHT'S DREAMING" PAINTED BY AMANO
TM AND ©1999 DC COMICS. ALL RIGHTS RESERVED • PRODUCED BY GRAPHITTI DESIGNS

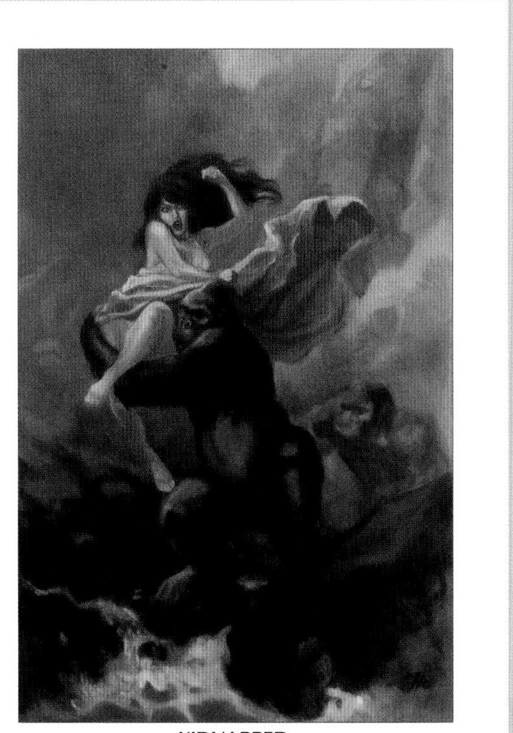
KIDNAPPED
by Frank Cho
2001 COMIC BOOK EXPO
• SAN DIEGO

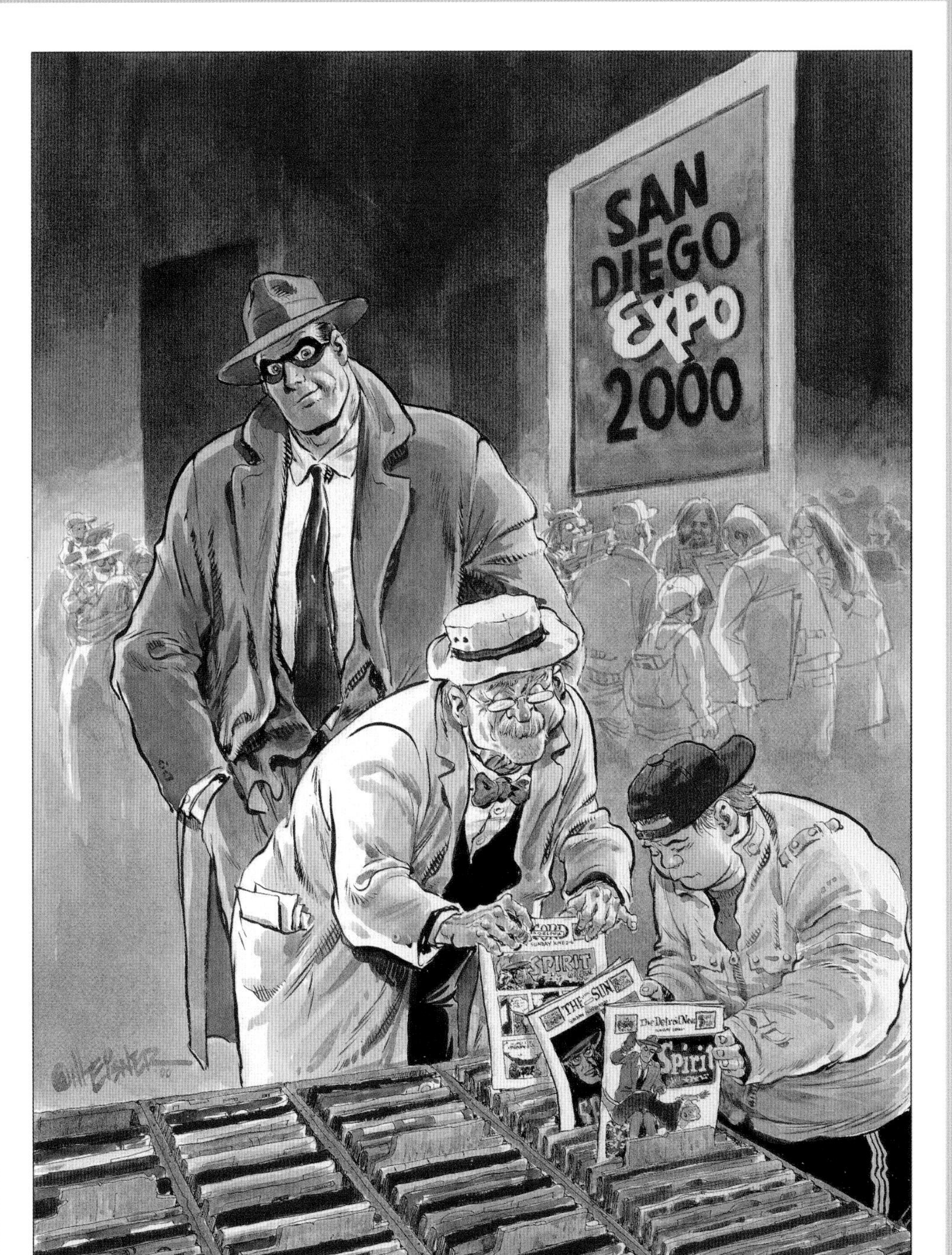
SAN DIEGO EXPO 2000
THE SUN
SPIRIT
WILL EISNER
THE SPIRIT OF COLLECTING
by Will Eisner
2000 COMIC BOOK EXPO
• SAN DIEGO
THE SPIRIT TM AND © 2000 WILL EISNER. ALL RIGHTS RESERVED
PRODUCED BY GRAPHITTI DESIGNS

OPPOSITE, TOP ROW, FROM LEFT: 1995: Stardust, by Charles Vess; 1996: Sin City by Frank Miller **BOTTOM ROW, FROM LEFT:** 1997: U.S. (Uncle Sam), by Alex Ross; 1999: Spider-Man & Thor by John Romita Jr. and John Romita **ABOVE, CLOCKWISE FROM TOP LEFT:** 1999: The Sandman: The Dream Hunters, by Yoshitaka Amano; 2000: The Spirit of Collecting, by Will Eisner; 2001: Kidnapped, by Frank Cho

MASQUERADE

Comic-Con's Masquerade is much more than just a display of individually crafted costumes. It includes a touch of theater—a portrayal of characters often with bits of drama, comedy, and sometimes song and dance. For many attendees it is a way not only to immerse themselves in a character or genre they love but also to exercise their creativity and have fun.

Comic-Con added a Masquerade costume contest to its events at the El Cortez Hotel in 1974. The first one was held on Friday night, and cartoon voice actress June Foray (*The Rocky and Bullwinkle Show*) was its first mistress of ceremonies. Even in those early days, the audience of a few hundred would line up well before the show for prime seating. Along with the comic book–inspired costumes and science fiction movie re-creations, entries based on *The Rocky Horror Picture Show* were common, and fans were guaranteed to see at least one lip-synched rendition of "Time Warp." Audience participation soon became common as they sang along with the costumers. Never shy, they usually let the contestant know whether they were impressed with an entry or felt the contestants were on stage too long. For many years musical entertainment was provided by Dr. Raoul Duke and His All-Human Orchestra during "halftime" while the judges decided which contestants would get prizes.

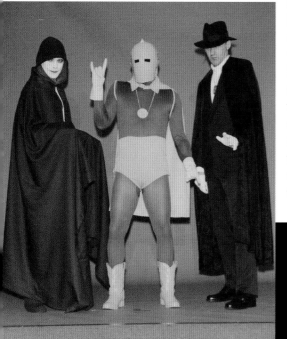

Throughout the 1980s and 1990s, the Masquerade moved among a number of venues. When Comic-Con moved to the Convention and Performing Arts Center in 1980, the Masquerade's new home was Golden Hall, giving it more stage and seating space. In 1988 the Masquerade (now on Saturday nights) moved to CPAC's three-thousand-seat Civic Theatre for a few years. With a real stage, theatrical lighting, dressing rooms, and more, the costumes and presentations became more elaborate and the show more polished. In 1992 and 1993, after Comic-Con had moved to the new San Diego Convention Center, the event was staged at Symphony Hall, with buses ferrying the audience to and from the venue. Halftime entertainment became exclusive movie previews and behind-the-scenes films provided by Hollywood studios. During this time, Hugo Award–winning artist and writer Phil Foglio became the Masquerade's MC in residence, hosting the event nearly every year thereafter. Before him, MCs had included television personality Gary Owens, radio DJ Gabriel Wisdom (dressed as the Mighty Thor), artist Scott Shaw!, and *MAD* magazine's Sergio Aragonés, among others.

Throughout the late 1990s, audience size continued to climb, more contestants sought to be in the show, and more companies began offering generous prizes to supplement the impressive custom-designed trophies now being given to winners. In 1998 the Masquerade moved into the convention center. Large projection screens hanging overhead, fed by multiple cameras, provided close-up views to audiences of more than thirty-five hundred. As Japanese animation blossomed, it started to inspire a great many costumes, and more original designs began to appear as well. After the convention center expanded in 2001, the Masquerade settled into its current venue of Ballroom 20, with even more advancements of lighting,

TOP LEFT: Space Ghost (1994) **TOP RIGHT:** Alien, winner of the Best Novice Award (2006); **BOTTOM:** (from left): the Spectre, Dr. Fate, and the Phantom Stranger (2000) **OPPOSITE, CLOCKWISE FROM TOP LEFT:** Gary Owens, the Masquerade's MC, with a participant in 1980; the Golden Age's Flash and Hourman (1996); Transformers (1997); Thor vs. Hercules (1994); the 2006 Best in Show entry, "Dancing with Celebrities from the Stars"; 2007's Best Re-creation, Beetlejuice

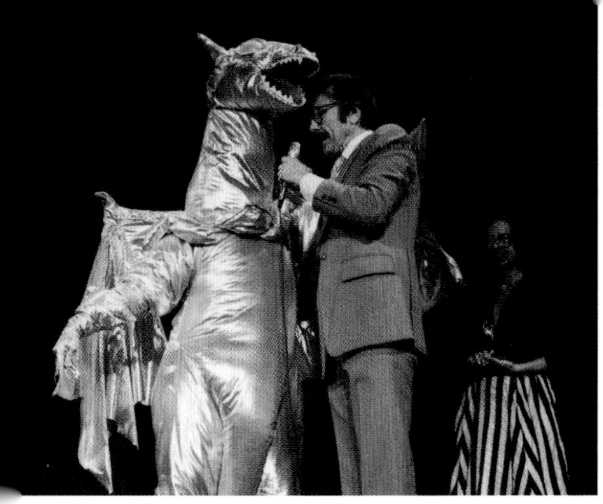

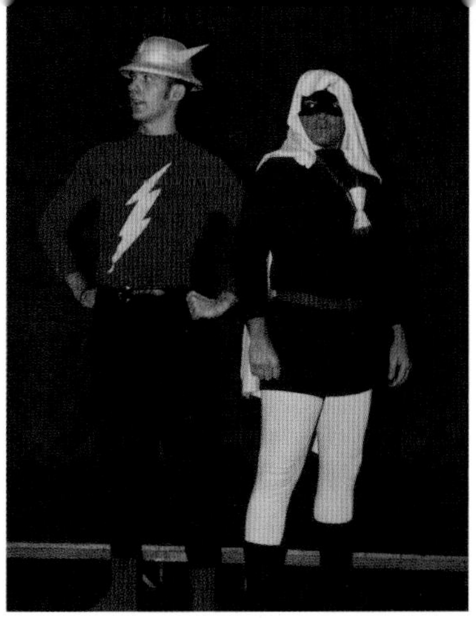

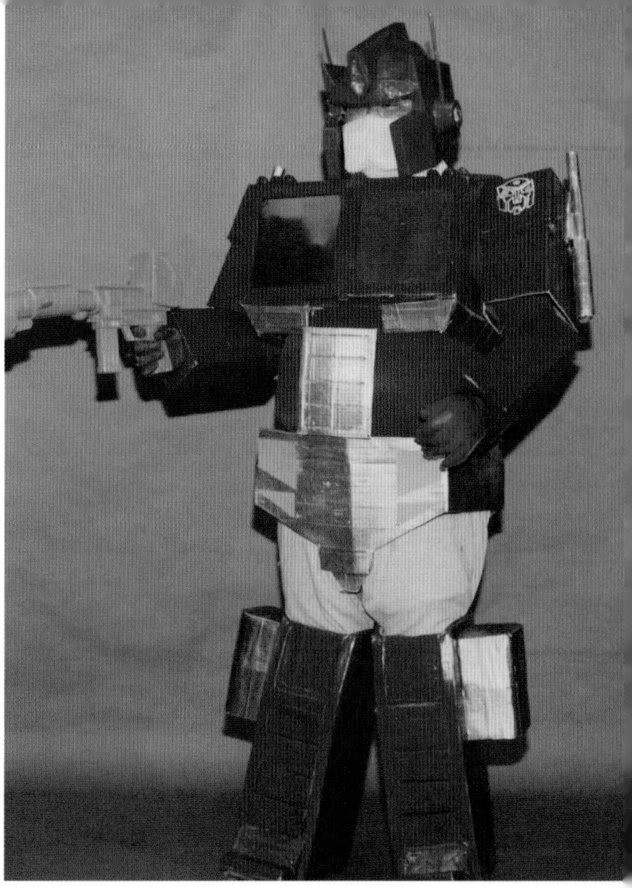

sound, and staging and with larger screens and more cameras.

What was once a simple costume show consisting of mostly fabric-based solo entries now features simulated armor cast from specialized plastics, built-in electrical effects, custom music recorded on computer, and costume groups that can number fifteen or more. It is a common sight on Saturday afternoon to see fans claiming a space in line as early as five or six hours before the show starts. With the ballroom filled to capacity and the event broadcast into overflow rooms, nearly seven thousand attendees now watch close to fifty entries participate each year in the Masquerade.

Why do the contestants do it? There are many reasons: the thrill of creation; the quest for recognition; and the display of one's hard work, craftsmanship, and diligence. But most contestants do it out of the sheer love they have for comics, movies, science fiction and fantasy, and, of course, costuming. That love shows in every person—and the costumes they wear—when they take the Masquerade stage.

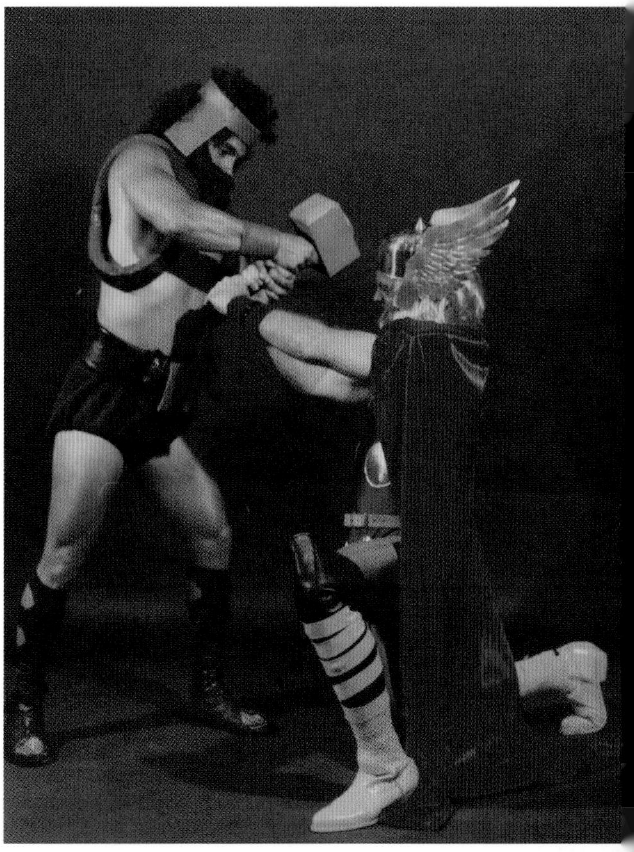

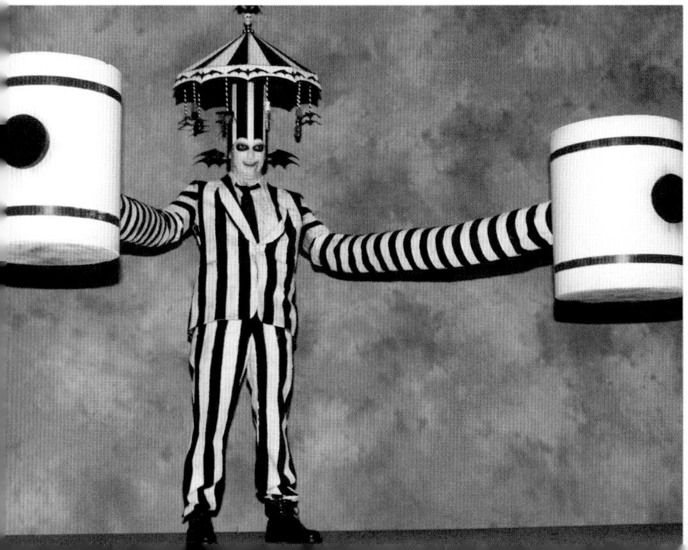

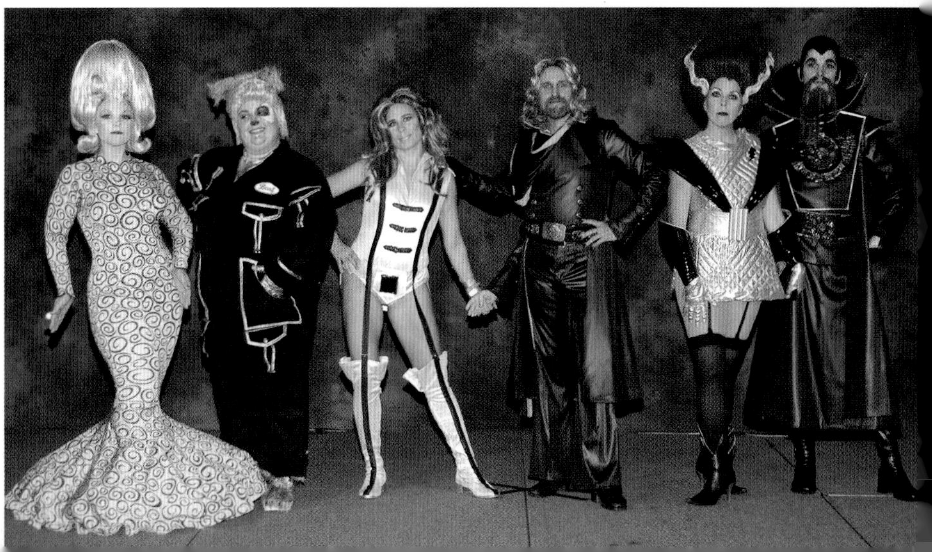

NOTABLE GUESTS

PEOPLE MAKING THEIR FIRST APPEARANCES AS SPECIAL GUESTS AT COMIC-CON IN THE 1980s . . .

1980
COMIC-CON 11

JOHN BYRNE: comic book writer/artist, *The Fantastic Four, X-Men*

CHRIS CLAREMONT: comic book writer, *X-Men*

MIKE GRELL: comic book writer/artist, *Superboy and the Legion of Super-Heroes, Warlord*

PAUL GULACY: comic book artist, *Shang-Chi: Master of Kung Fu, Sabre* graphic novel

GO NAGAI: manga writer/artist, *Mazinger Z, Cutie Honey, Devilman*

LARRY NIVEN: science fiction author, *Ringworld*; co-author (with Jerry Pournelle) of *Inferno, Lucifer's Hammer, The Mote in God's Eye*

JOE ORLANDO: EC Comics artist; DC Comics writer, artist, editor, and vice president

JERRY POURNELLE: science fiction author, *Janissaries*; co-author (with Larry Niven) of *Inferno, Lucifer's Hammer, The Mote in God's Eye*

MONKEY PUNCH: manga writer/artist, *Lupin III*

OSAMU TEZUKA: the father of anime and manga in Japan, creator of *Astro Boy, Kimba the White Lion, Phoenix, Buddha, Black Jack*

ADAM WEST: actor, *Batman* television series

WALLY WOOD: comic book artist, EC Comics and *MAD* magazine, *Will Eisner's The Spirit, T.H.U.N.D.E.R. Agents, Daredevil, Creepy, Eerie*

1981
COMIC-CON 12

JERRY BAILS: writer/editor, regarded as the father of comics fandom

DAVE BERG: comics writer/artist, *MAD* magazine

L. B. COLE: dean of Golden Age comic book cover artists

DICK GIORDANO: artist/editor, Charlton Comics, DC Comics; co-founder (with Neal Adams) of Continuity Associates

BIL KEANE: syndicated cartoonist and creator, *Family Circus*

JULIUS SCHWARTZ: DC Comics editor, credited with heralding the Silver Age of comics

JIM SHOOTER: comic book writer, editor in chief, Marvel Comics (1978–1987)

DAVE SIM: comic book writer/artist/creator, *Cerebus*

1982
COMIC-CON 13

BRIAN BOLLAND: British comic book artist, *Camelot 3000*

MAX ALLAN COLLINS: writer, *Ms. Tree* comic book, *Dick Tracy* syndicated newspaper strip

HANK KETCHAM: syndicated cartoonist/creator, *Dennis the Menace*

FRANK MILLER: comic book writer/artist, *Daredevil*

LEONARD STARR: syndicated cartoonist/creator, *Mary Perkins, On Stage*

ROBERT WILLIAMS: painter, underground comix artist/illustrator, *Zap, Coochie Cootie*

BILL WOGGON: writer/artist/creator, *Katy Keene*

1983
COMIC-CON 14

DOUGLAS ADAMS: science fiction author, *The Hitchhiker's Guide to the Galaxy*

FLOYD GOTTFREDSON: syndicated cartoonist, *Mickey Mouse*

NORMAN MAURER: comic book writer/artist/publisher; movie producer, *The Three Stooges*

GEORGE PÉREZ: comic book writer/artist, *The New Teen Titans, The Avengers*

1984
COMIC-CON 15

STAN DRAKE: syndicated cartoonist/creator, *The Heart of Juliet Jones*

OLLIE JOHNSTON AND FRANK THOMAS: animators, Walt Disney classic features

ROBERT SHAYNE: actor, Inspector Henderson on the *Adventures of Superman* television series

DAVE STEVENS: comic book writer/artist, *The Rocketeer*

CURT SWAN: comic book artist, *Superman*

AL WILLIAMSON: comic book artist, EC Comics; syndicated cartoonist, *Secret Agent X-9* and *Star Wars* comic strips

1985
COMIC-CON 16

BEN BOVA: science fiction author, *The Winds of Altair, City of Darkness*

JACK DAVIS: artist, EC Comics, *MAD* magazine; illustrator, movie posters, magazine covers

ALAN MOORE: comic book writer, *Swamp Thing*

DAN O'BANNON: movie writer/director, *Dark Star, Alien*

ALEX SCHOMBURG: Golden Age comic book artist, science fiction illustrator famed for his covers

LOUISE SIMONSON: editor, Warren Publications, Marvel; writer/co-creator, *Power Pack*

WALT SIMONSON: comic book writer/artist, *Manhunter, The Mighty Thor*

1986

COMIC-CON 17

POUL ANDERSON: science fiction/fantasy author, *Brain Wave*, *The Star Fox*

MARION ZIMMER BRADLEY: fantasy author, Avalon and Darkover series

JEAN "MOEBIUS" GIRAUD: French comic book artist, *Blueberry*, *Heavy Metal* magazine

MART NODELL: Golden Age comic book artist; co-creator, *Green Lantern*

HARVEY PEKAR: writer, *American Splendor*

DOUG WILDEY: comic book artist, *Rio*; animation director, co-creator of *Johnny Quest*, *Herculoids*, and *Jana of the Jungle*

1987

COMIC-CON 18

HARLAN ELLISON: author, *I Have No Mouth, and I Must Scream*; *Paingod and Other Delusions*; "A Boy and His Dog"

WARD KIMBALL: animator, one of Walt Disney's "Nine Old Men"

FRANÇOISE MOULY: artist/editor/publisher, *RAW* magazine

BILL MUMY: actor, *Lost in Space*

MIKE PETERS: syndicated and editorial cartoonist, *Mother Goose & Grimm*

ROBERT SILVERBERG: science fiction author, *The Stochastic Man*, *Lord Valentine's Castle*

ART SPIEGELMAN: underground comix writer/artist, *RAW* magazine, *Maus*

BERNIE WRIGHTSON: illustrator, comic book artist, and co-creator of Swamp Thing

1988

COMIC-CON 19

ROBERT ASPRIN: science fiction/fantasy author, *MythAdventures* series

JULES FEIFFER: comic book writer, *Will Eisner's The Spirit*; syndicated cartoonist, *Village Voice*; screenwriter, *Popeye*, *Carnal Knowledge*

DAVID GERROLD: science fiction author; writer, *Star Trek* original television series

MATT GROENING: cartoonist/creator, *Life in Hell*, *The Simpsons*

GEORGE R. R. MARTIN: science fiction author, *Sandkings*, *The Skin Trade*; editor, Wild Cards series

MATT WAGNER: comic book writer/artist, *Mage*, *Grendel*

1989

COMIC-CON 20

PAUL CHADWICK: writer/artist/creator, *Concrete*

HOWARD CRUSE: underground cartoonist, *Barefootz*, *Wendel*, *Gay Comix*

RON GOULART: science fiction author, *When the Waker Sleeps*, *The Robot in the Closet*; pop culture historian

GILBERT AND JAIME HERNANDEZ: writers/artists/creators, *Love and Rockets*

SYD MEAD: film designer, *Blade Runner*, *Aliens*, *Tron*

JERRY ROBINSON: Golden Age comic book artist, *Batman*; co-creator, the Joker

BILL SIENKIEWICZ: comic book artist, *Moon Knight*, *New Mutants*, *Elektra: Assassin*

GAHAN WILSON: magazine cartoonist, the *New Yorker*, *Playboy*, *National Lampoon*

> "My favorite Comic-Con moment was sometime in the early '80s when I saw a chance encounter between Jack Kirby, Jerry Siegel, and Joe Shuster in the dealers' room in the old San Diego Convention Center. As they stood there chatting, I couldn't help wondering, if it weren't for them, would there even be a comics industry, which inspired a convention like this? Would I even be doing this for a living? I felt I owed a lot to those gentlemen."
>
> **—STEVE LEIALOHA**
> ARTIST, *FABLES*, *COYOTE*

THE 1990s

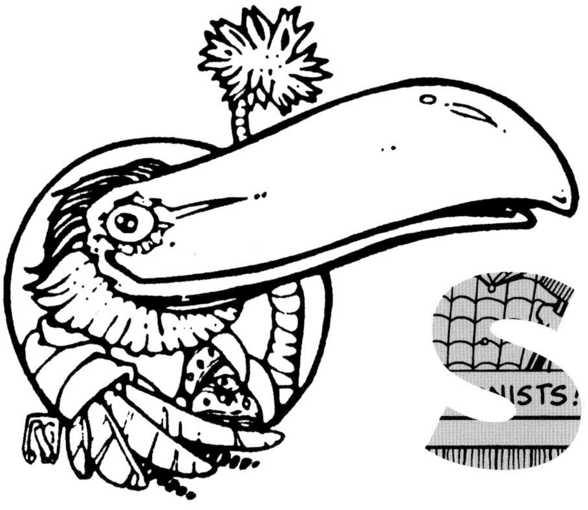

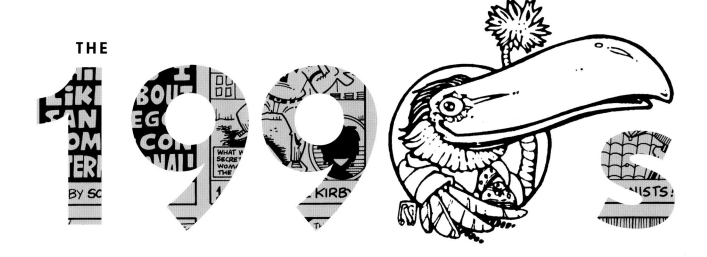

The 1990s were boom years for Comic-Con. Attendance nearly quadrupled, going from thirteen thousand in 1990 to more than forty-eight thousand in 1999. Fortunately, the city of San Diego had just built a brand-new convention center, and Comic-Con moved there in 1991, after one last year at CPAC.

Accompanying the move to the San Diego Convention Center was a renewed focus on public relations and marketing for Comic-Con. At the end of the 1980s, more professionally produced commercials appeared on San Diego television stations, but the 1990s saw those commercials air nationally. While San Diego city buses had featured advertising for Comic-Con in previous years, it wasn't until the 1990s that text-only ads were replaced by colorful artwork featuring comics superheroes and characters from popular animated television shows. Banners on downtown streets began to appear on Harbor Drive, then Broadway, and eventually a major portion of the Gaslamp Quarter. Advertising appeared before movie screenings at local theaters as well. In 1995 the board of directors adopted its mission statement, the name of the event was officially changed to Comic-Con International: San Diego, and the toucan logo was replaced with the current eye design.

POPULAR ENTERTAINMENT

One contributing factor to the popularity of Comic-Con in the 1990s was increased interest in comic books in general. By the early 1990s, the comics direct market—thousands of stores around the country specializing in comics—was in full swing, and publishers had shifted their marketing focus to these stores and the fans who frequented them. Events like the "Death of Superman" storyline also captured the attention of the general public. Comics sales soared as

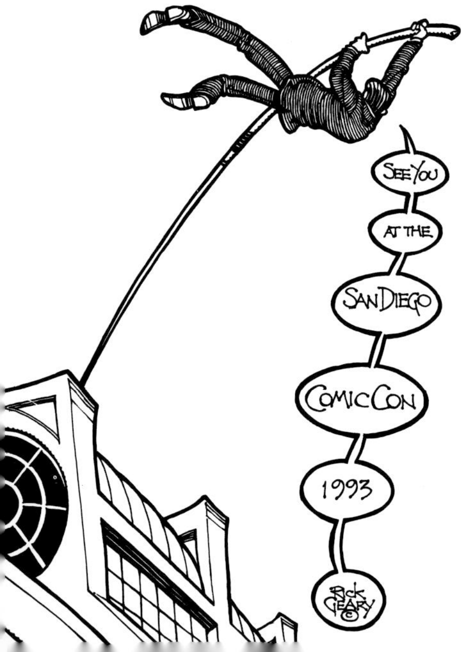
SEE YOU
AT THE
SAN DIEGO
COMIC CON
1993
RICK GEARY

ABOVE: Rick Geary's toucan logo **LEFT:** Geary's contribution to the 1993 Souvenir Book, featuring the new San Diego Convention Center **OPPOSITE:** Frank Miller's original art for the cover of the 1993 Souvenir Book, colored by Lynn Varley

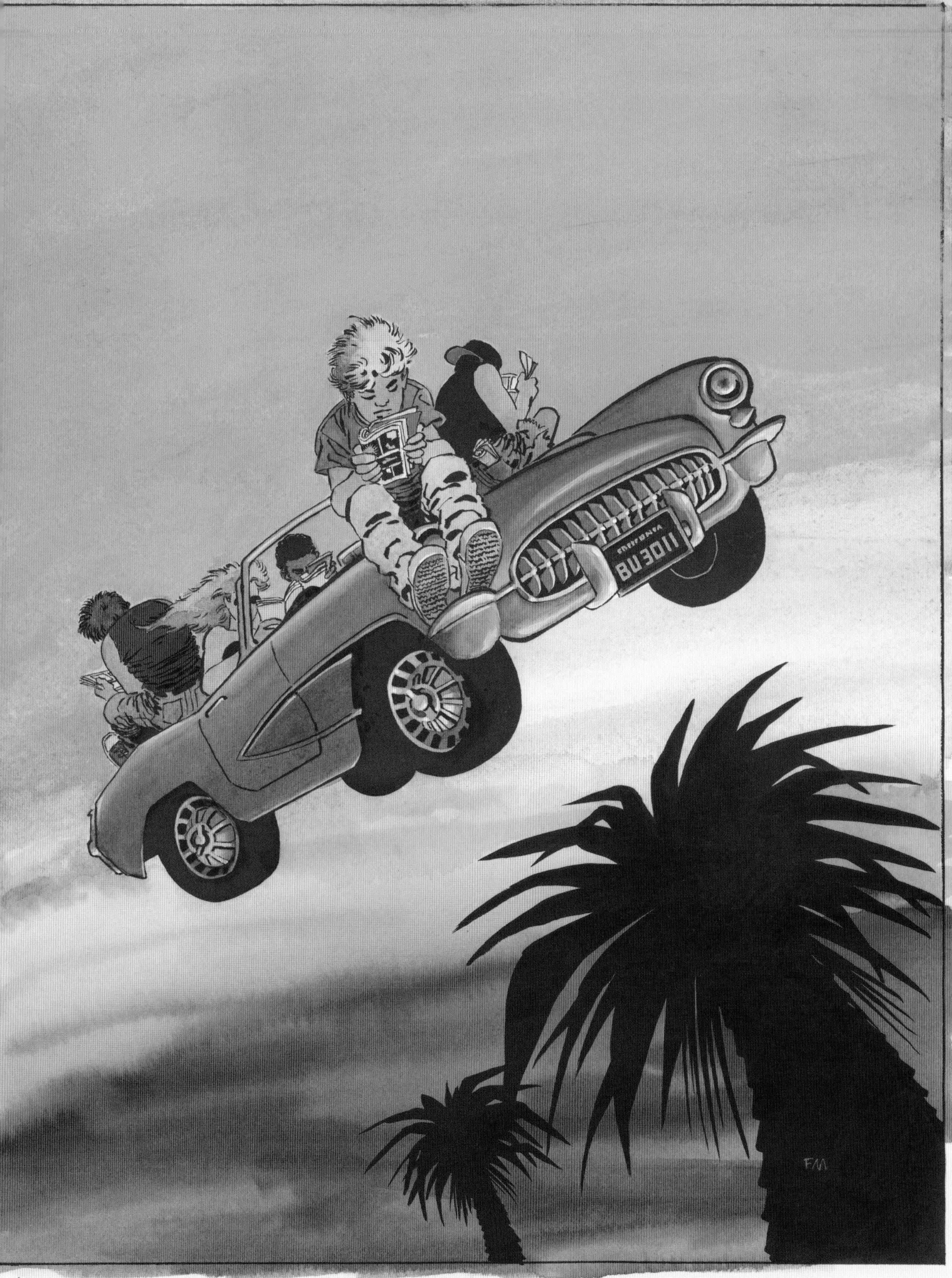
FM

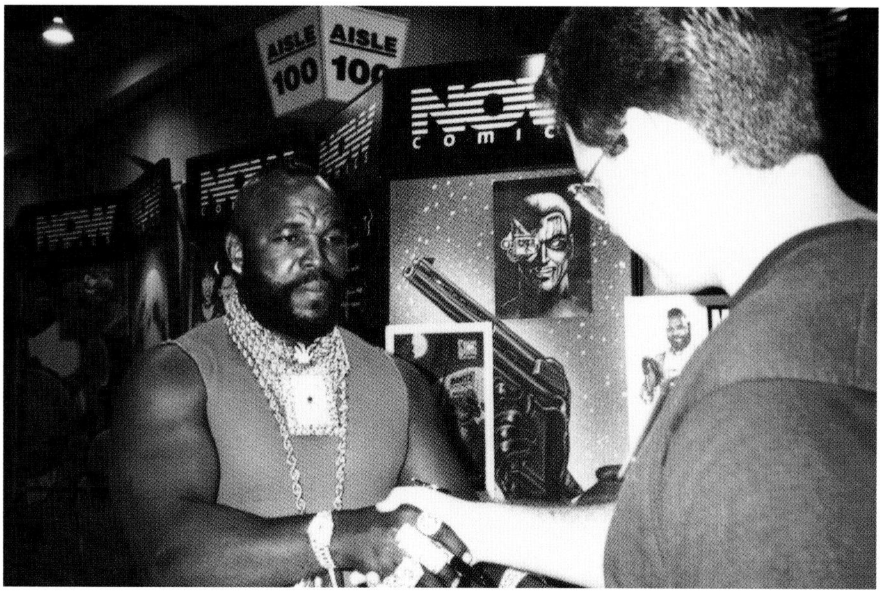
AISLE
100

fans (and speculators) sought out hot titles and hot artists, often buying multiple copies of individual issues or copies with variant covers. Additionally, the industry was rocked when some of the most popular artists at Marvel left to form their own company, Image Comics, in 1992. Fans stood in lines for hours at Comic-Con to get autographs from the new company's founders Todd McFarlane, Jim Lee, Rob Liefeld, Mark Silvestri, Erik Larsen, Whilce Portacio, and Jim Valentino.

Other new comics companies sprang up to cater directly to this expanding audience, and they knew they had to make a splash at Comic-Con to attract attention. Not only did they build flashy booths for the Exhibit Hall floor (perhaps inspired by the debut in 1993 of DC's megabooth, dubbed "Wayne's World" after DC marketing manager Bob Wayne), they brought in special guests to attract attendees to these booths, from William Shatner and Leonard Nimoy to Mickey Spillane and Mr. T.

In addition, companies that specialized in alternative comics and graphic novels used the opportunity of exhibiting at Comic-Con to reach the audience for their quirkier independent and literary titles. The self-publishing and small press movement also came into its own in the mid-1990s, with such creators as Jeff Smith (*Bone*), Terry Moore (*Strangers in Paradise*), and David Lapham (*Stray Bullets*) leading the way. These companies were represented on the Exhibit Hall floor with the creation of both a Small Press Area and an Independent Publishers' Pavilion. In 1997 three self-publishers—Jeff Smith, Charles Vess (*The Book of Ballads and Sagas*), and Linda Medley (*Castle Waiting*)—made a splash on the floor with their elaborate "Trilogy Tour" setup, which featured a giant tree and sculptures of some of their signature characters. The display grew even larger in 1998 with the addition of artists Jill Thompson (*Scary Godmother*), Stan Sakai (*Usagi Yojimbo*), and Mark Crilley (*Akiko*).

Comic-Con also threw the spotlight on the literary aspect of comics by including such guests as Dan Clowes (*Eightball*), the Hernandez Brothers (*Love and Rockets*), Chris Ware (*Acme Novelty Library*), Roberta Gregory (*Naughty Bits*), Charles Burns (*Black Hole*), and Art Spiegelman (*Maus*).

ABOVE: We have to say it: We pity the poor fool who missed Mr. T at his first appearance at Comic-Con in 1993, when his very own comic book came out from Now Comics

SOMETHING FOR EVERYONE

Many areas of Comic-Con besides the Exhibit Hall expanded in the 1990s. While the new center allowed for an increase in programming space, Comic-Con still occupied only a fraction of the new rooms available, but by the end of the decade the event was occupying most of the rooms on both the mezzanine and upper level of the convention center. Special areas were added for autograph signings and portfolio reviews, and the Art Show got more real estate. Feature films were screened at both the convention center and the official convention hotels, which also featured late-into-the-night gaming. And speaking of gaming, role-playing game companies were expanding their presence at the event as games such as Magic: The Gathering became ultrapopular. The mid-1990s also saw two special art exhibits during Comic-Con: M. C. Escher and Robert Williams. In 1995 the Eisner Awards and Inkpots were combined into one Friday night event, and the banquet was no more. The big Saturday night event, the Masquerade, finally moved to the convention center in 1998.

The increase in Comic-Con attendance didn't go unnoticed by Hollywood. While only select studios and production companies had participated in Comic-Con up until this point, the 1990s would see an increase in attention paid to the popular arts event, as evidenced by Matt Groening's brand-new *Simpsons* TV series in 1990 and an appearance by Francis Ford Coppola in 1992 to promote his version of *Dracula*. Celebrities on hand in 1994 included Jean-Claude Van Damme (promoting *Timecop*) in addition to William Shatner and Leonard Nimoy, and special screenings were held for *The Mask* and *Natural Born Killers*. Cult filmmaker Lloyd Kaufman (Troma Studios) and rocker Glen Danzig (who was promoting his fledgling comics line) both had a presence at the 1995 show, while 1997 brought appearances by director Paul Verhoeven (*Starship Troopers*), actors David Hasselhoff (*Nick Fury*, a made-for-television film), John Leguizamo and Michael Jai White (*Spawn*), and Hong Kong film legend Sammo Hung, as well as the first guest turn by Kevin Smith. In 1998 a panel and autograph signing by *Buffy the Vampire Slayer* writer/creator Joss Whedon and most of the show's cast caused a Beatles-like fan frenzy, while John Carpenter was on hand to talk about his film *Vampires*. In 1999 fans were treated to such varied fare as *The Blair Witch Project* (with star Heather Donahue), behind the scenes on *Farscape* (with Claudia Black and Rockne O'Bannon), and the making of *Iron Giant* (with Brad Bird and Vin Diesel, the voice of the Iron Giant).

The 1990s also saw a huge surge of interest in all things Japanese, especially manga and anime. More and more fans were wearing costumes from their favorite manga series to Comic-Con. What had previously been referred to as "hall costumes" (as opposed to costumes created strictly for competing in the Masquerade) was now entering the era of cosplay. And fans got a chance to meet such manga superstars as Rumiko Takahashi (1994), Ryoichi Ikegami (1995), *Sailor Moon*'s Naoko Takeuchi (1998), and Pokémon creator Toshihiro Ono (1999).

It was also during the 1990s that Comic-Con began to make an even greater effort to locate and invite writers, artists, and editors from the Golden and Silver Ages of comics. Many of these creators, who had much to tell about the early days of the medium, had never been to a comic convention. Comic-Con also continued with its tradition of having science fiction/fantasy guests and programming (with writers such as Joe Haldeman, Roger Zelazny, Clive Barker, and Samuel R. Delany and artists such as Rowena, the Brothers Hildebrandt, and Michael Whalen). Comic strip creators such as Lynn Johnston (*For Better or For Worse*), Patrick McDonnell (*Mutts*), and Tom Batiuk (*Funky Winkerbean*) also took center stage at the event. And the "International" in Comic-Con International took on new meaning, as more creators from Europe, South America, and elsewhere (in addition to Japan) were invited to the show as special guests (SEE Comic-Con Is Truly International, page 106).

Throughout the 1990s, Comic-Con continued to grow and prosper. The stage was set, but no one could anticipate what would happen to the convention in the new millennium.

ABOVE: Hawaiian shirts were popular with pros at Comic-Con in the late 1980s and early 1990s. Here at a late-night party in 1990 are (from left) cartoonist Bob Burden, artist Michael Kaluta, writer Len Wein, and cartoonist Scott Shaw! **OPPOSITE:** This ad for the 1998 show included art by Chris Ware (bottom left)

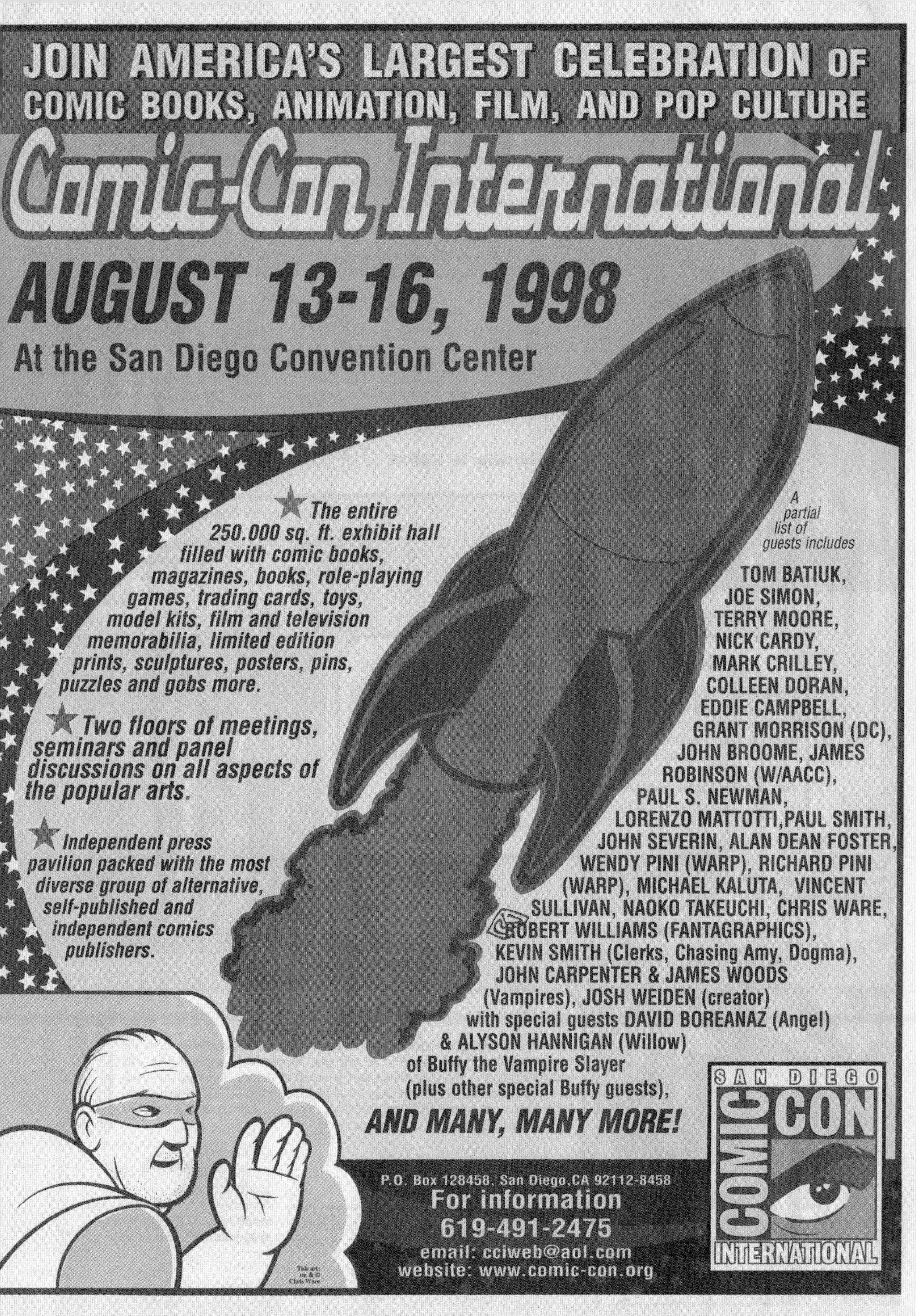

JOIN AMERICA'S LARGEST CELEBRATION OF COMIC BOOKS, ANIMATION, FILM, AND POP CULTURE
Comic-Con International
AUGUST 13-16, 1998
At the San Diego Convention Center
The entire 250.000 sq. ft. exhibit hall filled with comic books, magazines, books, role-playing games, trading cards, toys, model kits, film and television memorabilia, limited edition prints, sculptures, posters, pins, puzzles and gobs more.
Two floors of meetings, seminars and panel discussions on all aspects of the popular arts.
Independent press pavilion packed with the most diverse group of alternative, self-published and independent comics publishers.
A partial list of guests includes
TOM BATIUK, JOE SIMON, TERRY MOORE, NICK CARDY, MARK CRILLEY, COLLEEN DORAN, EDDIE CAMPBELL, GRANT MORRISON (DC), JOHN BROOME, JAMES ROBINSON (W/AACC), PAUL S. NEWMAN, LORENZO MATTOTTI,PAUL SMITH, JOHN SEVERIN, ALAN DEAN FOSTER, WENDY PINI (WARP), RICHARD PINI (WARP), MICHAEL KALUTA, VINCENT SULLIVAN, NAOKO TAKEUCHI, CHRIS WARE, ROBERT WILLIAMS (FANTAGRAPHICS), KEVIN SMITH (Clerks, Chasing Amy, Dogma), JOHN CARPENTER & JAMES WOODS (Vampires), JOSH WEIDEN (creator) with special guests DAVID BOREANAZ (Angel) & ALYSON HANNIGAN (Willow) of Buffy the Vampire Slayer (plus other special Buffy guests),
AND MANY, MANY MORE!
SAN DIEGO COMIC CON INTERNATIONAL
P.O. Box 128458, San Diego,CA 92112-8458
For information
619-491-2475
email: cciweb@aol.com
website: www.comic-con.org
This art: tm & © Chris Ware

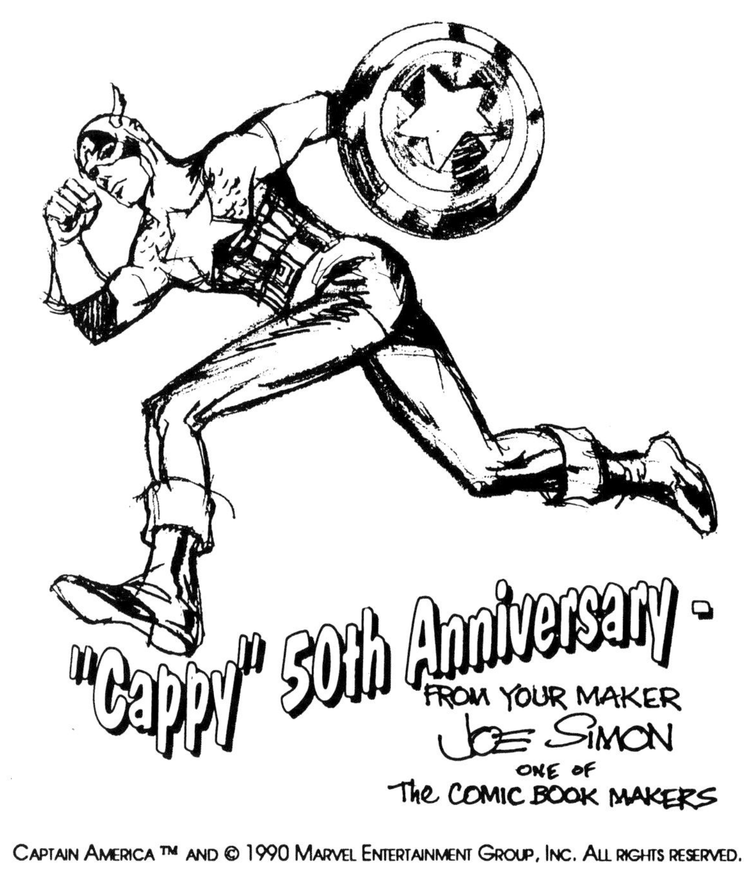
"Cappy" 50th Anniversary -
FROM YOUR MAKER
JOE SIMON
ONE OF
The COMIC BOOK MAKERS
CAPTAIN AMERICA ™ AND © 1990 MARVEL ENTERTAINMENT GROUP, INC. ALL RIGHTS RESERVED.

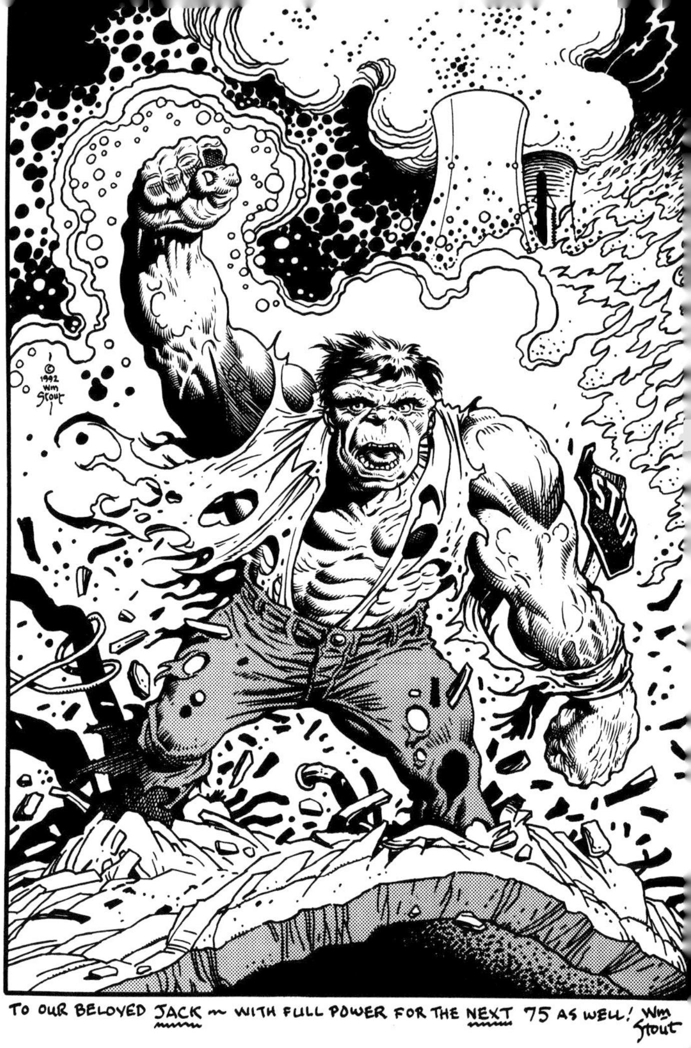
TO OUR BELOVED JACK ~ WITH FULL POWER FOR THE NEXT 75 AS WELL! Wm Stout

CLOCKWISE FROM ABOVE LEFT: Co-creator Joe Simon's celebration of the fiftieth anniversary of Captain America; artist William Stout's commemoration of Jack Kirby's seventy-fifth birthday in 1992; Slave Labor Graphics publisher Dan Vado at a 1991 Comic-Con party; a 1991 ad for a live Comic-Con performance of Harvey Pekar's *American Splendor* stage play, starring Dan Castellaneta (the voice of Homer Simpson) **OPPOSITE, LEFT, TOP TO BOTTOM:** Neil Gaiman at the 2007 Comic-Con; Gaiman with Comic-Con president John Rogers in 1995; Top comics powerhouses—(from left) Frank Miller (*Sin City*), Neil Gaiman, Bill Sienkiewicz (*Elektra: Assassin*), Bernie Wrightson (*Swamp Thing*), and Dave Gibbons (*Watchmen*)—bonding at a party in the early 1990s; Gaiman and British TV personality Jonathan Ross at the 2007 Eisner Awards **TOP RIGHT:** Gaiman accepting the Comic-Con Icon Award on national TV in 2007 **BOTTOM RIGHT:** The 1999 Comic-Con badge with art celebrating the tenth anniversary of Gaiman's signature creation, *The Sandman*

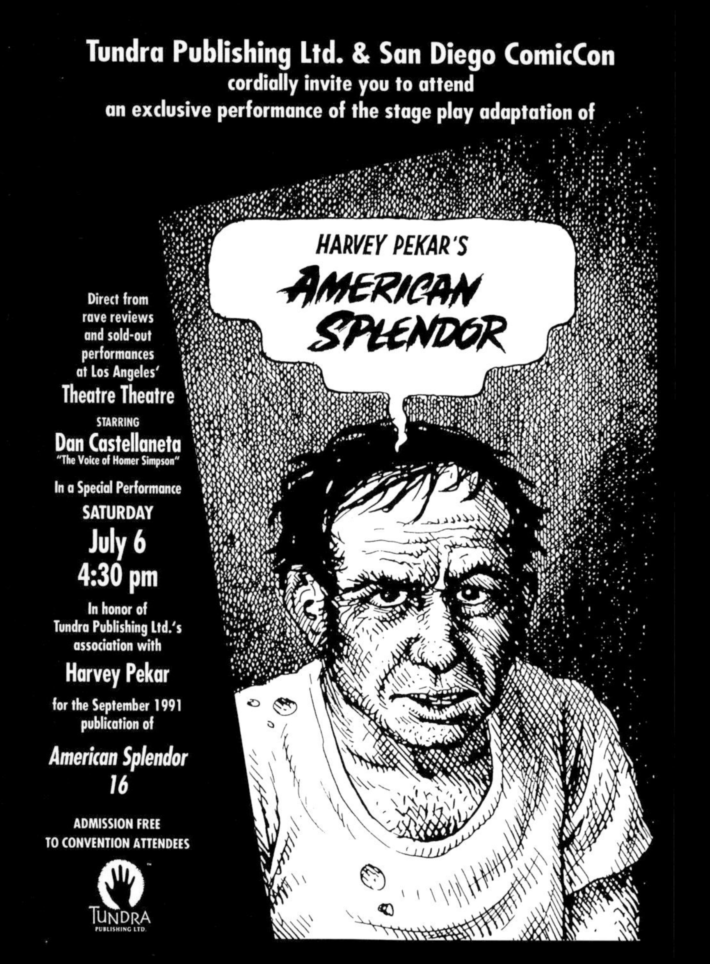
Tundra Publishing Ltd. & San Diego ComicCon
cordially invite you to attend
an exclusive performance of the stage play adaptation of
HARVEY PEKAR'S
AMERICAN SPLENDOR
Direct from rave reviews and sold-out performances at Los Angeles' Theatre Theatre
STARRING
Dan Castellaneta
"The Voice of Homer Simpson"
In a Special Performance
SATURDAY
July 6
4:30 pm
In honor of Tundra Publishing Ltd.'s association with
Harvey Pekar
for the September 1991 publication of
American Splendor 16
ADMISSION FREE
TO CONVENTION ATTENDEES
TUNDRA
PUBLISHING LTD.

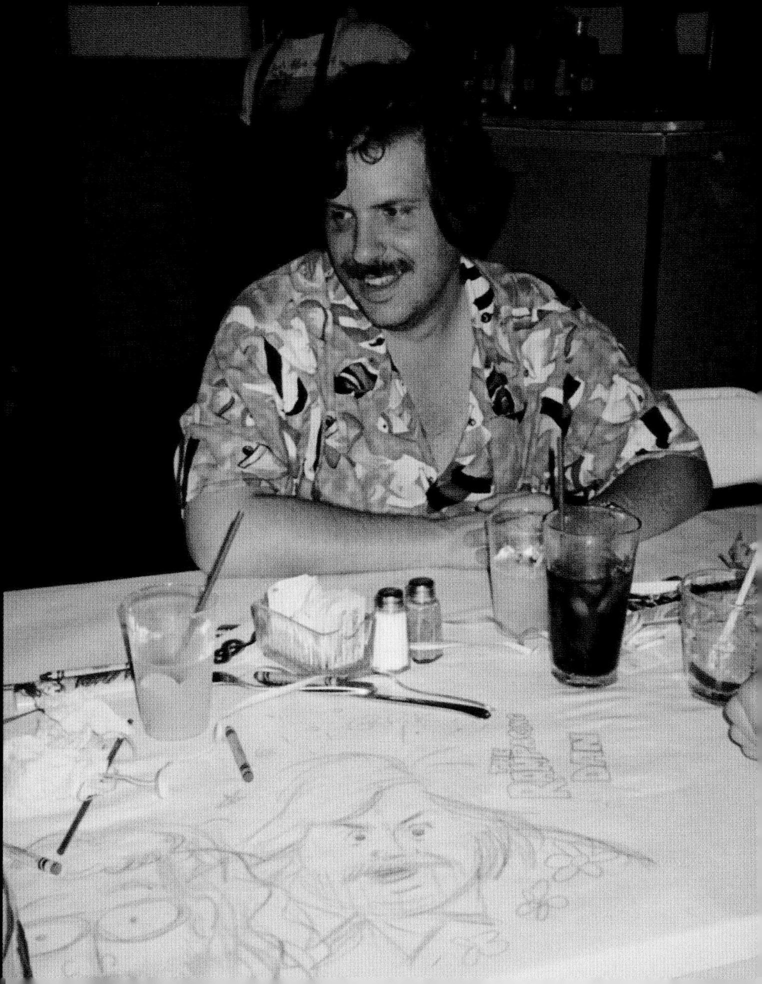

NEIL GAIMAN

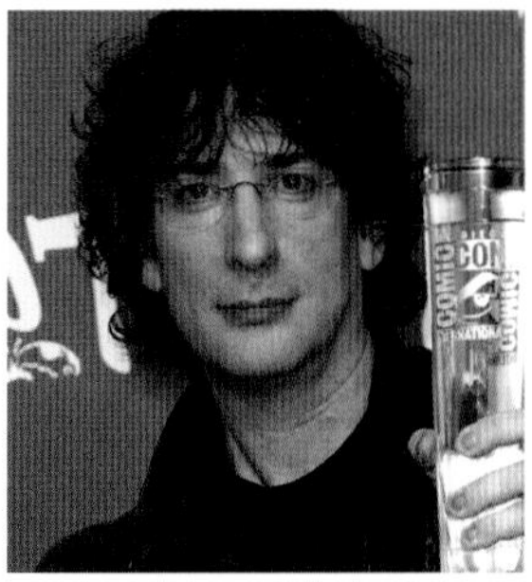

NEIL GAIMAN is the closest thing the comics industry has to a rock star. When he appears at Comic-Con, he speaks to packed audiences, fans wait in long lines to get his autograph, and he is mobbed whenever he attempts to walk around the Exhibit Hall.

A best-selling novelist today (*American Gods*, *Anansi Boys*, *Coraline*), Gaiman first climbed to popularity as a writer in the comic book world in the late 1980s with *Black Orchid* for the Vertigo imprint of DC Comics and *Miracleman* for Eclipse Comics. But it was *The Sandman* that captured fans' imaginations. This Vertigo series, which ran seventy-five issues (plus a few spin-offs) up through 1996, wove tales of Morpheus, Lord of Dreams. Aided by a variety of artists, Gaiman drew on mythology and literature to explore a number of classic fantasy themes. And in so doing he garnered a readership that was 50 percent female—pretty much unheard of in the comic book world at that time. *The Sandman* has gone on to be collected in numerous trade paperback and deluxe editions that remain best-sellers.

While still living in his native Great Britain, Neil made his first visit to Comic-Con in 1989. In 1991 he was a special guest for the first time and received an Inkpot Award. Over the following years he continued to write occasional comics and graphic novels (*Violent Cases*, *Mr. Punch*, and *Signal to Noise*) but became better known as a novelist. Neil returned regularly to Comic-Con to present programs, appear at film screenings, promote movies for which he wrote screenplays such as *Stardust* and *Beowulf*, and sign autographs for hours at a time.

Neil has also been a fixture at the Eisner Awards, having been the recipient of twelve since 1991. One of Gaiman's most memorable appearances at the awards ceremony occurred in 2007, when he copresented an award with old friend and British celebrity Jonathan Ross. Mimicking what presenters Alison Bechdel and Ellen Forney had done earlier in the evening, Ross planted a big kiss on a surprised Gaiman, who could only muster the response, "And the nominees are . . ."

Gaiman has also received Comic-Con's Bob Clampett Humanitarian Award for his fund-raising efforts for a variety of charities including the Comic Book Legal Defense Fund, and the second Comic-Con Icon Award, which is presented to an individual or organization that has been instrumental in bringing comics and/or the popular arts to a wider audience.

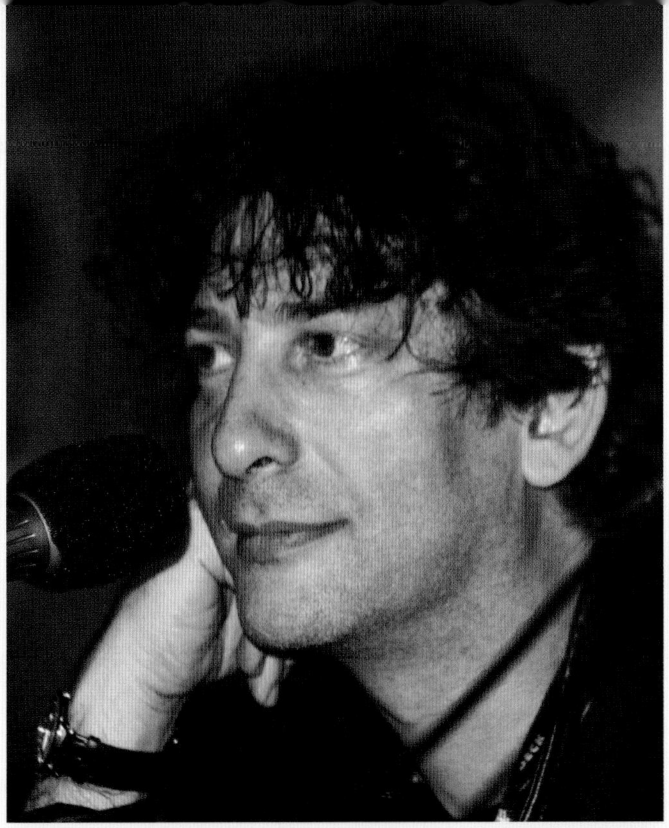

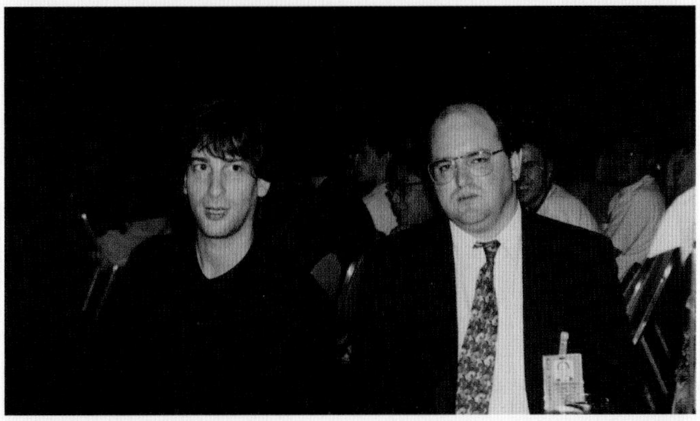

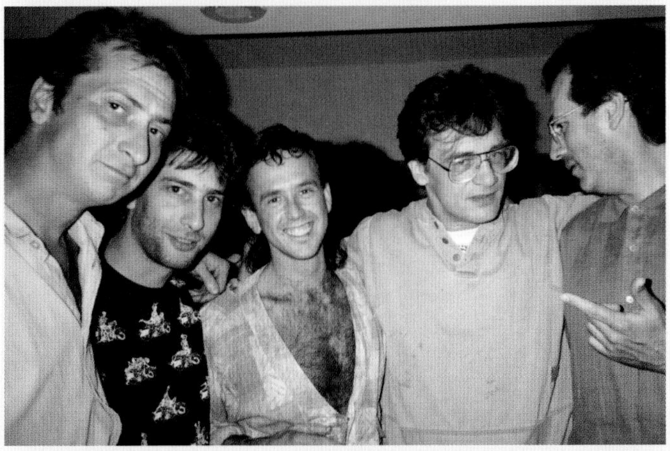

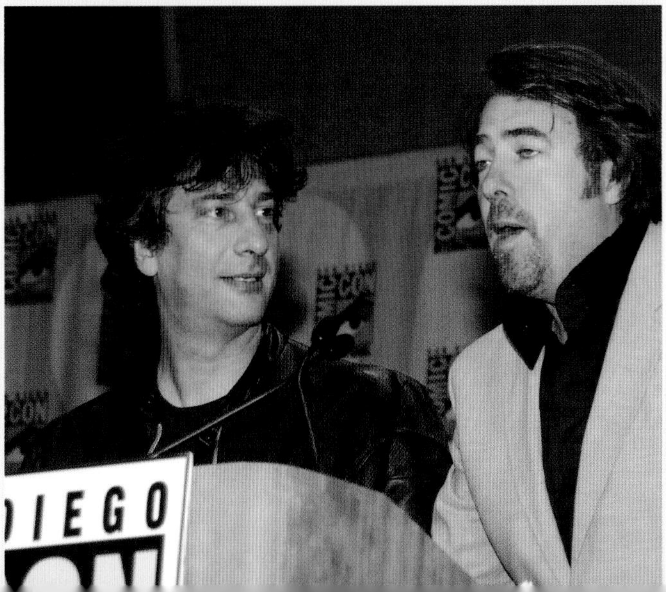

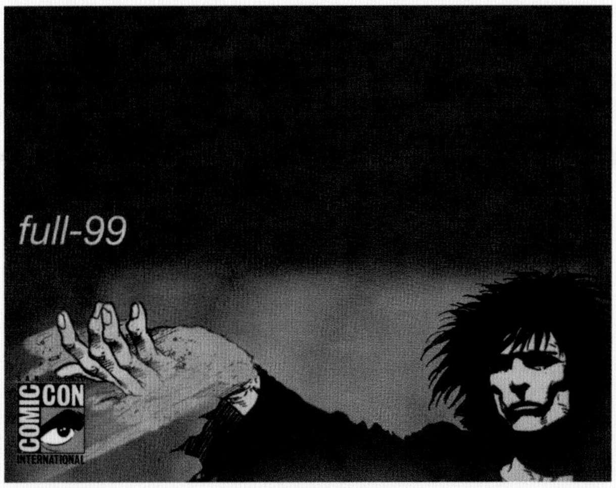
full-99
COMIC CON
INTERNATIONAL

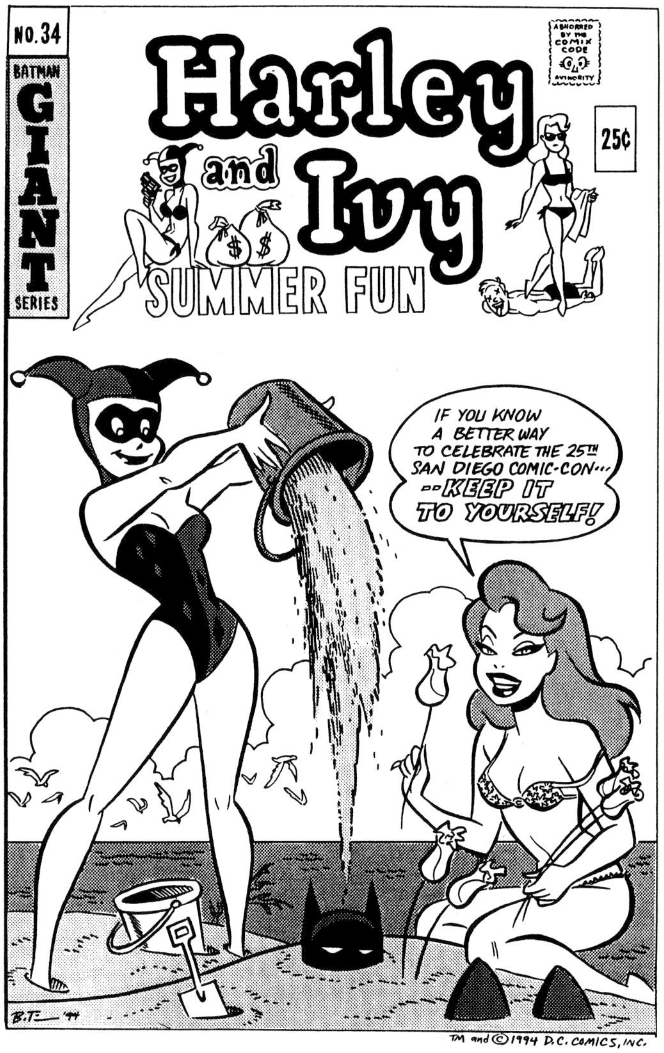
NO. 34
BATMAN GIANT SERIES
Harley and Ivy
SUMMER FUN
25¢
IF YOU KNOW A BETTER WAY TO CELEBRATE THE 25TH SAN DIEGO COMIC-CON... --KEEP IT TO YOURSELF!
B.T. '94
TM and © 1994 D.C. COMICS, INC.

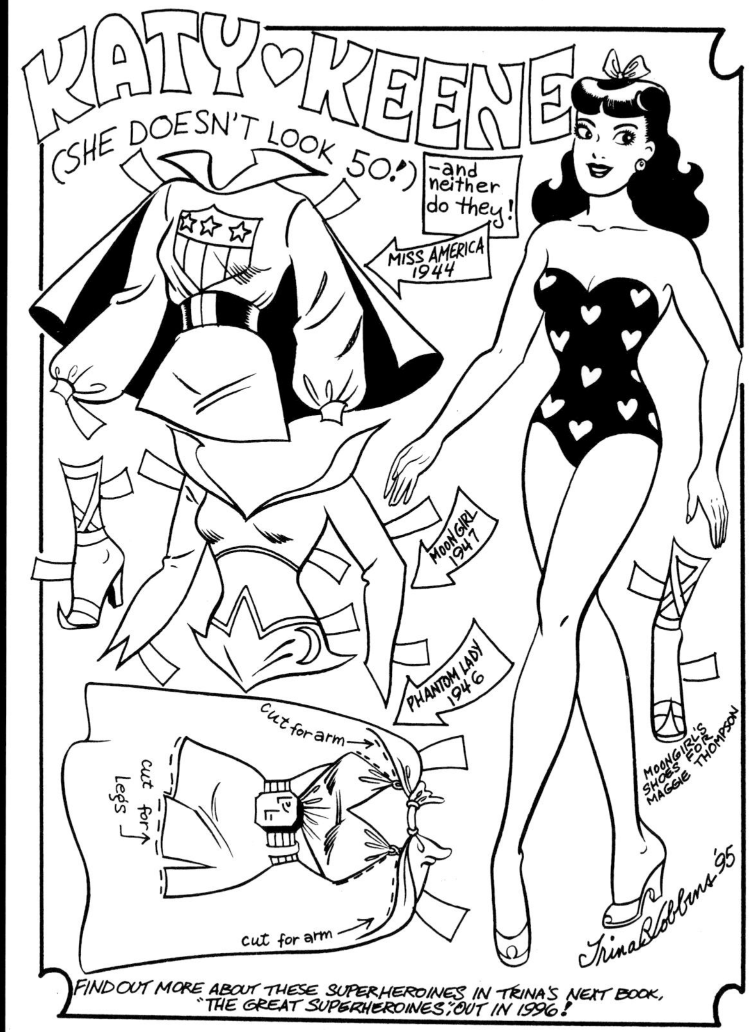
KATY♥KEENE
(SHE DOESN'T LOOK 50!)
-and neither do they!
MISS AMERICA 1944
MOON GIRL 1947
PHANTOM LADY 1946
cut for arm
cut for legs
cut for arm
MOONGIRL'S SHOES FOR MAGGIE THOMPSON
Trina Robbins '95
FIND OUT MORE ABOUT THESE SUPERHEROINES IN TRINA'S NEXT BOOK, "THE GREAT SUPERHEROINES", OUT IN 1996!

CLOCKWISE FROM ABOVE LEFT: A quartet of Souvenir Book art pieces: Bruce Timm's Harley and Ivy at the beach (1994); Trina Robbins's Katy Keene paper doll (1995); Golden and Silver Ages great Sheldon Moldoff's depiction of four of the DC characters he's most famous for (1995); syndicated cartoonist Patrick McDonnell (*Mutts*) taking the dogs for a walk in 1997, the twentieth anniversary of *Star Wars*

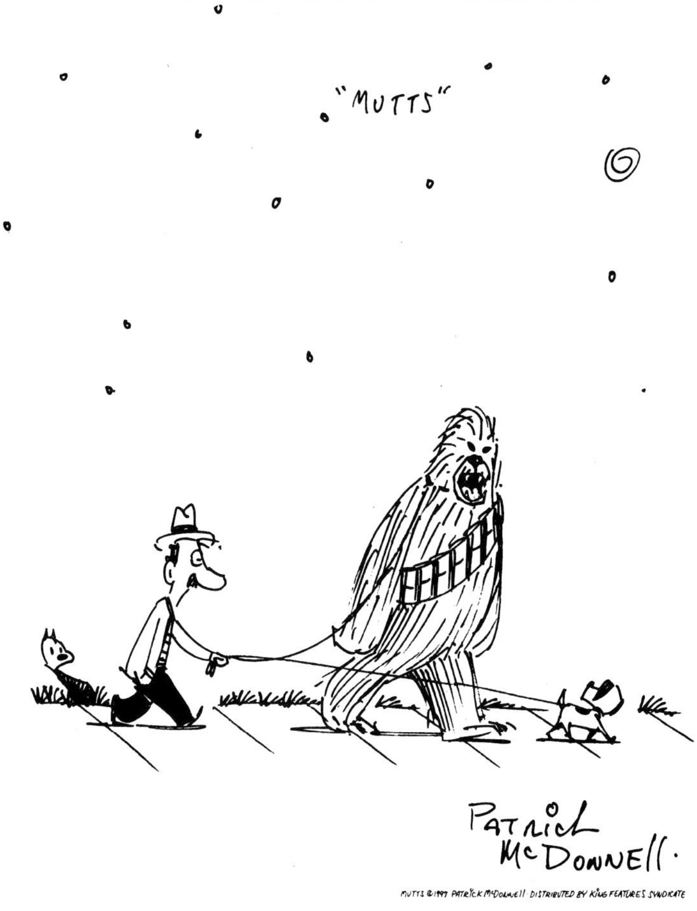
"MUTTS"
PATRICK McDONNELL
MUTTS ©1997 PATRICK McDONNELL DISTRIBUTED BY KING FEATURES SYNDICATE

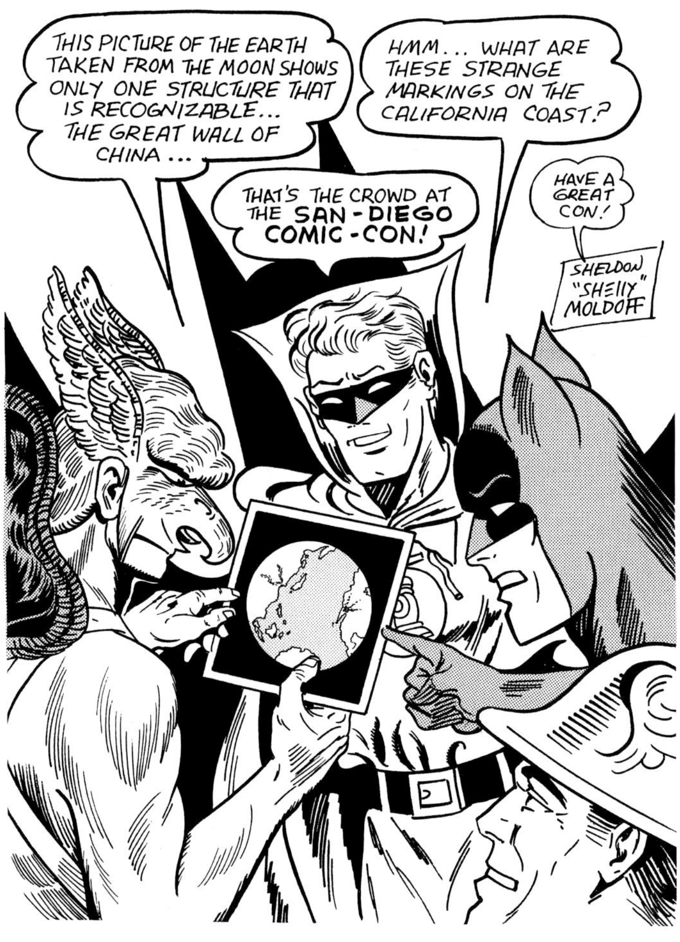
THIS PICTURE OF THE EARTH TAKEN FROM THE MOON SHOWS ONLY ONE STRUCTURE THAT IS RECOGNIZABLE... THE GREAT WALL OF CHINA...
HMM... WHAT ARE THESE STRANGE MARKINGS ON THE CALIFORNIA COAST?
THAT'S THE CROWD AT THE SAN-DIEGO COMIC-CON!
HAVE A GREAT CON!
SHELDON "SHELLY" MOLDOFF

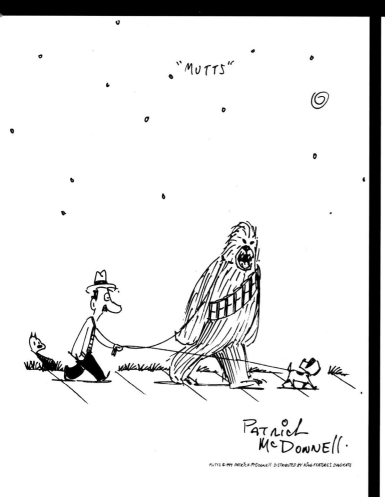

CON/FUSION

1st AVE. ROLL-UP DOORS
PLAZA HALL
STAIRS TO PARKING
ART SHOW
Programming Office
Kreed Hall (Seminars)
WOMEN
DEALERS AREA
Lounge
Ylum Room
Food Service
Barsoom Room (Gaming Area)
MEN
REGISTRATION
NeoTokyo Room
Metropolis Room
Darkover Room
Ashbless Room
B.O.
Information
Pre Reg
ELEVATORS
STAIRS TO PARKING
ELEVATORS
Entrance

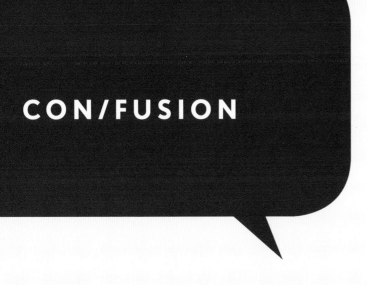

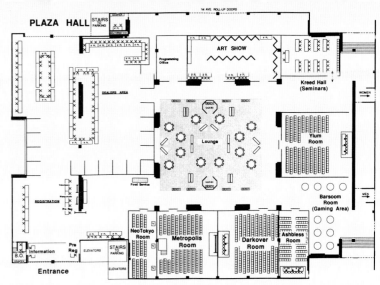

In 1991 Comic-Con added a winter convention to the calendar: Con/Fusion. Billed as a "fusion of the best aspects of a science fiction convention with the best attributes of a comic book convention," the three-day event was held on President's Day weekend, February 16-18, 1991, at the Convention and Performing Arts Center (CPAC) in downtown San Diego, with additional events at the nearby Kingston Hotel.

Chaired by Janet Tait, along with co-chairs Mark Stadler (events) and Mark Yturralde (operations), the convention had attendance limited to one thousand members. The rare winter show involved the rest of the Comic-Con crew and featured science fiction and fantasy author Tim Powers (*Last Call*, *Declare*), comic artist Steve Rude (*Nexus*), and Jim and Doreen Webbert, two noted members of science fiction's "Second Fandom," among the earliest fans of the genre. The show included all the Comic-Con staples: an exhibit hall with a small but impressive Artists' Alley (featuring famed science fiction artist Kelly Freas and what would soon become some of Image Comics' founders: Jim Lee, Whilce Portacio, and Jim Valentino, among others), gaming, a masquerade, an art show, film screenings, and a complete programming schedule.

That programming schedule took place in rooms named after some of the most famous locations in science fiction and comics—the Metropolis Room, the Barsoom Room, and Kreed Hall—and featured panels and workshops. In addition to the special guests, participants included fantasy author Marion Zimmer Bradley, (who had her own "lost art of plotting" workshop, appropriately held in the "Darkover Room"), cartoonist Trina Robbins, Comic-Con mainstay Scott Shaw!, and many more.

It was hoped that the new event would bridge the gap between comics and science fiction fandom. Many Comic-Con committee members were science fiction fans and wanted to introduce more science fiction–oriented programming into Comic-Con without diluting the show's comics-heavy appeal. The thought behind the show was to add an event at the opposite side of the calendar and also continue to utilize CPAC as Comic-Con prepared to move to the brand new San Diego Convention Center for the first time in July 1991.

Con/Fusion lasted for only one year, a noble experiment from the Comic-Con committee. With the move to the new Convention Center, the original show would begin to experience an unprecedented growth spurt that would keep everyone more than busy.

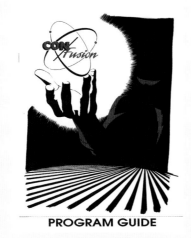

CON Fusion
PROGRAM GUIDE

ABOVE: The convention map shows CPAC's Plaza Hall divided into the many worlds of Con/Fusion **LEFT:** Steve Rude's atmospheric cover for the Con/Fusion program guide, showcasing his signature character Nexus, co-created with writer Mike Baron

COMIC-CON IS TRULY INTERNATIONAL

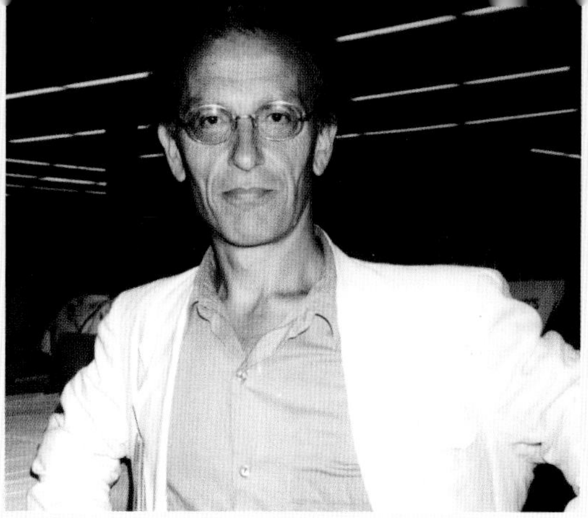

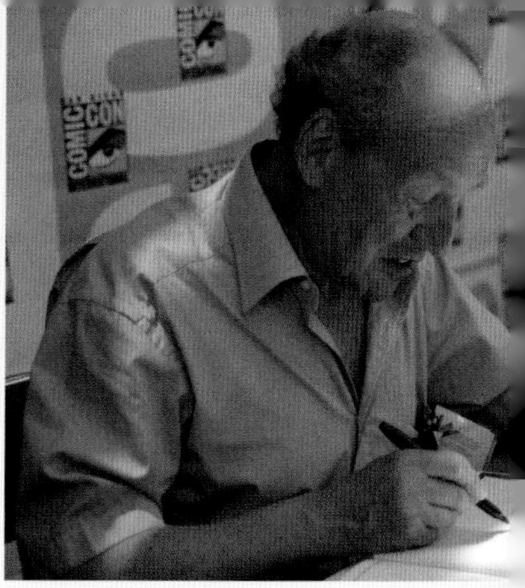
COMIC-CON

Comic-Con's international flavor began in the mid-1970s with an influx of top Filipino artists including Alex Niño, Nestor Redondo, Alfredo Alcala, and Ernie Chan. They were all legendary comics artists in the Philippines who moved to the United States to work for companies like Warren Publishing, DC Comics, and Marvel. Niño drew stories for *House of Mystery* and *House of Secrets*, Redondo and Alcala had memorable runs on *Swamp Thing*, and Chan inked *Conan* at Marvel. Other Filipino artists who attended in subsequent years included Rudy Nebres, Dell Barras, Tony DeZuñiga, and Romeo Tanghal. More recently, the Philippines has been well represented at Comic-Con by such artists as Jay Anacleto, Leinil Francis Yu, and Rod Espinosa.

Japan came next. In 1980 several dozen fans and some manga superstars descended on Comic-Con in a special tour. Having the great Osamu Tezuka (*Astro Boy*, *Black Jack*) in San Diego was akin to Jack Kirby making an appearance at a Japanese fan event. Tezuka's compatriots included cartoonists Go Nagai (*Cutie Honey*, *Devilman*) and Monkey Punch (*Lupin III*), and the tour group held a special reception to encourage communication between American and Japanese comics creators. Although anime screenings had their own programming track beginning in 1978, it wasn't until the 1990s that manga and anime began to really catch on at San Diego and other Japanese superstars began to appear at Comic-Con. They included Rumiko Takahashi in 1994 and again in 2000, Ryoichi Ikegami in 1995, and Naoko Takeuchi in 1998. Manga, anime, and Japanese toys were mainstays in the Exhibit Hall for years, but in the new century the floor exploded with giant booths devoted to all things Japanese. Several manga publishers sponsored Japanese creators at their booths, and Comic-Con special guests included Kazuo Koike, Yoshihiro Tatsumi, and Tite Kubo.

In music, the British Invasion was in the 1960s, but for comics it started in the 1980s and continued into the 1990s. DC had discovered a number of writers from the United Kingdom who became fan favorites in the United States, especially on titles for DC's Vertigo imprint. Alan Moore (doing *Swamp Thing* at the time) made his only U.S. comic convention appearance in San Diego in 1985; he was later followed by Grant Morrison, Garth Ennis, Peter Milligan, and Neil Gaiman. Popular U.K. artists at Comic-Con during this period included Brian Bolland, Alan Davis, Steve Dillon, Dave Gibbons, Simon Bisley, and Dave McKean. Many of those creators returned several times over the next decade. In the 2000s, the British invasion continued with Bryan Talbot, Mike Carey, Kevin O'Neill, Mark Buckingham, and Warren Ellis. In categories by themselves are Eddie Campbell, a Scotsman who lives in Australia, and cartoonist Roger Langridge, a New Zealander who lives in England. Comic-Con has also featured British authors and fantasy artists, from Douglas Adams and Clive Barker to Roger Dean and Brian and Wendy Froud.

THIS SPREAD, LEFT TO RIGHT: Comics creators from around the world who have been guests at Comic-Con: France's Jean "Moebius" Giraud (*The Airtight Garage*, *Arzach*) and Jean-Claude Mézières (*Valerian*); Japan's Rumiko Takahashi (*InuYasha*, *Urusei Yatsura*) and Ryoichi Ikegami (*Crying Freeman*); Israel's Rutu Modan (*Exit Wounds*); and the Philippines' Alfredo Alcala (*Conan the Barbarian*, *Swamp Thing*)

The popularity of *Heavy Metal* magazine led to an interest in European comics creators in the 1980s and several panels on the topic at Comic-Con, often spearheaded by Jean-Marc and Randy Lofficier. One of the first European greats to appear at Comic-Con was Jean Giraud (a.k.a. "Moebius") in 1986, and he made several return appearances. Subsequent European guests have included Belgian artist François Schuiten, Italian painter Lorenzo Mattotti, French cartoonist Lewis Trondheim, Norwegian cartoonist Jason, French graphic novelist David B., French artist Jean-Claude Mézières, and French writer-artist team Philippe Dupuy and Charles Berbérian. A number of exhibitors now specialize in European graphic novels and albums.

Comic-Con fans have also been treated to appearances by Spanish artist Luis Royo, Argentinian artists Eduardo Risso and Luis Dominguez, Hungarian-Israeli graphic novelist Miriam Katin, Bulgarian artist Alexander Maleev, and Israeli writer/artist Rutu Modan, to name a few.

Closer to home, Comic-Con has always welcomed creators and fans from Mexico and Canada. Sergio Aragonés (who was born in Spain, raised in Mexico, and moved to the United States in 1962) has encouraged many Mexican creators to attend. In 1988 a group of Mexican cartoonists, headed by Oscar González Loyo and Carlos Tron, made the trip to Comic-Con. Canadian guests over the years have ranged from indie/alternative creators such as Dave Sim, Julie Doucet, and Guy Delisle to popular mainstream comics creator Darwyn Cooke and syndicated cartoonist Lynn Johnston.

More recently, Comic-Con has hosted nearly three thousand press representatives each year from many nations, and people from all over the world both attend and are now kept up-to-date on this truly international event.

SAN DIEGO
COMIC CON COMICS
3

1994

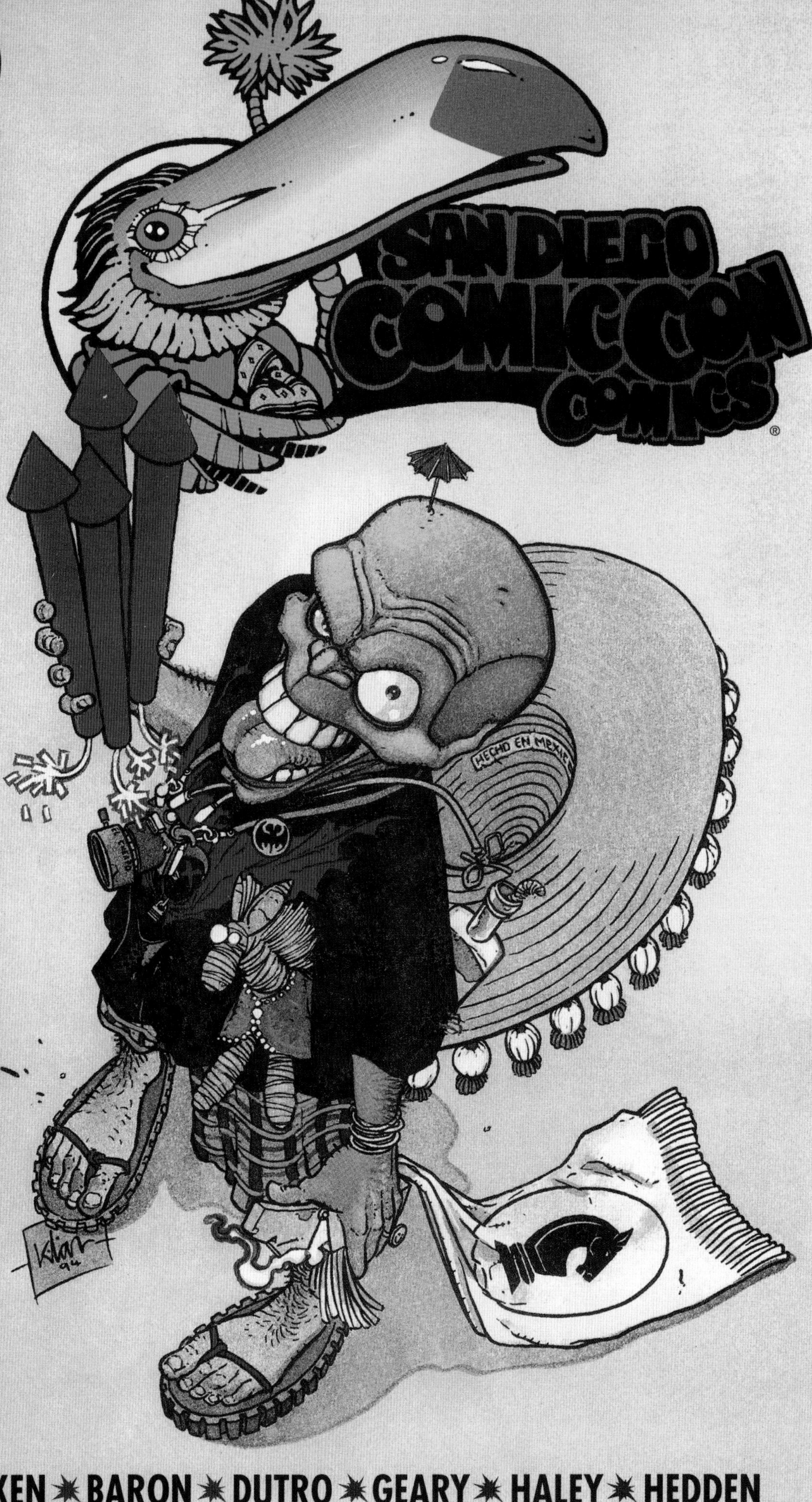
SAN DIEGO COMIC CON COMICS
HECHO EN MEXICO

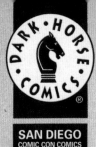

AIKEN ✷ BARON ✷ DUTRO ✷ GEARY ✷ HALEY ✷ HEDDEN
LUKE ✷ PLUNKETT ✷ ROBINSON ✷ ROYAL ✷ SILKE ✷ SIMMONS
THOMPSON ✷ WAGNER ✷ WARREN ✷ WILLIAMS

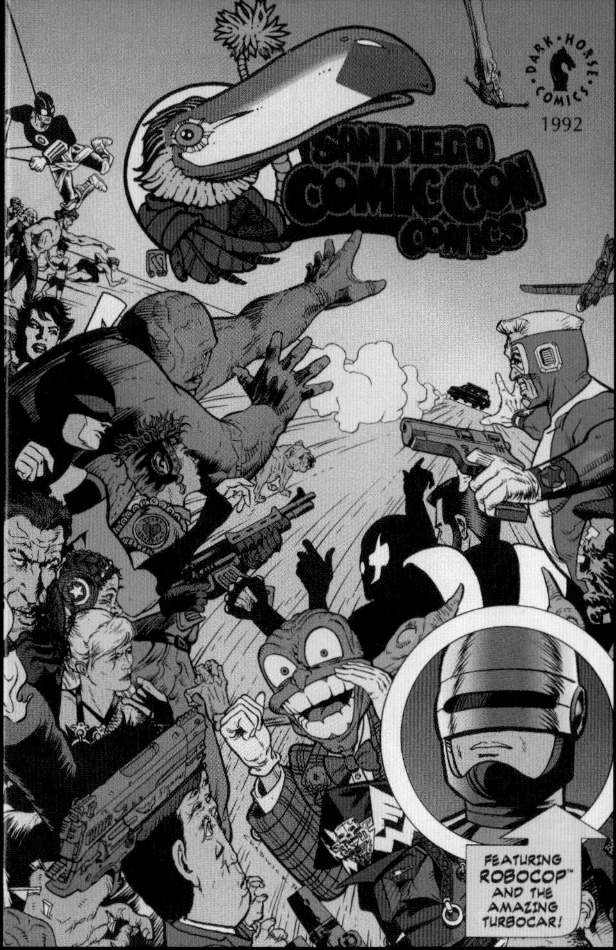
DARK HORSE COMICS
1992
SAN DIEGO COMIC CON COMICS
FEATURING ROBOCOP™ AND THE AMAZING TURBOCAR!

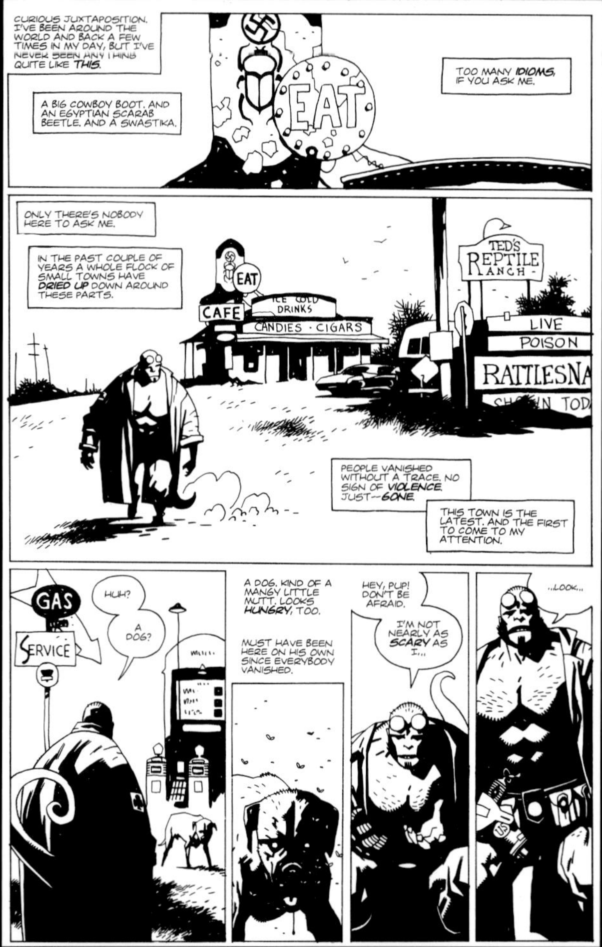
CURIOUS JUXTAPOSITION. I'VE BEEN AROUND THE WORLD AND BACK A FEW TIMES IN MY DAY, BUT I'VE NEVER SEEN ANYTHING QUITE LIKE THIS.
A BIG COWBOY BOOT, AND AN EGYPTIAN SCARAB BEETLE, AND A SWASTIKA.
EAT
TOO MANY IDIOMS, IF YOU ASK ME.
ONLY THERE'S NOBODY HERE TO ASK ME.
IN THE PAST COUPLE OF YEARS A WHOLE FLOCK OF SMALL TOWNS HAVE DRIED UP DOWN AROUND THESE PARTS.
EAT
CAFE
ICE COLD DRINKS
CANDIES · CIGARS
TED'S REPTILE RANCH
LIVE
POISON
RATTLESNA
PEOPLE VANISHED WITHOUT A TRACE. NO SIGN OF VIOLENCE. JUST--GONE.
THIS TOWN IS THE LATEST, AND THE FIRST TO COME TO MY ATTENTION.
GAS
SERVICE
HUH?
A DOG?
A DOG. KIND OF A MANGY LITTLE MUTT. LOOKS HUNGRY, TOO.
MUST HAVE BEEN HERE ON HIS OWN SINCE EVERYBODY VANISHED.
HEY, PUP! DON'T BE AFRAID.
I'M NOT NEARLY AS SCARY AS I...
...LOOK...

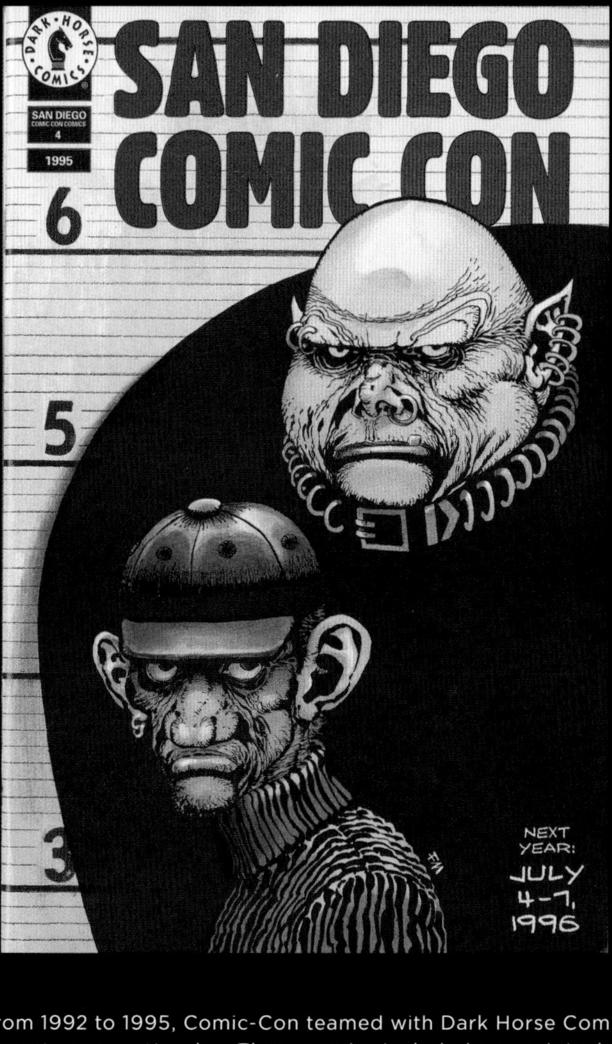
DARK HORSE COMICS
SAN DIEGO COMIC CON COMICS 4
1995
SAN DIEGO COMIC CON
6
5
3
NEXT YEAR: JULY 4-7, 1996

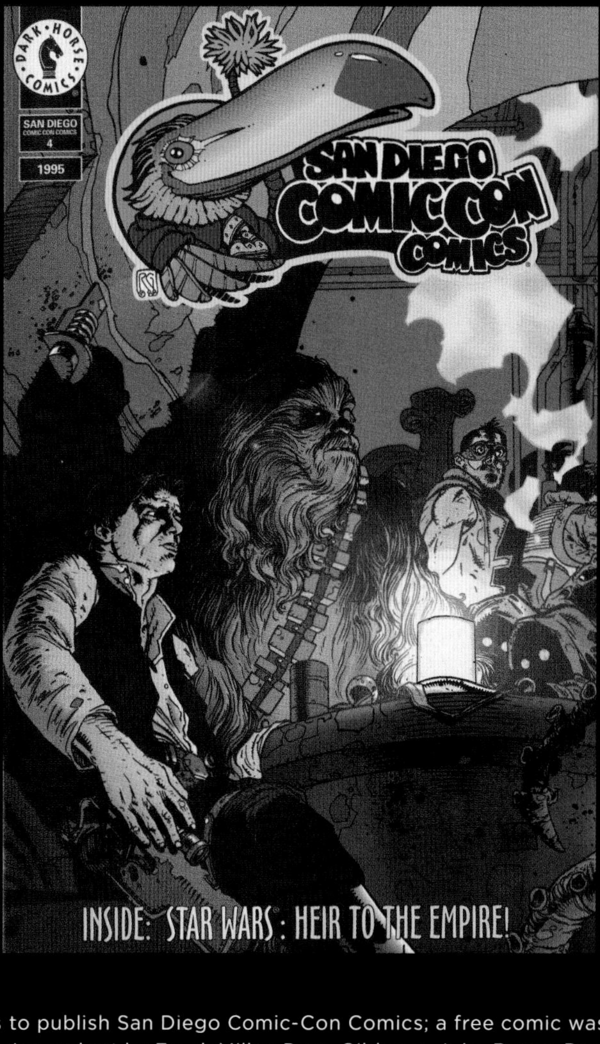
DARK HORSE COMICS
SAN DIEGO COMIC CON COMICS 4
1995
SAN DIEGO COMIC CON COMICS
INSIDE: STAR WARS : HEIR TO THE EMPIRE!

From 1992 to 1995, Comic-Con teamed with Dark Horse Comics to publish San Diego Comic-Con Comics; a free comic was given to every attendee. These comics included rare original stories and art by Frank Miller, Dave Gibbons, John Byrne, Paul Chadwick, Rick Geary, Art Adams, Matt Wagner, and Mike Mignola, who contributed the first appearance of Hellboy (issue no. 2, **TOP RIGHT**). Cover artists include Kilian Plunkett (no. 3, **OPPOSITE**), Paul Chadwick (no. 1, **TOP LEFT**), Frank Miller (**ABOVE LEFT**), and Kilian Plunkett (**ABOVE RIGHT**) on the flip-book covers for no. 4.

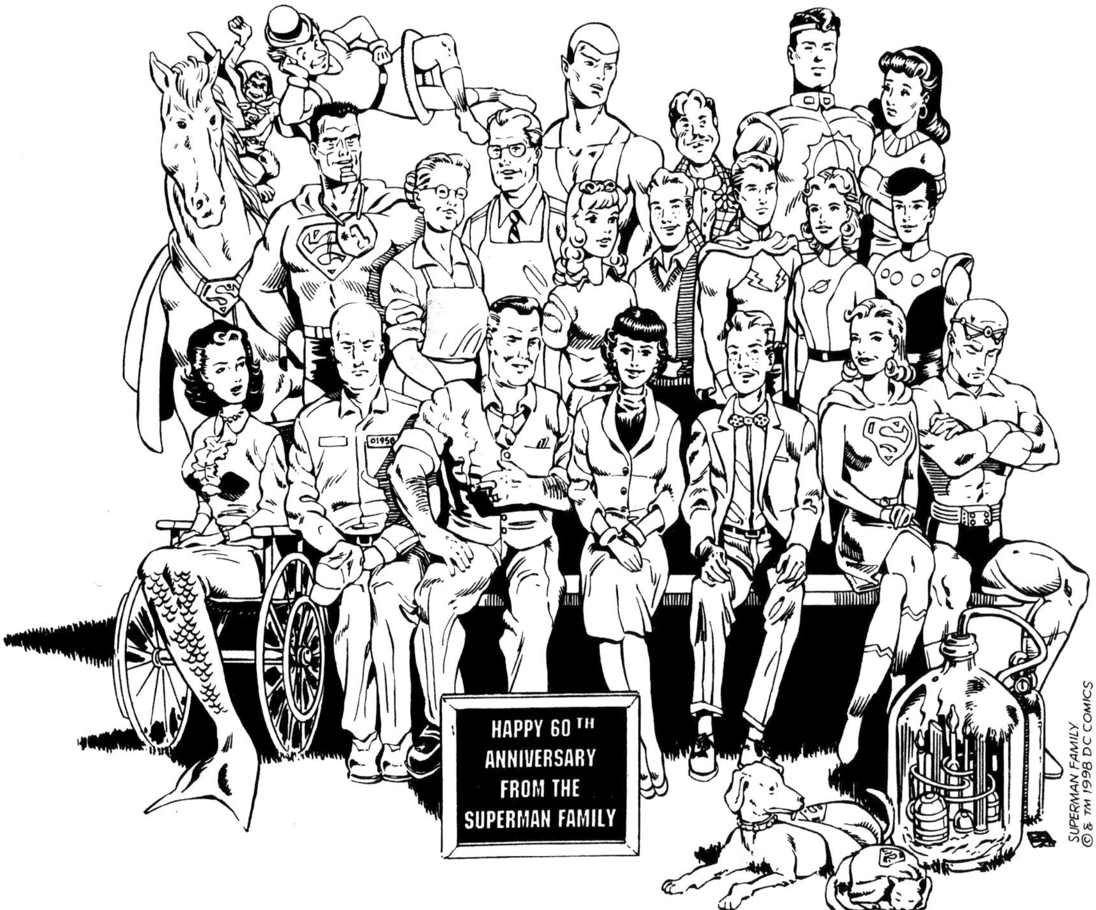
HAPPY 60TH
ANNIVERSARY
FROM THE
SUPERMAN FAMILY
SUPERMAN FAMILY
© & TM 1998 DC COMICS

ABOVE: Wes Abbott's piece for the 1998 Souvenir Book, celebrating Superman's sixtieth anniversary **BELOW LEFT:** Stan Sakai's observation that the thirtieth anniversary of Comic-Con in 1999 was also the fifteenth of his Usagi Yojimbo **BELOW RIGHT:** The Golden Age Green Lantern and co-creator/artist Mart Nodell celebrating the fact that the 1991 Comic-Con fell on the Fourth of July

OPPOSITE, CLOCKWISE FROM TOP LEFT: The fortieth anniversary of EC Comics in 1990 marked by Jaime and Gilbert Hernandez with *Love and Rockets'* Maggie the Mechanic; Hilary Barta's honoring of the fiftieth anniversary of Will Eisner's *The Spirit*; writer Charles Novinskie and artist Lon T. Roberts's exploration of "the fine line between fan and pro" in a 1990 piece; George Pérez saluting the fiftieth anniversary of Captain America

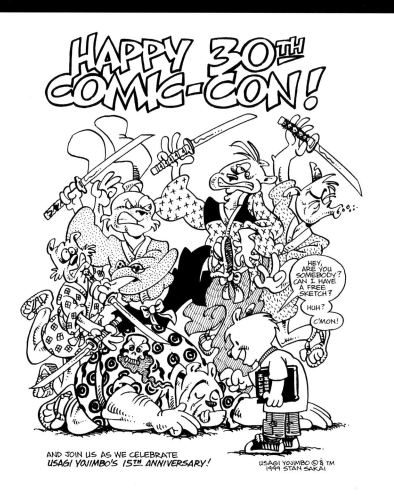

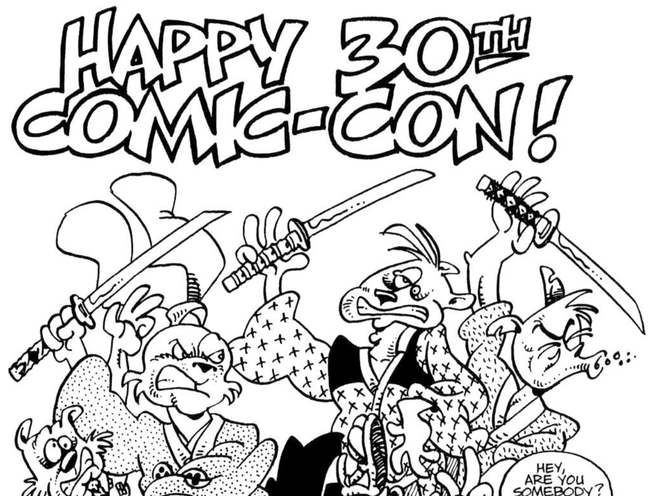
HAPPY 30TH
COMIC-CON!
HEY, ARE YOU SOMEBODY? CAN I HAVE A FREE SKETCH?
HUH?
C'MON!
AND JOIN US AS WE CELEBRATE
USAGI YOJIMBO'S 15TH ANNIVERSARY!
USAGI YOJIMBO © & TM
1999 STAN SAKAI

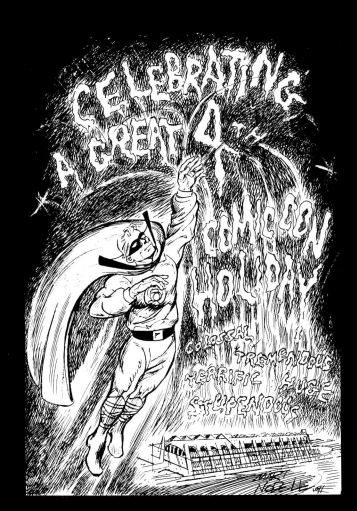

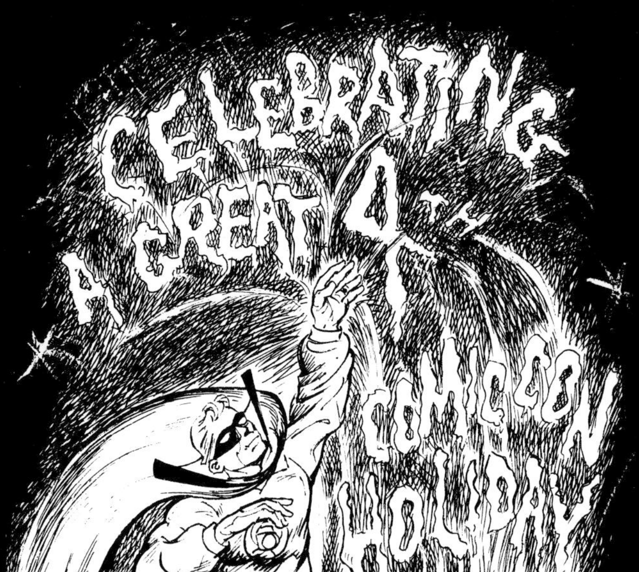
CELEBRATING
A GREAT 4TH
COMIC-CON
HOLIDAY
COLOSSAL
TREMENDOUS
TERRIFIC HUGE
STUPENDOUS

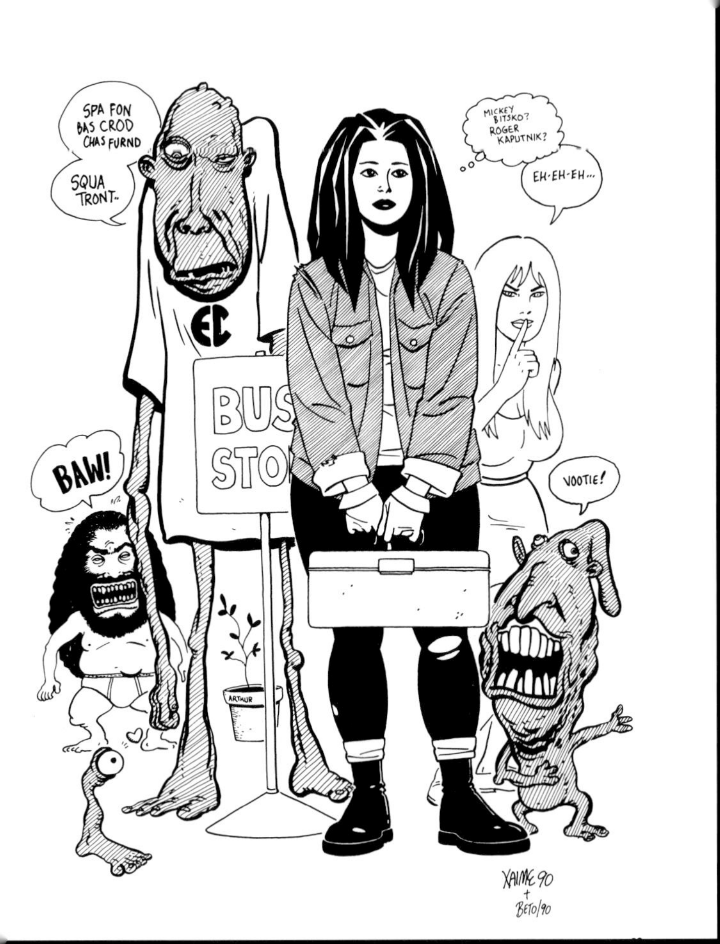
SPA FON BAS CROD CHAS FURND
SQUA TRONT..
MICKEY BITSKO? ROGER KAPUTNIK?
EH-EH-EH...
EC
BUS STO
BAW!
VOOTIE!
ARTHUR
XAIME 90 + BETO/90

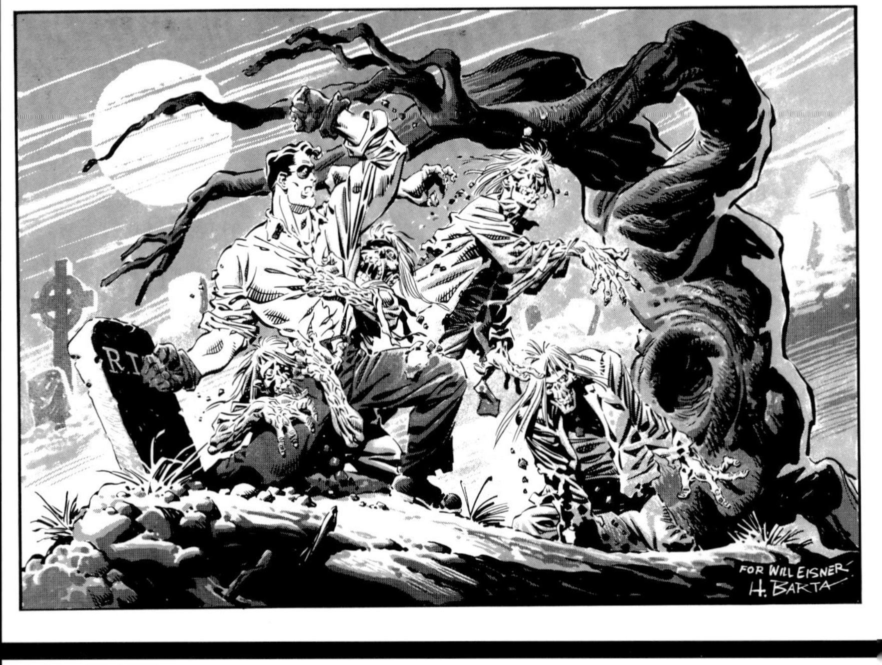
R.I.
FOR WILL EISNER
H. BARTA

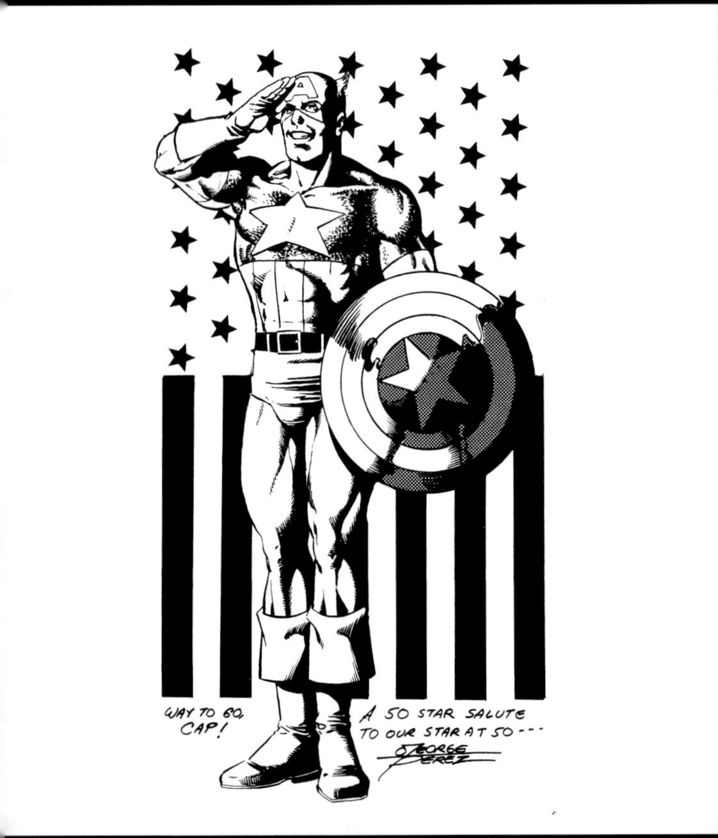
WAY TO GO, CAP!
A 50 STAR SALUTE TO OUR STAR AT 50---
GEORGE PEREZ

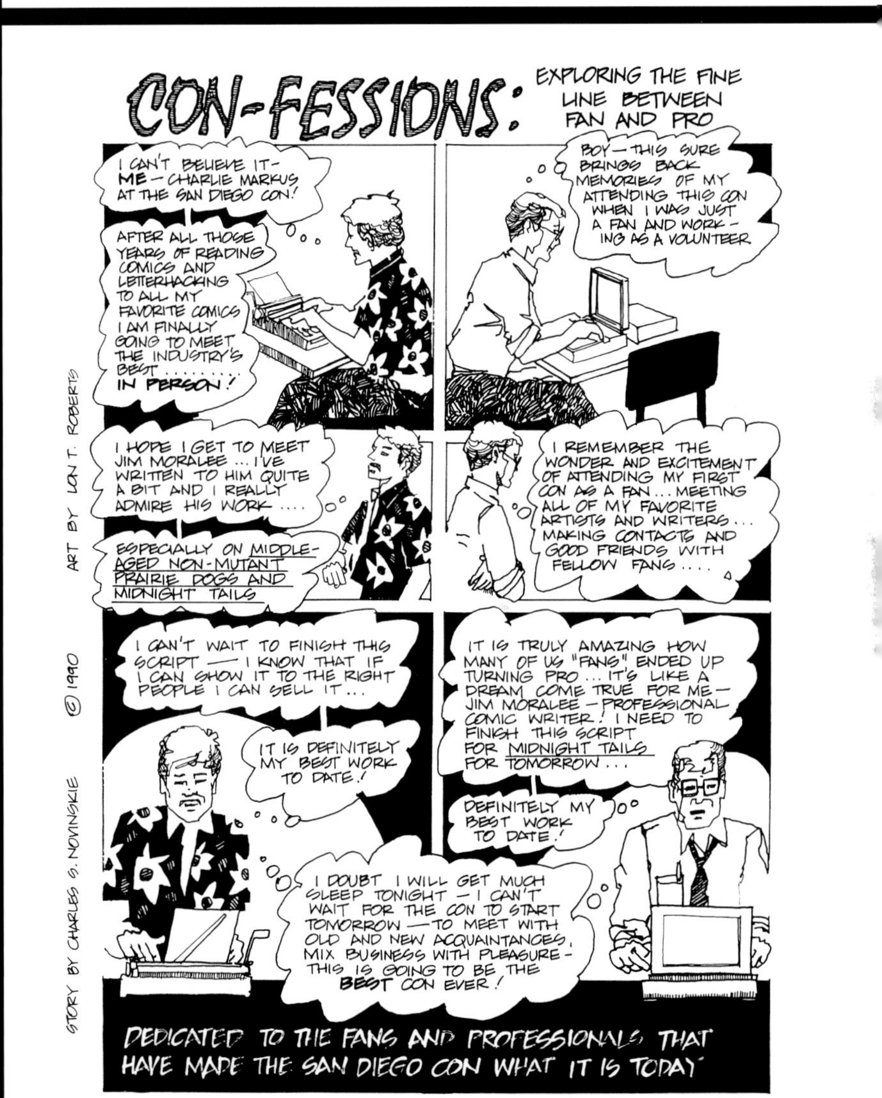
CON-FESSIONS:
EXPLORING THE FINE LINE BETWEEN FAN AND PRO
I CAN'T BELIEVE IT— ME—CHARLIE MARKUS AT THE SAN DIEGO CON!
AFTER ALL THOSE YEARS OF READING COMICS AND LETTERHACKING TO ALL MY FAVORITE COMICS I AM FINALLY GOING TO MEET THE INDUSTRY'S BEST .... IN PERSON!
BOY—THIS SURE BRINGS BACK MEMORIES OF MY ATTENDING THIS CON WHEN I WAS JUST A FAN AND WORKING AS A VOLUNTEER
I HOPE I GET TO MEET JIM MORALEE ... I'VE WRITTEN TO HIM QUITE A BIT AND I REALLY ADMIRE HIS WORK ....
ESPECIALLY ON MIDDLE-AGED NON-MUTANT PRAIRIE DOGS AND MIDNIGHT TAILS
I REMEMBER THE WONDER AND EXCITEMENT OF ATTENDING MY FIRST CON AS A FAN ... MEETING ALL OF MY FAVORITE ARTISTS AND WRITERS ... MAKING CONTACTS AND GOOD FRIENDS WITH FELLOW FANS ....
I CAN'T WAIT TO FINISH THIS SCRIPT — I KNOW THAT IF I CAN SHOW IT TO THE RIGHT PEOPLE I CAN SELL IT ...
IT IS DEFINITELY MY BEST WORK TO DATE!
IT IS TRULY AMAZING HOW MANY OF US "FANS" ENDED UP TURNING PRO ... IT'S LIKE A DREAM COME TRUE FOR ME—JIM MORALEE—PROFESSIONAL COMIC WRITER! I NEED TO FINISH THIS SCRIPT FOR MIDNIGHT TAILS FOR TOMORROW ...
DEFINITELY MY BEST WORK TO DATE!
I DOUBT I WILL GET MUCH SLEEP TONIGHT — I CAN'T WAIT FOR THE CON TO START TOMORROW — TO MEET WITH OLD AND NEW ACQUAINTANCES, MIX BUSINESS WITH PLEASURE—THIS IS GOING TO BE THE BEST CON EVER!
DEDICATED TO THE FANS AND PROFESSIONALS THAT HAVE MADE THE SAN DIEGO CON WHAT IT IS TODAY
STORY BY CHARLES S. NOVINSKIE © 1990 ART BY LON T. ROBERTS

“You can't talk about Comic-Con as if it was a convention. It's actually many different conventions under one roof. If you're into videogames, you can spend the entire con focusing just on that. If you're a TV person, movie fan, science fiction reader, or a gamer, you can spend your entire convention pursuing that interest. And if you're into comics, well, that's what Comic-Con is still about. But if you're like me and you like a little of everything, it's all right there for the picking.”

—MARV WOLFMAN

WRITER/EDITOR, *TOMB OF DRACULA*, *TEEN TITANS*

APE: THE ALTERNATIVE PRESS EXPO

APE

ALTERNATIVE PRESS EXPO

APE, the Alternative Press Expo, showcases the incredibly diverse and vibrant world of alternative and self-published comic books, fanzines, magazines, art books, and other forms of artistic expression.

Founded by writer and comics publisher Dan Vado of SLG (Slave Labor Graphics) Publishing, APE got its start in 1994 as a one-day convention in San Jose, California. Vado's vision was to create an event that would spotlight small publishing companies, self-publishers, and creators working in the alternative and independent side of the comics industry. This show also allowed greater interaction between attendees and creators and added fuel to the DIY (do-it-yourself) comics movement growing around the world. The first APE tied in to a series of like-minded gatherings around the country, coming off the "Spirits of Independence" tour of Dave Sim, creator of *Cerebus*, and is one of the few—along with the Small Press Expo (SPX) in Bethesda, Maryland—that survived and flourished beyond the first year.

With APE's second year, Comic-Con International came on board and has maintained the show ever since, with Vado in the role of founder and his SLG Publishing anchoring the Exhibit Hall with a large presence. The event expanded to two days in 1998. In 2000 it moved to San Francisco's Herbst Pavilion in Fort Mason Center for a one-day trial run. That venue proved to be successful enough not only to keep APE in the city, but also to return it to being a two-day show in 2001. In 2004 APE moved to the much larger Concourse Exhibition Center, also in San Francisco. Attendance has grown to more than five thousand, with more than 350 tables available for exhibitors.

In addition to a large Exhibit Hall, APE features special guests and programming devoted to alternative and self-published comics. Guests have included Jessica Abel, Mike Allred, Alison Bechdel, Paige Braddock, Charles Burns, Dan Clowes, Howard Cruse, Justin Green, Kevin Huizenga, Megan Kelso, Keith Knight, David Lapham, Hope Larson, Batton Lash, Carol Lay, Matt Madden, Terry Moore, Françoise Mouly, Bryan Lee O'Malley, Paul Pope, Alex Robinson, Dave Sim, Jeff Smith, Art Spiegelman, Raina Telgemeier, Adrian Tomine, Carol Tyler, Jhonen Vasquez, Chris Ware, Robert Williams, and Gene Yang.

A walk through the APE Exhibit Hall reveals many fascinating sides to comics publishing. From mini-comics to full-fledged art books, from comics as art objects to graphic novels, the work represented at the Alternative Press Expo is personal, cutting-edge, and exciting in a way that traditional mainstream publishers can't duplicate. APE remains one of the true bastions of personal creativity and ingenuity in publishing today.

ABOVE: (Left to right) graphic novelists Art Spiegelman (*Maus*), Kevin Huizenga (*Ganges*), Hope Larson (*Gray Horses*), and Bryan Lee O'Malley (*Scott Pilgrim*) at APE 2007 **OPPOSITE, TOP ROW, FROM LEFT:** Tiki-inspired cover for the APE VI program book in 1999; writer/artist Chris Ware (*The ACME Novelty Library*) making his second-ever U.S. convention appearance at APE in 2008; the poster for APE 2004, with illustration by cartoonist Batton Lash (*Supernatural Law*) **MIDDLE ROW, FROM LEFT:** APE 2007 illustration by Gene Yang (*American Born Chinese*); APE 2006 illustration by Keith Knight (*The K Chronicles*); the cover for the APE 1995 program book; illustration by Paige Braddock (*Jane's World*) for APE 2008 **BOTTOM:** The busy APE exhibit hall at the Concourse Exhibition Center in San Francisco in 2007

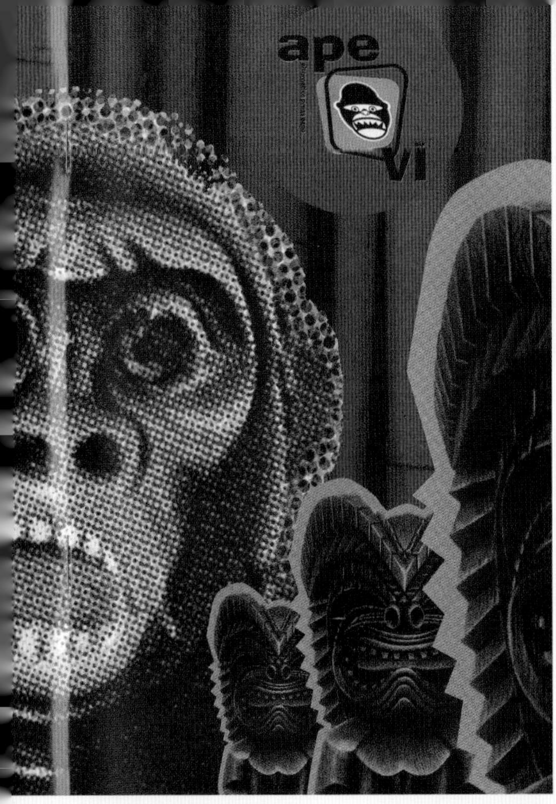
ape
VI

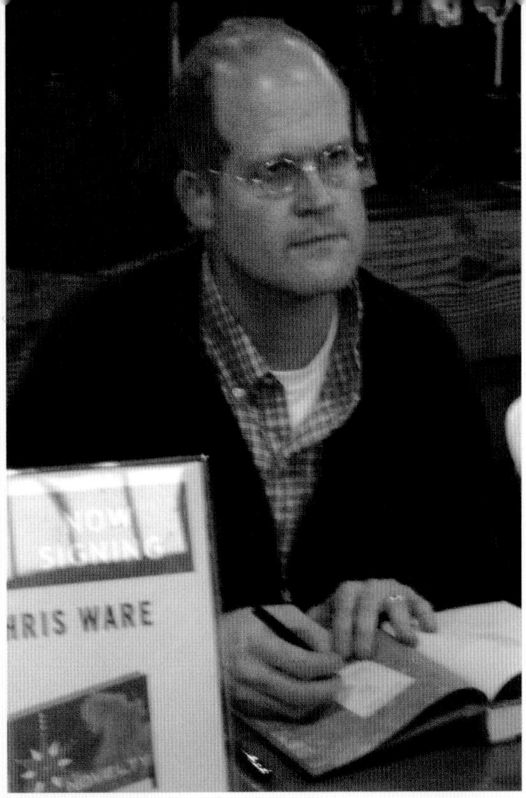
NOW SIGNING
HRIS WARE

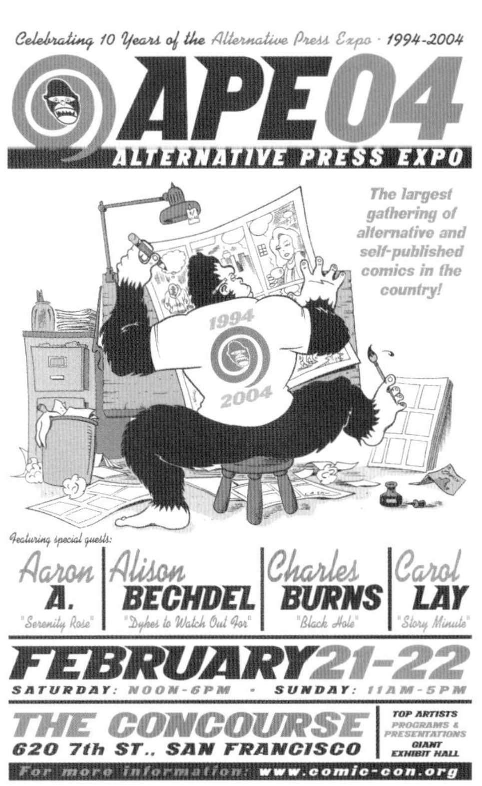
Celebrating 10 Years of the Alternative Press Expo · 1994-2004
APE04
ALTERNATIVE PRESS EXPO
The largest gathering of alternative and self-published comics in the country!
1994
2004
Featuring special guests:
Aaron A. "Serenity Rose"
Alison BECHDEL "Dykes to Watch Out For"
Charles BURNS "Black Hole"
Carol LAY "Story Minute"
FEBRUARY21-22
SATURDAY: NOON-6PM · SUNDAY: 11AM-5PM
THE CONCOURSE
620 7th ST., SAN FRANCISCO
TOP ARTISTS
PROGRAMS & PRESENTATIONS
GIANT EXHIBIT HALL
For more information: www.comic-con.org

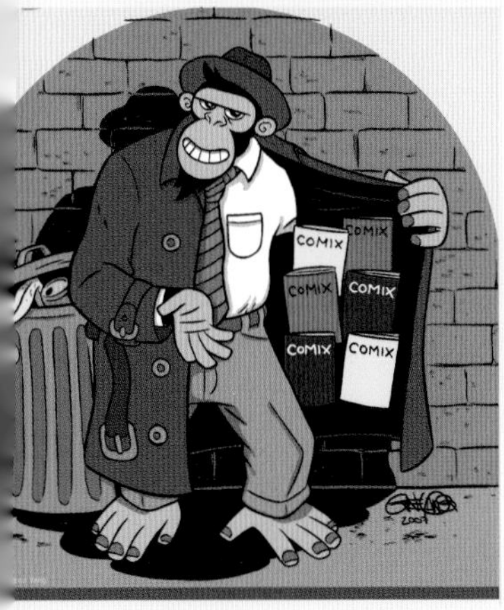
COMIX
COMIX
COMIX
COMIX
COMIX
COMIX

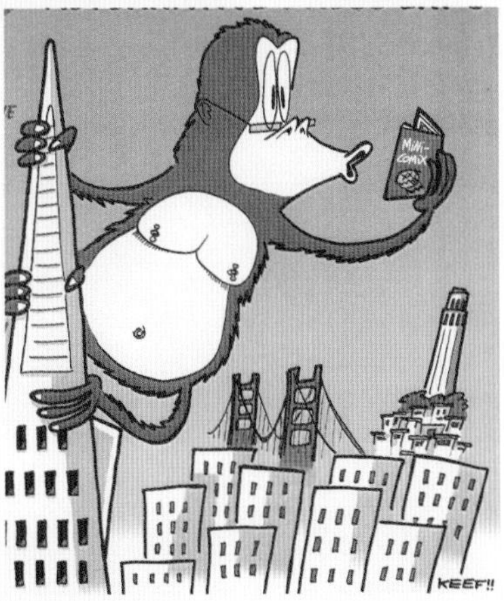
KEEF!!

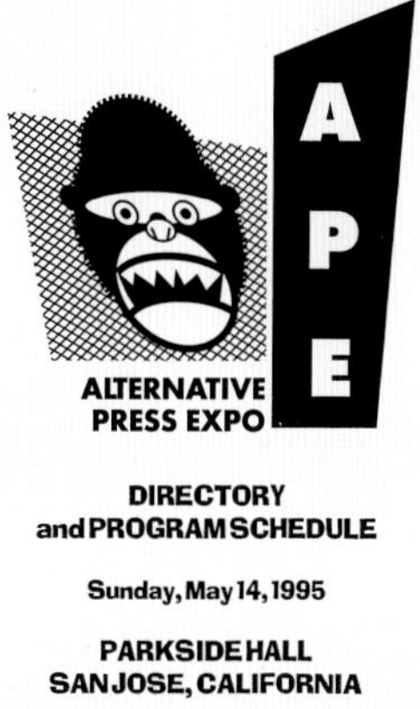
APE
ALTERNATIVE PRESS EXPO
DIRECTORY
and PROGRAM SCHEDULE
Sunday, May 14, 1995
PARKSIDE HALL
SAN JOSE, CALIFORNIA

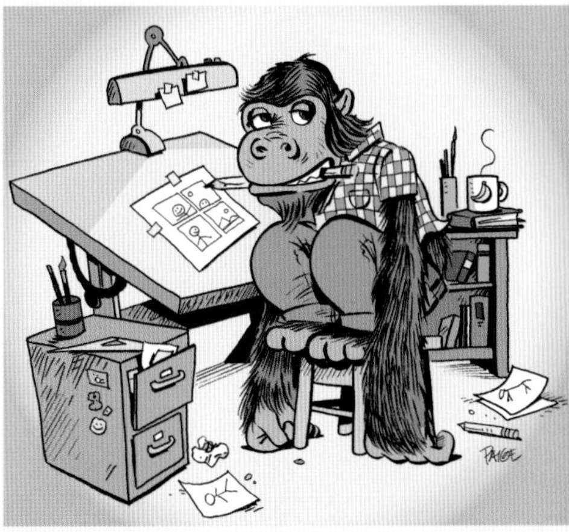

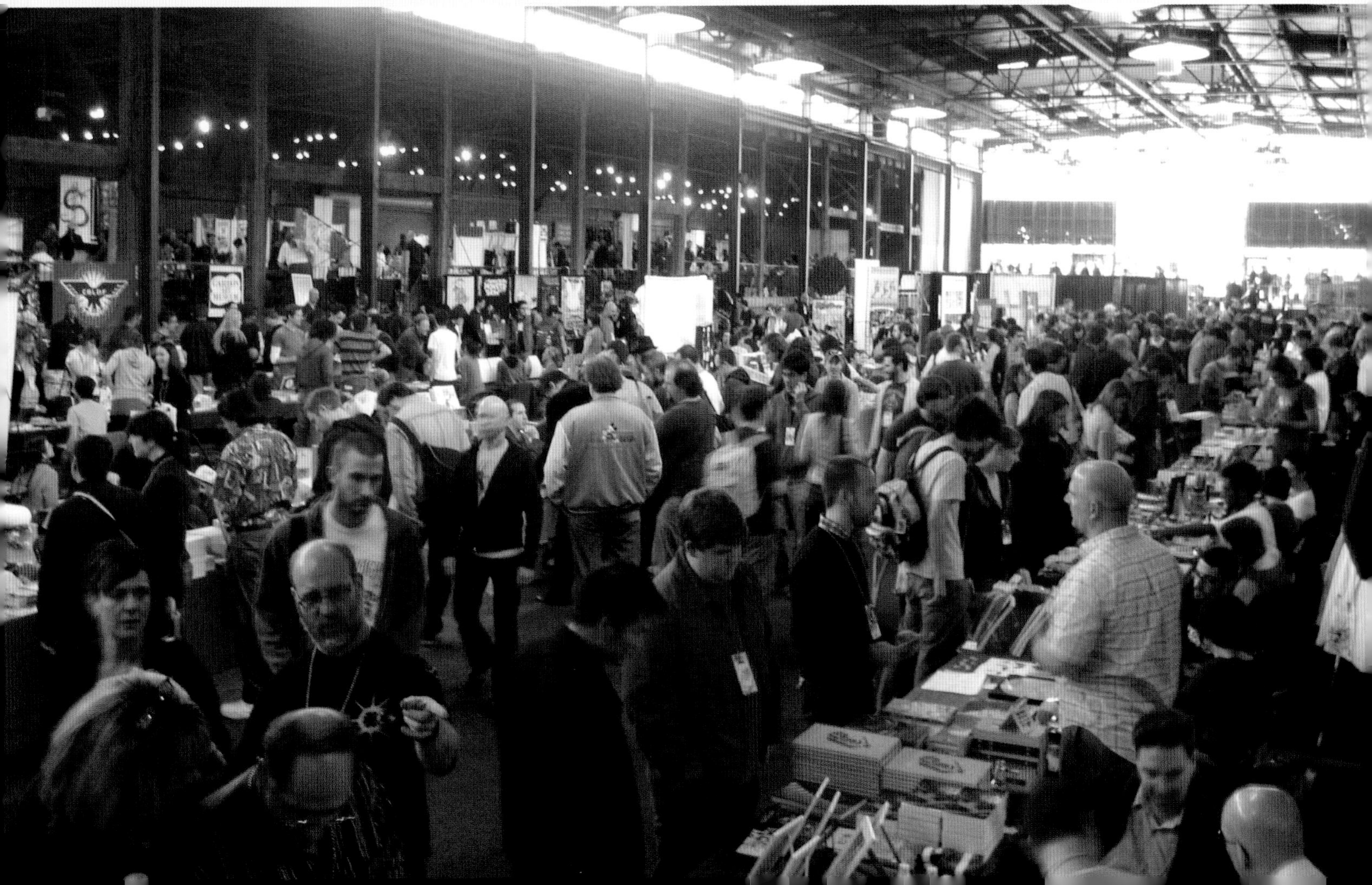

FRANK MILLER

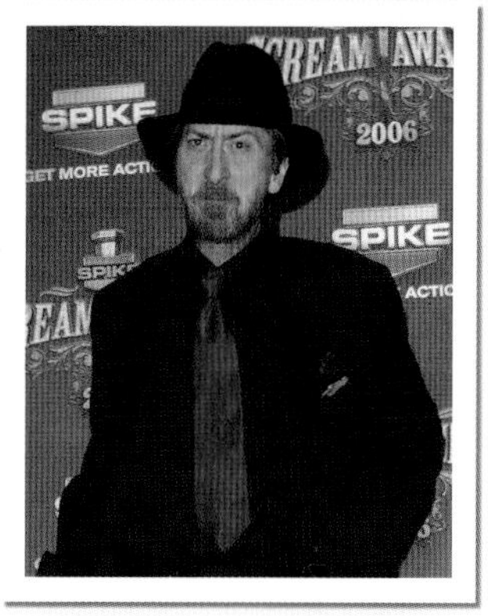
SPIKE
2006
SPIKE

FRANK MILLER, one of the most influential comics creators in the history of the medium, first appeared as a special guest at Comic-Con in 1982. Still in his early twenties, Frank was already a fan favorite for his work on Marvel's *Daredevil*. He had started drawing the book with issue #158 and soon began writing it as well. Miller's Daredevil was a new kind of comic book hero, one steeped in the dark traditions of film noir. Miller introduced compelling characters such as the tragic Elektra, a ninja assassin and former love of Daredevil's.

Miller's subsequent career in some ways seemed to parallel what was happening with Comic-Con itself. As he became more and more successful in the comics world, he became increasingly involved in the movie industry and garnered greater name recognition with the general public.

In 1986 Frank reinvented the Caped Crusader in *Batman: The Dark Knight Returns*, a miniseries collected into a graphic novel that has been one of the most influential superhero works of all time. That work is credited (along with another 1986 landmark, Alan Moore and Dave Gibbons's *Watchmen*) as ushering in the "grim and gritty" approach to superheroes. Miller's follow-up series, *Batman: Year One* (with art by David Mazzucchelli) also influenced future takes on the character, including the 2008 blockbuster *The Dark Knight*.

The appeal of Miller's writing and popularity was not lost on Hollywood, and in the early 1990s Frank ended up writing screenplays for *RoboCop 2* and *RoboCop 3*. Not too happy with that experience, Miller went back to his comics work full time, producing the award-winning *Sin City* series, writing *Hard Boiled* (with art by Geof Darrow) and *Give Me Liberty* (with art by Dave Gibbons), and writing and drawing *300* (with colors by Lynn Varley), a retelling of the story of the three hundred Spartans. All these projects garnered numerous Will Eisner Comic Industry nominations and awards, as well as the 1998 Bob Clampett Humanitarian Award, given in part for his work on behalf of the Comic Book Legal Defense Fund. Miller was also the recipient of the first Comic-Con Icon Award, which is given to an organization or individual who has been instrumental in bringing comics and/or popular arts to a wider audience. He received the award during the nationally televised Scream Awards on the Spike cable network.

With the new millennium, Frank revisited Batman with *The Dark Knight Strikes Again*, a flamboyant miniseries offering an over-the-top view of the DC superhero universe. At this point, he had been vocal in his views against Hollywood "strip-mining" comics and refused to even speak to producers who wanted to option his books. But then Robert Rodriguez sent him a short film that showed how *Sin City* could be adapted for the screen, and Frank ended up collaborating with Rodriguez on the feature film that was truly faithful to the comic book source material. That film—along with the success of Zack Snyder's movie adaptation of *300*—factored into Miller getting his first solo job writing and directing a feature motion picture: the big-screen adaptation of Will Eisner's *The Spirit*.

For more than two decades, Miller has been a presence at Comic-Con, whether speaking on panels about his comics work and his films, doing signings and booth appearances, or being onstage to accept awards. In 2008 Miller gave the keynote speech at the Will Eisner Comic Industry Awards, reminding professionals in the audience that creating "damn good comic books" should be their first priority, not movies, not games, "and in time, who knows what will happen?"

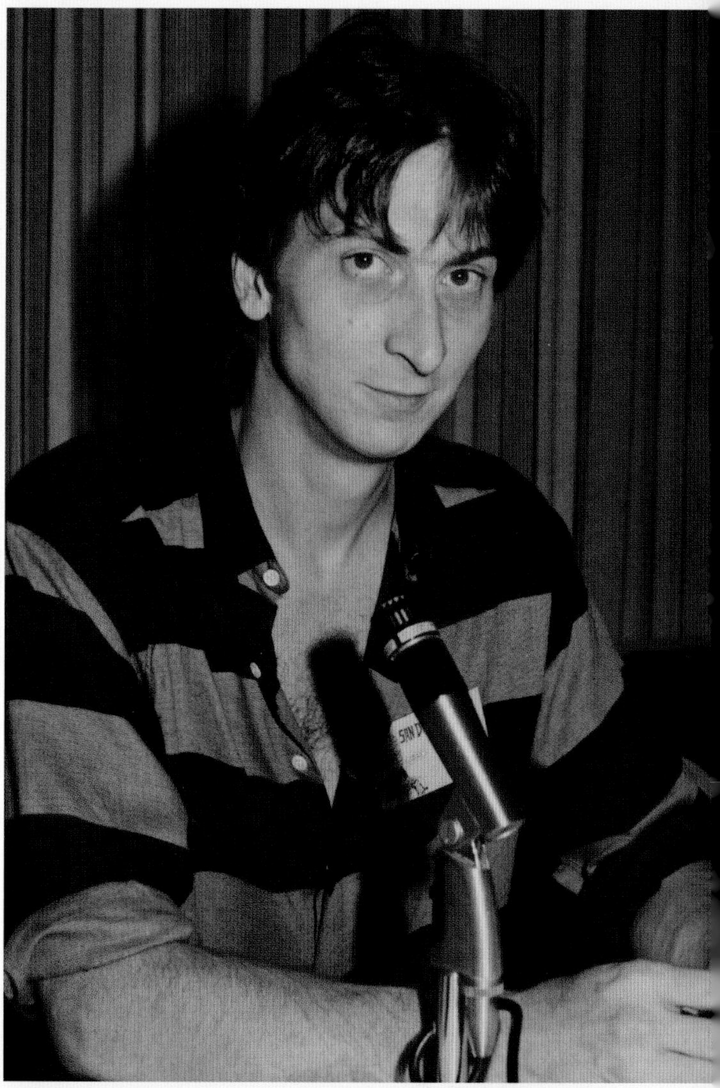

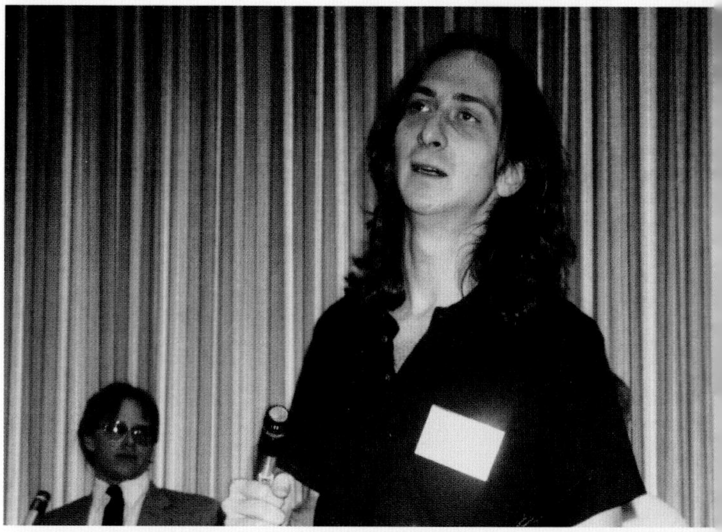

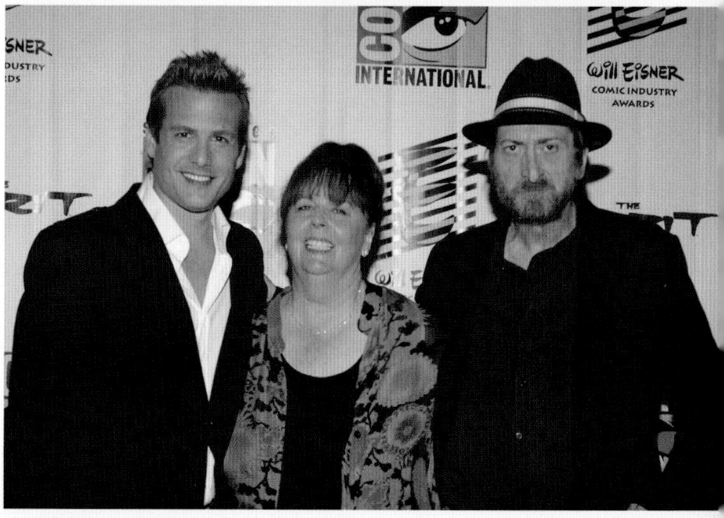
INTERNATIONAL
Will Eisner
COMIC INDUSTRY AWARDS

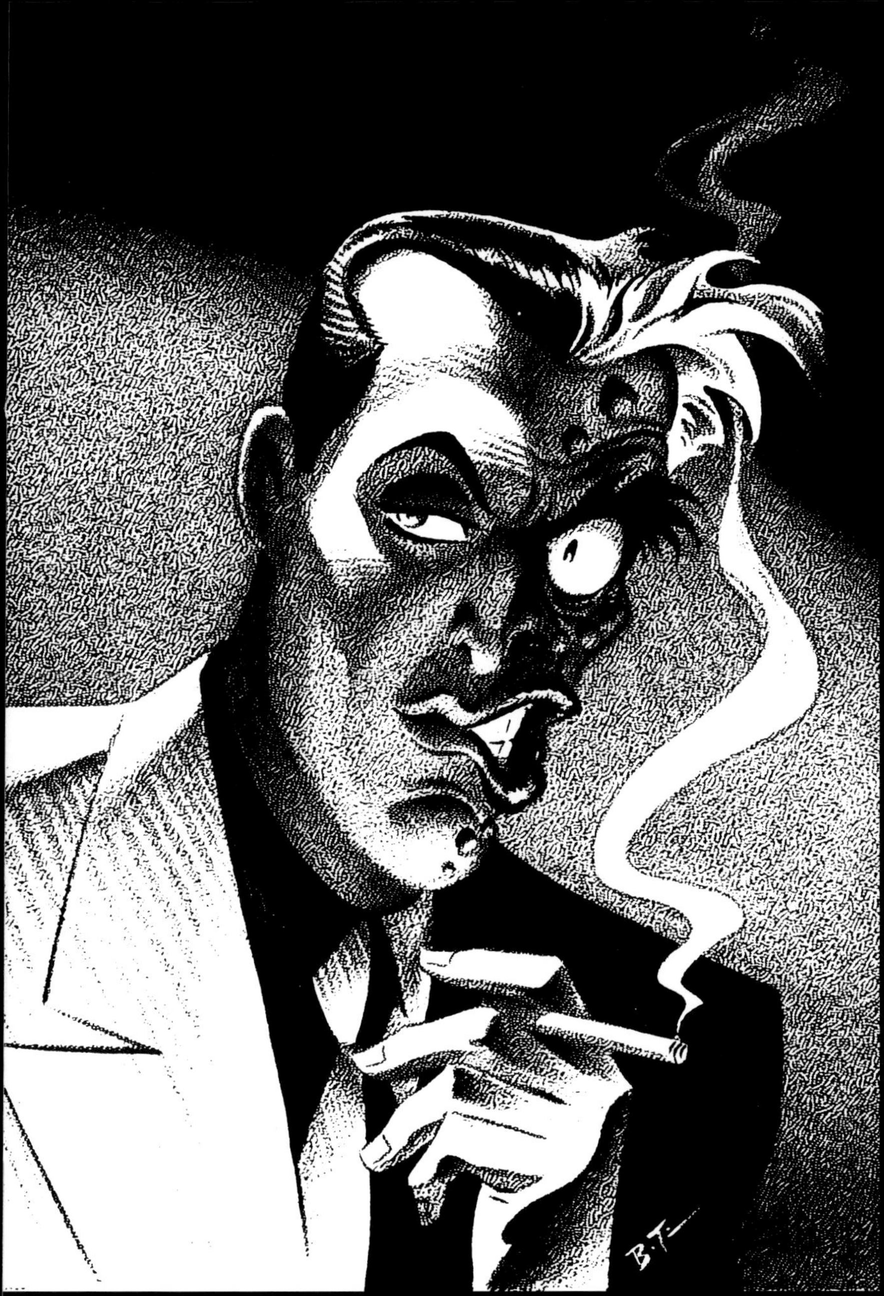
B.T.

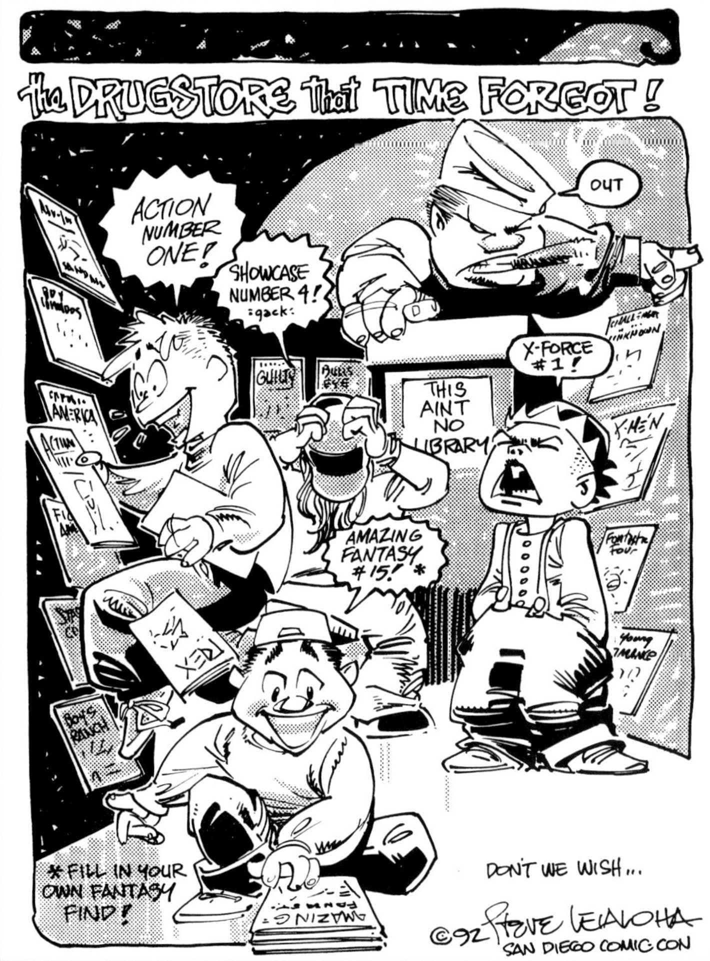
the DRUGSTORE that TIME FORGOT!
OUT
ACTION NUMBER ONE!
SHOWCASE NUMBER 4! :gack:
X-FORCE #1!
THIS AINT NO LIBRARY
AMAZING FANTASY #15! *
X-MEN
* FILL IN YOUR OWN FANTASY FIND!
DON'T WE WISH...
©92 STEVE LEIALOHA
SAN DIEGO COMIC CON

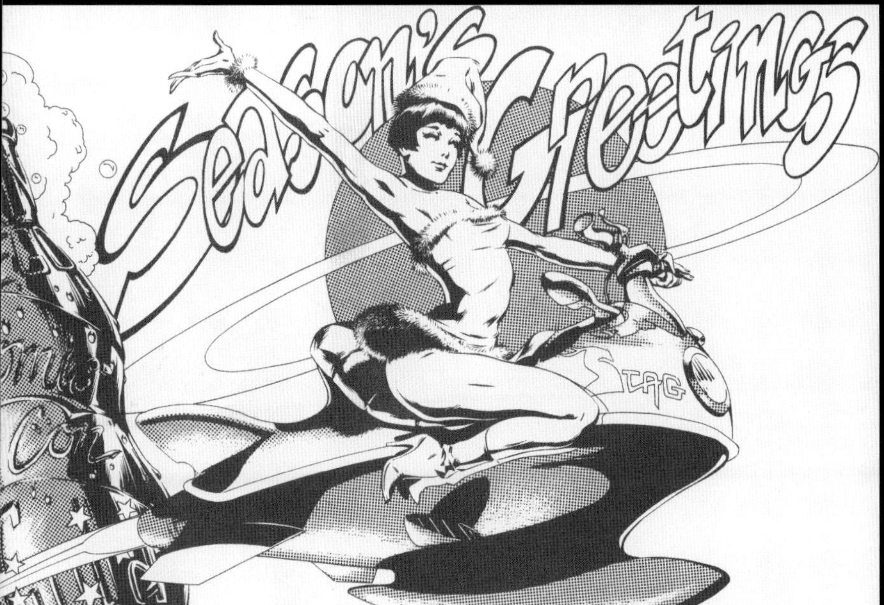
Season's Greetings
STAG
From San Diego... To EARTH

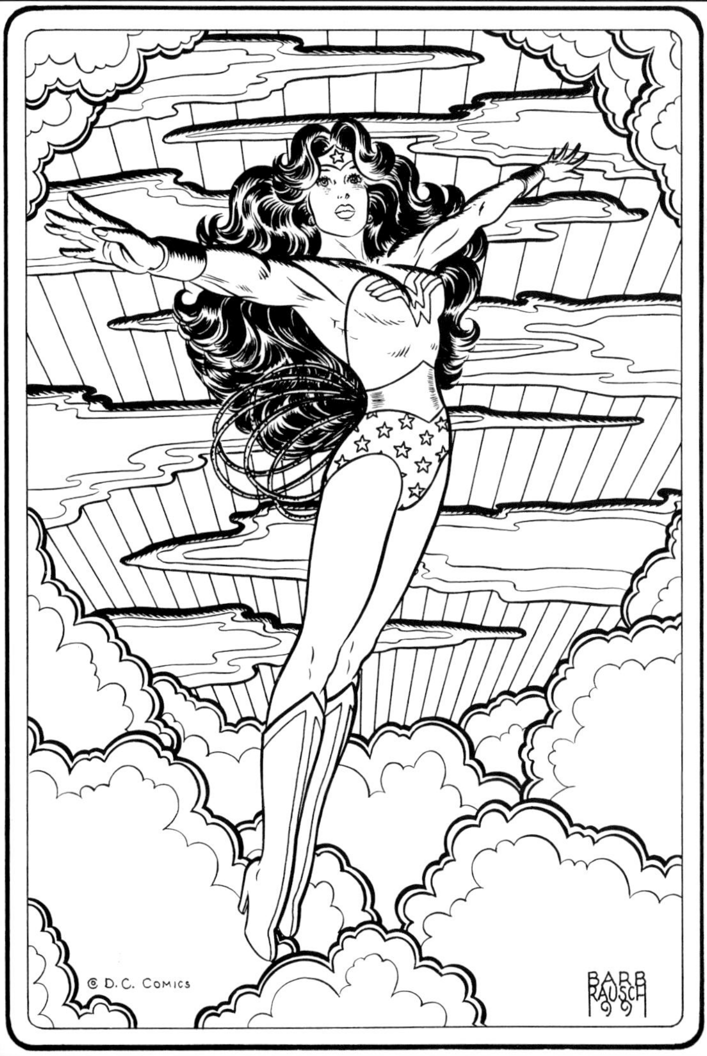
© D.C. COMICS
BARB RAUSCH 91

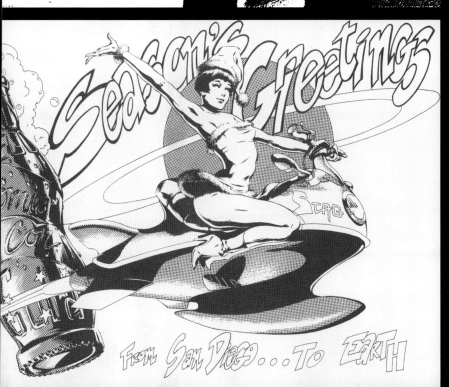

OPPOSITE, CLOCKWISE FROM TOP LEFT: Frank Miller at the Scream Awards in 2006, where he was presented with the first Comic-Con Icon Award; Miller at Comic-Con in 1985; Miller in 1986, the year *Batman: The Dark Knight Returns* debuted; Miller (far right) with the star of *The Spirit* movie, Gabriel Macht (left), and producer Deborah Del Prete (center) at the 2008 Eisner Awards ceremony **CLOCKWISE FROM TOP LEFT:** Bruce Timm's atmospheric Two-Face rendering from 1992; Steve Leialoha's look at a different comics-buying era (1992); Barb Rausch's beautiful Wonder Woman drawing celebrating the character's fiftieth anniversary; Nghia Lam's Comic-Con Christmas card for 1994

TOP ROW, FROM LEFT: Troma Entertainment at Comic-Con in 1995, represented by Toxie and Sgt. Kabukiman; director Francis Ford Coppola, a guest in 1992, promoting *Bram Stoker's Dracula* **MIDDLE ROW, FROM LEFT:** Leonard Nimoy appearing in 1994 to promote Tekno Comix's *Primortals*; everyone's favorite horror hostess, Elvira (Cassandra Peterson), in 1995; the Thing making a friend in 1995 **BOTTOM ROW, FROM LEFT:** Metamorpho co-creators Ramona Fradon (left) and Bob Haney (right) in 1997; Seduction of the Innocent, a band organized specifically to play at Comic-Con, consisting of actor Bill Mumy (front) plus (back, left to right) author Max Allan Collins, actor Miguel Ferrer, comics artist Steve Leialoha, and musician/record producer John "Chris" Christensen (who joined them in 1990) **OPPOSITE:** Spidey meeting his maker, co-creator Stan Lee, at Comic-Con in 1990

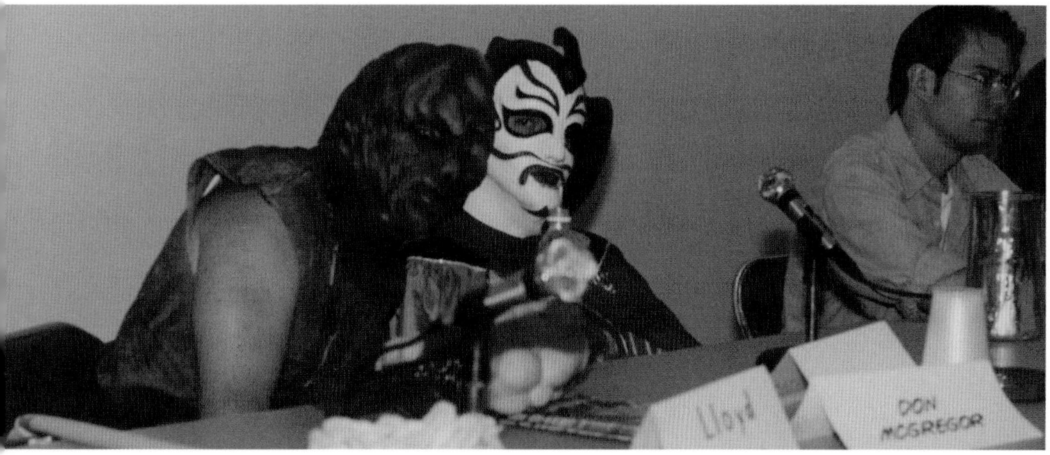
Lloyd
DON MCGREGOR

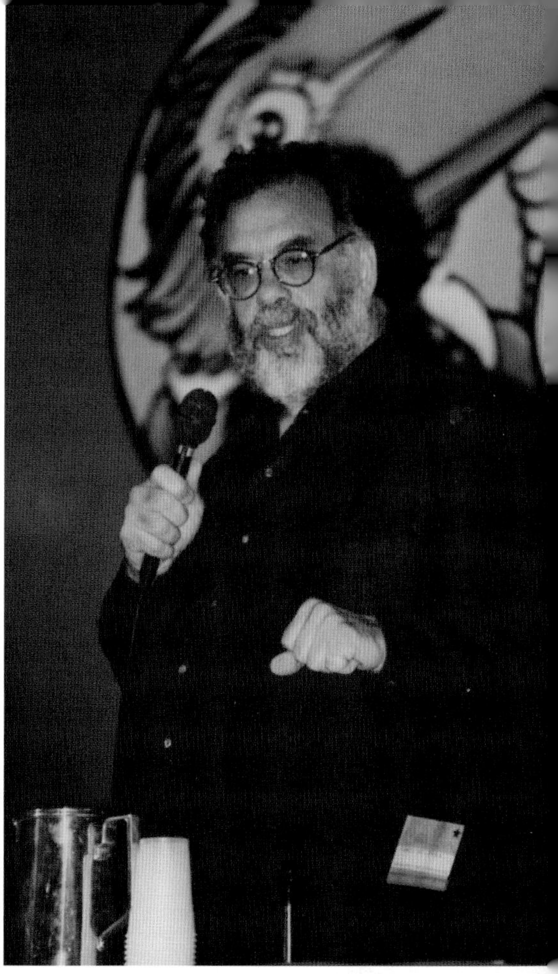

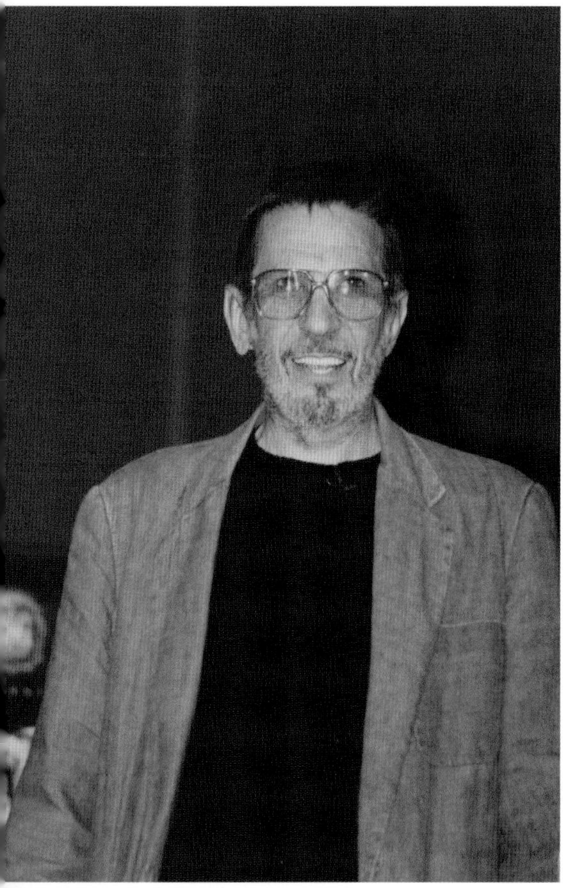

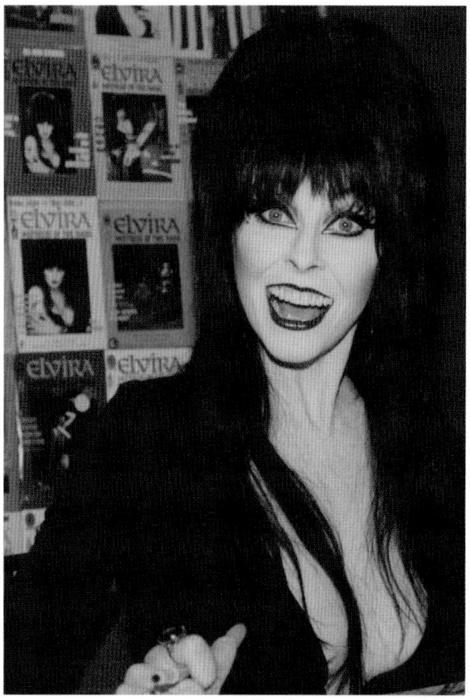
ELVIRA
ELVIRA
ELVIRA
ELVIRA

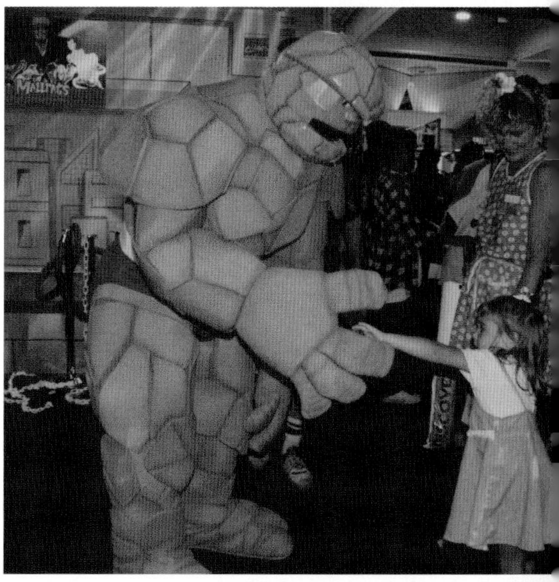

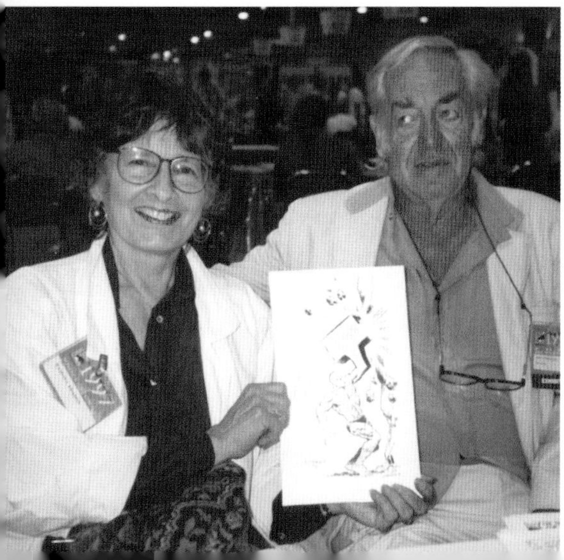

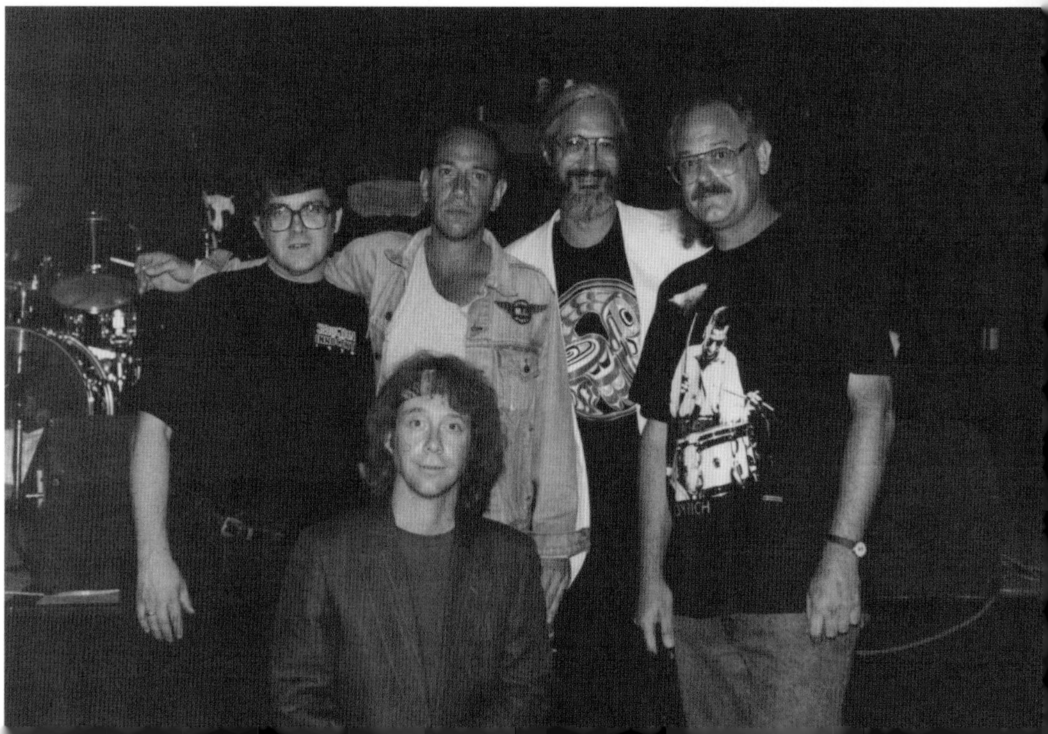

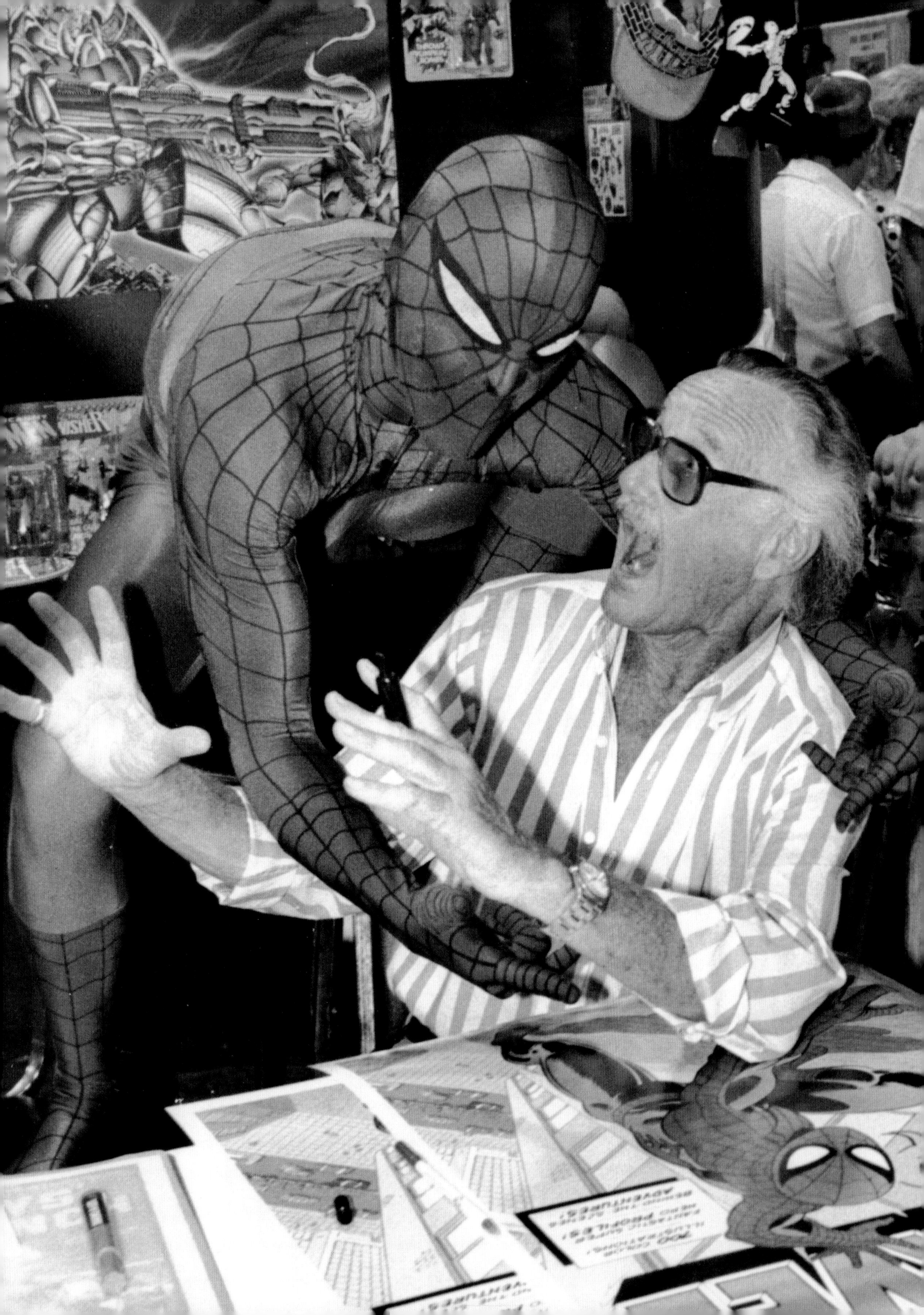

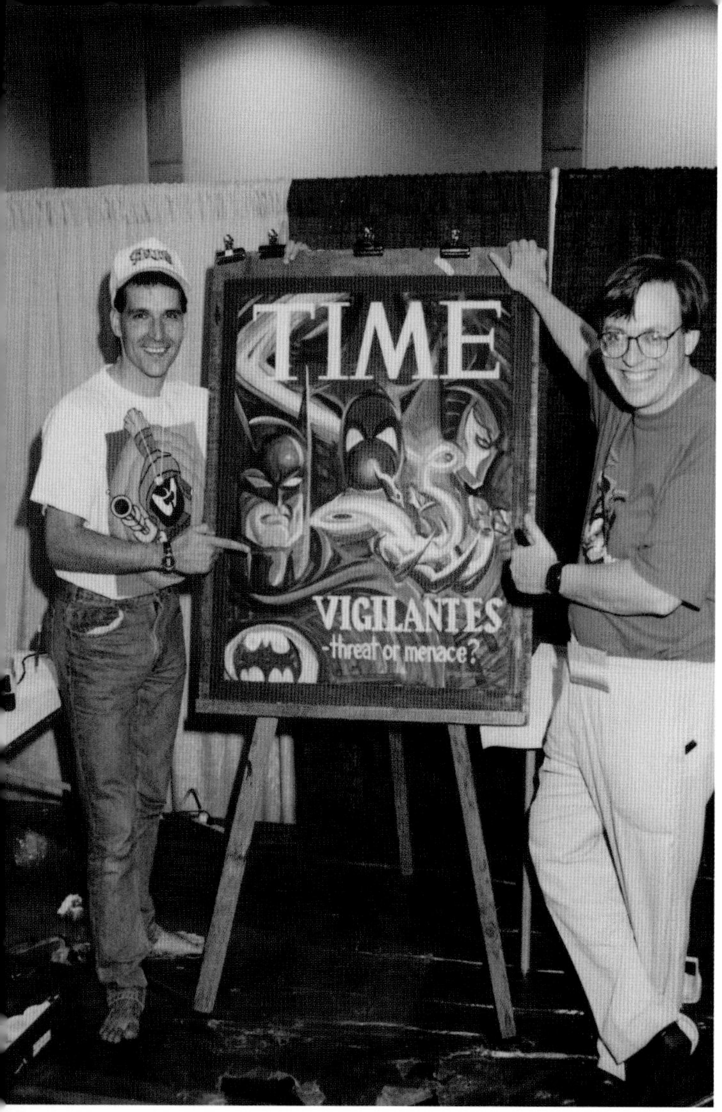
TIME
VIGILANTES
-threat or menace?

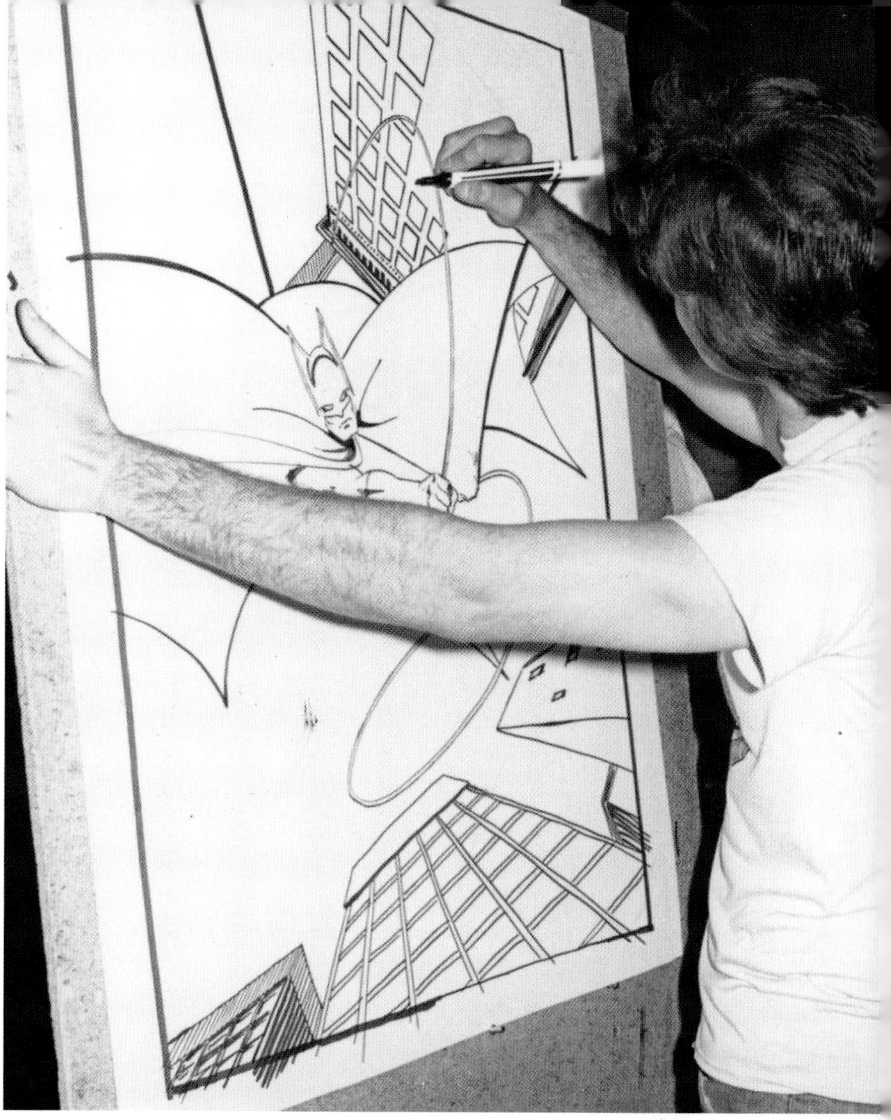

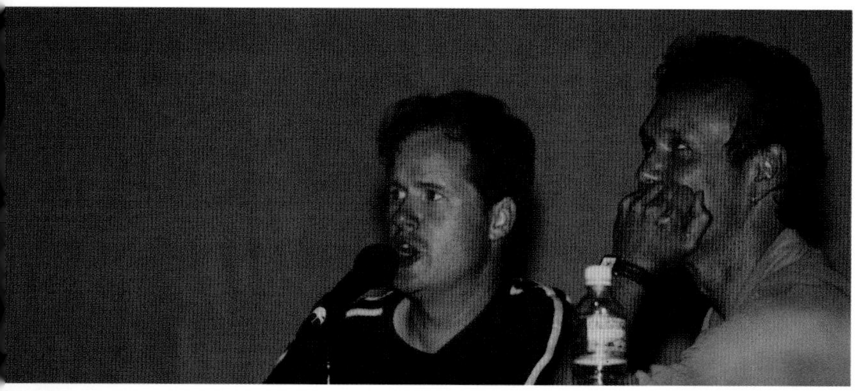

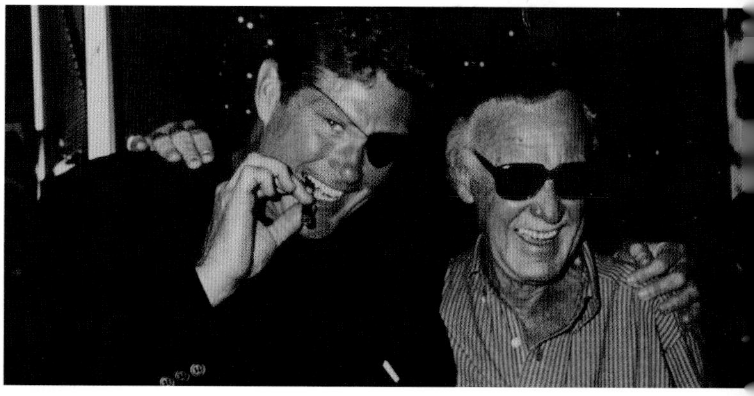

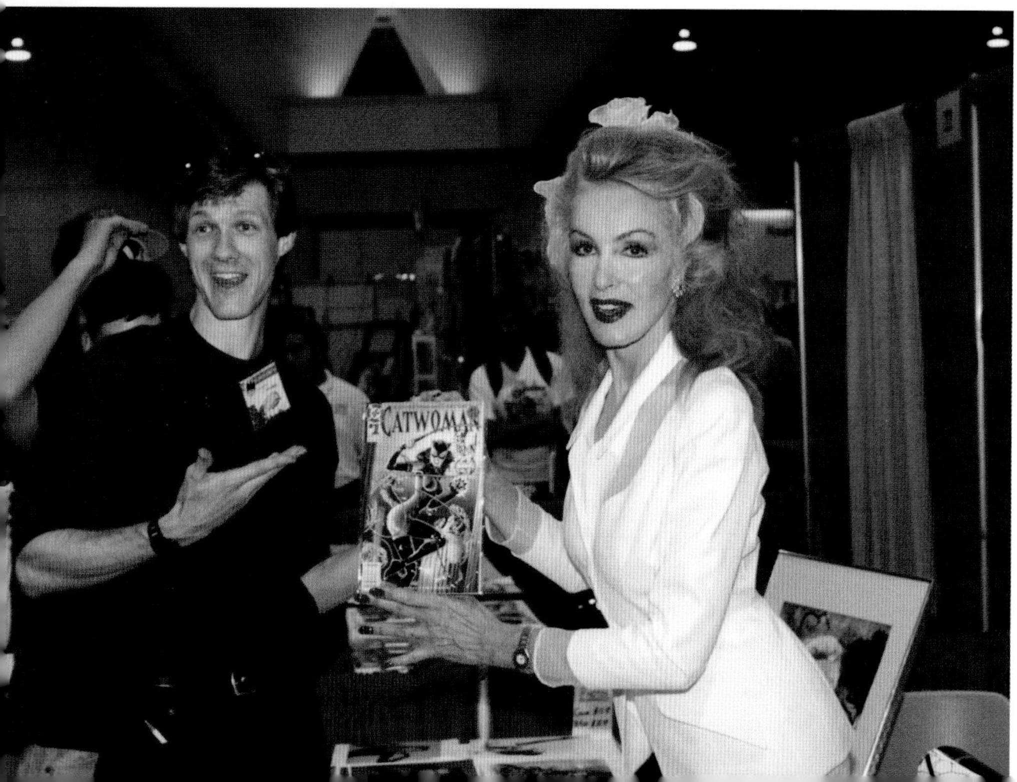

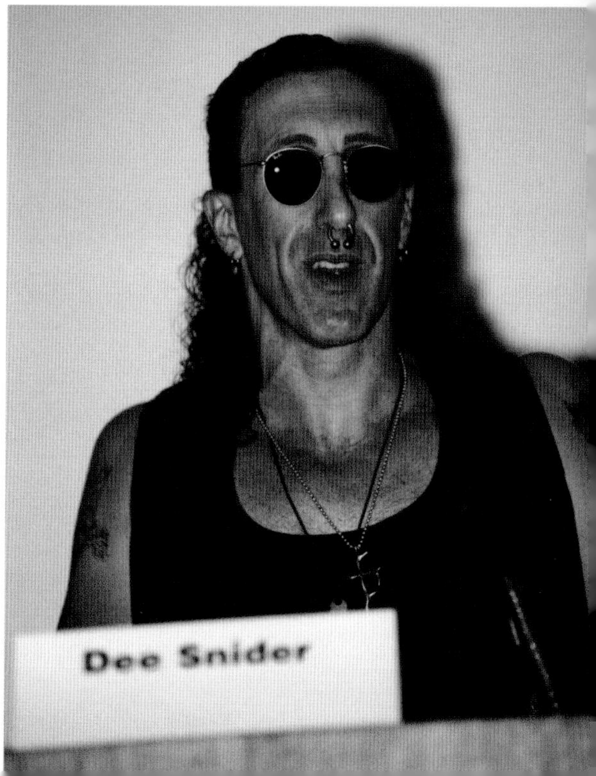
Dee Snider

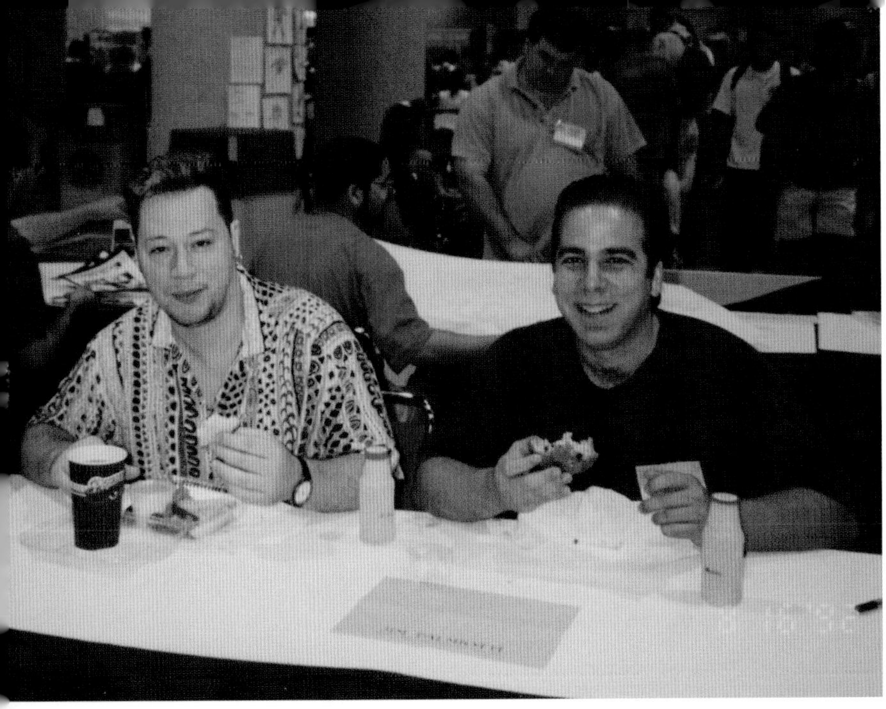

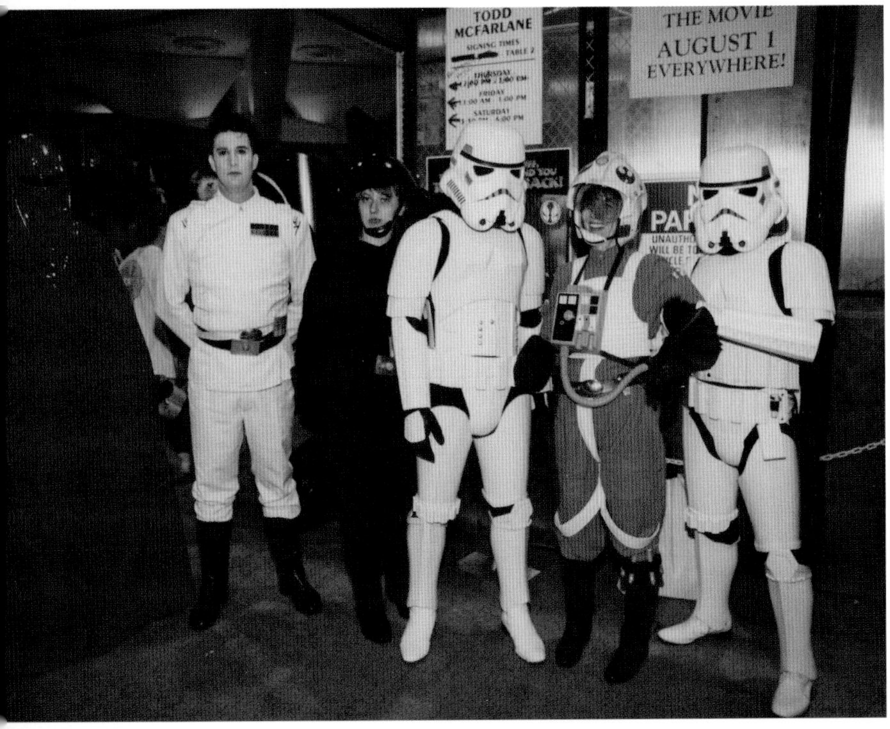
TODD
MCFARLANE
THE MOVIE
AUGUST 1
EVERYWHERE!

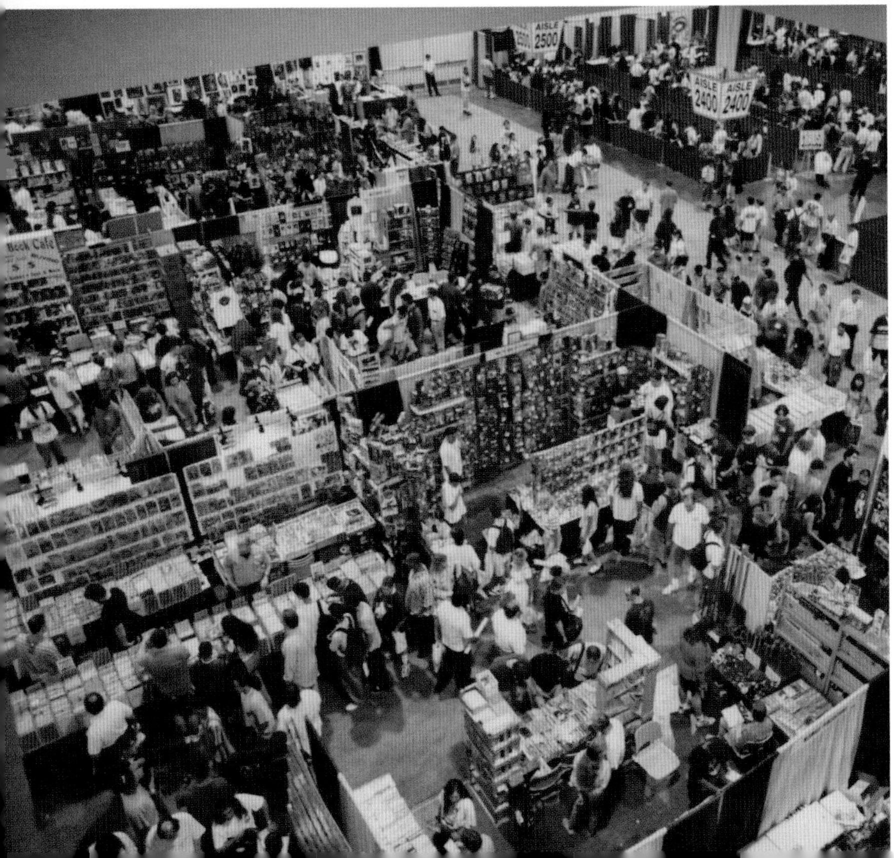
AISLE 2500
AISLE 2400
AISLE 2400

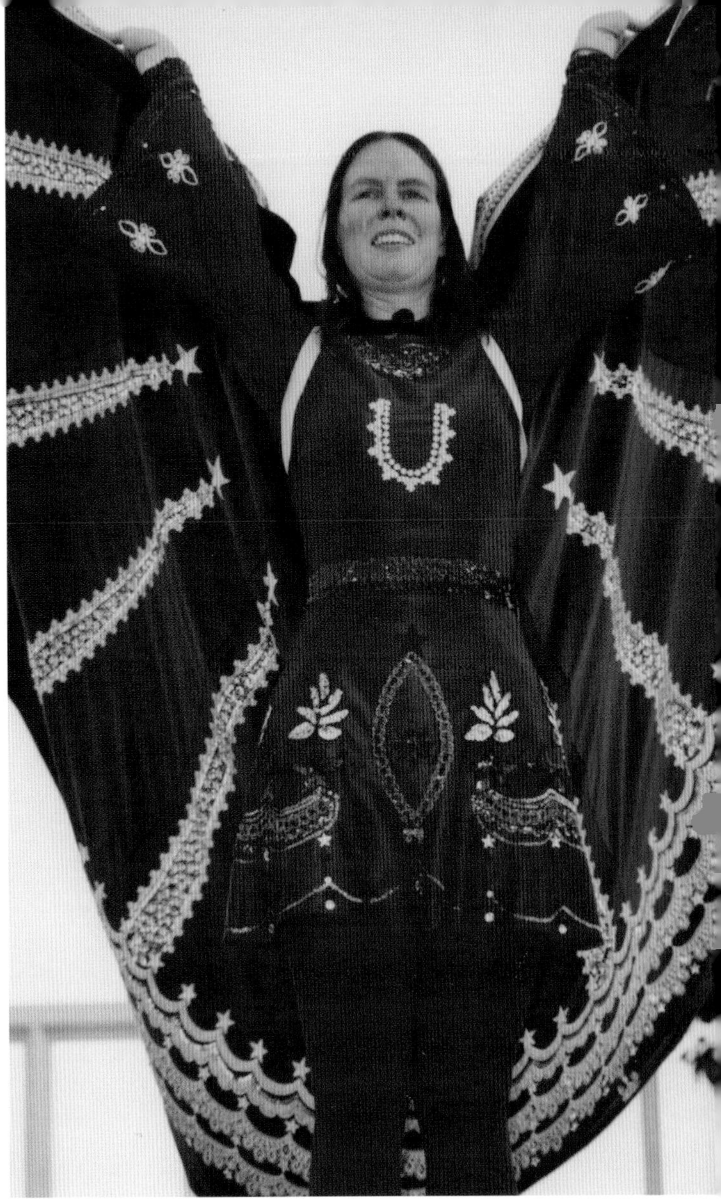

OPPOSITE, CLOCKWISE FROM TOP LEFT: Todd McFarlane (left) and Ken Steacy (right) with Steacy's painting created for the Comic-Con Art Auction; Marshall Rogers sketching Batman in the early 1990s; David Hasselhoff (left) as *Nick Fury, Agent of S.H.I.E.L.D.*, with Stan Lee (right) in 1997; Twisted Sister's Dee Snider at the show in 1998; *Catwoman* artist Jim Balent (left) meeting the real thing, Julie Newmar (right), in 1995; *Buffy the Vampire Slayer*'s Joss Whedon (left) and Anthony Stewart Head (right), who, with others from the cast, inspired Beatles-like mania when they appeared in 1998 **LEFT, TOP TO BOTTOM:** Joe Quesada (soon to be editor-in-chief of Marvel Comics, left) and writer/inker Jimmy Palmiotti (right) grabbing lunch in Artists' Alley in the mid-1990s; Storm Troopers, a common sight at Comic-Con since *Star Wars* debuted in 1977; a bird's-eye view of the Exhibit Hall in 1997 **ABOVE:** Suzanne Muldowney, who gained fame as Underdog, both at Comic-Con (shown here in 1994) and later on *The Howard Stern Show*

COMIC-CON PUBLICATIONS

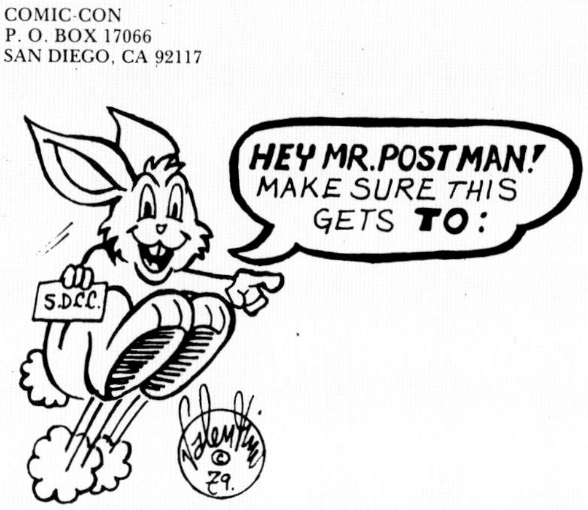
COMIC-CON
P. O. BOX 17066
SAN DIEGO, CA 92117
HEY MR. POSTMAN! MAKE SURE THIS GETS TO:
S.D.C.C.

Comics are a print medium, so it makes sense that Comic-Con itself has produced hundreds of publications over its forty-year history.

The first publications were advertising flyers, adorned with original art by committee members such as cartoonist Scott Shaw! and often hand-lettered by Shel Dorf.

Starting with the first Comic-Con, the show's program book has been a showcase for art and articles. The contents include artwork done specifically for the convention, exclusive articles and photos devoted to special guests and themes, and much more. Even the comics company advertisements appearing in the books contained art and content seen only at Comic-Con.

The first program books were digest-size, but they expanded to magazine-size in the mid-1970s, complete with color covers by the likes of Will Eisner and Sergio Aragonés. Pinups and special art were added, contributed by major comic artists (Carl Barks and Steve Ditko to name just a few) and Comic-Con's invited guests.

As the convention evolved, so did its publications. The program book split in two, and became the Souvenir Book and the Events Guide. The Comic-Con Souvenir Book of the past twenty-some years is a high-end trade paperback filled with art and articles devoted to the event's programming themes, including diverse topics ranging from underground comix to Superman's fiftieth anniversary. The Events Guide became a separate show schedule featuring a complete rundown of all the programming, events, and other timely information, including an Exhibit Hall map and directory.

In addition to the on-site publications available to attendees, Comic-Con also puts out a quarterly magazine. What had started as "Progress Reports"—information about what was happening at the next show sent to attendees on the mailing list—evolved through several formats (folded-over flyer, eight-page digest, newsprint tabloid) into a comic-size, full-color publication titled *Update* by the early 2000s. In 2008 *Update* metamorphosed into *Comic-Con Magazine*, a full-size quarterly (which counts the event's yearly Souvenir Book as one of its four issues). Each issue of *Comic-Con Magazine* has a print run of more than two hundred thousand copies, the majority of which are distributed free to the Comic-Con mailing list, with the rest going through the direct comics market and to various venues throughout California. The new incarnation of the magazine contains information on upcoming events and exclusive content, including interviews with special guests.

In addition to all of these publications, Comic-Con maintains a Web site—www.comic-con.org—that keeps fans and attendees up to date on details concerning all three of the Comic-Con events.

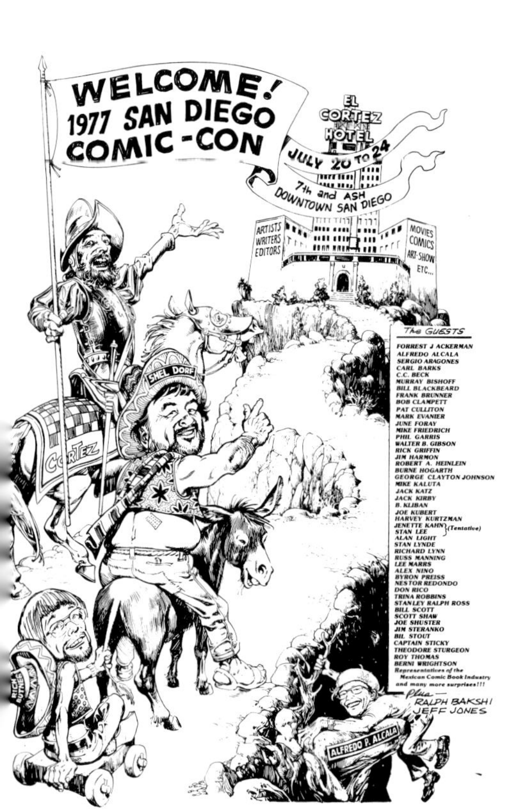
WELCOME!
1977 SAN DIEGO
COMIC-CON
EL CORTEZ HOTEL
JULY 20 TO 24
7th and ASH
DOWNTOWN SAN DIEGO
ARTISTS WRITERS EDITORS
MOVIES COMICS ART-SHOW ETC...
The GUESTS
FORREST J ACKERMAN
ALFREDO ALCALA
SERGIO ARAGONES
CARL BARKS
C.C. BECK
MURRAY BISHOFF
BILL BLACKBEARD
FRANK BRUNNER
BOB CLAMPETT
PAT CULLITON
MARK EVANIER
JUNE FORAY
MIKE FRIEDRICH
PHIL GARRIS
WALTER B. GIBSON
RICK GRIFFIN
JIM HARMON
ROBERT A. HEINLEIN
BURNE HOGARTH
GEORGE CLAYTON JOHNSON
MIKE KALUTA
JACK KATZ
JACK KIRBY
B. KLIBAN
JOE KUBERT
HARVEY KURTZMAN
JENETTE KAHN
STAN LEE
(Tentative)
ALAN LIGHT
STAN LYNDE
RICHARD LYNN
RUSS MANNING
LEE MARRS
ALEX NINO
BYRON PREISS
NESTOR REDONDO
DON RICO
TRINA ROBBINS
STANLEY RALPH ROSS
BILL SCOTT
SCOTT SHAW
JOE SHUSTER
JIM STERANKO
BIL STOUT
CAPTAIN STICKY
THEODORE STURGEON
ROY THOMAS
BERNI WRIGHTSON
Representatives of the Mexican Comic Book Industry and many more surprises!!!
Plus — RALPH BAKSHI JEFF JONES
ALFREDO P. ALCALA

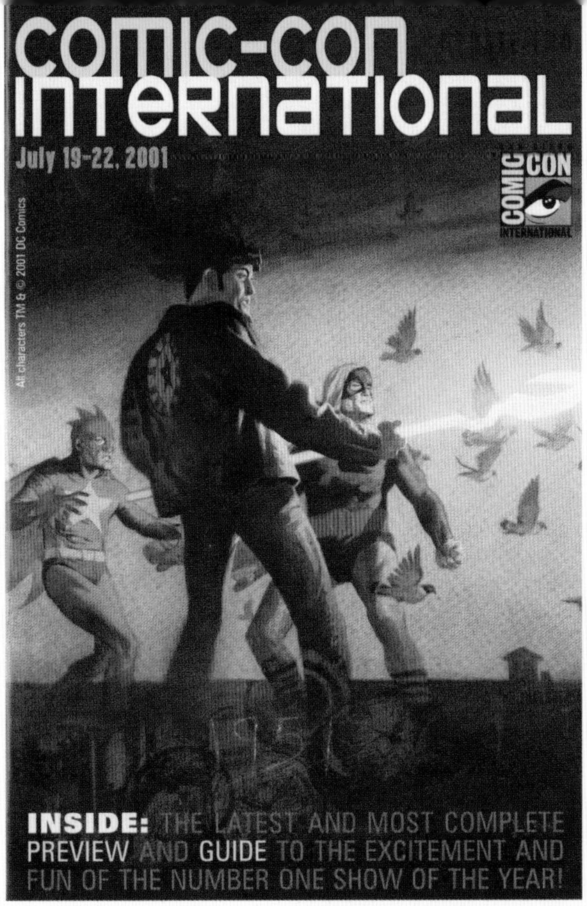
COMIC-CON INTERNATIONAL
July 19-22, 2001
COMIC CON INTERNATIONAL
At characters TM & © 2001 DC Comics
INSIDE: THE LATEST AND MOST COMPLETE PREVIEW AND GUIDE TO THE EXCITEMENT AND FUN OF THE NUMBER ONE SHOW OF THE YEAR!

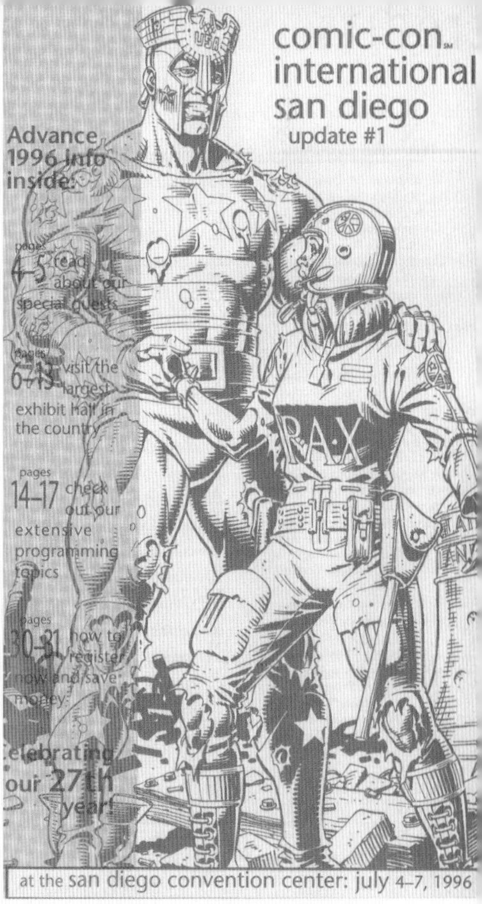
comic-con international san diego
update #1
Advance 1996 info inside:
pages 4–5 read about our special guests
pages 6–13 visit the largest exhibit hall in the country
pages 14–17 check out our extensive programming topics
pages 30–31 how to register now and save money
celebrating our 27th year!
at the san diego convention center: july 4–7, 1996

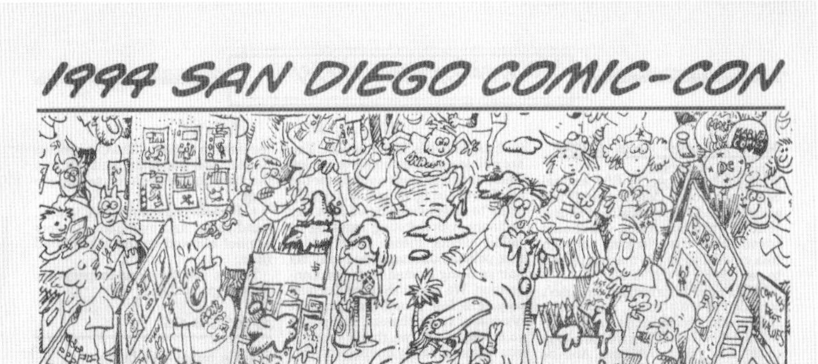
1994 SAN DIEGO COMIC-CON
SAN DIEGO COMIC CON '94
ARAGONES '94
EVENTS GUIDE

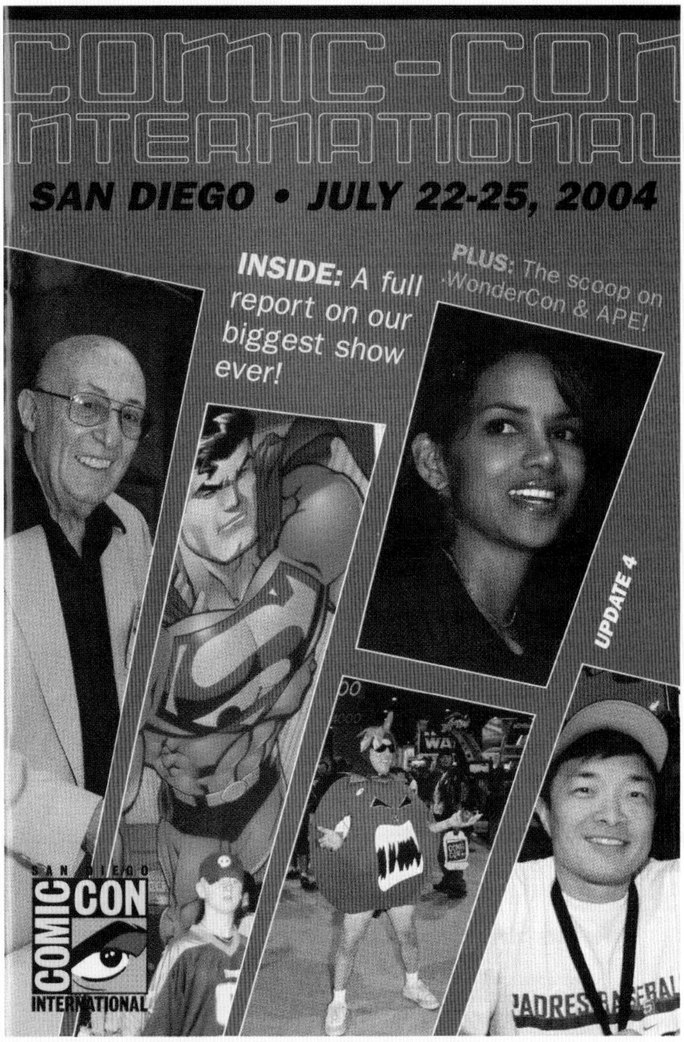
COMIC-CON INTERNATIONAL
SAN DIEGO • JULY 22-25, 2004
INSIDE: A full report on our biggest show ever!
PLUS: The scoop on WonderCon & APE!
UPDATE 4
SAN DIEGO COMIC CON INTERNATIONAL

OPPOSITE: Jim Valentino art for a Progress Report's mailing label from 1979 **TOP ROW, FROM LEFT:** A 1977 flyer featuring Comic-Con's Richard Butner and Shel Dorf, illustrated by artist Alfredo P. Alcala; the cover to the second 2001 *Update* magazine, with a painting of DC's Starman by Andrew Robinson; *Update* no. 1 from 1996 with a Dave Gibbons Martha Washington cover **BOTTOM, FROM LEFT:** Sergio Aragonés's 1994 Events Guide cover, celebrating Comic-Con's twenty-fifth anniversary; a 2003 *Update* cover, featuring a look back at that year's Comic-Con

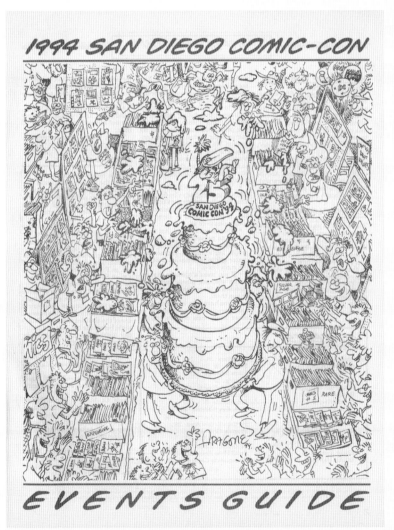

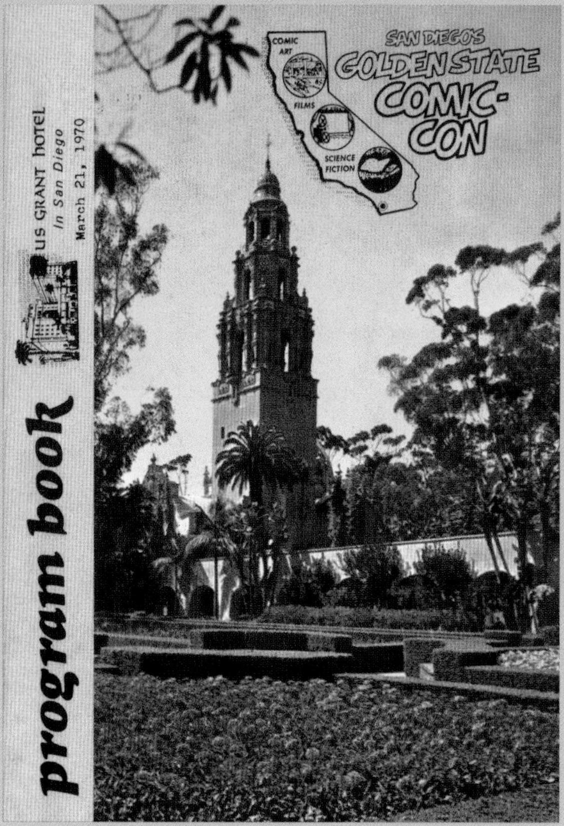
program book
US GRANT hotel
In San Diego
March 21, 1970
SAN DIEGO'S
GOLDEN STATE
COMIC-
CON
COMIC
ART
FILMS
SCIENCE
FICTION

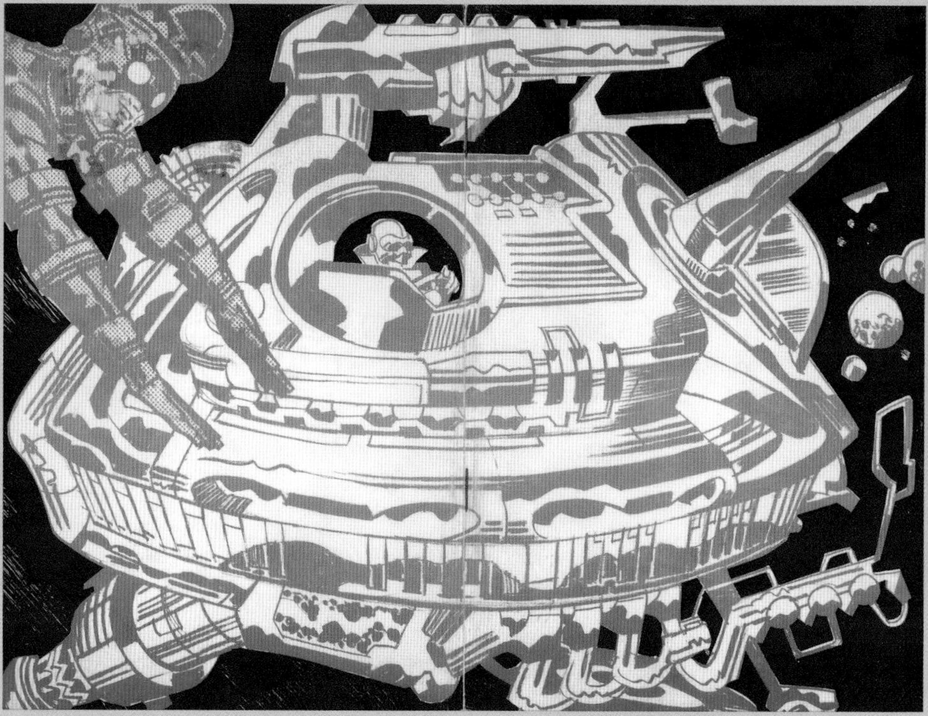

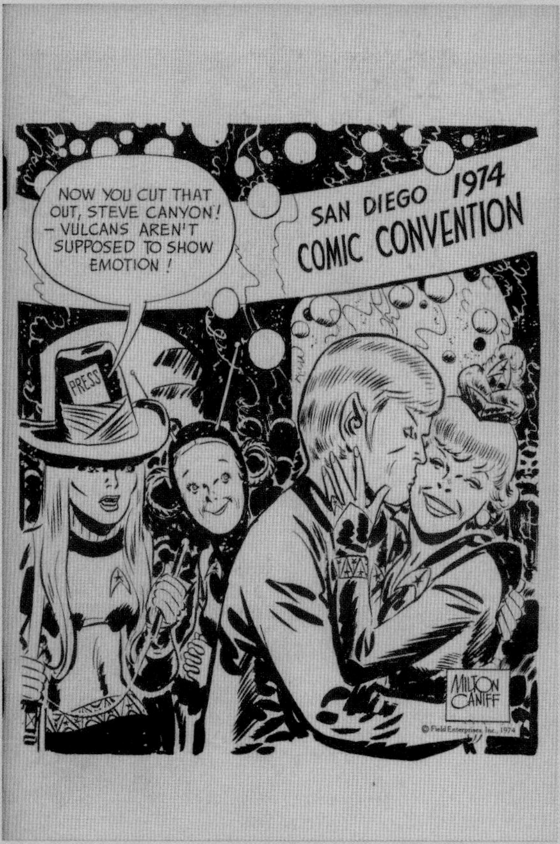
NOW YOU CUT THAT OUT, STEVE CANYON! – VULCANS AREN'T SUPPOSED TO SHOW EMOTION!
SAN DIEGO 1974
COMIC CONVENTION
PRESS
MILTON CANIFF
© Field Enterprises, Inc., 1974

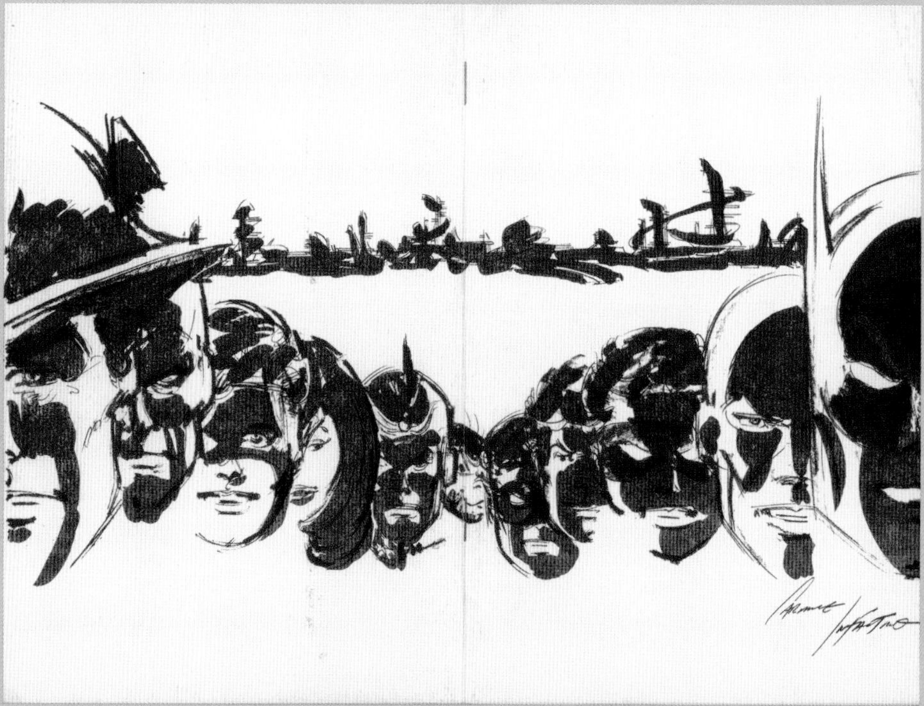

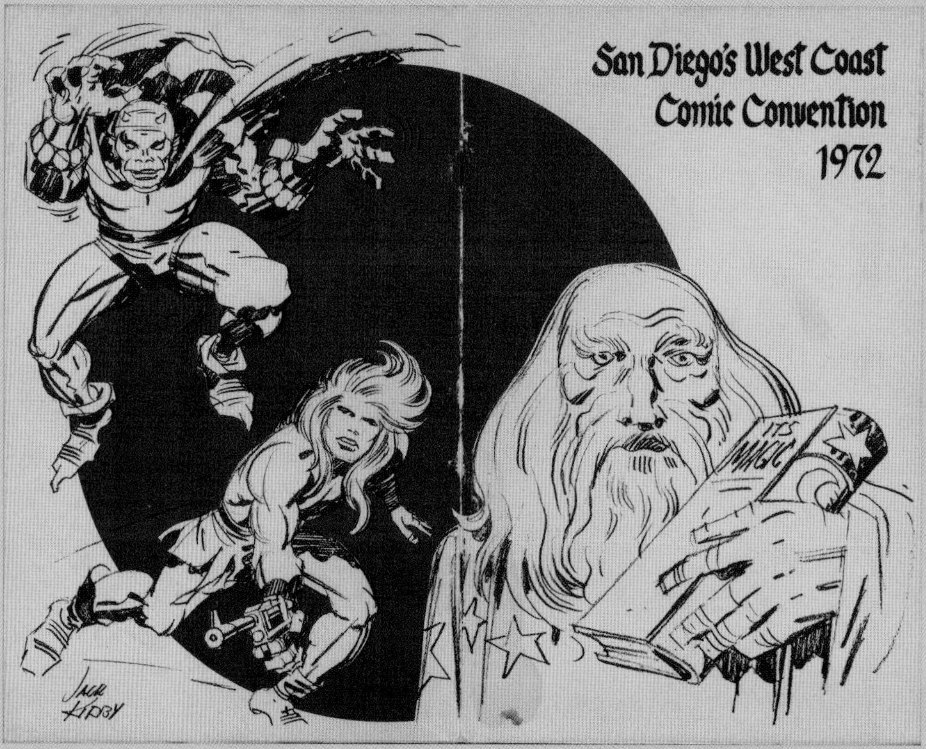
San Diego's West Coast
Comic Convention
1972
JACK KIRBY

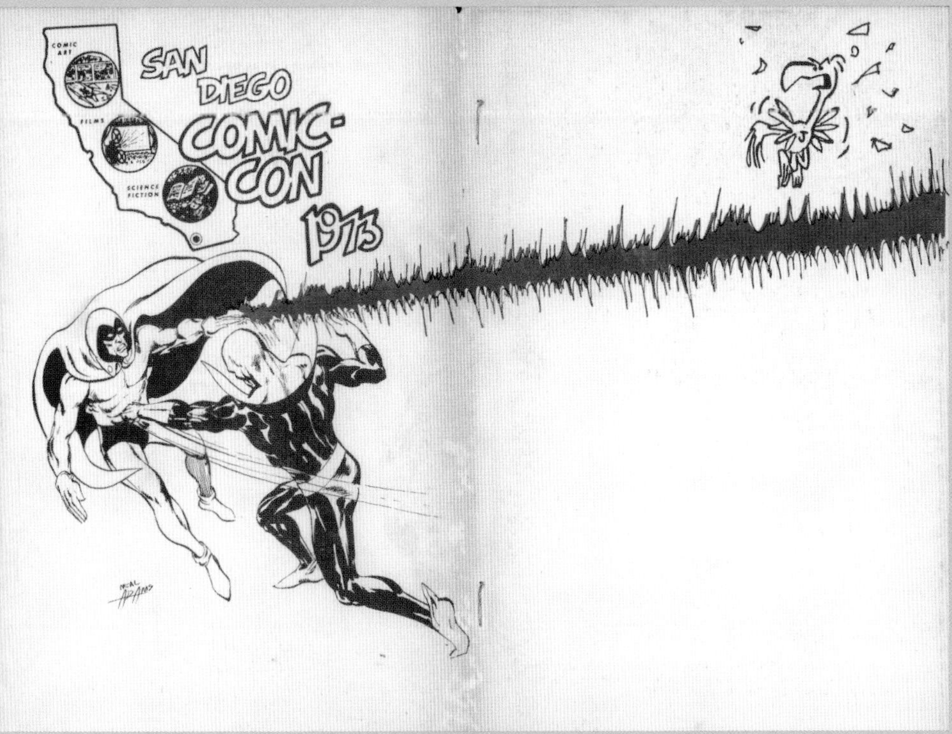
SAN DIEGO
COMIC-CON
1973
COMIC ART
FILMS
SCIENCE FICTION

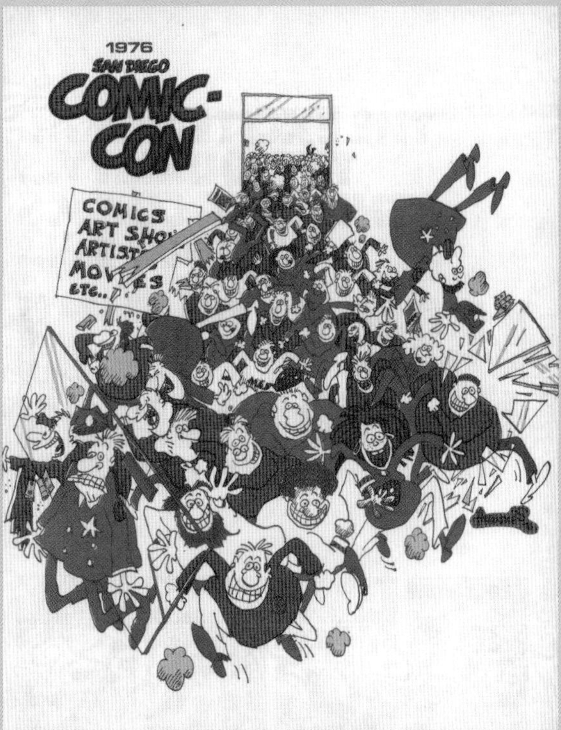
1976
SAN DIEGO
COMIC-CON

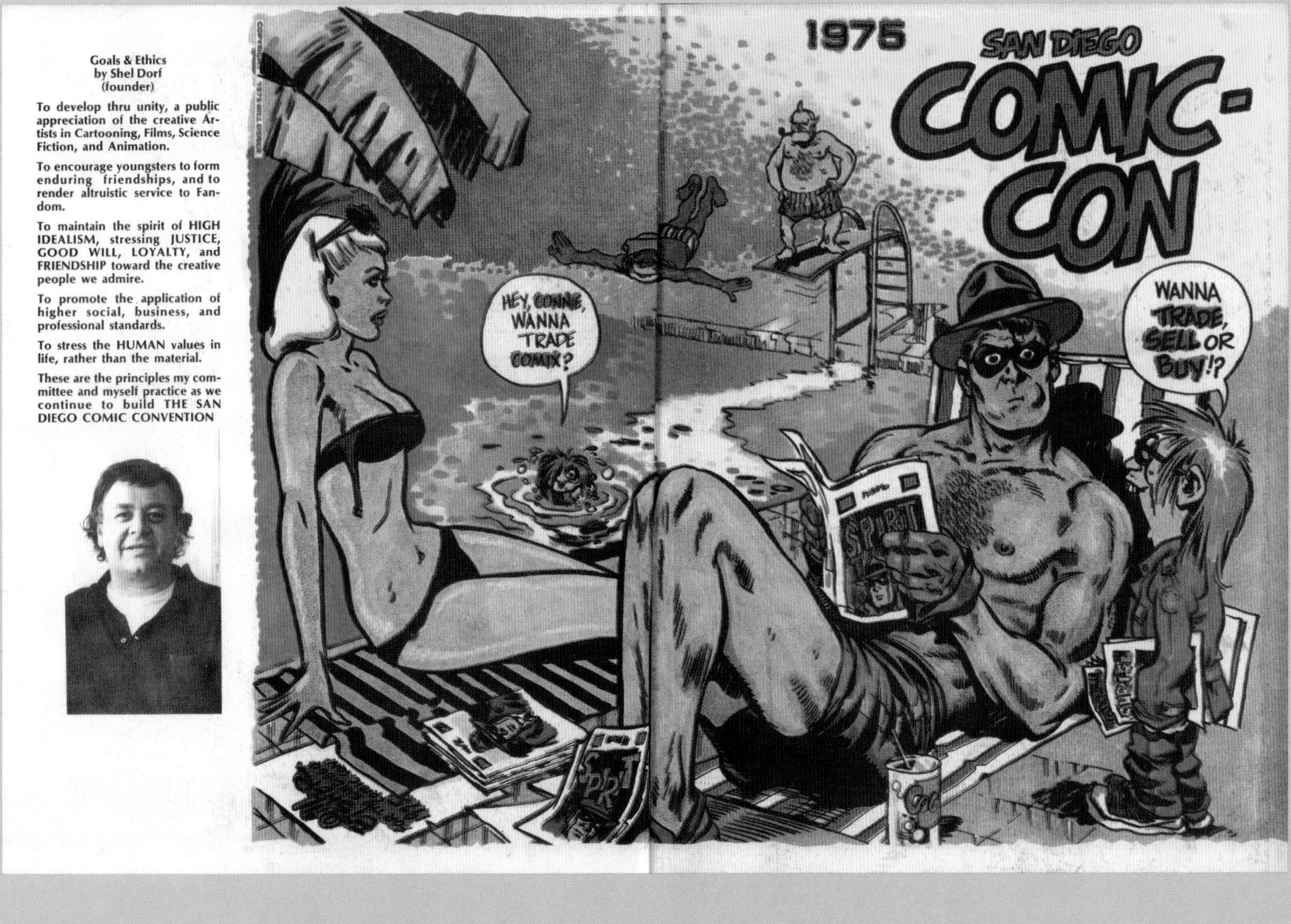
Goals & Ethics
by Shel Dorf
(founder)
To develop thru unity, a public appreciation of the creative Artists in Cartooning, Films, Science Fiction, and Animation.
To encourage youngsters to form enduring friendships, and to render altruistic service to Fandom.
To maintain the spirit of HIGH IDEALISM, stressing JUSTICE, GOOD WILL, LOYALTY, and FRIENDSHIP toward the creative people we admire.
To promote the application of higher social, business, and professional standards.
To stress the HUMAN values in life, rather than the material.
These are the principles my committee and myself practice as we continue to build THE SAN DIEGO COMIC CONVENTION
1975
SAN DIEGO
COMIC-CON
HEY, CONNIE, WANNA TRADE COMIX?
WANNA TRADE, SELL OR BUY!?

OPPOSITE, CLOCKWISE FROM TOP LEFT: 1970's program book cover featured a stock photo of Balboa Park; 1970, by Jack Kirby; 1971, by Carmine Infantino; 1972, by Jack Kirby; 1974, by Milton Caniff
ABOVE, CLOCKWISE FROM TOP LEFT: 1973, by Neal Adams (back cover art); 1976, by Sergio Aragonés; 1975, by Will Eisner

PAGE 124, CLOCKWISE FROM TOP LEFT: 1977, by Alex Nino; 1978, by Boris Vallejo; 1980, by Jack Katz; 1983, by Rick Geary; 1982, by Frank Brunner; 1981, by Dick Giordano **PAGE 125:** 1979's special newspaper-like edition featured Sunday comic strips by Mort Walker (*Beetle Bailey*, top) and Russ Manning (*Star Wars*, bottom)

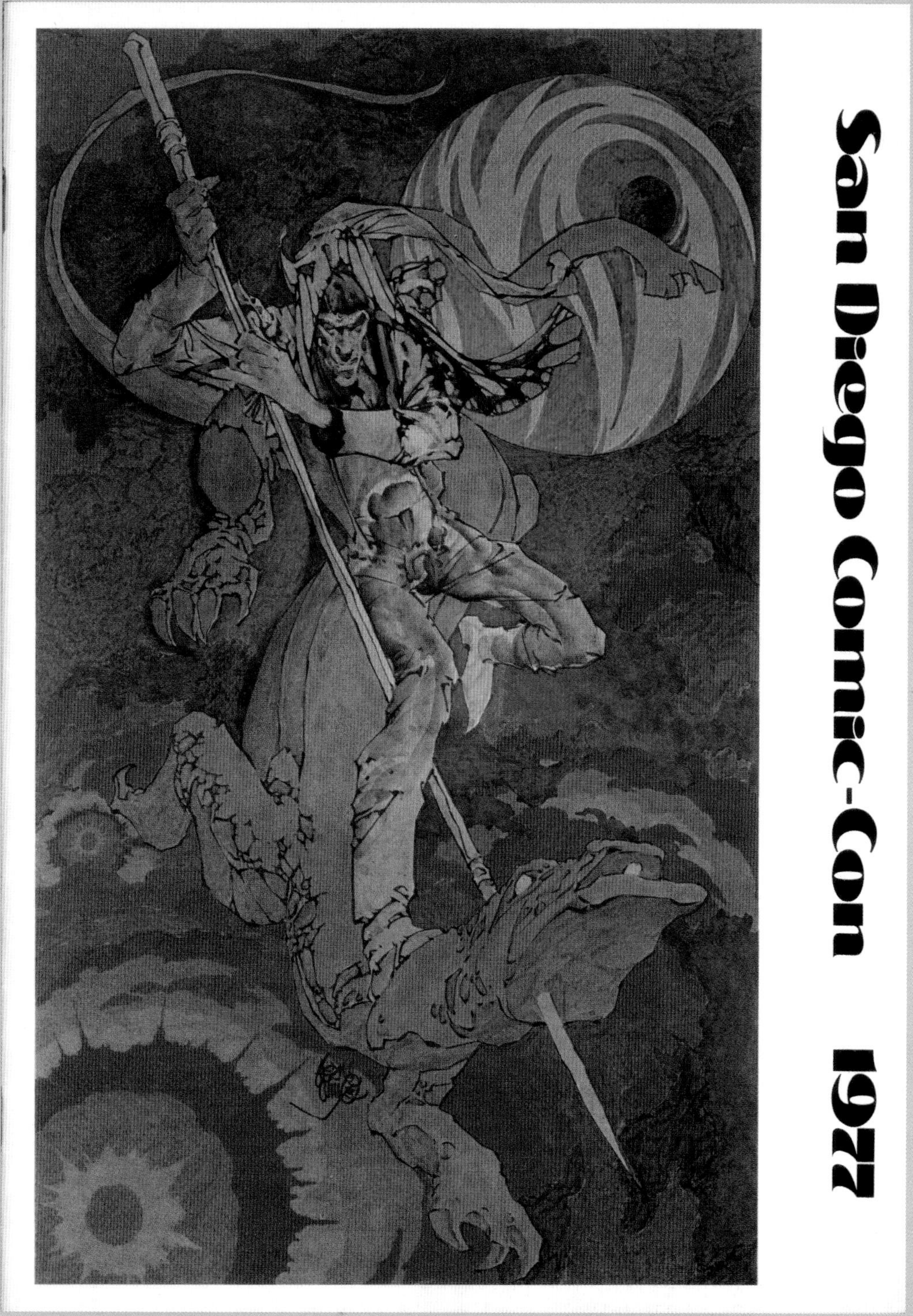
San Diego Comic-Con 1977

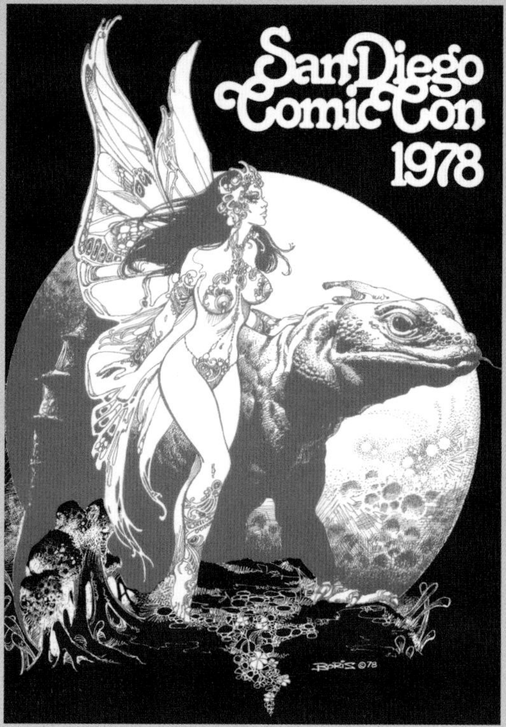
San Diego Comic Con 1978

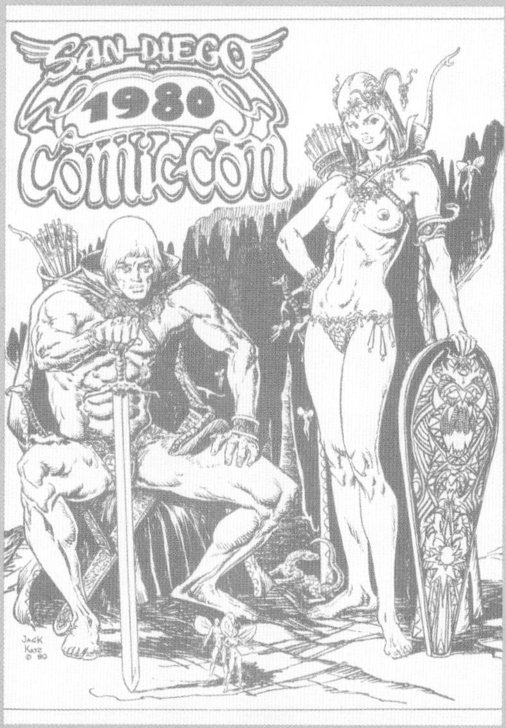
SAN DIEGO
1980
COMIC-CON

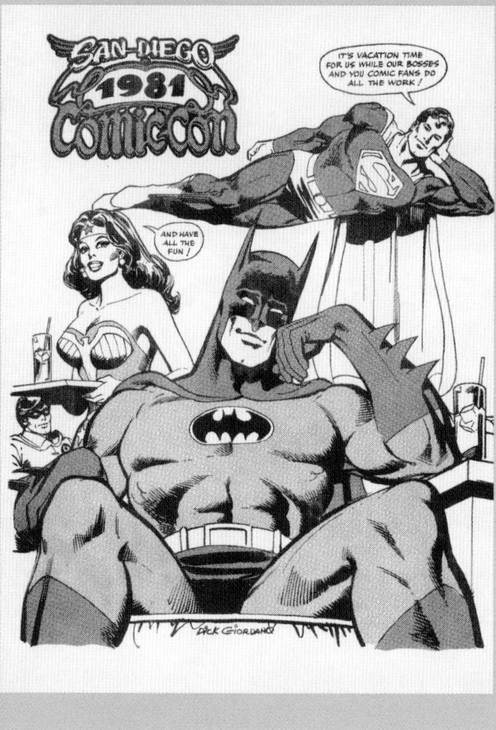
SAN DIEGO
1981
COMIC-CON
IT'S VACATION TIME FOR US WHILE OUR BOSSES AND YOU COMIC FANS DO ALL THE WORK!
AND HAVE ALL THE FUN!

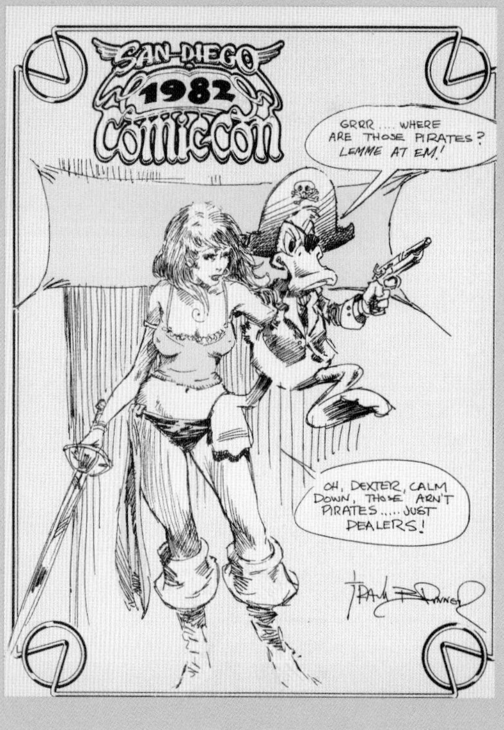
SAN DIEGO
1982
COMIC-CON
GRRR.... WHERE ARE THOSE PIRATES? LEMME AT EM!
OH, DEXTER, CALM DOWN, THOSE ARN'T PIRATES..... JUST DEALERS!

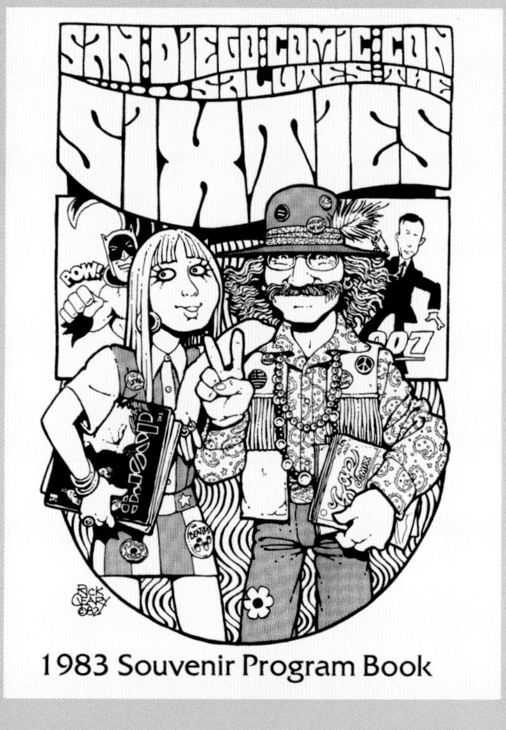
SAN DIEGO COMIC CON SALUTES THE SIXTIES
POW!
1983 Souvenir Program Book

The San Diego Comic-Con

SOUVENIR BOOK
TENTH ANNIVERSARY DELUXE EDITION

FREE to Convention Attendees

VOLUME X NUMBER 10 VALENTINO/OLSHEVSKY, EDITORS
AUGUST 2-5, 1979

$2.00 to Non-Attendees

BEETLE BAILEY

by Mort Walker

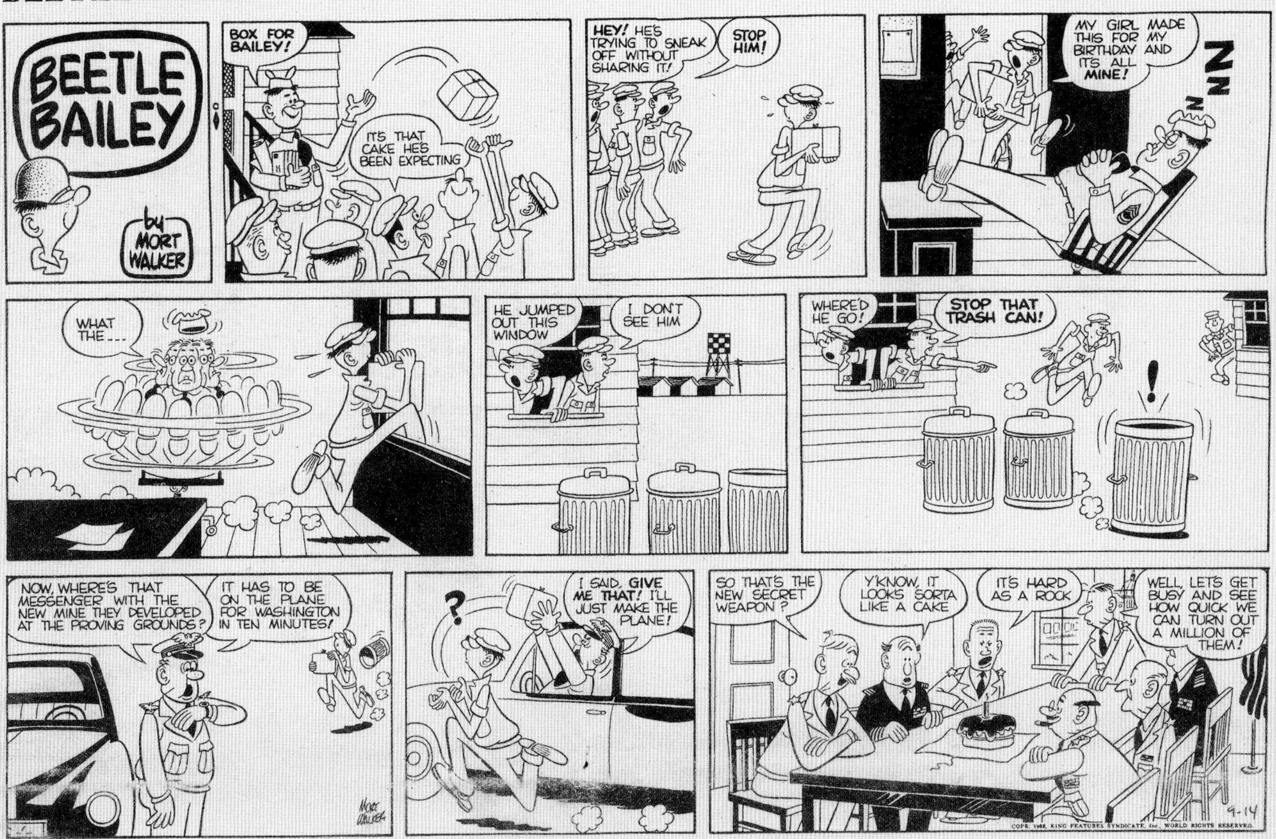

BEETLE BAILEY
by MORT WALKER
BOX FOR BAILEY!
IT'S THAT CAKE HE'S BEEN EXPECTING
HEY! HE'S TRYING TO SNEAK OFF WITHOUT SHARING IT!
STOP HIM!
MY GIRL MADE THIS FOR MY BIRTHDAY AND IT'S ALL MINE!
Z Z Z
WHAT THE ...
HE JUMPED OUT THIS WINDOW
I DON'T SEE HIM
WHERE'D HE GO!
STOP THAT TRASH CAN!
!
NOW, WHERE'S THAT MESSENGER WITH THE NEW MINE THEY DEVELOPED AT THE PROVING GROUNDS?
IT HAS TO BE ON THE PLANE FOR WASHINGTON IN TEN MINUTES!
?
I SAID, GIVE ME THAT! I'LL JUST MAKE THE PLANE!
SO THAT'S THE NEW SECRET WEAPON?
Y'KNOW, IT LOOKS SORTA LIKE A CAKE
IT'S HARD AS A ROCK
WELL, LET'S GET BUSY AND SEE HOW QUICK WE CAN TURN OUT A MILLION OF THEM!
MORT WALKER
9-14
COPR. 1968, KING FEATURES SYNDICATE, Inc., WORLD RIGHTS RESERVED.

STAR WARS

by Russ Manning

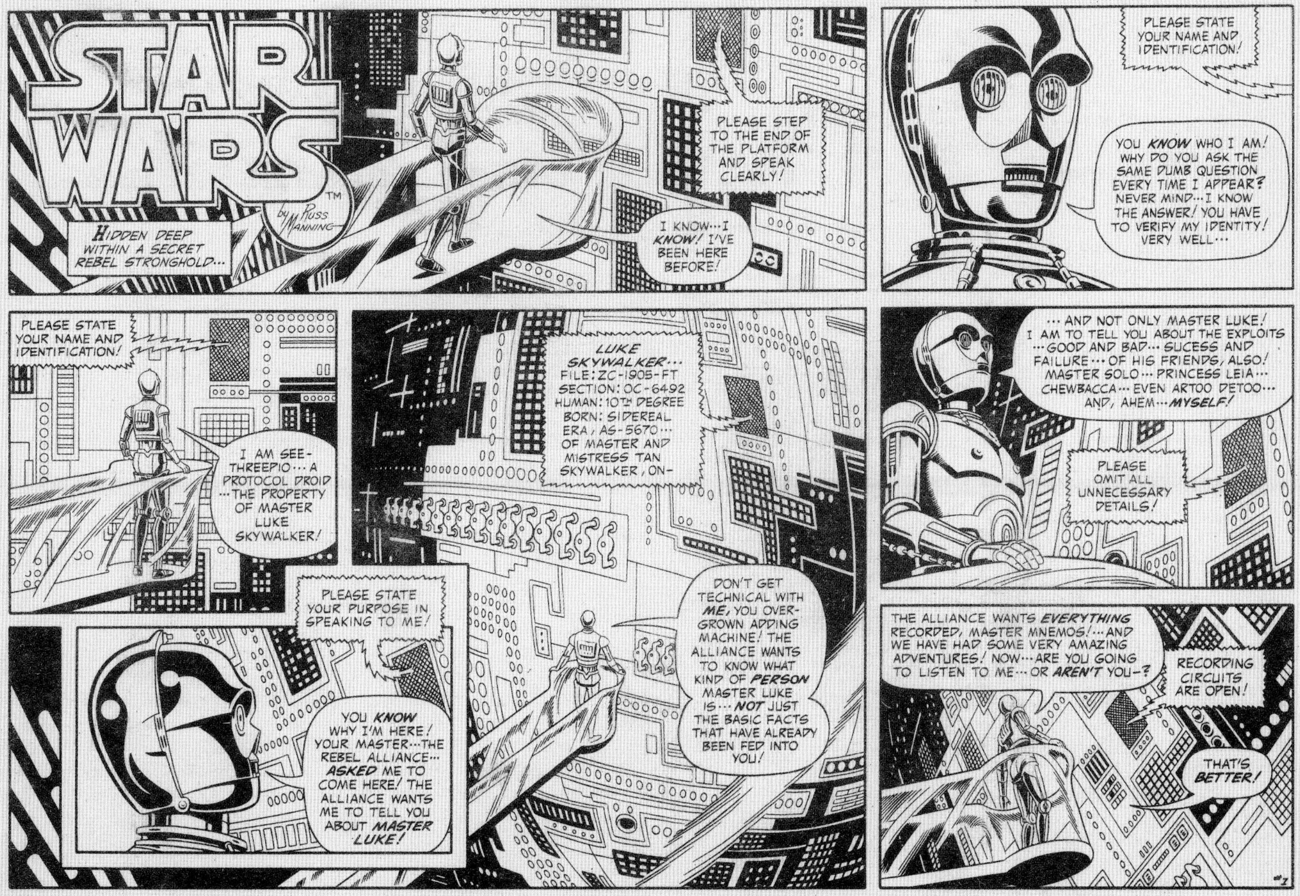

STAR WARS
by RUSS MANNING
HIDDEN DEEP WITHIN A SECRET REBEL STRONGHOLD...
PLEASE STEP TO THE END OF THE PLATFORM AND SPEAK CLEARLY!
I KNOW... I KNOW! I'VE BEEN HERE BEFORE!
PLEASE STATE YOUR NAME AND IDENTIFICATION!
YOU KNOW WHO I AM! WHY DO YOU ASK THE SAME DUMB QUESTION EVERY TIME I APPEAR? NEVER MIND... I KNOW THE ANSWER! YOU HAVE TO VERIFY MY IDENTITY! VERY WELL...
PLEASE STATE YOUR NAME AND IDENTIFICATION!
I AM SEE-THREEPIO... A PROTOCOL DROID ... THE PROPERTY OF MASTER LUKE SKYWALKER!
LUKE SKYWALKER... FILE: ZC-1905-FT SECTION: OC-6492 HUMAN: 10TH DEGREE BORN: SIDEREAL ERA, AS-5670... OF MASTER AND MISTRESS TAN SKYWALKER, ON-
... AND NOT ONLY MASTER LUKE! I AM TO TELL YOU ABOUT THE EXPLOITS ... GOOD AND BAD... SUCESS AND FAILURE... OF HIS FRIENDS, ALSO! MASTER SOLO... PRINCESS LEIA... CHEWBACCA... EVEN ARTOO DETOO... AND, AHEM... MYSELF!
PLEASE OMIT ALL UNNECESSARY DETAILS!
PLEASE STATE YOUR PURPOSE IN SPEAKING TO ME!
YOU KNOW WHY I'M HERE! YOUR MASTER... THE REBEL ALLIANCE... ASKED ME TO COME HERE! THE ALLIANCE WANTS ME TO TELL YOU ABOUT MASTER LUKE!
DON'T GET TECHNICAL WITH ME, YOU OVER-GROWN ADDING MACHINE! THE ALLIANCE WANTS TO KNOW WHAT KIND OF PERSON MASTER LUKE IS... NOT JUST THE BASIC FACTS THAT HAVE ALREADY BEEN FED INTO YOU!
THE ALLIANCE WANTS EVERYTHING RECORDED, MASTER MNEMOS! ... AND WE HAVE HAD SOME VERY AMAZING ADVENTURES! NOW... ARE YOU GOING TO LISTEN TO ME... OR AREN'T YOU--?
RECORDING CIRCUITS ARE OPEN!
THAT'S BETTER!

BELOW, LEFT TO RIGHT: 1984, by Marshall Rogers and Howard Chaykin; 1985, art provided by DC Comics in celebration of the company's fiftieth anniversary; 1987, by Jean "Moebius" Girard; 1988, by Wayne Boring; 1990, by Bill Morrison; 1986, by John Romita; 1991, by William Stout
OPPOSITE, CLOCKWISE FROM TOP LEFT: 1992, by Ken Steacy; 1993, by Frank Miller and Lynn Varley; 1989, by Bill Sienkiewicz

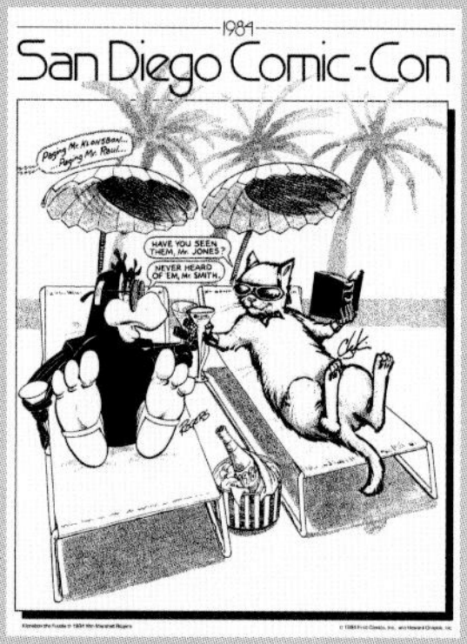
1984
San Diego Comic-Con

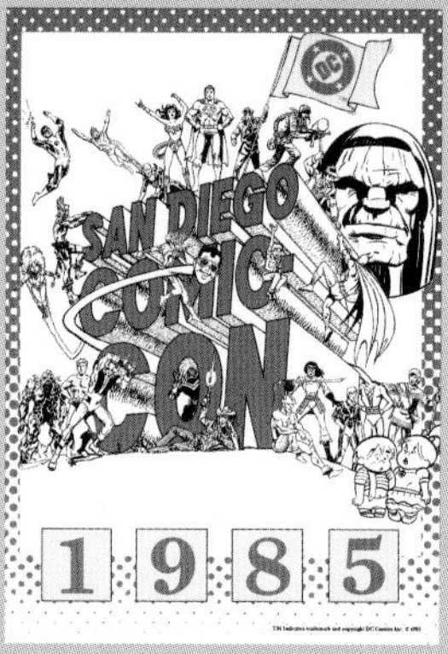
SAN DIEGO COMIC-CON
1985

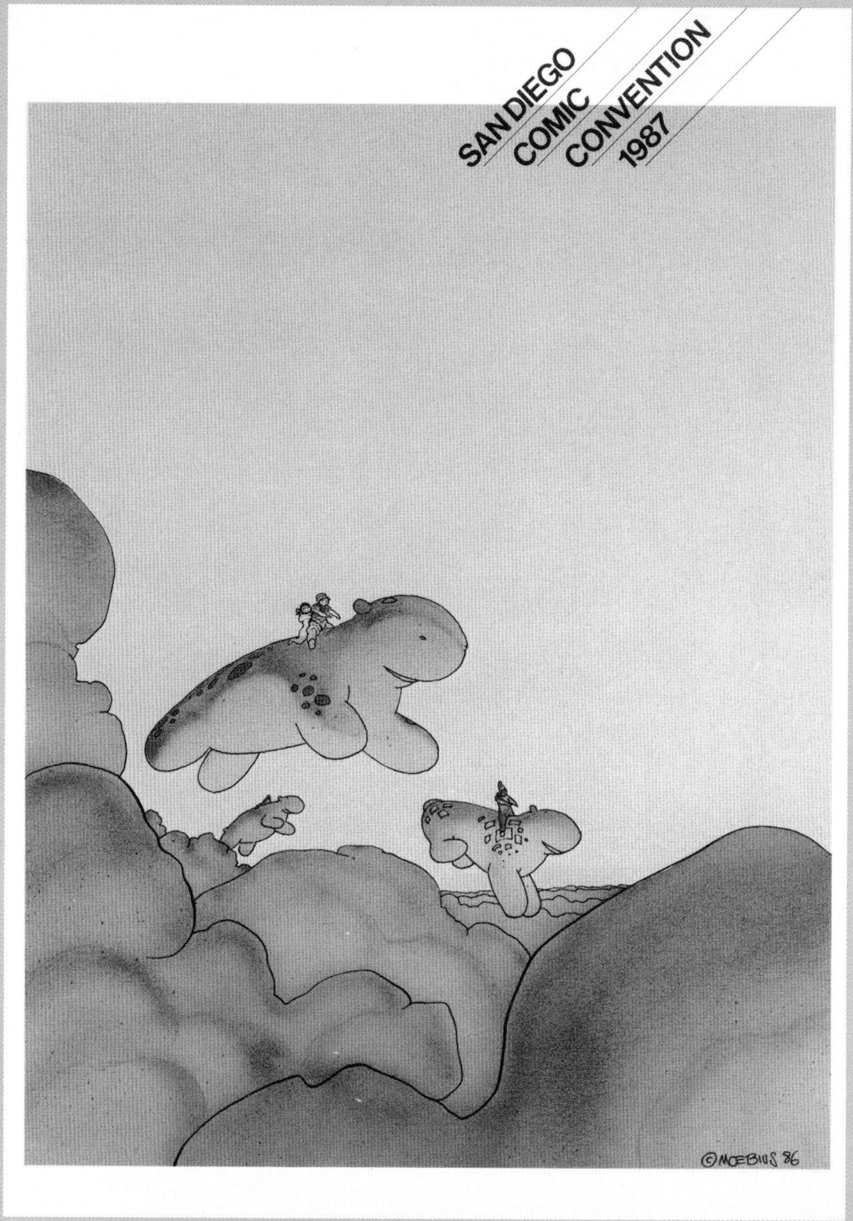
SAN DIEGO
COMIC
CONVENTION
1987
©MOEBIUS 86

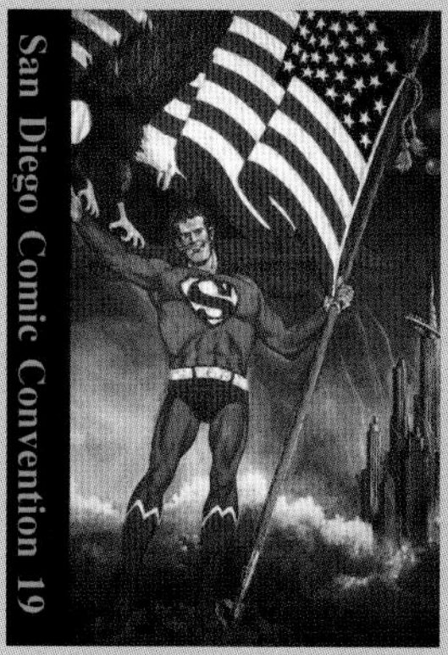
San Diego Comic Convention 19

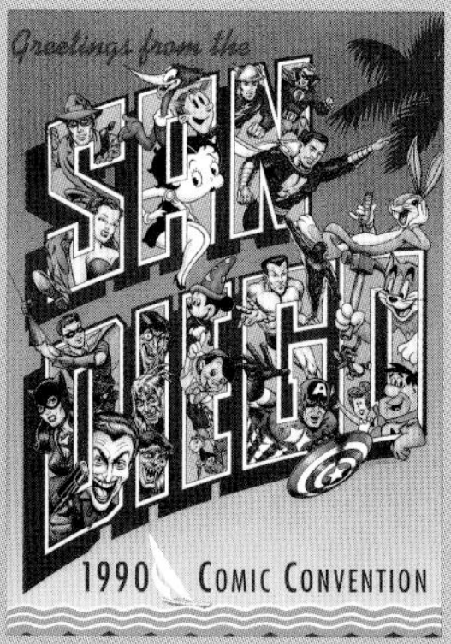
Greetings from the
SAN DIEGO
1990 COMIC CONVENTION

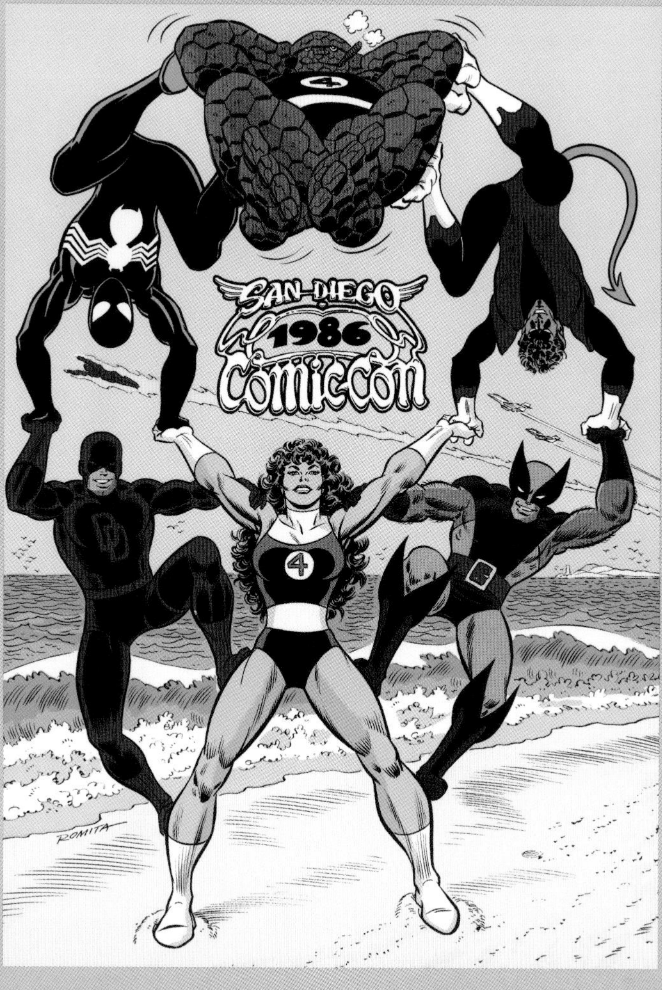
SAN DIEGO
1986
COMIC-CON
ROMITA

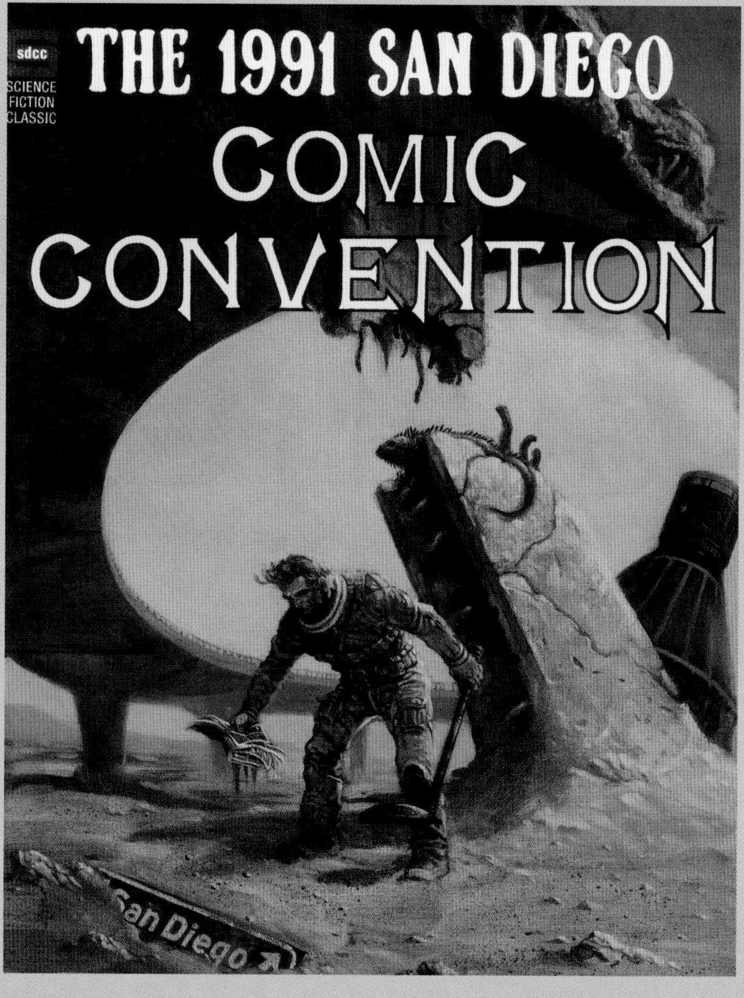
sdcc
SCIENCE FICTION CLASSIC
THE 1991 SAN DIEGO
COMIC
CONVENTION
San Diego

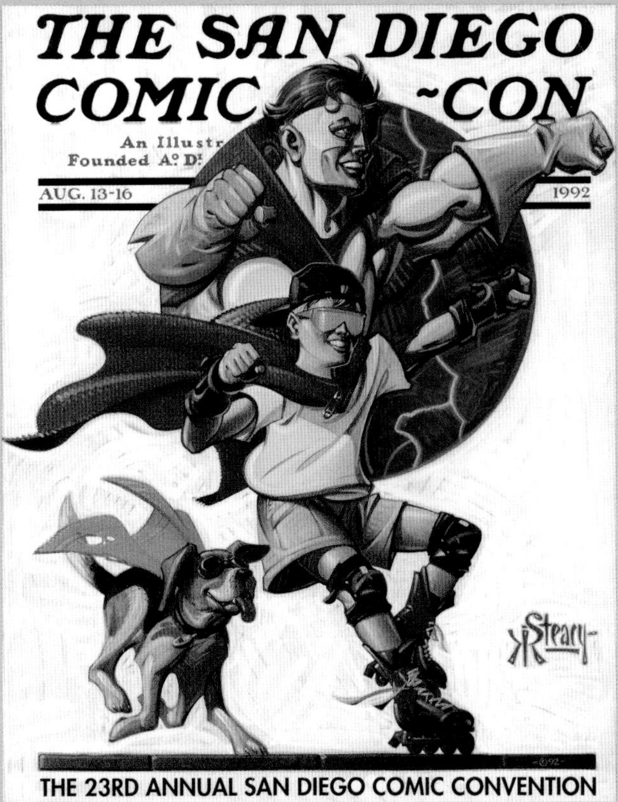
THE SAN DIEGO
COMIC-CON
An Illustr
Founded A.D.
AUG. 13-16
1992
Steacy
THE 23RD ANNUAL SAN DIEGO COMIC CONVENTION

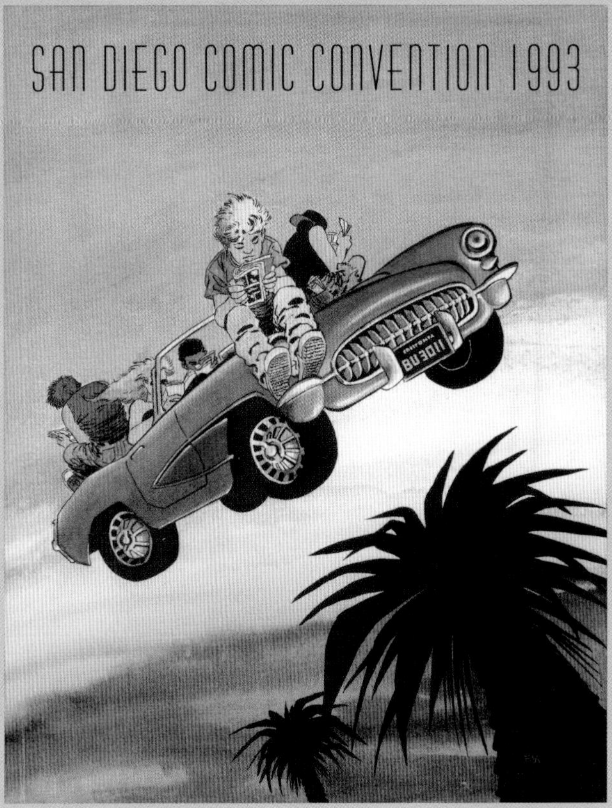
SAN DIEGO COMIC CONVENTION 1993

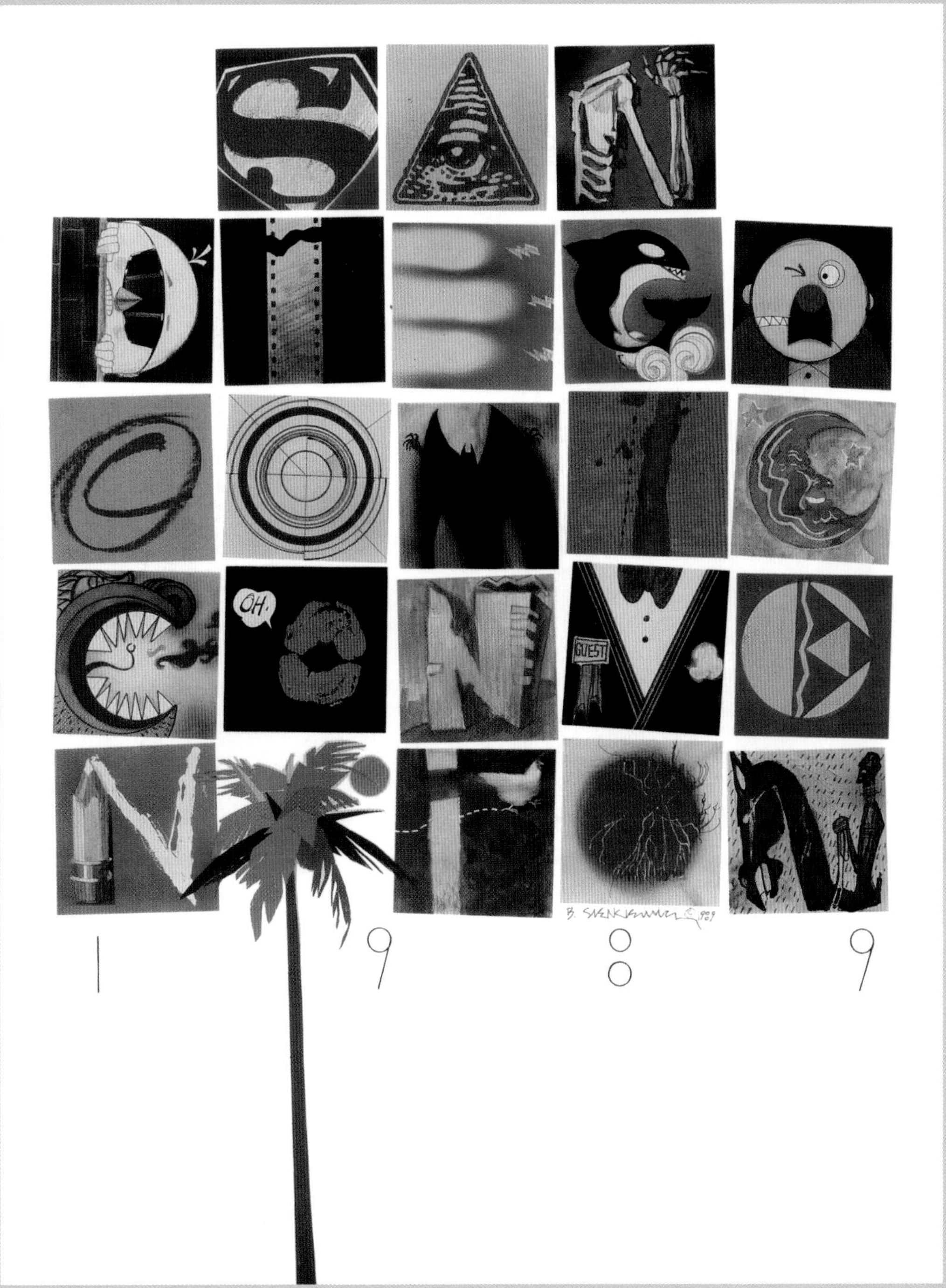
OH!
GUEST
1 9 8 9

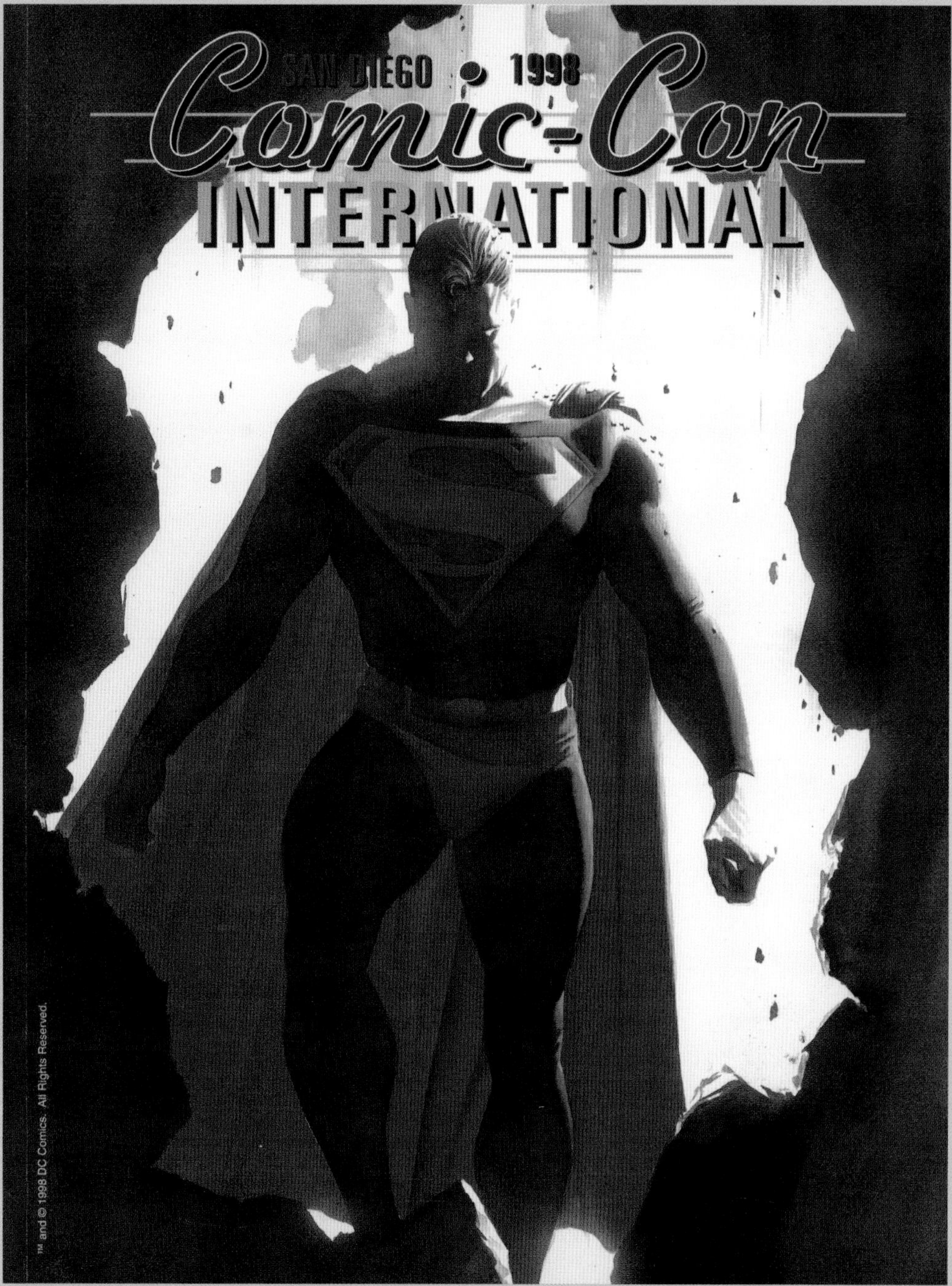
SAN DIEGO • 1998
Comic-Con
INTERNATIONAL
™ and © 1998 DC Comics. All Rights Reserved.

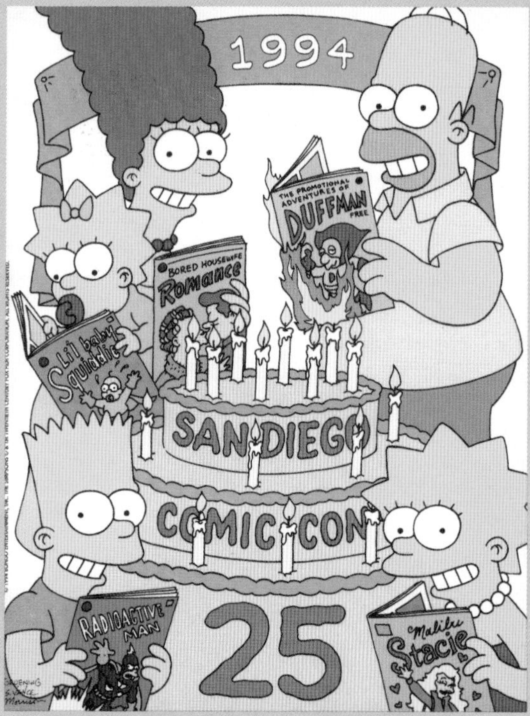
1994
THE PROMOTIONAL ADVENTURES OF DUFFMAN FREE
BORED HOUSEWIFE Romance
Li'l baby Squishie
SAN DIEGO
COMIC CON
25
RADIOACTIVE MAN
Malibu Stacie

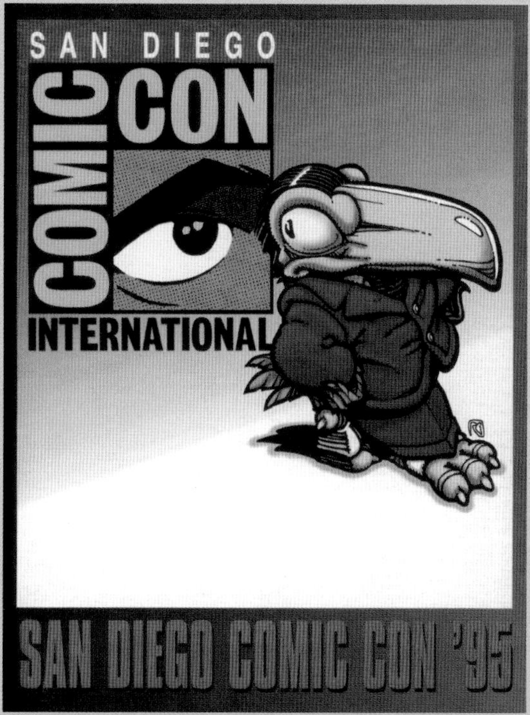
SAN DIEGO
COMIC CON
INTERNATIONAL
SAN DIEGO COMIC CON '95

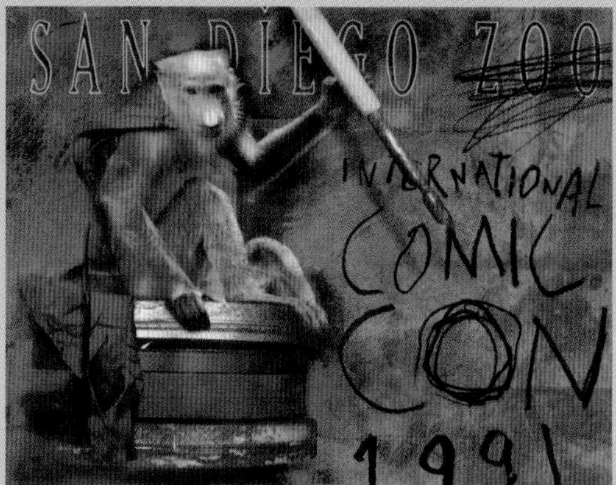
SAN DIEGO ZOO
INTERNATIONAL
COMIC
CON
1996
See strange and bewildering creatures at play in their natural habitats.

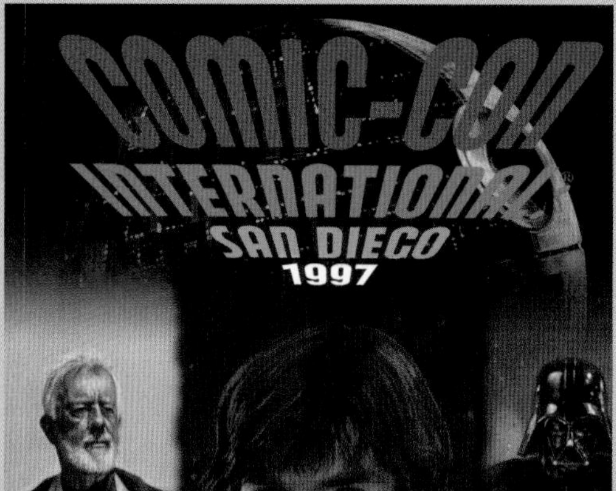
COMIC-CON
INTERNATIONAL
SAN DIEGO
1997

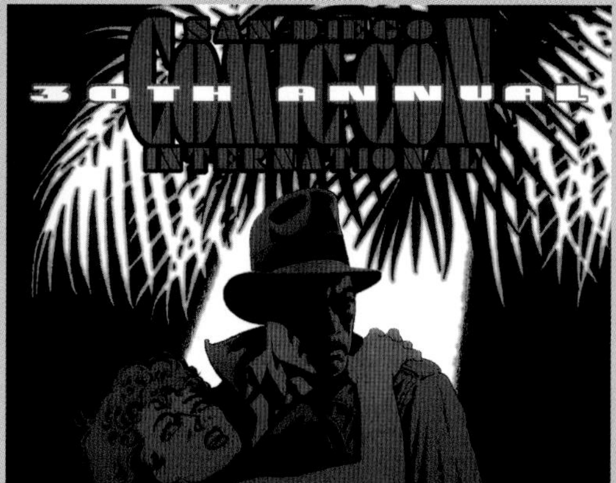
SAN DIEGO
COMIC-CON
30TH ANNUAL
INTERNATIONAL
STERANKO

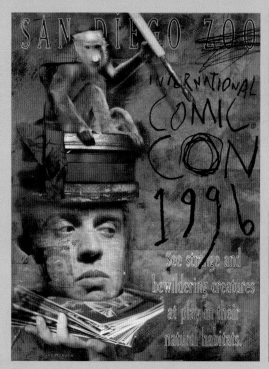

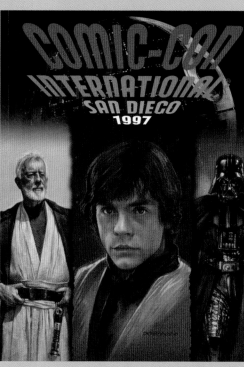

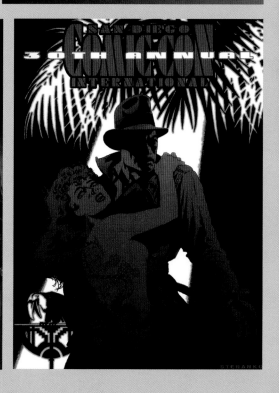

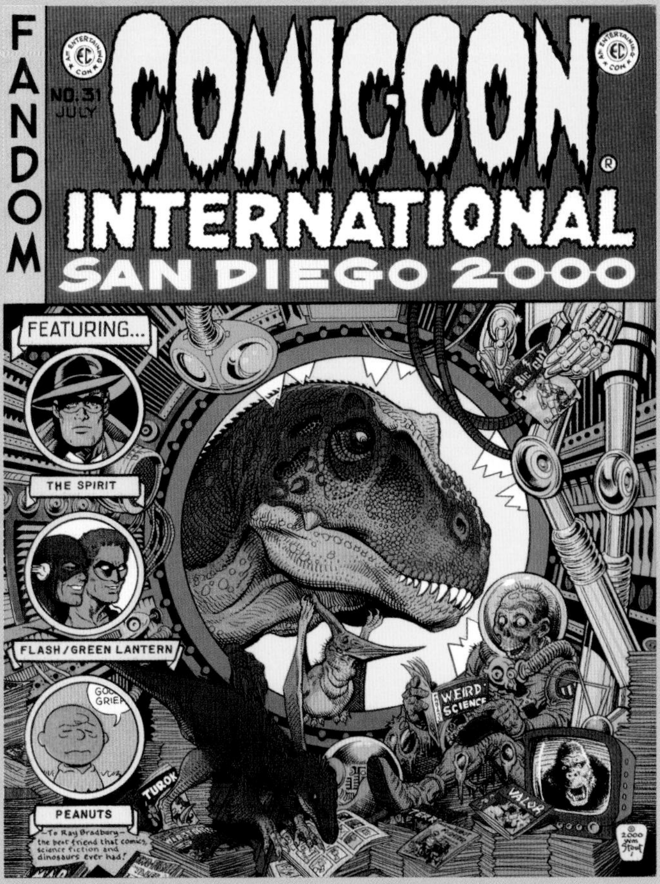
FANDOM
COMIC-CON
NO.31 JULY
INTERNATIONAL
SAN DIEGO 2000
FEATURING...
THE SPIRIT
FLASH/GREEN LANTERN
PEANUTS
WEIRD SCIENCE
TUROK

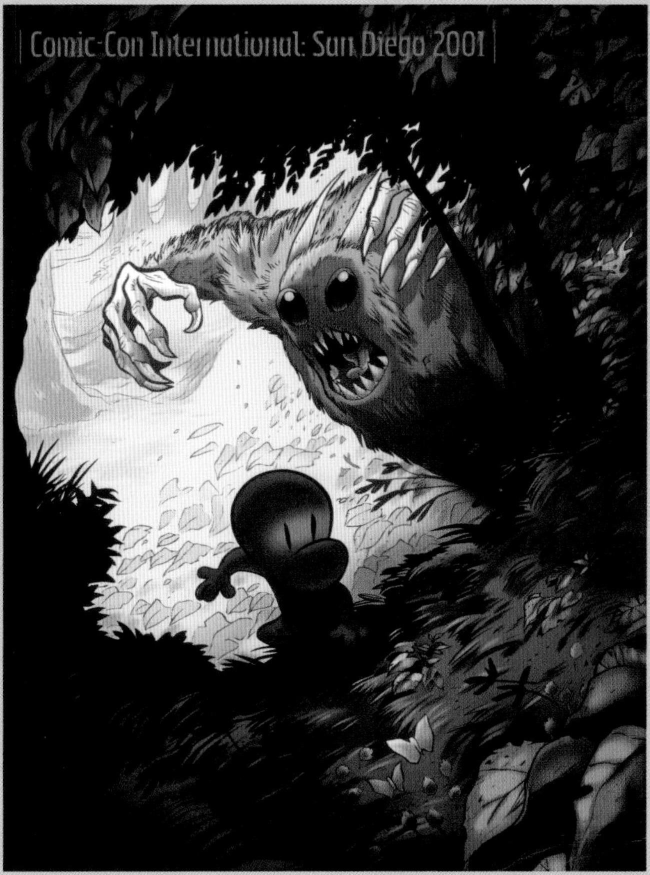
Comic-Con International: San Diego 2001

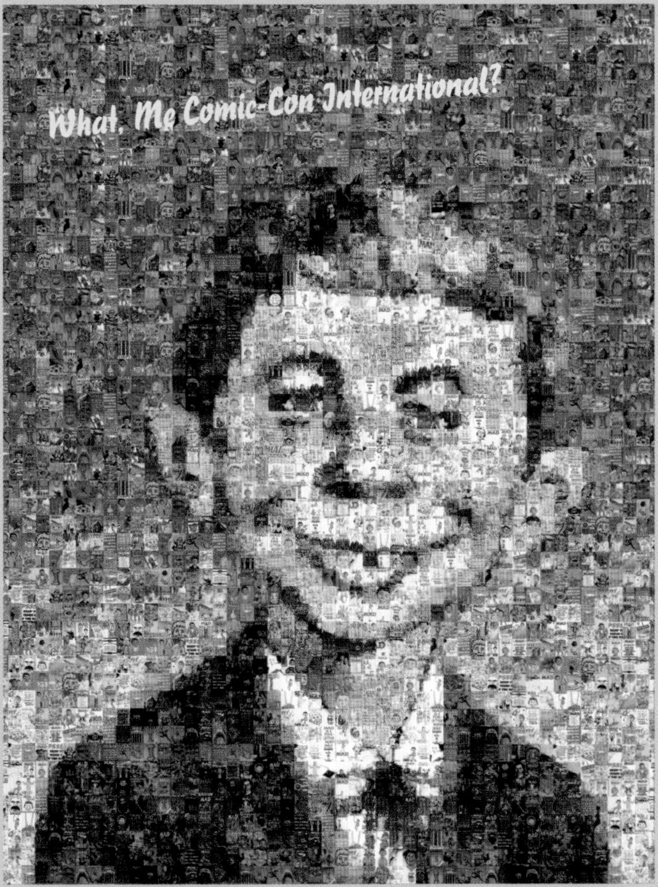
What, Me Comic-Con International?

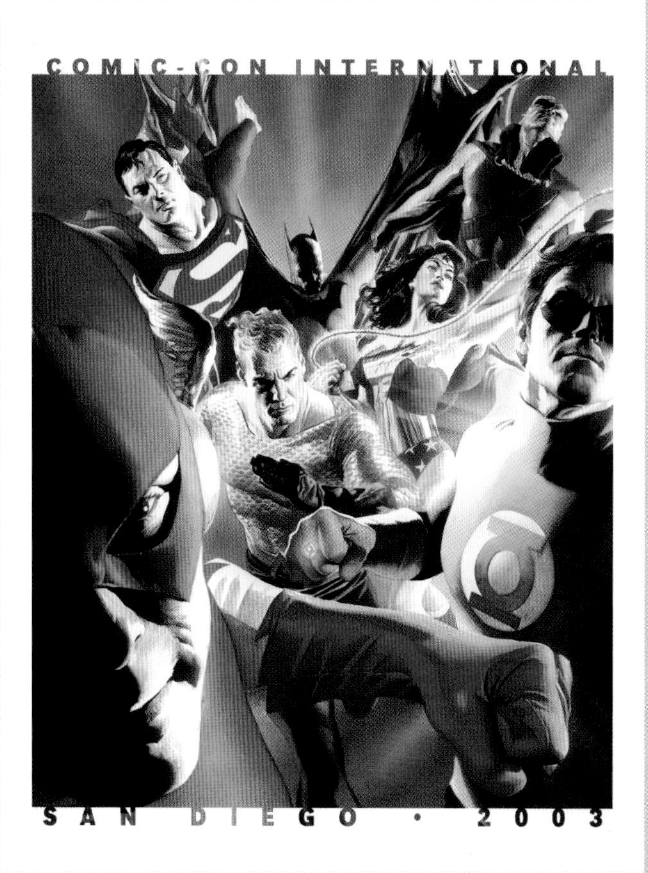
COMIC-CON INTERNATIONAL
SAN DIEGO · 2003

OPPOSITE, CLOCKWISE FROM TOP LEFT: 1998, by Alex Ross; 1994, by Matt Groening; 1995, by Rick Geary; 1999, by Jim Steranko; 1997, by Dave Dorman; 1996, by Dave McKean
TOP ROW, FROM LEFT: 2000, by William Stout; 2001, Fone Bone and Rat Creature chase in forest, by Jeff Smith **ABOVE, FROM LEFT:** 2002, MAD magazine's fiftieth (artist unknown); 2003, by Alex Ross

PAGE 130, CLOCKWISE FROM TOP LEFT: 2004, by Jack Kirby and Michael Thibodeaux; 2005, by Will Eisner; 2008, by Alex Ross; 2006, by Frank Miller and Lynn Varley
PAGE 131: 2007, by Adam Hughes
PAGES 132–135: A plethora of Comic-Con publications from over the years

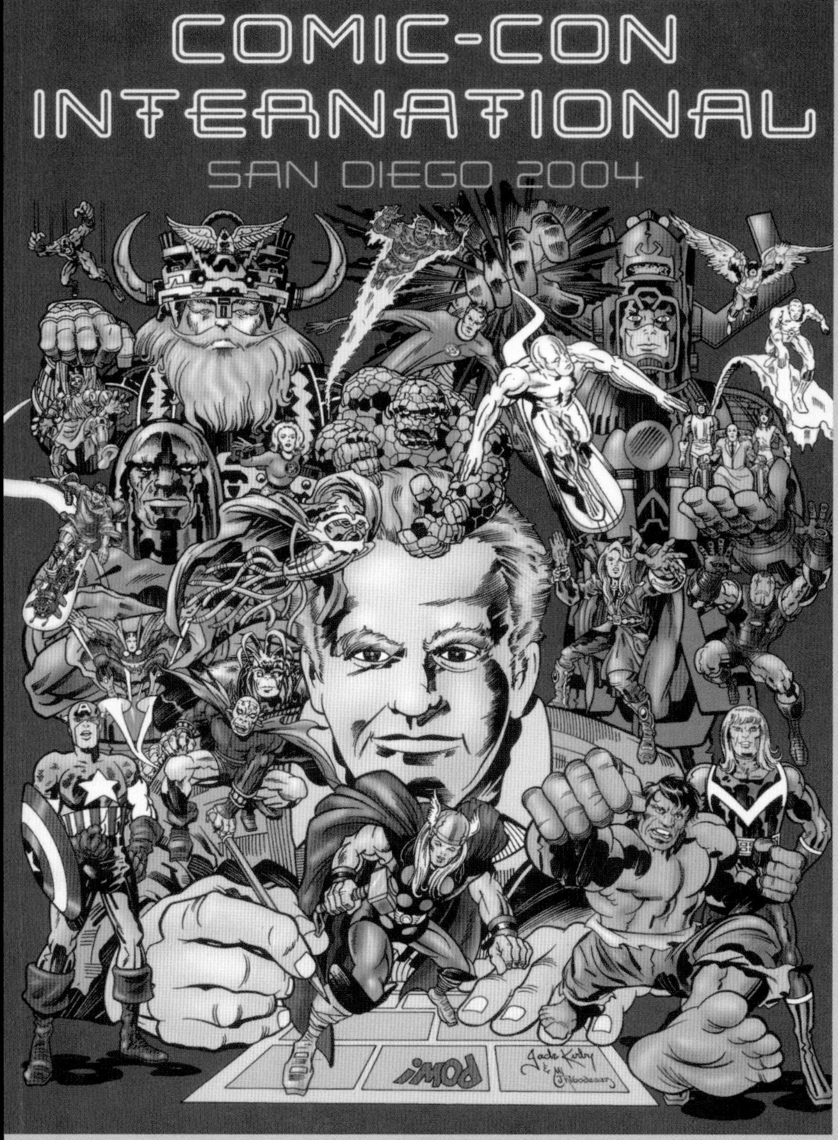
COMIC-CON
INTERNATIONAL
SAN DIEGO 2004
POW!

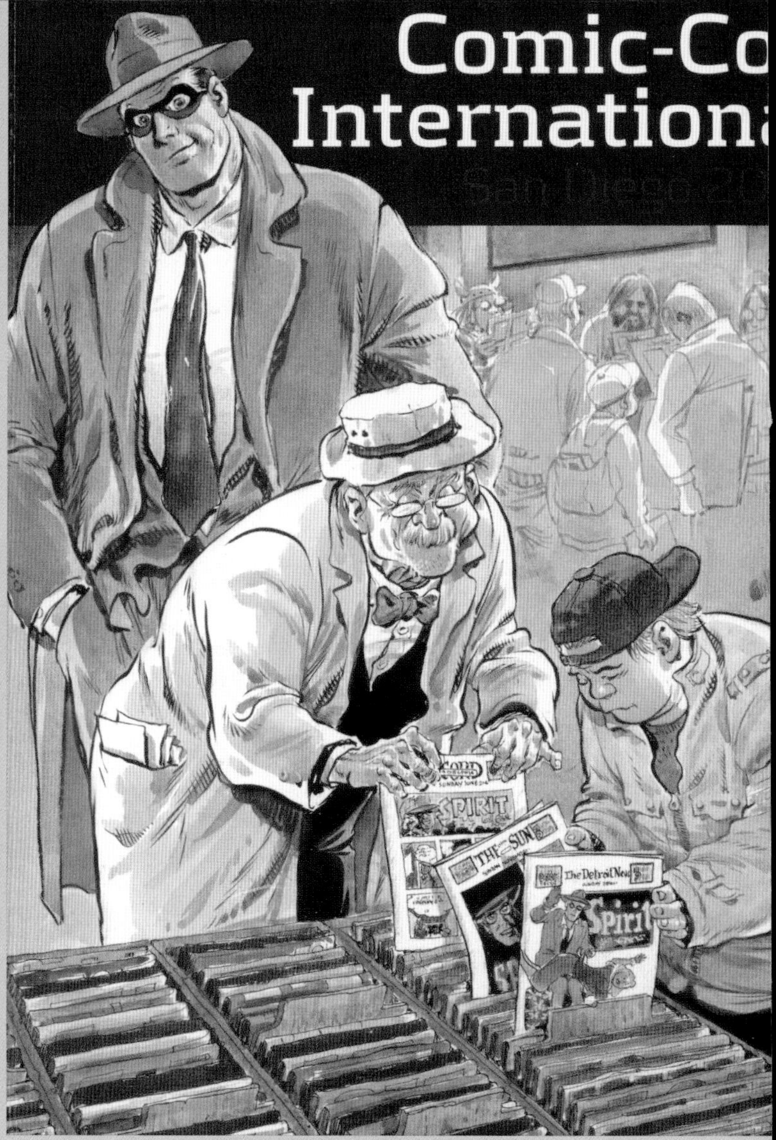
Comic-Co
Internationa

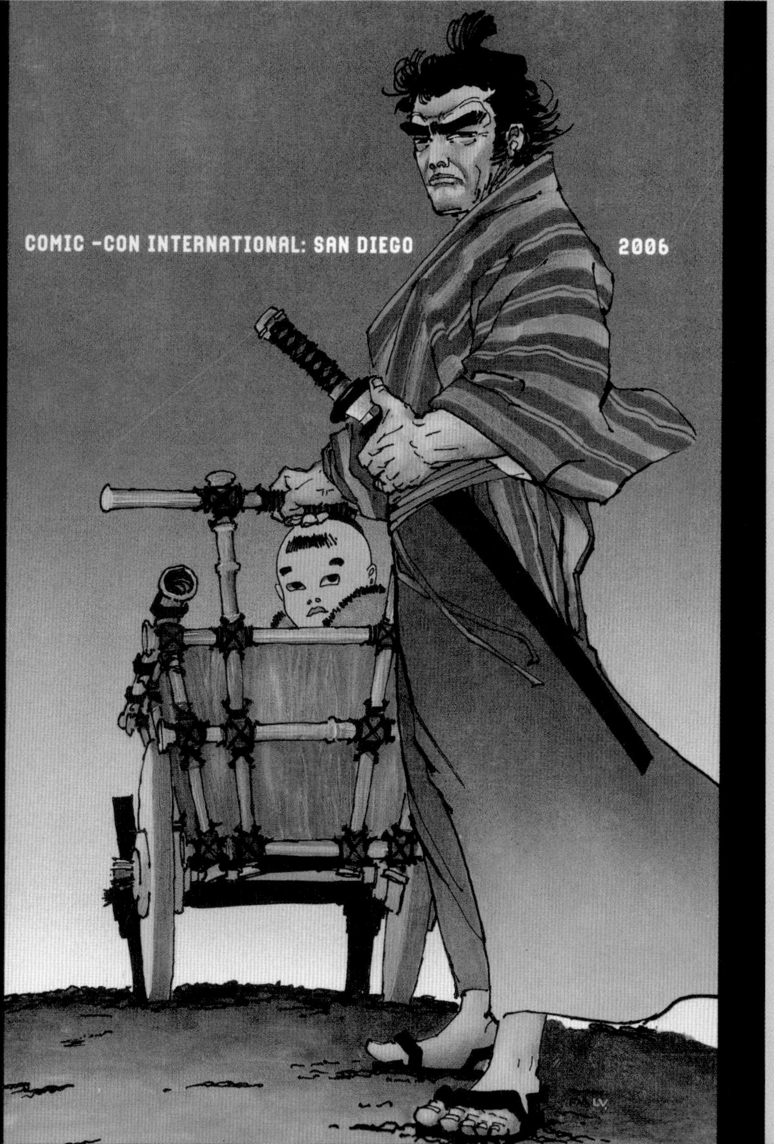
COMIC -CON INTERNATIONAL: SAN DIEGO
2006

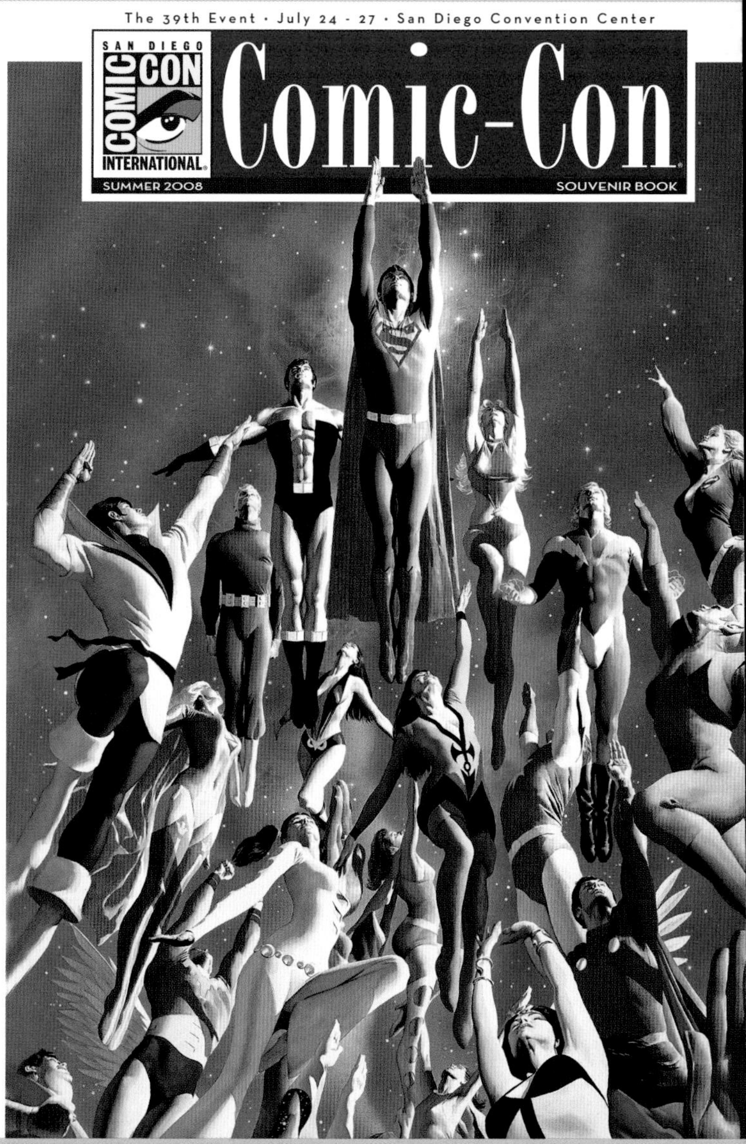
The 39th Event · July 24 - 27 · San Diego Convention Center
SAN DIEGO COMIC CON INTERNATIONAL
Comic-Con
SUMMER 2008
SOUVENIR BOOK

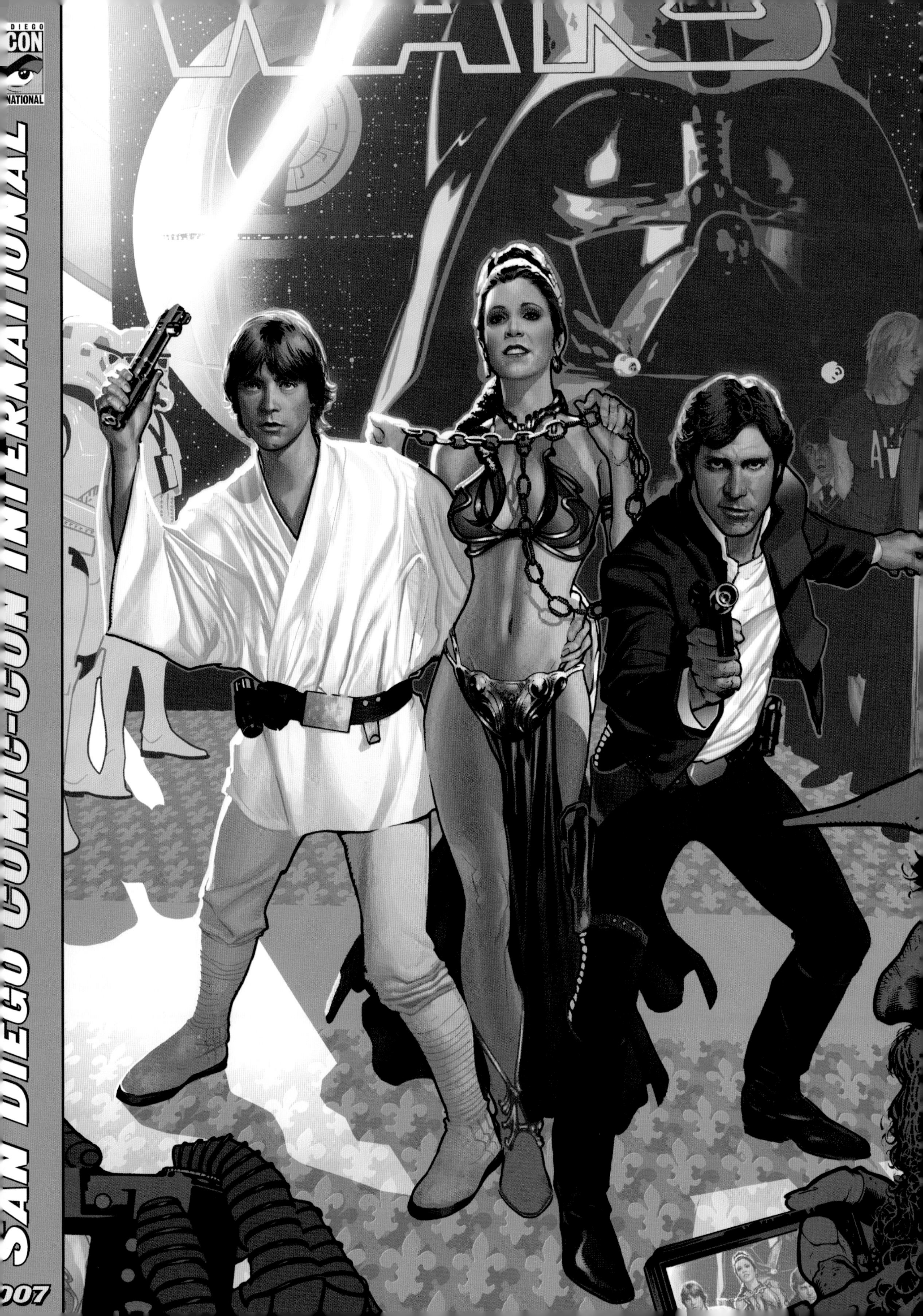
SAN DIEGO COMIC-CON INTERNATIONAL

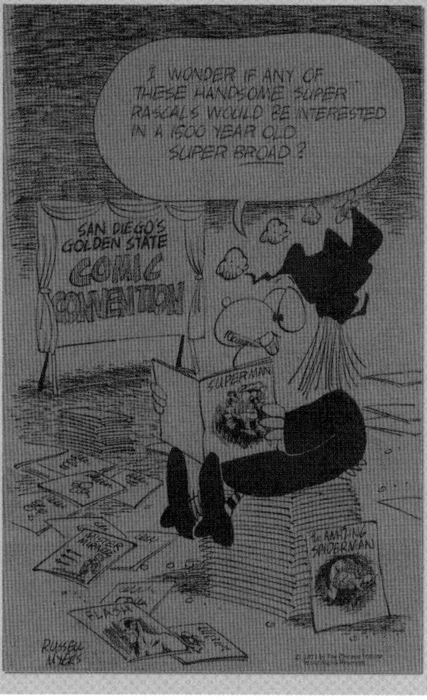
I WONDER IF ANY OF THESE HANDSOME SUPER RASCALS WOULD BE INTERESTED IN A 1500 YEAR OLD SUPER BROAD?
SAN DIEGO'S GOLDEN STATE COMIC CONVENTION
SUPERMAN
RUSSELL MYERS

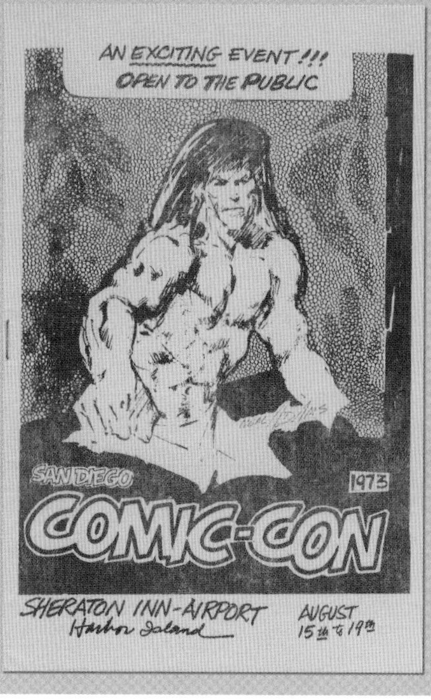
AN EXCITING EVENT!!!
OPEN TO THE PUBLIC
SAN DIEGO
1973
COMIC-CON
SHERATON INN-AIRPORT
Harbor Island
AUGUST
15th to 19th

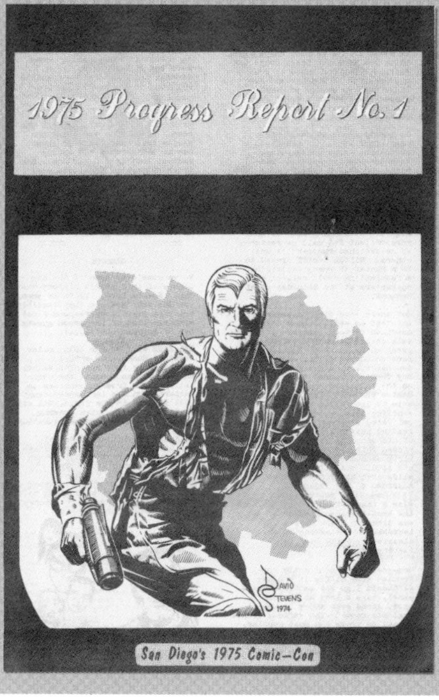
1975 Progress Report No. 1
David Stevens 1974
San Diego's 1975 Comic-Con

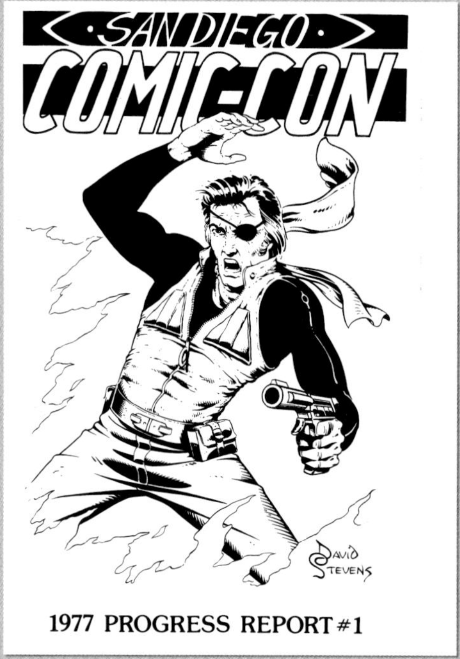
SAN DIEGO
COMIC-CON
David Stevens
1977 PROGRESS REPORT #1

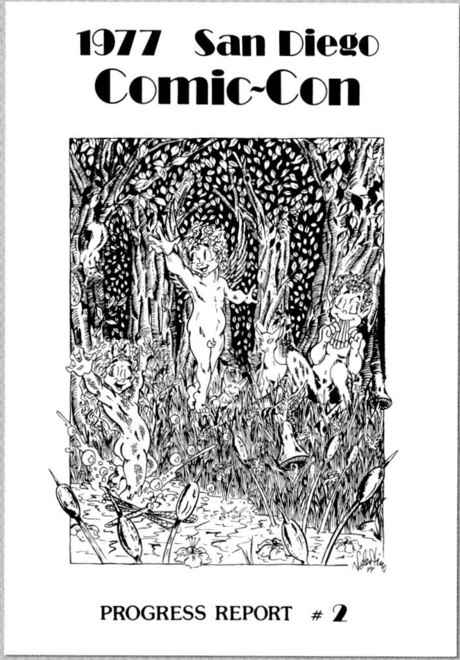
1977 San Diego
Comic-Con
PROGRESS REPORT # 2

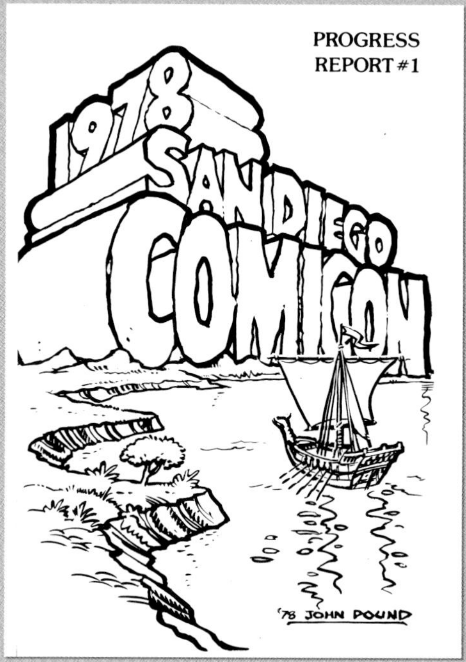
PROGRESS
REPORT #1
1978
SAN DIEGO
COMICON
'78 JOHN POUND

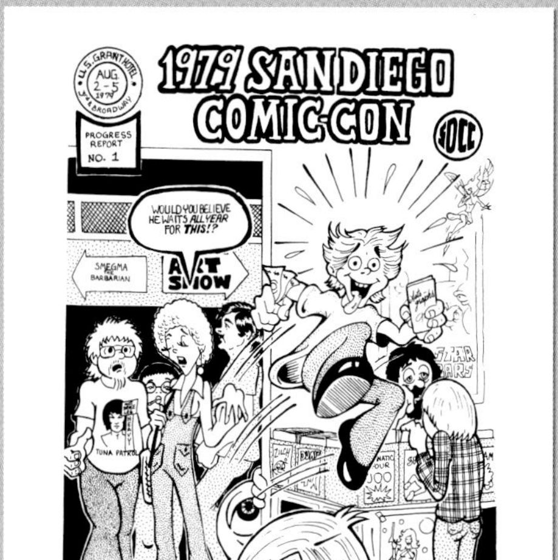
1979 SAN DIEGO
COMIC-CON
PROGRESS REPORT
NO. 1
SDCC
WOULD YOU BELIEVE HE WAITS ALL YEAR FOR THIS!?
ART SHOW
BARBARIAN

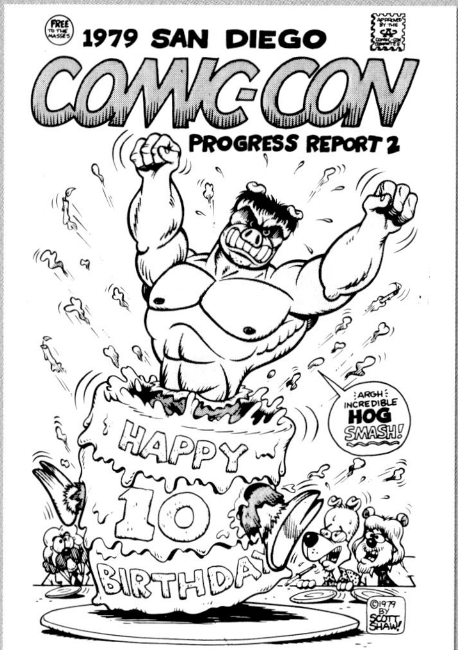
FREE TO THE MASSES
1979 SAN DIEGO
COMIC-CON
PROGRESS REPORT 2
ARGH! INCREDIBLE HOG SMASH!
HAPPY
10
BIRTHDAY
©1979 BY SCOTT SHAW!

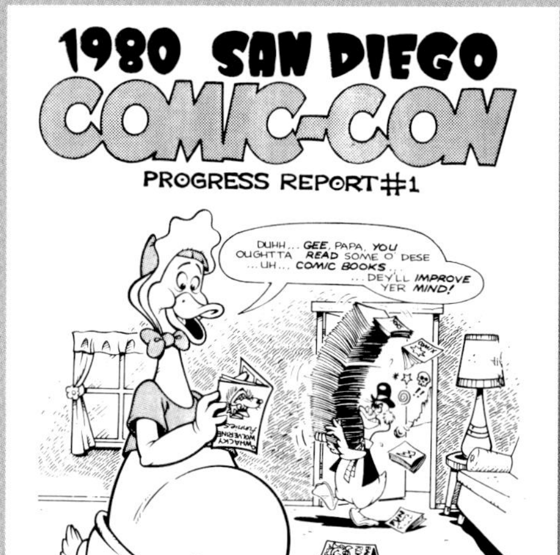
1980 SAN DIEGO
COMIC-CON
PROGRESS REPORT #1
DUHH... GEE, PAPA, YOU OUGHTTA READ SOME O DESE ...UH... COMIC BOOKS... DEY'LL IMPROVE YER MIND!
SCOTT SHAW!
FEBRUARY, 1980

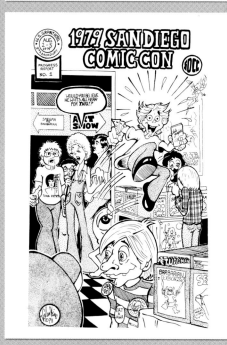

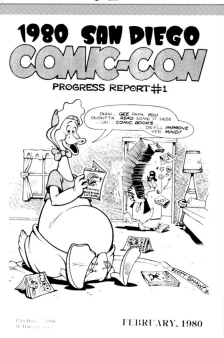

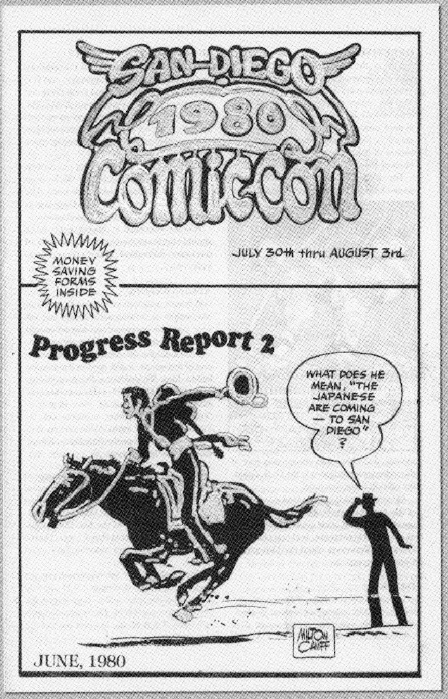
SAN DIEGO
1980
COMIC-CON
MONEY SAVING FORMS INSIDE
JULY 30th thru AUGUST 3rd
Progress Report 2
WHAT DOES HE MEAN, "THE JAPANESE ARE COMING — TO SAN DIEGO"?
JUNE, 1980

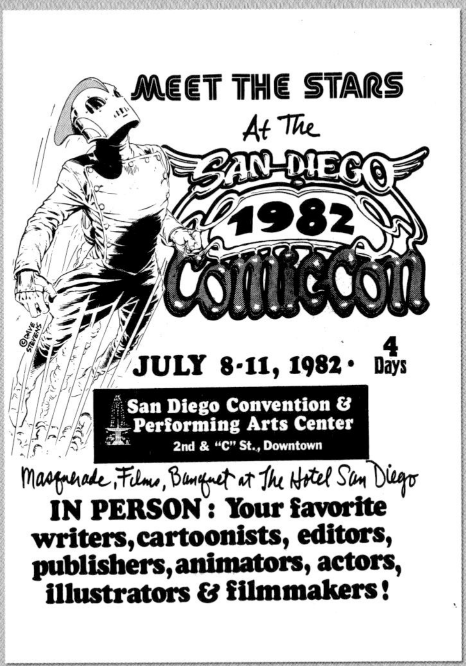
MEET THE STARS
At The
SAN DIEGO
1982
COMIC-CON
JULY 8-11, 1982 • 4 Days
San Diego Convention & Performing Arts Center
2nd & "C" St., Downtown
Masquerade, Films, Banquet at The Hotel San Diego
IN PERSON : Your favorite writers, cartoonists, editors, publishers, animators, actors, illustrators & filmmakers!

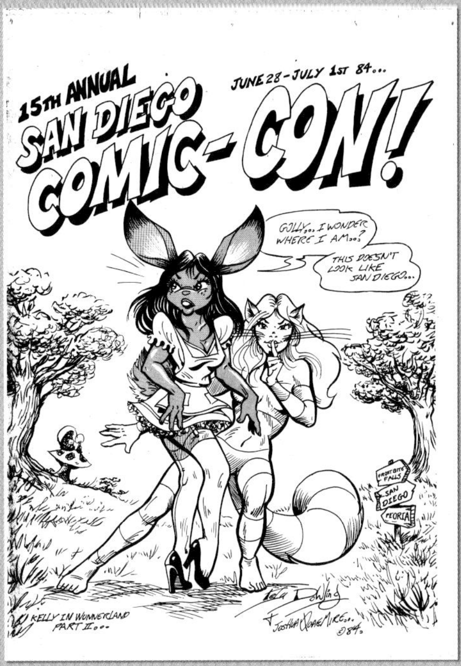
15TH ANNUAL
SAN DIEGO
COMIC-CON!
JUNE 28 - JULY 1ST 84...
GOLLY... I WONDER WHERE I AM...?
THIS DOESN'T LOOK LIKE SAN DIEGO...
SAN DIEGO
KELLY IN WONDERLAND PART II...

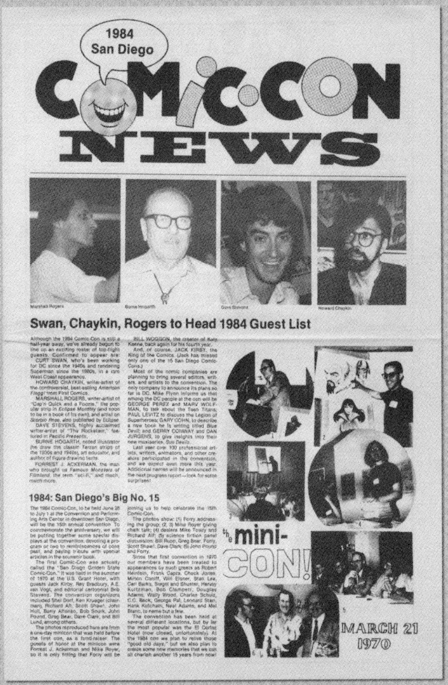
1984 San Diego
COMIC-CON
NEWS
Marshall Rogers
Burne Hogarth
Dave Stevens
Howard Chaykin
Swan, Chaykin, Rogers to Head 1984 Guest List
1984: San Diego's Big No. 15
the mini-CON!
MARCH 21 1970

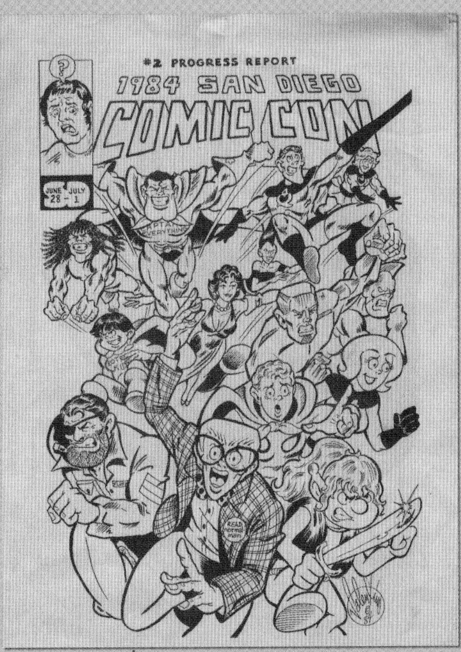
#2 PROGRESS REPORT
1984 SAN DIEGO
COMIC CON
JUNE 28 - JULY 1

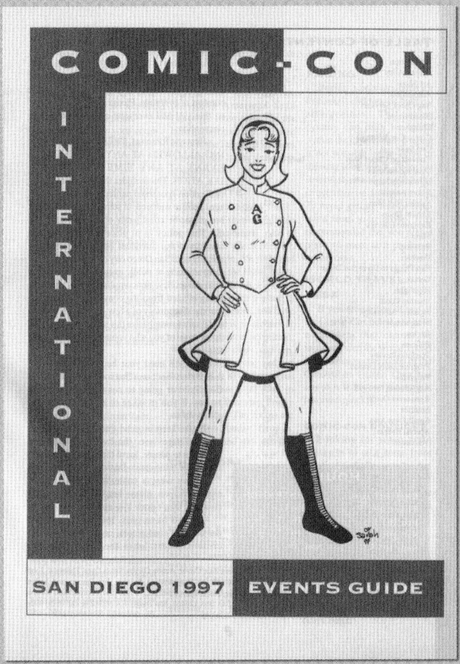
COMIC-CON
INTERNATIONAL
SAN DIEGO 1997
EVENTS GUIDE

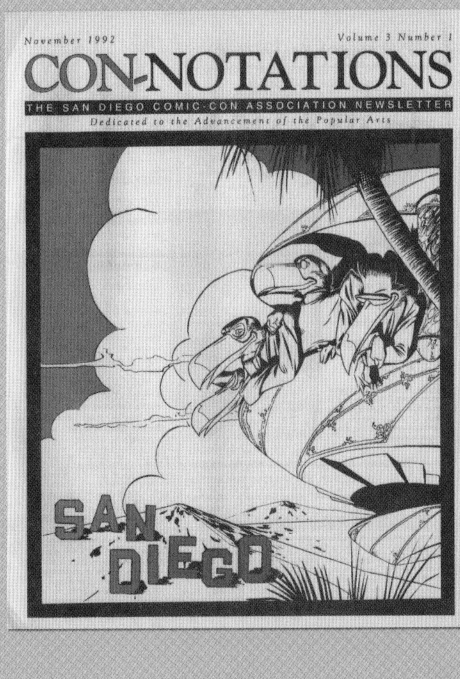
November 1992
Volume 3 Number 1
CON-NOTATIONS
THE SAN DIEGO COMIC-CON ASSOCIATION NEWSLETTER
Dedicated to the Advancement of the Popular Arts
SAN DIEGO

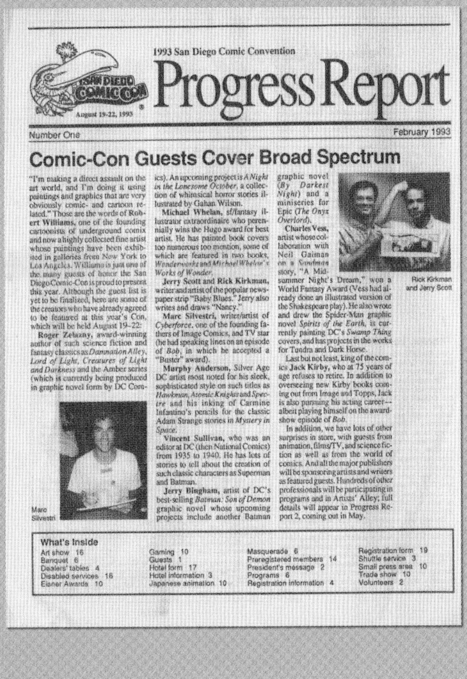
1993 San Diego Comic Convention

SAN DIEGO COMIC-CON August 19-22, 1993

Progress Report

Number One — February 1993

Comic-Con Guests Cover Broad Spectrum

"I'm making a direct assault on the art world, and I'm doing it using paintings and graphics that are very obviously comic- and cartoon related." Those are the words of **Robert Williams**, one of the founding cartoonists of underground comix and now a highly collected fine artist whose paintings have been exhibited in galleries from New York to Los Angeles. Williams is just one of the many guests of honor the San Diego Comic-Con is proud to present this year. Although the guest list is yet to be finalized, here are some of the creators who have already agreed to be featured at this year's Con, which will be held August 19–22:

Roger Zelazny, award-winning author of such science fiction and fantasy classics as *Damnation Alley*, *Lord of Light*, *Creatures of Light and Darkness* and the Amber series (which is currently being produced in graphic novel form by DC Comics). An upcoming project is *A Night in the Lonesome October*, a collection of whimsical horror stories illustrated by Gahan Wilson.

Michael Whelan, sf/fantasy illustrator extraordinaire who perennially wins the Hugo award for best artist. He has painted book covers too numerous too mention, some of which are featured in two books, *Wonderworks* and *Michael Whelan's Works of Wonder*.

Jerry Scott and Rick Kirkman, writer and artist of the popular newspaper strip "Baby Blues." Jerry also writes and draws "Nancy."

Marc Silvestri, writer/artist of *Cyberforce*, one of the founding fathers of Image Comics, and TV star (he had speaking lines on an episode of *Bob*, in which he accepted a "Buster" award).

Murphy Anderson, Silver Age DC artist most noted for his sleek, sophisticated style on such titles as *Hawkman*, *Atomic Knights* and *Spectre* and his inking of Carmine Infantino's pencils for the classic Adam Strange stories in *Mystery in Space*.

Vincent Sullivan, who was an editor at DC (then National Comics) from 1935 to 1940. He has lots of stories to tell about the creation of such classic characters as Superman and Batman.

Jerry Bingham, artist of DC's best-selling *Batman: Son of Demon* graphic novel whose upcoming projects include another Batman graphic novel (*By Darkest Night*) and a miniseries for Epic (*The Onyx Overlord*).

Charles Vess, artist whose collaboration with Neil Gaiman on a *Sandman* story, "A Midsummer Night's Dream," won a World Fantasy Award (Vess had already done an illustrated version of the Shakespeare play). He also wrote and drew the Spider-Man graphic novel *Spirits of the Earth*, is currently painting DC's *Swamp Thing* covers, and has projects in the works for Tundra and Dark Horse.

Last but not least, king of the comics **Jack Kirby**, who at 75 years of age refuses to retire. In addition to overseeing new Kirby books coming out from Image and Topps, Jack is also pursuing his acting career—albeit playing himself on the award-show episode of *Bob*.

In addition, we have lots of other surprises in store, with guests from animation, films/TV, and science fiction as well as from the world of comics. And all the major publishers will be sponsoring artists and writers as featured guests. Hundreds of other professionals will be participating in programs and in Artists' Alley; full details will appear in Progress Report 2, coming out in May.

Rick Kirkman and Jerry Scott

Marc Silvestri

What's Inside

Art show 16	Gaming 10	Masquerade 6	Registration form 19
Banquet 6	Guests 1	Preregistered members 14	Shuttle service 3
Dealers' tables 4	Hotel form 17	President's message 2	Small press area 10
Disabled services 16	Hotel information 3	Programs 6	Trade show 10
Eisner Awards 10	Japanese animation 10	Registration information 4	Volunteers 2

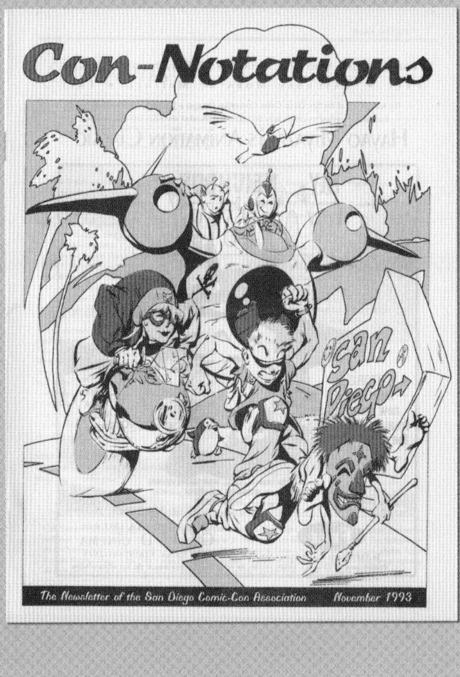
Con-Notations
San Diego
The Newsletter of the San Diego Comic-Con Association November 1993

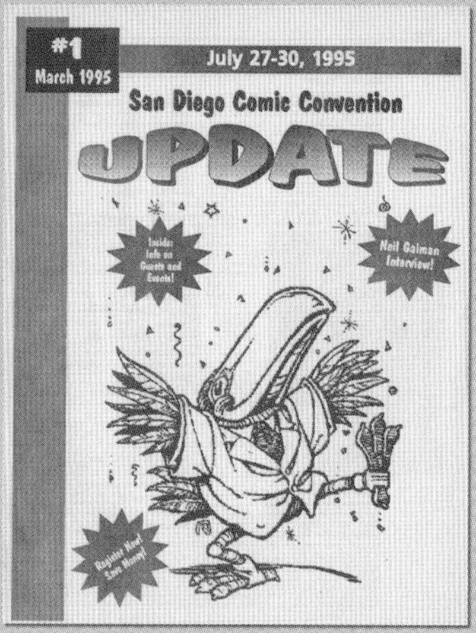
#1
March 1995
July 27-30, 1995
San Diego Comic Convention
UPDATE
Neil Gaiman Interview!

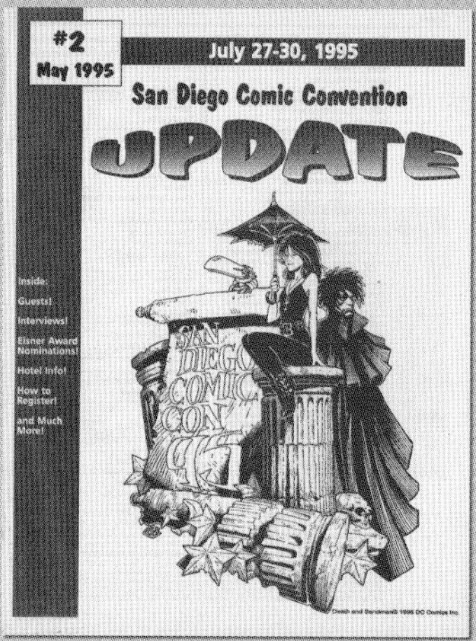
#2
May 1995
July 27-30, 1995
San Diego Comic Convention
UPDATE
Inside:
Guests!
Interviews!
Eisner Award Nominations!
Hotel Info!
How to Register!
and Much More!

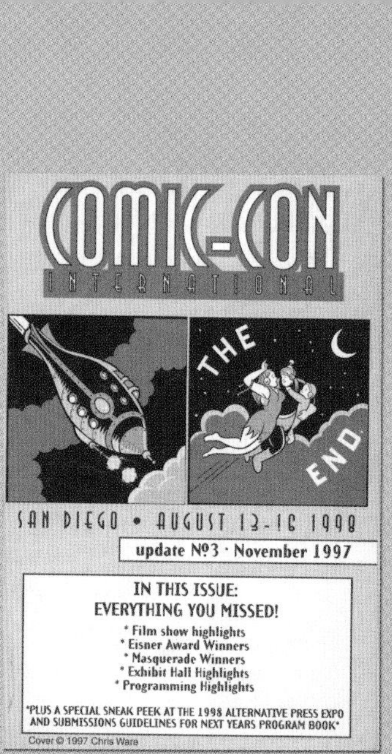
COMIC-CON
INTERNATIONAL
THE
END
SAN DIEGO • AUGUST 13-16 1998
update №3 · November 1997
IN THIS ISSUE:
EVERYTHING YOU MISSED!
* Film show highlights
* Eisner Award Winners
* Masquerade Winners
* Exhibit Hall Highlights
* Programming Highlights
PLUS A SPECIAL SNEAK PEEK AT THE 1998 ALTERNATIVE PRESS EXPO AND SUBMISSIONS GUIDELINES FOR NEXT YEARS PROGRAM BOOK
Cover © 1997 Chris Ware

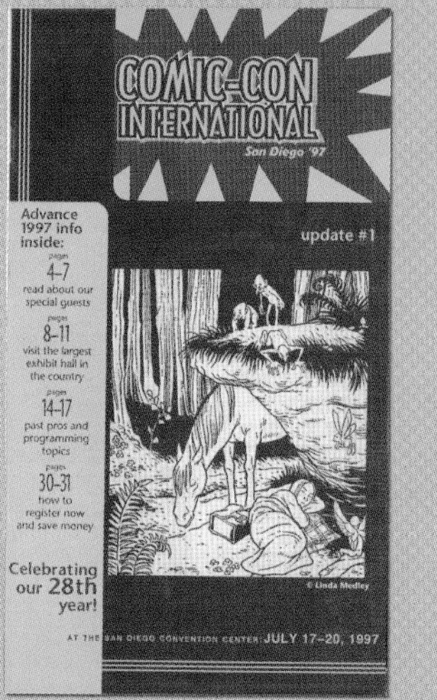
COMIC-CON
INTERNATIONAL
San Diego '97
update #1
Advance 1997 info inside:
4-7
8-11
14-17
30-31
Celebrating our 28th year!
JULY 17-20, 1997

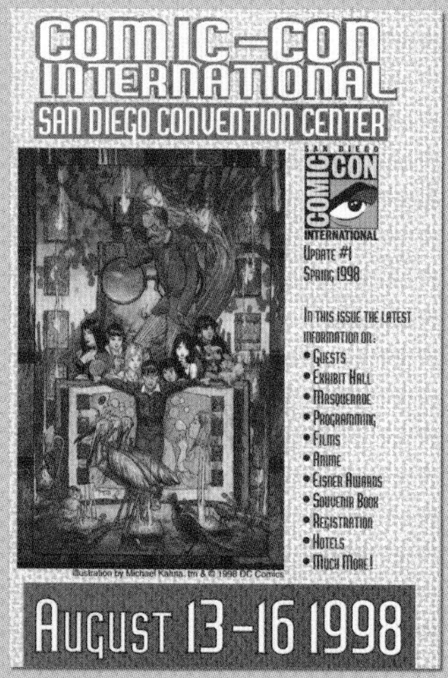
COMIC-CON
INTERNATIONAL
SAN DIEGO CONVENTION CENTER
COMIC CON INTERNATIONAL
UPDATE #1
SPRING 1998
IN THIS ISSUE THE LATEST INFORMATION ON:
• GUESTS
• EXHIBIT HALL
• MASQUERADE
• PROGRAMMING
• FILMS
• ANIME
• EISNER AWARDS
• SOUVENIR BOOK
• REGISTRATION
• HOTELS
• MUCH MORE!
AUGUST 13-16 1998

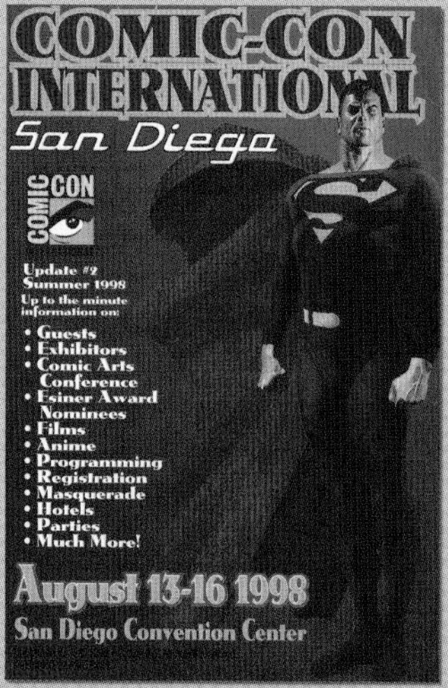
COMIC-CON
INTERNATIONAL
San Diego
Update #2
Summer 1998
Up to the minute information on:
• Guests
• Exhibitors
• Comic Arts Conference
• Esiner Award Nominees
• Films
• Anime
• Programming
• Registration
• Masquerade
• Hotels
• Parties
• Much More!
August 13-16 1998
San Diego Convention Center

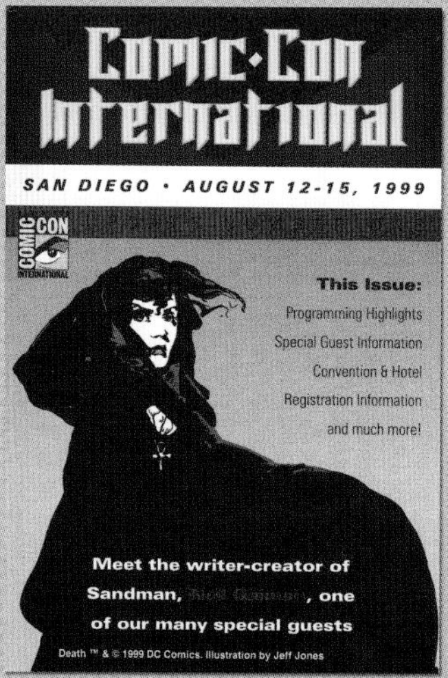
Comic-Con
International
SAN DIEGO • AUGUST 12-15, 1999
This Issue:
Programming Highlights
Special Guest Information
Convention & Hotel
Registration Information
and much more!
Meet the writer-creator of
Sandman,
one
of our many special guests
Death ™ & © 1999 DC Comics. Illustration by Jeff Jones

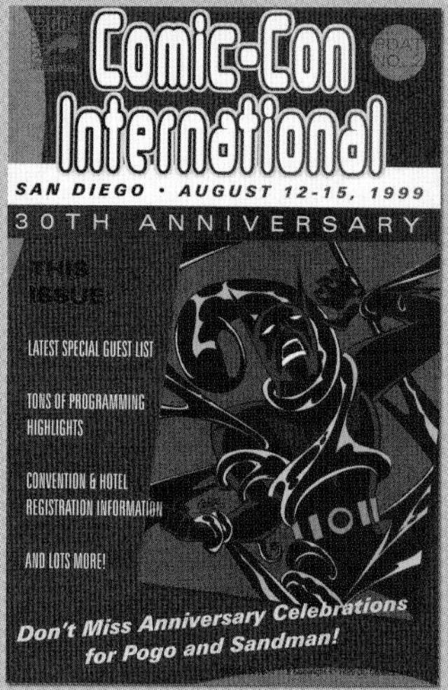
Comic-Con
International
SAN DIEGO • AUGUST 12-15, 1999
30TH ANNIVERSARY
THIS ISSUE
LATEST SPECIAL GUEST LIST
TONS OF PROGRAMMING HIGHLIGHTS
CONVENTION & HOTEL REGISTRATION INFORMATION
AND LOTS MORE!
Don't Miss Anniversary Celebrations for Pogo and Sandman!

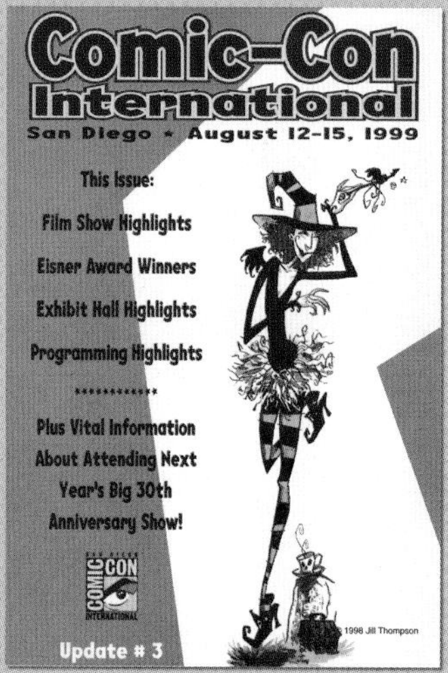
Comic-Con
International
San Diego • August 12-15, 1999
This Issue:
Film Show Highlights
Eisner Award Winners
Exhibit Hall Highlights
Programming Highlights
Plus Vital Information About Attending Next Year's Big 30th Anniversary Show!
Update # 3
1998 Jill Thompson

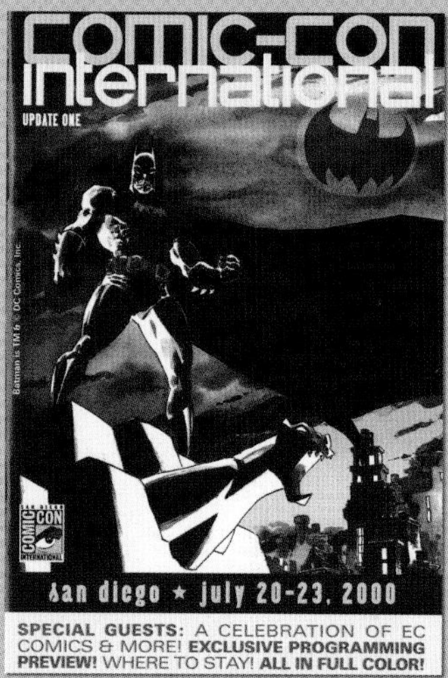
COMIC-CON
INTERNATIONAL
UPDATE ONE
san diego ★ july 20-23, 2000
SPECIAL GUESTS: A CELEBRATION OF EC COMICS & MORE! EXCLUSIVE PROGRAMMING PREVIEW! WHERE TO STAY! ALL IN FULL COLOR!

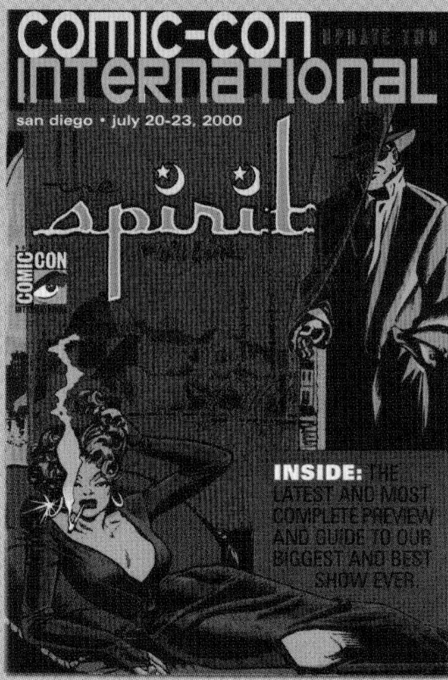
COMIC-CON
INTERNATIONAL
san diego • july 20-23, 2000
spirit
INSIDE: THE LATEST AND MOST COMPLETE PREVIEW AND GUIDE TO OUR BIGGEST AND BEST SHOW EVER.

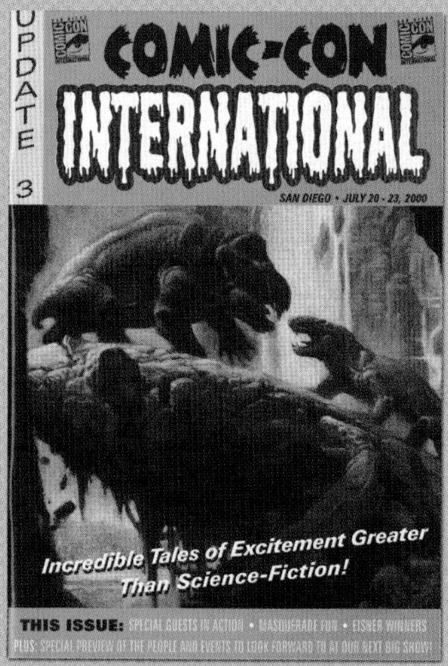
UPDATE 3
COMIC-CON
INTERNATIONAL
SAN DIEGO • JULY 20-23, 2000
Incredible Tales of Excitement Greater Than Science-Fiction!
THIS ISSUE:

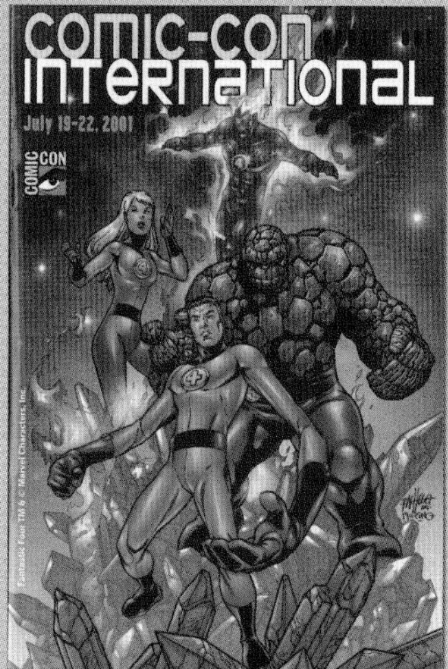
COMIC-CON
INTERNATIONAL
July 19-22, 2001

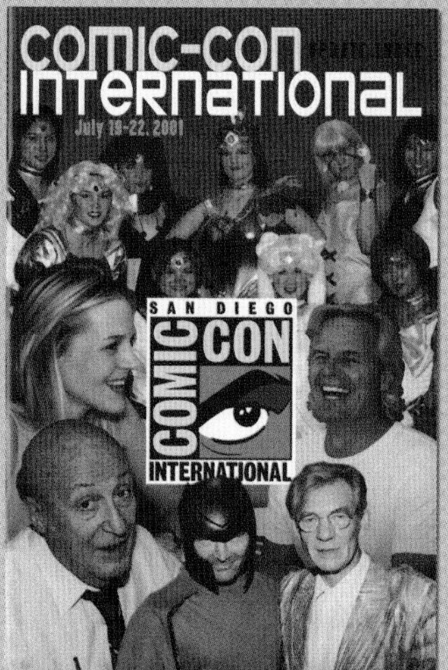
COMIC-CON
INTERNATIONAL
July 19-22, 2001
SAN DIEGO
COMIC CON
INTERNATIONAL

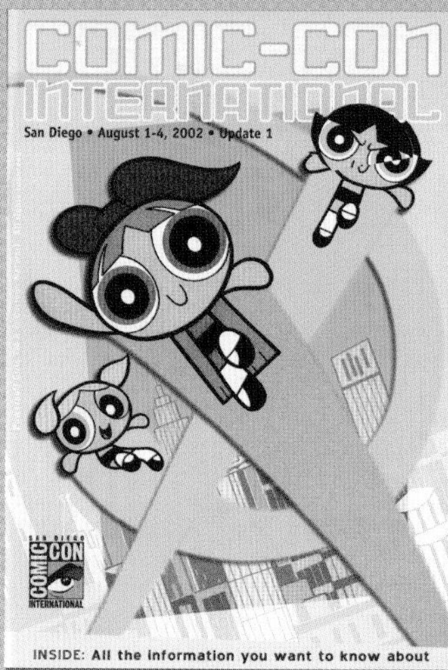
COMIC-CON
INTERNATIONAL
San Diego • August 1-4, 2002 • Update 1
INSIDE: All the information you want to know about

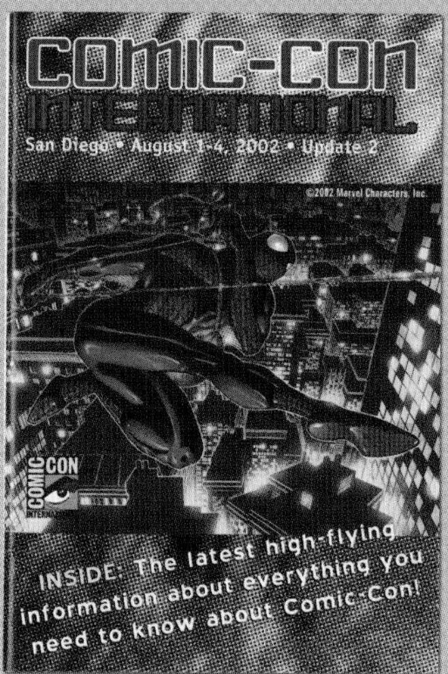
COMIC-CON
INTERNATIONAL
San Diego • August 1-4, 2002 • Update 2
©2002 Marvel Characters, Inc.
INSIDE: The latest high-flying information about everything you need to know about Comic-Con!

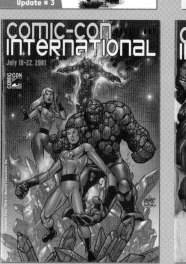

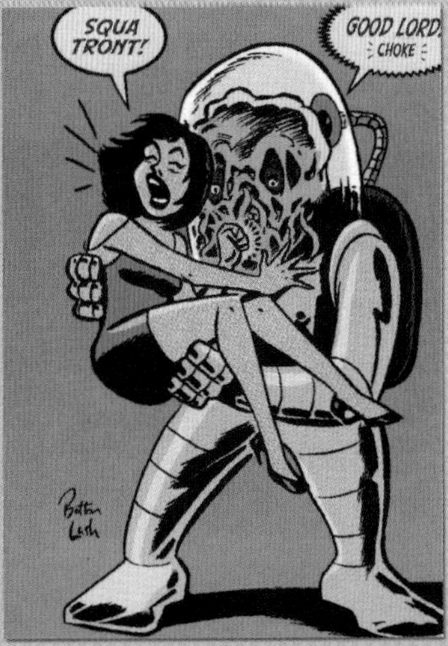
SQUA TRONT!
GOOD LORD! CHOKE

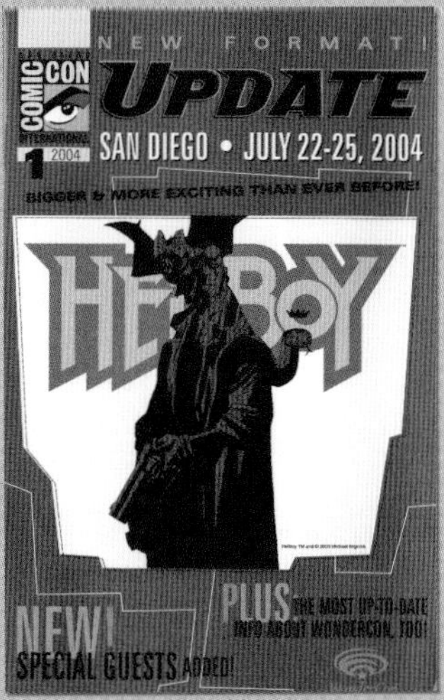
NEW FORMAT!
COMIC-CON INTERNATIONAL
UPDATE
1 2004
SAN DIEGO • JULY 22-25, 2004
BIGGER & MORE EXCITING THAN EVER BEFORE!
HELLBOY
NEW! SPECIAL GUESTS ADDED!
PLUS THE MOST UP-TO-DATE INFO ABOUT WONDERCON, TOO!

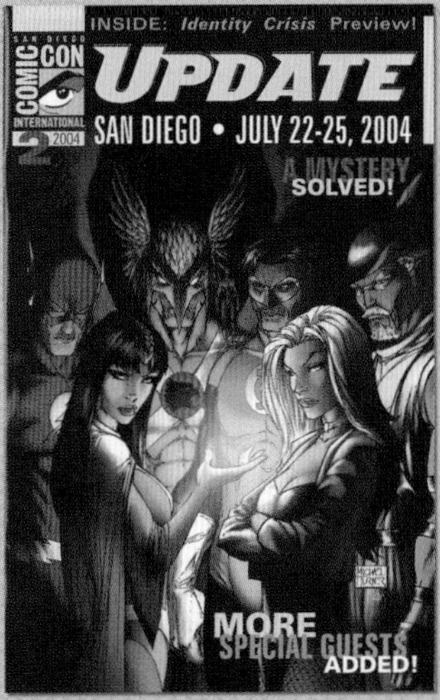
INSIDE: Identity Crisis Preview!
COMIC-CON INTERNATIONAL
UPDATE
2 2004
SAN DIEGO • JULY 22-25, 2004
A MYSTERY SOLVED!
MORE SPECIAL GUESTS ADDED!

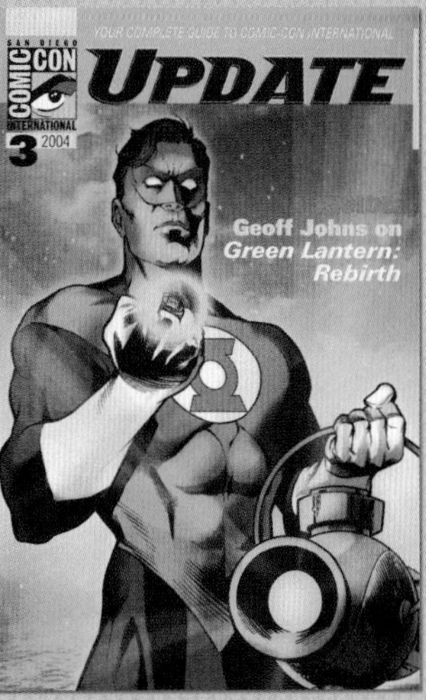
YOUR COMPLETE GUIDE TO COMIC-CON INTERNATIONAL
COMIC-CON INTERNATIONAL
UPDATE
3 2004
Geoff Johns on Green Lantern: Rebirth

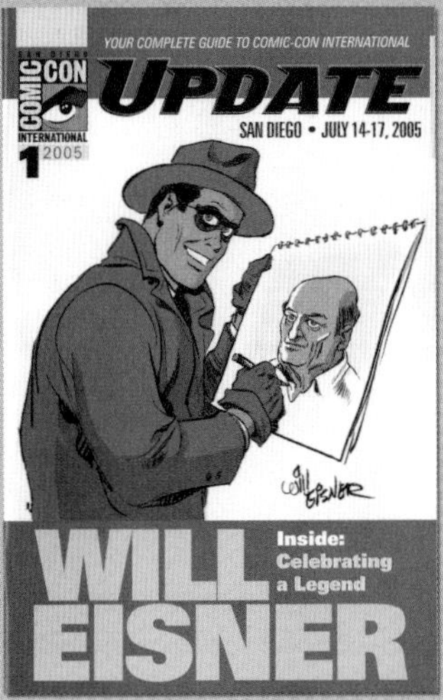
YOUR COMPLETE GUIDE TO COMIC-CON INTERNATIONAL
COMIC-CON INTERNATIONAL
UPDATE
1 2005
SAN DIEGO • JULY 14-17, 2005
WILL EISNER
Inside: Celebrating a Legend

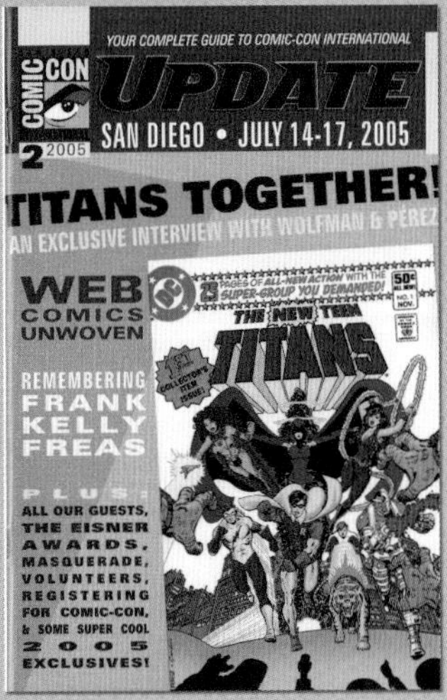
YOUR COMPLETE GUIDE TO COMIC-CON INTERNATIONAL
COMIC-CON INTERNATIONAL
UPDATE
2 2005
SAN DIEGO • JULY 14-17, 2005
TITANS TOGETHER!
AN EXCLUSIVE INTERVIEW WITH WOLFMAN & PEREZ
WEB COMICS UNWOVEN
REMEMBERING FRANK KELLY FREAS
PLUS: ALL OUR GUESTS, THE EISNER AWARDS, MASQUERADE, VOLUNTEERS, REGISTERING FOR COMIC-CON, & SOME SUPER COOL 2005 EXCLUSIVES!
THE NEW TEEN TITANS

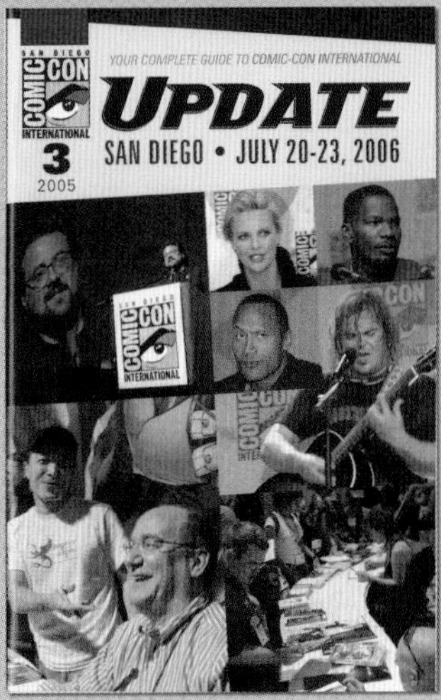
YOUR COMPLETE GUIDE TO COMIC-CON INTERNATIONAL
COMIC-CON INTERNATIONAL
UPDATE
3 2005
SAN DIEGO • JULY 20-23, 2006

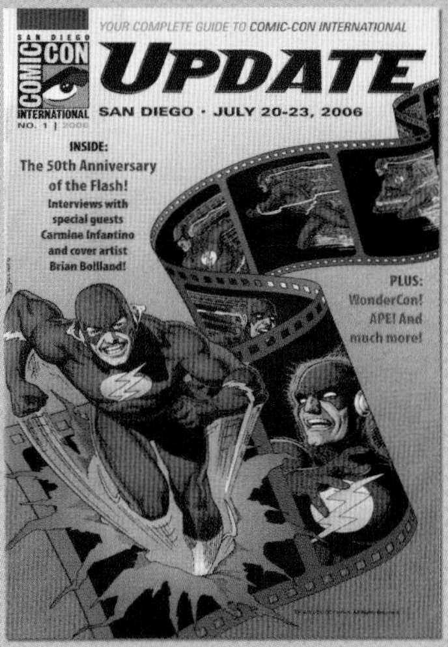
YOUR COMPLETE GUIDE TO COMIC-CON INTERNATIONAL
COMIC-CON INTERNATIONAL
UPDATE
NO. 1 | 2006
SAN DIEGO • JULY 20-23, 2006
INSIDE: The 50th Anniversary of the Flash! Interviews with special guests Carmine Infantino and cover artist Brian Bolland!
PLUS: WonderCon! APE! And much more!

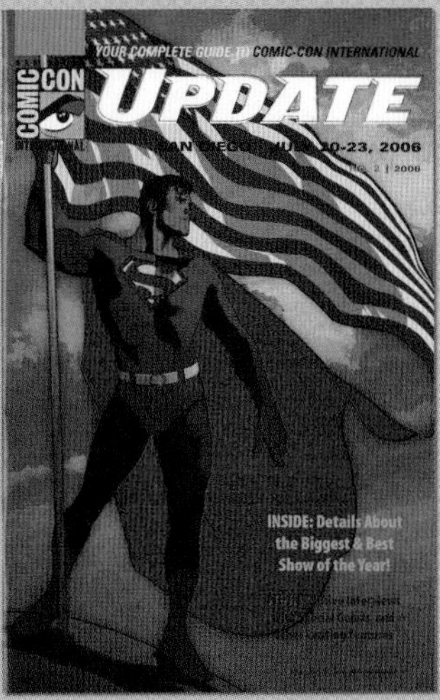
YOUR COMPLETE GUIDE TO COMIC-CON INTERNATIONAL
COMIC-CON INTERNATIONAL
UPDATE
SAN DIEGO • JULY 20-23, 2006
INSIDE: Details About the Biggest & Best Show of the Year!

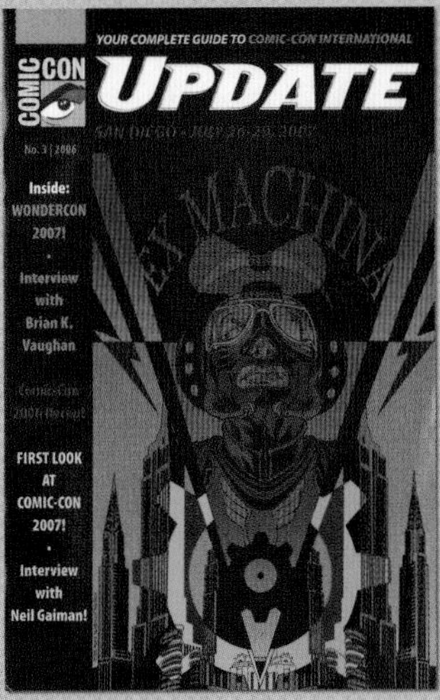
YOUR COMPLETE GUIDE TO COMIC-CON INTERNATIONAL
COMIC-CON INTERNATIONAL
UPDATE
No. 3 | 2006
Inside: WONDERCON 2007!
Interview with Brian K. Vaughan
FIRST LOOK AT COMIC-CON 2007!
Interview with Neil Gaiman!
EX MACHINA

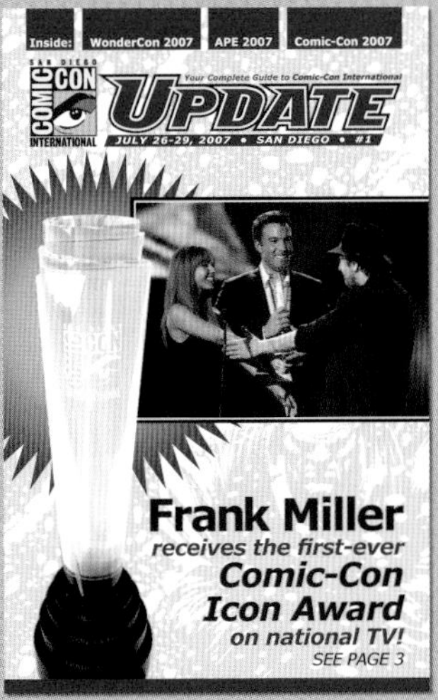
Inside: WonderCon 2007 | APE 2007 | Comic-Con 2007
Your Complete Guide to Comic-Con International
COMIC-CON INTERNATIONAL
UPDATE
JULY 26-29, 2007 • SAN DIEGO • #1
Frank Miller receives the first-ever Comic-Con Icon Award on national TV!
SEE PAGE 3

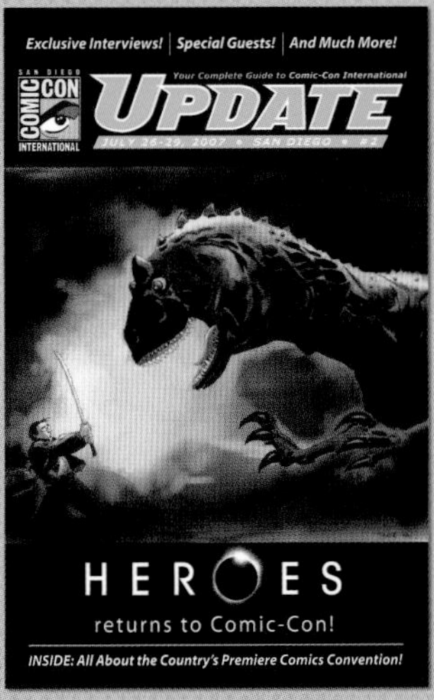
Exclusive Interviews! | Special Guests! | And Much More!
Your Complete Guide to Comic-Con International
COMIC-CON INTERNATIONAL
UPDATE
JULY 26-29, 2007 • SAN DIEGO • #2
HEROES
returns to Comic-Con!
INSIDE: All About the Country's Premiere Comics Convention!

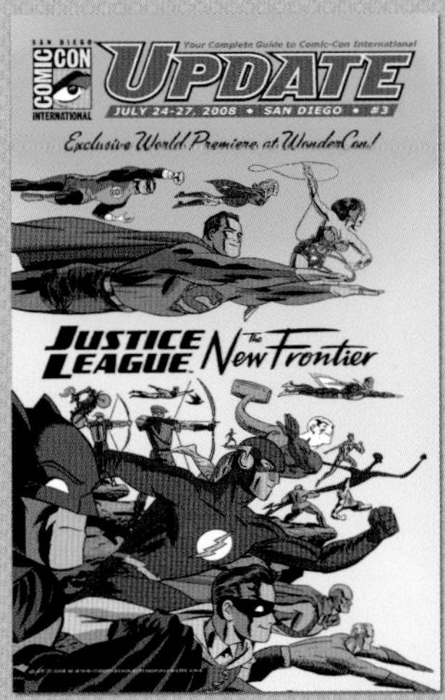
Your Complete Guide to Comic-Con International
COMIC-CON INTERNATIONAL
UPDATE
JULY 24-27, 2008 • SAN DIEGO • #3
Exclusive World Premiere at WonderCon!
JUSTICE LEAGUE The New Frontier

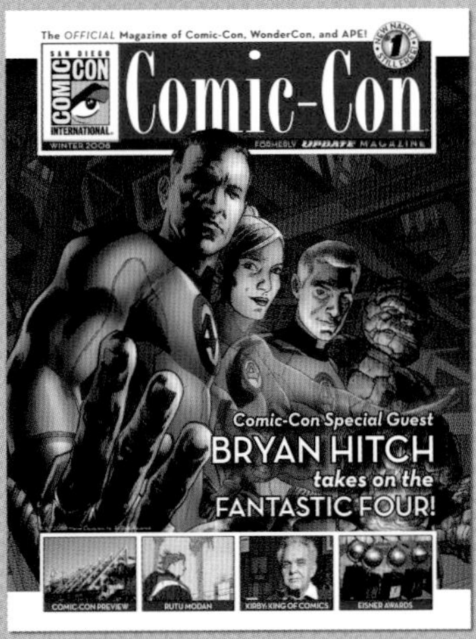
The OFFICIAL Magazine of Comic-Con, WonderCon, and APE!
COMIC-CON INTERNATIONAL
Comic-Con
WINTER 2008
FORMERLY UPDATE MAGAZINE
Comic-Con Special Guest BRYAN HITCH takes on the FANTASTIC FOUR!
COMIC-CON PREVIEW
RUTU MODAN
KIRBY: KING OF COMICS
EISNER AWARDS

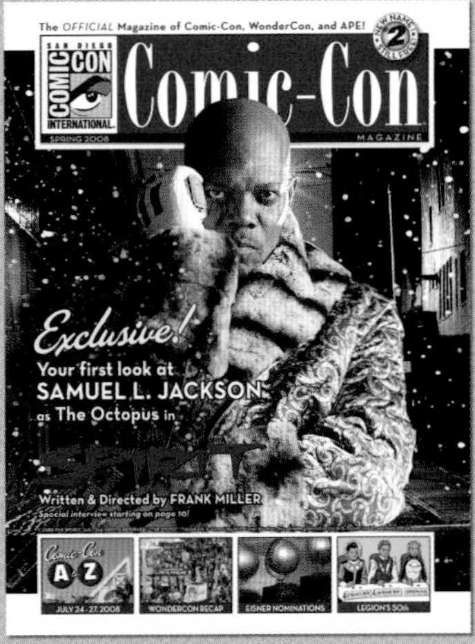
The OFFICIAL Magazine of Comic-Con, WonderCon, and APE!
COMIC-CON INTERNATIONAL
Comic-Con
SPRING 2008
MAGAZINE
Exclusive! Your first look at SAMUEL L. JACKSON as The Octopus in
Written & Directed by FRANK MILLER
A-Z
JULY 24-27, 2008
WONDERCON RECAP
EISNER NOMINATIONS
LEGION'S 50th

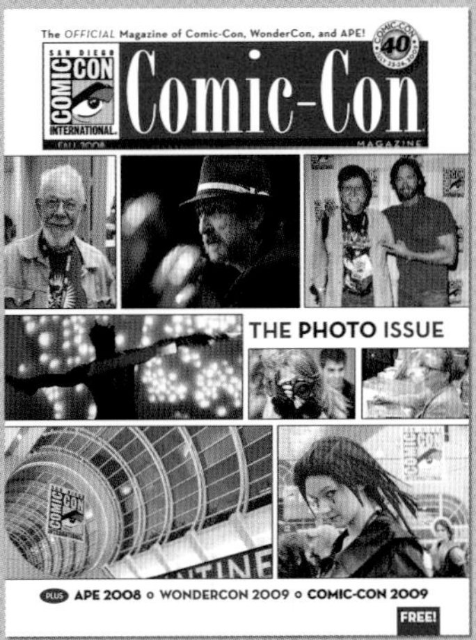
The OFFICIAL Magazine of Comic-Con, WonderCon, and APE!
COMIC-CON INTERNATIONAL
Comic-Con
MAGAZINE
40
THE PHOTO ISSUE
PLUS APE 2008 ○ WONDERCON 2009 ○ COMIC-CON 2009
FREE!

THE OFFICIAL COMIC-CON T-SHIRT

One of Comic-Con's most popular items is the official Con T-shirt, produced by Bob Chapman and Graphitti Designs.

Each year since 1981, an "official" Comic-Con shirt has been produced. The shirts are limited editions, featuring art and designs exclusive to Comic-Con. The first shirt featured a stunning image of Sheena, Queen of the Jungle, by fan-favorite artist Dave Stevens. That initial shirt not only started a Comic-Con tradition but also inadvertently laid the foundation for what was to become Graphitti Designs.

After first attending Comic-Con in 1980 to sell his childhood comics collection, Bob Chapman attended a committee meeting the following year and proposed producing an official event T-shirt. A screen printer by trade, Chapman walked away from that meeting with that fateful Sheena image by Stevens. That image and his later meeting with Stevens in his Los Angeles studio would have a life-changing effect. After successfully selling the shirts at the 1981 Comic-Con,

Chapman went on to develop a diverse line of quality licensed comic book and pop culture–related products, including apparel, cold-cast statues and bronzes, limited-edition hardcover books and prints, and action figures. Stevens continued to play an important role in the development of the Graphitti product line's look and style. Many of Graphitti Designs' first offerings were based on Stevens's art and characters. For instance, Stevens's *The Rocketeer* was the subject of the first book and initial cloisonné pin Chapman produced. A statue and high-quality print, both based on Dave Stevens's designs, soon followed.

Twenty-eight years later, Graphitti Designs remains an important partner of Comic-Con, having designed and sold twenty-nine shirts for attendees to date (two designs were offered in 1991). In addition to the annual event shirt, the company has also produced twenty-two shirts for Comic-Con's volunteers (SEE page 173). Each year since 1988, all four-day volunteers have received an exclusive shirt (different from the attendee shirt available for sale) as a reward for all their hard work. The shirts—both attendee and volunteer—have become sought-after collectibles and an important part of Comic-Con's image.

ABOVE: Graphitti Designs' Bob and Donna Chapman, selling the first Comic-Con T-shirt in 1981

OPPOSITE, CLOCKWISE FROM TOP LEFT: The first four official Comic-Con T-shirts: Sheena, by Dave Stevens (1981); Captain Victory, by Jack Kirby (1982); The Foozle and Raul the Cat, by Marshall Rogers and Howard Chaykin (1984); George Pérez's superfamily (1983)

PAGE 138: FIRST ROW, FROM LEFT: Death and the Sandman, by Chris Bachalo (1995); Timberland Tales, by B. K. Taylor (1985); Lady Blackhawk, by Brian Bolland (1986) **SECOND ROW, FROM LEFT:** Lone Wolf and Cub, by Goseki Kojima (1987); Superman, by Joe Shuster (1988) **THIRD ROW, FROM LEFT:** Batman, by Jerry Robinson (1989); Captain America, by Kevin Maguire (1990); The Rocketeer, by Dave Stevens (1991); X-Men, by Jim Lee (1991)

FOURTH ROW, FROM LEFT: Lobo, by Simon Bisley (1992); Sin City, by Frank Miller (1993); DC 0 to 25, by Dan Jurgens and Butch Guice (1994); Captain America, by Rob Liefeld (1996)

PAGE 139: FIRST ROW, FROM LEFT: DC and MAD, by Sergio Aragonés (front and back of shirt, 1997); Green Lantern, by Gil Kane (1998); Wonder Woman, by Adam Hughes (1999) **SECOND ROW, FROM LEFT:** Flash of Two Worlds, by Carmine Infantino and Murphy Anderson (2000); Green Arrow, by Matt Wagner (2001); Sgt. Rock, by Joe Kubert (2002); Justice League, by Alex Ross (2003) **THIRD ROW, FROM LEFT:** Superman, by Jim Lee (2004); All-Star Batman and Robin the Boy Wonder, by Jim Lee (2005) **FOURTH ROW, FROM LEFT:** Star Wars, by Adam Hughes (2007); Final Crisis, by J. G. Jones (2008); Superman, by Adam Hughes (2006)

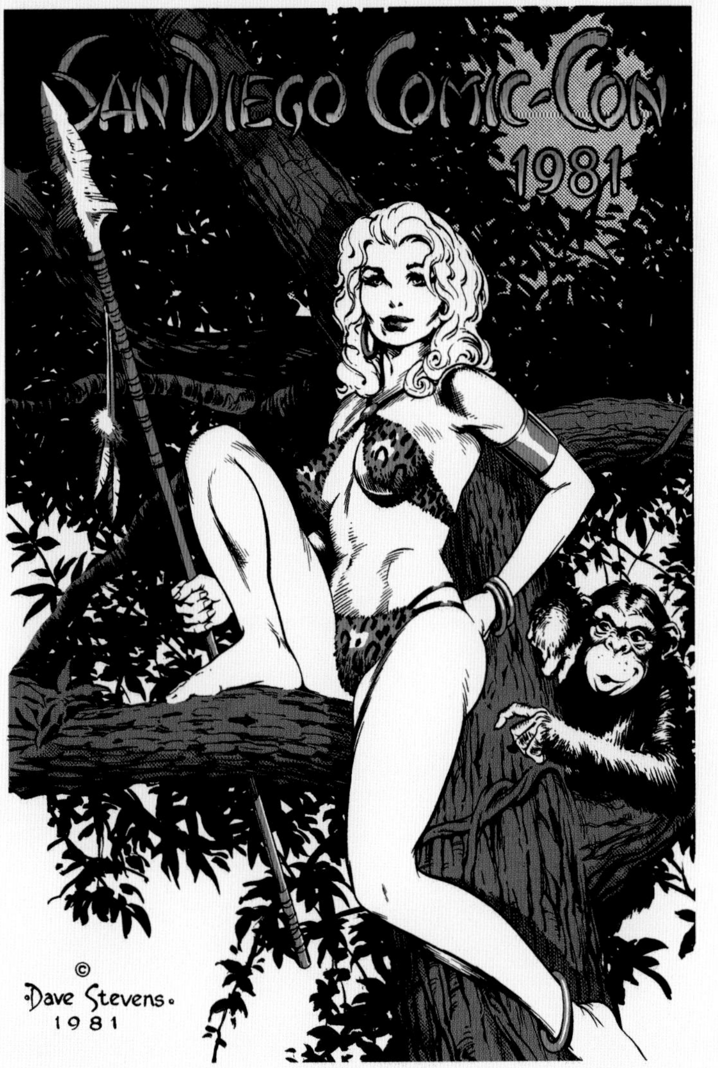
SAN DIEGO COMIC-CON
1981
© Dave Stevens 1981

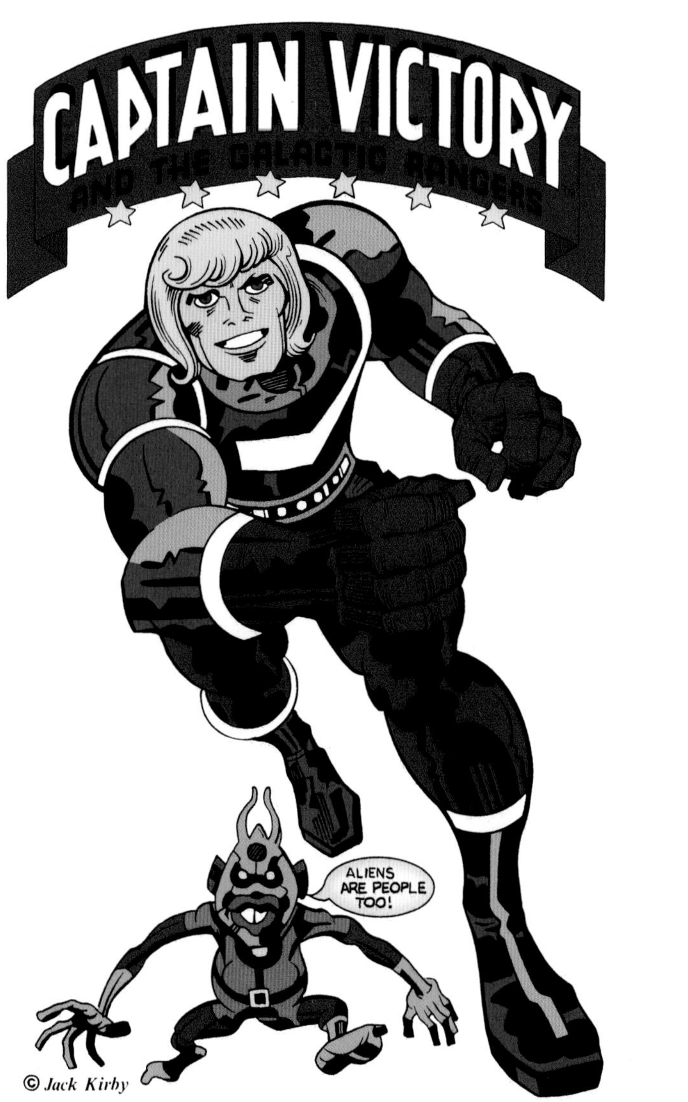
CAPTAIN VICTORY
AND THE GALACTIC RANGERS
ALIENS ARE PEOPLE TOO!
© Jack Kirby

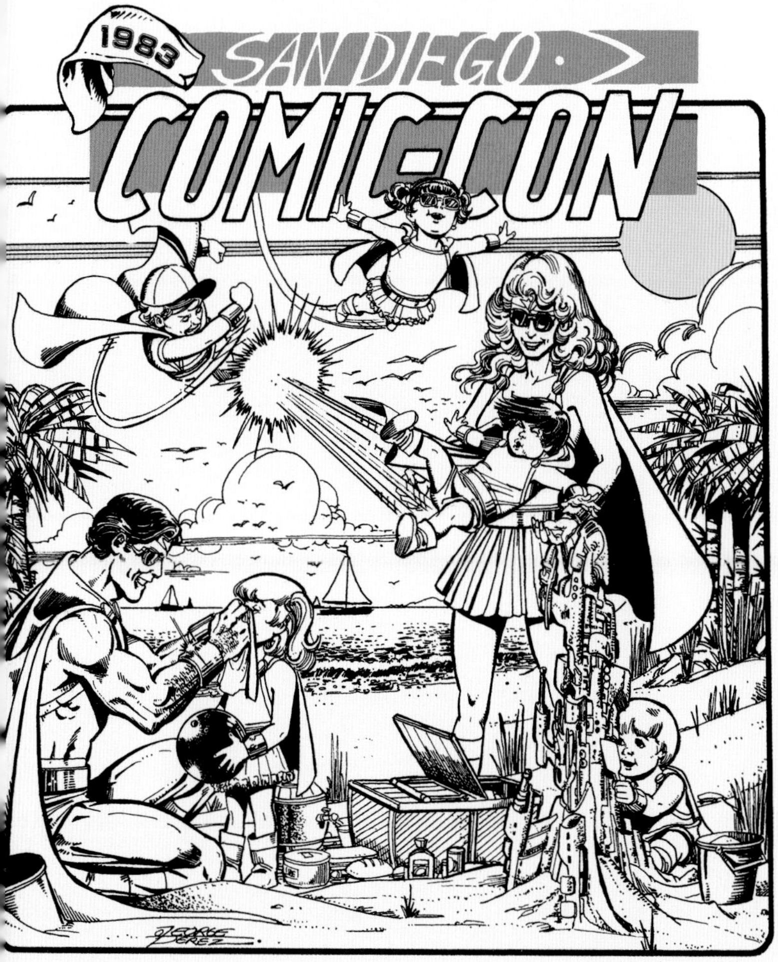
1983
SAN DIEGO
COMIC-CON

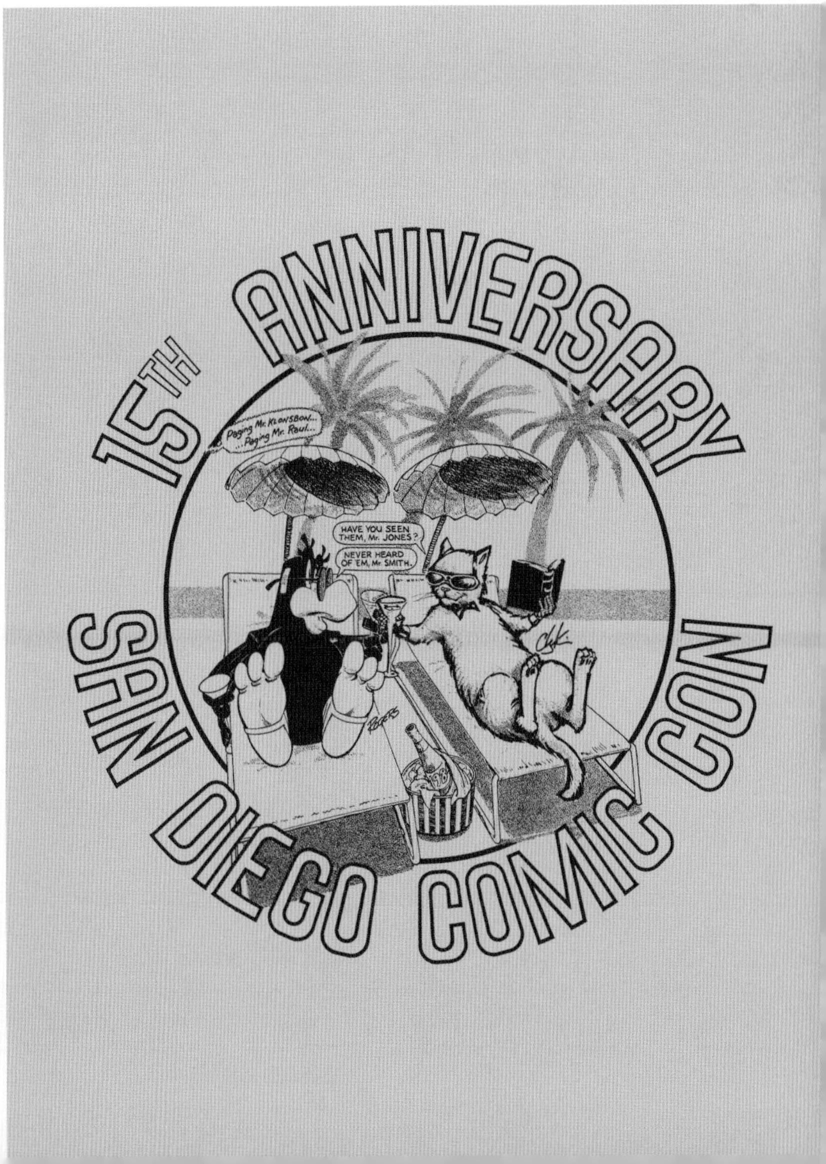
15TH ANNIVERSARY
HAVE YOU SEEN THEM, Mr. JONES?
NEVER HEARD OF 'EM, Mr. SMITH.
SAN DIEGO COMIC CON

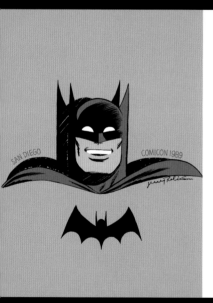

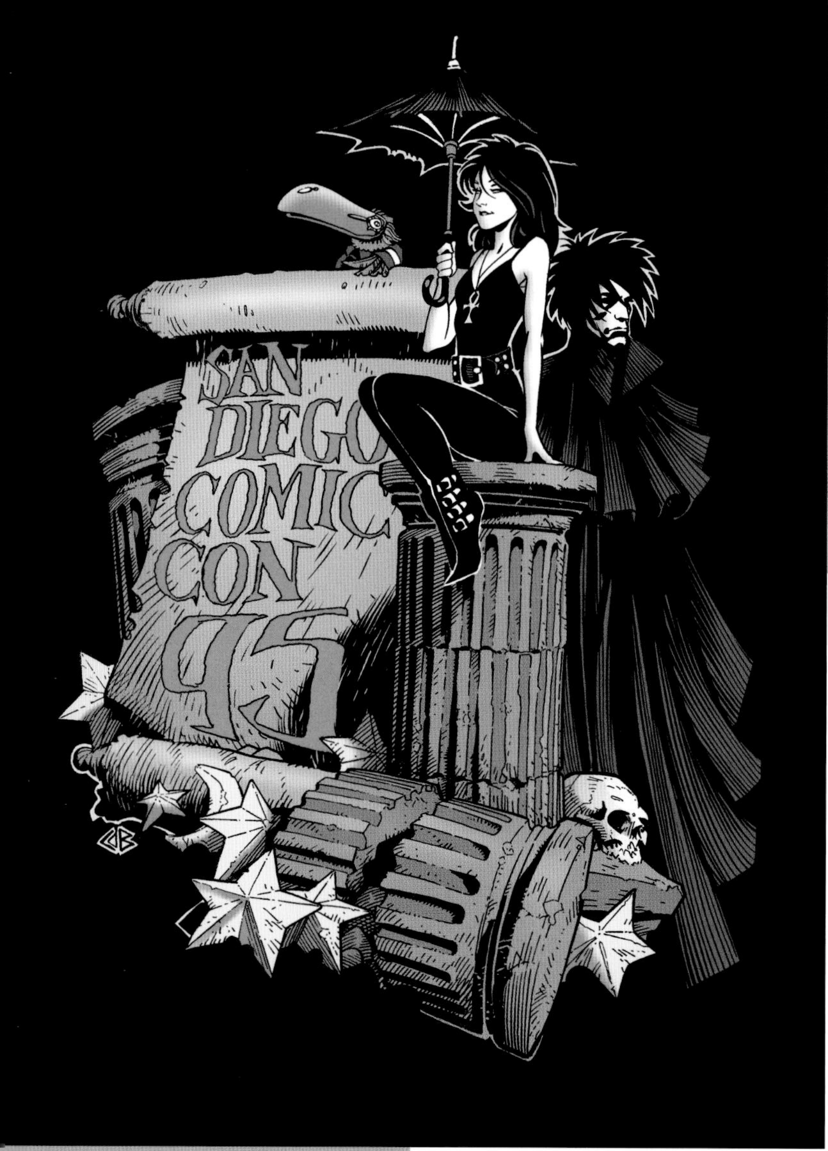
SAN DIEGO COMIC CON 95

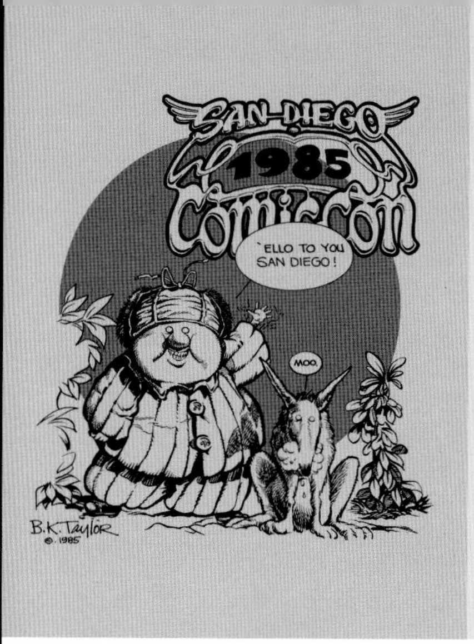
SAN DIEGO
1985
COMIC-CON
"ELLO TO YOU SAN DIEGO!
MOO.
B.K. Taylor
© 1985

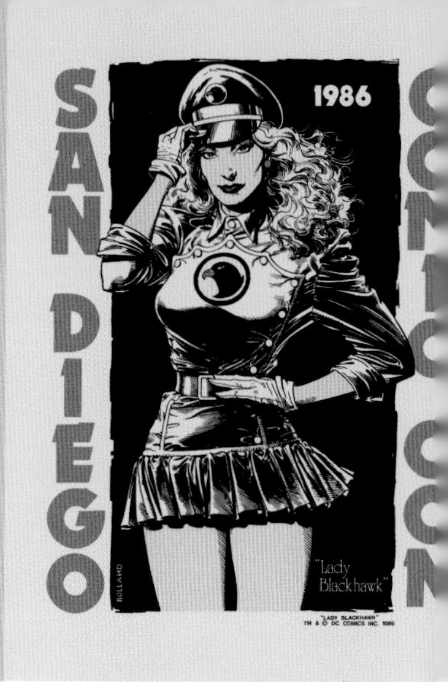
1986
SAN DIEGO
COMIC CON
"Lady Blackhawk"

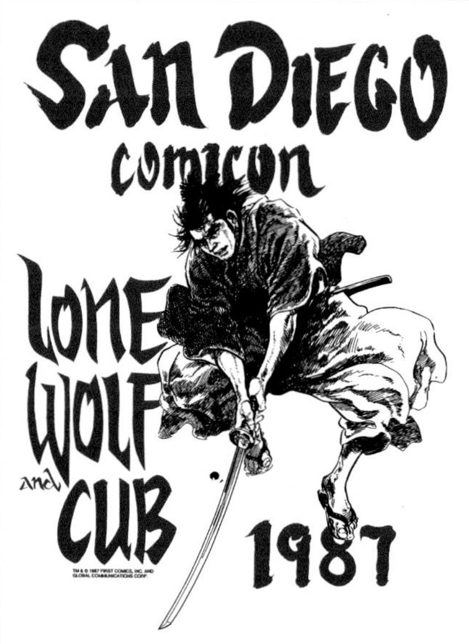
SAN DIEGO
comicon
LONE WOLF and CUB
1987

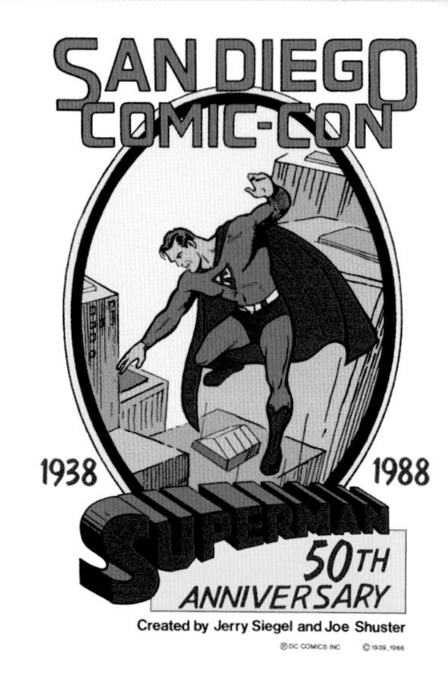
SAN DIEGO
COMIC-CON
1938
1988
SUPERMAN
50TH ANNIVERSARY
Created by Jerry Siegel and Joe Shuster

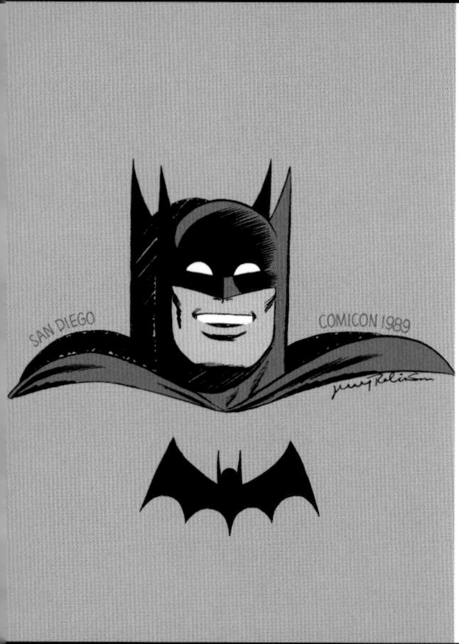
SAN DIEGO
COMICON 1989

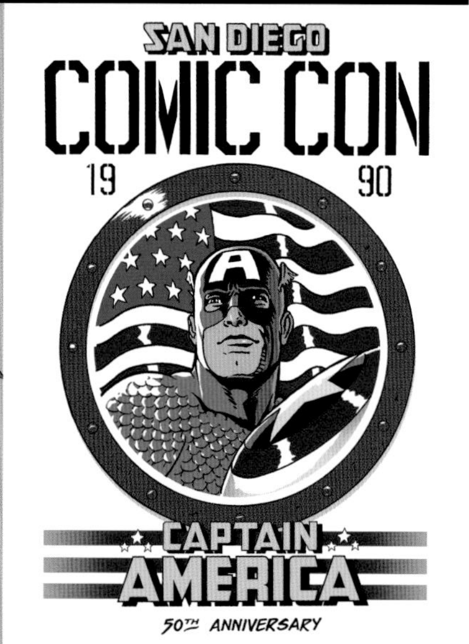
SAN DIEGO
COMIC CON
19
90
CAPTAIN AMERICA
50TH ANNIVERSARY

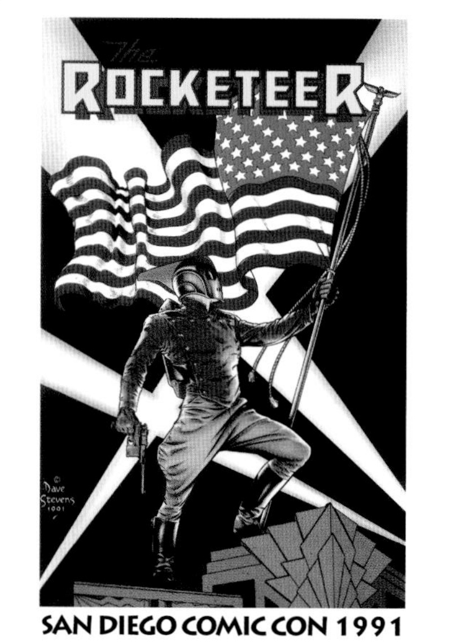
The ROCKETEER
Dave Stevens 1991
SAN DIEGO COMIC CON 1991

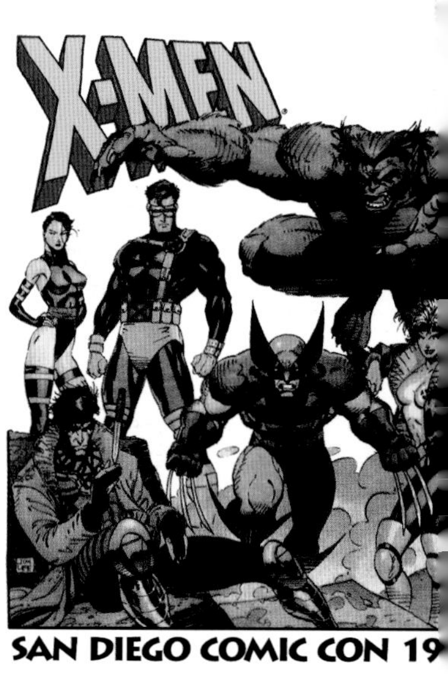
X-MEN
SAN DIEGO COMIC CON 19

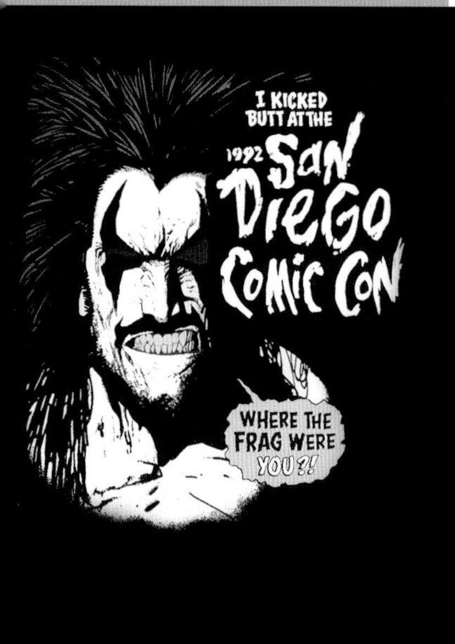
I KICKED BUTT AT THE
1992 SAN DIEGO COMIC CON
WHERE THE FRAG WERE YOU?!

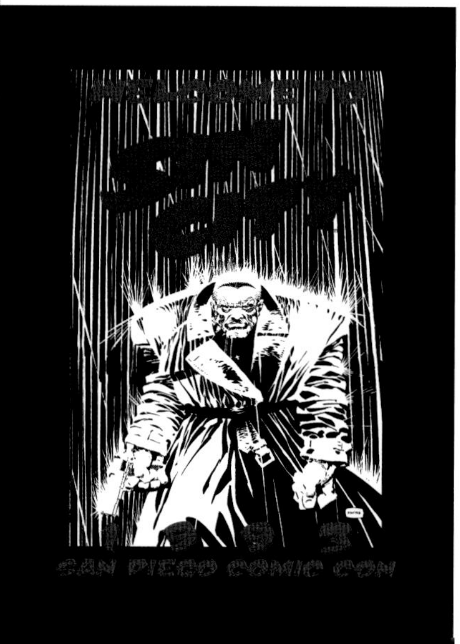
SAN DIEGO COMIC CON

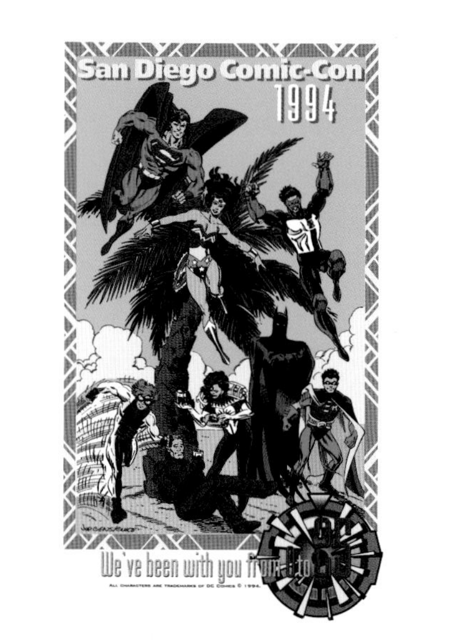
San Diego Comic-Con
1994
We've been with you from the start

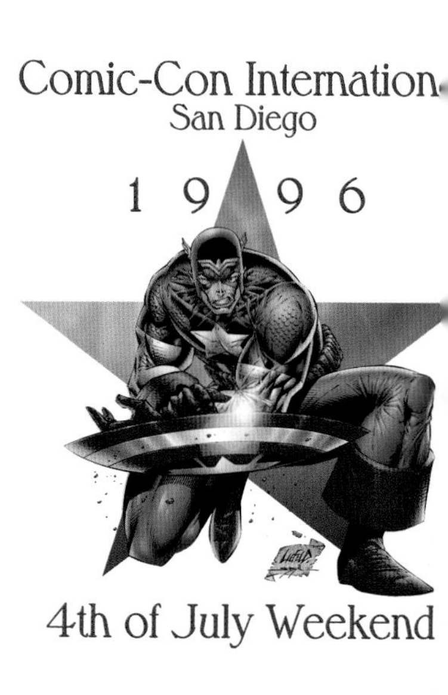
Comic-Con International
San Diego
1 9 9 6
4th of July Weekend

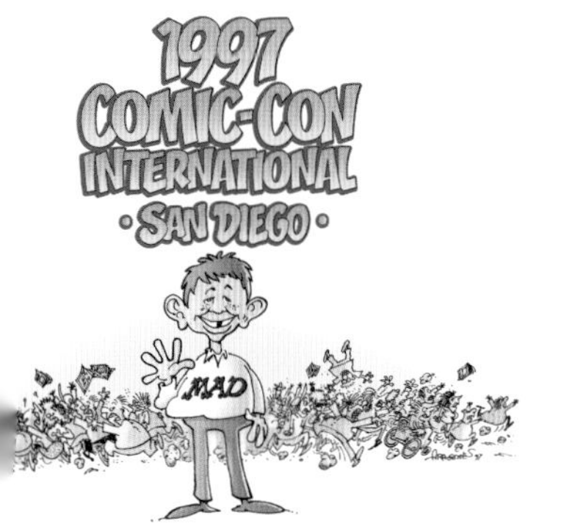
1997
COMIC-CON
INTERNATIONAL
SAN DIEGO
MAD

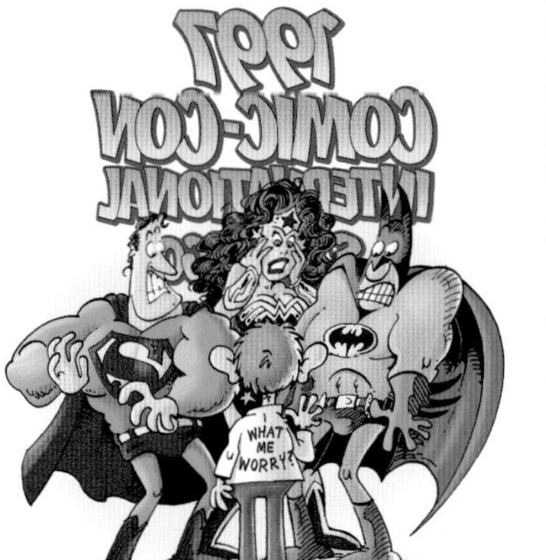
WHAT ME WORRY?

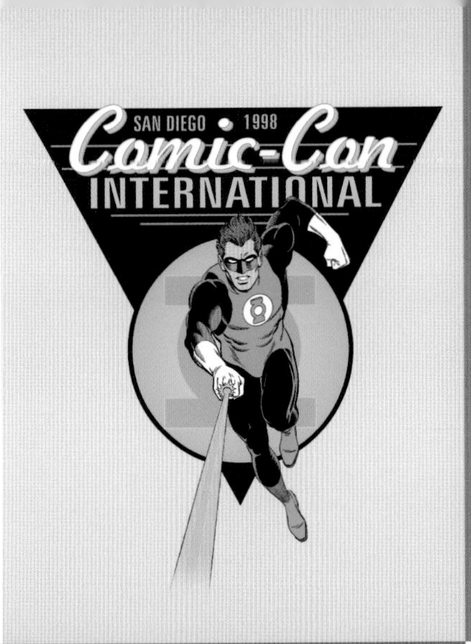
SAN DIEGO • 1998
Comic-Con
INTERNATIONAL

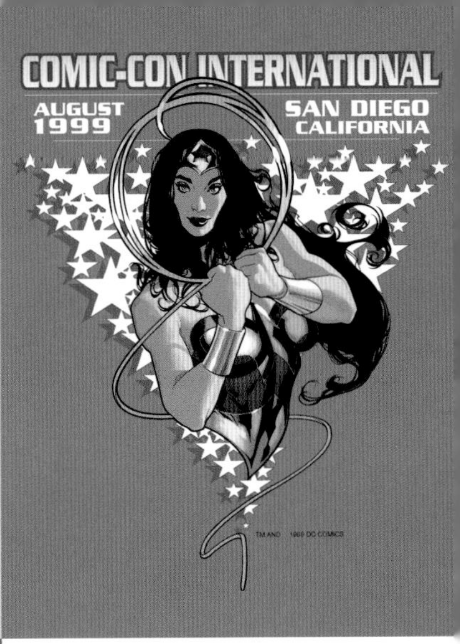
COMIC-CON INTERNATIONAL
AUGUST 1999
SAN DIEGO CALIFORNIA

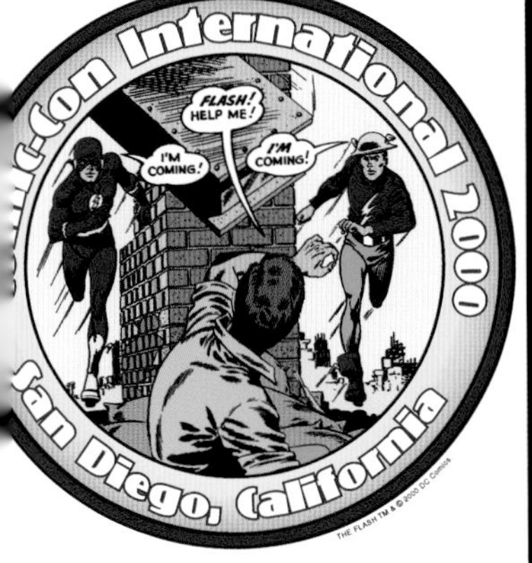
Comic-Con International 2000
FLASH! HELP ME!
I'M COMING!
I'M COMING!
San Diego, California

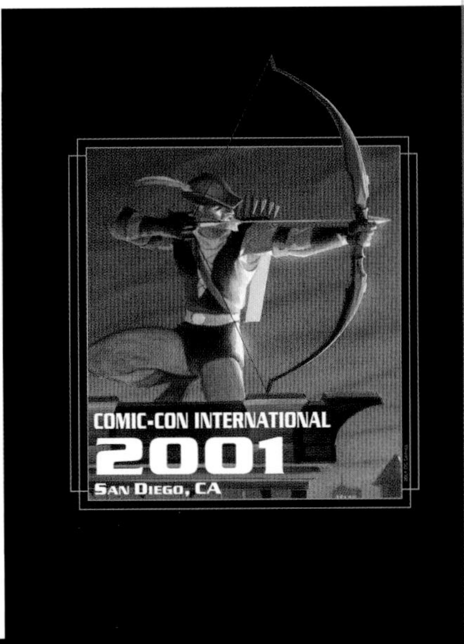
COMIC-CON INTERNATIONAL
2001
SAN DIEGO, CA

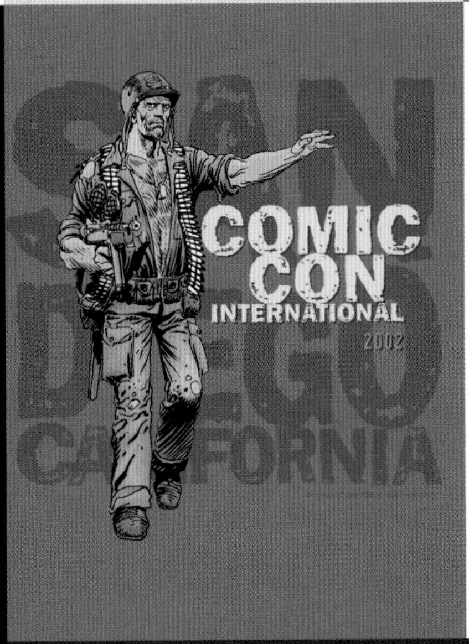
SAN DIEGO CALIFORNIA
COMIC CON
INTERNATIONAL
2002

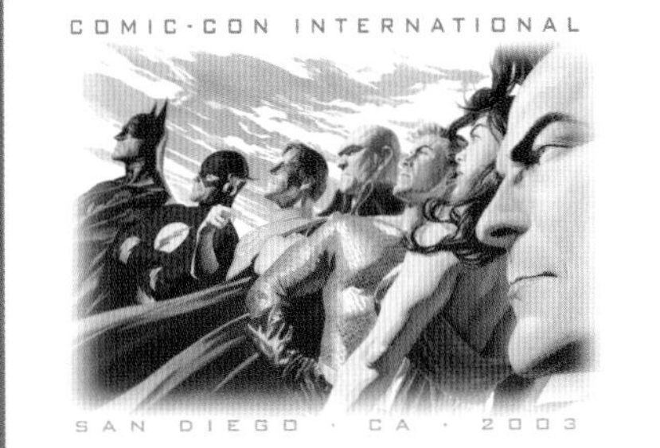
COMIC-CON INTERNATIONAL
SAN DIEGO · CA · 2003

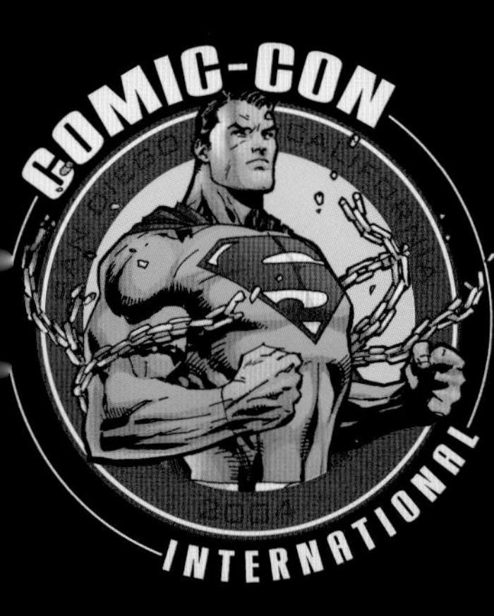
COMIC-CON
INTERNATIONAL

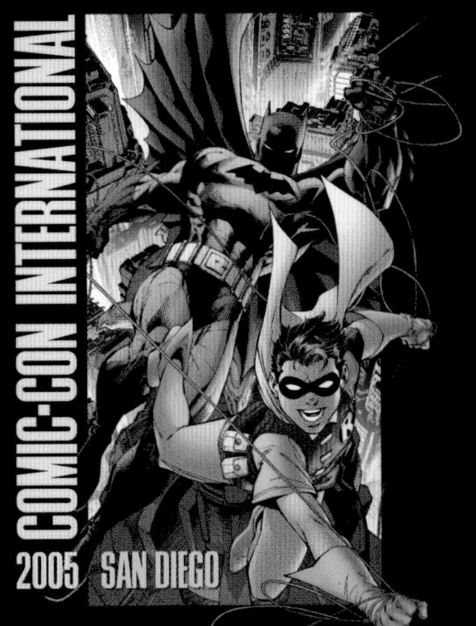
COMIC-CON INTERNATIONAL
2005 SAN DIEGO

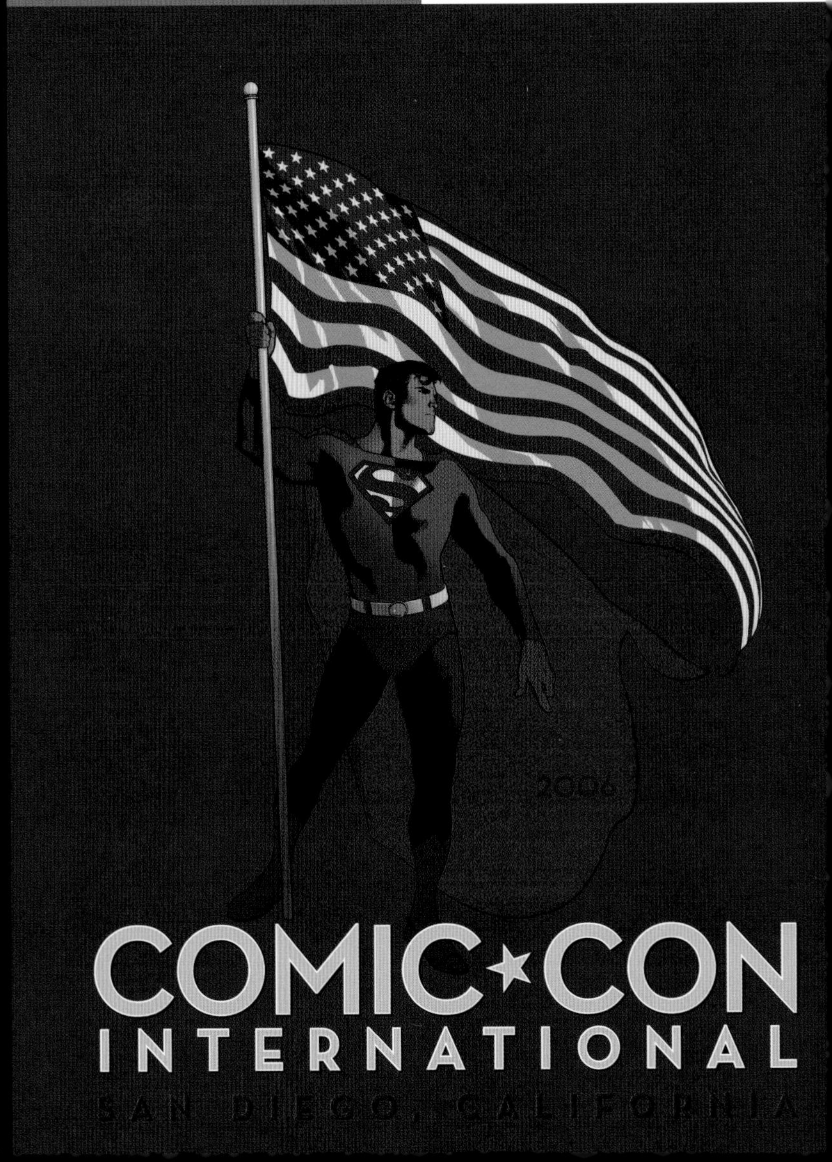
COMIC★CON
INTERNATIONAL
SAN DIEGO, CALIFORNIA

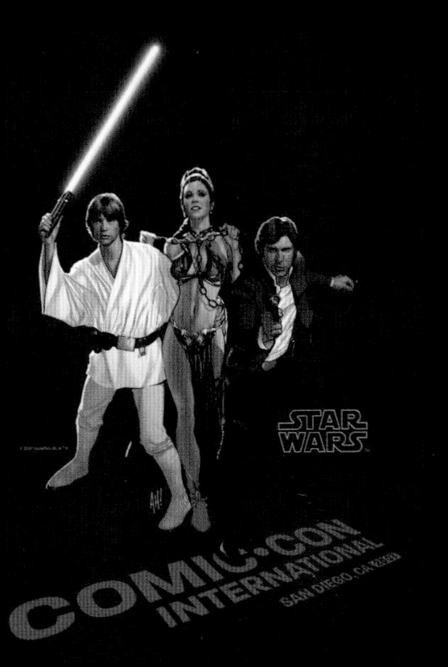
STAR WARS
COMIC•CON
INTERNATIONAL

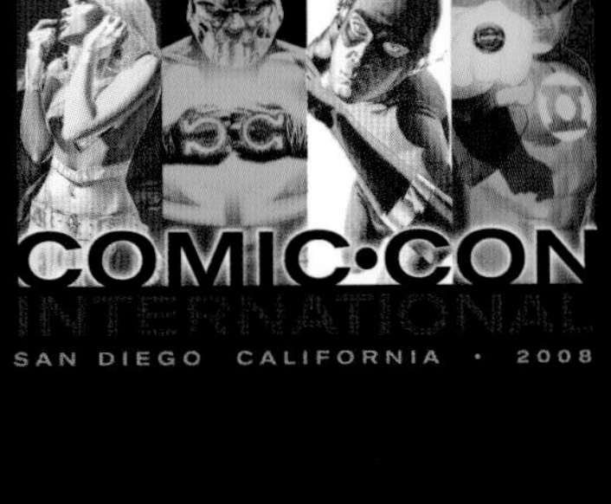
COMIC•CON
INTERNATIONAL
SAN DIEGO CALIFORNIA • 2008

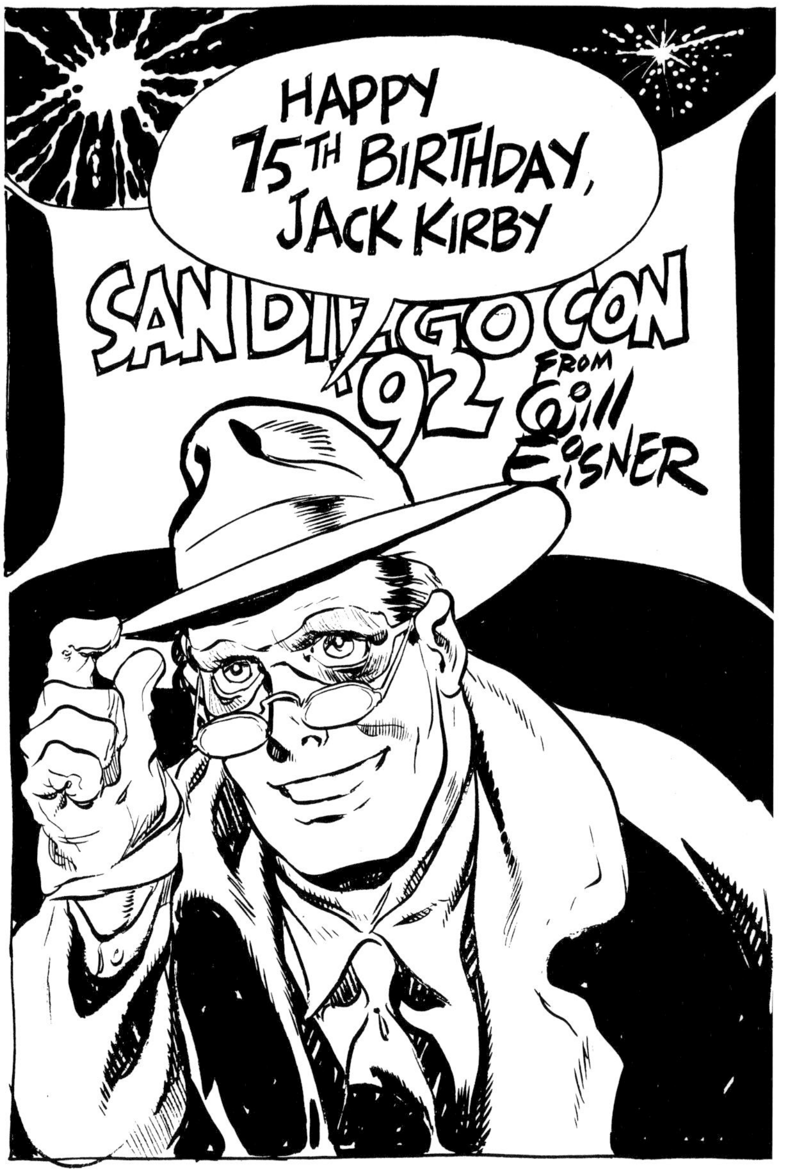
HAPPY 75TH BIRTHDAY, JACK KIRBY
SAN DIEGO CON '92
FROM Will Eisner

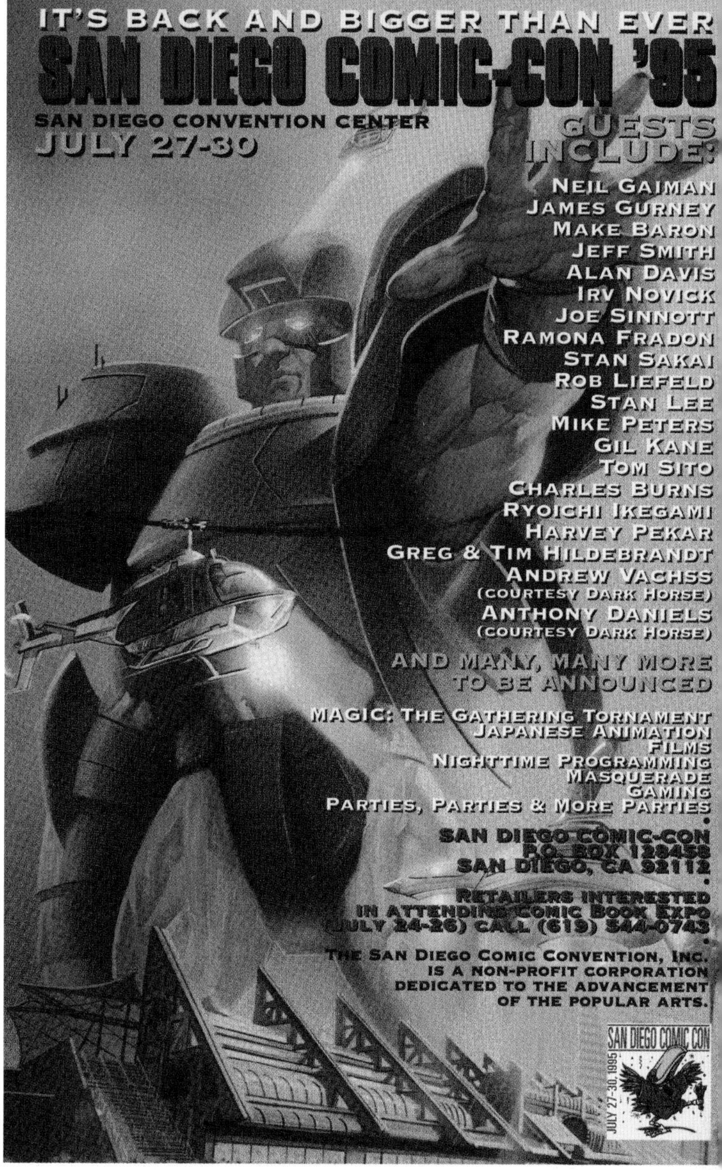
IT'S BACK AND BIGGER THAN EVER
SAN DIEGO COMIC-CON '95
SAN DIEGO CONVENTION CENTER
JULY 27-30
GUESTS INCLUDE:
NEIL GAIMAN
JAMES GURNEY
MAKE BARON
JEFF SMITH
ALAN DAVIS
IRV NOVICK
JOE SINNOTT
RAMONA FRADON
STAN SAKAI
ROB LIEFELD
STAN LEE
MIKE PETERS
GIL KANE
TOM SITO
CHARLES BURNS
RYOICHI IKEGAMI
HARVEY PEKAR
GREG & TIM HILDEBRANDT
ANDREW VACHSS
(COURTESY DARK HORSE)
ANTHONY DANIELS
(COURTESY DARK HORSE)
AND MANY, MANY MORE TO BE ANNOUNCED
MAGIC: THE GATHERING TORNAMENT
JAPANESE ANIMATION FILMS
NIGHTTIME PROGRAMMING
MASQUERADE
GAMING
PARTIES, PARTIES & MORE PARTIES
SAN DIEGO COMIC-CON
P.O. BOX 128458
SAN DIEGO, CA 92112
RETAILERS INTERESTED IN ATTENDING COMIC BOOK EXPO (JULY 24-26) CALL (619) 544-0743
THE SAN DIEGO COMIC CONVENTION, INC. IS A NON-PROFIT CORPORATION DEDICATED TO THE ADVANCEMENT OF THE POPULAR ARTS.
SAN DIEGO COMIC CON
JULY 27-30, 1995

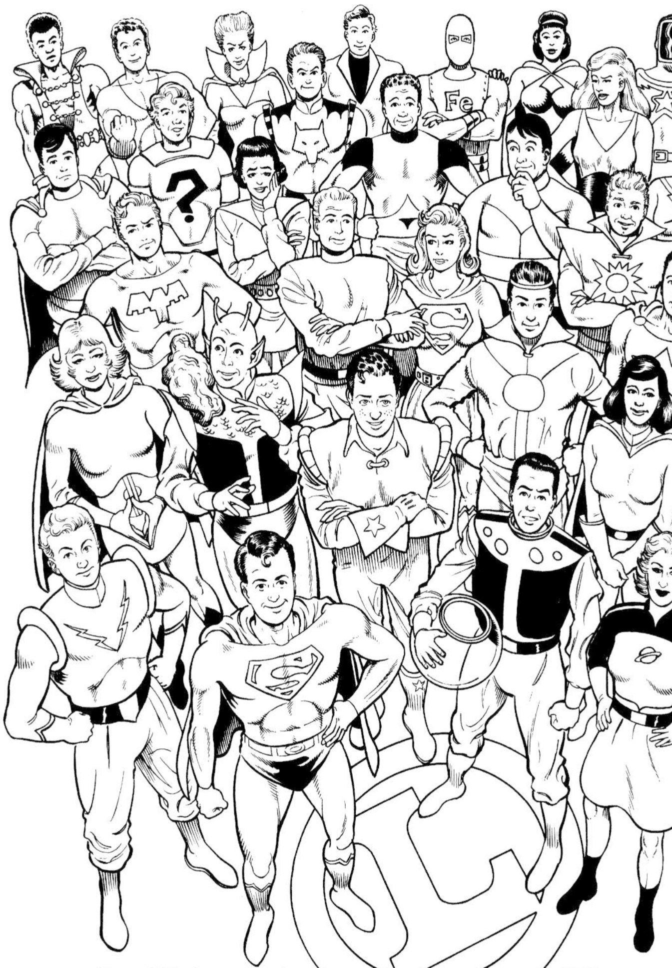
Happy 40th Anniversary!
S. Blue 1998

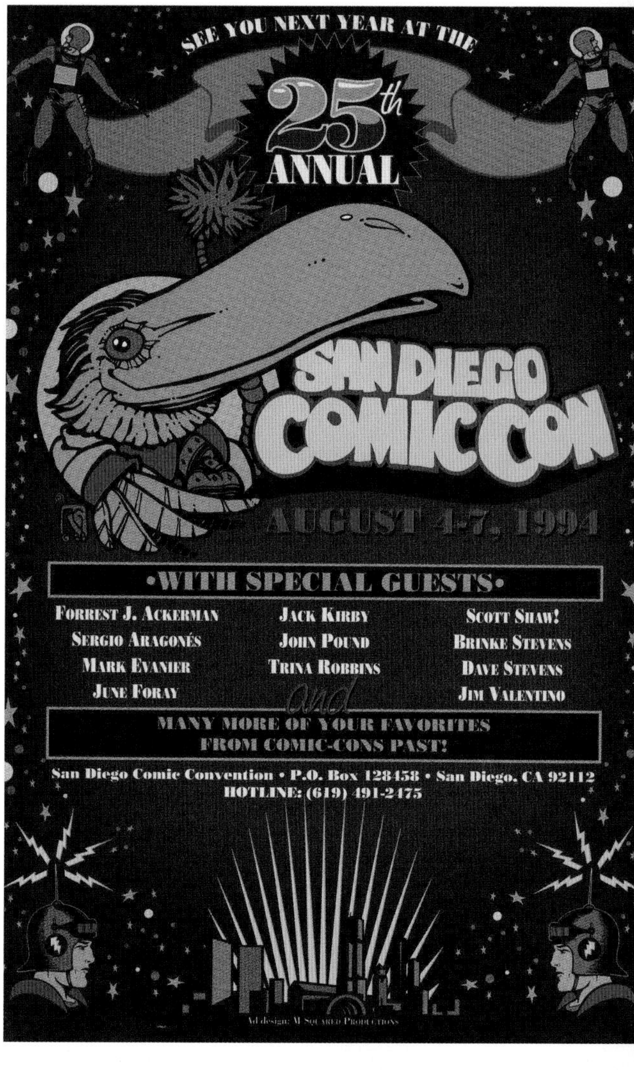
SEE YOU NEXT YEAR AT THE
25th ANNUAL
SAN DIEGO COMIC CON
AUGUST 4-7, 1994
•WITH SPECIAL GUESTS•
FORREST J. ACKERMAN
SERGIO ARAGONÉS
MARK EVANIER
JUNE FORAY
JACK KIRBY
JOHN POUND
TRINA ROBBINS
SCOTT SHAW!
BRINKE STEVENS
DAVE STEVENS
JIM VALENTINO
and
MANY MORE OF YOUR FAVORITES FROM COMIC-CONS PAST!
San Diego Comic Convention • P.O. Box 128458 • San Diego, CA 92112
HOTLINE: (619) 491-2475

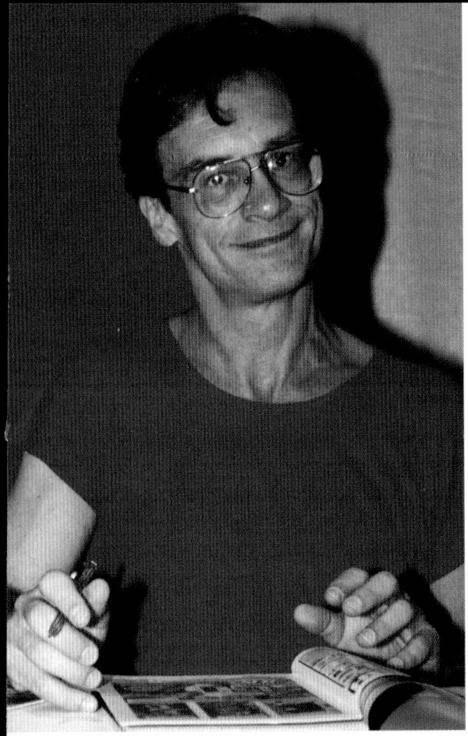

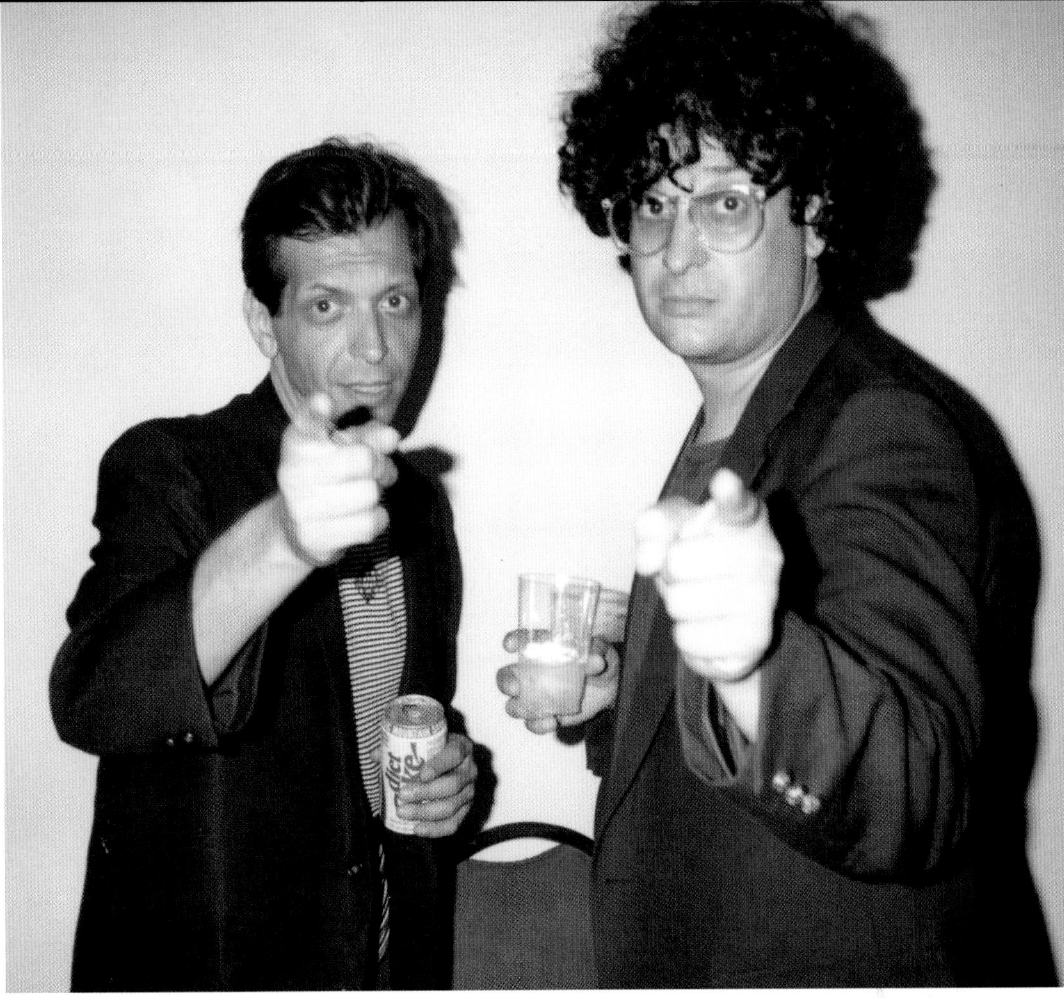

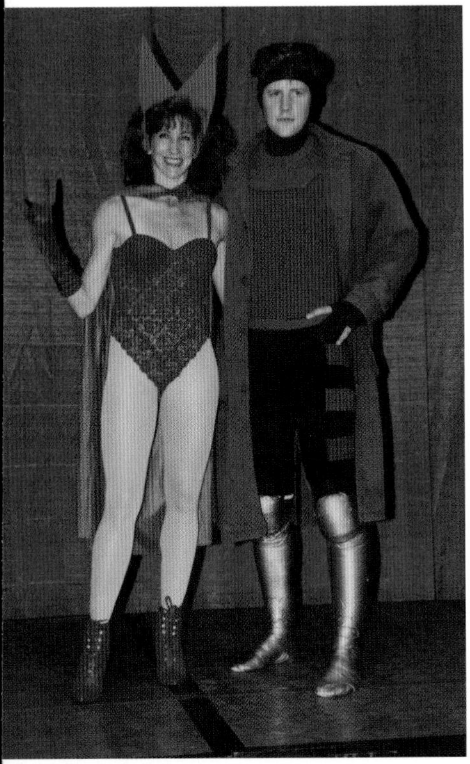

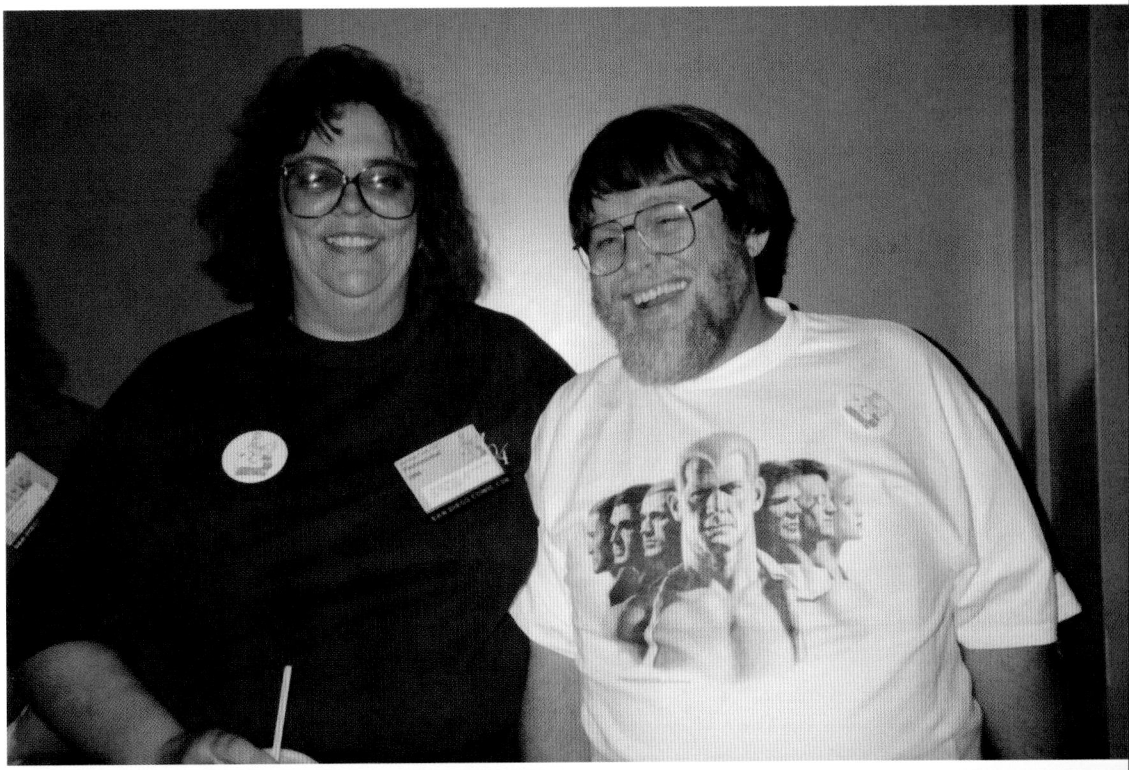

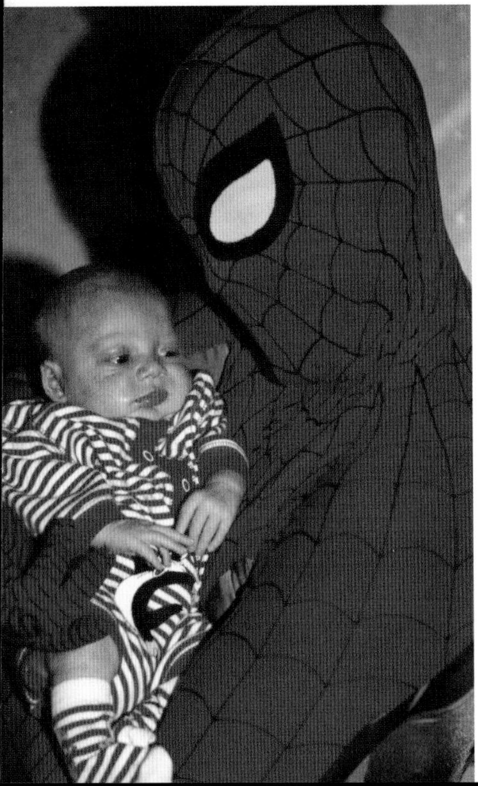

OPPOSITE, CLOCKWISE FROM TOP LEFT: Will Eisner's salute to Jack Kirby's seventy-fifth birthday at the 1992 Comic-Con; ads for both the 1995 and 1994 Comic-Cons that appeared in Dark Horse comics; a salute to the fortieth anniversary of the *Legion of Super-Heroes* in 1998, by Stephen Blue

CLOCKWISE FROM TOP LEFT: Bernie Wrightson signing at the 1994 Comic-Con; cartoonist Batton Lash (left) and animation director Russell Calabrese (right) at a party for Will Eisner in 1990; Maeheah Alzmann (left) and former Comic-Con vice president Richard Butner (right) helping to celebrate the show's twenty-fifth anniversary in 1994; Spider-Man and the littlest of comics fans; the Scarlet Witch and Gambit (Susie Brooks and Steve Pearson), a pair of 1994 Masquerade entries

OVERLEAF: An article from the 1994 Souvenir Book in which Rick Marschall looks back at the great comic strips that started in 1934

The Class of '34

by Rick Marschall

Sixty years ago, in a remarkable burst of fecundity, several of the most memorable quality newspaper strips commenced. More significantly, 60 years ago a new type of comic strip achieved dominance.

In its early days the American comic strip evolved through definite periods of thematic preoccupation and stylistic convention. For a while, new waves crashed to shore approximately once a decade. The decade or so following comics' birth around 1895 made up the experimental period; after that the daily strip was standardized, and syndication brought formulas and categories (kid strips, family strips). The 1920s saw more types, with suburban and working-women themes, and the advent of the continuity strip. And the 1930s brought the zenith of the adventure strip.

The protean influences of early comics and their distinguishing periods all brought the adventure strip to maturity right around 1934. Mixtures of continuity, humor, adventure, melodrama, and fantasy (which had been a staple of comics in their first decade) resulted in an impressive list of creations that included *Secret Agent X-9, Flash Gordon, Jungle Jim, Terry and the Pirates, Mandrake the Magician,* and *Li'l Abner.* These strips are the most representative—fondly and lately recalled or even still running—of a larger, varied group of comics that debuted that year.

Notice that most of these seminal strips were adventure strips (even *Li'l Abner* had its adventurous moments). Why was it that they became so dominant 60 years ago?

The quick, easy, and traditional answer is that, with the United States in the throes of a deep economic depression, adventure strips provided escapist entertainment. Yet, if you think about it the lighter and vicarious aspects of *any* comic strip, especially humor strips, provide escapism enough in difficult times.

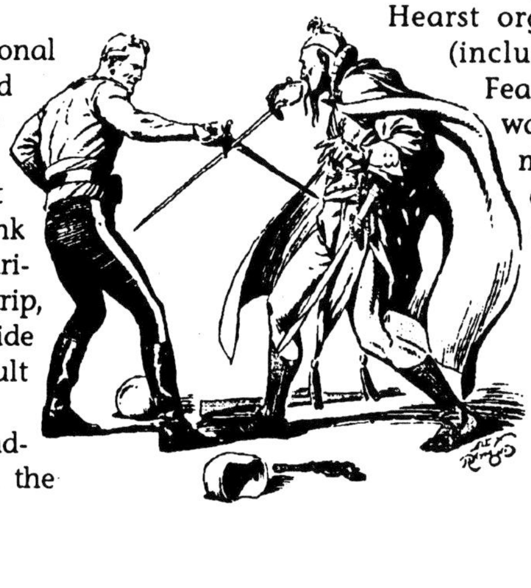

Another answer is that readers took special interest in the mature stories with more complex characters and continuing plots. But these elements weren't new to adventure strips in 1934. 'Way back, the Yellow Kid and Mutt and Jeff starred in loose continuities; so did Happy Hooligan, and Little Nemo's adventures often continued week to week. *Just-Kids* was a mediocre humor strip from the 1920s to the 1950s, but it was a creditable, and surprising, kids' adventure strip in 1916. And even though *Little Orphan Annie* and *Phil Hardy* (by George Storm) weren't drawn realistically back in the 1920s, they featured real adventure. *Wash Tubbs* showcased humor and adventure; *The Gumps,* melodrama and adventure; *Tim Tyler's Luck,* travelogue and adventure; *Gasoline Alley,* domestic adventure; *Apple Mary,* soap opera and adventure.

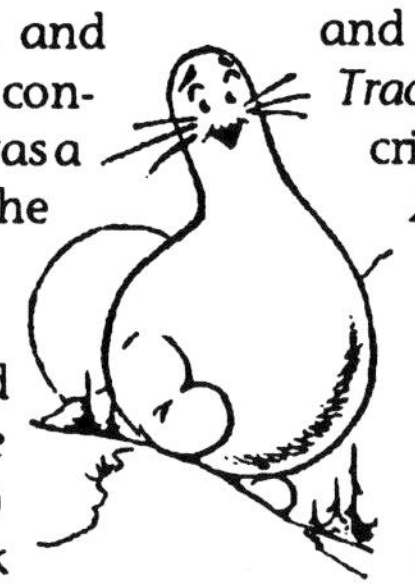

Nevertheless, going into 1934 there were only three major strips that could be termed straight adventure strips without qualifiers: the somewhat Baroque *Buck Rogers* (which began on the first day of 1929); Hal Foster's *Tarzan* (also January 1, 1929), with its captions instead of balloons that reinforced its literary source, the adventure novels of Edgar Rice Burroughs; and Chester Gould's *Dick Tracy* (1931), with an art style more Expressionist than realist and stories that can only be described as adventure with a capital A.

So what happened in 1934? One factor was actually *Dick Tracy* itself. Gould was an artist who through the 1920s had failed with several strips with the Hearst organization (including King Features) and was not much more successful with either the *Daily News* or the *Tribune* in Chicago until *Tracy* clicked. King Features president Joe Connolly regretted "one getting away" and also genuinely admired hard-boiled crime strips. Lee Falk told me that in 1934 he served as unofficial comics editor under Connolly and helped fashion competition to *Tracy*—not one but ultimately five crime-adventure strips: *Secret Agent X-9, Red Barry, Sergeant Pat of the Radio Patrol, Inspector Wade,* and *Mandrake the Magician,* whose sophisticated mysteries set a different tone for readers.

So in 1934 it was figured that crime would pay. Here were stories from the front pages—and emotions from concerned readers' hearts—translated directly to comics pages. But during Prohibition in the 20s, the gangsterism hadn't inspired a new wave of comic strip themes. No, it was not specific current events or general economic malaise that caused a revolution in 1934.

Rather, we should look (as always with that most American of artforms, the comics) at commercial factors. Technical innovations in several fields combined with economic and social malaise to set the state for an explosion in the popular arts. Comic books happened in 1934, with the debut of *Famous Funnies;* a promotional risk became a surprise success. Big Little Books were a year old in 1934, and sales in the millions spread the appetite for comics. An explosion in sales for pulp magazines coincided tellingly with the decline in humor magazines—almost exclusively, they offered adventure, mystery, and science fiction fare.

Movie serials, a staple of Saturday mornings since the teens, now had sound and increasingly more sophisticated production values. Radio serials were catching the public's fancy, with adventures like *Little Orphan Annie* and *Jack Armstrong, All-American Boy* rivaling comedies like *Amos 'n' Andy.*

Miniature golf and bingo games were national fads and rampant in every neighborhood. Moving-picture theaters—as if their attendance wasn't already at an all-time high—beckoned audiences with Bank Nights ("Match

Why was it that adventure strips became so dominant 60 years ago?

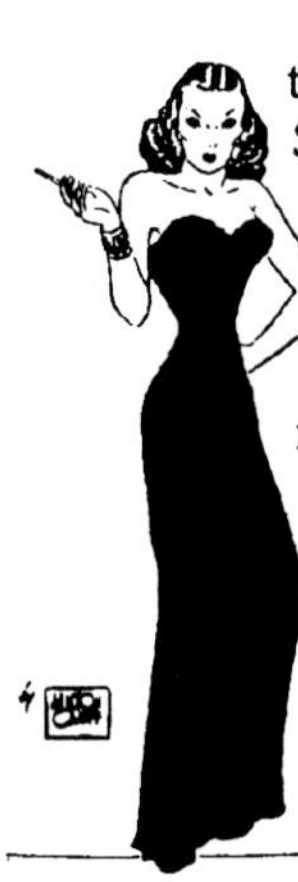

The DRAGON LADY

the number on your ticket for $1,000!"), Free Dish Nights, and other promotions. Concurrently, the number of primitive fast-food joints, already threatening Pullman car–style diners, proliferated during the 30s, mostly pushing hamburgers for a nickel.

With all the competition for escapists in the market, the comic strip business had to innovate and expand in order to survive. Coupled with the thematic departures was an expansion of formats. Sunday comics sections increased their pages in 1934 in spite of hard times. The previous year the Chicago Tribune–New York News Syndicate introduced eight features simultaneously, and the following year the Hearst chain introduced a gaggle of new strips that filled its new tabloid format color supplement (which in itself might have been a response to the popularity of the comic book format).

Having given commercialism its due, we can escape once again to the valid role of escapist themes. There was much to escape during the Depression, and both adults and kids did it in three-minute, half-hour, and 100-minute doses via comic strips, radio shows, and movies (all with equal enthusiasm, we note, while today's comic strip syndicates bemoan the effect of TV and movies on the insipid remnants of adventure strips). Why the sudden appearance of exotic locales and science fiction themes, as in *Flash Gordon*? In part this was due to the movies' growing ability to produce special effects, but across the media another reason is the spirit of the times.

Factories might have been rusting, but advertisements nonetheless promised a brave new world of technology: gadgets would not only help us but be our salvation. Meanwhile, the enormously perfervid political atmosphere around the world convinced perhaps a majority of the public that ultramodern dictatorships were in the offing.

So in 1934 there was a heady mix of new technologies, new hopes, and new fears. The public was hungry for wellsprings and new amounts of entertainment. Cross-pollination was happily rife in the popular arts. The political ferment was such that strips simultaneously advocated rugged individualism and collectivism, nativism and wanderlust, traditional values and technological fantasies, violence as a curse and a cure.

Was there something in the water at King Features in 1934? Bullpen grunt Alex Raymond was tapped first to draw Dashiel Hammett's *Secret Agent X-9,* then two other classics: *Flash Gordon* and *Jungle Jim.* As with *Dick Tracy* leading to *X-9,* there might have been a creative, uh, inspiration for *Flash Gordon* as King Features beheld *Buck Rogers.* In his first months, Raymond engaged in *Buck Rogers*'s patented anachronisms (medieval trappings in a high-tech future-world) in a pulp magazine dry-brush style, but then he broke through with exciting settings (the Water World), compelling character types (although Flash's squeeze Dale Arden was the dippiest heroine since Buster Keaton's foils), and the handsomest artwork in the funnies—a sensual wetbrush look, experimentation with panel arrangements, dialogue in balloons or running captions, and so forth. Raymond was having fun, and so were his readers. *Jungle Jim* was—dare we suggest?—an answer to *Tarzan,* but in Raymond's jungle there was more cogitation than vine swinging, more foreign smugglers than roaring lions.

Mandrake the Magician was another strip that emphasized the cerebral over the muscular, although Lee Falk and artist Phil Davis structured a heavy and heady portion of suspense and excitement. Mandrake was a modern-day Sherlock with added portions of fantasy and magic, As in *Tracy,* the villains were physically and psychically bizarre; and if Mandrake resembled the movies' John Gilbert, then his girlfriend Narda resembled Myrna Loy.

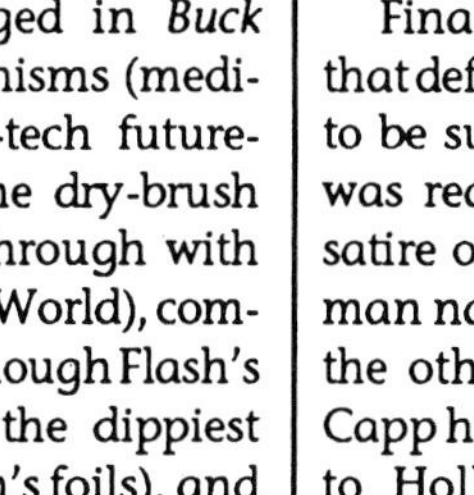

In another 1934 entry, movie stars inspired characters, but then Milton Caniff's *Terry and the Pirates* was itself to inspire later filmmakers in its pacing and staging, its mood, evocation, and atmosphere. The earliest sequences of *Terry* resemble the later sequences of Caniff's 1933 *Dickie Dare,* but he was experimenting throughout 1934 and the rest of the 30s. Arguably the greatest of all adventure strips, *Terry* was set in the exotic Far East, offering a menu of vicarious delights with a boy protagonist, a handsome hero, and a cast of stunning women whose personalities ranged from pure evil to virginal innocence. Caniff was the comics' master of characterization, dialogue, and design—his "camera angles" and visual storytelling have inspired succeeding generations of cartoonists but have never been equaled.

Finally, there was *Li'l Abner,* a strip that defies categorization. A humor strip, to be sure, but Al Capp's hillbilly saga was really a satire. And more than a satire of current events, it satirized human nature. If we look to similarities in the other popular arts (and why not? Capp himself did), *Li'l Abner* was similar to Hollywood's screwball comedies, where impoverished rustic types frequently found themselves in urban high-society settings. And we should look beyond Hollywood to literature in Dickens, Twain, and Swift for the likes of Capp's characterizations and observations.

There have been other periods of innovation and change in comic strip history, but only the period of 1949–1951, when *Pogo, Peanuts, Dennis the Menace,* and *Beetle Bailey* debuted, comes close to rivaling the short period in 1934 that produced landmark strips of a new sort that changed the artform and have withstood the passage of time in their quality and appeal.

Sixty years have passed, and the Class of '34 still exhibits just that: Class.

Rick Marschall is the editor-in-chief of Hogan's Alley, *a new magazine devoted to the comic arts, especially comic strips.*

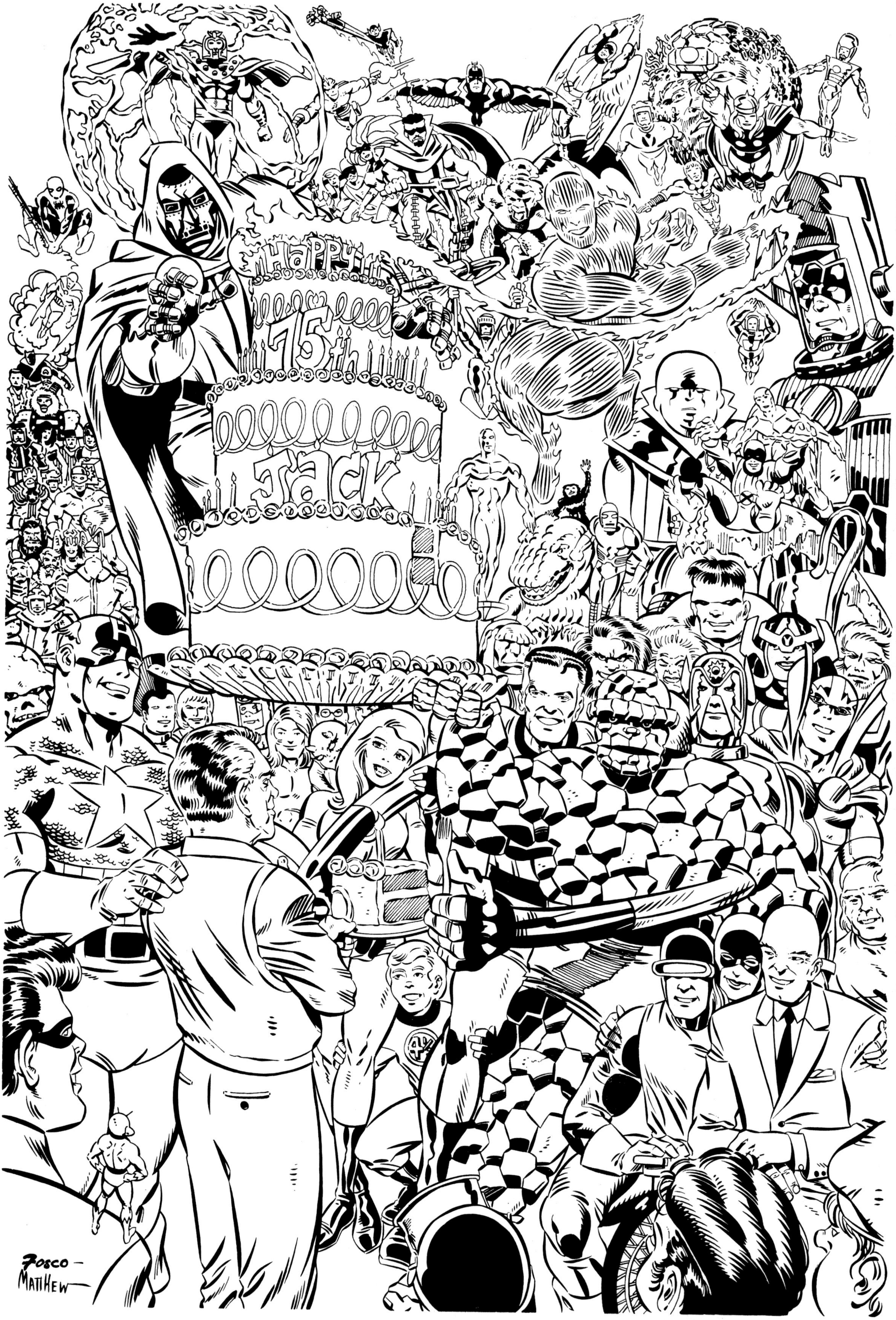
HaPPY
75th
Jack
FOSCO-
MATHEW

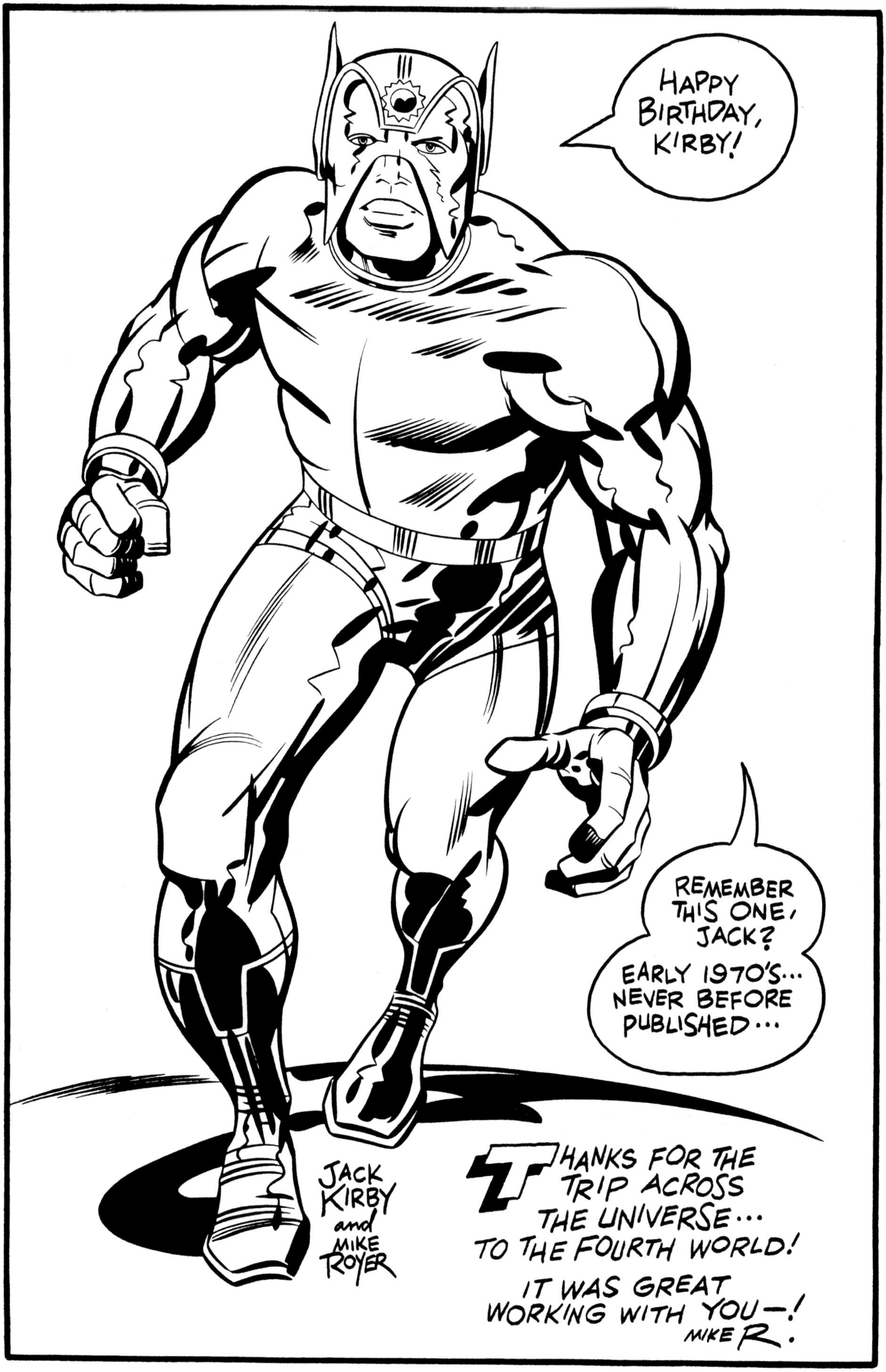
HAPPY BIRTHDAY, KIRBY!
REMEMBER THIS ONE, JACK?
EARLY 1970'S... NEVER BEFORE PUBLISHED...
JACK KIRBY and MIKE ROYER
THANKS FOR THE TRIP ACROSS THE UNIVERSE... TO THE FOURTH WORLD!
IT WAS GREAT WORKING WITH YOU—!
MIKE R.

OPPOSITE: Fosco and Matthew's birthday salute to Jack Kirby, featuring a plethora of his characters
ABOVE: Longtime collaborator Mike Royer's inked version of an early 1970s Kirby sketch of Orion, from the *New Gods*

A BRIEF HISTORY OF UNDERGROUND COMICS

BY JAY KENNEDY

In November 1967, while living in the Haight Ashbury district of San Francisco, Robert Crumb put the finishing touches on *Zap Comix* #1. In February 1968, Don Donahue financed the printing of 5,000 copies by trading a reel-to-reel tape recorder to the printer and beat poet, Charles Plymell.

The cover bore the words, "FAIR WARNING: FOR ADULT INTELLECTUALS ONLY!" It was a succinct and cleverly satiric declaration that this wasn't a typical comic book. Inside were bold, irreverent stories that questioned societal roles and norms. Permeating the book was a hope that there was more to life than a steady job, a spouse, two kids, and a car. There was a sense that a profound, meaningful and enlightening cultural change was afoot and that it could be had by opening one's mind. There was a sense that reading this comic was a part of that process.

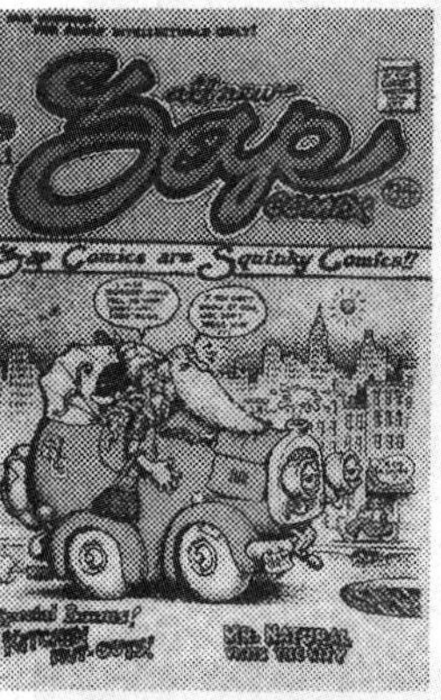
Zap
Zap Comics are Squinky Comics!

Zap's unbridled creativity was electrifying to dozens of other artists living in the Haight at that time and to hundreds of other artists around the world in the years that followed. In retrospect, *Zap Comix* #1 was a seminal comic book. Although there had been a handful of earlier publications that can legitimately lay claim to being part of the underground comix movement,* *this* was the comic that widely inspired other artists and thus triggered the advent of the underground comix movement.

Underground comix (spelled with an "x" to distinguish them from mainstream newsstand comic books) acquired the label ***underground*** from the newspapers in which many of the cartoonists had honed their skills. In 1965, newspapers such as *The East Village Other* and *The Berkeley Barb* expressed antiestablishment sentiments and quickly became romantically referred to as the "underground press." The label stuck and would be "officially" adopted in 1967 when these and other underground newspapers banded together to form the Underground Press Syndicate, a hip wire service.

**The Adventures of Jesus* (Frank Stack, 1962), *Das Kampf* (Vaughn Bode, 1963), *God Nose* (Jack Jackson, 1964), *Lenny of Laredo* (Joel Beck, 1965), *S. Clay Wilson's Twenty Drawings* (S. Clay Wilson, 1967), and others.

For many people the phrase "underground comix" is synonymous with "hippy comics." Indeed, underground comix grew out of a countercultural milieu and are most renowned for their explicit and frequent references to sex, drugs, music, and radical politics. The status of early undergrounds as nostalgic sixties artifacts is itself reason enough for many people to collect them today. But to see the comix solely in that light is to ignore the significance of the fundamental changes they made in how comic books are produced and viewed.

Underground comix marked a radical change in the direction of comic book art. They shifted the reason for doing a comic book from the telling of a plot-centered fantasy adventure story to unrestrained personal expression. Underground cartoonists started doing comic books about things relevant to their lives. No subject matter or image was off limits. From the Vietnam war to sexual obsessions, they questioned the society around them and the neuroses within them. In short, the cartoonists were doing highly individualistic comix for themselves and, by extension, other adults who shared their interests.

In the initial years of underground comix (1968 and 1969), the artists became enraptured (some would say seduced) by the possibilities of complete artistic freedom. They did more than just stretch accepted notions of what comic books could be—they aggressively confronted such notions. They broke taboos, experimented with the form, and established new channels of production and distribution.

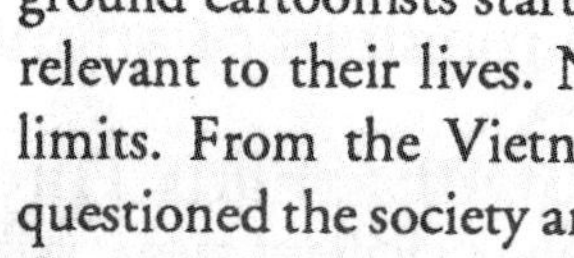
FREAK
BROTHERS

They used comix to work out and push beyond their own ingrained sense of what was proper. S. Clay Wilson's work most vividly exemplified this approach. He drew graphic scenes of pirates, dykes, and motorcycle gangs dismembering each other. Crumb drew pocket-sized parodies of smut books and went past the point authorities could tolerate. His *Snatch Comics* #1 (Oct. 1968) was busted as obscene, but lengthy court cases upheld artists' rights to freedom of the press.

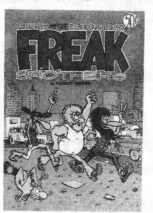

Underground comix shifted the reason for doing a comic book from the telling of a plot-center fantasy adventure story to unrestrained personal expression.

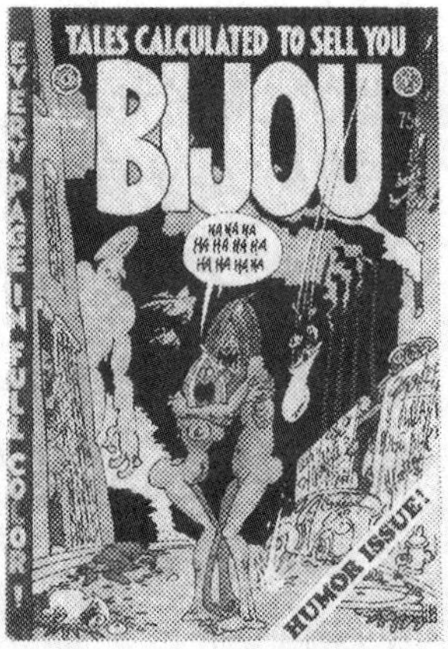
TALES CALCULATED TO SELL YOU
BIJOU
EVERY PAGE IN FULL COLOR!
HUMOR ISSUE!

1968 and 1969 also saw the development of the publishing end of underground comix and it, too, was unique. Publishers sprung up with names like The Print Mint, Apex Novelties, Krupp Comics Work, (now Kitchen Sink Press), the Rip Off Press, Bijou Publishing Company, The San Francisco Comic Book Company and in 1970, Last Gasp Eco-Funnies and Company & Sons. Unlike mainstream comic book publishers, these publishers bought only one-time printing rights, not the copyrights to the work.

Barred from the newsstands because they didn't meet the standards of the Comics Code Authority, underground comix publishers relied heavily on distributing their wares through a network of local headshops where their books sold well, by comix standards. Print runs of 10,000–20,000 copies were the norm and sold out in three or four months. Unlike mainstream comics, which are removed from the racks each month when the new issue comes along, most underground comix were intentionally published as one-shots. Like regular hardcover books, each comix title would remain on the shelves until it sold out. If it sold out fast enough, additional printings were done until demand was exhausted.

1970 to 1973 were the boom years for underground comix. Comix were selling as fast as they could be produced. While their popularity still largely stemmed from reinforcing the countercultural values that the cartoonists shared with their customers, the artists' fascination with breaking taboos waned and the range of their subject matter expanded. There were, for example, ecological comix (*Slow Death Funnies*), women's comix (*Wimmen's Comix*), back-to-the-land comix (*Truckin'*), and self-analytic comix (*Binky Brown Meets the Holy Virgin Mary*). The total body of underground comix was becoming as diverse as the people who created it.

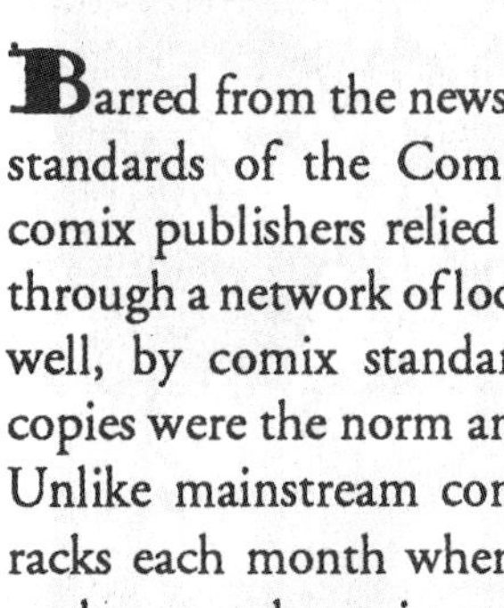
WIMMEN'S COMIX

Late 1973 brought the end of the heyday of underground comix. The rebellious youth of the sixties who had been the primary audience for underground comix began to be assimilated back into mainstream society. A U.S. Supreme Court ruling shifted the definition of pornography from national to local standards, causing many retailers to drop underground comix from their inventories for fear of being arrested by the local sheriff. And in a series of events that was to be repeated in 1987 with the black-and-white independent comic books, a glut of artistically inferior comix had a deleterious effect on sales when they tainted people's overall opinion of underground comix.

Throughout the remainder of the seventies, underground comix publishers retrenched. They reprinted old material that had sold well and limited the release of new material to work by well known artists.

It wasn't until the 1980s that sales of underground comix began to rebound. The emergence of the retail comic book speciality shop provided a new audience comprised of comic book fans whose interests in comics had continued past adolescence.

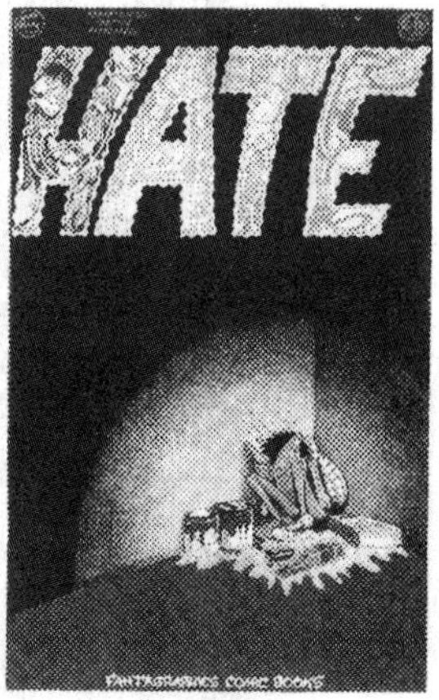
HATE

Today, classic underground comix continue to be reprinted, but the distinctions between new undergrounds and many of the new independent comic books have become negligible. Comics like Peter Bagge's *Hate* and Wayno's *Beer Nutz* would certainly have been considered underground twenty years ago. Regardless of how books like these are classified, it is clear that they owe their existence to the strides made by underground comix.

Underground comix changed the understanding of what a comic book can be. Artists, and increasingly the general public, now realize that comic books can be an adult medium of personal expression.

Jay Kennedy is comics editor for King Features Syndicate and author of The Underground and Newwave Comix Price Guide.

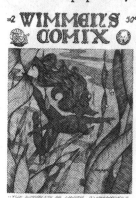

COMICS ARTS CONFERENCE

"Racial and Gender Ambiguity in Krazy Kat." "Criticism in Action: Scholars Interpret Kurt Busiek's Astro City (with a response by Busiek)." "The Metaphorical Structuring of McCloud's Webcomics." If these panels sound a bit unusual for Comic-Con, you probably haven't been attending the Comics Arts Conference, a full-fledged academic conference that takes place each year within Comic-Con International: San Diego.

The conference began in 1992 when Peter M. Coogan, a graduate student at Michigan State University, and Randy Duncan, Communication Department chair at Henderson State University, decided it was time for an academic conference devoted solely to the study of comics and to hold it at Comic-Con to facilitate the involvement of comics professionals and fans.

Comic-Con International made the first conference possible by donating the use of a conference room at the nearby Marriott. Will Eisner and Robert C. Harvey, the leading practitioner-theorists of the day, acted as respondents. The highlight of the day was Scott McCloud's preview of his groundbreaking book *Understanding Comics*, which focuses on the complexity and depth of the comics medium and its unique integration of words and sequential art to tell a story.

After another year in San Diego, the Comics Arts Conference (CAC) was held at the Chicago Comicon for two years, but it returned to San Diego for good

in 1996. The conference was on a one-year hiatus in 1997 when Comic-Con approached Duncan and Coogan about making the CAC an official part of the convention, joining its seminars, programs, panel discussions, and hands-on workshops in helping to fulfill its educational mission. Since 1998 the conference has gradually expanded to offer four full days of programming.

Part of the unique mission of the conference is the involvement of comics professionals in the critical analysis of the art form. Melding an academic conference with the massive Comic-Con has allowed for professionals such as Paul Levitz, Michael Chabon, Trina Robbins, Steve Englehart, Danny Fingeroth, Kurt Busiek, Jeff Smith, Chip Kidd, and others to engage in serious discussions of comics with scholars. In 2002 the conference reunited Eisner, McCloud, and Harvey for a "Ten Years Later" panel to reflect on the progress of comics in academia.

The conference has been a wellspring of comics scholarship. Presenters have included comics studies pioneers Thomas Andrae, John A. Lent, and Tom Roberts as well as such leading lights of the next generation of scholars as Amy Kiste Nyberg (*Seal of Approval*), Bart Beaty (*Fredric Wertham and the Critique of Mass Culture*), Neil Cohn (*Early Writings on Visual Language*), and Stanford Carpenter (*The Work of Imagining Identity in Comic Books*). Many of the presentations given at CAC have led to articles in the *International Journal of Comic Art* and other academic journals. Through conference presentations, Peter Coogan developed the concepts that were the basis of his book *Superhero: The Secret Origin of a Genre*, and Matthew Smith and Randy Duncan have since co-authored *The Power of Comics: An Introduction to Graphic Storytelling*.

ABOVE: The CAC logo **OPPOSITE:** Just one of many Comics Arts Conference seminars at Comic-Con over the years. This one focused on the lasting appeal of Superman on his seventieth birthday in 2008 and was moderated by scholar Ben Saunders.

Since partnering with Comic-Con, the conference has continued to grow and diversify. In 2006 Coogan and Duncan were joined by a third conference organizer, Kathleen McClancy of Duke University. The reach of the conference expanded in 2007 with the addition of academic panels at Comic-Con's sister show, WonderCon in San Francisco. Wittenberg University even offers a summer course, "The Culture of Popular Things: Ethnographic Examination of Comic-Con," designed around CCI and CAC. In 2008 the annual Comics Studies Forum debuted to provide comics scholars an opportunity to discuss the current and future state of the field of comics studies and form collaborations to launch new academic projects.

The CAC offers a decidedly different, and often exciting, type of academic conference. The Comics Arts Conference organizers and Comic-Con are dedicated to continuing their mission of bringing scholars and professionals together to discuss comics in a public forum and invigorating the study of comics as a medium and an art form.

NOTABLE GUESTS

PEOPLE MAKING THEIR FIRST APPEARANCES AS SPECIAL GUESTS AT COMIC-CON IN THE 1990s . . .

1990
COMIC-CON 21

PETER DAVID: comic book writer, *The Spectacular Spider-Man, The Incredible Hulk, Aquaman: Atlantis Chronicles*

GRANT MORRISON: Scottish comic book writer, *Animal Man, Doom Patrol, Arkham Asylum*

JOHN ROMITA JR.: comic book artist, *The Amazing Spider-Man, Daredevil*

VAN WILLIAMS: actor, *Green Hornet* television series

1991
COMIC-CON 22

CLIVE BARKER: horror author, *Books of Blood, Cabal, The Great and Secret Show*

DAN DECARLO: comic book artist, *Betty and Veronica*; co-creator, *Josie and the Pussycats*

NEIL GAIMAN: British comic book writer, *The Sandman, The Books of Magic*

KEITH GIFFEN: comic book writer, *Legion of Super-Heroes, Lobo*; writer/artist, *Ambush Bug*

JOE HALDEMAN: science fiction author, *The Forever War, Worlds, All My Sins Remembered*

LYNN JOHNSTON: syndicated cartoonist/creator, *For Better or For Worse*

JIM LEE: comic book artist, *Uncanny X-Men*

1992
COMIC-CON 23

FRANCIS FORD COPPOLA: film writer/director, *The Godfather, Apocalypse Now, Dracula*

CREIG FLESSEL: Golden Age comic book artist, *Adventure Comics, Detective Comics*

BILL GRIFFITH: underground comix writer/artist, *Zippy the Pinhead*

TODD MCFARLANE: comic book writer/artist, *Spider-Man, Spawn*

DIANE NOOMIN: underground comix writer/artist, *Didi Glitz*; editor, *Twisted Sisters*

ROWENA (MORRILL): fantasy illustrator, book cover artist

WILLIAM SHATNER: actor, *Star Trek, T. J. Hooker*; author, *TekWar*

VERNOR VINGE: science fiction author, *Marooned in Realtime, The Peace War, A Fire Upon the Deep*

1993
COMIC-CON 24

MURPHY ANDERSON: Silver Age comic book artist, *Hawkman, Adam Strange, Superman*

JIM APARO: Silver Age comic book artist, *Aquaman, Phantom Stranger, Batman and the Outsiders*

PETER BAGGE: alternative comics writer/artist/creator, *Hate*

DAN CLOWES: alternative comics writer/artist/creator, *Eightball, Lloyd Llewelyn*

PAUL DINI: comic book and animation writer, *Batman: The Animated Series*

GARTH ENNIS: Irish comic book writer, *Hellblazer, The Demon*

RICK KIRKMAN AND JERRY SCOTT: syndicated cartoonists, *Baby Blues*

DON MARTIN: *MAD* magazine's maddest cartoonist

OLIVIA (DEBERARDINIS): fantasy illustrator/painter

MARC SILVESTRI: comic book artist, *Uncanny X-Men, Wolverine*

VINCENT SULLIVAN: Golden Age editor at National Periodical Publications (DC Comics)

MICHAEL WHALEN: science fiction/fantasy artist, book cover illustrator

ROGER ZELAZNY: science fiction/fantasy author, *Lord of Light, The Chronicles of Amber* series

1994
COMIC-CON 25

MICHAEL ALLRED: comic book writer/artist, *Madman*

DAVID BRIN: science fiction author, *The Postman, Startide Rising, Earth*

AL FELDSTEIN: Golden Age EC Comics writer/artist and editor; *MAD* magazine editor (1956–1984)

STAN GOLDBERG: Silver Age Marvel bullpen; artist, Archie Comics

ROBERTA GREGORY: alternative comics writer/artist; creator, *Naughty Bits*

JAMES O'BARR: comic book writer/artist/creator, *The Crow*

LUCIUS SHEPARD: science fiction/fantasy author, *Life During Wartime, The Golden*

J. MICHAEL STRACZYNSKI: comic book writer, *The Amazing Spider-Man*; movie and television writer/producer/creator, *Babylon 5*

RUMIKO TAKAHASHI: Japanese manga writer/artist, *Urusei Yatsura, Ranma ½, InuYasha*

JEAN-CLAUDE VAN DAMME: action movie actor, *Timecop*

1995
COMIC-CON 26

CHARLES BURNS: alternative comics writer/artist, *RAW* magazine, *Black Hole*

ALAN DAVIS: British comic book artist, *D.R. & Quinch, Captain Britain, Excalibur*

RAMONA FRADON: Silver Age comic book artist, *Aquaman, Metamorpho*

JAMES GURNEY: author/illustrator, *Dinotopia*

TIM AND GREG HILDEBRANDT (THE BROTHERS HILDEBRANDT): fantasy illustrators/painters, *The Lord of the Rings* trilogy

RYOICHI IKEGAMI: Japanese manga artist, *Crying Freeman, Mai the Psychic Girl*

IRV NOVICK: Golden and Silver Age artist, *The Shield, Batman, The Brave and the Bold*

JOE SINNOTT: Silver Age comic book artist/inker, *The Fantastic Four, The Mighty Thor*

TOM SITO: storyboard artist/animator, *Pocahontas, Osmosis Jones*

JEFF SMITH: comic book writer/artist/creator, *Bone*

ANDREW VACHSS: crime fiction author, *Flood, Strega, Hard Candy*

1996
COMIC-CON 27

STEVE DILLON: British comic book artist, *Hellblazer, Preacher*

MORT DRUCKER: cartoonist, *MAD* magazine

BEN EDLUND: writer/artist/creator, *The Tick*

DAVE GIBBONS: British comic book artist, *Watchmen*

DAVE MCKEAN: British comic book artist/illustrator, *Violent Cases, Black Orchid, Arkham Asylum*; *The Sandman* covers

KURT SCHAFFENBERGER: Silver Age comic book artist, *Lois Lane*

FRANÇOIS SCHUITEN: Belgian comic book artist, *Cities of the Fantastic* series

MARIE SEVERIN: Golden and Silver Age comic book artist/colorist, EC Comics, *The Incredible Hulk, Kull the Conqueror, Not Brand Ecch*

1997
COMIC-CON 28

DICK AYERS: Silver Age comic book artist/inker, *The Fantastic Four, Sgt. Fury and His Howling Commandos*

TERRY BROOKS: fantasy author, *Shannara* series

KURT BUSIEK: comic book writer, *Marvels, Kurt Busiek's Astro City*

PETER KUPER: alternative cartoonist, *Bleeding Heart, Comics Trips, World War 3 Illustrated*

DAVID LAPHAM: comic book writer/artist/creator, *Stray Bullets*

JOSEPH MICHAEL LINSNER: comic book writer/artist, *Dawn*

RALPH MCQUARRIE: movie designer/futurist, *Star Wars, E. T.: The Extra-Terrestrial*

LINDA MEDLEY: comic book writer/artist/creator, *Castle Waiting*

MICHAEL MOORCOCK: British science fiction/fantasy author, *Elric of Melniboné* stories, *Jerry Cornelius* series

ALEX ROSS: comic book artist, *Marvels, Kingdom Come*

R. A. SALVATORE: fantasy author, *Forgotten Realms* series

KEVIN SMITH: movie writer/director, *Clerks, Chasing Amy*

GEORGE TUSKA: Golden and Silver Age comic book artist, *Crime Does Not Pay, Ghost Rider, The Invincible Iron Man*

PAUL VERHOEVEN: movie director, *RoboCop, Total Recall, Starship Troopers*

MARK WAID: comic book writer, *The Flash, Captain America, Kingdom Come*

1998
COMIC-CON 29

JOHN BROOME: Silver Age comic book writer, *Green Lantern, Flash*

EDDIE CAMPBELL: Scottish comic book writer/artist, *Alec, Bacchus*; artist, *From Hell*

NICK CARDY: Silver Age comic book artist, *Aquaman, Teen Titans, Bat Lash*

LORENZO MATTOTTI: Italian painter, comic book writer/artist, *Fires, Murmur*

TERRY MOORE: comic book writer/artist/creator, *Strangers in Paradise*

JOHN SEVERIN: Silver Age comic book artist and inker, EC Comics, *MAD, Sgt. Fury and His Howling Commandos, Kull the Conqueror*

JOE SIMON: Golden Age comic book writer/artist/publisher, co-creator of *Captain America*

NAOKO TAKEUCHI: Japanese manga artist, *Sailor Moon*

CHRIS WARE: alternative comics writer/artist/creator, *Acme Novelty Library*

1999
COMIC-CON 30

TOM BATIUK: syndicated cartoonist, *Funky Winkerbean*

SAMUEL R. DELANEY: science fiction author, *Babel-17, The Einstein Intersection, Dhalgren*

ARNOLD DRAKE: Silver Age comic book writer/co-creator, *Deadman, Doom Patrol*

LARRY GONICK: alternative comics writer/artist, *Cartoon History of the Universe*

IRWIN HASEN: Golden Age comic book artist, *Green Lantern, The Flash*; syndicated cartoonist, *Dondi*

PATRICK MCDONNELL: syndicated cartoonist, *Mutts*

MIKE MIGNOLA: comic book writer/artist/creator, *Hellboy*

MARK MOTHERSBAUGH: musician/composer, film and television scores and theme songs

JILL THOMPSON: comic book artist, *The Sandman, The Invisibles*; writer/artist/creator, *Scary Godmother*

BRUCE TIMM: artist/animator, *Batman: The Animated Series*

BARRY WINDSOR-SMITH: comic book artist, *Conan the Barbarian, Wolverine: Weapon X, Archer & Armstrong*

When I first came to San Diego, I had somewhat vague ambitions of working as a cartoonist. A career in comics was very far from my mind. Attending Comic-Con introduced me to a new world, brought me in contact with terrific people, and set me on a path of very rewarding work.

—RICK GEARY
WRITER/CARTOONIST, NUMEROUS GRAPHIC NOVELS, INCLUDING *THE LINDBERGH CHILD*

2000s

As the new decade began and progressed, it was becoming more and more apparent that comics had finally reached a mainstream audience. Graphic novels, arguably around since 1976 or even earlier, gained amazing ground in bookstores, with Borders and Barnes & Noble devoting entire sections to the books sprouting up. The incredible popularity of manga and anime contributed to this new-found respect for comics. Exciting new types of comics grew and shined in the 2000s: Webcomics, published online rather than printed on paper, took a strong hold on the public's imagination, and special guests such as Scott Kurtz (*PvP*) and Steve Purcell (*Sam & Max: Freelance Police*) helped celebrate the burgeoning medium. The DIY publishing movement took off and more and more small press and independent publishers started appearing at all three of the Comic-Con events, including WonderCon and APE, the Alternative Press Expo. Greater emphasis was placed on manga and international guests, with superstars such as Tite Kubo (*Bleach*), Kazuko Koike (*Lone Wolf and Cub*), and Jean-Claude Mézières (*Valérian and Laureline*), visiting the show for the first time. Comics had become an accepted art form. As comics and movie writer David Goyer put it, "We won": Comics had gained the mainstream acceptance and recognition the medium so justly deserved.

THE SPIRIT ©2005 WILL EISNER
ARTWORK ©2005 BENTON JEW

BENTON JEW 2005

LEFT: Artist Benton Jew's tribute to Will Eisner from the 2005 Comic-Con Souvenir Book (Eisner died in January 2005) **OPPOSITE:** A giant robot across from the Convention Center in 2004, used to promote the film *Sky Captain and the World of Tomorrow*

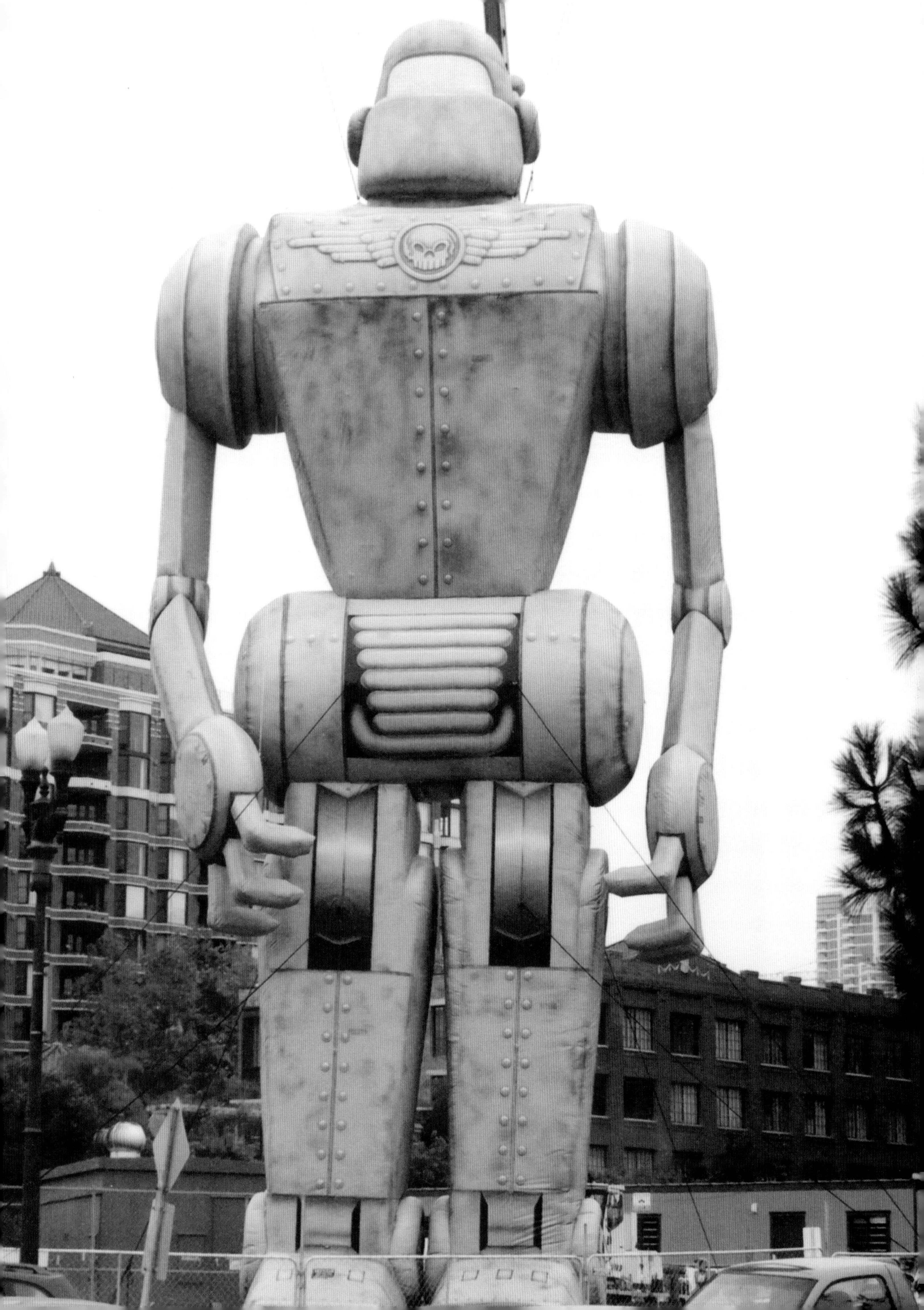

LEAPS AND BOUNDS

The new century also saw Comic-Con's attendance grow almost exponentially. From 2000 to 2007, attendance more than doubled, going from 48,500 in the first year of the new decade to more than 125,000 seven years later. In fact, in 2007, Comic-Con experienced its first-ever completely sold-out days. In 2008 all the memberships for the event—four days and single days—sold out online weeks before anyone set foot in the building.

In 2001 the San Diego Convention Center—Comic-Con's home for ten years—added a major expansion, doubling the size of the facility. Accounting for growth, the original plan was to add a new hall to the Comic-Con floor plan every two years. But attendance increased at an incredible rate, and that plan quickly went out the window. Within two years, Comic-Con's Exhibit Hall rapidly grew from two hundred fifty thousand square feet to more than four hundred sixty thousand square feet, the equivalent of about nine football fields laid side by side.

Along with the expansion came added meeting space upstairs, including Ballroom 20, a venue large enough to seat more than 4,250 people. Comic-Con immediately earmarked that room for both the Will Eisner Comic Industry Awards and the Masquerade. Additional major events on Thursday night were added in Ballroom 20, including the *Star Wars* Fan Film Awards and the world premieres of films such as *Superman Doomsday*. In 2004 Comic-Con took the extraordinary step of utilizing the one remaining Exhibit Hall space on the ground floor of the convention center, Hall H, as a sixty-five-hundred-seat programming room. The obvious question—Will we fill it?—was answered with a capacity crowd for the very first program in Hall H on Friday, July 23, 2004, a Warner Bros. presentation featuring *Batman Begins* (with screenwriter David Goyer and star Cillian Murphy) and *Constantine* (with stars Keanu Reeves and Djimon Housou and director Francis Lawrence).

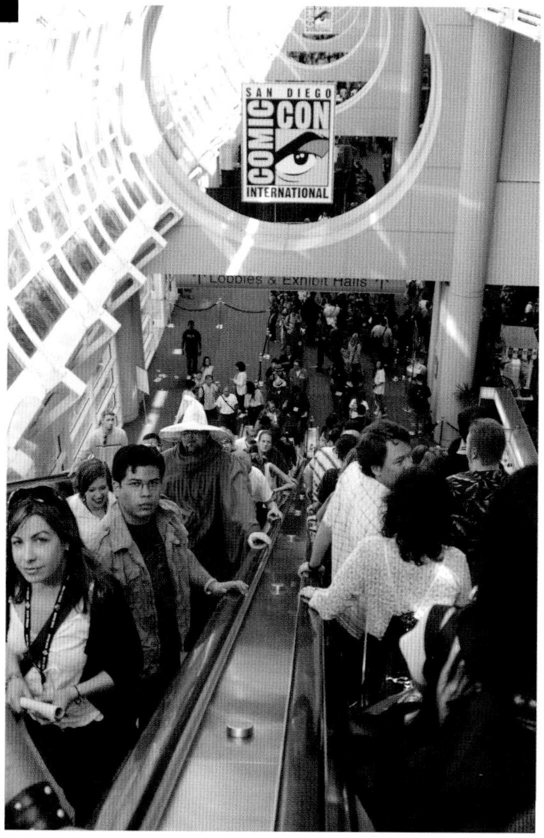
SAN DIEGO
COMIC CON
INTERNATIONAL

WHERE THE COOL KIDS ARE

Hall H became home to another area of growth in the new decade: Hollywood's increased interest. Of course, movie-oriented programming at the event goes back to the first Comic-Con in 1970. Comic-Con proved to be the launching pad for many popular films, especially those with their roots in comic books, such as the *X-Men* and *Spider-Man* films, *Iron Man*, *Superman Returns*, *Hellboy*, *Sin City*, *300*, *The Spirit*, and *Watchmen*, to name just a few. Most of these films were showcased in panels and events many months before they premiered in local movie theaters. One constant throughout the years: Lucasfilm and *Star Wars*. The studio has been part of Comic-Con since 1976, when Charlie Lippincott provided the first look at an unheard-of new film by director George Lucas. Since then, *Star Wars* has continued to capture the hearts and minds

LEFT: The crowd going to and from programs on the second level of the Convention Center of Comic-Con attendees in both programming and the giant Lucasfilm Pavilion in the Exhibit Hall.

In the new decade, television studios began to view Comic-Con as a "testing ground" for new shows. It started with the debut of *Lost* at Comic-Con in 2004, featuring stars Matthew Fox, Evangeline Lilly, and Dominic Monaghan. Panels for other shows followed, including *Heroes, Chuck, Reaper, Pushing Daisies, Battlestar Galactica*, and many more. The producers for shows such as *Lost* and *Heroes* view Comic-Con as the place they began and return year after year to the event for fan feedback. Animated shows such as *The Simpsons, Futurama, Family Guy, American Dad*, and many Nickelodeon and Cartoon Network programs—including the Adult Swim shows—are also a part of Comic-Con's programming, with voice actors, writers, producers, and directors showing clips, never-before-seen episodes and bonus features, and even doing live "table readings" of scripts.

All of this increased attention brought Comic-Con center stage in the entertainment industry and added intensive mainstream press coverage. Starting with such industry publications as the *Hollywood Reporter* and *Variety*, reporting quickly spread to mainstream magazines, including *Entertainment Weekly* and *TV Guide*. Newspaper coverage began on a national level with *USA Today*, the *New York Times*, and the *Los Angeles Times*, and wire service reports filtered down to local papers around the world. Television programs such as *Entertainment Tonight* covered the show and the online world reported and blogged about every aspect of Comic-Con. The secret was clearly out: Comics were cool and Comic-Con was *the* place to be to catch the cutting edge of what was hot and what was next.

Comic-Con relaunched its film festival during this decade. The new incarnation became the Comic-Con International Independent Film Festival (CCI-IFF). In 2002 the festival grew to cover all four days of the event and added the Comic-Con Film School, a series of panels featuring nuts-and-bolts information on how to make your own films, from getting started to postproduction and marketing. The CCI-IFF includes films in seven categories (action/adventure, animation, comics-oriented, pop-culture oriented documentary, horror/suspense, humor/parody, and science fiction/fantasy), and does not accept films that have distribution deals in place. One such film, *9*, written and directed by Shane Acker (winner of a CCI-IFF award), went on to an Academy Award nomination for Best Animated Short Film and a big-budget movie produced by Tim Burton. The festival became a juried event in 2005, with trophies and prizes given to the films deemed best by the judges in all seven categories, plus an additional "Judges' Choice" award to the film considered the best in the festival. Past judges include Mark Altman (*CFQ Magazine*), Amber Benson (*Buffy the Vampire Slayer*), Max Allan Collins (*Road to Perdition*), Tom DeSanto (*Transformers*), Chris Gore (*Film Threat*), Thomas Jane (*The Punisher*), Borys Kit (*The Hollywood Reporter*), Tom McLean (*Variety*), Sean Rourke (visual effects artist), and Scott Zakarin (*Comic Book: The Movie*). The festival has become a popular stand-alone event at Comic-Con.

BACK TO THE FUTURE

In the 2000s, Comic-Con continues to do what it does best: present the entire world of comics to its attendees and, by extension, the rest of the world. All the major comics publishers come to the show and participate in both the giant Exhibit Hall and programming. But Comic-Con also focuses on other areas of the medium, inviting numerous guests from the indie and alternative comic scene and international comics creators, including manga artists. Comic-Con aims the spotlight on Webcomics, editorial cartooning, the Golden and Silver Ages of comics, art comics, and syndicated newspaper strips. In this "brave new world" of popularity, Comic-Con continues its mission of creating awareness of and appreciation for comics and related popular arts to an ever-widening audience, one that is more eager and receptive than ever before.

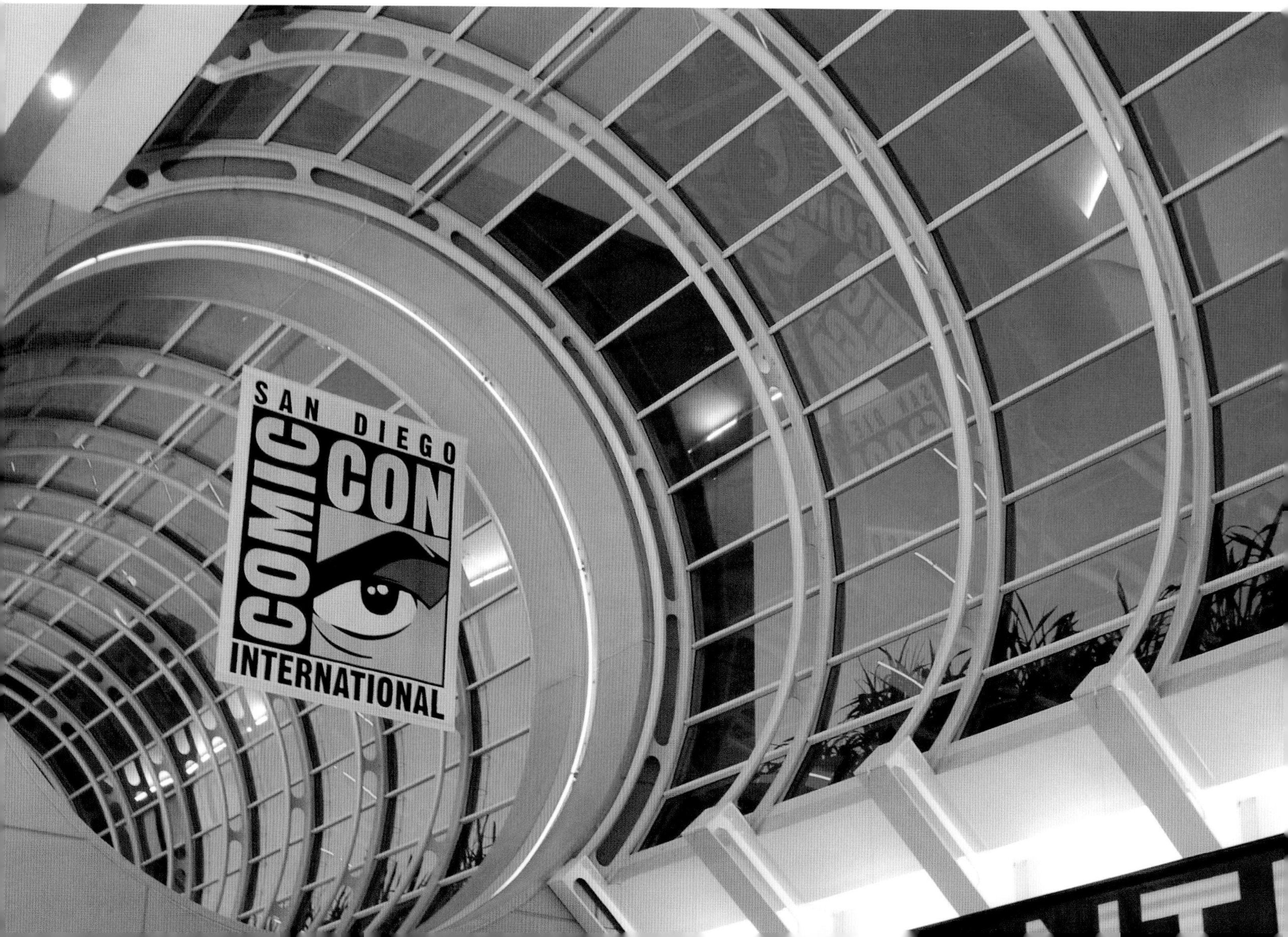
SAN DIEGO
COMIC
CON
INTERNATIONAL

WILL EISNER SPIRIT OF COMICS RETAILER AWARD

Comic Relief
PLEASE
LEAVE
ALL BAGS AT
THE
FRONT
COUNTER
THANKS!!
PAPRIKA

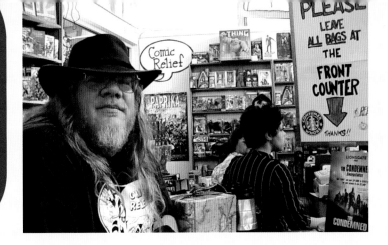

In the mid-1990s, visionary comics creator Will Eisner (*The Spirit, Contract with God*) approached Comic-Con about creating a new award. He wanted to acknowledge and celebrate the incredible contribution retailers make to the comic book industry by providing the crucial link between creator and reader in getting comics into the hands of the public. The resulting award was named in his honor: the Will Eisner Spirit of Comics Retailer Award.

Starting in 1993 with the first recipients—Moondog's of Chicago, The Beguiling of Toronto, and Comic Relief of Berkeley and San Francisco—the award has been given to comics stores and retailers around the globe, including Canada, Holland, Australia, and across the United States. It is given to individual retailers who have done an outstanding job of supporting the comics art medium both in the community and within the industry at large.

SAN DIEGO
COMIC CON

The criteria include:

- **SUPPORT OF A WIDE VARIETY OF INNOVATIVE MATERIAL**
  Providing opportunities for creators' material to reach buyers and stocking a diverse inventory.
- **KNOWLEDGE**
  Working to stay informed on retailing as well as on the comics field
- **COMMUNITY ACTIVITY**
  Promoting comics to the community, including maintaining relationships with schools and libraries and keeping active in social, business, and arts community organizations
- **QUALITY OF STORE IMAGE**
  Utilizing innovative display approaches and store design creatively
- **ADHERENCE TO STANDARD ETHICAL BUSINESS PRACTICES**

Eisner's vision of recognizing that the comics retailer is the direct link between creator and public—and an extremely important factor in how writers and artists connect to their fans—continues to this day. For more than fifteen years, a panel of industry judges including creative professionals, retailers, and comics company luminaries has selected what many regard as the finest comics shops in the world. The award was originally bestowed during a ceremony at Comic Book Expo; it is now presented each year as part of the Will Eisner Comic Industry Awards in a gala ceremony at Comic-Con International.

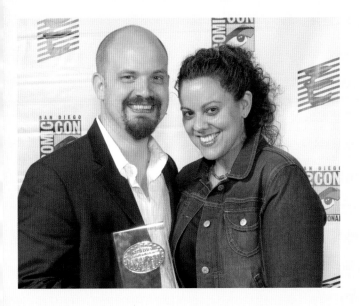

OPPOSITE: The San Diego Convention Center at dusk
ABOVE: The late Rory Root in his Berkeley, California, store, Comic Relief. Rory was one of the first Spirit Award recipients in 1993.
LEFT: Atom! and Portlyn Freeman, of Brave New World Comics in Newhall, California, the 2008 recipients

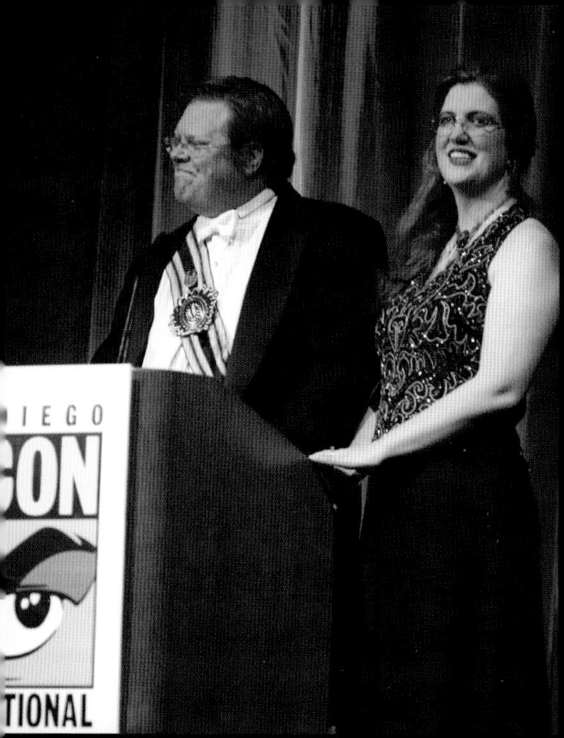
CON

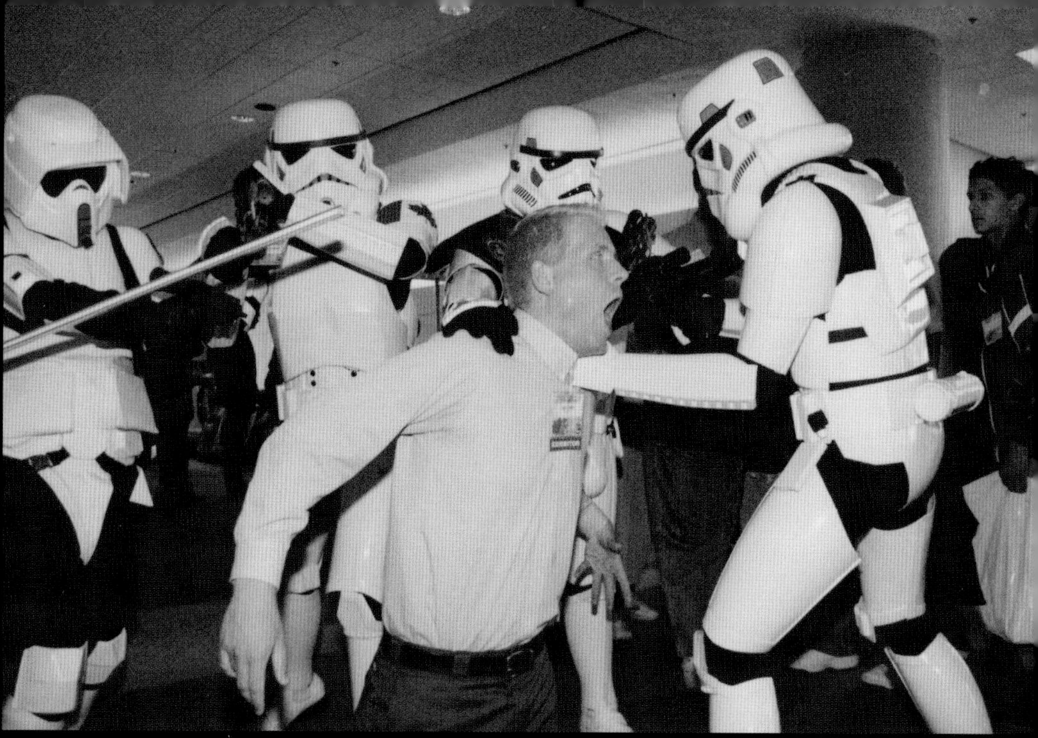

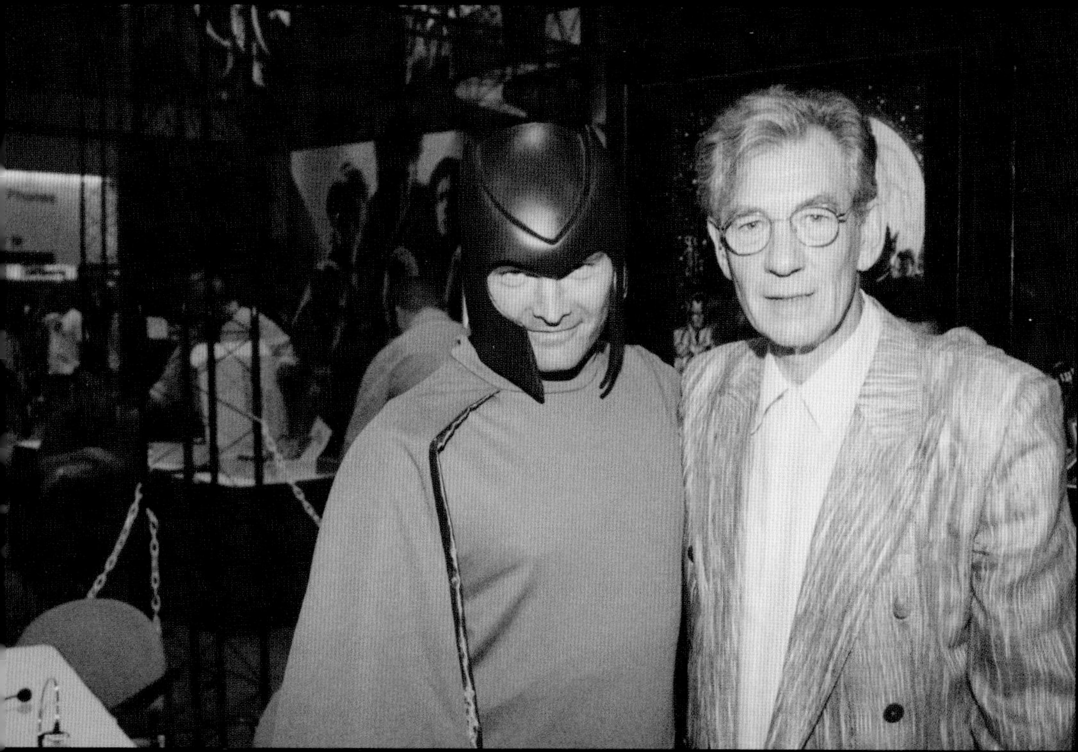

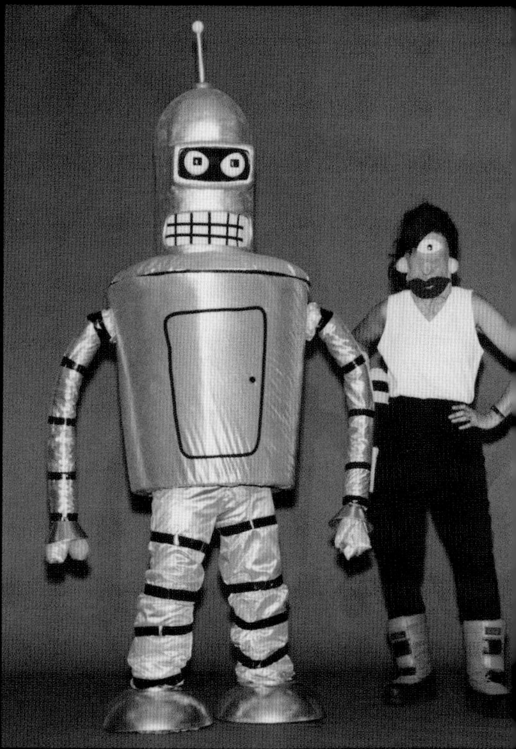

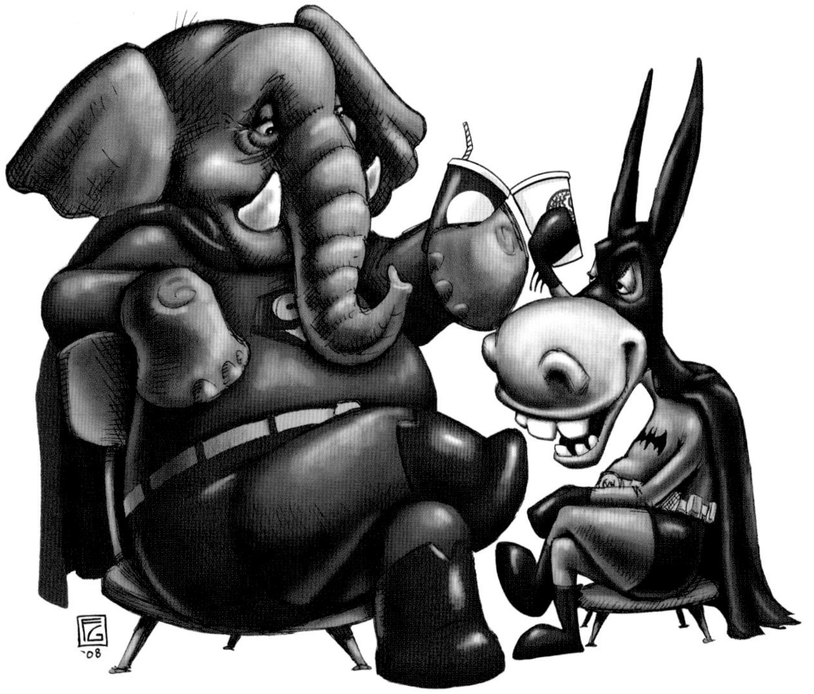
'08

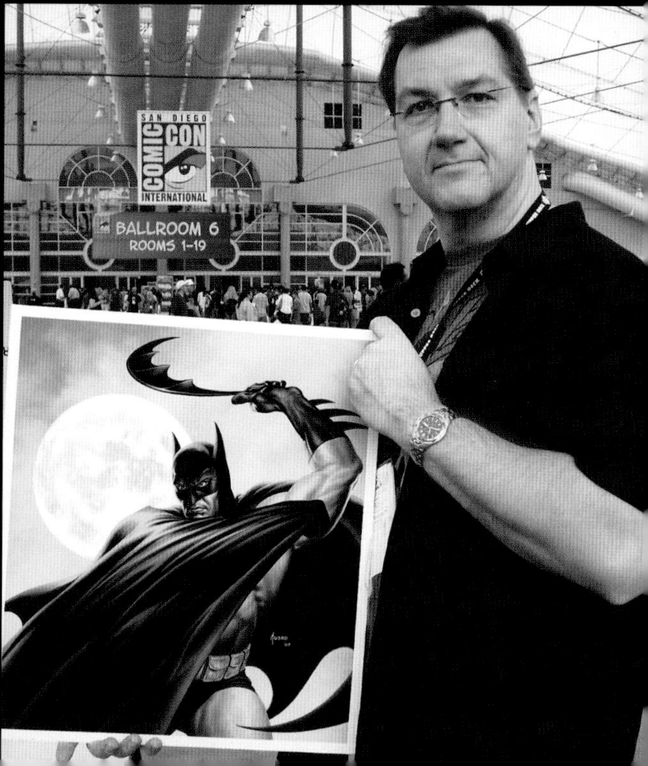
SAN DIEGO
COMIC CON
INTERNATIONAL
BALLROOM 6
ROOMS 1-19

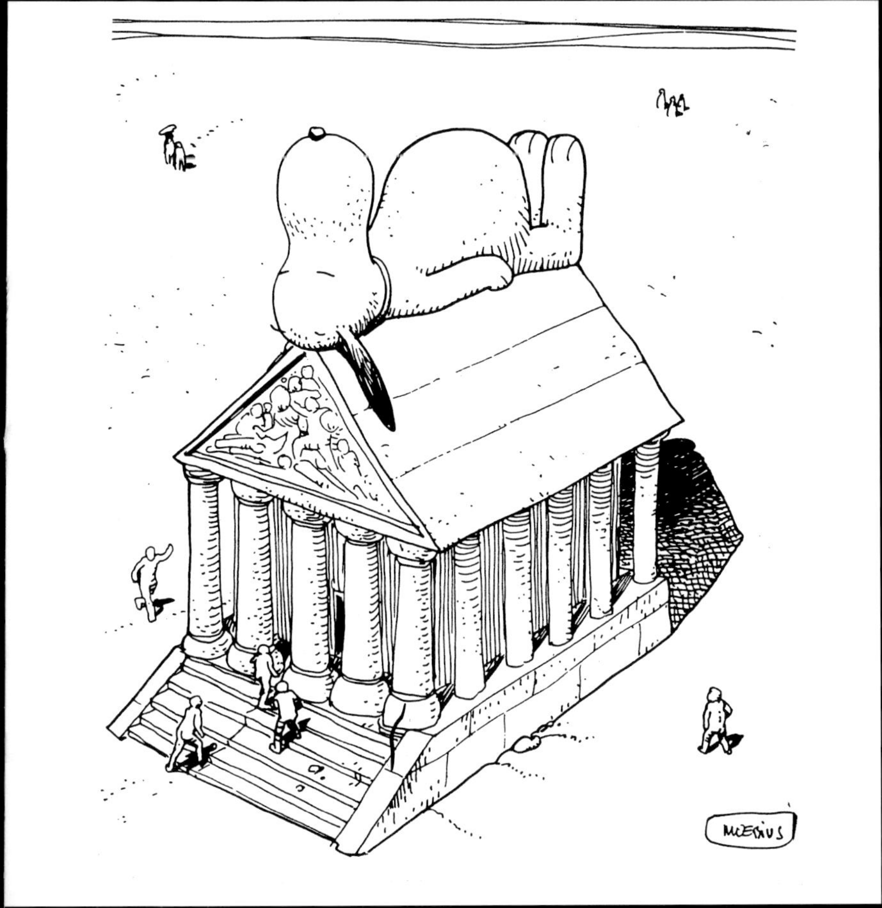
MŒBIUS

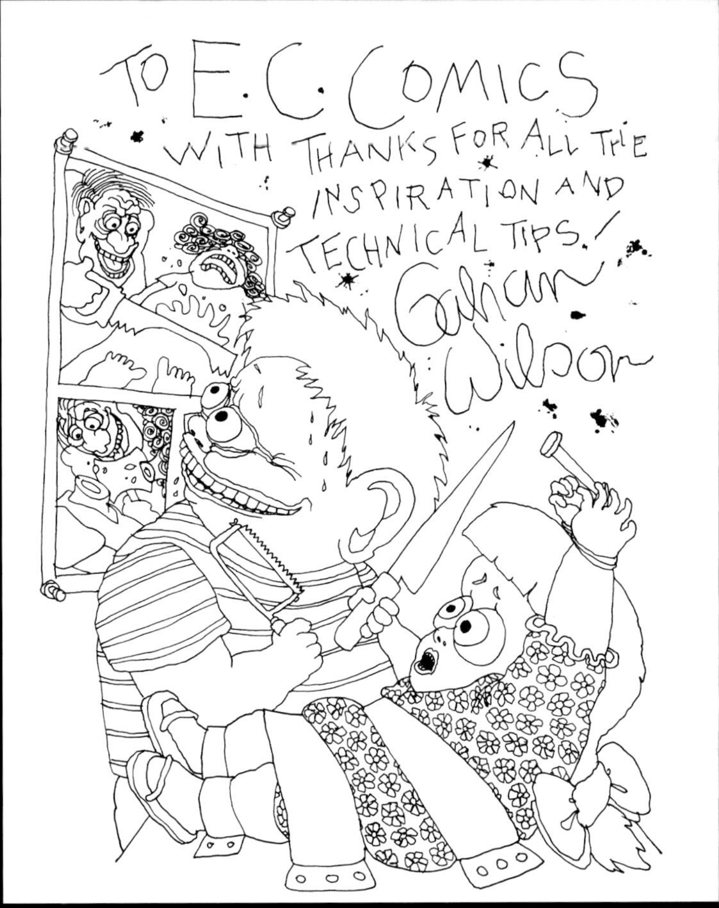
TO E.C. COMICS
WITH THANKS FOR ALL THE INSPIRATION AND TECHNICAL TIPS!
Gahan Wilson

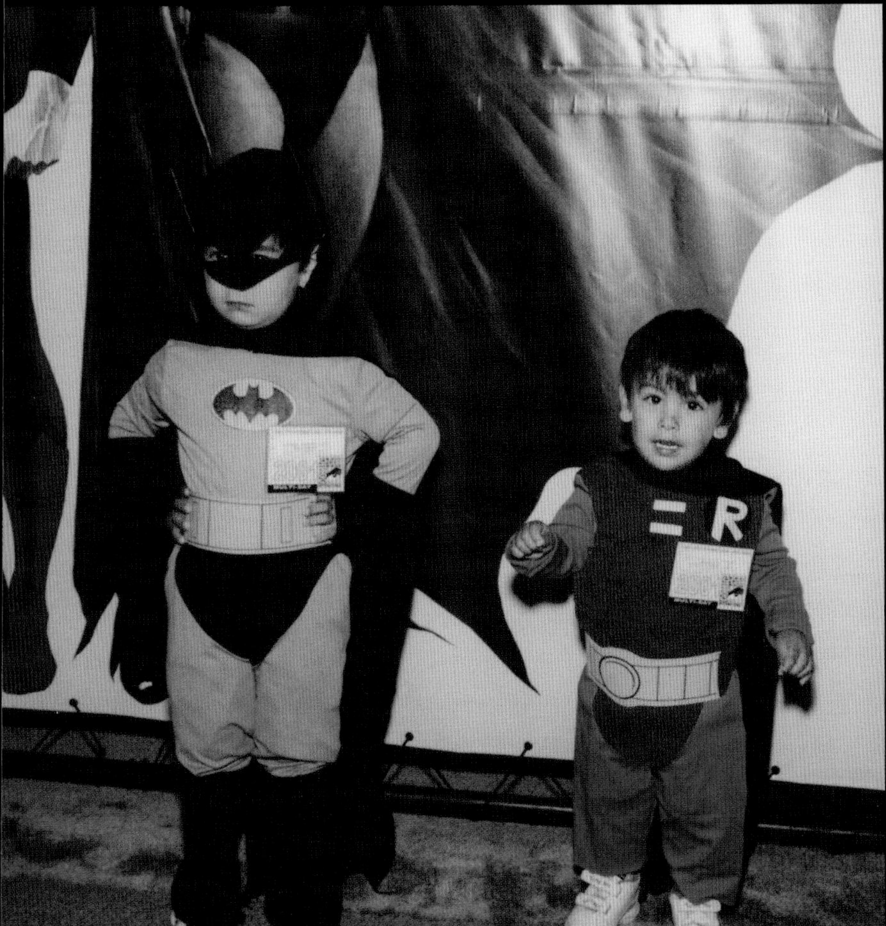

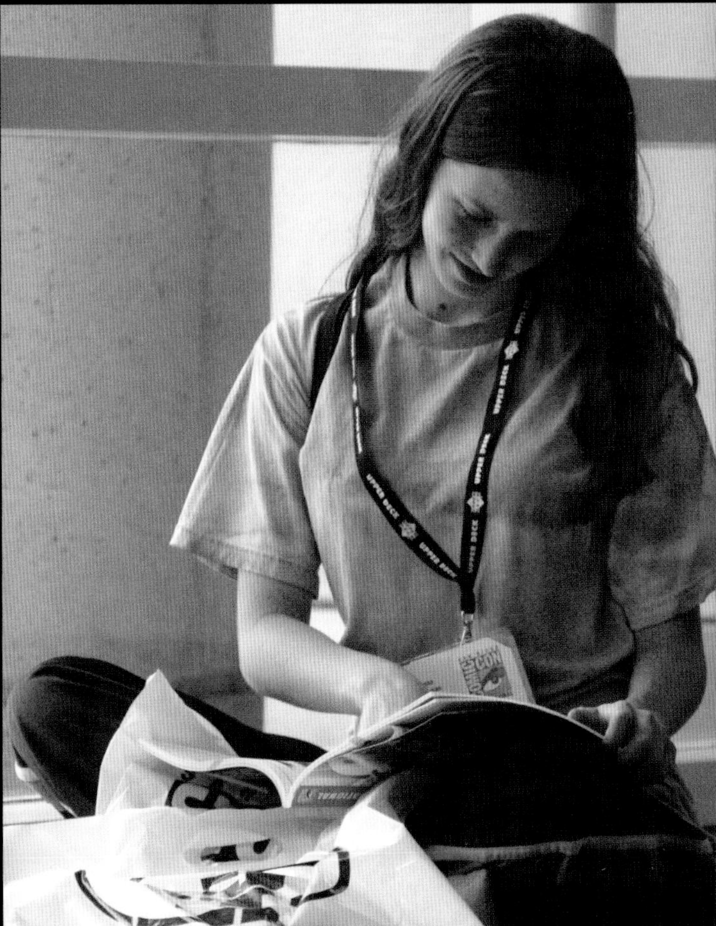

OPPOSITE, CLOCKWISE FROM TOP LEFT: Perennial Masquerade masters of ceremonies Phil and Kaja Foglio start the show in 2008; the Storm Troopers are normally really very nice; *Futurama* entry in the 2000 Masquerade; artist Joe Jusko with his Batman painting for Comic-Con's Art Auction; art by Frank Grau for the cover of the 2008—election year—edition of the Comic-Con Events Guide; Sir Ian McKellen (right) with Magneto (left) in 2000, just a few days after *X-Men* was released **CLOCKWISE FROM TOP LEFT:** Moebius's tribute to the timelessness of *Peanuts* in 2000, the strip's fiftieth anniversary and the year creator Charles M. Schulz died; Gahan Wilson's thank-you to EC Comics in a 2000 tribute to the comics company's fiftieth; two familiar sights at Comic-Con: people reading everywhere and kids in costumes

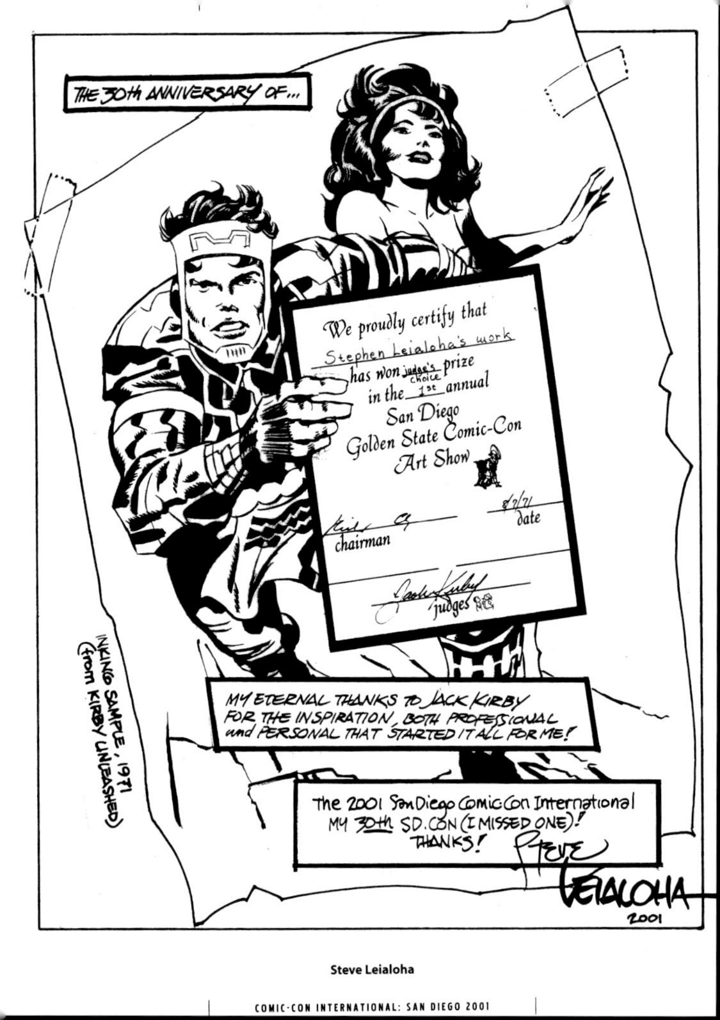
THE 30th ANNIVERSARY OF...
We proudly certify that
Stephen Leialoha's work
has won judge's choice prize
in the 1st annual
San Diego
Golden State Comic-Con
Art Show
chairman
date
judges
MY ETERNAL THANKS TO JACK KIRBY FOR THE INSPIRATION, BOTH PROFESSIONAL and PERSONAL THAT STARTED IT ALL FOR ME!
The 2001 San Diego Comic-Con International
MY 30th SD.CON (I MISSED ONE)!
THANKS! STEVE LEIALOHA 2001
INKING SAMPLE, 1971 (from KIRBY UNLEASHED)
Steve Leialoha
COMIC-CON INTERNATIONAL: SAN DIEGO 2001

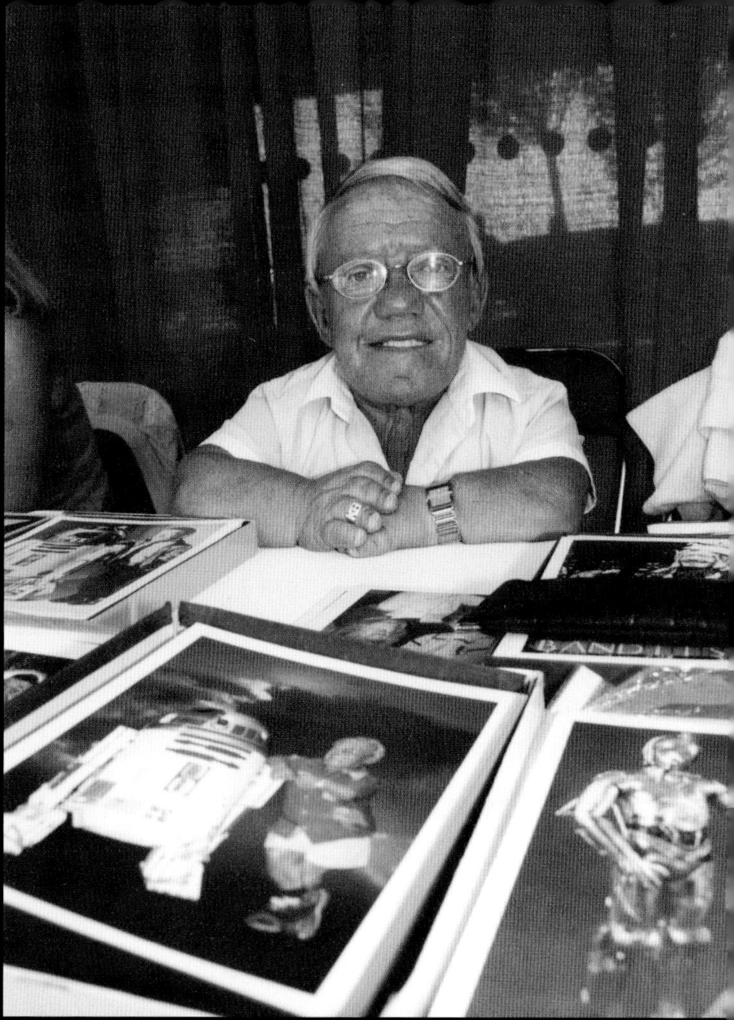

CLOCKWISE FROM ABOVE LEFT: Steve Leialoha's 2001 look back at his 1971 prizewinning entry in a Jack Kirby–judged art contest; R2-D2 actor Kenny Baker in Comic-Con's Autograph Area in 2001; artist Jill Thompson sketching in 2001; Green Lantern and Aquaman teaming up with the Atom for a 2001 Masquerade entry

OPPOSITE, TOP TO BOTTOM: Mark Evanier (left) interviewing legendary comics artists Nick Cardy (center) and Gene Colan (right) at WonderCon in 2007; Evanier (left) with Bill Finger Award–winner Larry Lieber (center) and award founder Jerry Robinson (right) in 2008; Evanier with Marv Wolfman at Comic-Con in the early 1970s; Evanier in 1983

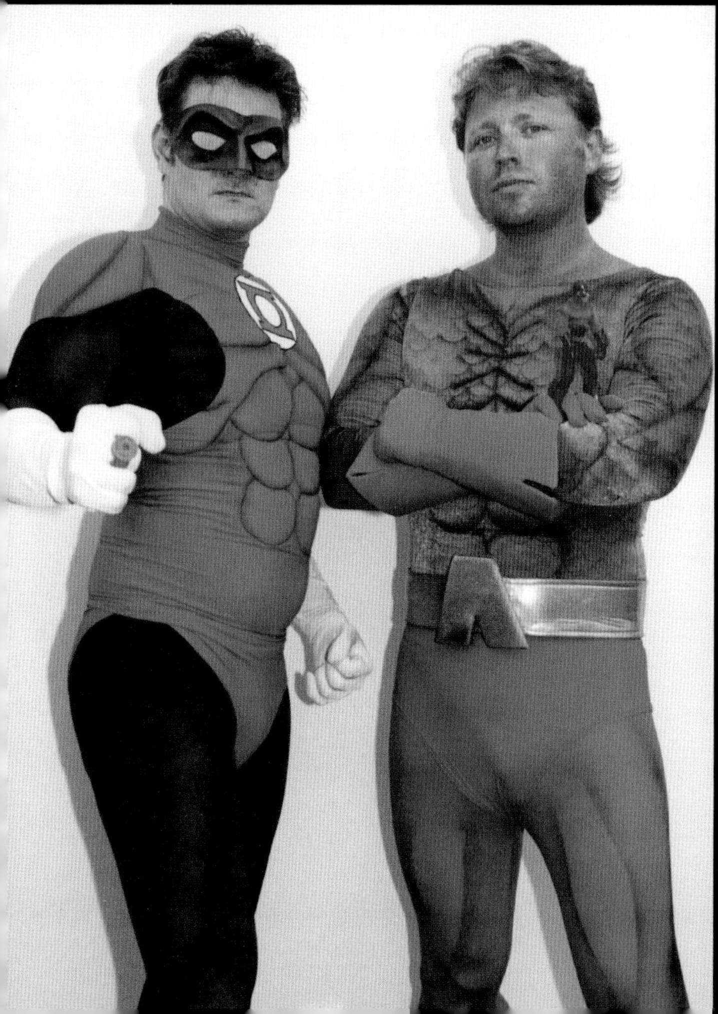

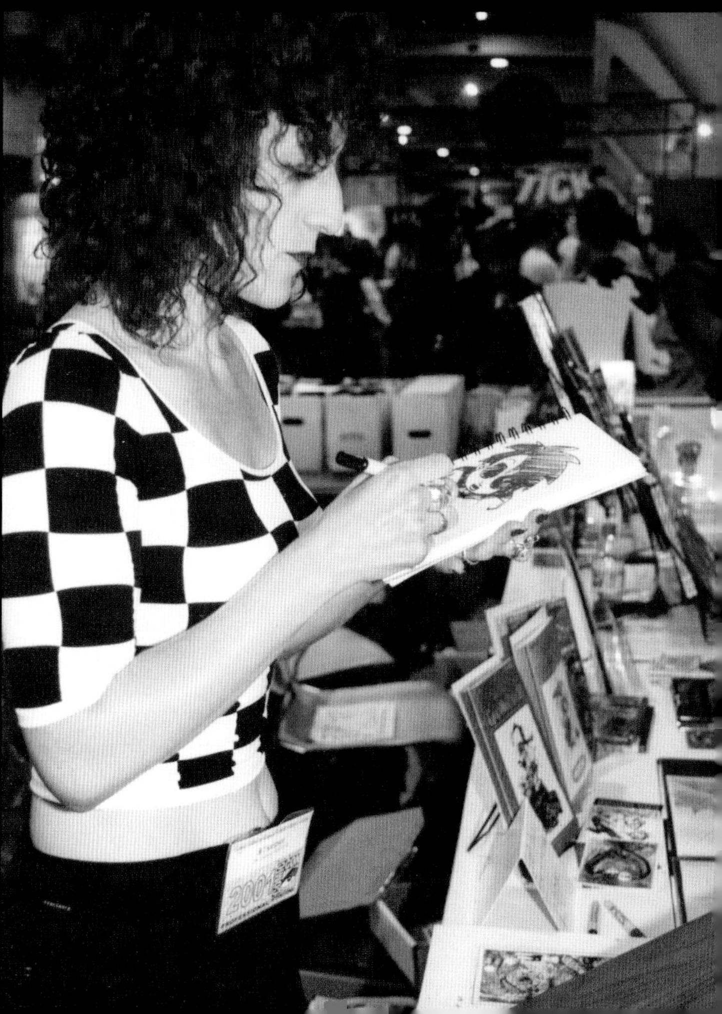

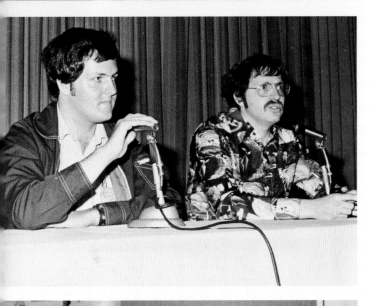

MARK EVANIER

THE MAN partially known for hosting more panels at any given Comic-Con than was thought humanly possible is also a gifted writer of comics, television, and animation.

Mark Evanier, born in 1952, grew up seeing his father work at a job he hated; as a result, Mark decided to have a career doing something he loved: writing. He sold his first professional work to magazines in 1969. A week later he met Jack Kirby and soon after became one of his assistants. Kirby remained a mentor and close friend until his death in 1994. In 2008 Evanier authored a major art book about the life and career of his friend, *Kirby: King of Comics*.

Evanier has written for many comics companies and publications, including his longtime collaboration with Sergio Aragonés. Their best-known work together is *Groo the Wanderer*, the ongoing tale of a dim-witted barbarian and his adventures, which has been published continuously for more than twenty-five years. Evanier has also written for animation and television, including such shows as *Garfield and Friends*; *Scooby Doo, Where Are You!*; *Superman: The Animated Series*; and *Welcome Back, Kotter*, among others. He's also one of the first bloggers to emerge from the comic industry, writing daily entries on www.newsfromme.com.

By his own admission, he has attended at least one day of every Comic-Con over the past thirty-nine years and was present for all four days during most of them. Evanier started his panel-moderating chores in year two or three of Comic-Con by presiding over a writers' panel. Since 2000 his hosting duties have taken off, and Evanier regularly moderates a number of panels at the show, including "Golden and Silver Age of Comics," the "Jack Kirby Tribute," "Cartoon Voices," and the popular "Quick Draw" event, in which artists Sergio Aragonés, Scott Shaw!, and a different third cartoonist each year are put through their paces by the host, who throws out topics for them to draw as quickly as they can. Evanier has also hosted numerous panels at Comic-Con's sister show, WonderCon, in San Francisco, and at other conventions around the country.

Evanier is the recipient of three Eisner Awards. In 2001 he was given the Bob Clampett Humanitarian Award for his work in mentoring talent and helping comics creators. In 2005 he became the chair of the Bill Finger Award for Excellence in Comic Book Writing. Named for the unheralded co-creator of such seminal comics characters as Batman and Green Lantern, the award was started by Finger's friend and colleague Jerry Robinson. It is given out each year at Comic-Con to two writers, one living and one deceased. When Evanier isn't writing, blogging, or moderating panels, he continues to work on a more in-depth biography of Jack Kirby.

> **In 1998 a fan named Richard Morrissey raised the money to bring veteran DC writer John Broome to his first and only appearance at any comic convention. I interviewed Broome on a panel in a room that was not only packed, but packed with other professional comic book writers. They'd all come to learn from the master.**
>
> **—MARK EVANIER**
> **COMICS, ANIMATION, AND TELEVISION WRITER,**
> ***GROO THE WANDERER*, *CROSSFIRE***
> **(On his most memorable Comic-Con moment)**

WONDERCON

Comic-Con's sister show, WonderCon, was started in 1987 in Oakland, California, as "The Wonderful World of Comics Convention." The brainchild of Bay Area comics retailer John Barrett, the show was to shed light on the local comics community. Barrett called on a number of friends and associates to help realize his vision, including Bob Borden, Bryan Uhlenbrock, Rory Root, and Mike Friedrich, all founders of the event. With the third year, "WonderCon" became the official name of the convention. The original show included all the classic comic convention features: an Exhibit Hall with dealers selling old and new comics and other items, programming, anime screenings, and gaming. In 2001, after the fifteenth event, then co-owners Mike Friedrich and Joe Field (another prominent Bay Area comics retailer) decided to sell the show.

Realizing that WonderCon is not only an important event on the comic convention calendar, but also right in line with Comic-Con's mission statement— "to create awareness of and appreciation for comics and related popular arts"— Comic-Con International was offered the reins in 2002. The show stayed at the Oakland Convention Center for that first year, but the size constraints of that venue limited the event's growth. In 2003 WonderCon moved across the bay to Moscone Center, in the heart of San Francisco.

WonderCon's reputation for being a fan-friendly event continued. A more intimate setting than Comic-Con allowed fans greater access to some of the most popular creators in comics. Guests since 2002 have included such comic book superstars as Neal Adams, Sergio Aragonés, Brian Azzarello, Darwyn Cooke, Mark Evanier, Dave Gibbons, Adam Hughes, Joe Kubert, Mike Mignola, Frank Miller, Grant Morrison, John Romita and John Romita Jr., Alex Ross, Gail Simone, Jeff Smith, Kevin Smith, J. Michael Straczynski, Jim Steranko, Jill Thompson, Bruce Timm, and Matt Wagner.

WonderCon, now in its larger Moscone Center headquarters, has added more programs and events over the years. In addition to a complete slate of comics-oriented programming, including some of the best-known writers, artists, and companies in the industry, WonderCon attendees have seen major movie and television panels. Presentations have been devoted to *Batman Begins* (with Christian Bale in a rare convention appearance), *Spider-Man 2* (with star Tobey Maguire), *300* (with director Zack Snyder and stars Gerard Butler and Lena Headey), *The X-Files: I Want to Believe* (with stars David Duchovny and Gillian Anderson in their first-ever convention appearance together), and many more. The event also instituted a WonderCon Masquerade; this costume competition, featuring prizes and trophies for the winning entries as selected by a panel of judges, has grown each year to become a popular Saturday night event.

Not unlike Comic-Con, WonderCon is a fun, fan-oriented show held in the heart of one of the country's most beautiful and vibrant cities. For more than two decades it has carved out a niche not only as a comic convention but also as a Bay Area institution.

ABOVE: Darwyn Cooke (left) and Bruce Timm (right) talking about *Justice League: The New Frontier* at the world premiere of the animated film at WonderCon 2008 **OPPOSITE, TOP ROW, FROM LEFT:** Sergio Aragonés sketching for a young fan at WonderCon 2008; writer/artist Matt Wagner in 2007; writer Grant Morrison in 2006 **MIDDLE ROW, FROM LEFT:** Steve Carell and Anne Hathaway promoting *Get Smart* in 2008; the cover of the 2008 program book by Darwyn Cooke; Masquerade entry from 2008 **BOTTOM ROW, FROM LEFT:** The packed Exhibit Hall in 2007; winning Masquerade entry from 2007 featuring *Star Wars*/LEGO figures

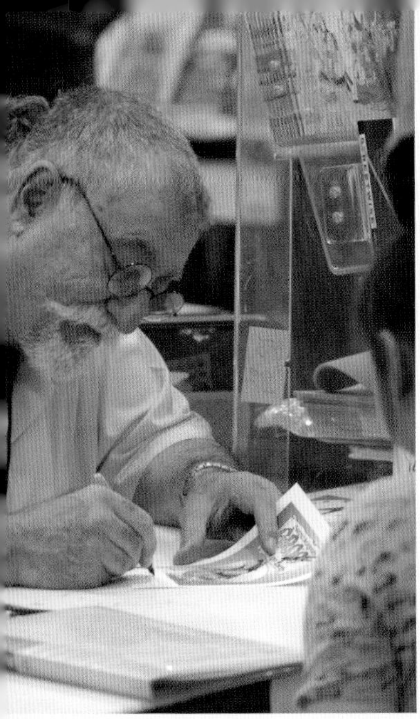

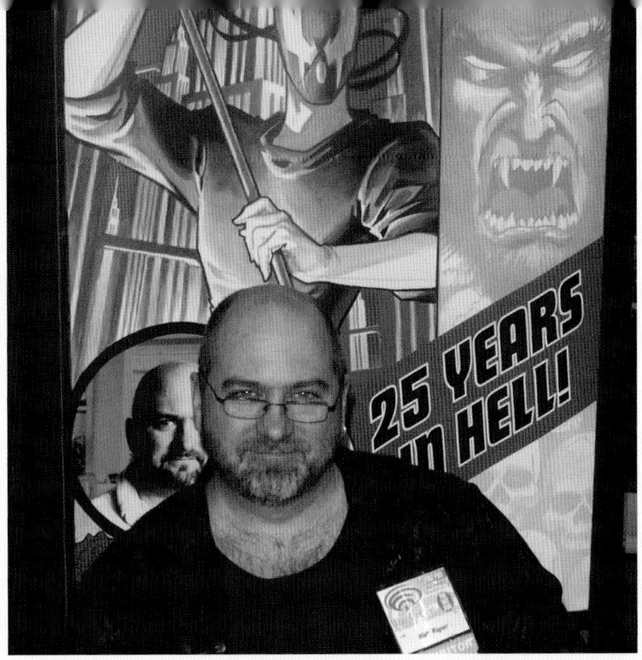
25 YEARS IN HELL!

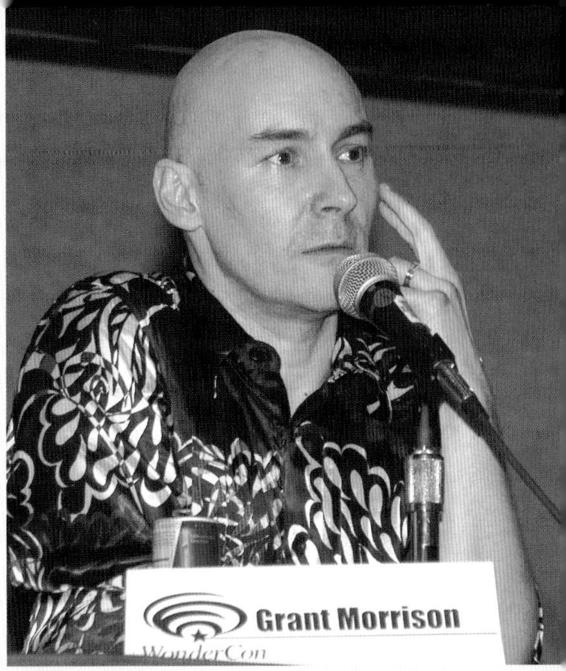
Grant Morrison
WonderCon

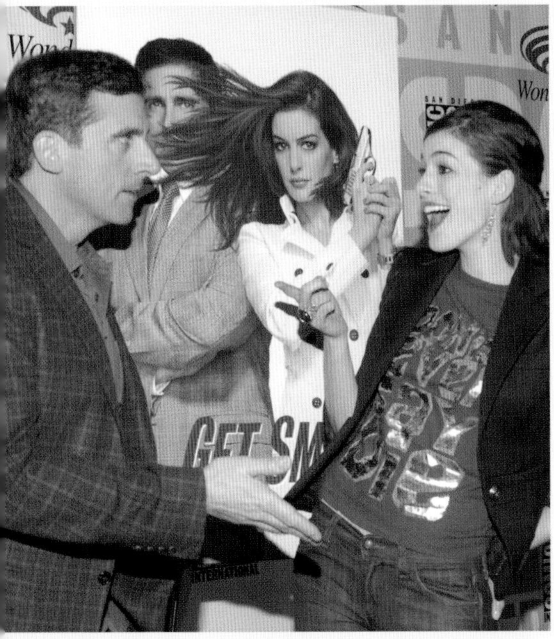

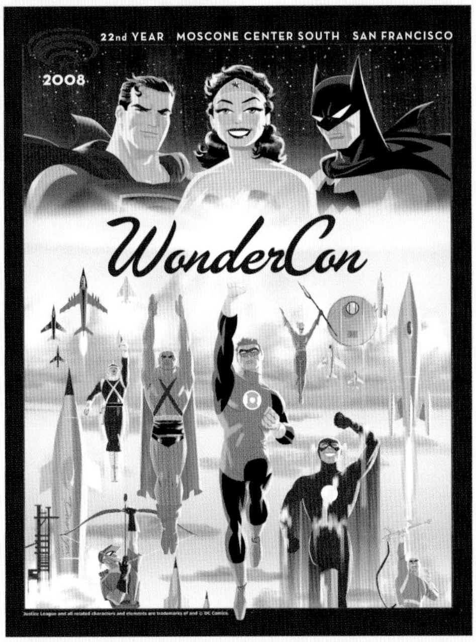
22nd YEAR MOSCONE CENTER SOUTH SAN FRANCISCO
2008
WonderCon

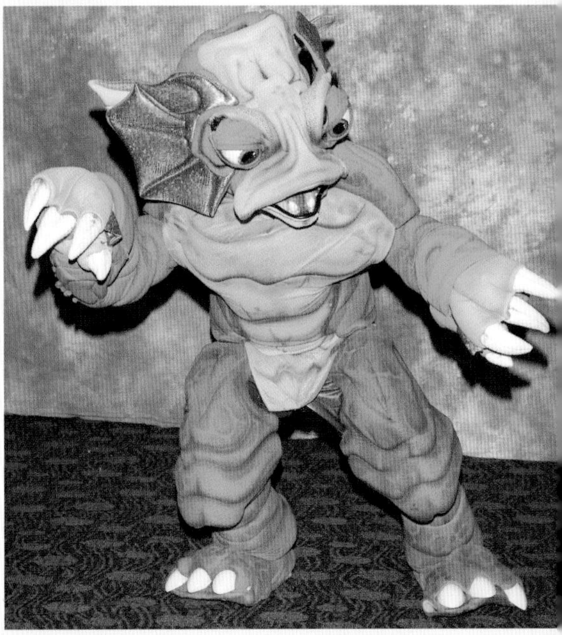

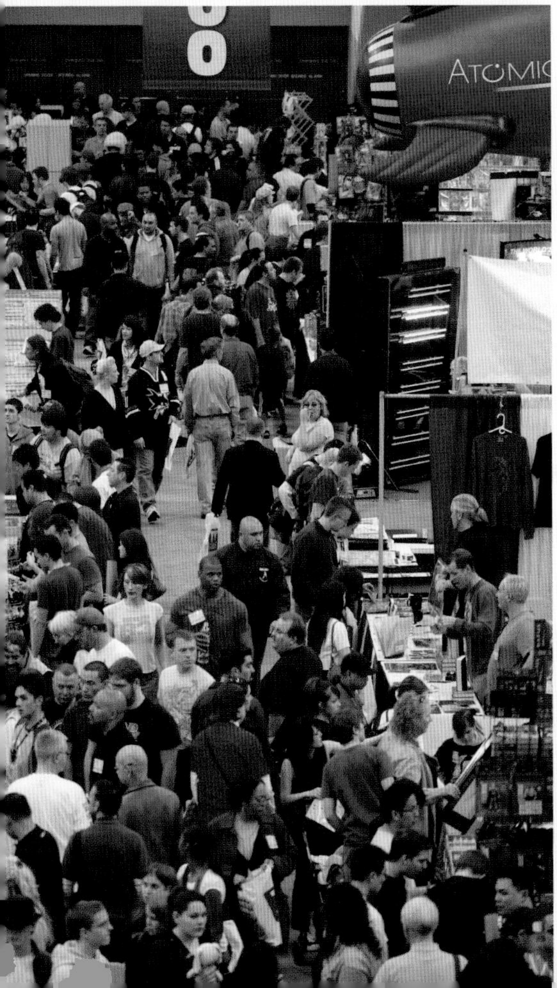

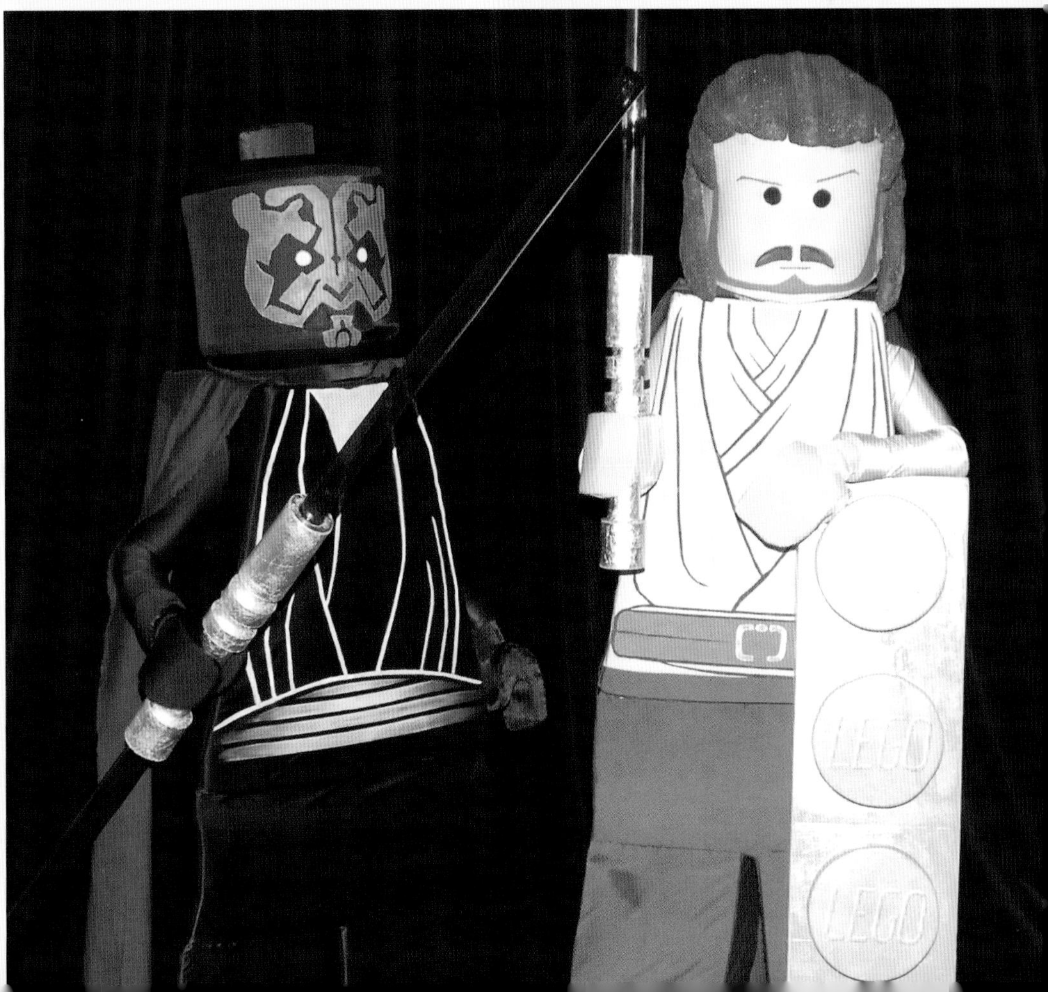
LEGO
LEGO

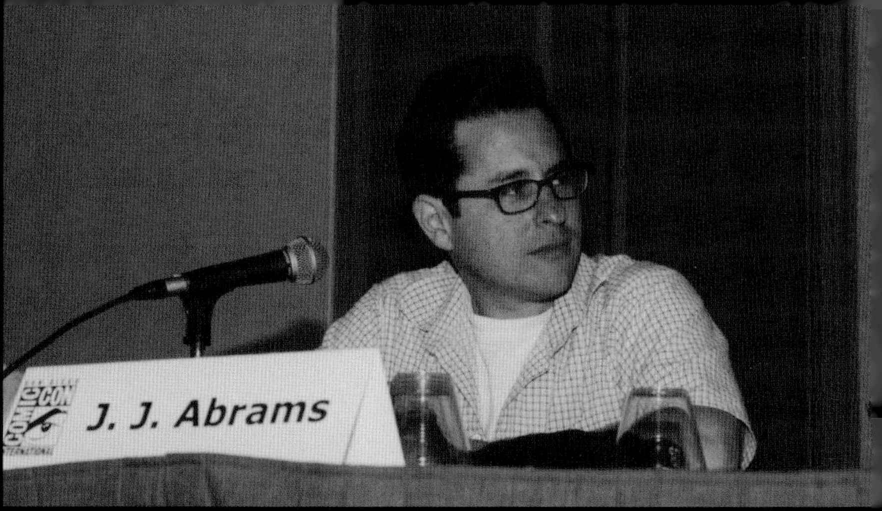
J. J. Abrams

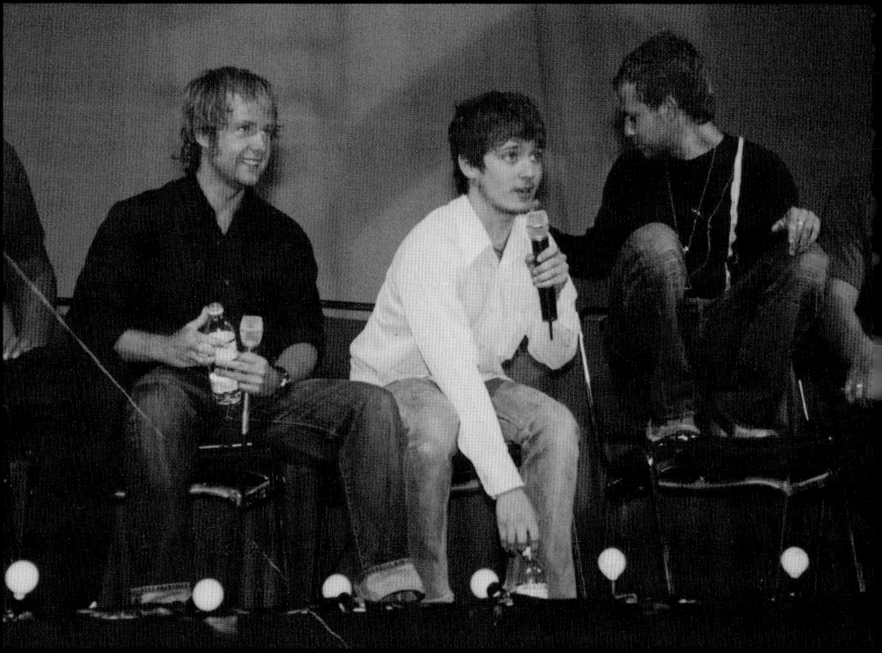

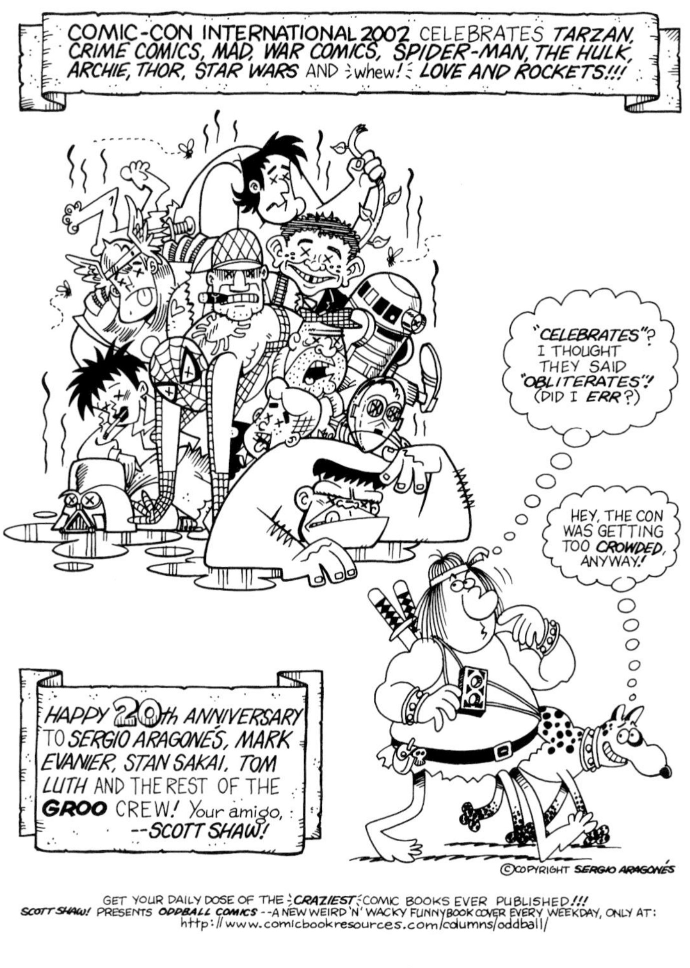
COMIC-CON INTERNATIONAL 2002 CELEBRATES TARZAN, CRIME COMICS, MAD, WAR COMICS, SPIDER-MAN, THE HULK, ARCHIE, THOR, STAR WARS AND whew! LOVE AND ROCKETS!!!
"CELEBRATES"? I THOUGHT THEY SAID "OBLITERATES"! (DID I ERR?)
HEY, THE CON WAS GETTING TOO CROWDED, ANYWAY!
HAPPY 20th ANNIVERSARY TO SERGIO ARAGONÉS, MARK EVANIER, STAN SAKAI, TOM LUTH AND THE REST OF THE GROO CREW! Your amigo, --SCOTT SHAW!
©COPYRIGHT SERGIO ARAGONÉS
GET YOUR DAILY DOSE OF THE CRAZIEST COMIC BOOKS EVER PUBLISHED!!!
SCOTT SHAW! PRESENTS ODDBALL COMICS --A NEW WEIRD 'N' WACKY FUNNYBOOK COVER EVERY WEEKDAY, ONLY AT:
http://www.comicbookresources.com/columns/oddball/

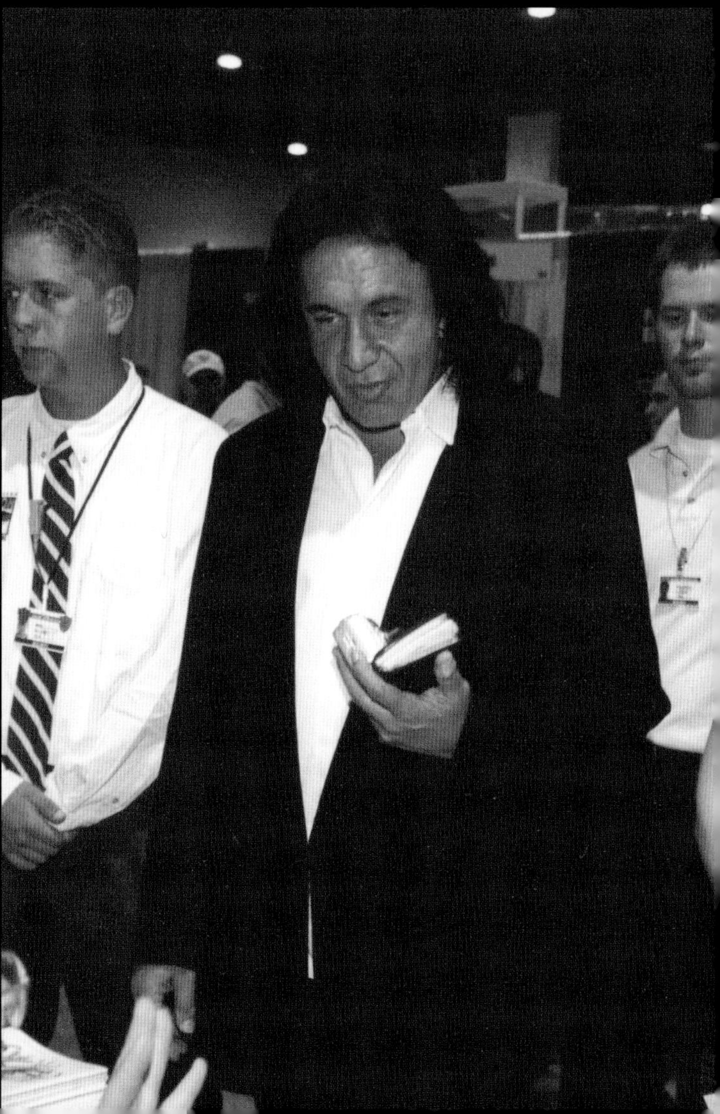

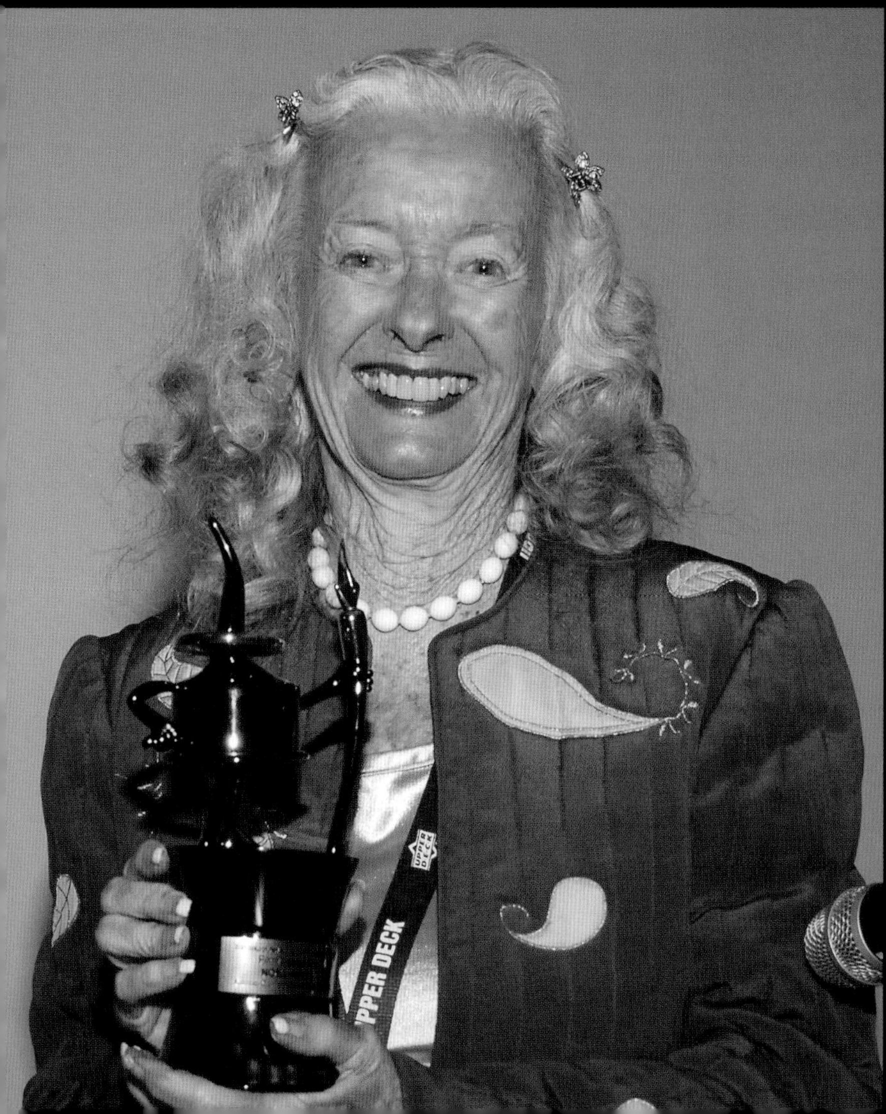
UPPER DECK

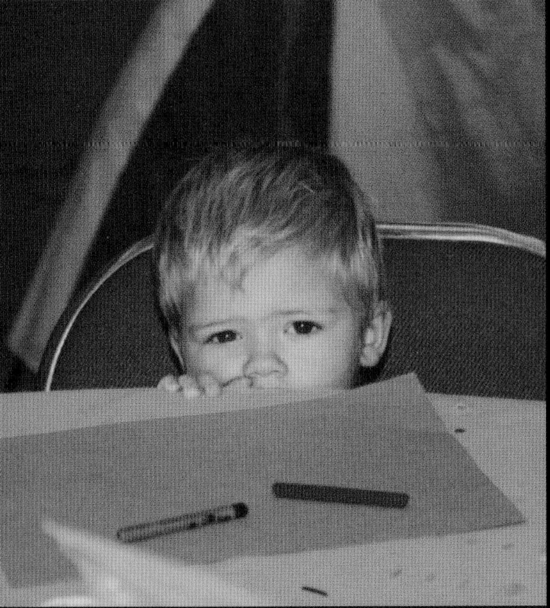

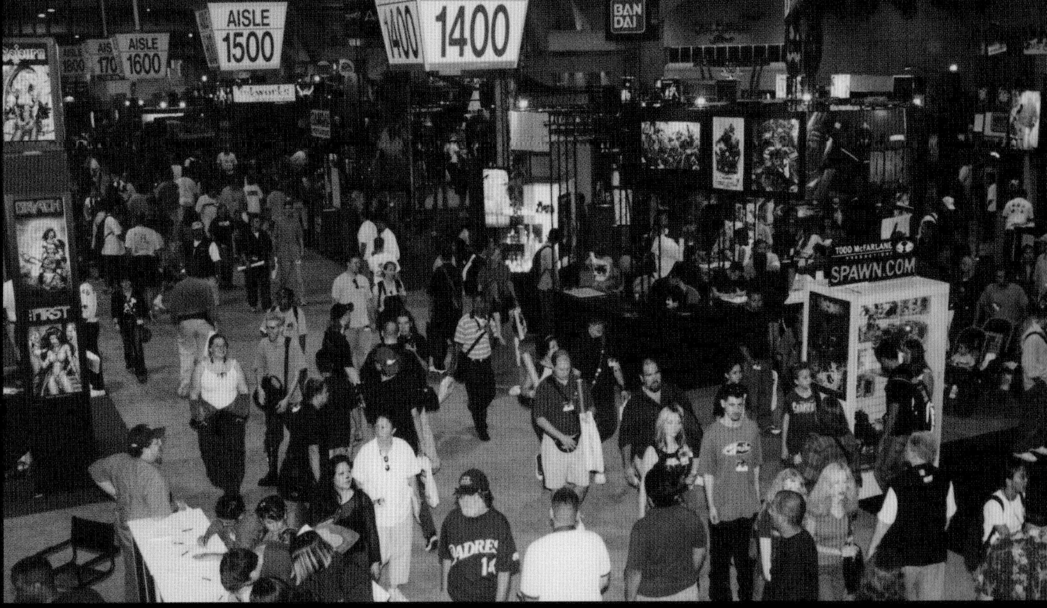
AISLE
1500
1400
AISLE
1600
BAN
DAI
SPAWN.COM

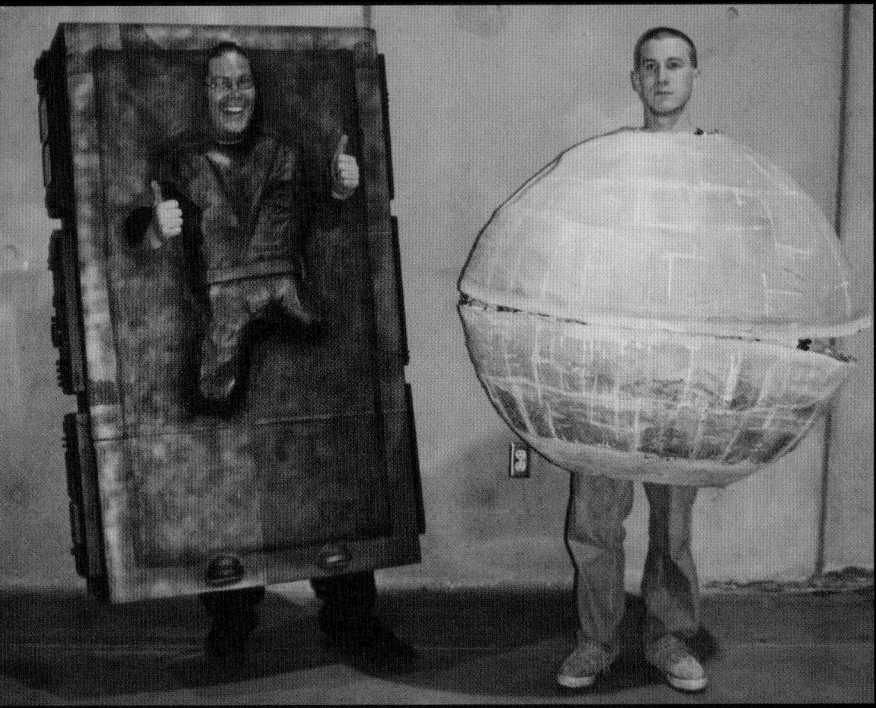

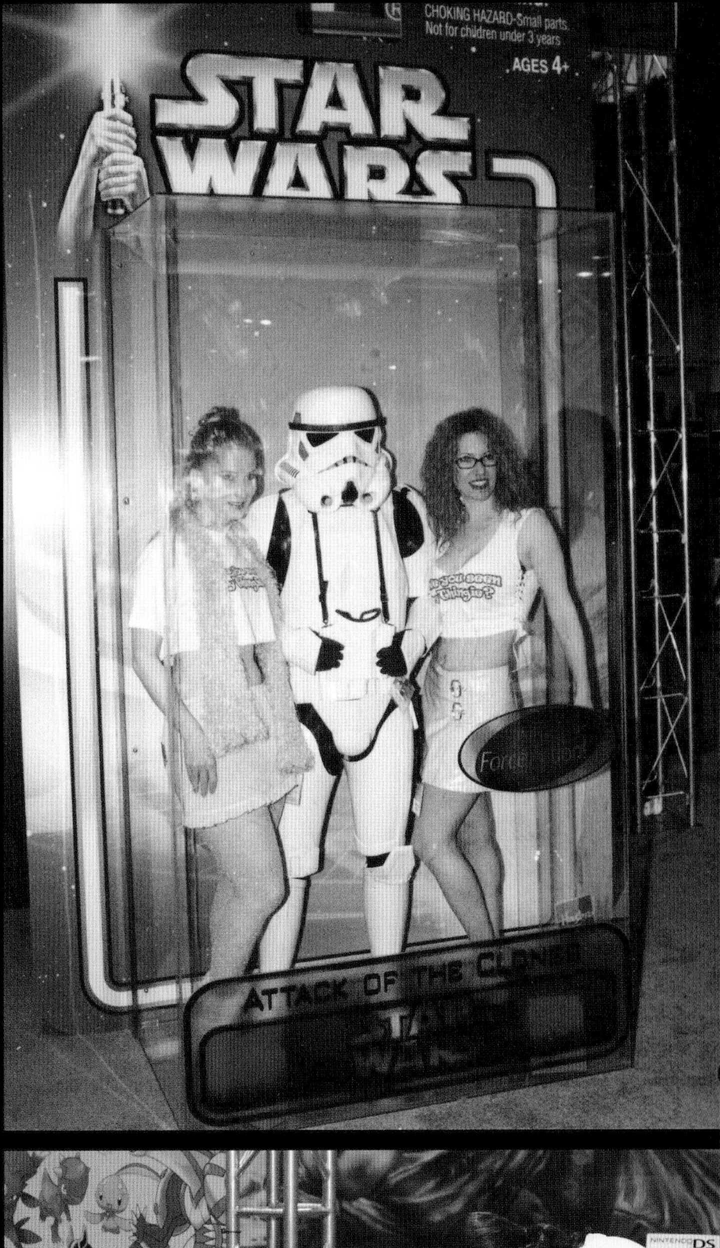
CHOKING HAZARD-Small parts.
Not for children under 3 years
AGES 4+
STAR
WARS
ATTACK OF THE CLONES

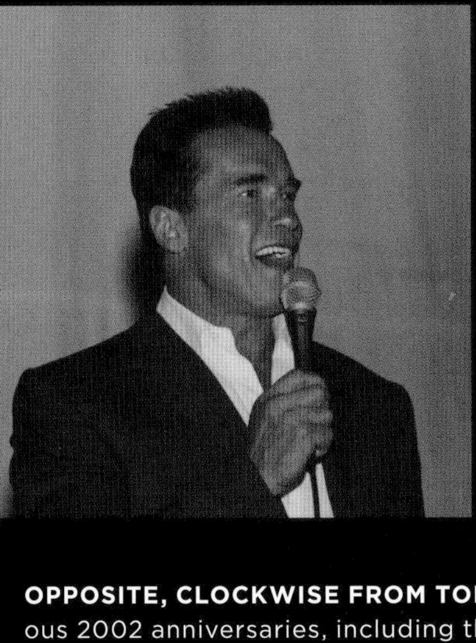

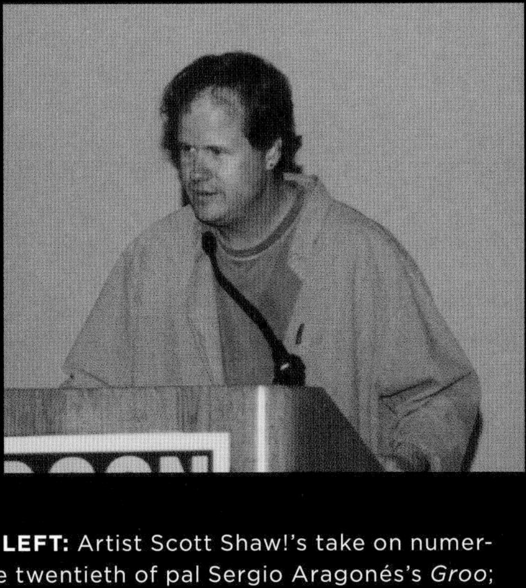

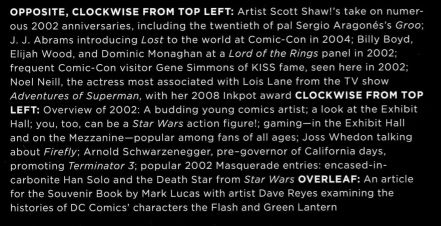

OPPOSITE, CLOCKWISE FROM TOP LEFT: Artist Scott Shaw!'s take on numerous 2002 anniversaries, including the twentieth of pal Sergio Aragonés's *Groo*; J. J. Abrams introducing *Lost* to the world at Comic-Con in 2004; Billy Boyd, Elijah Wood, and Dominic Monaghan at a *Lord of the Rings* panel in 2002; frequent Comic-Con visitor Gene Simmons of KISS fame, seen here in 2002; Noel Neill, the actress most associated with Lois Lane from the TV show *Adventures of Superman*, with her 2008 Inkpot award **CLOCKWISE FROM TOP LEFT:** Overview of 2002: A budding young comics artist; a look at the Exhibit Hall; you, too, can be a *Star Wars* action figure!; gaming—in the Exhibit Hall and on the Mezzanine—popular among fans of all ages; Joss Whedon talking about *Firefly*; Arnold Schwarzenegger, pre-governor of California days, promoting *Terminator 3*; popular 2002 Masquerade entries: encased-in-carbonite Han Solo and the Death Star from *Star Wars* **OVERLEAF:** An article for the Souvenir Book by Mark Lucas with artist Dave Reyes examining the histories of DC Comics' characters the Flash and Green Lantern

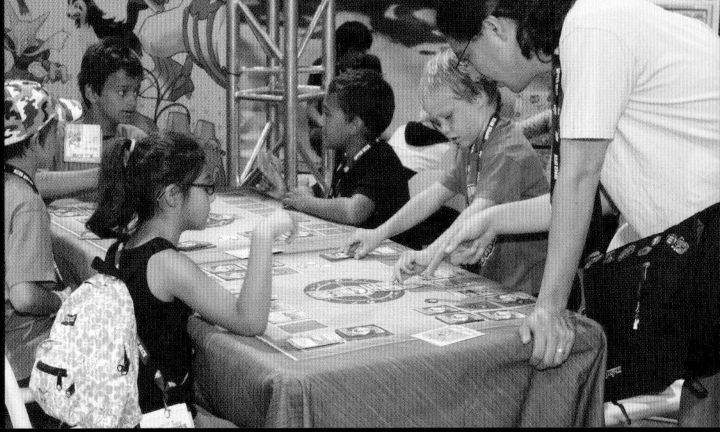

Sixty Years of Archetypes

HAPPY BIRTHDAY FLASH & GREEN LANTERN

BY MARK LUCAS

Sixty may seem like an old age to most comics fans. When we think of sixties, we may imagine grandfathers, World Wars, and an age seemingly more innocent. 1940 was anything but an innocent year, with the madness of the world slowly creeping into America's isolationism. The economy was emerging from the Great Depression, while both sides of the Atlantic were engulfed in passionate struggles against fascism. What America needed was an escape. A pair of years earlier, the comics medium was revolutionized when a man of steel flew into the four color world. With the success of Superman, everyone wanted their own super-hero. The comics industry was booming and costumed heroes were the rage.

In January 1940, *Flash Comics* #1 introduced the Flash by Harry Lampert. Featuring Jay Garrick, "the fastest man alive," this Mercury-like character sped faster than a speeding bullet. Intriguingly, this issue also marked the first appearance of the Hawkman. Six months later, *All-American Comics* #14 introduced the Green Lantern by Martin Nodell. Inspired by Aladdin's lamp, Alan Ladd (a.k.a Alan Scott) found a magic lanterm that gave him incredible powers, charged through a magic ring.

Both of these characters caught the public's attention and soon became lead features in their magazines and founding members of the Justice Society (and solo) in *All-Star Comics*. These mythical, magical characters tapped into the nation's unconscious at a time when the world needed to escape for awhile and imagine what it would be like for men who have the power of gods to solve the nation's problems. Taking popular mythical images and updating them to a post-industrial society, these characters provided fantasy for millions during a difficult period in the nation's history.

By the late 1940s, however, these characters and their images had diminished in the public's eye. The war was over and prosperity and peace were around the corner. With the looming Cold War, America's entertainment turned inward toward more horror and science fiction elements during the 1950s. It wasn't until the end of the decade when National Publications chose to experiment and revive these classic heroes in a modern format. In

September 1956 in *Showcase* #4, Editor Julie Schwartz, writer Robert Kanigher, and artist Carmine Infantino revived the Flash in a new world. This Flash was Barry Allen, a police scientist who was struck by lightning and could run at the speed of light. However, rather than fight crime and war, this Flash fought more colorful super-powered costume villains and more scientific threats. Intriguingly, this success spawned more revivals and is generally considered the beginning of the second great era in comics, the Silver Age.

With the success of this revival, three years later in *Showcase* #22, the Green Lantern was reintroduced. Hal Jordan, a test pilot, found a dying alien who gave him a magical ring and lantern. With a more science fiction and space age element, this character used his ring to battle threats to Coast City. What these two revived characters illustrated was a reaction to the Cold War threats that plagued the nation. Again, it was necessary for America to imagine super-powered characters protecting us against threats from the sky and beyond. Following the lead of the 1940s heroes, these two became part of the 1960s super-team, the Justice League of America.

By the early 1980s, the comics industry found itself in a recession along with the rest of the nation. Post-Vietnam and -Watergate malaise had struck America. Inflationary pressures were piercing consumers' pocketbooks. The comics industry itself was at a low point sales-wise. While the Flash had survived, Green Lantern was relegated to a back-up strip in *Flash* comics. What seemed like these familiar characters' sunset years was actually only the seeds of a third relaunch.

Crisis on Infinite Earths, the 1986 DC mega-crossover series that redefined that universe and comics themselves, saw the death of the Barry Allen Flash. However, quickly taking on his role as the third Flash was his nephew Wally West, formerly known as Kid Flash, Barry Allen's occasional sidekick. Grown-up and soon emerging with his own new *Flash* series, Wally originally began as a 1990s slacker trying to find his way in the world. This is generally viewed as the beginning of comics' third great era, the Modern Age (for lack of a better defining term). What was different about this Flash was an emphasis on technology, extra-dimensional threats, and an exploration of the very concept of "speed." The series saw a variety of speed characters serve supporting roles as villains and fellow heroes, with the creators focusing on our hero surviving the modern world's fast-paced pressures.

It wasn't until 1994 that DC Comics got around to updating the Green Lantern for this new era. Given a power ring similar to that of his predecessor, Kyle Rayner, a twentysomething freelance artist, found himself in receipt of a strange and powerful gift. Redefining himself as a new-era Green Lantern, this character quickly differentiated himself from his predecessors in his imaginative uses for the ring and the unique threats he faced. Like his colleague the Flash, this Green Lantern struggled with his personal life's pressures, which were often as difficult as those he faced in costume. In a new world of technology, it is the human pressures that exert the greatest struggles, as our hero seeks a life of balance. As before, these two characters soon joined the Justice League and have fought side-by-side.

What is amazing and appears unintended is the way each of these pairs of characters define their individual era. In the 1940s, their Flash and Green Lantern are remnants of a country redefining myths in a post-industrial world that needed protection. In the 1960s, their heroes represented a bastion of safety against Cold War threats and fears. Once this subsided in the early 1990s, the characters were redefined again with the focus more inward, exploring at what cost our new fast-paced world of technology is doing to us. What is more amazing is how these characters remain primal archetypes in our collective unconscious, echoing ancient myths of Mercury and Aladdin (and others). Perhaps we do all seeks protection and dream our saviors are among us, granting our wishes. We live vicariously through them and, in doing so, dream of what we may become. There may always be a Flash or Green Lantern, and for that, sixty years does not seem so long at all.

Mark Lucas is a freelance writer and editor residing in Los Angeles

FLASH & GREEN LANTERN SIXTIETH ANNIVERSARY   DAVE REYES

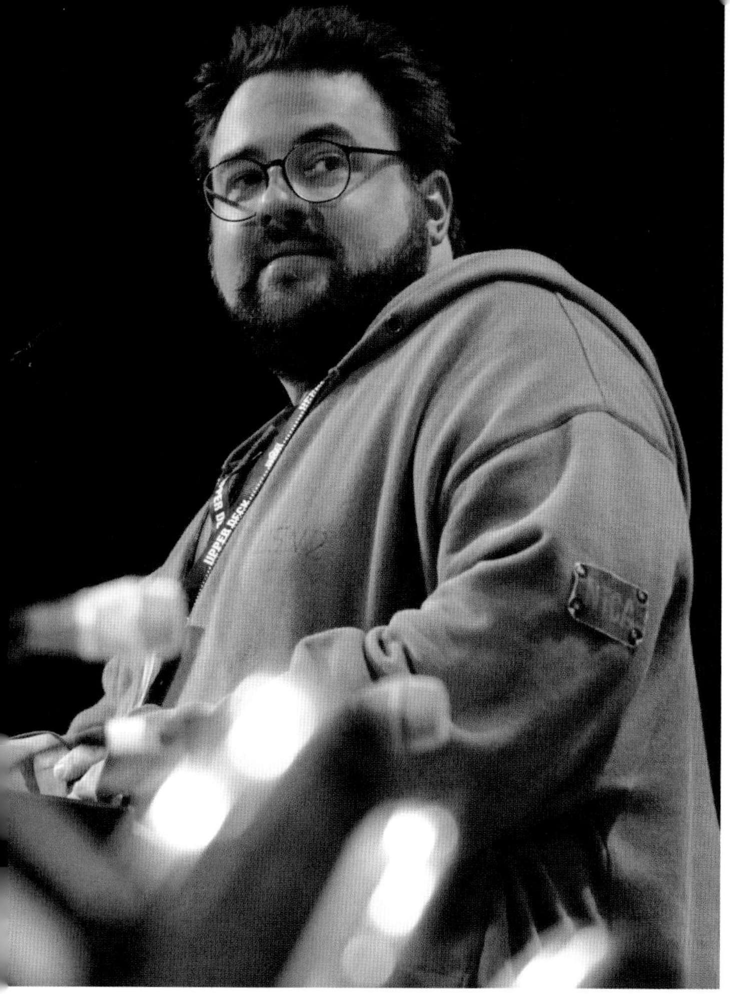

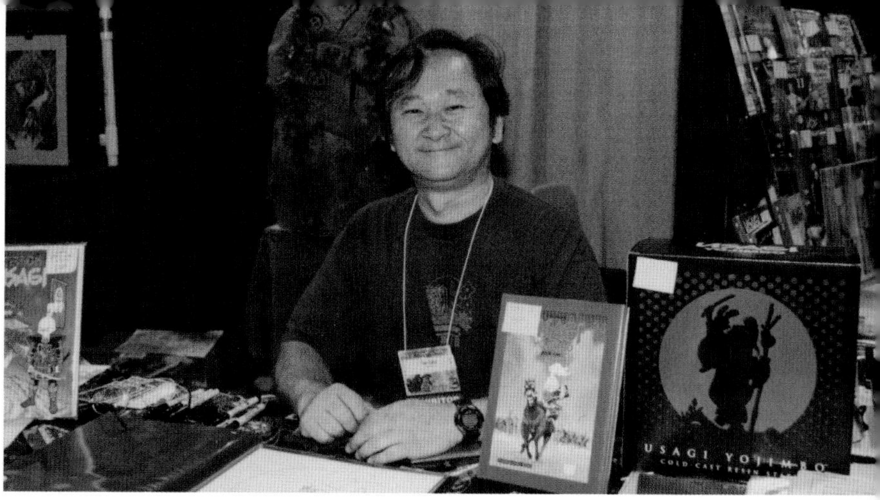
USAGI YOJIMBO

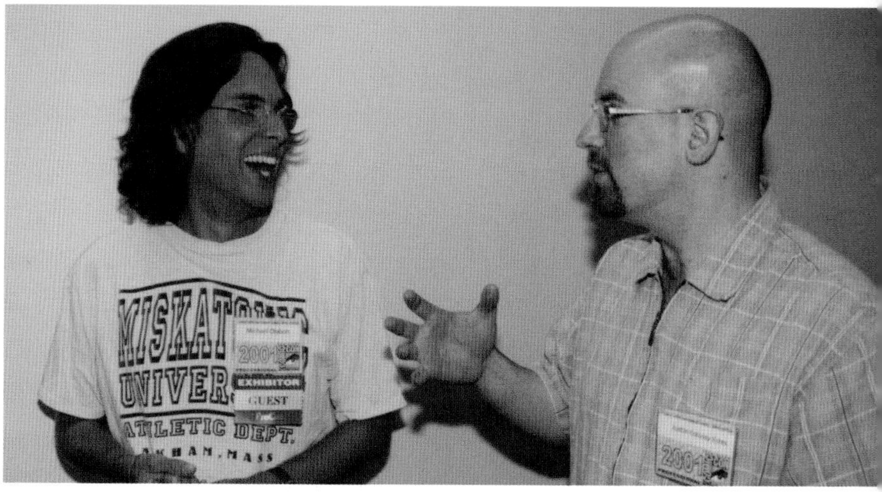

> "Look around you at all the movies, TV shows, videogames, and toys out there today. Even if they do not represent a current comic property, you can see how comics influenced their very existence. The comics industry is a petri dish for many creative ideas, and Comic-Con is the manifestation of the positive, creative influence comics has had on pop culture."
>
> **—BOB CHAPMAN**
>
> **OWNER, GRAPHITTI DESIGNS**

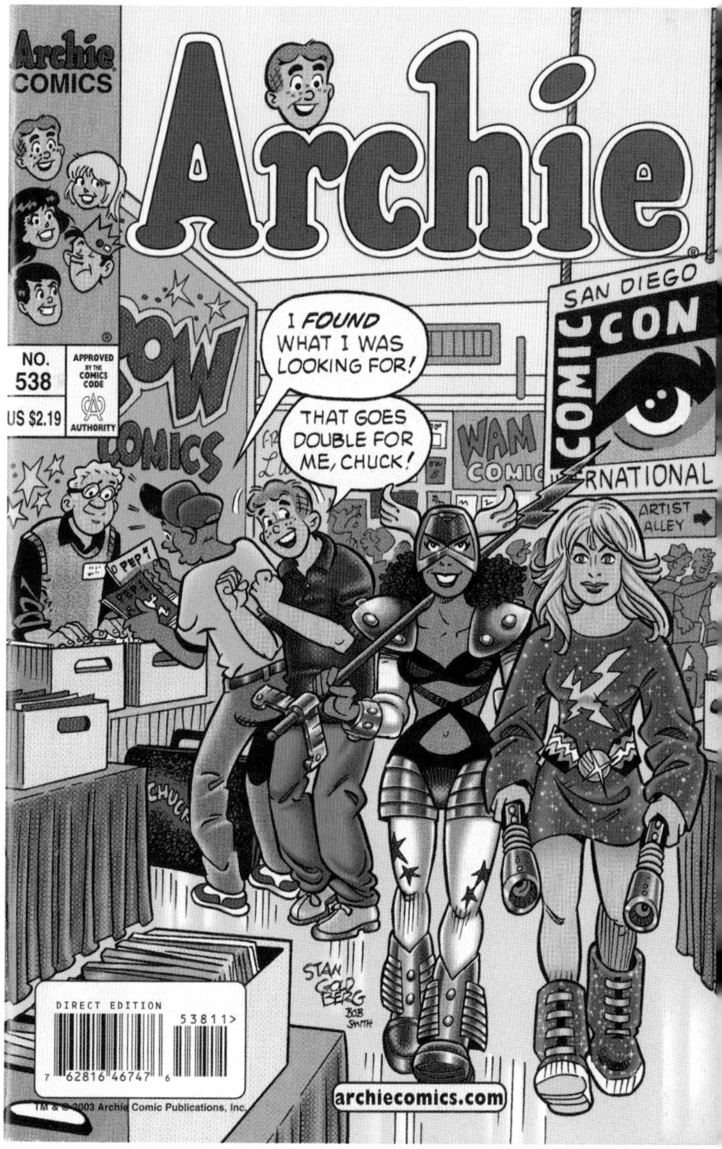
Archie COMICS
Archie
NO. 538
APPROVED BY THE COMICS CODE AUTHORITY
US $2.19
I FOUND WHAT I WAS LOOKING FOR!
THAT GOES DOUBLE FOR ME, CHUCK!
SAN DIEGO COMIC CON
RNATIONAL
ARTIST ALLEY
WAM
COMICS
STAN GOLDBERG
BOB SMITH
DIRECT EDITION
archiecomics.com
TM & © 2003 Archie Comic Publications, Inc.

CLOCKWISE FROM TOP LEFT: Kevin Smith talking *Zack and Miri* at the 2008 Comic-Con; artist Stan Sakai, the creator of *Usagi Yojimbo* and a longtime presence at the show; Michael Chabon (left), author of *The Amazing Adventures of Kavalier and Clay*, talking with Justin Colussy Estes after his 2001 "Spotlight" panel; Archie and friends visited Comic-Con again in 2003 as shown on this *Archie* cover **OPPOSITE:** Two incredible group costumes created for the Masquerade: the X-Men with Captain America, from 2003 (top) and characters from Hayao Miyazaki's *Spirited Away* (bottom)

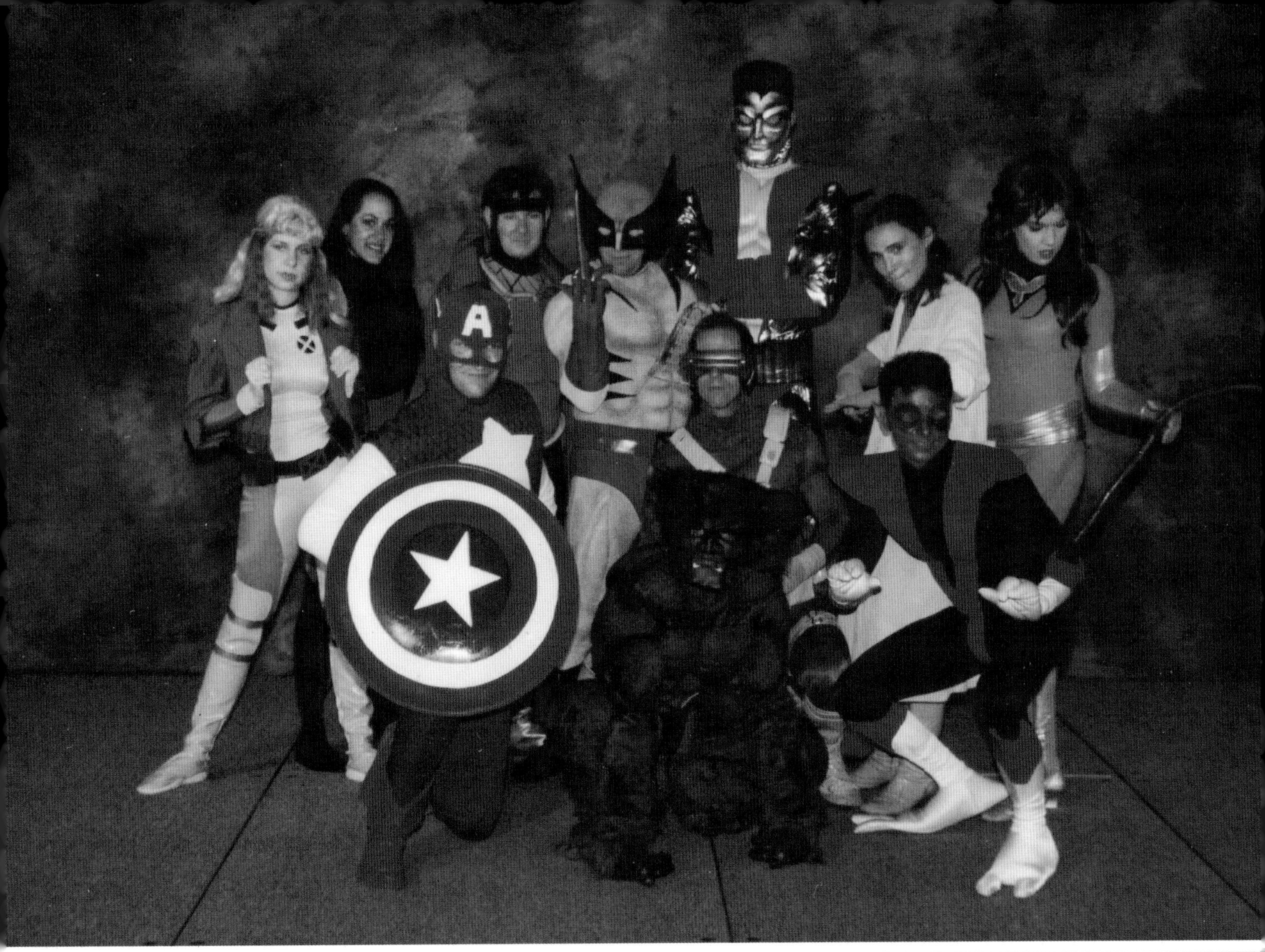

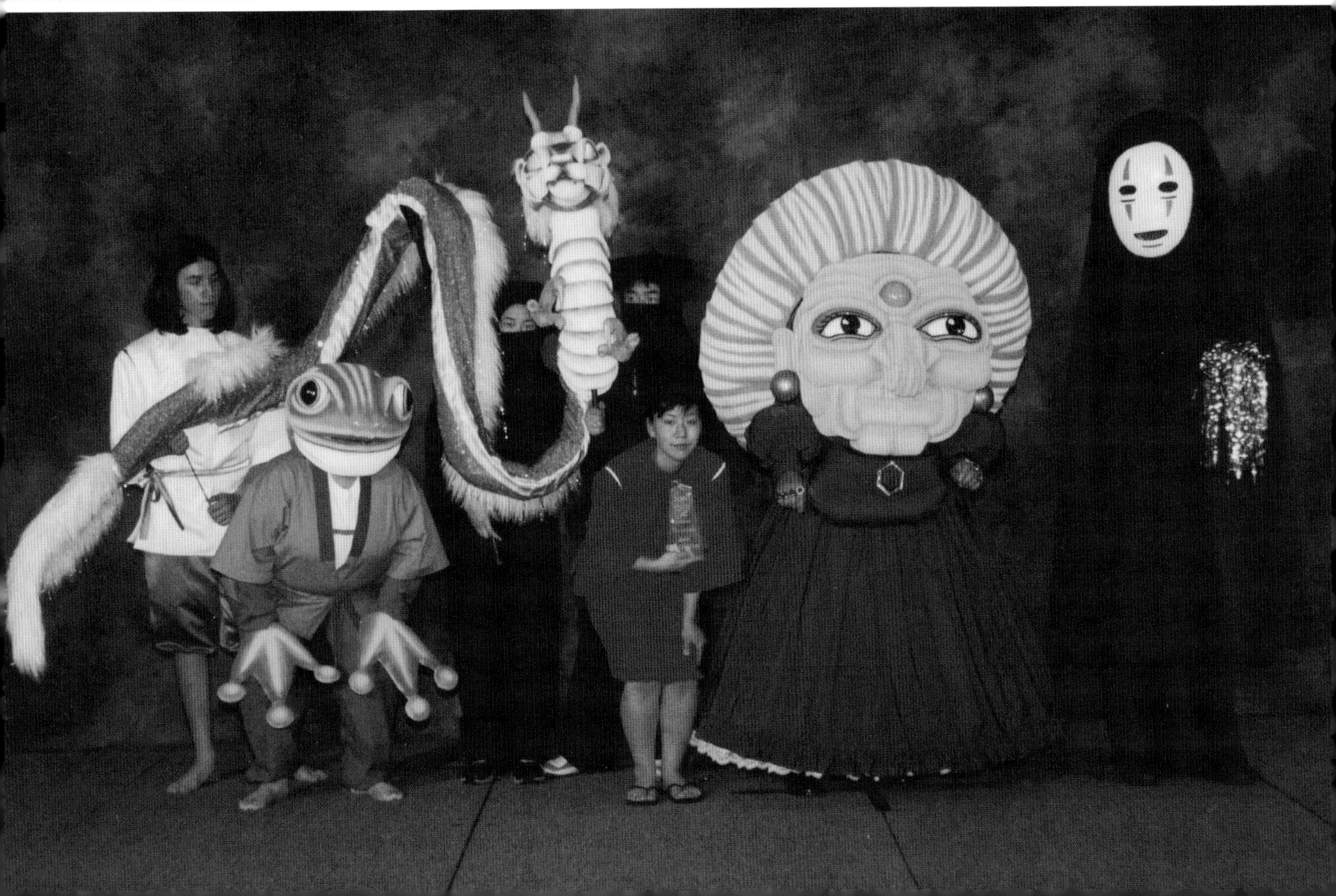

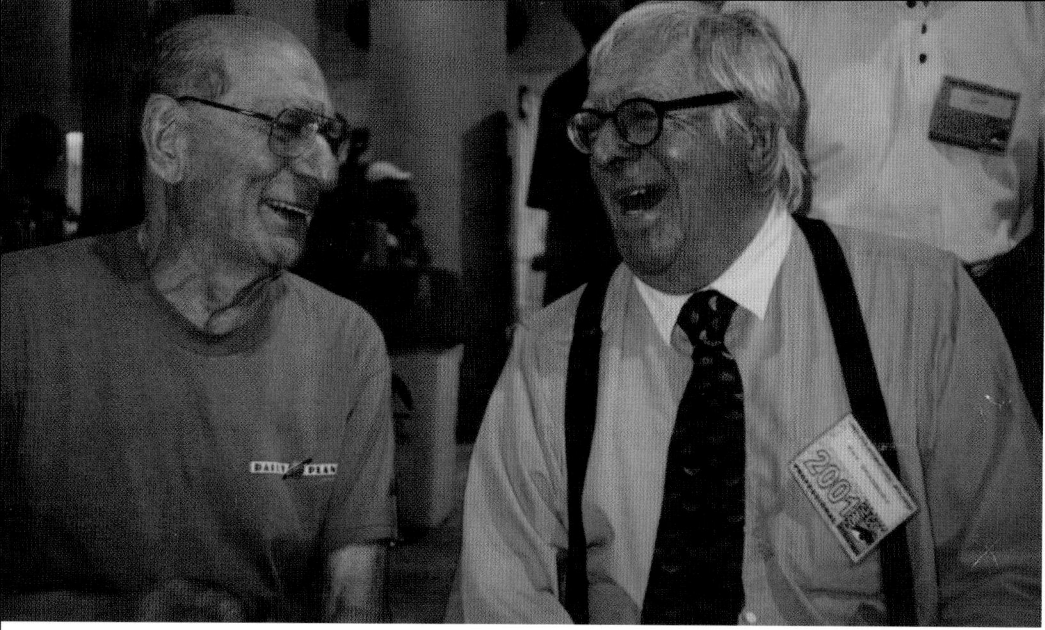
2001

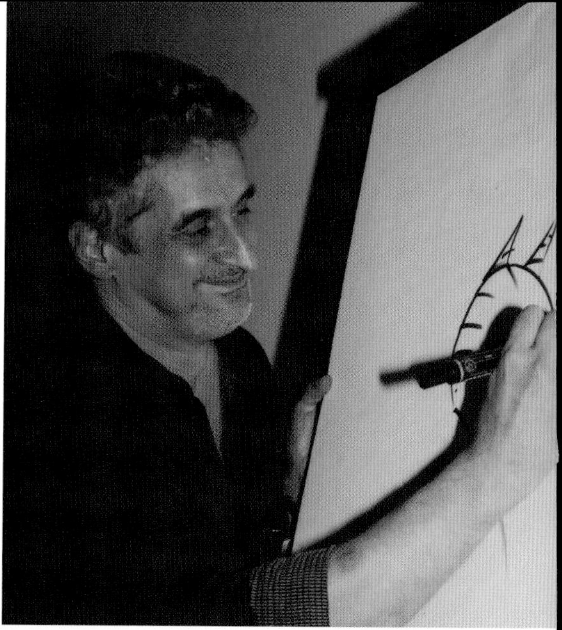

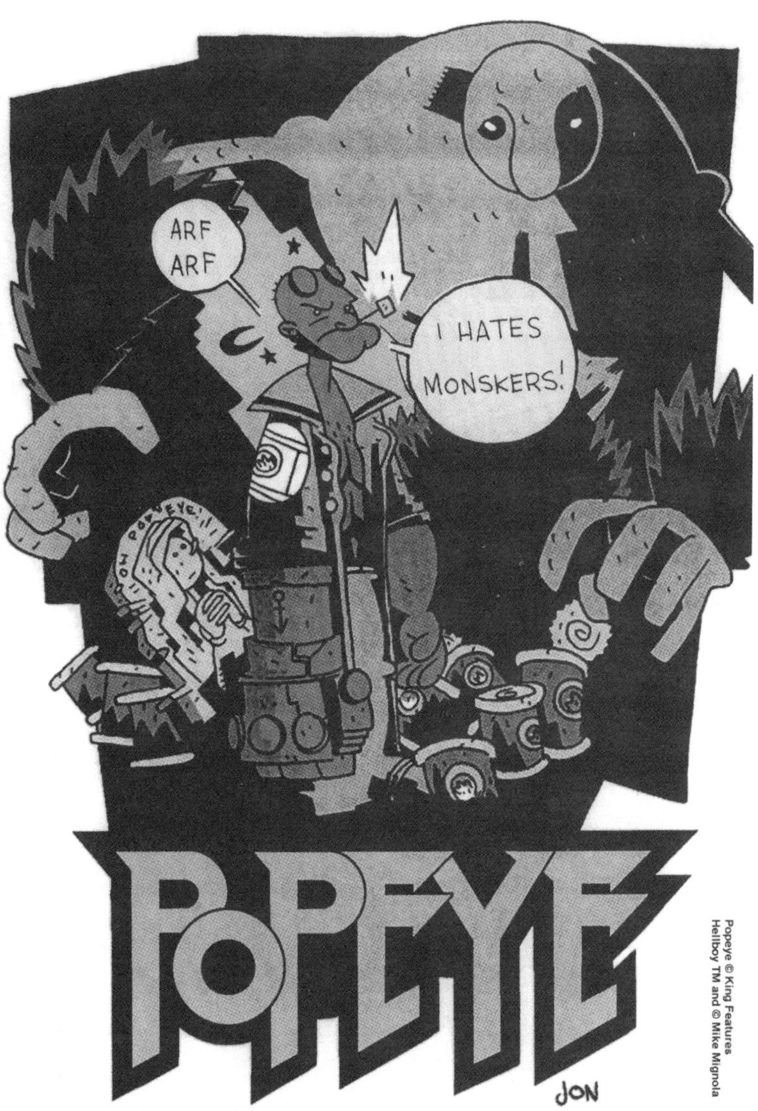
ARF
ARF
I HATES
MONSKERS!
POPEYE
JON

Popeye © King Features
Hellboy TM and © Mike Mignola

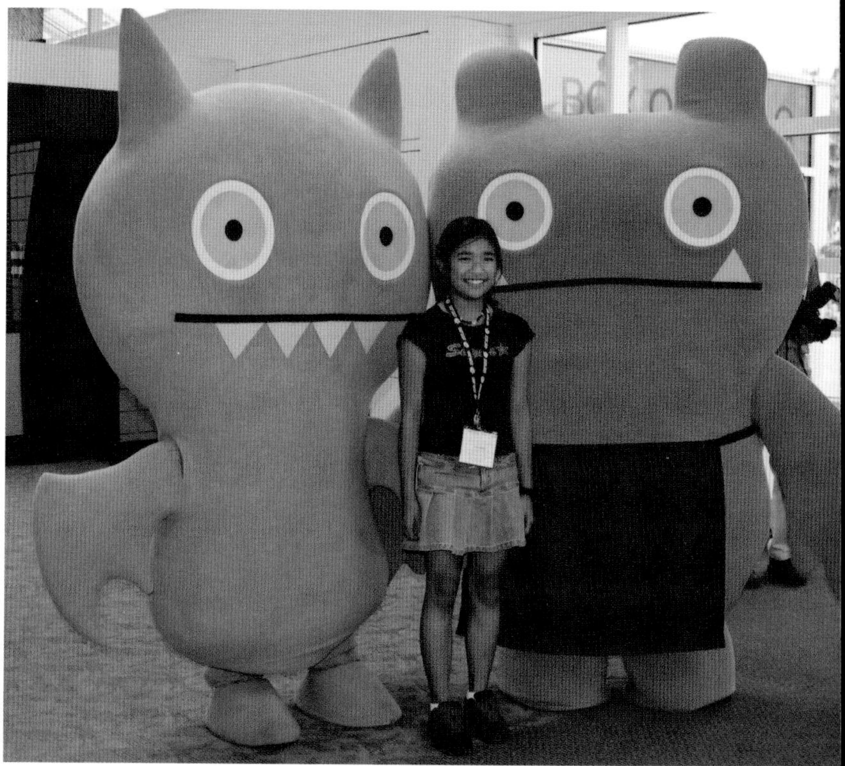

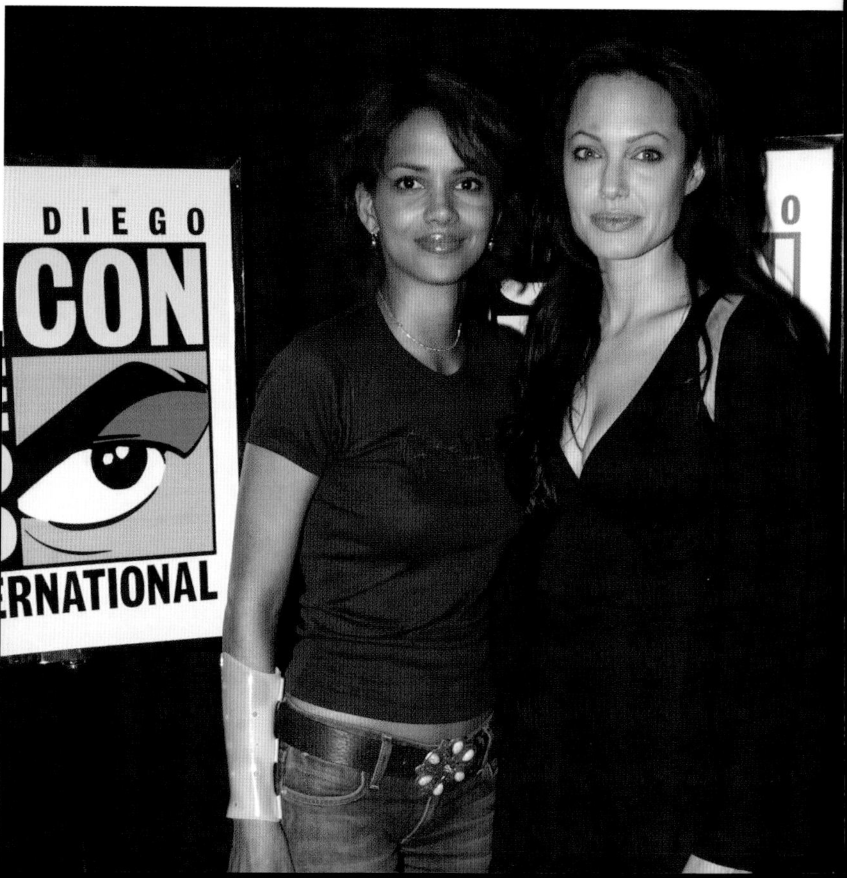
DIEGO
CON
ERNATIONAL

CLOCKWISE FROM TOP LEFT: Lifelong friends Julius Schwartz (left) and Ray Bradbury (right) at Comic-Con in 2001; cartoonist Patrick McDonnell sketching Mooch from *Mutts* in 2004; the Uglydolls always generate spontaneous picture taking; Halle Berry and Angelina Jolie at Comic-Con in 2003 promoting their new films (Berry's *Gothika* and Jolie's *Lara Croft Tomb Raider: Cradle of Life*); Jon Morris's 2004 art celebrating the seventy-fifth anniversary of Popeye and the tenth of *Hellboy*
OPPOSITE, CLOCKWISE FROM TOP LEFT: Wolverine co-creator Len Wein (left) with *Wolverine* star Hugh Jackman (right) backstage in Hall H in 2008; *Elfquest* creator Wendy Pini with her contribution to the 2006 Art Auction; Scott Saavedra's playful depiction of the Universal Monsters for their seventy-fifth anniversary in 2006; popular writer/artist Kyle Baker signing at his booth in 2006

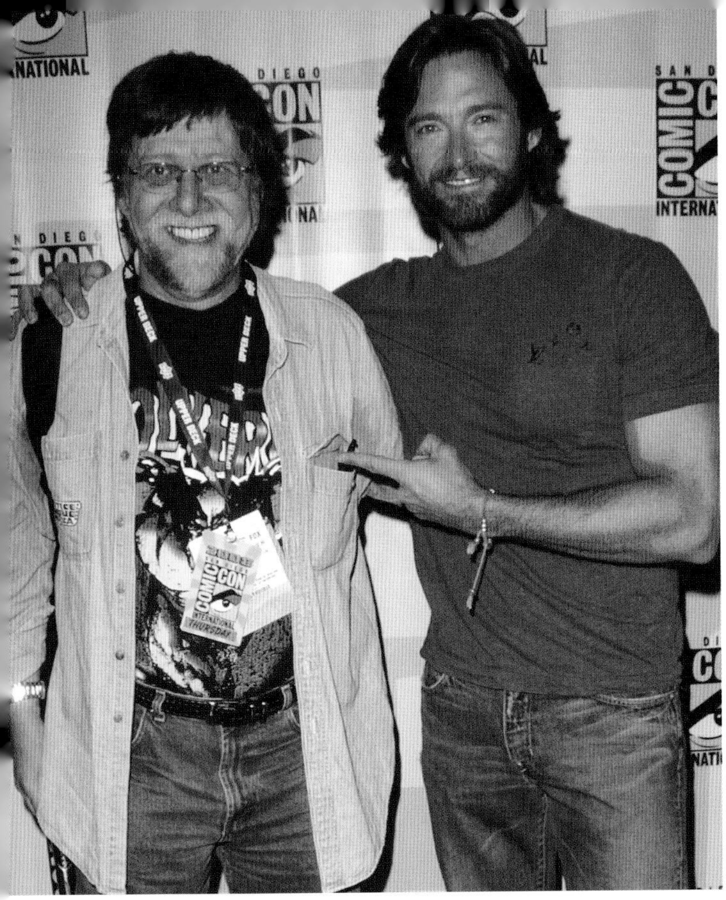

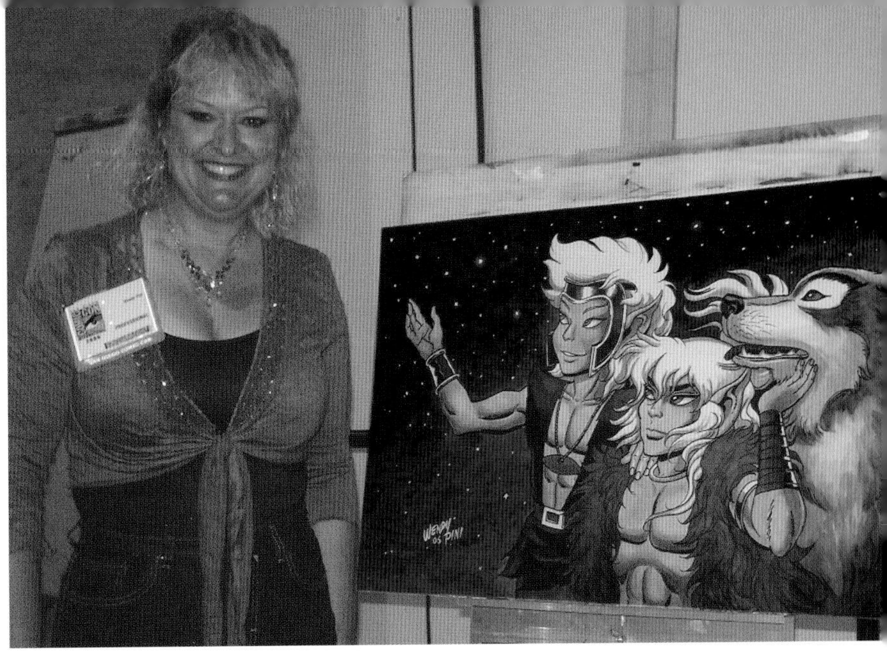

> The hijacking of the *Van Helsing* presentation by a half dozen stripped-down Wolverines who rushed the front of the stage.
>
> **—HUGH JACKMAN**
>
> ACTOR/PRODUCER, X-MEN MOVIES, *X-MEN ORIGINS: WOLVERINE*, *VAN HELSING*
>
> (On his most memorable Comic-Con moment)

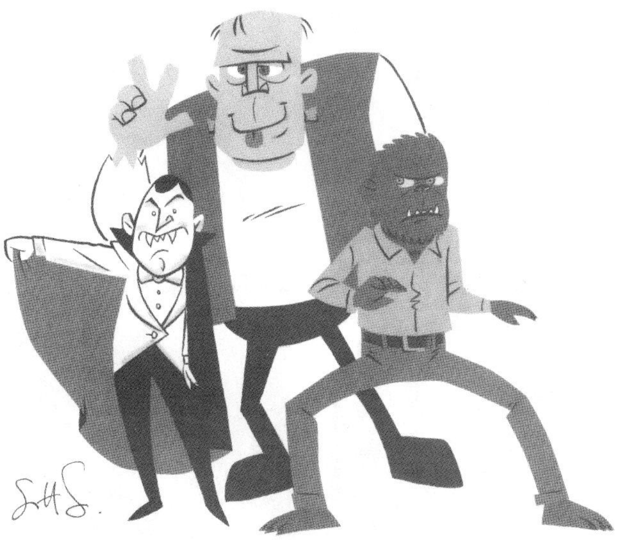

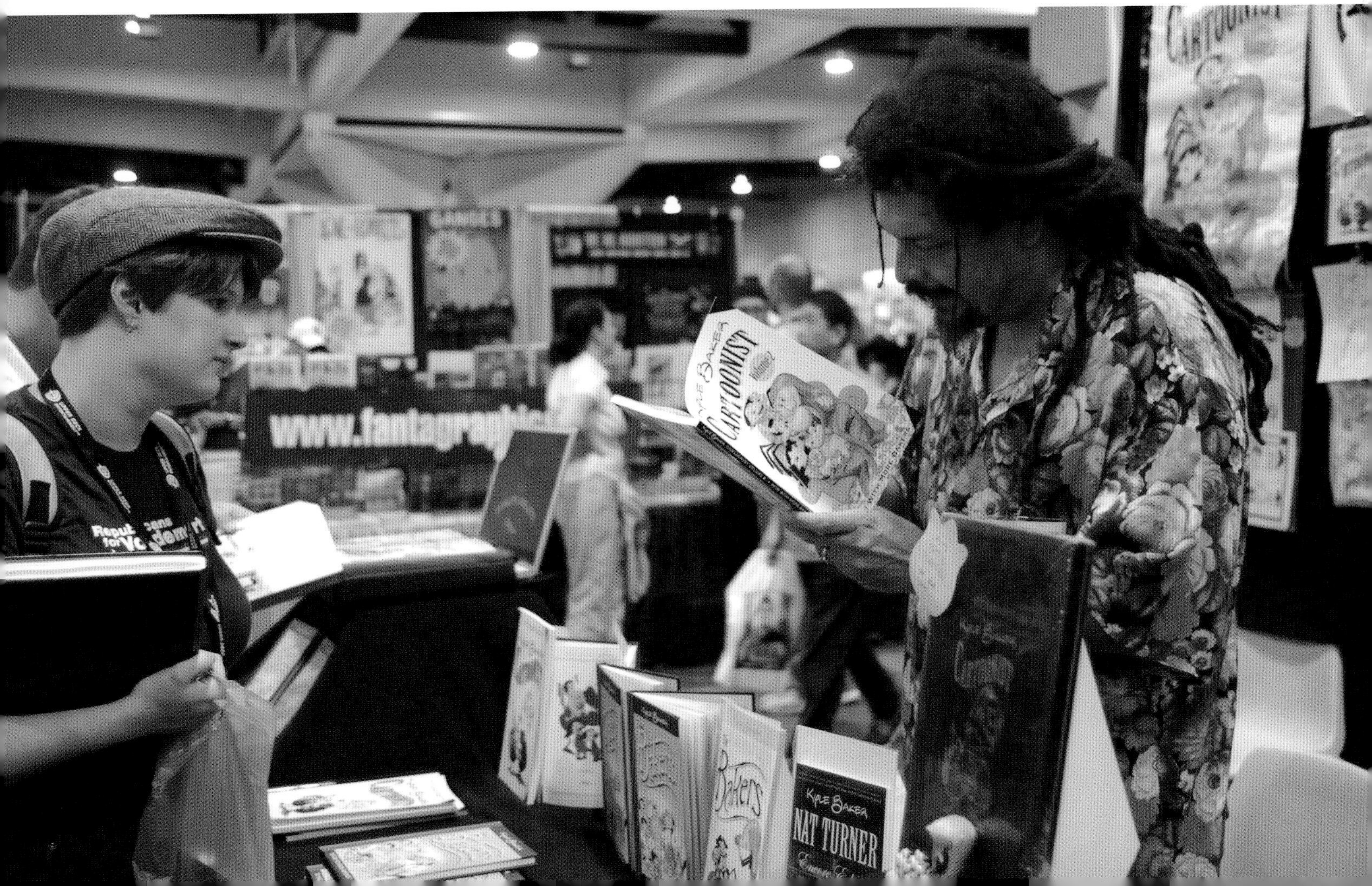
KYLE BAKER
NAT TURNER

VOLUNTEERS

Without the efforts of a dedicated band of volunteers, Comic-Con would not be the world-class event it is today.

From the very beginning, volunteers have helped make the show happen. The group of fans who started Comic-Con in 1970 were all volunteers, and even after incorporation as a nonprofit educational organization in 1975, the convention continued to be run first and foremost by fans. In the mid-1980s, Comic-Con hired an executive director to oversee the day-to-day management of the event, and other full-time staff positions followed over the years. But the show continues to be supported by an extensive volunteer staff on-site. More than two thousand people worked as volunteers at Comic-Con 2008.

The organization is run by an elected thirteen-member board of directors including a president, two vice presidents, a secretary, a treasurer, and eight at-large members. A full-time office staff of about twenty people handles exhibits, programming, publications, marketing, publicity, and the daily operations of all three events. A core committee of about sixty people, plus a few hundred more long-time volunteers, handles specific areas such as the Art Show, Anime, the Masquerade, Disabled Services, guest relations, the Autograph Area, logistics, and

gaming. The people who fill these roles include a fairly even balance of men and women in a variety of professions, including teachers, research scientists, and telecommunication executives.

Becoming a volunteer is a simple process: You commit to a certain amount of time—usually a three-hour shift—and you get into Comic-Con free for that day. Those who volunteer for all four days get a rare and extremely limited Comic-Con volunteer T-shirt that is different each year—making the shirts instant collectors' items.

All of the current department heads and board members started off in humble positions—as gofers, room-sitters, or projectionists. This experience proves invaluable, as there are few better ways to learn the details of the event than from the ground up. Some volunteers have now been with Comic-Con for twenty or thirty years. And all originally came to Comic-Con for the same reason: They were fans, and they loved everything the event has to offer.

Twenty years of exclusive Comic-Con volunteer T-shirts **OPPOSITE, FIRST ROW, FROM LEFT:** Usagi Yojimbo, by Stan Sakai (1988); Comic-Con Toucan, by Rick Geary (1989); Starstruck, by Michael Kaluta (1990); X-Men, by Jim Lee (1991) **SECOND ROW, FROM LEFT:** Spider-Man/Carnage, by Aaron Lopresti (1992); Spider-Man, by Mark Bagley (1994); Velocity (1995); Groo, by Sergio Aragonés (1996) **THIRD ROW, FROM LEFT:** WILDC.A.T.s/X-Men, by Travis Charest (1997); Roswell, by Bill Morrison (1998); Big Guy and Rusty the Boy Robot, by Geof Darrow (2000); Lone Wolf and Cub, by Goseki Kojima (2001) **FOURTH ROW, FROM LEFT:** Speed Racer (2002); Hellboy, by Mike Mignola (2003); Mutts, by Patrick McDonnell (2004); Teen Titans animated TV show (2005) **FIFTH ROW, FROM LEFT:** Gumby, by Rick Geary (2006); Superman/Doomsday (2007); Legion of Super-Heroes, by Alex Ross (2008)

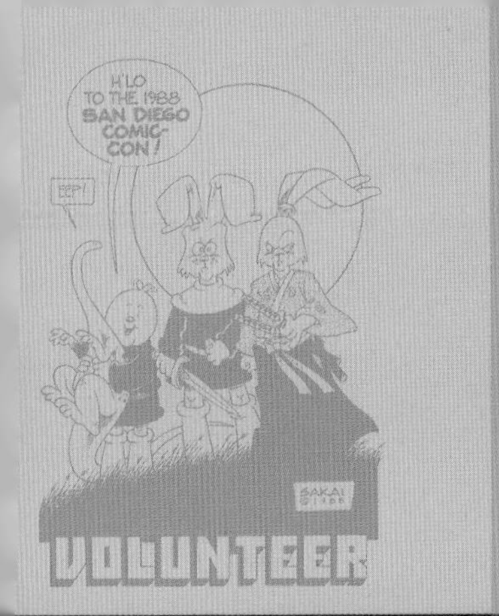
H'LO TO THE 1988 SAN DIEGO COMIC-CON!
VOLUNTEER

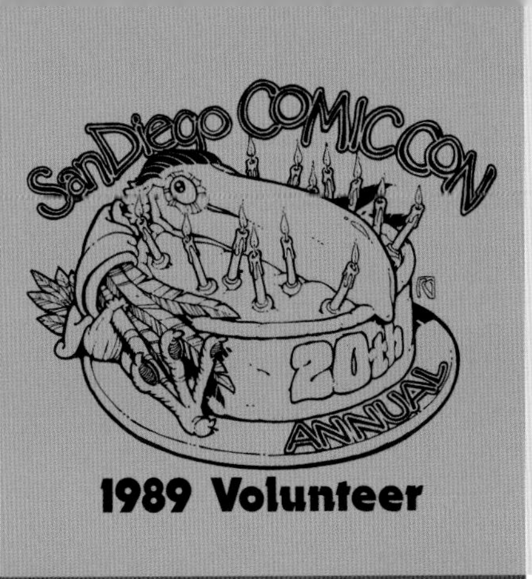
San Diego COMIC CON
20th ANNUAL
1989 Volunteer

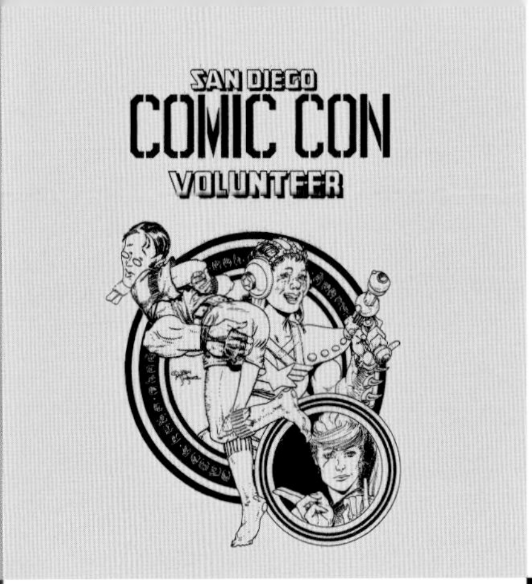
SAN DIEGO
COMIC CON
VOLUNTEER

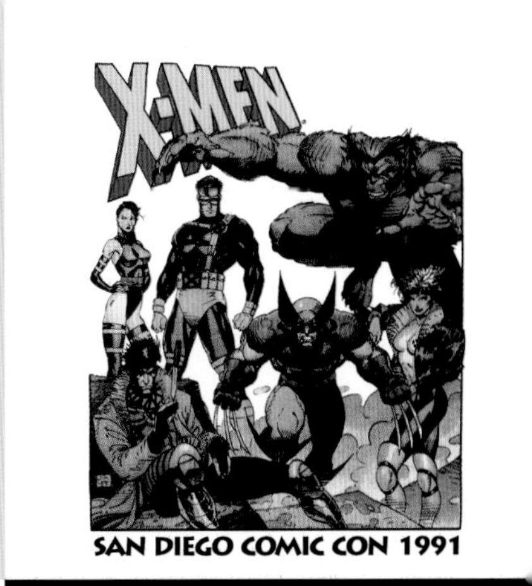
X-MEN
SAN DIEGO COMIC CON 1991

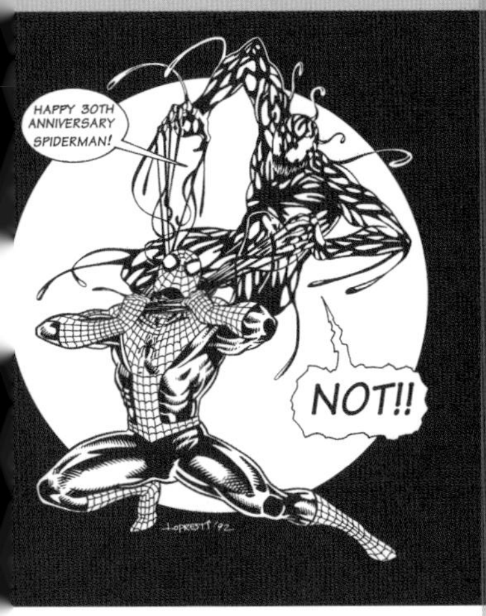
HAPPY 30TH ANNIVERSARY SPIDERMAN!
NOT!!

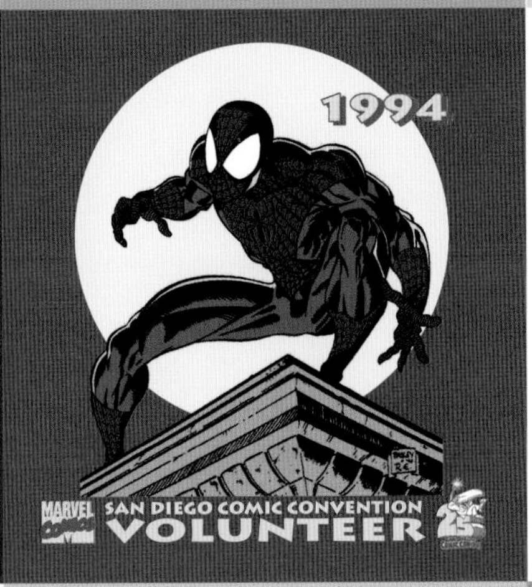
1994
MARVEL
SAN DIEGO COMIC CONVENTION
VOLUNTEER

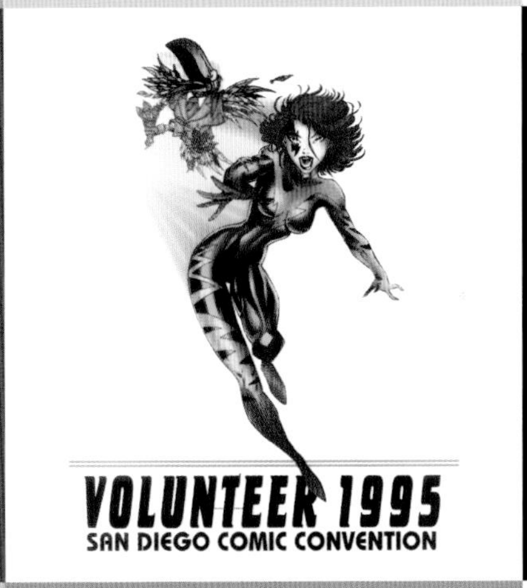
VOLUNTEER 1995
SAN DIEGO COMIC CONVENTION

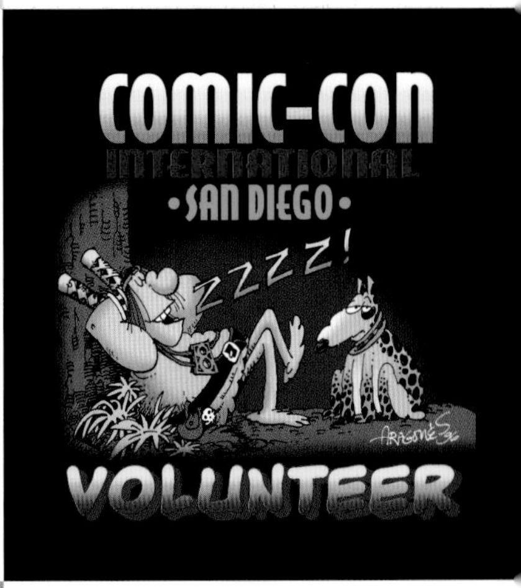
COMIC-CON
INTERNATIONAL
•SAN DIEGO•
ZZZZ!
VOLUNTEER

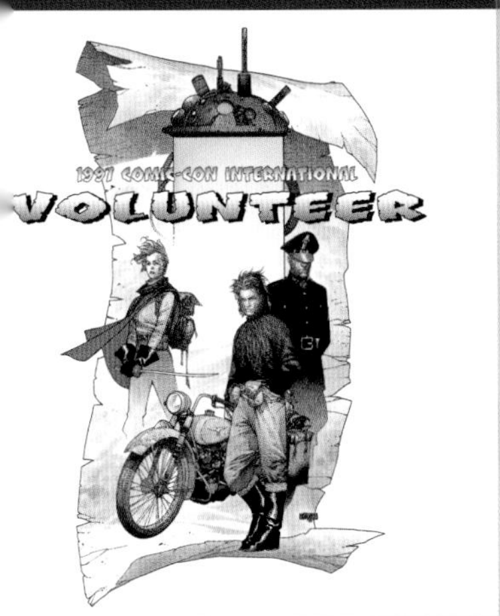
1997 COMIC-CON INTERNATIONAL
VOLUNTEER

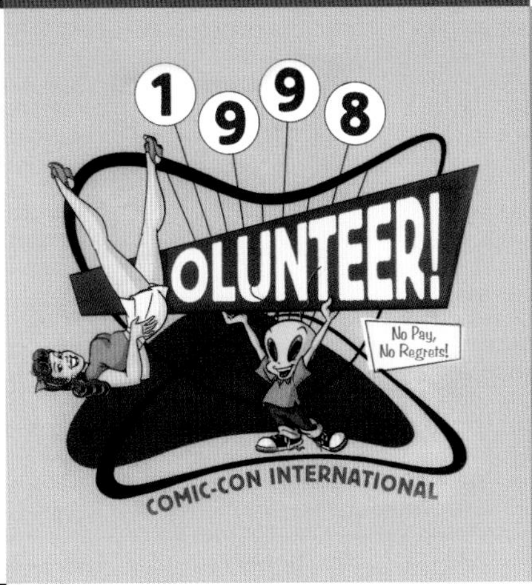
1998
VOLUNTEER!
No Pay, No Regrets!
COMIC-CON INTERNATIONAL

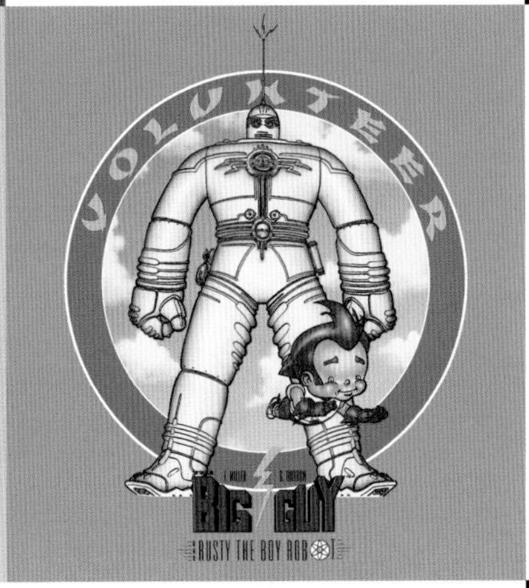
VOLUNTEER
BIG GUY
RUSTY THE BOY ROBOT

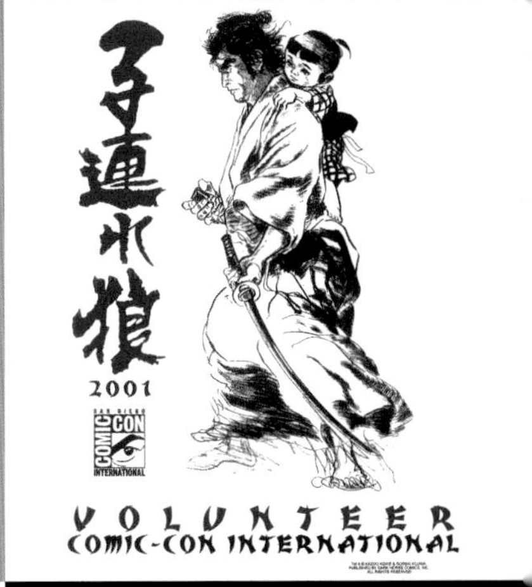
2001
SAN DIEGO COMIC CON INTERNATIONAL
VOLUNTEER
COMIC-CON INTERNATIONAL

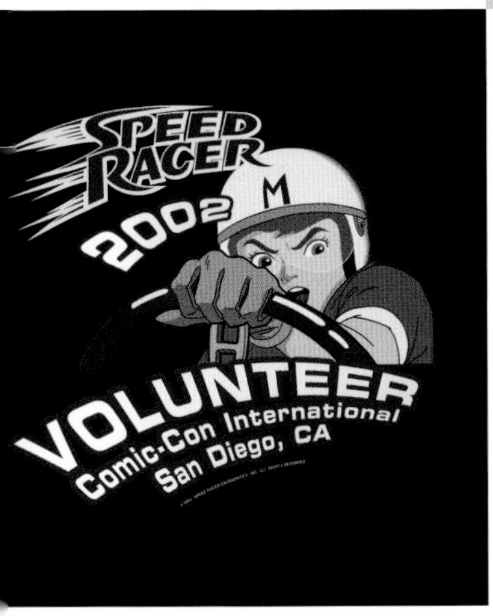
SPEED RACER
2002
M
VOLUNTEER
Comic-Con International
San Diego, CA

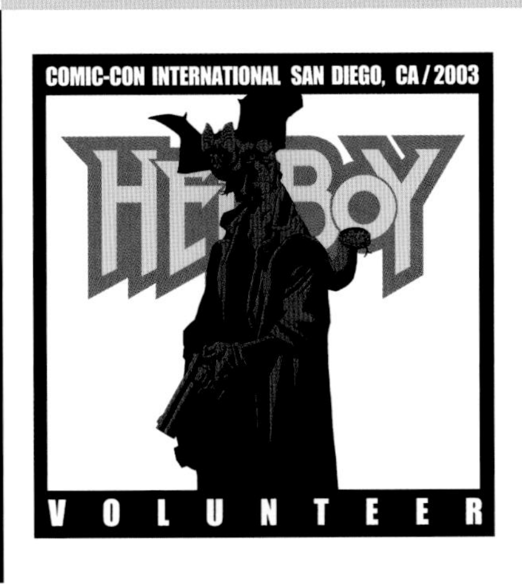
COMIC-CON INTERNATIONAL SAN DIEGO, CA / 2003
VOLUNTEER

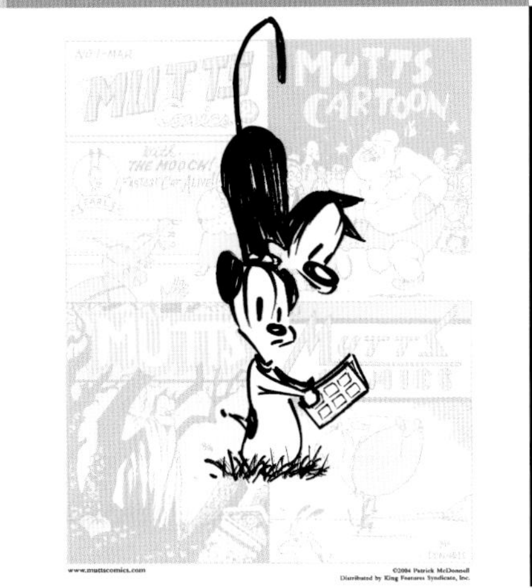
MUTTS CARTOON
www.muttscomics.com
©2004 Patrick McDonnell
Distributed by King Features Syndicate, Inc.

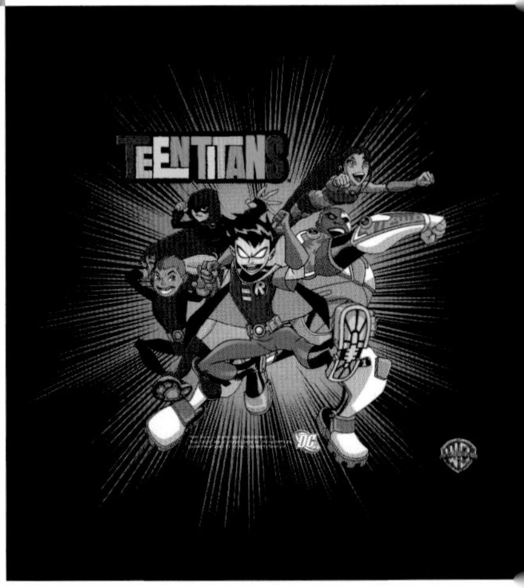
TEEN TITANS

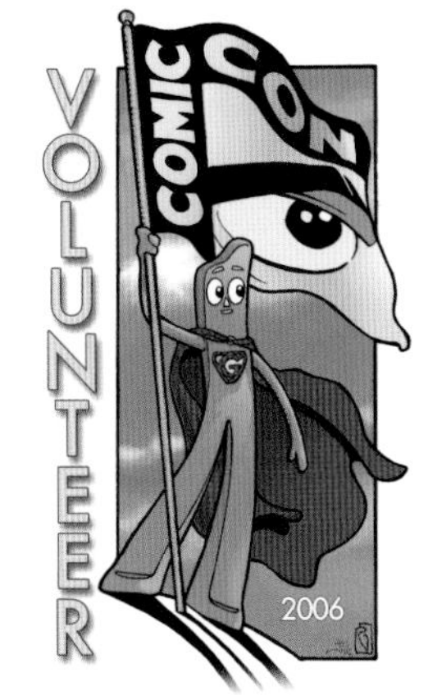
VOLUNTEER
COMIC CON
2006

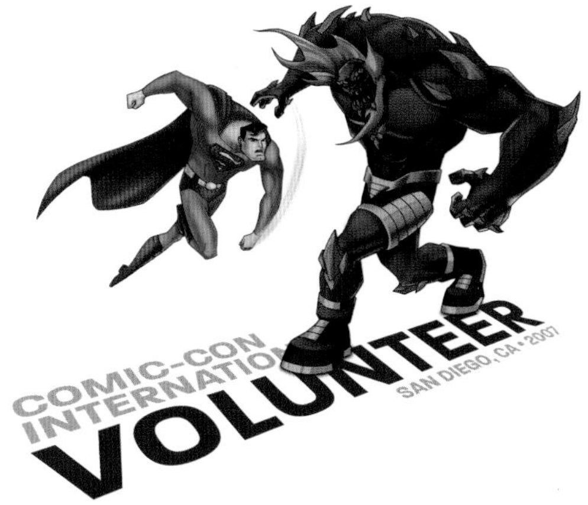
COMIC-CON INTERNATIONAL
VOLUNTEER
SAN DIEGO, CA • 2007

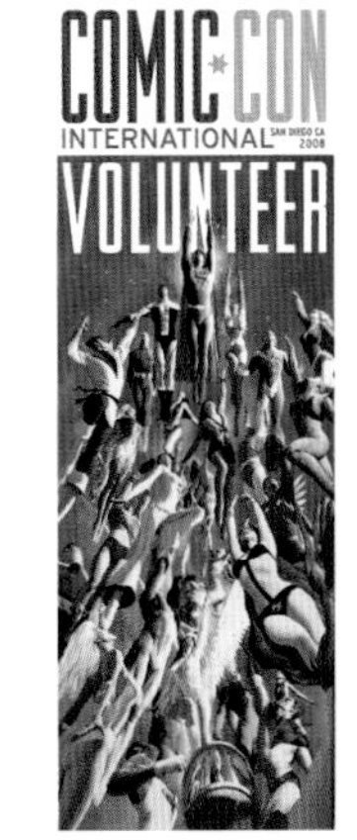
COMIC CON
INTERNATIONAL
SAN DIEGO CA 2008
VOLUNTEER

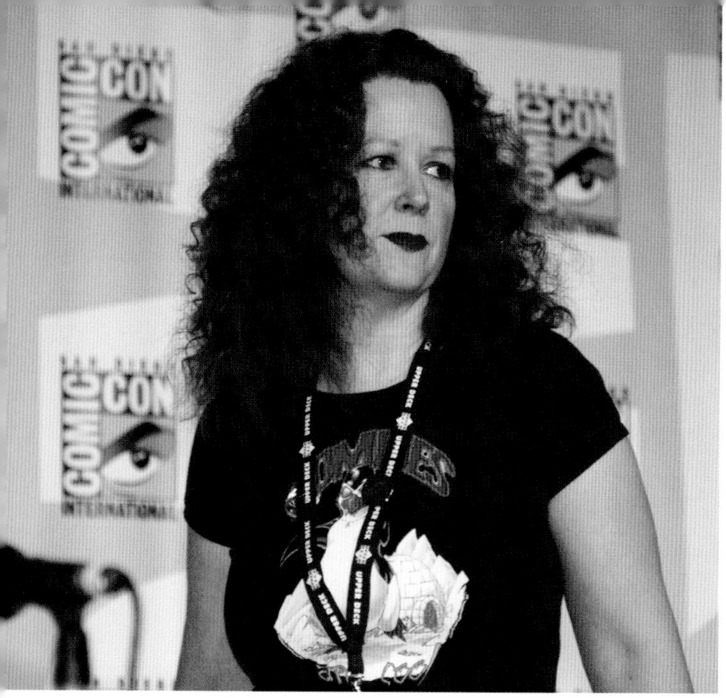
COMIC CON INTERNATIONAL
UPPER DECK

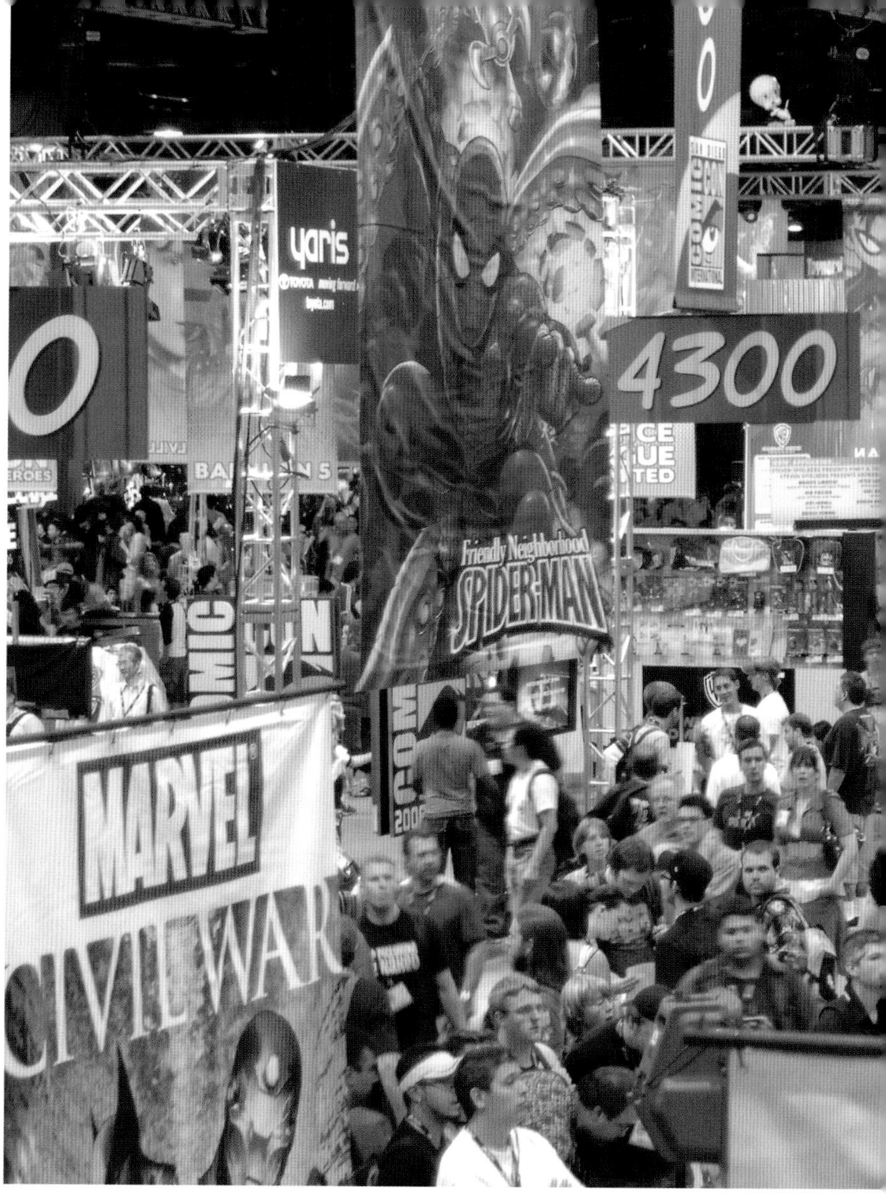
yaris
4300
Friendly Neighborhood
SPIDER-MAN
MARVEL
CIVIL WAR

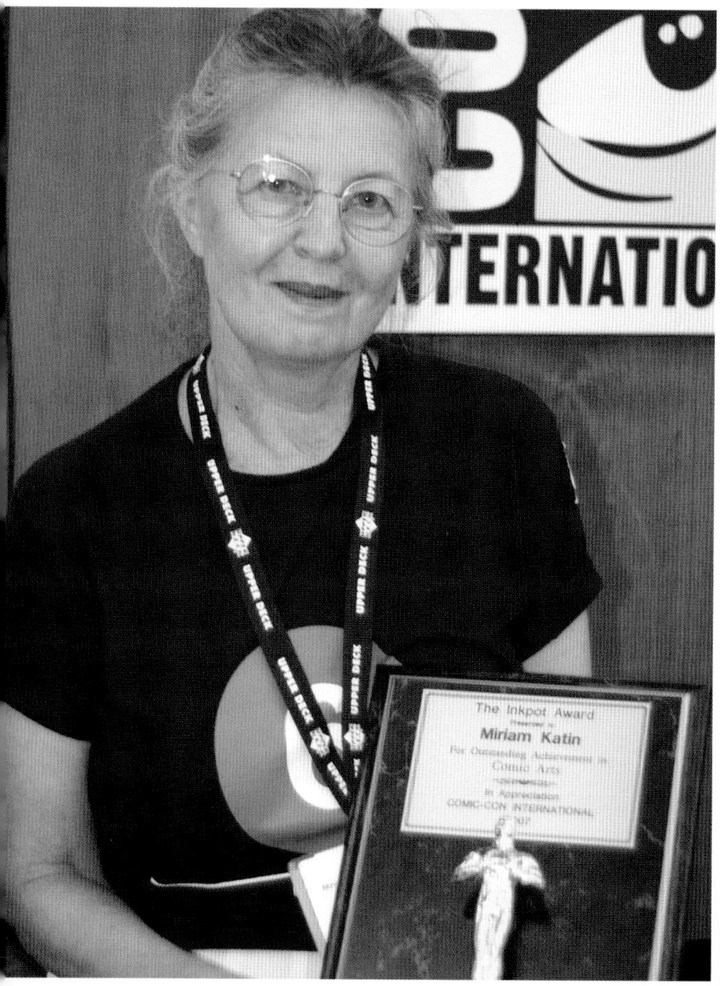
INTERNATIO
UPPER DECK
The Inkpot Award
Presented to
Miriam Katin
For Outstanding Achievement in
Comic Arts
In Appreciation
COMIC-CON INTERNATIONAL

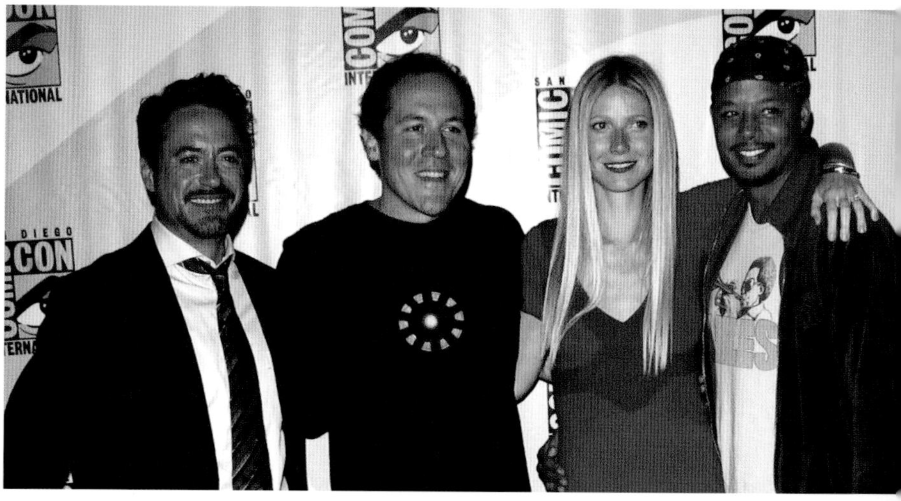
SAN DIEGO COMIC CON INTERNATIONAL

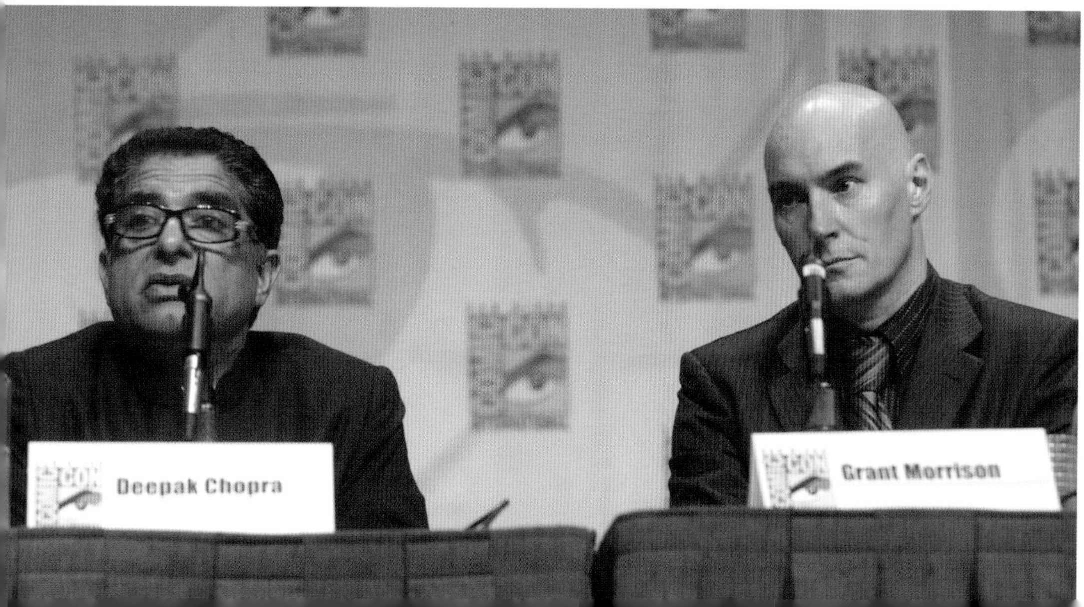
Deepak Chopra
Grant Morrison

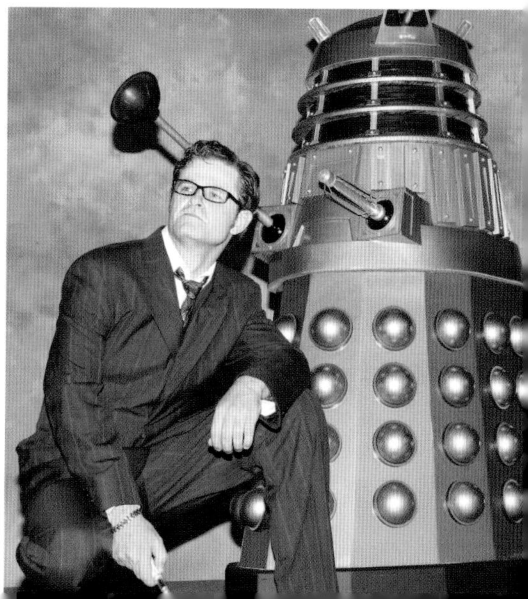

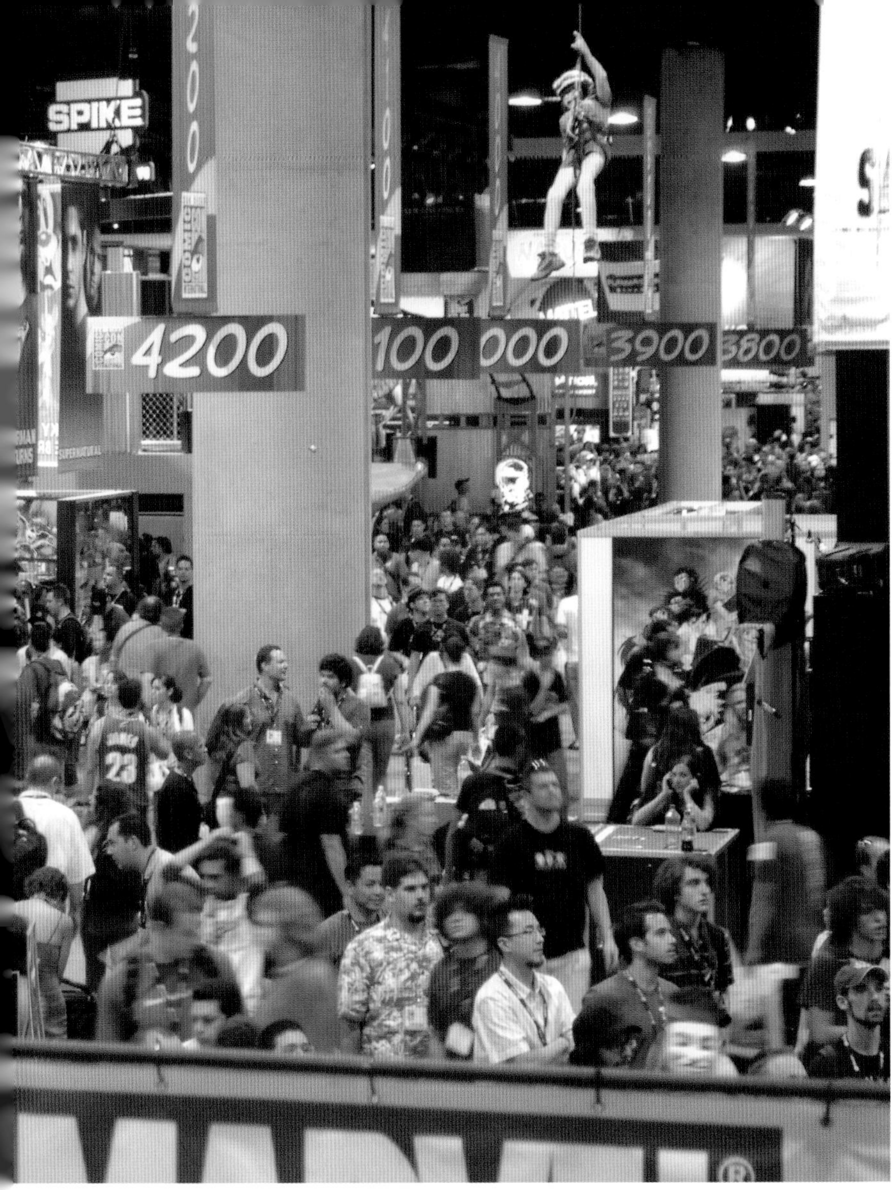
SPIKE
4200
100 000
3900
3800

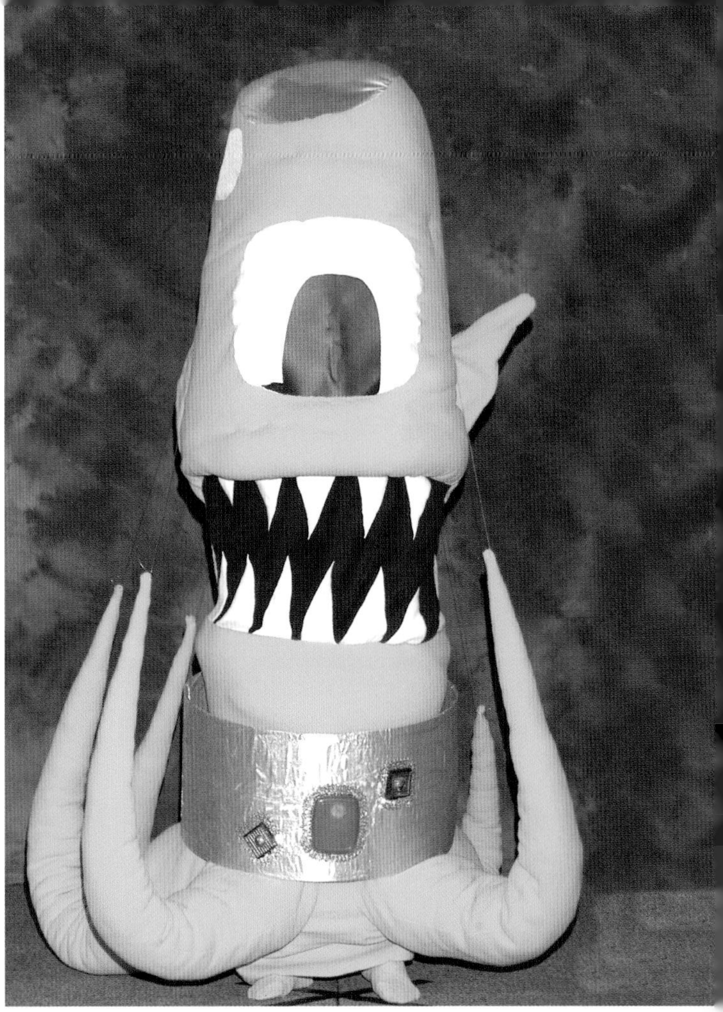

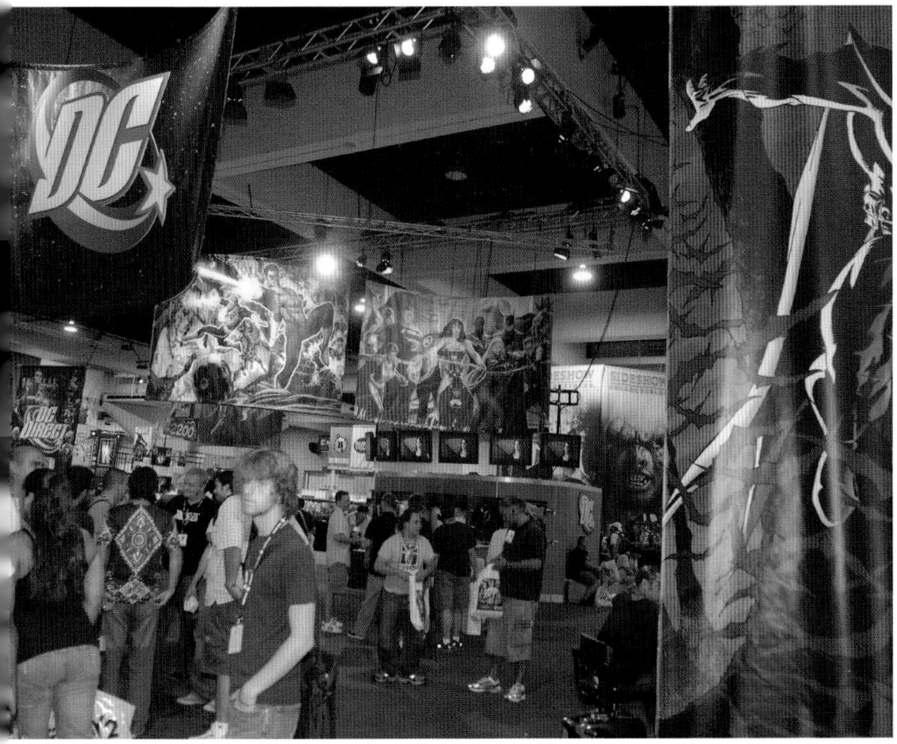
DC

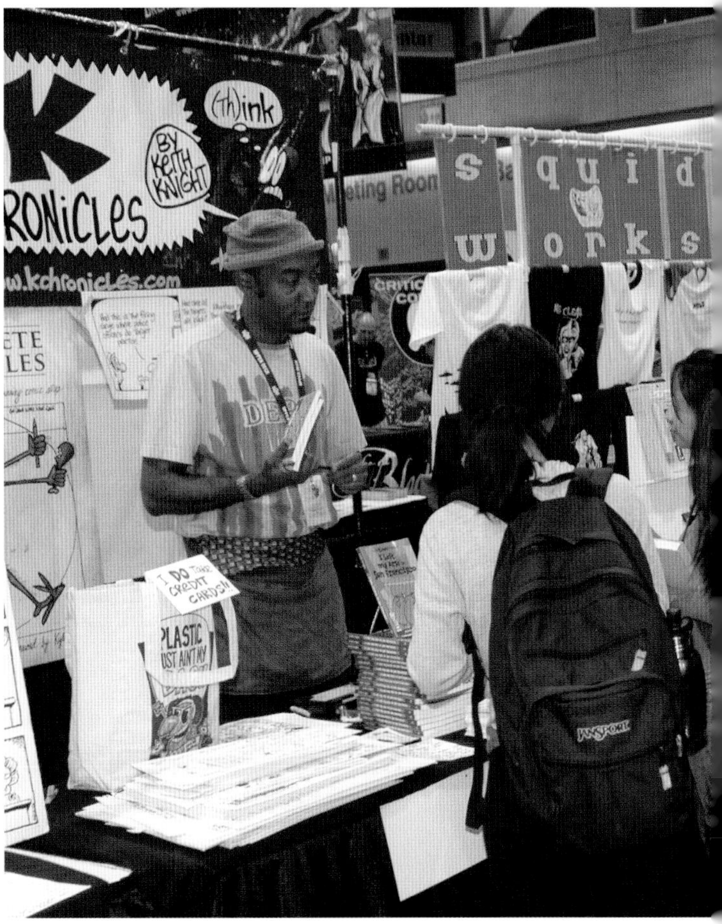
(th)ink
BY KEITH KNIGHT
RONICLES
www.kchronicles.com
squid works

OPPOSITE, CLOCKWISE FROM TOP LEFT: Author Laurell K. Hamilton making her first Comic-Con appearance, in 2007; just a portion of the massive Exhibit Hall in 2007; the *Iron Man* movie folks backstage at Comic-Con 2007: (from left) Robert Downey Jr., director Jon Favreau, Gwyneth Paltrow, and Terrence Howard; an award-winning *Dr. Who* entry in the 2007 Masquerade; Deepak Chopra with Grant Morrison in 2006; graphic novelist Miriam Katin with her Inkpot Award in 2007 **CLOCKWISE FROM TOP RIGHT:** Another amazing Masquerade costume, from 2006; cartoonist Keith Knight at his booth in 2008; part of the giant DC Comics booth in 2007

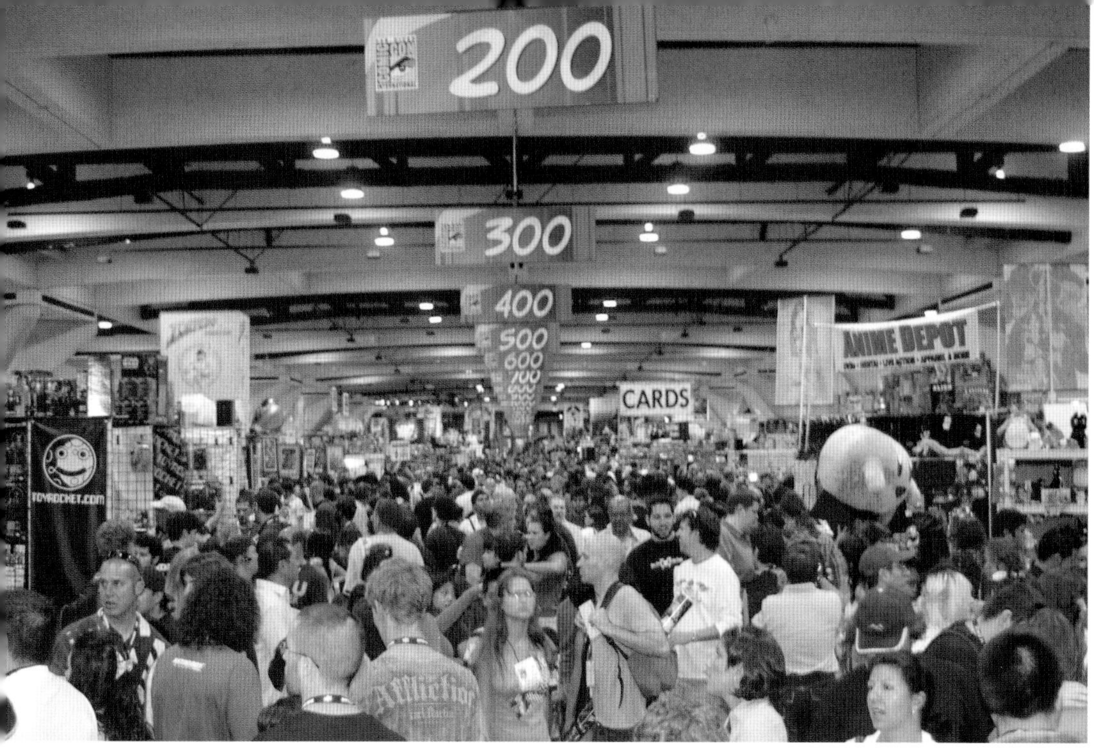
200
300
400
500
600
ANIME DEPOT
CARDS
TOYROCKET.COM
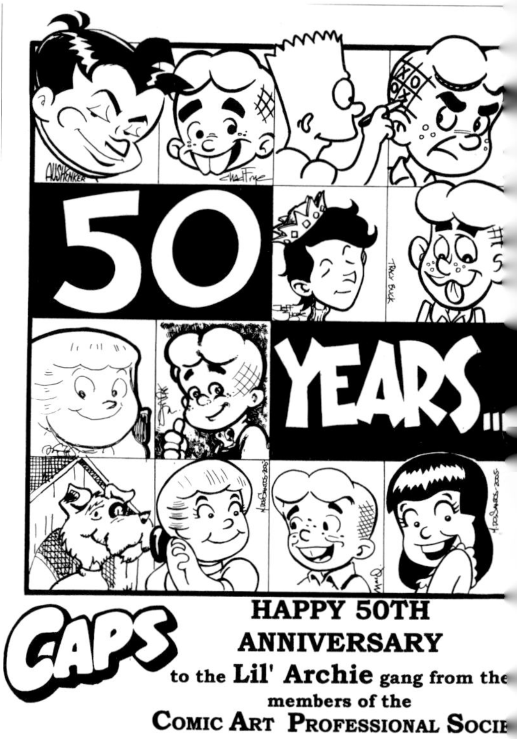
50
YEARS...
CAPS
HAPPY 50TH
ANNIVERSARY
to the Lil' Archie gang from the
members of the
COMIC ART PROFESSIONAL SOCIE
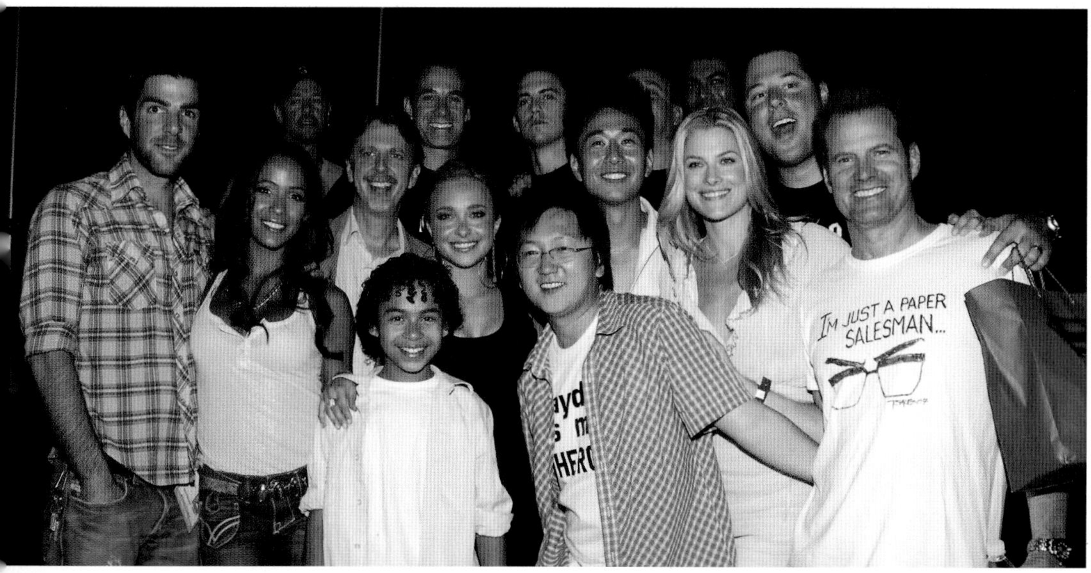
I'M JUST A PAPER
SALESMAN...
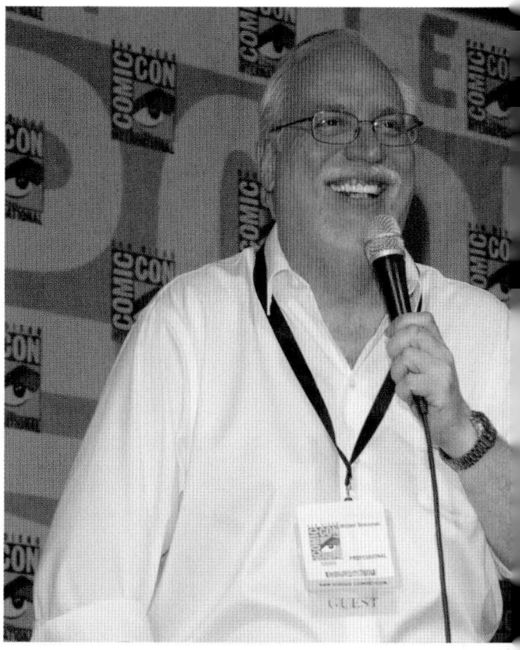
COMIC CON
GUEST
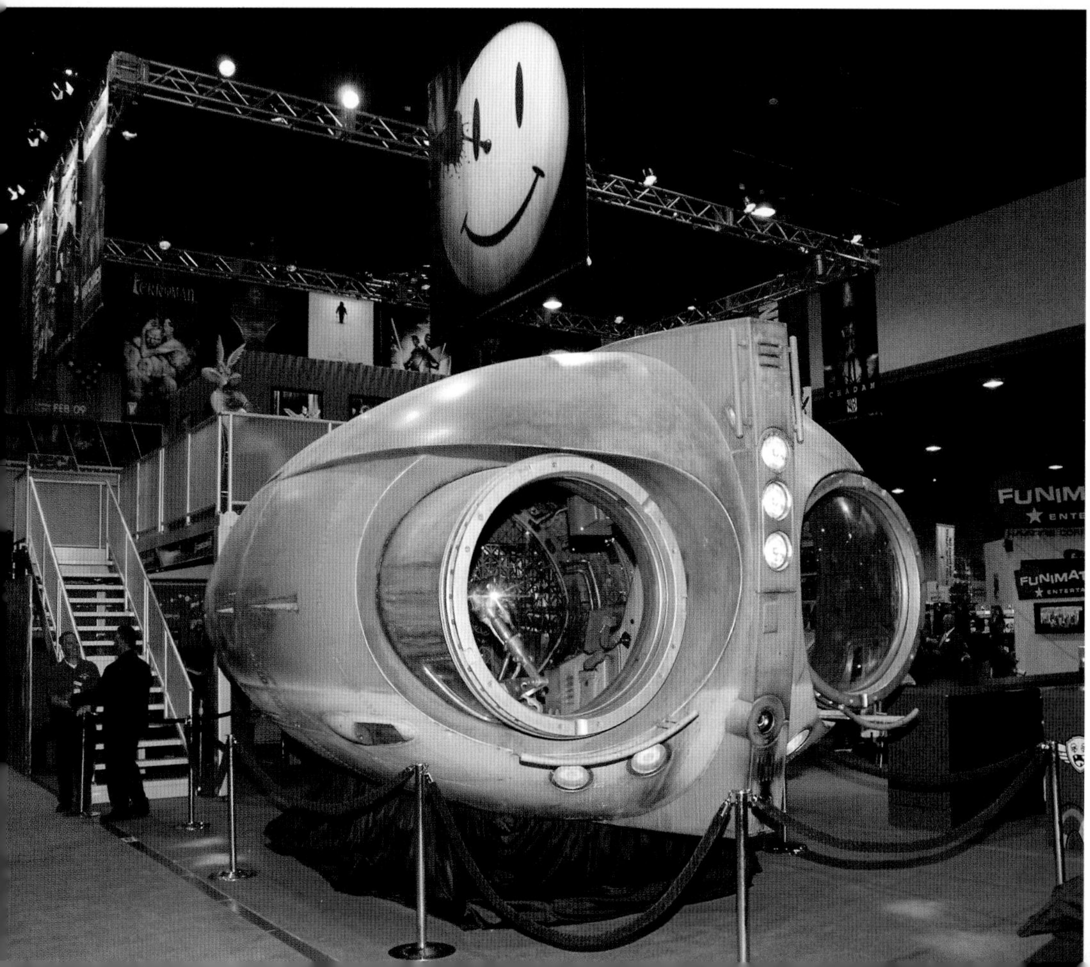
FUNIMATION
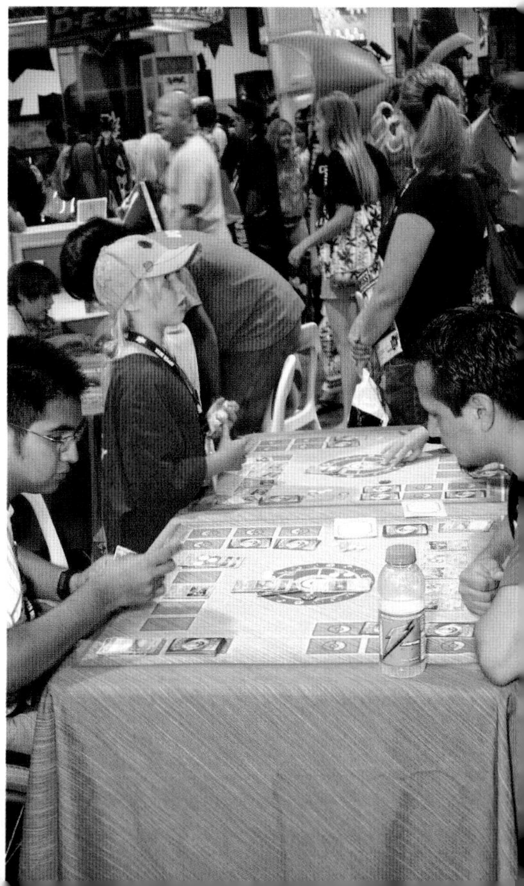

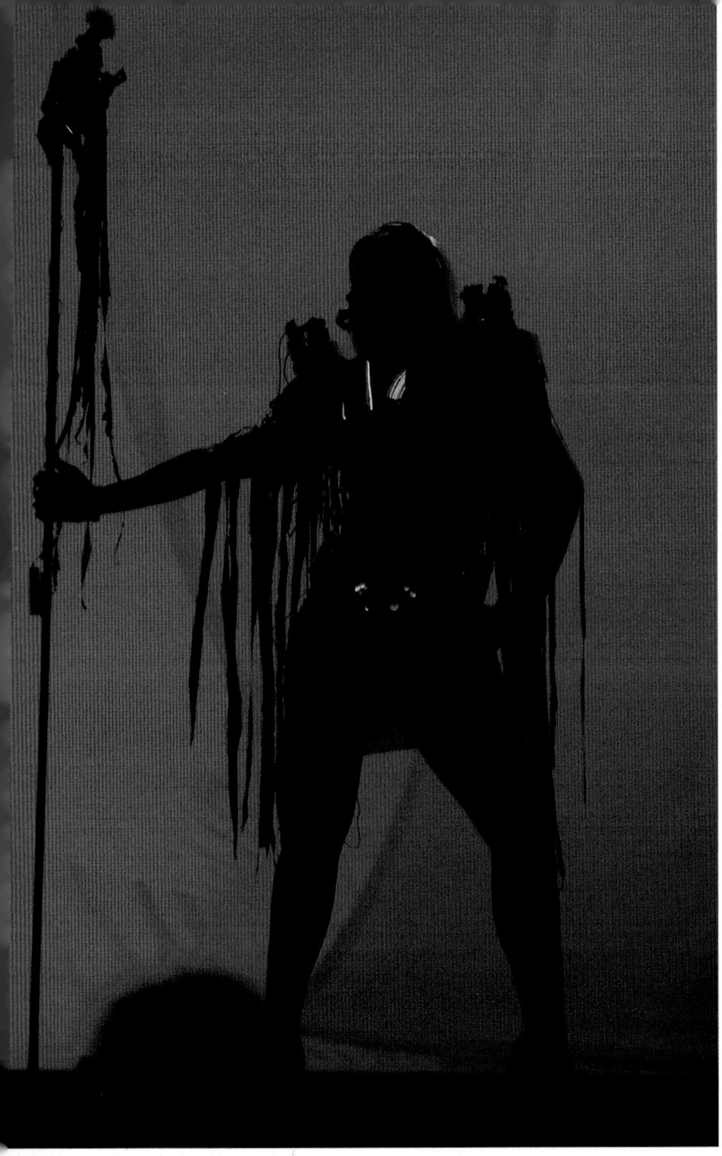

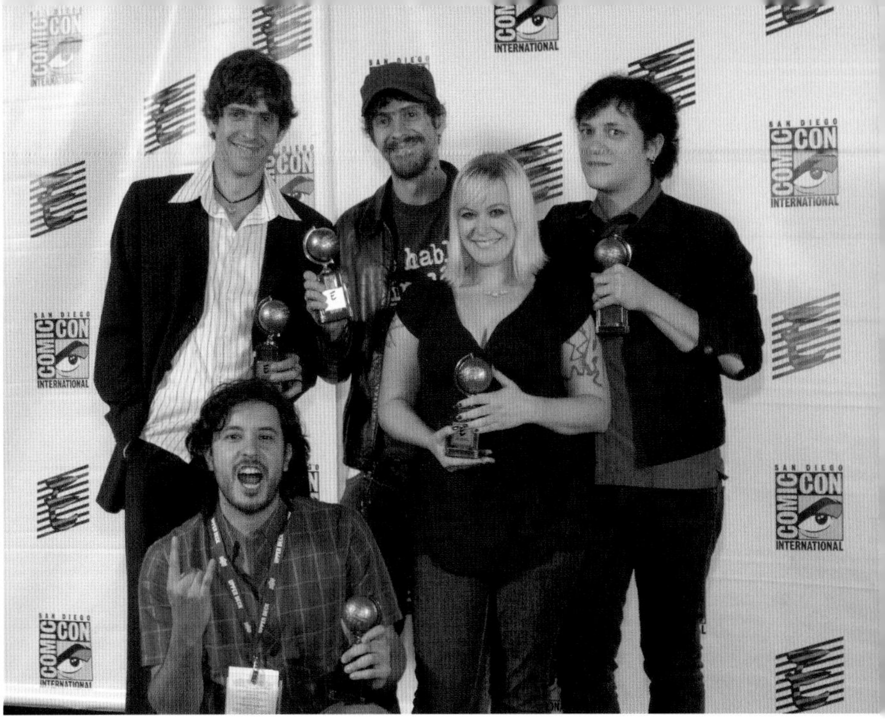
COMIC CON INTERNATIONAL

OPPOSITE, CLOCKWISE FROM TOP LEFT: A view of the Exhibit Hall in 2008 appearing to go on forever; the Comic Art Professional Society paying tribute to *Little Archie's* fiftieth birthday in 2005; the always popular writer and producer J. Michael Straczynski in 2008; more gaming for all ages; the impressive Owl Ship from *Watchmen* in the Warner Bros. booth in 2008; the cast of *Heroes* in 2007
CLOCKWISE FROM UPPER LEFT: A hint, in this 2008 photo, of how colorful and atmospheric the live performances of the Masquerade can be; Eisner Award winners (for Best Anthology, *5*): (clockwise from bottom left) Rafael Grampá, Fabio Moon, Gabriel Bá, Becky Cloonan, and Vasilis Lolos; the Exhibit Hall from the 2008 Comic-Con looking like Times Square on a Saturday night

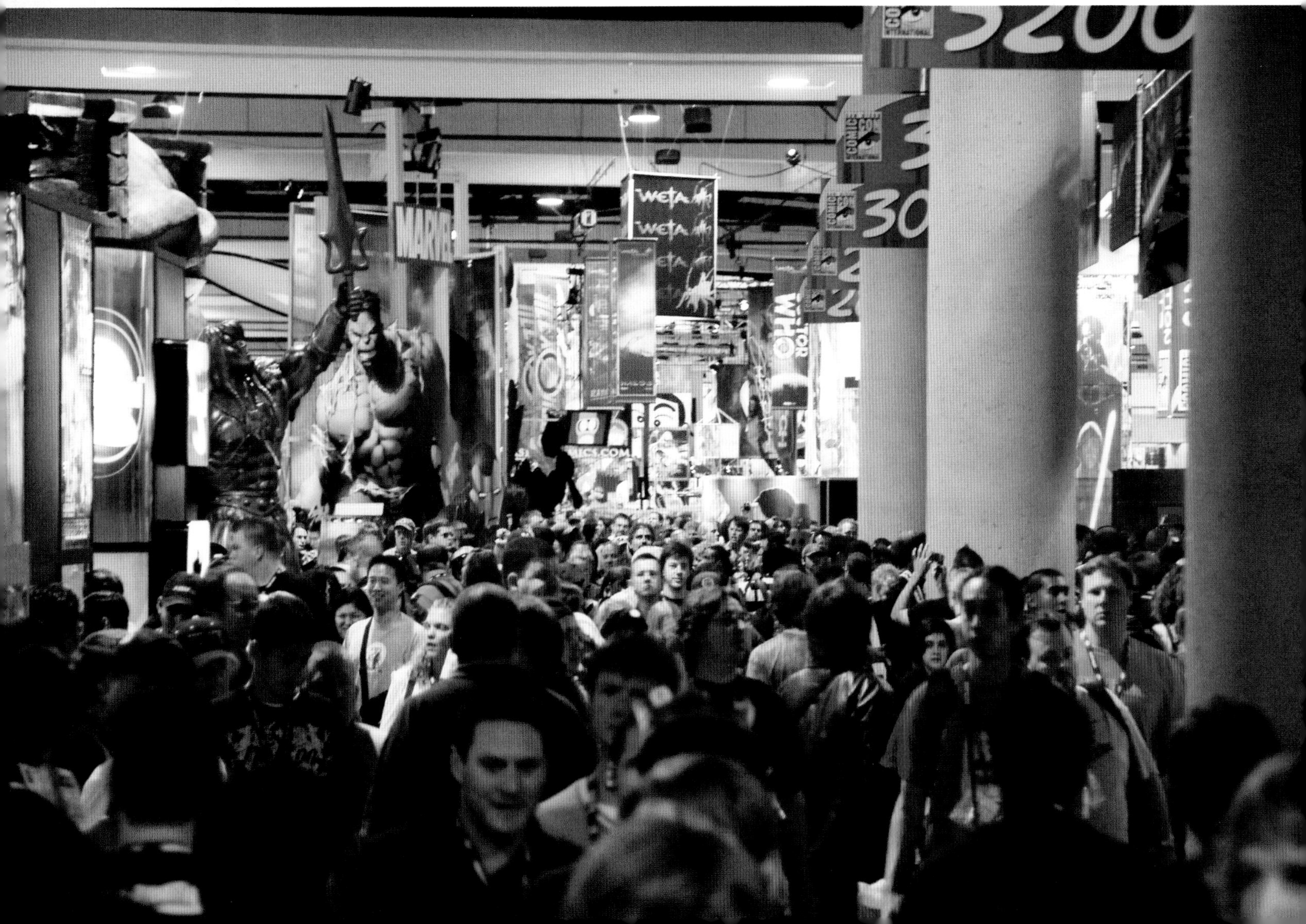
MARVEL
WETA

JIM LEE

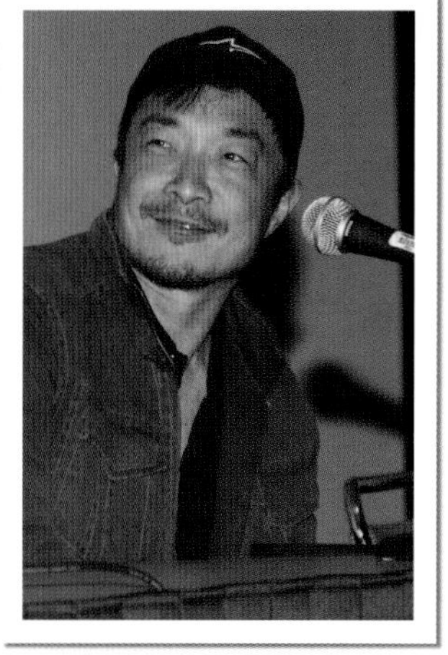

ONE OF the most dynamic and popular artists working in comics today, Jim Lee is a mainstay at both Comic-Con and WonderCon.

Born in South Korea in 1964, Lee was raised in St. Louis, Missouri. After attending Princeton University as a premed student, he found that his talents and interests lay more in the art and illustration world. After moving to La Jolla, California, Jim started his comics career at Marvel with work on *Alpha Flight* and *Punisher War Journal* in the late 1980s. But it was his stunning art on *Uncanny X-Men* that put him squarely into the sights of comics readers everywhere. Lee's heroic figures, fluid storytelling, and amazing design skills garnered him legions of fans. In 1991 he launched a new Marvel mutant title, simply titled *X-Men*, and the first issue went on to become the best-selling comic book of all time, selling more than eight million copies. In 1992 he was one of the original seven artists who formed Image Comics, with his own imprint, WildStorm Productions, based in La Jolla. His first comic for the fledgling company was *WildC.A.T.s*, which he co-wrote and drew.

In 1998 Lee sold WildStorm to DC Comics, where he became an integral part of the company. He collaborated with writer Jeph Loeb on the immensely popular *Batman: Hush* storyline. This led to a similar collaboration with writer Brian Azzarello on *Superman: For Tomorrow* and later with writer Frank Miller on the launch of a new Batman book, *All-Star Batman & Robin, the Boy Wonder*. In recent years, in addition to his editorial duties running WildStorm, Lee has been the executive creative director behind the new DC Universe Online game, which debuted at Comic-Con in 2008.

As a San Diego–area resident, Jim has been appearing at Comic-Con for more than fifteen years. Lee often donates his time and art to the Comic Book Legal Defense Fund, not only at Comic-Con and WonderCon, but at other convention appearances around the country as well. Lee's exciting style of superhero art—along with his longtime inker and collaborator Scott Williams—continues to set a high bar for storytelling and puts him in constant demand as one of comics' top artists.

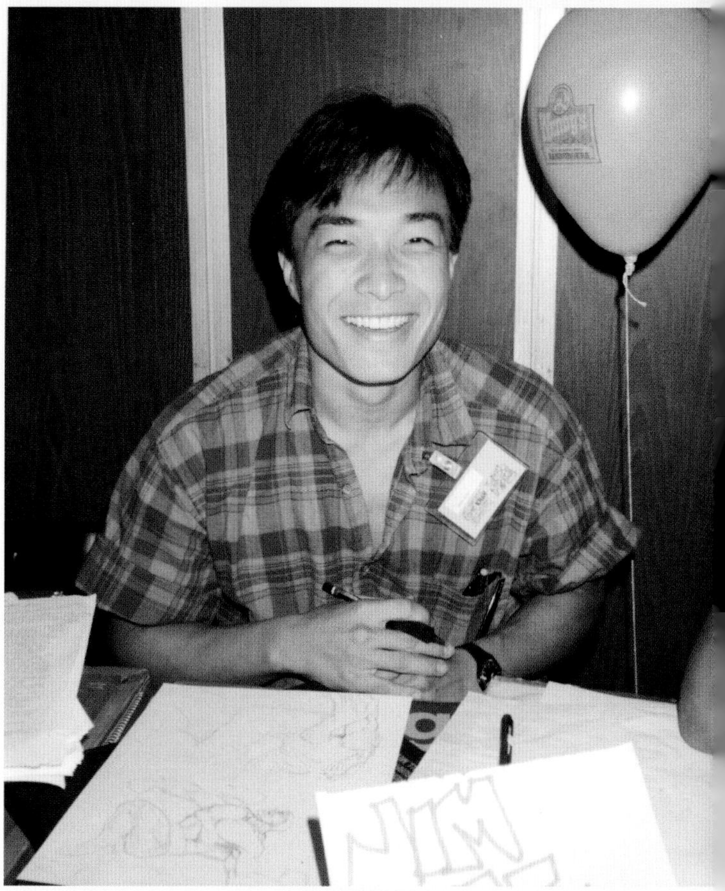

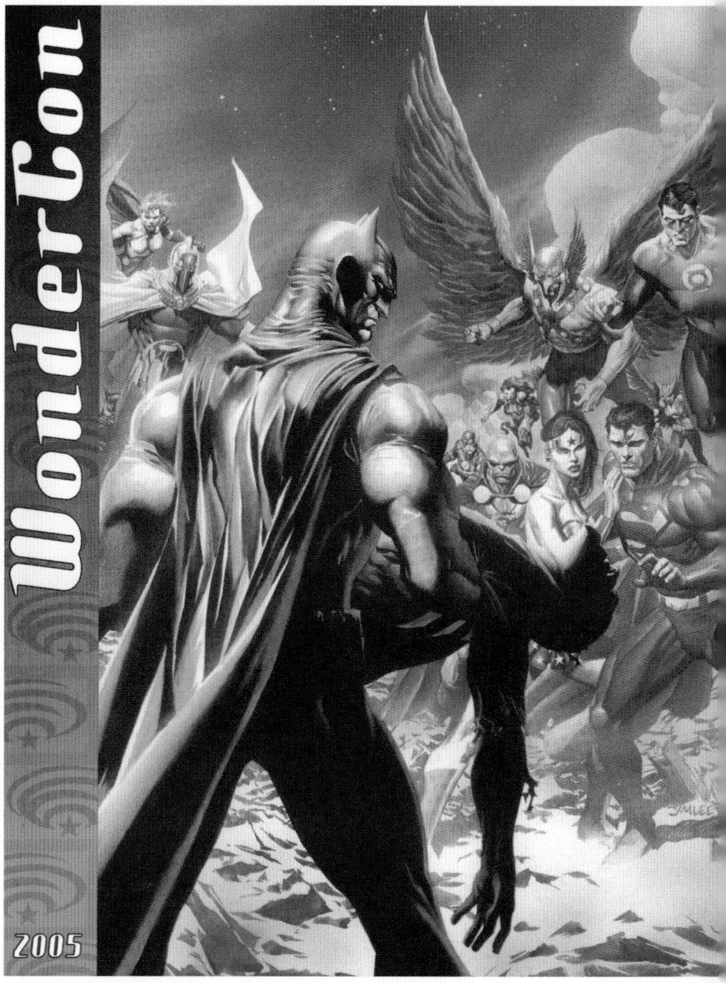
WonderCon
2005

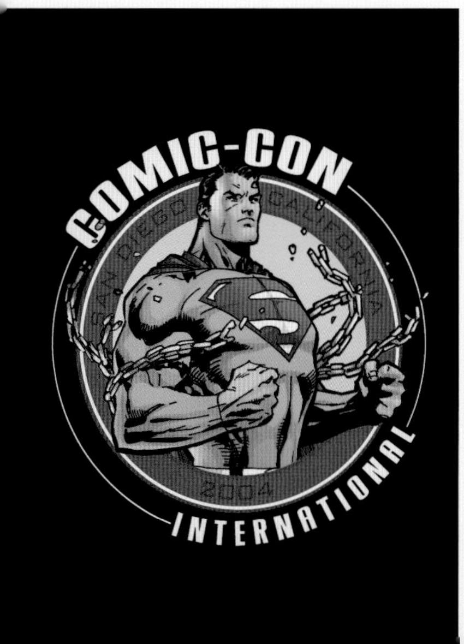
COMIC-CON
SAN DIEGO CALIFORNIA
2004
INTERNATIONAL

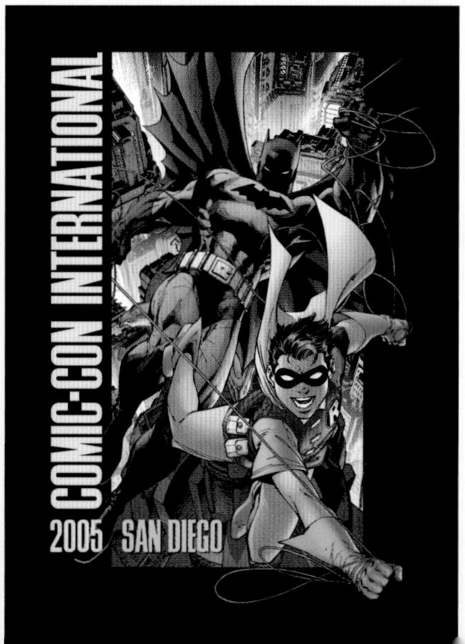
COMIC-CON INTERNATIONAL
2005 SAN DIEGO

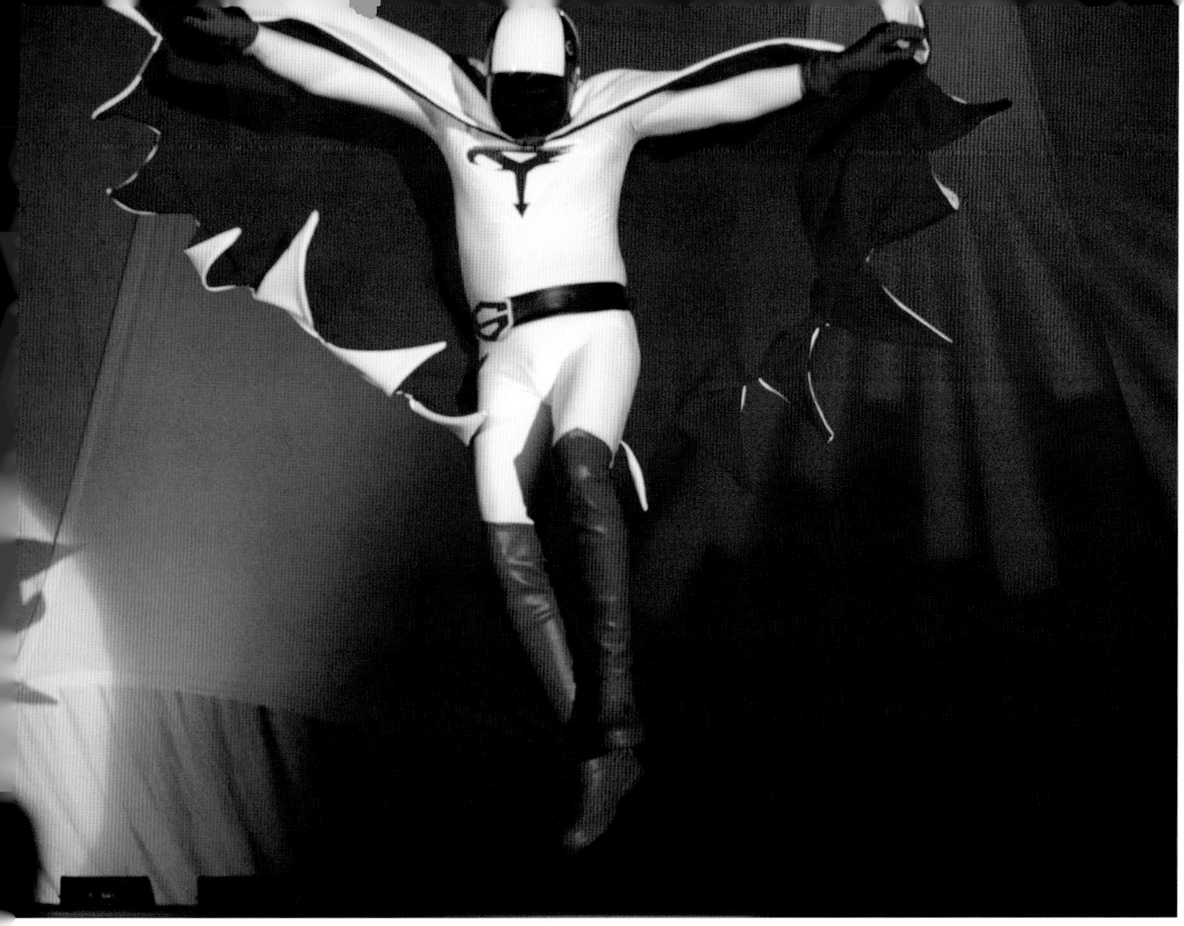

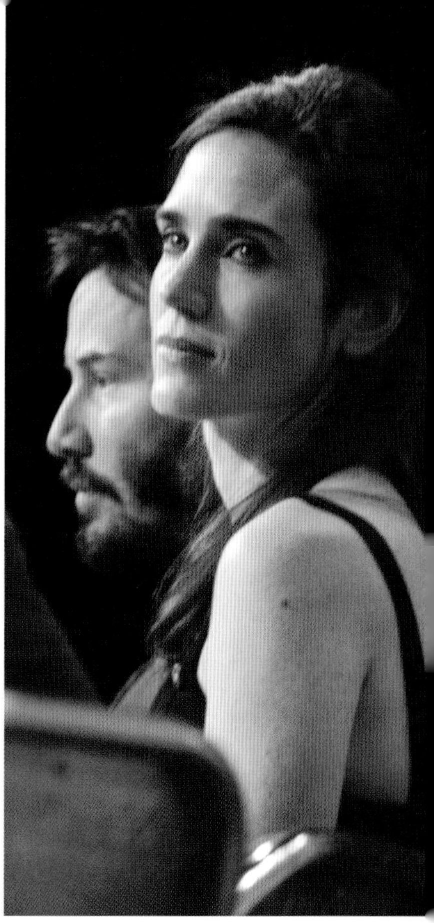

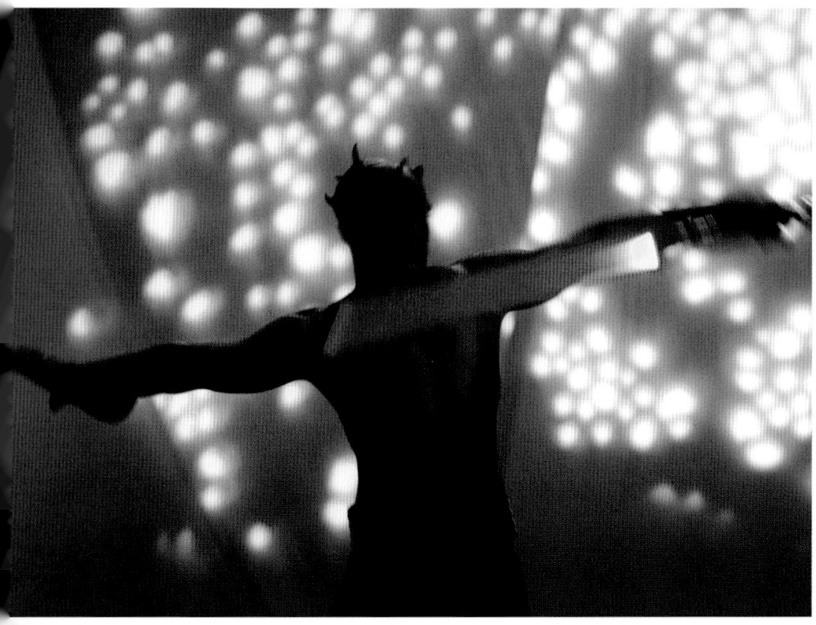

OPPOSITE, CLOCKWISE FROM TOP LEFT: Jim Lee at WonderCon in 2007; Jim in Artists' Alley in the late 1980s; Jim's cover pencils for the 2005 WonderCon program book, painted by Alex Ross; Jim Lee designs for the official Comic-Con T-shirts in 2005 (Batman and Robin) and 2004 (Superman)
CLOCKWISE FROM TOP LEFT: An amazing shot from the 2008 Masquerade, featuring an entry from *Battle of the Planets*; Keanu Reeves and Jennifer Connelly promoting *The Day the Earth Stood Still* in 2008; X-Wing Girl, the Best *Star Wars* entry in the 2008 Masquerade; shopping for back issues—still a top priority at Comic-Con; Darth Maul putting on a show at the 2008 Masquerade

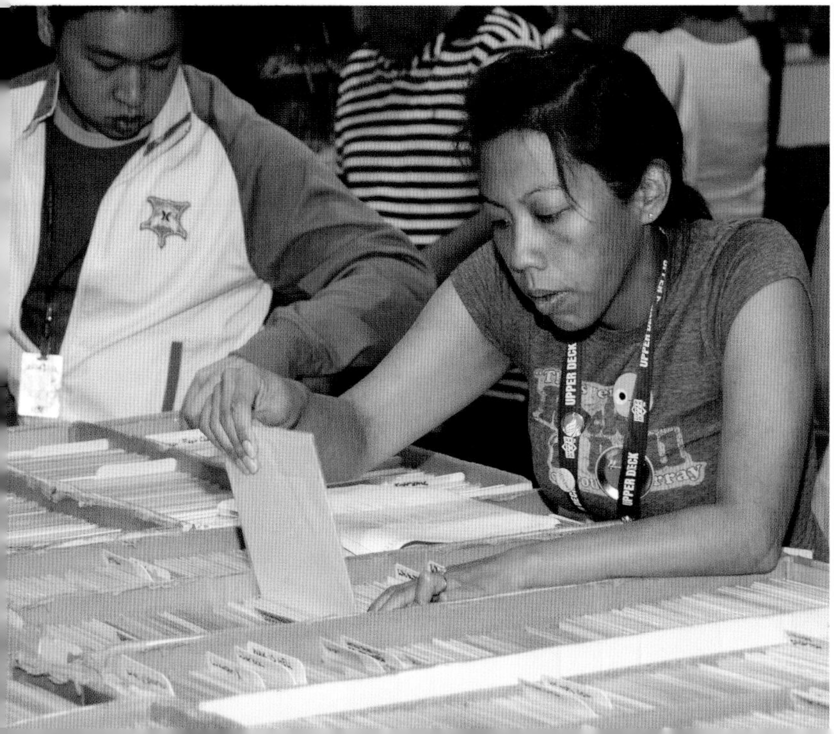
UPPER DECK

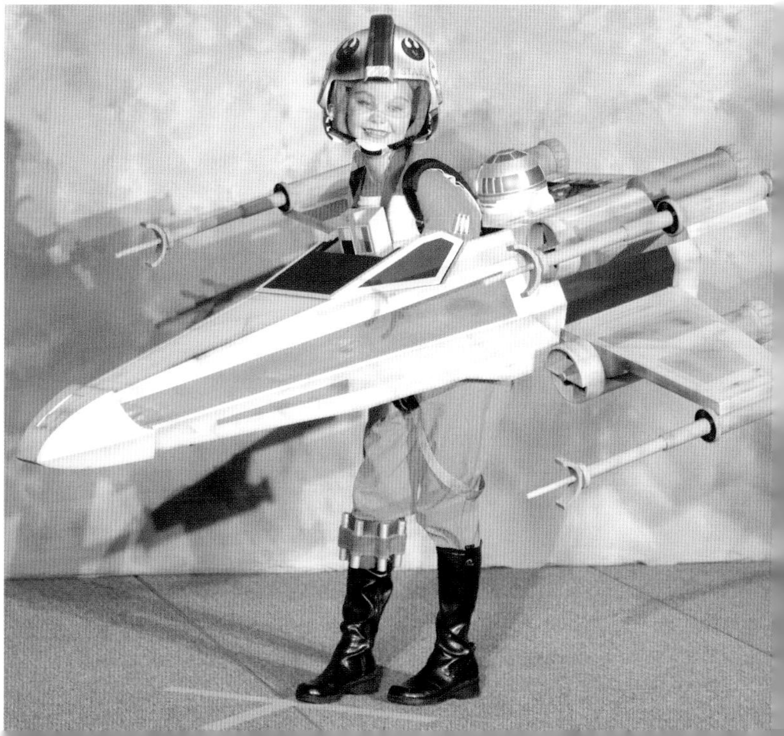

NOTABLE GUESTS

PEOPLE MAKING THEIR FIRST APPEARANCES AS SPECIAL GUESTS AT COMIC-CON IN THE 2000s...

2000
COMIC-CON 31

KYLE BAKER: cartoonist, graphic novelist, *The Cowboy Wally Show, Why I Hate Saturn, You Are Here*

PHOEBE GLOECKNER: alternative comics writer/artist, *A Child's Life and Other Stories*

BEN KATCHOR: cartoonist, *Julius Knipl, Real Estate Photographer*

HARRY KNOWLES: Internet writer and pop culture critic, Ain't It Cool News

HARRY LAMPERT: Golden Age comic book artist, *The Flash*; gag cartoonist

JEPH LOEB: comic book writer, *Batman: The Long Halloween, Superman for All Seasons*

SCOTT MCCLOUD: comic book writer/artist/creator, *Zot!*; author, *Understanding Comics, Reinventing Comics*

TIM SALE: comic book artist, *Batman: The Long Halloween, Superman for All Seasons*

BRYAN TALBOT: British comic book writer/artist, *The Adventures of Luther Arkwright; The Tale of One Bad Rat, Heart of Empire*

LEWIS TRONDHEIM: French cartoonist, *Harum Scarum; The Nimrod*

JANNY WURTS: fantasy author and illustrator, *Cycle of Fire* trilogy, *Wars of Light and Shadow* series

FIFTIETH ANNIVERSARY OF EC COMICS: Will Elder, Ric Estrada, Al Feldstein, Annie Gaines (wife of Bill), Jack Kamen, Adele Kurtzman (wife of Harvey), Marie Severin, Angelo Torres, Al Williamson

2001
COMIC-CON 32

BRIAN MICHAEL BENDIS: comic book writer, *Powers, Jinx, Torso, Fortune and Glory*

MICHAEL CHABON: author, *The Amazing Adventures of Kavalier & Clay*

FRANK CHO: comic book writer/artist, *Liberty Meadows*

JULIE DOUCET: French-Canadian alternative cartoonist, *Dirty Plotte, My New York Diary*

BRIAN AND WENDY FROUD: British fantasy illustrators/film designers, *The Dark Crystal, Labyrinth, Faeries*

GENE HA: comic book artist, *Top Ten*

KIM STANLEY ROBINSON: science fiction author, *The Wild Shore, Mars Trilogy*

SPIDER AND JEANNE ROBINSON: Canadian science fiction authors, *Starmind, Starseed*

P. CRAIG RUSSELL: comic book writer/artist, *Elric: Stormbringer, Fairy Tales of Oscar Wilde, Ring of the Nibelung*

ALVIN SCHWARTZ: Golden Age comic book writer, *Wonder Woman, The Flash, Green Lantern*

DAN SPIEGLE: Silver Age comic book artist, *Space Family Robinson, Blackhawk*

JHONEN VASQUEZ: comic book writer/artist/creator, *Johnny the Homicidal Maniac*

JUDD WINICK: comic book writer/artist, *The Adventures of Barry Ween, Boy Genius; Pedro and Me*

2002
COMIC-CON 33

DICK AYERS: Golden and Silver Age artist/inker, *Two-Gun Kid, Sgt. Fury and His Howling Commandos, Sgt. Rock*

MIKE CAREY: British comic book writer, *Lucifer, Hellblazer*

DEVIN GRAYSON: comic book writer, *Batman: Gotham Knights, Catwoman, The Titans*

FRANK JACOBS: writer/humorist, *MAD* magazine

JASON: Norwegian cartoonist, *Hey, Wait*

CHIP KIDD: book designer/author, *Batman Collected, Batman Animated*

BOB LUBBERS: Golden Age comic book "good girl" artist, *Fiction House*; artist, *Li'l Abner*

JASON LUTES: comic book writer/artist/creator, *Jar of Fools, Berlin*

CRAIG MCCRACKEN: artist/animator/creator, *The Powerpuff Girls, Dexter's Laboratory*

TONY MILLIONAIRE: alternative cartoonist, *Maakies, Sock Monkey*

BOB OKSNER: Golden and Silver Age comic book artist, *Binky, Adventures of Jerry Lewis, Adventures of Bob Hope, Angel and the Ape*

LEW SAYRE SCHWARTZ: Golden Age comic book artist, *Batman, Detective Comics, World's Finest Comics*

ERIC SHANOWER: comic book writer/artist, *Oz* graphic novels, *Age of Bronze*

HERB TRIMPE: Silver Age comic book artist, *The Incredible Hulk, G.I. Joe, Godzilla*

GEORGE WOODBRIDGE: cartoonist, *MAD* magazine

2003
COMIC-CON 34

BRIAN AZZARELLO: comic book writer/creator, *100 Bullets, Hellblazer*

SAL BUSCEMA: Silver Age comic book artist, *The Incredible Hulk, Peter Parker, The Spectacular Spider-Man*

PHILIPPE DUPUY AND CHARLES BERBÉRIAN: French cartoonist team, *Monsieur Jean* series

JACKSON "BUTCH" GUICE: comic book artist, *Action Comics, Birds of Prey, Ruse*

NALO HOPKINSON: Canadian-Jamaican fantasy author, *The Midnight Robber, Skin Folk*

STEVE JACKSON: game designer, *Car Wars*, *G.U.R.P.S.*

SID JACOBSON: longtime comic book editor at Harvey Comics, co-creator of Richie Rich

GEOFF JOHNS: comic book writer, *JSA*, *Flash*, *Hawkman*, *Teen Titans*

LARRY LIEBER: Silver Age comic book writer/artist, *The Rawhide Kid*; comic strip artist, *The Incredible Hulk*, *Spider-Man*

CARLA SPEED MCNEIL: comic book writer/artist/creator, *Finder*

KEVIN O'NEILL: British comic book artist and co-creator, *Marshall Law*, *League of Extraordinary Gentlemen*

HOWARD POST: comic book writer and artist, *Anthro*; syndicated cartoonist, *The Dropouts*

R. A. SALVATORE: science fiction author, *Demon Wars* trilogy, *Star Wars* novels

2004
COMIC-CON 35

JACK ADLER: Golden and Silver Age production artist, DC Comics; freelance artist/colorist

ROGER DEAN: British fantasy illustrator/painter, album cover artist

TOM GILL: Silver Age comic book artist, *The Lone Ranger*

BATTON LASH: comic book writer/artist/creator, *Supernatural Law*

CHUCK MCCANN: actor, films and television commercials; children's show host; voice actor

AARON MCGRUDER: syndicated cartoonist, *Boondocks*

BRAD MELTZER: fiction author, *The Tenth Justice*, *The Zero Game*; comic book writer, *Green Arrow*, *Identity Crisis*

BILL PLYMPTON: artist/animator, *Mutant Aliens*, *Idiots & Angels*, *The Tune*

EDUARDO RISSO: Argentinian comic book artist, *100 Bullets*

FRANK SPRINGER: comic book/comic strip artist, *Phoebe Zeit-Geist*, *National Lampoon*

CRAIG THOMPSON: graphic novel writer/artist, *Blankets*

JOHN TOTLEBEN: comic book artist, *Swamp Thing*, *Miracleman*, *The Dreaming*

2005
COMIC-CON 36

LALO ALCAREZ: syndicated cartoonist, *La Cucaracha*

DAVID B.: French comic book writer/artist, *Epileptic*

SY BARRY: comic strip artist, *The Phantom*

BOB BOLLING: Silver Age comic book writer/artist, *Little Archie*

BRUCE CAMPBELL: movie and television actor, *Evil Dead* series, *Briscoe County Jr.*; author, *If Chins Could Kill*

BOB FUJITANI: Golden Age comic book artist, *Black Condor*, *Dollman*, *The Ray*, *The Hangman*

PIA GUERRA: comic book artist, *Y: The Last Man*

RAY HARRYHAUSEN: movie producer/special effects artist, *The 7th Voyage of Sinbad*, *Clash of the Titans*

ROBERT JORDAN: fantasy author, *Wheel of Time* series

RICHARD MORGAN: British novelist, *Altered Carbon*, *Broken Angels*, *Market Forces*

GARY PANTER: underground comix writer/artist, *Jimbo*; television designer, *Pee-Wee's Playhouse*

ERIC POWELL: comic book writer/artist/creator, *The Goon*

J. J. SEDELMAIER: artist/animator, "TV Funhouse" on *Saturday Night Live*, *Harvey Birdman, Attorney at Law*

DEXTER TAYLOR: Silver Age comic book writer/artist, *Little Archie*

BRIAN K. VAUGHAN: comic book writer, *Y: The Last Man*, *Ex Machina*, *Runaways*, *Ultimate X-Men*

JAMES WARREN: comics and magazine publisher, *Famous Monsters of Filmland*, *Creepy*, *Eerie*

2006
COMIC-CON 37

PETER S. BEAGLE: fantasy author, *The Last Unicorn*, *A Fine and Private Place*

ART CLOKEY: animator/creator, *Gumby*

AMANDA CONNER: comic book artist, *Vampirella*, *Painkiller Jane*, *The Pro*

ROGER CORMAN: movie producer/director, *The Little Shop of Horrors*, *Tales of Terror*

BASIL GOGOS: painter/cover artist, *Famous Monsters of Filmland*

EVERETT RAYMOND KINSTLER: Golden Age comic book artist, pulp magazine illustrator, paperback cover artist

JAMES KOCHALKA: cartoonist, *American Elf*, *Peanutbutter & Jeremy*

KAZUO KOIKE: Japanese manga writer/co-creator, *Lone Wolf and Cub*, *Samurai Executioner*, *Lady Snowblood*

ROGER LANGRIDGE: New Zealand–British cartoonist, *Fred the Clown*, *Art D'Ecco*

JEAN-CLAUDE MÉZIÈRES: French comic book artist, *Valerian*; film designer, *The Fifth Element*

JIMMY PALMIOTTI: prolific comic book writer/penciller/inker, *Jonah Hex*, *The Pro*, *21 Down*; co-creator, *Painkiller Jane*

CHRISTOPHER PAOLINI: fantasy author, *Eragon*

ANDY RUNTON: comic book writer/artist/creator, *Owly*

SHAG (JOSH AGLE): pop illustrator/painter

YOSHIHIRO TATSUMI: Japan's godfather of alternative manga, *The Push Man*, *Abandon the Old in Tokyo*

2007
COMIC-CON 38

ALISON BECHDEL: cartoonist, *Fun Home*, *Dykes to Watch Out For*

DARWYN COOKE: comic book writer/artist, *DC: The New Frontier*

GUY DELISLE: Canadian graphic novel author, *Pyongyang*, *Schenzen*

CORY DOCTOROW: Canadian blogger, coeditor of *Boing Boing*; science fiction author, *Down and Out in the Magic Kingdom*

WARREN ELLIS: comic book writer, *Transmetropolitan, Planetary*; fiction author, *Crooked Little Vein*

RENÉE FRENCH: alternative cartoonist, *Grit Bath, Marbles in My Underpants, The Ticking*

LAURELL K. HAMILTON: fantasy author, *Anita Blake* and *Merry Gentry* series

MIRIAM KATIN: Hungarian-Israeli children's book illustrator; graphic novelist, *We Are on Our Own*

DAVID MORRELL: author, *First Blood, The Brotherhood of the Rose*

LILY RENÉE PHILLIPS: Golden Age comic book artist, *Senorita Rio*, Fiction House cover artist

GEORGE ROMERO: film writer and director, *Night of the Living Dead, Dawn of the Dead, Creepshow*

F. PAUL WILSON: author, *The Keep, Repairman Jack* series

2008
COMIC-CON 39

RALPH BAKSHI: artist/animator/director, *Fritz the Cat, Heavy Traffic, Fire and Ice*

LYNDA BARRY: cartoonist, *Ernie Pook's Comeek, What It Is*

JIM BUTCHER: fantasy author, *The Dresden Files* and *Codex Alera* series

KIM DEITCH: alternative comics writer/artist, *Alias the Cat, The Boulevard of Broken Dreams*

VICTOR GORELICK: Archie Comics editor in chief, at the company for more than fifty years

AL JAFFEE: *MAD* magazine cartoonist, creator of *MAD* fold-ins

DEAN KOONTZ: fiction author, *Odd Thomas* series

TITE KUBO: Japanese manga writer/artist/creator, *Bleach*

RUTU MODAN: Israeli illustrator, comics writer/artist, *Exit Wounds*

NOEL NEILL: movie/television actress, played Lois Lane on the *Adventures of Superman*

FLOYD NORMAN: storyboard artist/animator, *The Hunchback of Notre Dame, Toy Story 2*

ADRIAN TOMINE: alternative comics writer/artist, *Optic Nerve, Shortcomings*

JIM WOODRING: alternative comics writer/artist, *The Frank Book, The Book of Jim, Seeing Things*

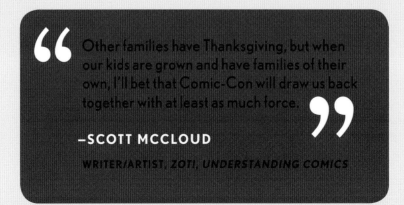

"Other families have Thanksgiving, but when our kids are grown and have families of their own, I'll bet that Comic-Con will draw us back together with at least as much force."

—SCOTT MCCLOUD
WRITER/ARTIST, ZOT!, UNDERSTANDING COMICS

APPENDICES

"Sitting by the pool at the old El Cortez listening to Jack Kirby and Sergio Aragonés tell tales in the evening hours after the con ... getting to know Dick Sprang over a meal he insisted on picking up the check for, after growing up on his Batman ... unveiling the DC stamps, and the breakfast we held before it for the talent who had created the art on the stamps, with Jim Lee and Carmine Infantino energetically comparing notes on what it meant to be a star artist in the field in different decades ... picking up the Hall of Fame Award for my mentor, Joe Orlando ... a breakfast with Will and Ann Eisner and Denis Kitchen, at which Will told me his view of where I fit in the world of comics ... Mark Evanier making sure I didn't leave the Eisners so I could receive the Bob Clampett Humanitarian Award ... and every year, watching the crowd as they come in at the beginning of the show, and their faces as they flow into the DC booth."

—PAUL LEVITZ
PRESIDENT AND PUBLISHER, DC COMICS
(On his most memorable Comic-Con moments)

ABOVE: Paul Levitz accepting the Inkpot Award for Golden and Silver Age artist Al Plastino in 2008

WILL EISNER COMIC INDUSTRY AWARDS

will Eisner
COMIC INDUSTRY
AWARDS

THE WILL EISNER COMIC INDUSTRY AWARDS are named after the visionary comics writer and artist Will Eisner (1917–2005), creator of *The Spirit*. Originally named for Jack Kirby, they're regarded as the comic book industry equivalent of the Oscars. The awards recognize creative achievement in a variety of categories and are given out each year. For more information on the awards, SEE page 84.

1985 KIRBY AWARDS
(for works published in 1984)

BEST SINGLE ISSUE: *Swamp Thing Annual* #2, by Alan Moore, Steve Bissette, and John Totleben (DC)

BEST CONTINUING SERIES: *Swamp Thing*, by Alan Moore, Steve Bissette, and John Totleben (DC)

BEST BLACK-AND-WHITE SERIES: *Cerebus*, by Dave Sim and Gerhard (Aardvark-Vanaheim)

BEST FINITE SERIES: *Crisis on Infinite Earths*, by Marv Wolfman and George Pérez (DC)

BEST NEW SERIES: *Zot!* by Scott McCloud (Eclipse)

BEST GRAPHIC ALBUM: *Beowulf*, by Jerry Bingham (First)

BEST WRITER: Alan Moore, *Swamp Thing* (DC)

BEST ARTIST: Dave Stevens, *Rocketeer* (Comico)

BEST ART TEAM: Steve Bissette and John Totleben, *Swamp Thing* (DC)

BEST COVER: *Swamp Thing* #34, by Steve Bissette and John Totleben (DC)

BEST COMICS PUBLICATION: *Comics Buyer's Guide*, edited by Don and Maggie Thompson (Krause Publications)

1986 KIRBY AWARDS
(for works published in 1985)

BEST SINGLE ISSUE: *Daredevil* #227, by Frank Miller and David Mazzucchelli (Marvel)

BEST CONTINUING SERIES: *Swamp Thing*, by Alan Moore, Steve Bissette, and John Totleben (DC)

BEST BLACK-AND-WHITE COMIC: *Love and Rockets*, by Jaime Hernandez and Gilbert Hernandez (Fantagraphics)

BEST FINITE SERIES: *Crisis on Infinite Earths*, by Marv Wolfman and George Pérez (DC)

BEST NEW SERIES: *Miracleman*, by Alan Moore and various artists (Eclipse)

BEST GRAPHIC ALBUM: *Rocketeer Graphic Album*, by Dave Stevens (Eclipse)

BEST WRITER: Alan Moore, *Swamp Thing* (DC)

BEST WRITER/ARTIST (SINGLE OR TEAM): Frank Miller and David Mazzucchelli, *Daredevil* (Marvel)

BEST ARTIST: Steve Rude, *Nexus* (First)

BEST ART TEAM: George Pérez and Jerry Ordway, for *Crisis on Infinite Earths* (DC)

1987 KIRBY AWARDS
(for works published in 1986)

BEST SINGLE ISSUE: *Batman: The Dark Knight Returns* #1, by Frank Miller and Klaus Janson (DC)

BEST CONTINUING SERIES: *Swamp Thing*, by Alan Moore, Steve Bissette, and John Totleben (DC)

BEST BLACK-AND-WHITE COMIC: *Cerebus*, by Dave Sim and Gerhard (Aardvark-Vanaheim)

BEST FINITE SERIES: *Batman: The Dark Knight Returns*, by Frank Miller and Klaus Janson (DC)

BEST NEW SERIES: *Watchmen*, by Alan Moore and Dave Gibbons (DC)

BEST GRAPHIC ALBUM: *Batman: The Dark Knight Returns*, by Frank Miller and Klaus Janson (DC)

BEST WRITER: Alan Moore, *Watchmen* (DC)

BEST WRITER/ARTIST (SINGLE OR TEAM): Alan Moore and Dave Gibbons, *Watchmen* (DC)

BEST ARTIST: Bill Sienkiewicz, *Elektra: Assassin* (Marvel)

BEST ART TEAM: Frank Miller, Klaus Janson, and Lynn Varley, *Batman: The Dark Knight Returns* (DC)

HALL OF FAME: Carl Barks, Will Eisner, Jack Kirby

NOTE: In 1988 the Kirby Awards were disbanded and replaced by two awards programs: the Harveys (named for Harvey Kurtzman) and the Eisners (named for Will Eisner).

1988 EISNER AWARDS
(for works published in 1987)

BEST SINGLE ISSUE: *Gumby Summer Fun Special* #1, by Bob Burden and Art Adams (Comico)

BEST CONTINUING SERIES: *Concrete*, by Paul Chadwick (Dark Horse)

BEST BLACK-AND-WHITE SERIES: *Concrete*, by Paul Chadwick (Dark Horse)

BEST FINITE SERIES: *Watchmen*, by Alan Moore and Dave Gibbons (DC)

BEST NEW SERIES: *Concrete*, by Paul Chadwick (Dark Horse)

BEST GRAPHIC ALBUM: *Watchmen*, by Alan Moore and Dave Gibbons (DC)

BEST WRITER: Alan Moore, *Watchmen* (DC)

BEST WRITER/ARTIST (SINGLE OR TEAM): Alan Moore and Dave Gibbons, *Watchmen* (DC)

BEST ARTIST: Steve Rude, *Nexus* (First)

BEST ART TEAM: Steve Rude, Willie Blyberg, and Ken Steacy, *Space Ghost Special* (Comico)

HALL OF FAME: Milton Caniff

1989 EISNER AWARDS
(for works published in 1988)

BEST SINGLE ISSUE: *Kings In Disguise* #1, by James Vance and Dan Burr (Kitchen Sink)

BEST CONTINUING SERIES: *Concrete*, by Paul Chadwick (Dark Horse)

BEST BLACK-AND-WHITE SERIES: *Concrete*, by Paul Chadwick (Dark Horse)

BEST FINITE SERIES: *Silver Surfer*, by Stan Lee and Jean "Moebius" Giraud (Marvel)

BEST NEW SERIES: *Kings In Disguise*, by James Vance and Dan Burr (Kitchen Sink)

BEST GRAPHIC ALBUM: *Batman: The Killing Joke*, by Alan Moore and Brian Bolland (DC)

BEST WRITER: Alan Moore, *Batman: The Killing Joke* (DC)

BEST WRITER/ARTIST: Paul Chadwick, *Concrete* (Dark Horse)

BEST ARTIST: Brian Bolland, *Batman: The Killing Joke* (DC)

BEST ART TEAM: Alan Davis and Paul Neary, *Excalibur* (Marvel)

HALL OF FAME: Harvey Kurtzman

NOTE: No awards were presented in 1990, a transition year when Comic-Con International took over administration of the awards.

1991 EISNER AWARDS
(for works published in 1990)

BEST STORY OR SINGLE ISSUE: *Concrete Celebrates Earth Day*, by Paul Chadwick, Charles Vess, and Jean "Moebius" Giraud (Dark Horse)

BEST CONTINUING SERIES: *Sandman*, by Neil Gaiman and various artists (DC)

BEST BLACK-AND-WHITE SERIES: *Xenozoic Tales*, by Mark Schultz (Kitchen Sink)

BEST FINITE SERIES: *Give Me Liberty*, by Frank Miller and Dave Gibbons (Dark Horse)

BEST GRAPHIC ALBUM–NEW: *Elektra Lives Again*, by Frank Miller and Lynn Varley (Marvel)

BEST GRAPHIC ALBUM–REPRINT: *The Sandman: The Doll's House*, by Neil Gaiman and various artists (DC)

BEST WRITER: Neil Gaiman, *The Sandman* (DC)

BEST WRITER/ARTIST OR WRITER/ARTIST TEAM: Frank Miller and Geof Darrow, *Hard Boiled* (Dark Horse)

BEST ARTIST: Steve Rude, *Nexus* (First)

BEST INKER: Al Williamson

HALL OF FAME: R. Crumb, Alex Toth

1992 EISNER AWARDS
(for works published in 1991)

NOMINATING JUDGES: JEFF GELB, ROCHON PERRY, LYNN PETERSON, SCOTT SHAW!, JANET TAIT

BEST SINGLE ISSUE OR STORY: *The Sandman* #22–#28: *Season of Mists*, by Neil Gaiman and various artists (DC)

BEST CONTINUING SERIES: *The Sandman*, by Neil Gaiman and various artists (DC)

BEST FINITE SERIES: *Concrete: Fragile Creature*, by Paul Chadwick (Dark Horse)

BEST ANTHOLOGY: *Dark Horse Presents*, edited by Randy Stradley (Dark Horse)

BEST GRAPHIC ALBUM–NEW: *To the Heart of the Storm*, by Will Eisner (Kitchen Sink)

BEST GRAPHIC ALBUM–REPRINT: *Maus II*, by Art Spiegelman (Pantheon Books)

BEST HUMOR PUBLICATION: *Groo the Wanderer*, by Mark Evanier and Sergio Aragonés (Marvel/Epic)

BEST COMIC STRIP COLLECTION: *Calvin and Hobbes: The Revenge of the Baby-Sat*, by Bill Watterson (Andrews McMeel)

BEST WRITER: Neil Gaiman, *The Books of Magic* (DC); *Miracleman* (Eclipse)

BEST WRITER/ARTIST OR WRITER/ARTIST TEAM: Peter David and Dale Keown, *The Incredible Hulk* (Marvel)

BEST ARTIST: Simon Bisley, *Batman/Judge Dredd: Judgment on Gotham* (DC)

BEST INKER: Adam Kubert, *Batman Versus Predator* (DC and Dark Horse)

BEST COLORIST: Steve Oliff, *Batman: Legends of the Dark Knight* (DC); *2112* (Dark Horse); *Akira* (Marvel)

BEST COVER ARTIST: Brian Bolland, *Animal Man* (DC)

BEST EDITOR: Karen Berger, *The Sandman*; *Shade, the Changing Man*; *Kid Eternity*; and *The Books of Magic* (DC)

BEST COMICS-RELATED PERIODICAL: *Comics Buyer's Guide*, edited by Don and Maggie Thompson (Krause Publications)

BEST COMICS-RELATED BOOK: *From Aargh! to Zap!: Harvey Kurtzman's Visual History of the Comics*, by Harvey Kurtzman, edited by Howard Zimmerman (Prentice Hall Press)

BEST COMICS-RELATED PRODUCT: Sandman statue, by Randy Bowen (DC)

HALL OF FAME: Joe Shuster, Jerry Siegel, Wally Wood

1993 EISNER AWARDS
(for works published in 1992)

NOMINATING JUDGES: BRIAN HIBBS, ROLF HOLBACH, BETH HOLLEY, HEIDI MACDONALD, ARLEN SCHUMER

BEST SINGLE ISSUE: *Nexus: The Origin*, by Mike Baron and Steve Rude (Dark Horse)

BEST SHORT STORY: "Two Cities," in *Xenozoic Tales* #12, by Mark Schultz (Kitchen Sink)

BEST SERIALIZED STORY: "From Hell," by Alan Moore and Eddie Campbell, in *Taboo* (SpiderBaby Graphix/Tundra)

BEST CONTINUING SERIES: *The Sandman*, by Neil Gaiman and various artists (DC)

BEST FINITE SERIES: *Grendel: War Child*, by Matt Wagner and Patrick McEown (Dark Horse)

BEST ANTHOLOGY: *Taboo*, edited by Steve Bissette (SpiderBaby Graphix/Tundra)

BEST GRAPHIC ALBUM–NEW: *Signal to Noise*, by Neil Gaiman and Dave McKean (VG Graphics/Dark Horse)

BEST GRAPHIC ALBUM–REPRINT: *Sin City*, by Frank Miller (Dark Horse)

BEST ARCHIVAL COLLECTION: *Carl Barks Library* album series (Gladstone)

BEST HUMOR PUBLICATION: *Bone*, by Jeff Smith (Cartoon Books)

BEST COMIC STRIP COLLECTION: *Calvin and Hobbes: Attack of the Deranged Mutant Killer Monster Snow Goons*, by Bill Watterson (Andrews McMeel)

BEST WRITER: Neil Gaiman, *Miracleman* (Eclipse) and *The Sandman* (DC)

BEST PAINTER: Dave Dorman, *Aliens: Tribes* (Dark Horse)

BEST PENCILLER: Steve Rude, *Nexus: The Origin* (Dark Horse)

BEST PENCILLER/INKER, BLACK-AND-WHITE PUBLICATION: Frank Miller, "Sin City," *Dark Horse Presents* (Dark Horse)

BEST PENCILLER/INKER, COLOR PUBLICATION: P. Craig Russell, *Fairy Tales of Oscar Wilde* (NBM); *Batman: Robin 3000, Batman: Legends of the Dark Knight: "Hothouse"* (DC)

BEST INKER: Kevin Nowlan, *Batman: Sword of Azrael* (DC)

BEST COLORIST: Steve Oliff/Olyoptics, *Batman: Legends of the Dark Knight* #28–#30, *Martian Manhunter: American Secrets* (DC); *James Bond 007: Serpent's Tooth* (Dark Horse); *Spawn* (Image)

BEST LETTERER: Todd Klein, *The Sandman, The Demon* (DC)

BEST WRITER/ARTIST: Frank Miller, "Sin City," *Dark Horse Presents* (Dark Horse)

BEST WRITER/ARTIST TEAM: Mike Baron/Steve Rude, *Nexus: The Origin* (Dark Horse)

BEST COVER ARTIST: Brian Bolland, *Animal Man, Wonder Woman* (DC)

BEST EDITOR: Archie Goodwin, *Batman: Legends of the Dark Knight, Batman: Sword of Azrael, Deadman: Exorcism* (DC)

BEST COMICS-RELATED PERIODICAL: *Comics Buyer's Guide*, edited by Don and Maggie Thompson (Krause Publications)

BEST PUBLICATION DESIGN: *The Sandman: Season of Mists*, designed by Dave McKean (DC)

HALL OF FAME: C. C. Beck, William Gaines

1994 EISNER AWARDS
(for works published in 1993)

NOMINATING JUDGES: MARK ASKWITH, MIMI CRUZ, MICHAEL T. GILBERT, BARRY SHORT, MARK YTURRALDE

BEST SINGLE ISSUE: *Batman Adventures: Mad Love*, by Paul Dini and Bruce Timm (DC)

BEST SHORT STORY: "The Amazing Colossal Homer," in *Simpsons Comics* #1, by Steve Vance, Cindy Vance, and Bill Morrison (Bongo)

BEST SERIALIZED STORY: *Bone* #8–#10: "The Great Cow Race," by Jeff Smith (Cartoon Books)

BEST CONTINUING SERIES: *Bone*, by Jeff Smith (Cartoon Books)

BEST FINITE/LIMITED SERIES: *Marvels*, by Kurt Busiek and Alex Ross (Marvel)

BEST ANTHOLOGY: *Dark Horse Presents*, edited by Randy Stradley (Dark Horse)

BEST GRAPHIC ALBUM–NEW: *A Small Killing*, by Alan Moore and Oscar Zarate (VG Graphics/Dark Horse)

BEST GRAPHIC ALBUM–REPRINT: *Cerebus: Mothers & Daughters 1: Flight*, by Dave Sim and Gerhard (Aardvark-Vanaheim)

BEST ARCHIVAL COLLECTION: *Complete Little Nemo in Slumberland*, vol. 6, by Winsor McCay (Fantagraphics)

BEST HUMOR PUBLICATION: *Bone*, by Jeff Smith (Cartoon Books)

BEST WRITER: Neil Gaiman, *The Sandman* (DC/Vertigo); *Death: The High Cost of Living* (DC/Vertigo)

BEST WRITER/ARTIST: Jeff Smith, *Bone* (Cartoon Books)

BEST PAINTER: Alex Ross, *Marvels* (Marvel)

BEST PENCILLER/INKER OR PENCILLER-INKER TEAM: P. Craig Russell, *The Sandman* #50 (DC/Vertigo)

BEST COLORIST: Steve Oliff and Reuben Rude (Olyoptics), *Spawn* (Image)

BEST LETTERER: Todd Klein, *The Shadow* (Dark Horse); *Dark Joker: The Wild* (DC); *The Sandman, The Demon, Jonah Hex: Two-Gun Mojo, Hellblazer* (DC/Vertigo)

BEST COVER ARTIST: Brian Bolland, *Animal Man* (DC/Vertigo); *Wonder Woman, Legends of the Dark Knight* #50 (DC)

BEST EDITOR (TIE): Karen Berger, *The Sandman, Death: The High Cost of Living* (DC/Vertigo) and Mike Carlin, *Superman* titles (DC)

BEST COMICS-RELATED BOOK: *Understanding Comics*, by Scott McCloud (Kitchen Sink)

BEST COMICS-RELATED PRODUCT/ITEM: Death statue, by Randy Bowen (DC)

BEST PUBLICATION DESIGN: *Marvels*, designed by Comicraft (Marvel)

HALL OF FAME: Steve Ditko, Stan Lee

1995 EISNER AWARDS
(for works published in 1994)

NOMINATING JUDGES: CARL DENBOW, TOM FASSBENDER, JOYCE GREENHOLDT, LARRY HOUSTON, CHRIS STURHANN

BEST SINGLE ISSUE: *Batman Adventures Holiday Special*, by Paul Dini, Bruce Timm, Ronnie Del Carmen, and others (DC)

BEST SHORT STORY: "The Babe Wore Red," by Frank Miller, in *Sin City: The Babe Wore Red and Other Stories* (Dark Horse/Legend)

BEST SERIALIZED STORY: "The Life and Times of Scrooge McDuck," by Don Rosa, in *Uncle Scrooge* #285–#296 (Gladstone)

BEST CONTINUING SERIES: *Bone*, by Jeff Smith (Cartoon Books)

BEST LIMITED SERIES: *Sin City: A Dame to Kill For*, by Frank Miller (Dark Horse/Legend)

BEST NEW SERIES: *Too Much Coffee Man*, by Shannon Wheeler (Adhesive)

BEST ANTHOLOGY: *Big Book of Urban Legends*, edited by Andy Helfer (Paradox Press)

BEST GRAPHIC ALBUM–NEW: *Fairy Tales of Oscar Wilde*, vol. 2, by P. Craig Russell (NBM)

BEST GRAPHIC ALBUM–REPRINT: *Hellboy: Seeds of Destruction*, by Mike Mignola (Dark Horse)

BEST ARCHIVAL COLLECTION: *The Christmas Spirit*, by Will Eisner (Kitchen Sink)

BEST HUMOR PUBLICATION: *Bone*, by Jeff Smith (Cartoon Books)

BEST WRITER: Alan Moore, *From Hell* (Kitchen Sink)

BEST WRITER/ARTIST: Mike Mignola, *Hellboy: Seeds of Destruction* (Dark Horse/Legend)

BEST WRITER/ARTIST–HUMOR: Jeff Smith, *Bone* (Cartoon Books)

BEST PAINTER: Jon J. Muth, *Mystery Play* (DC/Vertigo)

BEST PENCILLER/INKER OR PENCILLER/INKER TEAM: Dave Gibbons, *Martha Washington Goes to War* (Dark Horse)

BEST COLORING: Angus McKie, *Martha Washington Goes to War* (Dark Horse)

BEST LETTERING: Todd Klein, *Batman vs. Predator II* (DC/Dark Horse); *The Demon* (DC), *The Sandman* (DC/Vertigo); *Uncle Scrooge* (Gladstone)

BEST COVER ARTIST: Glenn Fabry, *Hellblazer* (DC/Vertigo)

TALENT DESERVING OF WIDER RECOGNITION: Evan Dorkin, *Milk and Cheese, Hectic Planet, Dork, Instant Piano*

BEST EDITOR: Karen Berger, *The Sandman, Sandman Mystery Theatre* (DC/Vertigo)

BEST COMICS-RELATED PUBLICATION: *Hero Illustrated* (Warrior Publications)

BEST COMICS-RELATED ITEM: Sandman Arabian Nights statue, designed by P. Craig Russell and sculpted by Randy Bowen (DC/Graphitti Designs)

BEST PUBLICATION DESIGN: *The Acme Novelty Library*, designed by Chris Ware (Fantagraphics)

HALL OF FAME: Frank Frazetta, Walt Kelly

1996 EISNER AWARDS
(for works published in 1995)

NOMINATING JUDGES: TOM DEHAVEN, NANCY FORD, MARK HERR, FRANK KURTZ, RORY ROOT

BEST SINGLE ISSUE: *Kurt Busiek's Astro City* #4: "Safeguards," by Kurt Busiek and Brent Anderson (Jukebox Productions/Image)

BEST SHORT STORY: "The Eltingville Comic-Book, Science-Fiction, Fantasy, Horror, and Role-Playing Club in Bring Me the Head of Boba Fett," by Evan Dorkin, in *Instant Piano* #3 (Dark Horse)

BEST SERIALIZED STORY: *Strangers in Paradise* #1-8, by Terry Moore (Abstract Studios)

BEST CONTINUING SERIES: *The Acme Novelty Library*, by Chris Ware (Fantagraphics)

BEST TITLE FOR YOUNGER READERS: *Batman & Robin Adventures*, by Paul Dini, Ty Templeton, and Rick Burchett (DC)

BEST LIMITED SERIES: *Sin City: The Big Fat Kill*, by Frank Miller (Dark Horse/Legend)

BEST NEW SERIES: *Kurt Busiek's Astro City*, by Kurt Busiek and Brent Anderson (Jukebox Productions/Image)

BEST ANTHOLOGY: *The Big Book of Conspiracies*, edited by Bronwyn Taggart (Paradox Press)

BEST GRAPHIC ALBUM–NEW: *Stuck Rubber Baby*, by Howard Cruse (Paradox Press)

BEST GRAPHIC ALBUM–REPRINT: *The Tale of One Bad Rat*, by Bryan Talbot (Dark Horse)

BEST ARCHIVAL COLLECTION: *The Complete Crumb Comics*, vol. 11, by R. Crumb (Fantagraphics)

BEST HUMOR PUBLICATION: *Milk & Cheese* #666, by Evan Dorkin (Slave Labor)

BEST WRITER: Alan Moore, *From Hell* (Kitchen Sink)

BEST WRITER/ARTIST, DRAMA: David Lapham, *Stray Bullets* (El Capitán)

BEST WRITER/ARTIST, HUMOR: Sergio Aragonés, *Groo the Wanderer* (Image)

BEST PAINTER: John Bolton, *Batman: Manbat* (DC)

BEST PENCILLER/INKER: Geof Darrow, *Big Guy and Rusty the Boy Robot* (Dark Horse/Legend)

BEST COVER ARTIST: Alex Ross, *Kurt Busiek's Astro City* (Jukebox Productions/Image)

BEST COLORING: Chris Ware, *The Acme Novelty Library* (Fantagraphics)

BEST LETTERING: Stan Sakai, *Groo the Wanderer* (Image); *Usagi Yojimbo* (Mirage)

TALENT DESERVING OF WIDER RECOGNITION: Stan Sakai, *Usagi Yojimbo*

BEST EDITOR (TIE): Stuart Moore, *Swamp Thing, The Invisibles, Preacher* (DC/Vertigo); Bronwyn Taggart, *The Big Book of Weirdos, The Big Book of Conspiracies, Brooklyn Dreams, Stuck Rubber Baby* (Paradox Press)

BEST COMICS-RELATED PUBLICATION–PERIODICAL: *The Comics Journal* (Fantagraphics)

BEST COMICS-RELATED PUBLICATION–BOOK: *Alex Toth*, edited by Manuel Auad (Kitchen Sink)

BEST COMICS-RELATED ITEM: Comic strip stamps (U.S. Postal Service)

BEST PUBLICATION DESIGN: *The Acme Novelty Library*, designed by Chris Ware (Fantagraphics)

HALL OF FAME: Hal Foster, Bob Kane, Winsor McCay, Alex Raymond

1997 EISNER AWARDS
(for works published in 1996)

NOMINATING JUDGES: JOE FIELD, PAUL GRANT, JANET HETHERINGTON, TONY ISABELLA, JESSE LEON MCCANN

BEST SHORT STORY: "Heroes," by Archie Goodwin and Gary Gianni, in *Batman: Black & White* #4 (DC Comics)

BEST SINGLE ISSUE: *Kurt Busiek's Astro City*, vol. 2, #1: "Welcome to Astro City," by Kurt Busiek, Brent Anderson, and Will Blyberg (Jukebox Productions/Homage)

BEST SERIALIZED STORY: *Starman* #20–#23: "Sand and Stars," by James Robinson, Tony Harris, Guy Davis, and Wade von Grawbadger (DC)

BEST CONTINUING SERIES: *Kurt Busiek's Astro City,* by Kurt Busiek, Brent Anderson, and Will Blyberg (Jukebox Productions/Homage)

BEST LIMITED SERIES: *Kingdom Come,* by Mark Waid and Alex Ross (DC)

BEST NEW SERIES: *Leave It to Chance,* James Robinson and Paul Smith (Homage)

BEST TITLE AIMED AT A YOUNGER AUDIENCE: *Leave It to Chance,* James Robinson and Paul Smith (Homage)

BEST HUMOR PUBLICATION: *Sergio Aragonés Destroys DC* (DC) and *Sergio Aragonés Massacres Marvel* (Marvel), by Mark Evanier and Sergio Aragonés

BEST ANTHOLOGY: *Batman: Black and White,* edited by Mark Chiarello and Scott Peterson (DC)

BEST GRAPHIC ALBUM–NEW: *Fax from Sarajevo,* by Joe Kubert (Dark Horse Books)

BEST GRAPHIC ALBUM–REPRINT: *Stray Bullets: Innocence of Nihilism,* by David Lapham (El Capitán)

BEST ARCHIVAL COLLECTION: *Tarzan: The Land That Time Forgot* and *The Pool of Time,* by Russ Manning (Dark Horse)

BEST WRITER: Alan Moore, *From Hell* (Kitchen Sink); *Supreme* (Maximum Press)

BEST WRITER/ARTIST–HUMOR: Don Rosa, *Walt Disney's Comics & Stories, Uncle Scrooge* (Gladstone)

BEST WRITER/ARTIST–DRAMA: Mike Mignola, *Hellboy: Wake the Devil* (Dark Horse/Legend)

BEST PENCILLER: Steve Rude, *Nexus: Executioner's Song* (Dark Horse)

BEST INKER: Al Williamson, *Spider-Man, Untold Tales of Spider-Man* #17–#18 (Marvel)

BEST PENCILLER/INKER OR PENCILLER/INKER TEAM: Charles Vess, *Book of Ballads and Sagas* (Green Man Press); *The Sandman* #75 (DC/Vertigo)

BEST PAINTER: Alex Ross, *Kingdom Come* (DC)

BEST COLORING: Matt Hollingsworth, *Preacher, Death: The Time of Your Life* (DC/Vertigo); *Dr. Strangefate, Challengers of the Unknown* (DC)

BEST LETTERING: Todd Klein, *The Sandman, Death: The Time of Your Life, House of Secrets, The Dreaming* (DC/Vertigo); *Batman, The Spectre; Kingdom Come* (DC)

BEST COVER ARTIST: Alex Ross, *Kingdom Come* (DC); *Kurt Busiek's Astro City* (Jukebox Productions/ Homage)

TALENT DESERVING OF WIDER RECOGNITION: Ricardo Delgado, *Age of Reptiles*

BEST EDITOR: Dan Raspler, *Kingdom Come; Hitman; The Spectre; Sergio Aragonés Destroys the DC Universe* (DC)

BEST COMICS-RELATED PERIODICAL: *The Comics Journal* (Fantagraphics)

BEST COMICS-RELATED BOOK: *Graphic Storytelling,* by Will Eisner (Poorhouse Press)

BEST COMICS-RELATED PRODUCT: Hellboy bust, by Randy Bowen (Bowen Designs)

BEST PUBLICATION DESIGN: *The Acme Novelty Library* #7, designed by Chris Ware (Fantagraphics)

HALL OF FAME: Gil Kane, Charles Schulz, Julius Schwartz, Curt Swan

1998 EISNER AWARDS
(for works published in 1997)

NOMINATING JUDGES: FRANK ALISON, STEVE BISSETTE, JOSH BRAUN, ERIC KIRSAMMER, BETH RIMMELS

BEST SHORT STORY: "The Eltingville Comic Book, Science-Fiction, Fantasy, Horror and Role-Playing Club In: The Marathon Men," by Evan Dorkin, in *Dork!* #4 (Slave Labor)

BEST SINGLE ISSUE: *Kurt Busiek's Astro City,* vol. 2, #10: "Show 'Em All," by Kurt Busiek, Brent Anderson, and Will Blyberg (Jukebox Productions/Homage)

BEST SERIALIZED STORY: *Kurt Busiek's Astro City* vol. 2, #4–#9: "Confession," by Kurt Busiek, Brent Anderson, and Will Blyberg (Jukebox Productions/Homage)

BEST CONTINUING SERIES: *Kurt Busiek's Astro City,* by Kurt Busiek, Brent Anderson, and Will Blyberg (Jukebox Productions/Homage)

BEST LIMITED SERIES: *Batman: The Long Halloween,* by Jeph Loeb and Tim Sale (DC)

BEST NEW SERIES: *Castle Waiting,* by Linda Medley (Olio)

BEST COMICS PUBLICATION FOR A YOUNGER AUDIENCE: *Batman & Robin Adventures,* by Ty Templeton, Brandon Kruse, Rick Burchett, and others (DC)

BEST HUMOR PUBLICATION: *Gon Swimmin',* by Masashi Tanaka (Paradox Press)

BEST ANTHOLOGY: *Hellboy Christmas Special,* edited by Scott Allie (Dark Horse)

BEST GRAPHIC ALBUM–NEW: *Batman & Superman Adventures: World's Finest,* by Paul Dini, Joe Staton, and Terry Beatty (DC)

BEST GRAPHIC ALBUM–REPRINT: *Sin City: That Yellow Bastard,* by Frank Miller (Dark Horse)

BEST ARCHIVAL COLLECTION: *Jack Kirby's New Gods,* by Jack Kirby (DC)

BEST U.S. EDITION OF FOREIGN MATERIAL: *Gon Swimmin',* by Masashi Tanaka (Paradox Press)

BEST WRITER: Garth Ennis, *Hitman* (DC); *Preacher, Unknown Soldier* (DC/Vertigo), *Blood Mary: Lady Liberty* (DC/Helix)

BEST WRITER/ARTIST: Mike Mignola, *Hellboy: Almost Colossus, Hellboy Christmas Special, Hellboy Jr. Halloween Special* (Dark Horse)

BEST WRITER/ARTIST–HUMOR: Jeff Smith, *Bone* (Cartoon Books)

BEST PENCILLER/INKER OR PENCILLER/INKER TEAM: P. Craig Russell, *Elric: Stormbringer* (Dark Horse/Topps); *Dr. Strange: What Is It That Disturbs You, Stephen?* (Marvel)

BEST PAINTER: Alex Ross, *Uncle Sam* (DC/Vertigo)

BEST COLORING: Chris Ware, *The Acme Novelty Library* (Fantagraphics)

BEST LETTERING: Todd Klein, Batman, *Batman: Poison Ivy* (DC); *The Dreaming, House of Secrets, The Invisibles, Uncle Sam* (DC/Vertigo); *Uncle Scrooge Adventures* (Gladstone); *Castle Waiting* (Olio)

BEST COVER ARTIST: Alex Ross, *Kurt Busiek's Astro City* (Jukebox Productions/Homage); *Uncle Sam* (DC/ Vertigo)

TALENT DESERVING OF WIDER RECOGNITION: Linda Medley, *Castle Waiting* (Olio)

BEST COMICS-RELATED PERIODICAL: *The Comics Journal* (Fantagraphics)

BEST COMICS-RELATED BOOK: *The R. Crumb Coffee Table Art Book*, edited by Pete Poplaski (Kitchen Sink)

BEST COMICS-RELATED PRODUCT: *The Acme Novelty Library* display stand, designed by Chris Ware (Fantagraphics)

BEST PUBLICATION DESIGN: *Kingdom Come* deluxe slipcover edition, art director Bob Chapman/DC design director Georg Brewer (DC Comics/Graphitti Designs)

HALL OF FAME: Neal Adams, Archie Goodwin, Joe Kubert, Jean "Moebius" Giraud

1999 EISNER AWARDS
(for works published in 1998)

NOMINATING JUDGES: JON COHEN, MIKE SCHIMMEL, LEN STRAZEWSKI, NANCY TREMPE, JONAH WEILAND

BEST SHORT STORY: "Devil's Advocate," by Matt Wagner and Tim Sale, in *Grendel: Black, White, and Red* #1 (Dark Horse)

BEST SINGLE ISSUE: *Hitman* #34: "Of Thee I Sing," by Garth Ennis, John McCrea, and Garry Leach (DC)

BEST SERIALIZED STORY: *Usagi Yojimbo* #13–#22: "Grasscutter," by Stan Sakai (Dark Horse)

BEST CONTINUING SERIES: *Preacher*, by Garth Ennis and Steve Dillon (DC/Vertigo)

BEST LIMITED SERIES: *300*, by Frank Miller and Lynn Varley (Dark Horse)

BEST NEW SERIES: *Inhumans*, by Paul Jenkins and Jae Lee (Marvel)

BEST TITLE FOR A YOUNGER AUDIENCE: *Batman: The Gotham Adventures*, by Ty Templeton, Rick Burchett, and Terry Beatty (DC)

BEST HUMOR PUBLICATION: *Groo the Wanderer*, by Sergio Aragonés and Mark Evanier (Dark Horse)

BEST ANTHOLOGY: *Grendel: Black, White, and Red*, by Matt Wagner, edited by Diana Schutz (Dark Horse)

BEST GRAPHIC ALBUM–NEW: *Superman: Peace on Earth*, by Paul Dini and Alex Ross (DC)

BEST GRAPHIC ALBUM–REPRINT: *Batman: The Long Halloween*, by Jeph Loeb and Tim Sale (DC)

BEST ARCHIVAL COLLECTION: *Plastic Man Archives*, vol. 1, by Jack Cole (DC)

BEST U.S. EDITION OF FOREIGN MATERIAL: *Star Wars: A New Hope—Manga*, by Hisao Tamaki (Dark Horse)

BEST WRITER: Kurt Busiek, *Kurt Busiek's Astro City* (Homage/WildStorm/Image); *Avengers* (Marvel)

BEST WRITER/ARTIST: Frank Miller, *300* (Dark Horse)

BEST WRITER/ARTIST–HUMOR: Kyle Baker, *You Are Here* (DC/Vertigo)

BEST PENCILLER/INKER OR PENCILLER/INKER TEAM: Tim Sale, *Superman for All Seasons* (DC); *Grendel: Black, White, and Red* #1 (Dark Horse)

BEST PAINTER: Alex Ross, *Superman: Peace on Earth* (DC)

BEST COLORING: Lynn Varley, *300* (Dark Horse)

BEST LETTERING: Todd Klein, *Castle Waiting* (Olio); *House of Secrets*, *The Invisibles*, *The Dreaming* (DC/Vertigo)

BEST COVER ARTIST: Brian Bolland, *The Invisibles* (DC/Vertigo)

TALENT DESERVING OF WIDER RECOGNITION: Brian Michael Bendis, writer/artist, *Jinx*, *Goldfish*, *Torso*

BEST COMICS-RELATED PERIODICAL: *The Comics Journal* (Fantagraphics)

BEST COMICS-RELATED BOOK: *Batman: Animated*, by Paul Dini and Chip Kidd (HarperCollins)

BEST COMICS-RELATED PRODUCT/ITEM: Sandman Pocketwatch, designed by Kris Ruotolo (DC/Vertigo)

BEST COMICS-RELATED SCULPTED FIGURES: Hellboy statue, sculpted by Randy Bowen, produced by Bowen Designs

BEST PUBLICATION DESIGN: *Batman Animated*, designed by Chip Kidd (HarperCollins)

HALL OF FAME: Murphy Anderson, Jack Cole, L. B. Cole, Bill Finger, Gardner Fox, Mac Raboy, Alex Schomburg, Joe Simon, Art Spiegelman, Dick Sprang

2000 EISNER AWARDS
(for works published in 1999)

NOMINATING JUDGES: ALEX AMADO, JOE FERRARA, BRIAN SANER LAMKEN, WAYNE MARKLEY, PAM NOLES

BEST SHORT STORY: "Letitia Lerner, Superman's Babysitter," by Kyle Baker, in *Elseworlds 80-Page Giant* (DC)

BEST SINGLE ISSUE: *Tom Strong* #1: "How Tom Strong Got Started" by Alan Moore, Chris Sprouse, and Al Gordon (ABC)

BEST SERIALIZED STORY: *Tom Strong* #4–#7 (Saveen/Ingrid Weiss time travel arc), by Alan Moore, Chris Sprouse, Al Gordon, and guest artists (ABC)

BEST CONTINUING SERIES: *The Acme Novelty Library*, by Chris Ware (Fantagraphics)

BEST LIMITED SERIES: *Whiteout: Melt*, by Greg Rucka and Steve Lieber (Oni)

BEST NEW SERIES: *Top Ten*, by Alan Moore, Gene Ha, and Zander Cannon (ABC)

BEST TITLE FOR A YOUNGER AUDIENCE: *Simpsons Comics*, by various (Bongo)

BEST HUMOR PUBLICATION: *Bart Simpson's Treehouse of Horror*, by Jill Thompson, Oscar González Loyo, Steve Steere Jr., Scott Shaw!, Sergio Aragonés, and Doug TenNapel (Bongo)

BEST ANTHOLOGY: *Tomorrow Stories*, by Alan Moore, Rick Veitch, Kevin Nowlan, Melinda Gebbie, and Jim Baikie (ABC)

BEST GRAPHIC ALBUM–NEW: *The Acme Novelty Library* #13, by Chris Ware (Fantagraphics)

BEST GRAPHIC ALBUM–REPRINT: *From Hell*, by Alan Moore and Eddie Campbell (Eddie Campbell Comics)

BEST ARCHIVAL COLLECTION/PROJECT: *Peanuts: A Golden Celebration*, by Charles Schulz (HarperCollins)

BEST U.S. EDITION OF FOREIGN MATERIAL: *Blade of the Immortal*, by Hiroaki Samura (Dark Horse)

BEST WRITER: Alan Moore, *League of Extraordinary Gentlemen*, *Promethea*, *Tom Strong*, *Tomorrow Stories*, *Top Ten* (ABC)

BEST WRITER/ARTIST: Dan Clowes, *Eightball* (Fantagraphics)

BEST WRITER/ARTIST–HUMOR: Kyle Baker, *I Die at Midnight* (DC/Vertigo); "Letitia Lerner, Superman's Babysitter," in *Elseworlds 80-Page Giant* (DC)

BEST PENCILLER/INKER OR PENCILLER/INKER TEAM: Kevin Nowlan, "Jack B. Quick," in *Tomorrow Stories* (ABC)

BEST PAINTER/MULTIMEDIA ARTIST: Alex Ross, *Batman: War on Crime* (DC)

BEST COLORING: Laura Dupuy, *The Authority, Planetary* (DC/WildStorm)

BEST LETTERING: Todd Klein, *Promethea, Tom Strong, Tomorrow Stories, Top Ten* (ABC); *The Dreaming, Gifts of the Night, The Invisibles, Sandman Presents: Lucifer* (DC/Vertigo)

BEST COVER ARTIST: Alex Ross, *Batman: No Man's Land, Batman: Harley Quinn, Batman: War on Crime, Kurt Busiek's Astro City* (Homage/DC/Wildstorm); *ABC* alternate #1 covers

TALENT DESERVING OF WIDER RECOGNITION: Tony Millionaire, *Sock Monkey*

BEST COMICS-RELATED PERIODICAL/PUBLICATION: *Comic Book Artist* (TwoMorrows)

BEST COMICS-RELATED BOOK: *The Sandman: The Dream Hunters*, by Neil Gaiman and Yoshitaka Amano (DC/Vertigo)

BEST COMICS-RELATED PRODUCT/ITEM: Lunch boxes: Milk & Cheese, Sin City, Bettie Page, Hellboy, Groo (Dark Horse)

BEST PUBLICATION DESIGN: *300*, designed by Mark Cox (Dark Horse)

HALL OF FAME: Bill Everett, George Herriman, Carmine Infantino, Sheldon Mayer, Al Williamson, Basil Wolverton

2001 EISNER AWARDS

(for works published in 2000)

NOMINATING JUDGES: ANINA BENNETT, KARON FLAGE, RALPH MATHIEU, CHRIS SCHAFF, DOUGLAS WOLK

BEST SHORT STORY: "The Gorilla Suit," by Sergio Aragonés, in *Streetwise* (TwoMorrows)

BEST SINGLE ISSUE: *Promethea* #10: "Sex, Stars, and Serpents," by Alan Moore, J. H. Williams III, and Mick Gray (ABC)

BEST SERIALIZED STORY: *100 Bullets* #15–#18: "Hang Up on the Hang Low," by Brian Azzarello and Eduardo Risso (Vertigo/DC)

BEST CONTINUING SERIES: *Top 10*, by Alan Moore, Gene Ha, and Zander Cannon (ABC)

BEST LIMITED SERIES: *The Ring of the Nibelung*, by P. Craig Russell, with Patrick Mason (Dark Horse Maverick)

BEST NEW SERIES: *Powers*, by Brian Michael Bendis and Michael Avon Oeming (Image)

BEST TITLE FOR A YOUNGER AUDIENCE: *Scary Godmother: The Boo Flu*, by Jill Thompson (Sirius)

BEST HUMOR PUBLICATION: *Sock Monkey*, vol. 3, by Tony Millionaire (Dark Horse Maverick)

BEST ANTHOLOGY: *Drawn & Quarterly*, vol. 3, edited by Chris Oliveros (Drawn & Quarterly)

BEST GRAPHIC ALBUM–NEW: *Safe Area Gorazde*, by Joe Sacco (Fantagraphics)

BEST GRAPHIC ALBUM–REPRINT: *Jimmy Corrigan*, by Chris Ware (Pantheon)

BEST ARCHIVAL COLLECTION/PROJECT: *The Spirit Archives*, vols. 1 and 2, by Will Eisner (DC)

BEST U.S. EDITION OF FOREIGN MATERIAL: *Lone Wolf and Cub*, by Kazuo Koike and Goseki Kojima (Dark Horse)

BEST WRITER: Alan Moore, *The League of Extraordinary Gentlemen, Promethea, Tom Strong, Top Ten, Tomorrow Stories* (ABC)

BEST WRITER/ARTIST: Eric Shanower, *Age of Bronze* (Image)

BEST WRITER/ARTIST–HUMOR: Tony Millionaire, *Maakies* (Fantagraphics), *Sock Monkey* (Dark Horse Maverick)

BEST PENCILLER/INKER OR PENCILLER/INKER TEAM: P. Craig Russell, *Ring of the Nibelung* (Dark Horse Maverick)

BEST PAINTER /MULTIMEDIA ARTIST (INTERIOR ART): Jill Thompson, *Scary Godmother* (Sirius)

BEST COLORING: Chris Ware, *The Acme Novelty Library* #14 (Fantagraphics)

BEST LETTERING: Todd Klein, *Promethea, Tom Strong, Tomorrow Stories, Top 10* (ABC); *The Invisibles, The Dreaming* (Vertigo/DC); *Castle Waiting* (Cartoon Books)

BEST COVER ARTIST: Brian Bolland, *Batman: Gotham Knights, The Flash* (DC); *The Invisibles* (Vertigo/DC)

TALENT DESERVING OF WIDER RECOGNITION: Alex Robinson, *Box Office Poison*

BEST COMICS-RELATED BOOK: *Wonder Woman: The Complete History*, by Les Daniels (Chronicle Books)

BEST PUBLICATION DESIGN: *Jimmy Corrigan*, designed by Chris Ware (Pantheon)

HALL OF FAME: Roy Crane, Chester Gould, Frank King, Dale Messick, E. C. Segar, Marie Severin

2002 EISNER AWARDS

(for works published in 2001)

NOMINATING JUDGES: MATT LEHMAN, LEE MARRS, GREG MCELHATTON, CALVIN REID, TIM STROUP

BEST SHORT STORY: "The Eltingville Club in 'The Intervention,'" by Evan Dorkin, in *Dork #9* (Slave Labor)

BEST SINGLE ISSUE: *Eightball* #22, by Dan Clowes (Fantagraphics)

BEST SERIALIZED STORY: *Amazing Spider-Man* #30–#35: "Coming Home," by J. Michael Straczynski, John Romita Jr., and Scott Hanna (Marvel)

BEST CONTINUING SERIES: *100 Bullets*, by Brian Azzarello and Eduardo Risso (Vertigo/DC)

BEST LIMITED SERIES: *Hellboy: Conqueror Worm*, by Mike Mignola (Dark Horse Maverick)

BEST NEW SERIES: *Queen & Country*, by Greg Rucka and Steve Rolston (Oni)

BEST TITLE FOR A YOUNGER AUDIENCE: *Herobear and the Kid*, by Mike Kunkel (Astonish Comics)

BEST HUMOR PUBLICATION: *Radioactive Man*, by Batton Lash, Abel Laxamana, Dan DeCarlo, Mike DeCarlo, and Bob Smith (Bongo)

BEST ANTHOLOGY: *Bizarro Comics*, edited by Joey Cavalieri (DC)

BEST GRAPHIC ALBUM–NEW: *The Name of the Game*, by Will Eisner (DC)

BEST GRAPHIC ALBUM–REPRINT: *Batman: Dark Victory*, by Jeph Loeb and Tim Sale (DC)

BEST ARCHIVAL COLLECTION/PROJECT: *Akira*, by Katsuhiro Otomo (Dark Horse)

BEST U.S. EDITION OF FOREIGN MATERIAL: *Akira*, by Katsuhiro Otomo (Dark Horse)

BEST WRITER: Brian Michael Bendis, *Powers* (Image); *Alias, Daredevil, Ultimate Spider-Man* (Marvel)

BEST WRITER/ARTIST: Dan Clowes, *Eightball* (Fantagraphics)

BEST WRITER/ARTIST–HUMOR: Evan Dorkin, *Dork* (Slave Labor)

BEST PENCILLER/INKER OR PENCILLER/INKER TEAM: Eduardo Risso, *100 Bullets* (Vertigo/DC)

BEST PAINTER/MULTIMEDIA ARTIST (INTERIOR ART): Charles Vess, *Rose* (Cartoon Books)

BEST COLORING: Laura DePuy, *Ruse* (CrossGen); *Ministry of Space* (Image)

BEST LETTERING: Todd Klein, *Promethea, Tom Strong's Terrific Tales, Tomorrow Stories, Top 10, Greyshirt* (ABC); *The Sandman Presents: Everything You Always Wanted to Know About Dreams But Were Afraid to Ask* (Vertigo/DC); *Detective Comics, The Dark Knight Strikes Again* (DC); *Castle Waiting* (Olio); *Universe X* (Marvel)

BEST COVER ARTIST: Dave Johnson, *Detective Comics* (DC); *100 Bullets* (Vertigo/DC)

TALENT DESERVING OF WIDER RECOGNITION: Dylan Horrocks, *Hicksville, Atlas*

BEST COMICS-RELATED PERIODICAL: *Comic Book Artist*, edited by Jon Cooke (TwoMorrows)

BEST COMICS-RELATED BOOK: *Peanuts: The Art of Charles M. Schulz*, edited by Chip Kidd (Pantheon)

BEST COMICS-RELATED ITEM: Dark Horse classic comic characters statuettes, sculpted by Yoe Studio (Dark Horse)

BEST PUBLICATION DESIGN: *The Acme Novelty Library* #15, designed by Chris Ware (Fantagraphics)

HALL OF FAME: Sergio Aragonés, Charles Biro, John Buscema, Dan DeCarlo, John Romita, Osamu Tezuka

2003 EISNER AWARDS
(for works published in 2002)

NOMINATING JUDGES: ANDREW ARNOLD, JEN CONTINO, STEVE LEAF, JEREMY SHORR, CHARLES VESS

BEST SHORT STORY: "The Magician and the Snake," by Katie Mignola and Mike Mignola, in *Dark Horse Maverick: Happy Endings* (Dark Horse)

BEST SINGLE ISSUE OR ONE-SHOT: *The Stuff of Dreams*, by Kim Deitch (Fantagraphics)

BEST SERIALIZED STORY: *Fables* #1–#5: "Legends in Exile," by Bill Willingham, Lan Medina, and Steve Leialoha (Vertigo/DC)

BEST CONTINUING SERIES: *Daredevil*, by Brian Michael Bendis and Alex Maleev (Marvel)

BEST LIMITED SERIES: *League of Extraordinary Gentlemen*, vol. 2, by Alan Moore and Kevin O'Neill (ABC)

BEST NEW SERIES: *Fables*, by Bill Willingham, Lan Medina, Mark Buckingham, and Steve Leialoha (Vertigo/DC)

BEST TITLE FOR A YOUNGER AUDIENCE: *Herobear and the Kid*, by Mike Kunkel (Astonish Comics)

BEST HUMOR PUBLICATION: *The Amazing Screw-On Head*, by Mike Mignola (Dark Horse)

BEST ANTHOLOGY: *SPX 2002* (CBLDF)

BEST GRAPHIC ALBUM–NEW: *One! Hundred! Demons!*, by Lynda Barry (Sasquatch Books)

BEST GRAPHIC ALBUM–REPRINT: *Batman: Black and White*, vol. 2, edited by Mark Chiarello and Nick J. Napolitano (DC)

BEST ARCHIVAL COLLECTION/PROJECT: *Krazy & Ignatz*, by George Herriman (Fantagraphics)

BEST U.S. EDITION OF FOREIGN MATERIAL: *Dr. Jekyll & Mr. Hyde*, by Robert Louis Stevenson, adapted by Jerry Kramsky and Lorenzo Mattotti (NBM)

BEST WRITER: Brian Michael Bendis, *Powers* (Image); *Alias, Daredevil, Ultimate Spider-Man* (Marvel)

BEST WRITER/ARTIST: Eric Shanower, *Age of Bronze* (Image)

BEST WRITER/ARTIST–HUMOR: Tony Millionaire, *House at Maakies Corner* (Fantagraphics)

BEST PENCILLER/INKER OR PENCILLER/INKER TEAM: Kevin O'Neill, *League of Extraordinary Gentlemen* (ABC)

BEST PAINTER/MULTIMEDIA ARTIST: George Pratt, *Wolverine: Netsuke* (Marvel)

BEST COLORING: Dave Stewart, *Hellboy: Third Wish, The Amazing Screw-on Head, Star Wars: Empire* (Dark Horse); *Human Target: Final Cut, Doom Patrol* (Vertigo/DC); *Tom Strong* (ABC); *Captain America* (Marvel)

BEST LETTERING: Todd Klein, *Dark Knight Strikes Again, Detective Comics, Wonder Woman: The Hiketeia* (DC); *Fables, Human Target: Final Cut* (Vertigo/DC); *Promethea, Tom Strong* (ABC); *Castle Waiting* (Olio)

BEST COVER ARTIST: Adam Hughes, *Wonder Woman* (DC)

TALENT DESERVING OF WIDER RECOGNITION: Jason Shiga, *Fleep* (Sparkplug)

BEST COMICS-RELATED PUBLICATION (PERIODICAL OR BOOK): *B. Krigstein*, vol. 1, by Greg Sadowski (Fantagraphics)

BEST PUBLICATION DESIGN: *Batman: Nine Lives*, designed by Amie Brockway-Metcalf (DC)

HALL OF FAME: Jack Davis, Will Elder, Al Feldstein, Hergé, Bernard Krigstein, John Severin

2004 EISNER AWARDS
(for works published in 2003)

NOMINATING JUDGES: GREG BENNETT, MARC BERNARDIN, MELONEY CRAWFORD CHADWICK, ANDREW FARAGO, FILIP SABLIK

BEST SHORT STORY: "Death," by Neil Gaiman and P. Craig Russell, in *The Sandman: Endless Nights* (Vertigo/DC)

BEST SINGLE ISSUE OR ONE-SHOT: (TIE) *Conan: The Legend* #0, by Kurt Busiek and Cary Nord (Dark Horse) and *The Goon #1*, by Eric Powell (Dark Horse)

BEST SERIALIZED STORY: *Gotham Central* #6–#10: "Half a Life," by Greg Rucka and Michael Lark (DC)

BEST CONTINUING SERIES: *100 Bullets*, by Brian Azzarello and Eduardo Risso (Vertigo/DC)

BEST LIMITED SERIES: *Unstable Molecules*, by James Sturm and Guy Davis (Marvel)

BEST NEW SERIES: *Plastic Man*, by Kyle Baker (DC)

BEST TITLE FOR A YOUNGER AUDIENCE: *Walt Disney's Uncle Scrooge*, by various (Gemstone)

BEST HUMOR PUBLICATION: *Formerly Known as the Justice League*, by Keith Giffen, J. M. DeMatteis, Kevin Maguire, and Joe Rubinstein (DC)

BEST ANTHOLOGY: *The Sandman: Endless Nights*, by Neil Gaiman and others, edited by Karen Berger and Shelly Bond (Vertigo/DC)

BEST GRAPHIC ALBUM–NEW: *Blankets*, by Craig Thompson (Top Shelf)

BEST GRAPHIC ALBUM–REPRINT: *Batman Adventures: Dangerous Dames and Demons*, by Paul Dini, Bruce Timm, and others (DC)

BEST ARCHIVAL COLLECTION/PROJECT: *Krazy and Ignatz, 1929–1930*, by George Herriman, edited by Bill Blackbeard (Fantagraphics)

BEST U.S. EDITION OF FOREIGN MATERIAL: *Buddha*, vols. 1–2, by Osamu Tezuka (Vertical)

BEST WRITER: Alan Moore, *The League of Extraordinary Gentlemen, Promethea, Smax, Tom Strong, Tom Strong's Terrific Tales* (ABC)

BEST WRITER/ARTIST: Craig Thompson, *Blankets* (Top Shelf)

BEST WRITER/ARTIST–HUMOR: Kyle Baker, *Plastic Man* (DC); *The New Bakers* (Kyle Baker Publishing)

BEST PENCILLER/INKER OR PENCILLER/INKER TEAM: John Cassaday, *Planetary, Planetary/Batman: Night on Earth* (WildStorm/DC); *Hellboy Weird Tales* (Dark Horse)

BEST PAINTER/MULTIMEDIA ARTIST: Jill Thompson, "Stray," in *The Dark Horse Book of Hauntings* (Dark Horse)

BEST COLORING: Patricia Mulvihill, *Batman, Wonder Woman* (DC); *100 Bullets* (Vertigo/DC)

BEST LETTERING: Todd Klein, *Detective Comics* (DC); *Fables, The Sandman: Endless Nights* (Vertigo/DC); *Tom Strong, Promethea* (ABC); *1602* (Marvel)

BEST COVER ARTIST: James Jean, *Batgirl* (DC); *Fables* (Vertigo/DC)

TALENT DESERVING OF WIDER RECOGNITION: Derek Kirk Kim, *Same Difference and Other Stories*

BEST COMICS-RELATED PERIODICAL: *Comic Book Artist*, edited by Jon B. Cooke (Top Shelf)

BEST COMICS-RELATED BOOK: *The Art of Hellboy*, by Mike Mignola (Dark Horse)

BEST PUBLICATION DESIGN: *Mythology: The DC Comics Art of Alex Ross*, designed by Chip Kidd (Pantheon)

HALL OF FAME: Otto Binder, Al Capp, Jules Feiffer, Kazuo Koike, Goseki Kojima, Don Martin, Jerry Robinson, John Stanley

2005 EISNER AWARDS
(for works published in 2004)

NOMINATING JUDGES: GIB BICKEL, STEVE CONLEY, KAT KAN, TOM MCLEAN, TOM RUSSO

BEST SHORT STORY: "Unfamiliar," by Evan Dorkin and Jill Thompson, in *The Dark Horse Book of Witchcraft* (Dark Horse Books)

BEST SINGLE ISSUE OR ONE-SHOT: *Eightball* #23: "The Death Ray," by Dan Clowes (Fantagraphics)

BEST SERIALIZED STORY: *Fables* #19–#27: "March of the Wooden Soldiers," by Bill Willingham, Mark Buckingham, and Steve Leialoha (Vertigo/DC)

BEST CONTINUING SERIES: *The Goon*, by Eric Powell (Dark Horse)

BEST LIMITED SERIES: *DC: The New Frontier*, by Darwyn Cooke (DC)

BEST NEW SERIES: *Ex Machina*, by Brian K. Vaughan, Tony Harris, and Tom Feister (WildStorm/DC)

BEST PUBLICATION FOR A YOUNGER AUDIENCE: *Plastic Man*, by Kyle Baker and Scott Morse (DC)

BEST HUMOR PUBLICATION: *The Goon*, by Eric Powell (Dark Horse)

BEST ANTHOLOGY: *Michael Chabon Presents The Amazing Adventures of the Escapist*, edited by Diana Schutz and David Land (Dark Horse)

BEST DIGITAL COMIC: *Mom's Cancer*, by Brian Fies

BEST GRAPHIC ALBUM–NEW: *The Originals*, by Dave Gibbons (Vertigo/DC)

BEST GRAPHIC ALBUM–REPRINT: *Bone* One Volume Edition, by Jeff Smith (Cartoon Books)

BEST ARCHIVAL COLLECTION/PROJECT: *The Complete Peanuts*, edited by Gary Groth (Fantagraphics)

BEST U.S. EDITION OF FOREIGN MATERIAL: *Buddha*, vols. 3–4, by Osamu Tezuka (Vertical)

BEST WRITER: Brian K. Vaughan, *Y: The Last Man* (Vertigo/DC); *Ex Machina* (WildStorm/DC); *Runaways* (Marvel)

BEST WRITER/ARTIST: Paul Chadwick, *Concrete: The Human Dilemma* (Dark Horse)

BEST WRITER/ARTIST–HUMOR: Kyle Baker, *Plastic Man* (DC); *Cartoonist* (Kyle Baker Publishing)

BEST PENCILLER/INKER: (TIE) John Cassaday, *Astonishing X-Men* (Marvel); *Planetary* (WildStorm/DC); *I Am Legion: The Dancing Faun* (Humanoids/DC); Frank Quitely, *WE3* (Vertigo/DC)

BEST PAINTER/MULTIMEDIA ARTIST (INTERIOR ART): Teddy Kristiansen, *It's a Bird . . .* (Vertigo/DC)

BEST COLORING: Dave Stewart, *Daredevil, Ultimate X-Men, Ultimate Six, Captain America* (Marvel); *Conan, BPRD* (Dark Horse); *DC: The New Frontier* (DC)

BEST LETTERING: Todd Klein, *Promethea, Tom Strong, Tom Strong's Terrific Tales* (ABC); *Wonder Woman* (DC); *Books of Magick: Life During Wartime, Fables, WE3* (Vertigo/DC); *Creatures of the Night* (Dark Horse)

BEST COVER ARTIST: James Jean, *Fables* (Vertigo/DC); *Green Arrow, Batgirl* (DC)

TALENT DESERVING OF WIDER RECOGNITION: Sean McKeever, *A Waiting Place, Mary Jane, Inhumans, Sentinels*

BEST COMICS-RELATED PERIODICAL: *Comic Book Artist*, edited by Jon B. Cooke (Top Shelf)

BEST COMICS-RELATED BOOK: *Men of Tomorrow: Geeks, Gangsters, and the Birth of the Comic Book*, by Gerard Jones (Basic Books)

BEST PUBLICATION DESIGN: *The Complete Peanuts*, designed by Seth (Fantagraphics)

HALL OF FAME: Nick Cardy, Gene Colan, Johnny Craig, Lou Fine, René Goscinny and Albert Uderzo, Hugo Pratt

2006 EISNER AWARDS
(for works published in 2005)

NOMINATING JUDGES: CHRISTOPHER ALLEN, JOHN GALLAGHER, NISHA GOPALAN, ROBERT RANDLE, ROBERT SCOTT

BEST SHORT STORY: "Teenage Sidekick," by Paul Pope, in *Solo* #3 (DC)

BEST SINGLE ISSUE OR ONE-SHOT: *Solo* #5, by Darwyn Cooke (DC)

BEST SERIALIZED STORY: *Fables* #36–#38, #40–#41: "Return to the Homelands," by Bill Willingham, Mark Buckingham, and Steve Leialoha (Vertigo/DC)

BEST CONTINUING SERIES: *Astonishing X-Men*, by Joss Whedon and John Cassaday (Marvel)

BEST LIMITED SERIES: *Seven Soldiers*, by Grant Morrison and various artists (DC)

BEST NEW SERIES: *All Star Superman*, by Grant Morrison and Frank Quitely (DC)

BEST PUBLICATION FOR A YOUNGER AUDIENCE: *Owly: Flying Lessons*, by Andy Runton (Top Shelf)

BEST ANTHOLOGY: *Solo*, edited by Mark Chiarello (DC)

BEST DIGITAL COMIC: *PVP*, by Scott Kurtz, www.pvponline.com

BEST REALITY-BASED WORK: *Nat Turner*, by Kyle Baker (Kyle Baker Publishing)

BEST GRAPHIC ALBUM–NEW: *Top Ten: The Forty-Niners*, by Alan Moore and Gene Ha (ABC)

BEST GRAPHIC ALBUM–REPRINT: *Black Hole*, by Charles Burns (Pantheon)

BEST ARCHIVAL COLLECTION/PROJECT–COMIC STRIPS: *The Complete Calvin & Hobbes*, by Bill Watterson (Andrews McMeel)

BEST ARCHIVAL COLLECTION/PROJECT–COMIC BOOKS: *Absolute Watchmen*, by Alan Moore and Dave Gibbons (DC)

BEST U.S. EDITION OF FOREIGN MATERIAL: *The Rabbi's Cat*, by Joann Sfar (Pantheon)

BEST WRITER: Alan Moore, *Promethea, Top Ten: The Forty-Niners* (ABC)

BEST WRITER/ARTIST: Geof Darrow, *Shaolin Cowboy* (Burlyman)

BEST WRITER/ARTIST–HUMOR: Kyle Baker, *Plastic Man* (DC); *The Bakers* (Kyle Baker Publishing)

BEST PENCILLER/INKER: John Cassaday, *Astonishing X-Men* (Marvel); *Planetary* (WildStorm/DC)

BEST PAINTER/MULTIMEDIA ARTIST: Ladronn, *Hip Flask: Mystery City* (Active Images)

BEST COVER ARTIST: James Jean, *Fables* (Vertigo/DC); *Runaways* (Marvel)

BEST COLORING: Chris Ware, *The Acme Novelty Library* #16 (ACME Novelty)

BEST LETTERING: Todd Klein, *Wonder Woman, Justice, Seven Soldiers* #0 (DC); *Desolation Jones* (WildStorm/DC); *Promethea, Top Ten: The Forty-Niners, Tomorrow Stories Special* (ABC); *Fables* (Vertigo); *1602: New World* (Marvel)

TALENT DESERVING OF WIDER RECOGNITION: Aaron Renier, *Spiral-Bound*

BEST COMICS-RELATED PERIODICAL: *Comic Book Artist*, edited by Jon B. Cooke (Top Shelf)

BEST COMICS-RELATED BOOK: *Eisner/Miller*, edited by Charles Brownstein and Diana Schutz (Dark Horse Books)

BEST PUBLICATION DESIGN: (TIE) *The Acme Novelty Library Annual Report to Shareholders*, designed by Chris Ware (Pantheon) and *Little Nemo in Slumberland: So Many Splendid Sundays*, designed by Philippe Ghielmetti (Sunday Press Books)

HALL OF FAME: Vaughn Bodé, Ramona Fradon, Floyd Gottfredson, Russ Manning, William Moulton Marston, Jim Steranko

2007 EISNER AWARDS
(for works published in 2006)

NOMINATING JUDGES: ROBIN BRENNER, WHITNEY MATHESON, CHRIS REILLY, JAMES SIME, JEFF VANDER MEER

BEST SHORT STORY: "A Frog's Eye View," by Bill Willingham and James Jean, in *Fables: 1001 Nights of Snowfall* (Vertigo/DC)

BEST SINGLE ISSUE OR ONE-SHOT: *Batman/The Spirit* #1: "Crime Convention," by Jeph Loeb and Darwyn Cooke (DC)

BEST CONTINUING SERIES: *All Star Superman*, by Grant Morrison and Frank Quitely (DC)

BEST LIMITED SERIES: *Batman: Year 100*, by Paul Pope (DC)

BEST NEW SERIES: *Criminal*, by Ed Brubaker and Sean Phillips (Marvel Icon)

BEST TITLE FOR A YOUNGER AUDIENCE: *Gumby*, by Bob Burden and Rick Geary (Wildcard)

BEST HUMOR PUBLICATION: *Flaming Carrot Comics*, by Bob Burden (Desperado/Image)

BEST ANTHOLOGY: *Fables: 1001 Nights of Snowfall*, by Bill Willingham and various (Vertigo/DC)

BEST DIGITAL COMIC: *Sam and Max*, by Steve Purcell

BEST REALITY-BASED WORK: *Fun Home*, by Alison Bechdel (Houghton Mifflin)

BEST GRAPHIC ALBUM–NEW: *American Born Chinese*, by Gene Luen Yang (First Second)

BEST GRAPHIC ALBUM–REPRINT: *Absolute DC: The New Frontier*, by Darwyn Cooke (DC)

BEST ARCHIVAL COLLECTION/PROJECT–STRIPS: *The Complete Peanuts, 1959–1960, 1961–1962*, by Charles Schulz (Fantagraphics)

BEST ARCHIVAL COLLECTION/PROJECT–COMIC BOOKS: *Absolute Sandman*, vol. 1, by Neil Gaiman and various (Vertigo/DC)

BEST U.S. EDITION OF INTERNATIONAL MATERIAL: *The Left Bank Gang*, by Jason (Fantagraphics)

BEST U.S. EDITION OF INTERNATIONAL MATERIAL–JAPAN: *Old Boy*, by Garon Tsuchiya and Nobuaki Minegishi (Dark Horse Manga)

BEST WRITER: Ed Brubaker, *Captain America, Daredevil* (Marvel); *Criminal* (Marvel Icon)

BEST WRITER/ARTIST: Paul Pope, *Batman: Year 100* (DC)

BEST WRITER/ARTIST–HUMOR: Tony Millionaire, *Billy Hazelnuts* (Fantagraphics); *Sock Monkey: The Inches Incident* (Dark Horse)

BEST PENCILLER/INKER OR PENCILLER/INKER TEAM: Mark Buckingham/Steve Leialoha, *Fables* (Vertigo/DC)

BEST PAINTER/MULTIMEDIA ARTIST: Jill Thompson, "A Dog and His Boy," in *The Dark Horse Book of Monsters*; "Love Triangle," in *Sexy Chix* (Dark Horse); "Fair Division," in *Fables: 1001 Nights of Snowfall* (Vertigo/DC)

BEST COVER ARTIST: James Jean, *Fables, Jack of Fables, Fables: 1001 Nights of Snowfall* (Vertigo/DC)

BEST COLORING: Dave Stewart, *BPRD, Conan, The Escapists, Hellboy* (Dark Horse); *Action Comics, Batman/The Spirit, Superman* (DC)

BEST LETTERING: Todd Klein, *Fables, Jack of Fables, Fables: 1001 Nights of Snowfall, Pride of Baghdad, Testament* (Vertigo/DC); *Fantastic Four: 1602, Eternals* (Marvel); *Lost Girls* (Top Shelf)

SPECIAL RECOGNITION: Hope Larson, *Gray Horses* (Oni)

BEST COMICS-RELATED PERIODICAL/JOURNALISM: *Alter Ego*, edited by Roy Thomas (TwoMorrows)

BEST COMICS-RELATED BOOK: *The Art of Brian Bolland*, edited by Joe Pruett (Desperado/Image)

BEST PUBLICATION DESIGN: *Absolute DC: The New Frontier*, designed by Darwyn Cooke (DC)

HALL OF FAME: Ross Andru, Dick Ayers, Wayne Boring, Mike Esposito, Robert Kanigher, Joe Orlando, Ogden Whitney

2008 EISNER AWARDS
(for works published in 2007)

NOMINATING JUDGES: JOHN DAVIS, PAUL DIFILIPPO, ATOM! FREEMAN, JEFF JENSEN, EVA VOLIN

BEST SHORT STORY: "Mr. Wonderful," by Dan Clowes, serialized in *New York Times Sunday Magazine*

BEST SINGLE ISSUE OR ONE-SHOT: *Justice League of America* #11: "Walls," by Brad Meltzer and Gene Ha (DC)

BEST CONTINUING SERIES: *Y: The Last Man*, by Brian K. Vaughan, Pia Guerra, and Jose Marzan Jr. (Vertigo/DC)

BEST LIMITED SERIES: *The Umbrella Academy*, by Gerard Way and Gabriel Bá (Dark Horse)

BEST NEW SERIES: *Buffy the Vampire Slayer*, Season 8, by Joss Whedon, Brian K. Vaughan, Georges Jeanty, and Andy Owens (Dark Horse)

BEST PUBLICATION FOR KIDS: *Mouse Guard: Fall 1152*, *Mouse Guard: Winter 1152*, by David Petersen (Archaia)

BEST PUBLICATION FOR TEENS: *Laika*, by Nick Abadzis (First Second)

BEST HUMOR PUBLICATION: *Perry Bible Fellowship: The Trial of Colonel Sweeto and Other Stories*, by Nicholas Gurewitch (Dark Horse)

BEST ANTHOLOGY: *5*, by Gabriel Bá, Becky Cloonan, Fabio Moon, Vasilis Lolos, and Rafael Grampa (self-published)

BEST DIGITAL COMIC: *Sugarshock!*, by Joss Whedon and Fabio Moon

BEST REALITY-BASED WORK: *Satchel Paige: Striking Out Jim Crow*, by James Sturm and Rich Tommaso (Center for Cartoon Studies/Hyperion)

BEST GRAPHIC ALBUM–NEW: *Exit Wounds*, by Rutu Modan (Drawn & Quarterly)

BEST GRAPHIC ALBUM–REPRINT: *Mouse Guard: Fall 1152*, by David Petersen (Archaia)

BEST ARCHIVAL COLLECTION/PROJECT–COMIC STRIPS: *Complete Terry and the Pirates*, vol. 1, by Milton Caniff (IDW)

BEST ARCHIVAL COLLECTION/PROJECT–COMIC BOOKS: *I Shall Destroy All the Civilized Planets!*, by Fletcher Hanks (Fantagraphics)

BEST U.S. EDITION OF INTERNATIONAL MATERIAL: *I Killed Adolf Hitler*, by Jason (Fantagraphics)

BEST U.S. EDITION OF INTERNATIONAL MATERIAL–JAPAN: *Tekkonkinkreet: Black & White*, by Taiyo Matsumoto (Viz)

BEST WRITER: Ed Brubaker, *Captain America, Criminal, Daredevil, Immortal Iron Fist* (Marvel)

BEST WRITER/ARTIST: Chris Ware, *The Acme Novelty Library* #18 (Acme Novelty)

BEST WRITER/ARTIST–HUMOR: Eric Powell, *The Goon* (Dark Horse)

BEST PENCILLER/INKER OR PENCILLER/INKER TEAM: Pia Guerra/Jose Marzan Jr., *Y: The Last Man* (Vertical/DC)

BEST PAINTER OR MULTIMEDIA ARTIST (INTERIOR ART): Eric Powell, *The Goon: Chinatown* (Dark Horse)

BEST COVER ARTIST: James Jean, *Fables* (Vertigo/DC); *The Umbrella Academy* (Dark Horse); *Process Recess 2, Superior Showcase 2* (AdHouse)

BEST COLORING: Dave Stewart, *BPRD, Buffy the Vampire Slayer, Cut, Hellboy, Lobster Johnson, The Umbrella Academy* (Dark Horse); *The Spirit* (DC)

BEST LETTERING: Todd Klein, *Justice, Simon Dark* (DC); *Fables, Jack of Fables, Crossing Midnight* (Vertigo/DC); *League of Extraordinary Gentlemen: The Black Dossier* (WildStorm/DC); *Nexus* (Rude Dude)

SPECIAL RECOGNITION: Chuck BB, *Black Metal* (artist, Oni)

BEST COMICS-RELATED PERIODICAL/JOURNALISM: *Newsarama*, produced by Matt Brady and Michael Doran, www.newsarama.com

BEST COMICS-RELATED BOOK: *Reading Comics: How Graphic Novels Work and What They Mean*, by Douglas Wolk (Da Capo Press)

BEST PUBLICATION DESIGN: *Process Recess 2*, designed by James Jean and Chris Pitzer (AdHouse)

HALL OF FAME: John Broome, Arnold Drake, R. F. Outcault, Len Wein, Major Malcolm Wheeler-Nicholson, Barry Windsor-Smith

WILL EISNER HALL OF FAME

THE **WILL EISNER HALL OF FAME** honors living and
deceased comics creators who have produced a significant
body of work in the medium.

NEAL ADAMS

MURPHY ANDERSON

ROSS ANDRU

SERGIO ARAGONÉS

DICK AYERS

CARL BARKS

C. C. BECK

OTTO BINDER

CHARLES BIRO

VAUGHN BODÉ

WAYNE BORING

JOHN BROOME

JOHN BUSCEMA

MILTON CANIFF

NICK CARDY

AL CAPP

GENE COLAN

JACK COLE

L. B. COLE

JOHNNY CRAIG

ROY CRANE

R. CRUMB

JACK DAVIS

DAN DECARLO

STEVE DITKO

ARNOLD DRAKE

WILL EISNER

MIKE ESPOSITO

BILL EVERETT

JULES FEIFFER

AL FELDSTEIN

LOU FINE

BILL FINGER

HAL FOSTER

GARDNER FOX

RAMONA FRADON

FRANK FRAZETTA

WILLIAM GAINES

JEAN "MOEBIUS" GIRAUD

ARCHIE GOODWIN

RENÉ GOSCINNY

FLOYD GOTTFREDSON

CHESTER GOULD

HERGÉ

GEORGE HERRIMAN

CARMINE INFANTINO

BOB KANE

GIL KANE

ROBERT KANIGHER

WALT KELLY

FRANK KING

JACK KIRBY

KAZUO KOIKE

GOSEKI KOJIMA

BERNARD KRIGSTEIN

JOE KUBERT

HARVEY KURTZMAN

STAN LEE

RUSS MANNING

WILLIAM MOULTON MARSTON

DON MARTIN

SHELDON MAYER

WINSOR MCCAY

DALE MESSICK

JOE ORLANDO

R. F. OUTCAULT

HUGO PRATT

MAC RABOY

ALEX RAYMOND

JERRY ROBINSON

JOHN ROMITA

ALEX SCHOMBURG

CHARLES M. SCHULZ

JULIUS SCHWARTZ

E. C. SEGAR

JOHN SEVERIN

MARIE SEVERIN

JOE SHUSTER

JERRY SIEGEL

JOE SIMON

ART SPIEGELMAN

DICK SPRANG

JOHN STANLEY

JIM STERANKO

CURT SWAN

OSAMU TEZUKA

ALEX TOTH

ALBERT UDERZO

LEN WEIN

MAJOR MALCOLM WHEELER-NICHOLSON

OGDEN WHITNEY

AL WILLIAMSON

BARRY WINDSOR-SMITH

BASIL WOLVERTON

WALLY WOOD

WILL EISNER SPIRIT OF COMICS RETAILER AWARD

THE WILL EISNER SPIRIT OF COMICS RETAILER AWARD is given to an individual retailer who has done an outstanding job of supporting the comics art medium both in the community and within the industry at large.

1993

MOONDOG'S
Gary Colobuono
Chicago, IL

THE BEGUILING
Sean Scoffield & Steve Solomos
Toronto, Ontario, Canada

COMIC RELIEF
Rory Root & Mike Patchen
Berkeley and San Francisco, CA

1994

GOLDEN APPLE
Bill Liebowitiz
Los Angeles, CA

DR. COMICS & MR. GAMES
Leon Cowen & Michael Pandolfo
Oakland, CA

1995

FLYING COLORS
Joe Field
Concord, CA

LAMBIEK
Kees Kousemaker
Amsterdam, Holland

1996

KINGS COMICS
George Vlastaras
Sydney, Australia

ATLANTIS FANTASYWORLD
Joe & Dottie Ferrara
Santa Cruz, CA

1997

CHICAGO COMICS
Eric Kirsammer
Chicago, IL

CENTRAL CITY COMICS
Steve Snyder
Columbus, OH

THAT'S ENTERTAINMENT
Paul Howley
Fitchburg and Worcester, MA

1998

HI DE HO COMICS
Mark & Robert Hennessey
Santa Monica, CA

MELTDOWN COMICS & COLLECTIBLES
Gaston Dominquez & Ilia Carson
Los Angeles, CA

1999

STAR CLIPPER COMICS & GAMES
Scott Thorne
St. Louis, MO

DREAMHAVEN
Greg Ketter
Minneapolis, MN

2000

GOLDEN AGE COLLECTABLES
Patrick Shaughnessy
Vancouver, British Columbia, Canada

2001

STRANGE ADVENTURES
Calum Johnston
Halifax, Nova Scotia, Canada

2002

SOURCE COMICS & GAMES
Nick Postilgione
Falcon Heights, MN

2003

ALL ABOUT BOOKS AND COMICS
Alan & Marsha Giroux
Phoenix, AZ

2004

ACME COMICS & COLLECTIBLES
Fran and Kevin McGarry
Sioux City, IA

2005

NIGHT FLIGHT COMICS
Mimi Cruz & Alan Carroll
Salt Lake City, UT

2006

ZEUS COMICS
Richard Neal
Dallas, TX

2007

EARTH 2 COMICS
Carr D'Angelo & Jud Meyers
Sherman Oaks, CA

2008

BRAVE NEW WORLD,
Atom! & Portlyn Freeman
Newhall, CA

INKPOT AWARDS

THE INKPOT AWARDS are Comic-Con's own special awards given to individuals for their contributions to the worlds of comics, science fiction/fantasy, film, television, animation, or fandom services.

1974

Forrest J Ackerman, Kirk Alyn, Ray Bradbury, Milton Caniff, Frank Capra, Bob Clampett, June Foray, Eric Hoffman, Chuck Jones, Jack Kirby, Bill Lund, Russ Manning, Russell Myers, Charles Schulz, Phil Seuling, Roy Thomas, Bjo Trimble

1975

Barry Alfonso, Brad Anderson, Robert Bloch, Vaughn Bodé (posthumous), Edgar Rice Burroughs (posthumous), Daws Butler, Richard Butner, Shel Dorf, Will Eisner, Mark Evanier, Gil Kane, Stan Lee, Alan Light, Dick Moores, George Pal, Rod Serling (posthumous), Joe Shuster, Jerry Siegel, Jim Starlin, Jim Steranko, Theodore Sturgeon, Larry (Seymour) Vincent, Barry Windsor-Smith

1976

Neal Adams, Sergio Aragonés, Mel Blanc, Frank Brunner, Tom French, Vicky Kelso Goulart, Rick Griffin, Johnny Hart, George Clayton Johnson, Jack Katz, Mell Lazarus, Dale Messick, Alex Niño, Don Rico, Noel Sickles, Don Thompson, Maggie Thompson

1977

Alfredo Alcala, Carl Barks, C. C. Beck, Howard Chaykin, Lester Dent (posthumous), Jackie Estrada, Hal Foster, Walter Gibson, Jim Harmon, Robert A. Heinlein, Eugene Henderson, Michael Kaluta, Joe Kubert, Harvey Kurtzman, George Lucas, Stan Lynde, Byron Preiss, Trina Robbins, Stanley Ralph Ross, Bill Scott, David Scroggy, Jay Ward

1978

John Buscema, Al Capp, Gene Colan, Gardner Fox, Virginia French, Steve Gerber, Chester Gould, Burne Hogarth, Bob Kane, Ken Krueger, Bernie Lansky, Gray Morrow, Clarence Nash, Grim Natwick, William Rotsler, Mike Royer, Gilbert Shelton, Dave Sheridan, Bill Stout, Frank Thorne, Boris Vallejo, Mort Weisinger (posthumous), Elmer Woggon (posthumous)

1979

Craig Anderson, Steve Englehart, Dale Enzenbacher, Kelly Freas, H. R. Giger, Gene Hazelton, Carl Macek, Victor Moscoso, Larry Niven, Dan O'Neill, Virgil Partch, Jerry Pournelle, Nestor Redondo, Marshall Rogers, John Romita Sr., Bill Spicer, Mort Walker, Len Wein, Marv Wolfman

1980

Terry Austin, Murray Bischoff, Pat Boyette, John Byrne, Ernie Chan, Chris Clarement, Film Board of Canada, Shary Flenniken, Mike Friedrich, Rick Geary, Don Glut, Sam Gross, Al Harley, B. Kliban, Jerry Muller, George Olshevsky, Joe Orlando, Fred Patten, Don Phelps, Richard Pini, Wendy Pini, David Raskin, Scott Shaw!, Jim Shooter, John Stanley, B. K. Taylor, Osamu Tezuka, Adam West, Wally Wood

1981

Jerry Bails, L. B. Cole, Jim Fitzpatrick, Dick Giordano, Dave Graue, Paul Gulacy, Mary Henderson, Karl Hubenthal, Bil Keane, Frank Miller, Doug Moench, Monkey Punch, Dennis O'Neill, Gary Owens, Richard W. Rockwell, Allen Saunders, Julius Schwartz, Mike Sekowsky, Bill Sienkiewicz, Dave Sim, Alex Toth, Morrie Turner, Doug Wildey, Bill Woggon

1982

Bob Bindig, Brian Bolland, Russ Cochran, Dave Cockrum, Max Allan Collins, Chase Craig, Archie Goodwin, Mike Grell, Bruce Hamilton, Howard Kazanjian, Hank Ketcham, Walter Koenig, Richard Kyle, Lee Marrs, Frank Marshall, John Pound, Tony Raiola, Steven Spielberg, Leonard Starr, Robert Williams

1983

Douglas Adams, Maeheah Alzmann, Don Bluth, Floyd Gottfredson, Norman Maurer, Rudy Nebres, George Pérez, Arn Saba, Dan Spiegel, Joe Staton, James Van Hise, cat yronwode

1984

Murphy Anderson, Roman Arambula, Greg Bear, Fae Desmond, Stan Drake, John Field, Rick Hoberg, Greg Jein, Ollie Johnston, Brant Parker, Robert Shayne, Curt Swan, Frank Thomas, Jim Valentino, Al Williamson

1985

Brent Anderson, Ben Bova, David Brin, Jack Cummings, Jack Davis, Sheldon Mayer, Alan Moore, Dan O'Bannon, Tom Orzechowski, John Rogers, Alex Schomburg, Walt Simonson

1986

Poul Anderson, Marian Zimmer Bradley, Dave Gibbons, Jean "Moebius" Giraud, Gilbert Hernandez, Jaime Hernandez, Denis Kitchen, Steve Leialoha, Mart Nodell, Harvey Pekar, Mark Stadler, Dave Stevens

1987

Harlan Ellison, Larry Geeck, Ward Kimball, Deni Loubert, William Messner-Loebs, Mike Peters, Bill Schanes, Steve Schanes, Robert Silverberg, Art Spiegelman, Bernie Wrightson, Ray Zone

1988

Robert Asprin, Mike Baron, Lynda Barry, John Bolton, Jules Feiffer, Raymond Feist, Matt Groening, Gary Groth, George R. R. Martin, Mike Pasqua, Steve Rude, Marie Severin, Matt Wagner

1989

Richard Alf, R. Crumb, Howard Cruse, Kevin Eastman, Lee Falk, Ron Goulart, Walt Kelly (posthumous), Peter Laird, Syd Mead, Andre Norton, Jerry Robinson, Diana Schutz, Janet Tait, Ron Turner, Gahan Wilson

1990

Karen Berger, Bob Burden, Tom De Falco, William Gaines, Jim Henson (posthumous), Jenette Kahn, Jean-Marc and Randi L'Officier, Grant Morrison, Robert Overstreet, Mikee (Reynante) Ritter, Bob Schreck, Ken Steacy, Rick Sternbach, Charles Vess

1991

Alicia Austin, Clive Barker, Dan Barry, Dan DeCarlo, Neil Gaiman, Ted (Dr. Seuss) Geisel, Keith Giffen, George Gladir, Joe Haldeman, Lynn Johnston, Carol Kalish, Don Maitz, Sheldon Moldoff, Steve Oliff, Julie Roloff, Stan Sakai

1992

John Bolton, Carina Burns-Chenelle, Bob Chapman, Francis Ford Coppola, Robin (Doig) Donlan, Creig Flessell, Alan Grant, Bill Griffith, Ray Harryhausen, Marc Hempel, Jim Lee, Milo Manara, Scott McCloud, Todd McFarlane, Rowena Morrill, Diane Noomin, Louise Simonson, Dick Sprang, Vernor Vinge, Mark Wheatley

1993

Jim Aparo, Gary Carter, Phil Foglio, Robert Goodwin, Ferd Johnson, Don Martin, Dave McKean, Clydene Nee, Paul Norris, Paul Power, P. Craig Russell, Mark Schultz, Vincent Sullivan, Michael Whelan, Roger Zelazny

1994

Mike Carlin, Paul Chadwick, Al Feldstein, Stan Goldberg, Chad Grothkopf, Roberta Gregory, Jerry Ordway, Bud Plant, Mike Richardson, John Romita Jr., Richard Rowell, Lucius Shepard, Mickey Spillane, J. Michael Stracyznski, Rumiko Takahashi

1995

Roger Corman, Ramona Fradon, Greg Hildebrandt, Tim Hildebrandt, Ryuichi Ikegami, Irv Novick, Joe Sinnott

1996

Donna Barr, Mort Drucker, Joe Giella, Jim Mooney, Kurt Schaffenberger, François Schuiten, David Siegel

1997

Dick Ayers, Steve Bissette, Terry Brooks, Bob Haney, Russ Heath, Carol Lay, Michael Moorcock, Janice Tobias, George Tuska

1998

Frank Alison, John Broome, Eddie Campbell, Nick Cardy, David Glanzer, Fred Guardineer, Lorenzo Mattotti, Paul S. Newman, John Severin, Joe Simon, Naoko Takeuchi, Mark Yturralde

1999

Tom Batiuk, Chuck Cuidera, Samuel R. Delaney, Arnold Drake, Sam Glanzman, Larry Gonick, Irwin Hasen, Sue Lord

2000

Will Elder, Ric Estrada, Phoebe Gloeckner, Beth Holley, Carmine Infantino, Jack Kamen, Ben Katchor, Harry Lampert, Bryan Talbot, Angelo Torres, Lewis Trondheim

2001

Henry Boltinoff, Irwin Donenfeld, Brian and Wendy Froude, Martin Jaquish, Kaiji Kawaguchi, Joe R. Lansdale, Spider and Jeanne Robinson, Alvin Schwartz, Jeff Smith, Kim Thompson

2002

Eddie Ibrahim, Frank Jacobs, Jason, Paul Levitz, Bob Lubbers, Bob Oksner, Lew Sayre Schwartz, Hal Sherman, Herb Trimpe, George Woodbridge, William Woolfolk

2003
Charles Berberian, Frank Bolle, Sal Buscema, John Davenport, Philippe Dupuy, Steve Jackson, Sid Jacobson, Larry Lieber, Terry Moore, Howard Post

2004
Jack Adler, Dan Davis, Tom Gill, Mark Hamill, Harry Harrison, Bruce Jones, Batton Lash, Mike Mignola, Bill Plympton, Frank Springer, John Totleben, Jim Warren

2005
Lee Ames, Barry Bard, Sy Barry, Bob Bolling, Taerie Bryant, Greg Evans, Bob Fujitani, Robert Jordan, David Lapham, Gary Panter, Dexter Taylor, Jhonen Vasquez

2006
Peter S. Beagle, Art Clokey, Dan Clowes, Luis Dominguez, Basil Gogos, Everett Raymond Kinstler, Kazuo Koike, Jean-Claude Mézières, Bill Pittman, Yoshihiro Tatsumi, John Wagner

2007
Kyle Baker, Allen Bellman, Renée French, Gary Friedrich, Adam Hughes, Miriam Katin, Mel Keefer, Joseph Michael Linsner, David Morrell, Lily Renée Phillips, Mike Ploog, Mary Sturhann, Dan Vado, Mark Verheiden, F. Paul Wilson

2008
Ralph Bakshi, Mike W. Barr, Ed Brubaker, Kim Deitch, Victor Gorelick, Al Jaffee, James Jira, Todd Klein, Dean Koontz, Tite Kubo, Noel Neill, Floyd Norman, Al Plastino, Jeff Watts, Bill Willingham, Connie Willis, Jim Woodring

BELOW: A 1979 article by then vice president of Comic-Con Richard Butner explaining the origin and significance of Comic-Con's Inkpot Award

THE INKPOT AWARD

by Richard Butner

EACH YEAR the Committee of the San Diego Comic Convention nominates and selects persons to receive the Inkpot Awards for achievement in the comic arts, the animation arts, the cinematic arts, science fiction and fandom projects and services.

The Inkpot Awards were presented for the first time at the 1974 San Diego Comic-Con Banquet. They were the brainchild of William Lund, then Comic-Con Chairman, Shel Dorf, and myself—who has long since recanted his original resistance to the presentation of a "special award for achievement" by the Convention. Little did we realize at the time that the Inkpot Award would become a traditional and important aspect of Convention activities and gain the respect of professionals and fans alike.

Several questions have arisen about the Inkpot Awards, primary among which is, Who selects the recipients of the Awards? As noted above, it is the Committee of the San Diego Comic-Con. There is no competition among nominees for the Award. Each nominee is considered on the basis of his merits and achievements in the categories described above, and if he—in our opinion—deserves recognition for his work, then he is awarded an Inkpot. It is as simple as that.

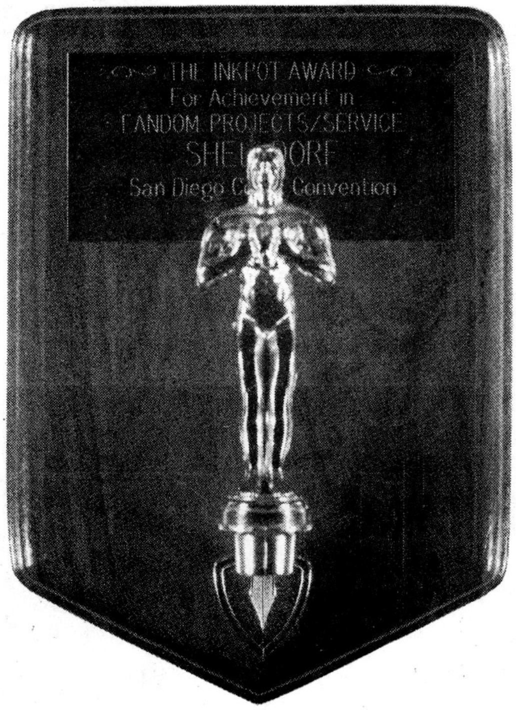
THE INKPOT AWARD
For Achievement in
FANDOM PROJECTS/SERVICE

Is it necessary for an Award winner to attend the Convention? No. Though we always hope the recipients will be in attendance at the Convention, there are times when this is not possible. Last year, both Al Capp and Chester Gould were voted Inkpot Awards, but neither was able to attend.

Why are the Awards not open to general fan balloting? First, to organize such a vote would be expensive and time-consuming. Second, the Inkpot Award was not conceived as an achievement award granted by fandom at large, but by those particular fans who organize the San Diego Comic Convention. Third, any such fandom-wide vote would degenerate into a popularity contest vulnerable to ballot box stuffing and all the other ills which normally plague such projects; and there is no guarantee in any case that we would reach a fair and representative selection of fandom.

The Inkpot Award, therefore, is our own personal way of expressing appreciation for the work of the person receiving the Award, an expression of our belief that the person merits recognition for the achievement of excellence in his field, and our hope that this work will continue to enrich the field in the future. ■

BOB CLAMPETT HUMANITARIAN AWARD

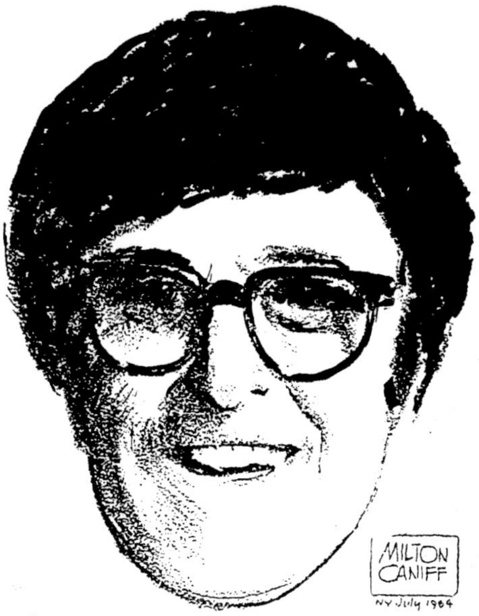
MILTON CANIFF

Bob Clampett portrait by Milton Caniff

THE BOB CLAMPETT HUMANITARIAN AWARD is presented in honor of the famed animator Bob Clampett (1913–1984), creator of *Beany and Cecil* and director of numerous popular Warner Bros. cartoons. Clampett was known for his work in helping others and serving as a mentor.

1984: Forrest J Ackerman

1985: Robert A. Heinlein

1986: Bernie Wrightson and Jim Starlin

1987: Ray Bradbury

1988: June Foray

1989: Phil Yeh

1990: Sergio Aragonés

1991: The Comic Book Legal Defense Fund

1992: Archie Goodwin

1993: Jack Kirby

1994: Will Eisner

1995: Maggie Thompson

1996: Andrew Vachss

1997: Joe Kubert

1998: Frank Miller

1999: Jerry Robinson

2000: Peter Laird

2001: Mark Evanier

2002: Herb Trimpe

2003: Alex Ross

2004: Mimi Cruz Carroll

2005: George Pérez

2006: Calvin Reid

2007: Neil Gaiman

2008: Paul Levitz

BILL FINGER AWARD FOR EXCELLENCE IN COMIC BOOK WRITING

Bill Finger portrait by
Jerry Robinson

THE BILL FINGER AWARD FOR EXCELLENCE IN COMIC BOOK WRITING is given each year to two writers—one living, one deceased—who have produced a significant body of work in the comics field. The award is named after William Finger (1914–1974), who was the first and, some say, most important writer of Batman. Many have called him the "unsung hero" of the character and have hailed his work not only on that iconic figure but on dozens of others, primarily for DC Comics.

2005: Jerry Siegel and Arnold Drake

2006: Harvey Kurtzman and Alvin Schwartz

2007: Gardner Fox and George Gladir

2008: Archie Goodwin and Larry Lieber

RUSS MANNING MOST PROMISING NEWCOMER AWARD

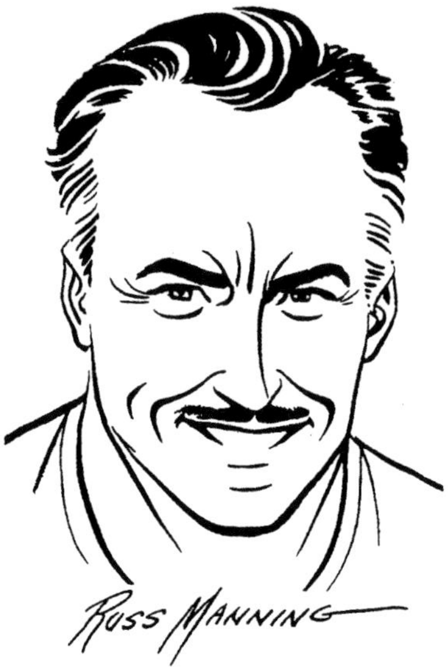
RUSS MANNING

Russ Manning self-portrait

THE RUSS MANNING MOST PROMISING NEWCOMER AWARD is named after legendary comics artist Russ Manning (1929–1981), whose work included the *Tarzan* and *Star Wars* newspaper comic strips. Given each year in conjunction with the West Coast Comics Club, the award recognizes Manning's commitment to finding and fostering new artistic talent.

1982: Dave Stevens

1983: Jan Duursema

1984: Steve Rude

1985: Scott McCloud

1986: Art Adams

1987: Eric Shanower

1988: Kevin Maguire

1989: Richard Piers Raynor

1990: Dan Brereton

1991: Daerick Gross

1992: Mike Okamoto

1993: Jeff Smith

1994: Gene Ha

1995: Edvin Biukovic

1996: Alexander Maleev

1997: Walt Holcomb

1998: Matt Vander Pool

1999: Jay Anceleto

2000: Alan Bunce

2001: Goran Sudzuka

2002: Tan Eng Huat

2003: Jerome Opeña

2004: Eric Wight

2005: Chris Bailey

2006: R. Kikuo Johnson

2007: David Petersen

2008: Cathy Malkasian

COMIC-CON ICON AWARD

COMIC
CON
INTERNATIONAL

THE COMIC-CON ICON AWARD is presented to an organization or individual that has been instrumental in bringing comics and/or the popular arts to a wider audience. The award has been presented on national television on the Spike cable network as part of the Scream Awards.

2006: Frank Miller

2007: Neil Gaiman

2008: George Lucas

AFTER WORDS

> " Comic-Con is a non-stop, high-stress, adrenaline-packed experience day after day. There's nothing else like it, and the best way I've found to experience it is to relax while you grab and hold onto every happy moment. "

MAGGIE THOMPSON
EXECUTIVE EDITOR, *COMICS BUYER'S GUIDE*

Comic-Con means a lot of different things to a lot of different people. Here's what some long-time professionals had to say when asked what they thought of the event and what was their most memorable Comic-Con moment. Other observations are scattered throughout the book.

> " My most memorable Comic-Con moment was when I appeared with Bob Kane to do the first convention presentation on Tim Burton's *Batman* in 1988. The fan response to Michael Keaton's casting was very negative then, so before leaving for San Diego, Bob had literally painted the bat-cowl over Michael's face from a still from *Clean and Sober*, and we projected it on screen to deafening boos. Once they got that out of their systems, we showed Anton Furst's production designs of Gotham City, Tim Burton touring the actual exterior sets, and first looks at both the bat suit and Batmobile. There was no more booing, and that day began the turnaround that ultimately led to phenomenal box office results. "

JEFF WALKER
HOLLYWOOD PUBLICIST/LONGTIME COMIC-CON ATTENDEE

> " The 2008 *Watchmen* panel was pretty amazing, but so was having my family in the audience when we won the Eisner for *Watchmen* in 1988 and, later, in 2005, for *The Originals*. "

DAVE GIBBONS
WRITER/ARTIST/CO-CREATOR, *WATCHMEN*

> " I was told if I was going to get anywhere in this business, I better head over to Comic-Con and start meeting people. That was the single best piece of advice I ever received. "

JIMMY PALMIOTTI
**WRITER/ARTIST, *JONAH HEX*,
*PAINKILLER JANE***

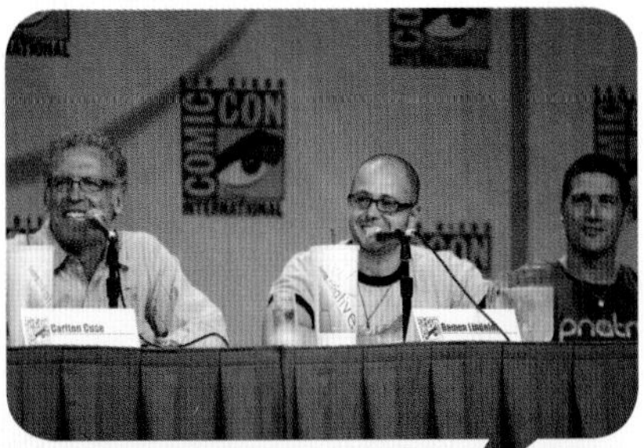

“The moment that I stepped out onto the stage after we screened the *Lost* premiere. It was just insanely surreal to suddenly be on a panel as opposed to being in the audience.”

DAMON LINDELOFF
WRITER/PRODUCER/CO-CREATOR, *LOST*

“Being at Comic-Con as a professional for the first time. I was pretty intimidated and remember going to dinner with Denny O'Neil, Jim Shooter, Archie Goodwin, and Steve Englehart. Me at the same table as all those other big shots! I guess I'd finally made good.”

TODD MCFARLANE
WRITER/ARTIST, *SPAWN*; PUBLISHER, IMAGE COMICS

“Comic-Con is a strange and fantastic freak show that has embraced *Heroes* from day one, and I think it's great.”

TIM KRING
WRITER/PRODUCER/CREATOR, *HEROES*

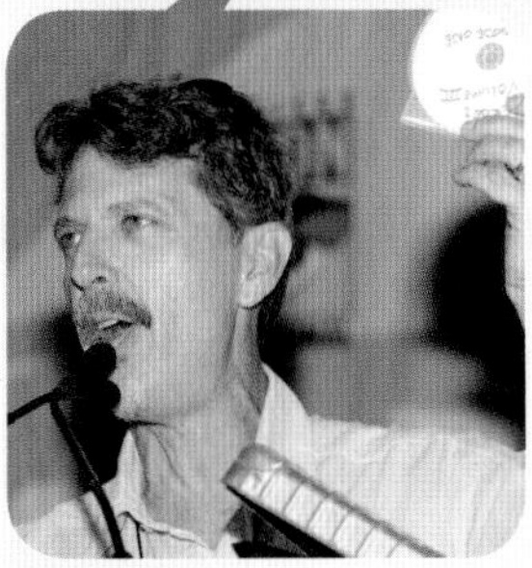

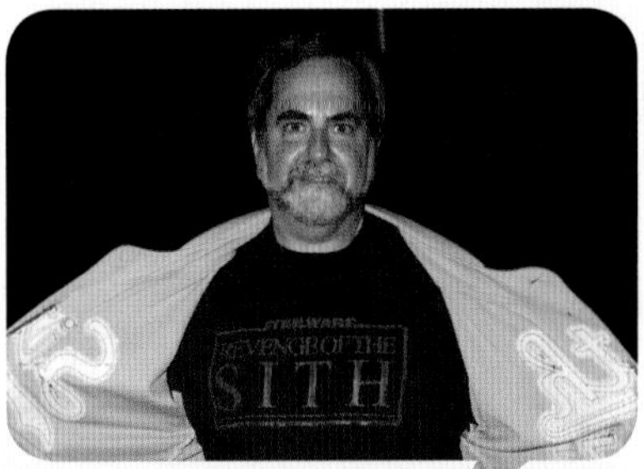
REVENGE OF THE SITH

“My really great experience came in 2004 in the humongous 6,500-seat hall, which was packed. I led up to a little announcement at the end of my presentation, presented as a video tease that steadily built: the name of the last *Star Wars* movie, *Revenge of the Sith*. To say it was a popular title is an understatement. There was a huge roar and some people jumped to their feet. As this was happening, I stepped out from behind the lectern, stripped off my overshirt, and showed off my new T-shirt sporting the movie's retro logo. I said, 'By the way, this has just gone on sale at the *Star Wars* shop booth in the Exhibit Hall.' Next thing I knew, hundreds of people were running out of the hall.”

STEVE SANSWEET
DIRECTOR OF FAN RELATIONS, LUCASFILM; CO-AUTHOR, *STAR WARS ENCYCLOPEDIA*

“Comic-Con is *the* comics industry event of each and every year. It has a weird *Twilight Zone* thing going on that when I am there, it seems that I have never left and the rest of my life is an illusion. Others report the same feeling.”

MIKE RICHARDSON
PUBLISHER, DARK HORSE COMICS

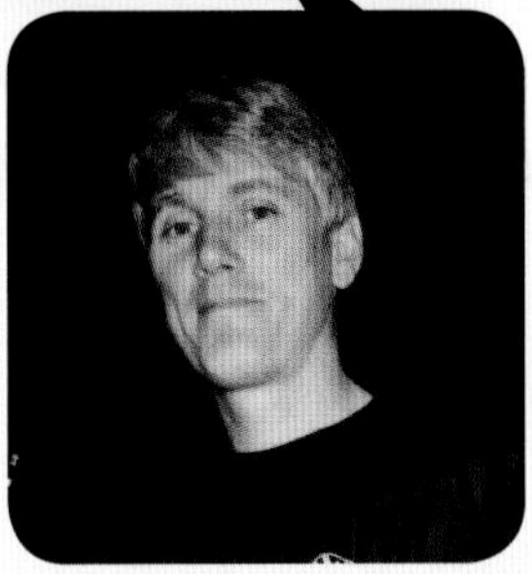

OPPOSITE, FROM TOP LEFT: Jeff Walker moderates an event in Hall H in 2008; Dave Gibbons at the *Watchmen* panel in 2008 **CLOCKWISE FROM TOP LEFT:** Damon Lindeloff (center) with co-executive producer Carlton Cuse (left) and actor Matthew Fox (right) at the *Lost* panel in 2008; Steve Sansweet revealing the big secret during the *Star Wars* panel in 2004; Dark Horse publisher Mike Richardson at Comic-Con in 1994; *Heroes* executive producer and creator Tim Kring with the sneak peek at *Heroes* season 3 episode 1, which premiered at Comic-Con in 2008

ACKNOWLEDGMENTS

THANK YOU to all the people who have served on the board and the committee and volunteered throughout the years, and to our staff and our families for understanding our commitment to Comic-Con.

CREDITS

WRITTEN BY
Gary Sassaman
Jackie Estrada

CONTRIBUTORS
John Rogers
Fae Desmond
David Glanzer
Martin Jaquish
Peter Coogan
Bob Chapman
Stephanie Ibrahim
Lisa Moreau
Matt Souza
Adam Neese

SCANS
Gary Sassaman
Tommy Goldbach
Digital One Color, San Diego, CA
  Mike Uriell and Mark Keller

SPECIAL THANKS
Sergio Aragonés
Mikayla Butchart
Bob Chapman
Dorothy Crouch
Andrea Fernandes
Denis Kitchen
Michael L. Lovitz
Tom Luth
Ron McFee
Michael Morris
Bill Schelly
Scott Shaw!
Kevin Toyama
Beth Weber

CURRENT BOARD OF DIRECTORS, OFFICE STAFF, AND DEPARTMENT HEADS

BOARD OF DIRECTORS
PRESIDENT
John Rogers

SECRETARY
Mary Sturhann

TREASURER
Mark Yturralde

VP, EVENTS
Robin Donlan

VP, OPERATIONS
William Pittman

DIRECTORS AT LARGE
Frank Alison
Ned Cato Jr.
Dan Davis
Craig Fellows
Eugene Henderson
Martin Jaquish
Lee Oeth
Chris Sturhann

EXECUTIVE DIRECTOR
Fae Desmond

DIRECTOR OF MARKETING AND PUBLIC RELATIONS
David Glanzer

DIRECTOR OF PRINT AND PUBLICATIONS
Gary Sassaman

DIRECTOR OF PROGRAMMING
Eddie Ibrahim

HR/OFFICE MANAGER
Sue Lord

TALENT RELATIONS MANAGER
Maija Gates

GUEST RELATIONS
Janet Goggins

EXHIBITS–DIRECTOR OF OPERATIONS
Justin Dutta

EXHIBITS–SALES
Rod Mojica

EXHIBITS–REGISTRATION
Sam Wallace

PROFESSIONAL REGISTRATION
Heather Lampron
Anna-Marie Villegas

EISNER AWARDS ADMINISTRATOR
Jackie Estrada

ASSISTANTS TO THE EXECUTIVE DIRECTOR
Lisa Moreau
Matt Souza

ASSISTANTS TO THE DIRECTOR OF MARKETING AND PUBLIC RELATIONS
Damien Cabaza
Marco Adames

ASSISTANT TO THE DIRECTOR OF PROGRAMMING
Tommy Goldbach

LINE CONTROL/ROOM ACCESS COORDINATOR
Adam Neese

OFFICE STAFF
Patty Campuzano
Ruben Mendez
Glenda Moreno
Colleen O'Connell

DEPARTMENTS

EVENTS
ANIME
John Davenport
Josh Ritter

AT-SHOW NEWSLETTER
Chris Sturhann

FILMS
Steve Brown
Josh Glaser

GAMES
Ken Kendall

MASQUERADE
Martin Jaquish

TECHNICAL SERVICES
Tristan Gates

EXHIBITS
ART AUCTION/ARTISTS' ALLEY
Clydene Nee

ART SHOW
LaFrance Bragg

AUTOGRAPH AREA
Katherine Morrison

CONVENTION SERVICES
Taerie Bryant

EXHIBIT FLOOR MANAGER
Andy Manzi

OPERATIONS
ARCHIVIST
Eugene Henderson

DISABLED SERVICES
William Curtis

HOSPITALITY SUITE
Mikee Ritter

LOGISTICS
Dan Davis

MATERIALS CHIEF/BLOOD DRIVE
Craig Fellows

REGISTRATION
Frank Alison
John Smith

VOLUNTEERS
Luigi Diaz
Jennifer Maturo

INFORMATION
Bruce Frankle

PHOTO CREDITS

Many talented photographers have donated their time and artistic talents over the years to document Comic-Con International. We have made every effort to include photo credits where known. Any errors that may have occurred are inadvertent and will be corrected in subsequent editions, provided notification is sent to the publisher. The photos included in this book are reproduced for historical reference and research purposes.

PAGES 4, 8-9, 14, 17, 29, 32, 33, 34 (Frank Capra), **51** (Bradbury/Ellison/Schwartz), **52, 53, 56, 57** (Heinlein sketching), **64** (Turner/Schwartz, Pournelle/Shooter), **66, 68-69, 70** (Laird, Groening) Image of Matt Groening reprinted by permission of Matt Groening Productions, Inc., **74** (Comic-Con committee, Moore/Kirby), **75** (Stevens), **78** (Thomas/Aragonés), **81** (Barks, Baker, Mignola, Jones), **85** (Kirby Awards), **98, 100, 102, 103** (Miller/Gaiman/Sinkiewicz/Wrightson/Gibbons), **106** (Moebius), **107** (Alcala), **114** (Miller 1985 & 1986), **116** (Fradon/Haney), **118** (Rogers), **141** (Lash/Calabrese), **161** (Evanier, bottom of page), **178** (Jim Lee with balloon), **205** (Richardson): Jackie Estrada

PAGE 31: Photo of boy outside door: Sam Churchill

PAGE 36: Walker: Shel Dorf

PAGE 42: Estrada/Butner: Shel Dorf

PAGE 48: Caniff: Shel Dorf

PAGE 49: Bradbury (bottom): Barry Brown

PAGE 50: Messick: Shel Dorf

PAGES 54-55: Photos © 2009 Clay Geerdes

PAGE 70: Pekar: Jeff Ferris

PAGE 71: McCloud: Jeff Ferris

PAGE 74: Spiegleman: Jeff Ferris

PAGE 81: Goodwin: Jeff Ferris

PAGE 85: Meltzer/Jackson, Eisner Award, Will Eisner, Todd Klein: Tom Deleon and Tony Amat

PAGE 87: Kalish: Jeff Ferris

PAGE 92: Space Ghost: Ralph Rawson Werner; Alien: Kevin Green

PAGE 93: Thor and Hercules: Russell Hedges; Beetlejuice: Jerry Shaw; Dancing with Celebrities from the Stars: Kevin Green

PAGE 103: Gaiman/2007: Tina Gill; Gaiman with Icon Award: Albert L. Ortega; Gaiman/Ross: Tom Deleon

PAGE 106: Modan: Johnakin Randolph

PAGE 107: Takahashi: Carla Van Wagoner

PAGES 112-113: Gary Sassaman

PAGE 114: Miller/Icon Award: Albert L. Ortega; Macht/Del Prete/Miller: Tom Deleon

PAGE 116: Nimoy: Ralph Rawson Werner; Coppola, Seduction of the Innocent: Carla Van Wagoner

PAGE 119: Underdog: Ralph Rawson Werner

PAGE 141: Wrightson: Carla Van Wagoner; Scarlet Witch/Gambit: Ralph Rawson Werner

PAGE 149: Tom Gurnee

PAGES 154 & 156: Kevin Green

PAGE 157: Rory Root: Fae Desmond; Atom! and Portlyn Freeman: Tom Deleon

PAGE 158: Joe Jusko: Clydene Nee

PAGE 159: Girl reading: Adrian Velazquez

PAGE 161: Evanier/Cardy/Colan: Tom Deleon; Evanier/Lieber/Robinson: Tom Deleon and Tony Amat

PAGE 162: Valerie Irene Perez

PAGE 163: Tom Deleon, Barry Brown (Masquerade photos)

PAGE 168: Kevin Smith: Austin Gorum

PAGE 171: Wein/Jackman: Albert L. Ortega; Wendy Pini: Clydene Nee

PAGE 174: Hamilton, Katin: Adrian Velazquez; *Iron Man* cast: Albert L. Ortega; Dr. Who: Jerry Shaw

PAGE 175: DC Booth: Austin Gorum; Masquerade: Kevin Green; Keith Knight: Scotty Oson

PAGE 176: Exhibit Hall: Sergio Palacios; Straczynski: Tom Deleon; Owl ship: Kevin Green

PAGE 177: Masquerade: Daniel Sakow; Eisner winners: Tom Deleon and Tony Amat; Exhibit Hall: Kevin Green

PAGE 178: Jim Lee (top left): Tom Deleon

PAGE 179: Masquerade: Daniel Sakow; Reeves/Connelly: Brian Wong; Back issues: Kevin Green; X-Wing girl: Goldie MacNeil

PAGE 204: Gibbons: Tina Gill

PAGE 205: Cuse/Lindeloff/Fox: Daniel Sakow; Tim Kring: Albert L. Ortega

TRADEMARK AND COPYRIGHT INFORMATION

Every effort has been made to trace the ownership of all copyrighted material included in this volume. Any errors that may have occurred are inadvertent and will be corrected in subsequent editions, provided notification is sent to the publisher. All illustrations contained herein are copyrighted by their respective copyright holders and are reproduced for historical reference and research purposes.

Entire editorial package © 2009 San Diego Comic Convention, Inc.

Cover art © 2009 Sergio Aragonés

PAGE 1: Superman, Wonder Woman ™ & © 2009 DC Comics; Spider-Man, Hulk, Silver Surfer ™ & © 2009 Marvel Characters, Inc.; other badge art © 2009 Patrick N. Cosgrove, Rick Geary, Carol Lay, John Pound, Schirm, Scott Shaw!, Dave Stevens Estate, William Stout, Carl Taylor, Jim Valentino

PAGE 2: Steve Canyon ™ & © 2009 Milton Caniff Estate; other badge art © 2009 Jim Cornelius, Dave Garcia, Rick Geary, Jason Greenhalgh, R. B. Lane, Bill Rotsler, Scott Shaw!, Sward, Dave Stevens Estate, Keith Widham, S. Woolley

PAGE 3: Mr. Monster ™ & © 2009 Michael T. Gilbert; Rusty Brown badge art © 2009 Chris Ware; other badge art © 2009 Berry, Jim Cornelius, J. Dooley, Don Dougherty, Michael Kelley, Louise and Morgan Rendich, Scott Shaw!, Sward, S. L. Woolley

PAGE 10: The Thing ™ & © 2009 Marvel Characters, Inc.; 2001: A Space Odyssey © 2009 Warner Bros. Entertainment Inc.; Batman ™ & © 2009 DC Comics

PAGE 13: Art © 2009 Ray Bradbury

PAGE 14: Batman and Robin ™ & © 2009 DC Comics

PAGE 19: Peanuts ™ & © 2009 United Features Syndicate, Inc.

PAGE 20: Superman ™ & © 2009 DC Comics; dinosaur art © 2009 John Pound

PAGE 21: Art © 2009 Jack Kirby Estate

PAGE 25: Art © 2009 Sergio Aragonés

PAGE 26: Star Wars COURTESY OF LUCASFILM LTD. ™ & © 2009 Lucasfilm Ltd. All rights reserved. Used under authorization. Unauthorized duplication is a violation of applicable law; Badge art © 2009 John Pound

PAGE 27: Dennis the Menace ® Used by permission of Hank Ketcham Enterprises and © North America Syndicate; DC Comics characters ™ & © 2009 DC Comics; Marvel Comics characters ™ & © 2009 Marvel Characters, Inc.

PAGE 28: Broom Hilda ™ & © 2009 Tribune Media Services, Inc.; Captain Marvel (Shazam) ™ & © 2009 DC Comics

PAGE 30: Badge art © 2009 Jim Valentino; Captain Marvel ™ & © 2009 Marvel Characters, Inc.; Broom Hilda ™ & © 2009 Tribune Media Services, Inc.; Peanuts ™ & © 2009 United Features Syndicate, Inc.; The Demon ™ & © 2009 DC Comics

PAGE 31: Superman ™ & © 2009 DC Comics; badge art © 2009 Scott Shaw!; Mr. Fantastic ™ & © 2009 Marvel Characters, Inc.; Broom Hilda ™ & © 2009 Tribune Media Services, Inc.

PAGE 32: The New Gods, Mister Miracle, The Forever People ™ & © 2009 DC Comics

PAGE 33: Silver Surfer, Captain America, Red Skull ™ & © 2009 Marvel Characters, Inc.

PAGE 35: Batman ™ & © 2009 DC Comics; Nancy and Sluggo ™ & © 2009 United Features Syndicate, Inc.

PAGE 36: Kirby art, Friends of Fandom art © 2009 Jack Kirby Estate; Darkseid ™ & © 2009 DC Comics

PAGE 38: Peanuts, Marmaduke ™ & © 2009 United Features Syndicate, Inc.; Kamandi ™ & 2009 DC Comics; Dragon Lady, Broom Hilda ™ & © 2009 Tribune Media Services, Inc.; Steve Canyon ™ & © 2009 Milton Caniff Estate; Mickey Mouse ™ & © 2009 The Walt Disney Company; Silver Surfer ™ & © 2009 Marvel Characters, Inc.; cartoon © 2009 Sergio Aragonés; "Alfred E. Neuman" (Boys Head Logo) and MAD ™ and © E.C. Publications, Inc.; 1975 San Diego Comic-Con record album © 2009 Alan L. Light

PAGE 39: Tarzan, John Carter ™ & © 2009 Edgar Rice Burroughs, Inc.; cartoon © 2009 Rick Geary; Stan Lee cartoon © 2009 Marvel Characters, Inc.; Hembeck cartoon © 2009 Fred Hembeck; The Avenger © 2009 Magazine Enterprises; Chronos, Gentleman Ghost ™ & © 2009 DC Comics; Black Bolt, Killraven ™ & © 2009 Marvel Characters, Inc.

PAGE 40: The Phantom Eagle ™ & © 2009 Marvel Characters, Inc.

PAGE 42: Mr. A © 2009 Steve Ditko; Captain America ™ & © 2009 Marvel Characters, Inc.

PAGE 43: Tarzan ™ & © 2009 Edgar Rice Burroughs, Inc.; Spider-Man, Peter Parker, Aunt May ™ & © 2009 Marvel Characters, Inc.

PAGE 44: Cartoon © 2009 Sergio Aragonés; Aquaman, Superman, Green Lantern, Batman ™ & © 2009 DC Comics

PAGE 47: Art © 2009 Rick Geary

PAGE 48: Art © 2009 William Stout; Captain Marvel (Shazam) ™ & © 2009 DC Comics

PAGE 49: Ray Bradbury sketch © 2009 Milton Caniff Estate

PAGE 51: Superman ™ & © 2009 DC Comics

PAGE 55: Pudge Girl Blimp ™ & © 2009 Lee Marrs

PAGE 57: Groo © 2009 Sergio Aragonés; Usagi Yojimbo ™ & © 2009 Stan Sakai; Urban Gorilla © 2009 Scott Shaw!

PAGE 60: Cartoon © 2009 Sergio Aragonés; "Alfred E. Neuman" (Boys Head Logo) and MAD ™ and © E.C. Publications, Inc.

PAGE 61: Archie ™ & © 2009 Archie Publications, Inc.

PAGE 63: Maggie and Hopey © 2009 Jaime Hernandez

PAGE 64: B. Kliban Cat ® © 2009 Judith K. Kliban, All Rights Reserved. Use by permission only.; Little Lulu and Tubby ™ & © 2009 Marjorie Henderson Buell; Kirby art © 2009 Jack Kirby Estate; Ward Kimball self-portrait © 2009 Ward Kimball Estate; Brenda Starr © 2009 Tribune Media Services, Inc.

PAGE 65: Odkin © 2009 Wallace Wood Estate; Elfquest ™ & © 2009 Warp Graphics, Inc.; Dick Tracy © 2009 Tribune Media Services, Inc.; badge art © 2009 Jim Cornelius

PAGE 66: Captain Victory ™ & © 2009 Jack Kirby Estate

PAGE 67: The Spirit ® is a registered trademark of Will Eisner Studios Inc.

PAGE 70: Teenage Mutant Ninja Turtles ™ & © 2009 Mirage Studios; Kurtzman sketch © 2009 Harvey Kurtzman Estate; Life in Hell © 2009 Matt Groening Productions, Inc. Used with permission

PAGE 71: Badge art © 2009 Rick Geary; Batman, Joker, Robin, Superman ™ & © 2009 DC Comics

PAGE 72: Art © 2009 Brent Anderson

PAGE 73: Art © 2009 Steve Purcell, Mike Mignola, Arthur Adams

PAGE 75: Sheena © 2009 Galaxy Publishing, Inc. art © 2009 Dave Stevens Estate

PAGES 76-77: Art © 2009 Scott Shaw!

PAGE 79: Art © 2009 Sergio Aragonés

PAGE 80: Art © 2009 Rick Geary

PAGE 82: California Girls © 2009 Trina Robbins

PAGE 83: Batman ™ & © 2009 DC Comics

PAGE 86: Art © 2009 Rick Geary

PAGE 87: Art © 2009 Rick Geary, Sergio Aragonés; The Spirit ® is a registered trademark of Will Eisner Studios Inc.

PAGE 88: The Rocketeer ™ & © 2009 Dave Stevens Estate; Mudwogs ™ & © 2009 Arthur Suydam; Bone ™ & © 2009 Jeff Smith

PAGE 89: Big Guy and Rusty the Boy Robot ™ & © 2009 Frank Miller and Geof Darrow

PAGE 90: Stardust ™ & © 2009 Neil Gaiman and Charles Vess; Sin City ™ & © 2009 Frank Miller; The Sandman ™ & © 2009 DC Comics; Spider-Man and Thor ™ & © 2009 Marvel Characters, Inc.

PAGE 91: Kidnapped © 2009 Frank Cho; Uncle Sam ™ & © 2009 DC Comics; The Spirit ® is a registered trademark of Will Eisner Studios Inc.

PAGE 96: Art © 2009 Rick Geary

PAGE 97: Art © 2009 Frank Miller

PAGE 101: Art © 2009 Rick Geary, Chris Ware

PAGE 102: Captain America, Hulk ™ & © 2009 Marvel Characters, Inc.; American Splendor ™ & © 2009 Harvey Pekar

PAGE 103: The Sandman ™ & © 2009 DC Comics

PAGE 104: Harley and Ivy, Hawkman, Green Lantern, Batman, Flash ™ & © 2009 DC Comics; Katy Keene © 2009 Archie Publications, Inc.; Mutts © 2009 Patrick McDonnell, Distributed by King Features Syndicate; Chewbacca COURTESY OF LUCASFILM LTD. ™ & © 2009 Lucasfilm Ltd. All rights reserved. Used under authorization. Unauthorized duplication is a violation of applicable law

PAGE 105: Nexus ™ & © 2009 Mike Baron and Steve Rude

PAGE 108: Issue 3: The Mask ™ & © 2009 Dark Horse Comics, Inc.

PAGE 109: Issue 1: Robocop ™ & © 2009 Orion Pictures Corporation; Argos ™ & © Leopoldo Duranova; Billi 99 ™ & © 2009 Sara Byam and Tim Sale; Concrete ™ & © 2009 Paul Chadwick; The Eyeball Kid ™ & © 2009 Eddie Campbell; The Creep ™ & © 2009 John Arcudi; Flaming Carrot ™ & © 2009 Bob Burden; Godzilla ™ & © 2009 TohoCo, Ltd; Grendel and The Aerialist ™ & © 2009 Matt Wagner; Harold Hound ™ & © 2009 Jim Bradrick; Heartbreakers ™ & © 2009 Anina Bennett and Paul Guinan; John Byrne's Next Men ™ & © 2009 John Byrne; Marshal Law ™ & © 2009 Pat Mills and Kevin O'Neill; Marv ™ & © 2009 Frank Miller Inc.; Trekker ™ & © 2009 Ron Randall; The American ™ & © 2009 Dark Horse; Nexus ™ & © 2009 Mike Baron and Steve Rude; Hellboy ™ & © 2009 Mike Mignola; Issue 4: Fat Man and Little Boy ™ & © 2009 Frank Miller; Star Wars COURTESY OF LUCASFILM LTD. ™ & © 2009 Lucasfilm Ltd. All rights reserved. Used under authorization. Unauthorized duplication is a violation of applicable law

PAGE 110: Superman Family, Green Lantern ™ & © 2009 DC Comics; Usagi Yojimbo ™ & © 2009 Stan Sakai

PAGE 111: Love and Rockets ™ & © 2009 Gilbert and Jaime Hernandez; The Spirit ® is a registered trademark of Will Eisner Studios Inc.; Captain America ™ & © 2009 Marvel Characters, Inc.; Con-Fessions © 2009 Charles S. Novinskie and Lon Roberts

PAGE 113: APE VI art © 2009 SLG Publishing; APE 2004 poster art © 2009 Batton Lash; 2007 poster art © 2009 Gene Yang; 2006 poster art © 2009 Keith Knight; 2008 poster art © 2009 Paige Braddock

PAGE 115: Two-Face ™ & © 2009 DC Comics; Drugstore That Time Forgot art © 2009 Steve Leialoha; Christmas card art © 2009 Nghia Lam; Wonder Woman ™ & © 2009 DC Comics

PAGE 118: Batman, Catwoman ™ & © 2009 DC Comics

PAGE 120: Art © 2009 Jim Valentino

PAGE 121: Art © 2009 Alfredo P. Alcala Estate; Starman ™ & © 2009 DC Comics; Captain America ™ & © 2009 Marvel Characters, Inc.

PAGE 122: 1970: Art © 2009 Jack Kirby Estate; 1971: Flash, Deadman, Kid Flash, Adam Strange, Detective Chimp, Green Lantern, Elongated Man, Robin, Flash, Batman ™ & © 2009 DC Comics; 1972: Demon, Kamandi, Merlin ™ & © 2009 DC Comics; 1974: Steve Canyon © 2009 Milton Caniff Estate

PAGE 123: 1973: Spectre, Deadman ™ & © 2009 DC Comics; 1976: art © 2009 Sergio Aragonés; 1975: The Spirit ® is a registered trademark of Will Eisner Studios Inc.

PAGE 124: 1977: Art © 2009 Alex Nino; 1978: art © 2009 Boris Vallejo; 1980: art © 2009 Jack Katz; 1981: Superman, Batman, Wonder Woman ™ & © 2009 DC Comics; 1982: Howard the Duck ™ & © 2009 Marvel Characters, Inc.; 1983: art © Rick Geary

PAGE 125: 1979: Beetle Bailey © 2009 King Features Syndicate, Inc.; Star Wars COURTESY OF LUCASFILM LTD. ™ & © 2009 Lucasfilm Ltd. All rights reserved. Used under authorization. Unauthorized duplication is a violation of applicable law

PAGE 126: 1984: The Foozle © 2009 Marshall Rogers Estate, Raul the Cat © 2009 Howard Chaykin; 1985: characters ™ & © 2009 DC Comics; 1986: Spider-Man, The Thing, Nightcrawler, Wolverine, She-Hulk, Daredevil ™ & © 2009 Marvel Characters, Inc.; 1987: art © 2009 Moebius (Jean Giraud); 1989: Superman ™ & © 2009 DC Comics; 1990: Characters © 2009 respective copyright holders; 1991: art © 2009 William Stout

PAGE 127: 1989: Art © 2009 Bill Sienkiewicz; 1992: art © 2009 Ken Steacy; 1993: art © 2009 Frank Miller.

PAGE 128: 1994 Comic-Con Souvenir Book cover image. © 1994 Matt Groening Productions, Inc. All Rights Reserved. The Simpsons. ™ and © Twentieth Century Fox Film Corporation. All Rights Reserved.; 1996: art © 2009 Dave McKean; 1998: Superman ™ & © 2009 DC Comics; 1997: Star Wars COURTESY OF LUCASFILM LTD. ™ & © 2009 Lucasfilm Ltd. All rights reserved. Used under authorization. Unauthorized duplication is a violation of applicable law; 1999: art © 2009 Steranko

PAGE 129: 2000: Art © 2009 William Stout; The Spirit ® is a registered trademark of Will Eisner Studios Inc.; Flash, Green Lantern ™ & © 2009 DC Comics; Peanuts ™ & © 2009 United Features Syndicate, Inc; 2001: Bone ™ & © 2009 Jeff Smith; 2002: "Alfred E. Neuman" (Boys Head Logo) and MAD ™ and © E.C. Publications, Inc.; 2003: Justice League ™ & © 2009 DC Comics

PAGE 130: 2004: Art © 2009 Jack Kirby Estate, characters ™ & © 2009 DC Comics and ™ & © 2009 Marvel Characters, Inc.; 2005: The Spirit ® is a registered trademark of Will Eisner Studios Inc.; 2006: Lone Wolf and Cub © 2009 Koike and Kojima; Superboy and the Legion of Super-Heroes ™ & © 2009 DC Comics

PAGE 131: Star Wars COURTESY OF LUCASFILM LTD. ™ & © 2009 Lucasfilm Ltd. All rights reserved. Used under authorization. Unauthorized duplication is a violation of applicable law

PAGE 132: Broom Hilda ™ & © 2009 Tribune Media Services; art © 2009 Neal Adams; Doc Savage is © and ™ Condé Nast. Used with permission; Nick Fury ™ & © 2009 Marvel Characters, Inc.; Baby Huey © 2009 Harvey Entertainment Inc.; art © 2009 John Pound, Scott Shaw!, Jim Valentino

PAGE 133: Art © 2008 Milton Caniff Estate; The Rocketeer © 2009 Dave Stevens Estate; art © 2009 Lela Dowling and Joshua Quagmire; Normalman © 2009 Jim Valentino; Action Girl © 2009 Sarah Dyer; Con-Notations art © 2009 Nghia Lam

PAGE 134: Sandman, Death, Books of Magic, Superman, Batman Beyond, Batman ™ & © 2009 DC Comics; art © 2009 Chris Ware; Castle Waiting © 2009 Linda Medley; Scary Godmother © 2009 Jill Thompson; The Spirit ® is a registered trademark of Will Eisner Studios Inc.; art © 2009 William Stout; POWERPUFF GIRLS used courtesy of Warner Bros. Entertainment, Inc. ™ & © Cartoon Network; Fantastic Four and Spider-Man ™ & © 2009 DC Comics

PAGE 135: Art © 2009 Batton Lash; Hellboy ™ & © 2009 Mike Mignola; Flash, Hawkman, Green Lantern, Green Arrow, Zatanna, Black Canary, Teen Titans, Superman, Justice League ™ & © 2009 DC Comics; The Spirit ® is a registered trademark of Will Eisner Studios Inc.; Ex Machina © 2009 Brian K. Vaughan and Tony Harris; Heroes © 2009 NBC/Universal; Fantastic Four ™ & © 2009 Marvel Characters, Inc.

PAGE 137: Sheena © 2009 Galaxy Publishing, Inc., art © 2009 Dave Stevens Estate; Captain Victory ™ & © 2009 Jack Kirby Estate; art © 2009 George Pérez; The Foozle © 2009 Marshall Rogers Estate; Raul the Cat © 2009 Howard Chaykin

PAGE 138: Death and The Sandman, Lady Blackhawk, Superman, Batman, Lobo, Justice League ™ & © 2009 DC Comics; Captain America, X-Men ™ & © 2009 Marvel Characters, Inc.; Timberland Tales © 2009 B. K. Taylor; The Rocketeer © 2009 Dave Stevens Estate; Lone Wolf and Cub © 2009 Koike and Kojima; Sin City © 2009 Frank Miller.

PAGE 139: "Alfred E. Neuman" (Boys Head Logo) and MAD ™ and © E.C. Publications, Inc.; Superman, Batman, Wonder Woman, Green Lantern, Flash, Green Arrow, Sergeant Rock, Justice League, Robin, Supergirl, Darkseid ™ & © 2009 DC Comics; Star Wars COURTESY OF LUCASFILM LTD. ™ & © 2009 Lucasfilm Ltd. All rights reserved. Used under authorization. Unauthorized duplication is a violation of applicable law

PAGE 140: The Spirit ® is a registered trademark of Will Eisner Studios Inc.; Superboy and the Legion of Super-Heroes ™ & © 2009 DC Comics

PAGES 142-143: Article © 2009 Rick Marschall; Shmoo © 2009 Capp Enterprises, Inc.; Flash Gordon, Ming the Merciless, Mandrake the Magician ™ & © 2009 King Features Syndicate, Inc.; Dragon Lady ™ & © 2009 Tribune Media Services

PAGE 144: Captain America, Fantastic Four, X-Men, and additional characters ™ & © 2009 Marvel Characters, Inc.; New Gods, Mister Miracle, Newsboy Legion, and additional characters ™ & © 2009 DC Comics

PAGE 145: Orion ™ & © 2009 DC Comics

PAGE 146-147: Article © 2009 Jay M. Kennedy. Reprinted by permission of Bruce C. Kennedy, Janet J. Kennedy, Mark W. Kennedy, Samuel Jewler, and Lenard Jewler; Fabulous Furry Freak Brothers © 2009 Gilbert Shelton; Hate © 2009 Peter Bagge; Zap Comix, Bijou Funnies, Wimmen's Comix © 2009 respective copyright owners

PAGE 152: The Spirit ® is a registered trademark of Will Eisner Studios Inc.

PAGE 158: Superman and Batman ™ & © 2009 DC Comics

PAGE 159: Peanuts ™ & © 2009 United Features Syndicate, Inc.; art © 2009 Gahan Wilson

PAGE 160: Forever People ™ & © 2009 DC Comics

PAGE 163: Justice League: New Frontier ™ & © 2009 DC Comics

PAGE 164: Groo © 2009 Sergio Aragonés, art © 2009 Scott Shaw!

PAGES 166-167: Article © 2009 Mark Lucas; Flash and Green Lantern ™ & © 2009 DC Comics

PAGE 168: Archie ™ & © 2009 Archie Publications, Inc.

PAGE 170: Popeye ™ & © 2009 King Features Syndicate, Inc.

PAGE 171: Elfquest ™ & © 2009 Warp Graphics, Inc.; art © 2009 Scott Saavedra

PAGE 173: Nilson Groundthumper and Hermy, Usagi Yojimbo ™ & © 2009 Stan Sakai; Starstruck © 2009 Michael Wm. Kaluta and Elaine Lee; X-Men, Spider-Man, Carnage, Wolverine ™ & © 2009 Marvel Characters, Inc.; Velocity © 2009 Top Cow Productions; Groo © 2009 Sergio Aragonés; Roswell © 2009 Bill Morrison; Big Guy and Rusty the Boy Robot © 2009 Frank Miller and Geof Darrow; Lone Wolf and Cub © 2009 Koike and Kojima; Speed Racer © 2009 Speed Racer Enterprises; Hellboy © 2009 Mike Mignola; Mutts © 2009 Patrick McDonnell, Distributed by King Features Syndicate; Teen Titans, Superman, Doomsday, Superboy and the Legion of Super-Heroes ™ & © 2009 DC Comics; Gumby ™ & © 2009 Wildcard Ink and Premavision

PAGE 176: Little Archie ™ & © 2009 Archie Publications, Inc.

PAGE 178: Superman, Batman, Robin, and other characters ™ & © 2009 DC Comics

PAGE 200: Bob Clampett sketch © 2009 Milton Caniff Estate

PAGE 201: Bill Finger sketch © 2009 Jerry Robinson

PAGE 202: Russ Manning sketch © 2009 Russ Manning Estate